Lecture Notes in Computer Scier

Commenced Publication in 1973
Founding and Former Series Editors:
Gerhard Goos, Juris Hartmanis, and Jan van Leeuwen

Jooseok Song   Taekyoung Kwon
Moti Yung (Eds.)

Information Security Applications

6th International Workshop, WISA 2005
Jeju Island, Korea, August 22-24, 2005
Revised Selected Papers

 Springer

Volume Editors

Jooseok Song
Yonsei University
Department of Computer Science
134 Shinchon-Dong, Seodaemun-Gu, Seoul, 120-749, Korea
E-mail: jssong@emerald.yonsei.ac.kr

Taekyoung Kwon
Sejong University
Department of Computer Engineering
98 Gunja-Dong, Kwangjin-Gu, Seoul, 143-747, Korea
E-mail: tkwon@sejong.ac.kr

Moti Yung
RSA Laboratories
and
Computer Science Department, Columbia University
Room 464, S.W. Mudd Building, New York, NY 10027, USA
E-mail: moti@cs.columbia.edu

Library of Congress Control Number: 2006920030

CR Subject Classification (1998): E.3, D.4.6, F.2.1, C.2, J.1, C.3, K.6.5

LNCS Sublibrary: SL 4 – Security and Cryptology

ISSN   0302-9743
ISBN-10   3-540-31012-6 Springer Berlin Heidelberg New York
ISBN-13   978-3-540-31012-9 Springer Berlin Heidelberg New York

Springer is a part of Springer Science+Business Media

springeronline.com

© Springer-Verlag Berlin Heidelberg 2006
Printed in Germany

Typesetting: Camera-ready by author, data conversion by Scientific Publishing Services, Chennai, India
Printed on acid-free paper   SPIN: 11604938   06/3142   5 4 3 2 1 0

Preface

The 6th International Workshop on Information Security Applications (WISA 2005) was held on Jeju Island, Korea, during August 22–24, 2005. The workshop was sponsored by the Korea Institute of Information Security and Cryptology (KIISC), the Electronics and Telecommunications Research Institute (ETRI) and the Ministry of Information and Communication (MIC).

The aim of the workshop is to serve as a forum for new conceptual and experimental research results in the area of information security applications, with contributions from the academic community as well as from industry. The workshop program covers a wide range of security aspects including network security, e-commerce, cryptography, cryptanalysis, applications and implementation aspects.

The Program Committee received 168 papers from 17 countries, and accepted 29 papers for a full presentation track and 16 papers for a short presentation track. Each paper was carefully evaluated through a peer-review process by at least three members of the Program Committee. This volume contains revised versions of 29 papers accepted and presented in the full presentation track. Short papers only appeared in the WISA 2005 pre-proceedings as preliminary versions, and their extended versions may be published elsewhere.

In addition to the contributed papers, the workshop had five special talks. Moti Yung gave a tutorial talk, entitled "Malware Meets Cryptography." Virgil Gligor and Michel Abdalla gave invited talks in the full presentation track, entitled "On the Evolution of Adversary Models in Security Protocols" and "Public-Key Encryption with Keyword Search," respectively. Finally, Shozo Naito and Jonguk Choi gave invited talks in the short presentation track, entitled "New RSA-Type Public-Key Cryptosystem and Its Performance Evaluation" and "A New Booming Era of DRM: Applications and Extending Business," respectively.

Many people helped and worked hard to make WISA 2005 successful. We would like to thank all the individuals involved in the Technical Program and in organizing the workshop. We are very grateful to the Program Committee members and the external referees for their time and efforts in reviewing the submissions and selecting the accepted papers. We also express our special thanks to the Organizing Committee members for making the workshop possible. Finally, we would like to thank all the authors of the submitted papers and the invited speakers for their contributions to the workshop.

December 2005

Jooseok Song
Taekyoung Kwon
Moti Yung

Preface

Organization

Advisory Committee

Man Young Rhee	Kyung Hee Univ., Korea
Hideki Imai	Tokyo Univ., Japan
Chu-Hwan Yim	ETRI, Korea
Bart Preneel	Katholieke Universiteit Leuven, Belgium

General Co-chairs

Dae Ho Kim	KIISC, Korea
Sung Won Sohn	ETRI, Korea

Steering Committee

Kil-Hyun Nam	Korea National Defense Univ., Korea
Sang Jae Moon	Kyungpook National Univ., Korea
Dong Ho Won	Sungkyunkwan Univ., Korea
Sehun Kim	KAIST, Korea
Pil-Joong Lee	POSTECH, Korea
Kyo-Il Chung	ETRI, Korea

Organization Committee

Chair:	Im Yeong Lee	Soonchunhyang Univ., Korea
Finance:	Dong-Il Seo	ETRI, Korea
Publication:	Ji Young Lim	Korean Bible Univ., Korea
Publicity:	Yoo-Jae Won	KISA, Korea
Registration:	Hyun-Gon Kim	Mokpo National Univ., Korea
Treasurer:	Hyung Woo Lee	Hanshin Univ., Korea
Local Arrangements:	Ki-Wook Sohn	NSRI, Korea
	Khi Jung Ahn	Cheju National Univ., Korea

Program Committee

Co-chairs:	Taekyoung Kwon	Sejong Univ., Korea
	Jooseok Song	Yonsei Univ., Korea
	Moti Yung	Columbia Univ., USA
Members:	Michel Abdalla	École Normale Superieure, France
	Dan Bailey	RSA Laboratories, USA

Feng Bao	Institute for Infocomm Research, Singapore
Colin Boyd	Queen's Univ. of Technology, Australia
Emmanuel Bresson	CELAR Technology Center, France
Liqun Chen	Hewlett-Packard, UK
Jung-Hee Cheon	Seoul National Univ., Korea
Kyo-Il Chung	ETRI, Korea
Mathieu Ciet	Gemplus, France
Bruno Crispo	Vrije Universiteit, Netherlands
Paulo D'Arco	Univ. of Salerno, Italy
Shlomi Dolev	Ben-Gurion University, Israel
Seungjoo Kim	Sungkyunkwan Univ., Korea
Yongdae Kim	Univ. of Minnesota at Twin Cities, USA
Chi Sung Laih	National Cheng Kung Univ., Taiwan
Moses Liskov	The College of William and Mary, USA
Kwok-Yan Lam	Tsinghua Univ., China
Dong Hoon Lee	CIST, Korea
Chae Hoon Lim	Sejong Univ., Korea
Javier Lopez	Malaga, Spain
Kanta Matsuura	Tokyo Univ., Japan
Atsuko Miyaji	JAIST, Japan
Fabian Monrose	Johns Hopkins University, USA
Gregory Neven	K.U. Leuven, Belgium
Daehun Nyang	Inha Univ., Korea
Sang-Woo Park	NSRI, Korea
Atul Prakash	Univ. of Michigan, USA
Jaechul Ryu	Chungnam National Univ., Korea
Kouichi Sakurai	Kyushu Univ., Japan
Stuart Schechter	Havard Univ., USA
Hovav Shacham	Stanford University, USA
Yannis C. Stamatiou	University of Ioannina, Greece
Willy Susilo	Univ. of Wollongong, Australia
William Whyte	NTRU System, USA
Yoo-Jae Won	KISA, Korea
Shouhuai Xu	Univ. of Texas, USA
Bulent Yener	Rensselaer Polytechnic Institute, USA
Kee Young Yoo	Kyungpook National University, Korea
Adam Young	MITRE, USA
Jianying Zhou	Institute for Infocomm Research, Singapore

Table of Contents

DRM/Software Security

Efficient HW Implementation

Side-Channel Attacks

Privacy/Anonymity

Efficient Implementation

Security Weakness in Ren et al.'s Group Key Agreement Scheme Built on Secure Two-Party Protocols*

Junghyun Nam, Seungjoo Kim, and Dongho Won

School of Information and Communication Engineering,
Sungkyunkwan University, Republic of Korea
jhnam@dosan.skku.ac.kr, skim@ece.skku.ac.kr, dhwon@dosan.skku.ac.kr

Abstract. A group key agreement protocol is designed to allow a group of parties communicating over an insecure, public network to agree on a common secret key. Recently, in WISA'04, Ren et al. proposed an efficient group key agreement scheme for dynamic groups, which can be built on any of secure two-party key establishment protocols. In the present work we study the main EGAKA-KE protocol of the scheme and point out a critical security flaw in the protocol. We show that the security flaw leads to a vulnerability to an active attack mounted by two colluding adversaries.

Keywords: Group key agreement, key authentication, collusion attack.

1 Introduction

Key establishment protocols are a critical building block for securing electronic communications over an untrusted, open network like the Internet. Even if it is computationally infeasible to break the cryptographic algorithm used, the whole system becomes vulnerable to all manner of attacks if the keys are not securely established. However, the experience has shown that the design of key establishment protocols that are secure against an active adversary is not an easy task to do, especially in a multi-party setting. Indeed, there is a long history of protocols for this domain being proposed and subsequently broken by some active attacks (e.g., [11, 15, 4, 18, 14]). Therefore, key establishment protocols must be subjected to the strictest scrutiny possible before they can be deployed into today's hostile networking environment.

The original idea of extending the two-party Diffie-Hellman scheme [8] to the multi-party setting dates back to the classical paper of Ingemarsson et al. [10], and is followed by many works [6, 2, 17, 12] offering various levels of complexity. Recently, in WISA 2004, Ren et al. [16] proposed an efficient group key agreement scheme for dynamic groups. Instead of building the scheme from the scratch, they

---

* This work was supported by the University IT Research Center Project funded by the Korean Ministry of Information and Communication.

J. Song, T. Kwon, and M. Yung (Eds.): WISA 2005, LNCS 3786, pp. 1–9, 2006.

construct it by utilizing an existing two-party key establishment protocol that is secure against an active adversary. The scheme consists of two sub-protocols: the key establishment protocol EGAKA-KE and the key update protocol EGAKA-KU. The main EGAKA-KE protocol allows a set of group members to establish a common secret key (called either *group key* or *session key*). The EGAKA-KU protocol aims to efficiently handle dynamic membership changes in the group. In this paper, we uncover a security flaw in the EGAKA-KE protocol and show that the security flaw leads to a vulnerability to an active attack mounted by two colluding adversaries.

2   Preliminaries

The EGAKA-KE protocol is based on a binary key tree structure [13], where every node is either a leaf or a parent of two nodes. The root is located at level 0 and all leaves are at level d or $d-1$, with d being the height of the key tree. Let $\mathcal{G} = \{M_1, \ldots, M_n\}$ be a set of group members wishing to agree on a group key. Group members are arranged at leaves of the tree; all interior nodes are logical nodes hosting no group members. We denote by $N_{l,r}$ the rth node from the left at level l and by $\hat{N}_{l,r}$ the sibling node of $N_{l,r}$. An illustrative example of the considered key tree is given in Fig. 1.

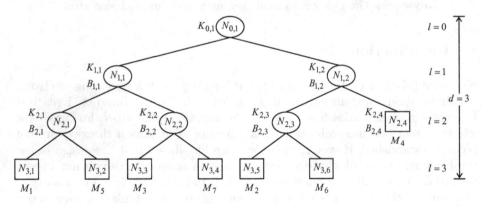

Fig. 1. An illustration of the key tree structure for $\mathcal{G} = \{M_1, \ldots, M_7\}$

Each node $N_{l,r}$, where $l \neq d$, in the key tree is associated with a key pair, the secret key $K_{l,r}$ and its corresponding blinded key $B_{l,r}$. Let $\mathcal{G}_{l,r}$ denote the subgroup consisting of the members in the subtree $T_{l,r}$ rooted at node $N_{l,r}$. Then, the secret key $K_{l,r}$ is shared only by the members in the subgroup $\mathcal{G}_{l,r}$, meaning that the root key $K_{0,1}$ serves as the group key shared by all the members in $\mathcal{G}$. To simplify the protocol description, we introduce some new notations through the following definitions.

Definition 1. *For each proper subtree of the key tree, there is a* designated negotiator (DN) *that is a group member at the leftmost leaf node of the subtree.*

By definition of DN, a group member can be a DN for multiple subtrees (up to d). For example, in Fig. 1, M_2 is the DN for the three subtrees $T_{3,5}$, $T_{2,3}$ and $T_{1,2}$, while M_4 is the DN only for the single-node subtree $T_{2,4}$.

Definition 2. *Let $\hat{T}_{l,r}$ denote the sibling subtree of $T_{l,r}$, i.e., the subtree rooted at $\hat{N}_{l,r}$. Let $M_{l,r}$ and $\hat{M}_{l,r}$ denote the DNs respectively for $T_{l,r}$ and $\hat{T}_{l,r}$. Then, we say that two DNs $M_{l,r}$ and $\hat{M}_{l,r}$ are partnered together, or equivalently, are partners of each other.*

As already mentioned, the EGAKA-KE protocol is built on an existing two-party protocol which is used to establish pairwise keys between group members. Each DN $M_{l,r}$ is designated as the representative of the subgroup $\mathcal{G}_{l,r}$, and is responsible for negotiating a pairwise key $k_{l,r}$ with his partner $\hat{M}_{l,r}$, hence the name of it.

3   A Review of the EGAKA-KE Protocol

In describing the protocol, we assume that group members have agreed on a two-party authenticated key agreement protocol that provides both perfect forward secrecy and known key security. One example of such a protocol is A-DH presented by Ateniese et al. [1]. We also assume that all members know the structure of the tree and their position within the tree. This can be done by letting one randomly chosen member generate these tree-related information and broadcast it to the other members. Despite the seemingly systematic arrangement of members in the example of Fig. 1, we note that there is no significance to the order of members' positions in the tree, but rather the members are placed in a random way as described in Section 4.1 of the original paper [16]; what really matters is that the tree should be "well-balanced" in the sense that the height of the two subtrees of a node should differ by at most one.

We now describe the details of the EGAKA-KE protocol. The operation of the protocol is broadly divided into two phases: phase one, pairwise key establishment; phase two, secret and blinded keys generation.

3.1   Phase One: Pairwise Key Establishment

During this phase, each pair of partnered DNs $M_{l,r}$ and $\hat{M}_{l,r}$ generates a pairwise key by performing the underlying two-party key agreement protocol. Note that there are $n-1$ such pairs in the key tree for the group of n members. For instance, in the tree of Fig. 1, there are 6 pairs of partnered DNs: (M_1, M_5), (M_3, M_7), (M_2, M_6), (M_1, M_3), (M_2, M_4) and (M_1, M_2). Since all the $n-1$ protocol executions can be run simultaneously, the number of communication rounds required in the first phase is the same as that needed to complete the underlying two-party protocol.

If instantiated with A-DH, this process can be made concrete as follows. Let $\mathbb{G} = \langle \alpha \rangle$ be a cyclic group of prime order q which is a subgroup of $\mathbb{Z}_p^*$ for a prime

p such that $p = kq + 1$ for some small $k \in \mathbb{N}$ (e.g., $k = 2$). Let (x_i, α^{x_i}) be the private/public key pair of M_i and let $\mathcal{P}_i$ be the set of all partners of M_i. Then, for all $M_i \in \mathcal{G}$ and for all $M_j \in \mathcal{P}_i$ such that $i < j$, M_i and M_j perform the following steps:

1. M_i chooses a random $r_i \in \mathbb{Z}_q^*$ and sends α^{r_i} to M_j.
2. M_j chooses a random $r_j \in \mathbb{Z}_q^*$ and sends $\alpha^{r_j f(\alpha^{x_i x_j})}$ to M_i. Here, f is a function mapping elements of $\mathbb{G}$ to elements of $\mathbb{Z}_q$. If p is a safe prime (i.e., $p = 2q + 1$), then a perfect mapping function would be $f(x) = x$ if $x \le q$, and $f(x) = p - x$ if $x > q$.
3. M_i and M_j compute the same pairwise key $\alpha^{r_i r_j}$.

These pairwise keys serve as key encryption keys used for securely exchanging the blinded keys between DNs in the second phase. In the sequel, we rule out the case $n = 2$ (i.e., $d = 1$) from consideration, since the group key for this special case is the pairwise key itself established between the two members in the first phase.

3.2   Phase Two: Secret and Blinded Keys Generation

Once group members have established a pairwise key with each of their partners, the secret and blinded keys of nodes are computed in a bottom-up manner, starting with the nodes at level $d - 1$ and proceeding towards the root at level 0. The blinded key of a node is always computed by applying a one-way hash function h to the secret key of the node, i.e., $B_{l,r} = h(K_{l,r})$. Although there are some exceptions, computing the secret key of a node requires the knowledge of two blinded keys, one for each of its two child nodes. More precisely, every $K_{l,r}$ for $l > d - 1$ (see below for the case $l = d - 1$) is computed recursively as follows:

$$K_{l,r} = h(B_{l+1,2r-1} \| B_{l+1,2r}).$$

In this manner, it requires d communication rounds for all the group members to determine the secret key of the root, i.e., the common group key; at the end of the ith round, the key pair of node $N_{l,r}$ at level $l = d - i$ becomes available to all the members of the subgroup $\mathcal{G}_{l,r}$. The details of each round are given below, where we assume $l = d - i$ for each l appearing in the description of the ith round.

Round 1: Let $l = d - 1$.

1. For each leaf node $N_{l,r}$, the secret key $K_{l,r}$ is just a random nonce chosen by the member at that node. For each internal node $N_{l,r}$, $K_{l,r}$ is the pairwise key itself shared between two members corresponding to the left and right children.
2. Each DN $M_{l,r}$ computes $B_{l,r}$ as $B_{l,r} = h(K_{l,r})$ and sends to his partner $\hat{M}_{l,r}$

$$\{B_{l,r} \| M_{l,r}\}_{k_{l,r}},$$

where $\{B_{l,r} \| M_{l,r}\}_{k_{l,r}}$ denotes the ciphertext of $B_{l,r} \| M_{l,r}$ encrypted using some secure symmetric cryptosystem under the pairwise key $k_{l,r}$.

Round i ($2 \leq i \leq d - 1$, for $d \geq 3$): Let $l = d - i$.

1. For each node $N_{l,r}$, consider the two partnered DNs $M_{l+1,2r-1}$ and $M_{l+1,2r}$ respectively for its left and right subtrees. We describe this step only for $M_{l+1,2r-1}$; $M_{l+1,2r}$ acts correspondingly. $M_{l+1,2r-1}$ recovers $B_{l+1,2r}$ by decrypting the message received from $M_{l+1,2r}$, and sends

$$\{B_{l+1,2r}\|M_{l+1,2r-1}\}_{K_{l+1,2r-1}}$$

to the rest of the subgroup $\mathcal{G}_{l+1,2r-1}$. Since all members in $\mathcal{G}_{l+1,2r-1}$ share the secret key $K_{l+1,2r-1}$, they can recover $B_{l+1,2r}$, and thus can compute $K_{l,r} = h(B_{l+1,2r-1}\|B_{l+1,2r})$ and $B_{l,r} = h(K_{l,r})$.

2. After computing $K_{l,r}$ and $B_{l,r}$, each DN $M_{l,r}$ sends $\{B_{l,r}\|M_{l,r}\}_{k_{l,r}}$ to his partner $\hat{M}_{l,r}$. Note that by definition of DN, one same member plays the role of both $M_{l+1,2r-1}$ and $M_{l,r}$.

Round d:

1. $M_{1,1}$ and $M_{1,2}$ recover respectively $B_{1,2}$ and $B_{1,1}$ by decrypting the message received from each other. $M_{1,1}$ then sends $\{B_{1,2}\|M_{1,1}\}_{K_{1,1}}$ to the other members of $\mathcal{G}_{1,1}$. Similarly, $M_{1,2}$ sends $\{B_{1,1}\|M_{1,2}\}_{K_{1,2}}$ to the rest of $\mathcal{G}_{1,2}$.

2. Finally, the members in $\mathcal{G}_{1,1}$ (respectively, $\mathcal{G}_{1,2}$) recover $B_{1,2}$ (respectively, $B_{1,1}$), and compute the group key as:

$$K_{0,1} = h(B_{1,1}\|B_{1,2}).$$

Consider, for example, the member M_2 in Fig. 1. At the end of the first phase, M_2 holds three pairwise keys $k_{3,5}$ ($= k_{3,6}$), $k_{2,3}$ ($= k_{2,4}$) and $k_{1,2}$ ($= k_{1,1}$) shared with M_6, M_4 and M_1, respectively. In round 1 of the second phase, M_2 first computes the secret and blinded keys of node $N_{2,3}$ as $K_{2,3} = k_{3,5}$ and $B_{2,3} = h(K_{2,3})$. M_2 then, as the DN $M_{2,3}$, sends $\{B_{2,3}\|M_2\}_{k_{2,3}}$ to M_4 who plays the role of the DN $M_{2,4}$. In round 2, M_2 obtains $B_{2,4}$ by decrypting $\{B_{2,4}\|M_4\}_{k_{2,4}}$ received from M_4 and sends $\{B_{2,4}\|M_2\}_{K_{2,3}}$ to M_6, the rest of subgroup $\mathcal{G}_{2,3}$. M_2 now computes the secret and blinded key pair of $N_{1,2}$ as $K_{1,2} = h(B_{2,3}\|B_{2,4})$ and $B_{1,2} = h(K_{1,2})$, and since he serves as $M_{1,2}$, sends $\{B_{1,2}\|M_2\}_{k_{1,2}}$ to M_1, the DN $M_{1,1}$. In round 3, M_2 recovers $B_{1,1}$ by decrypting $\{B_{1,1}\|M_1\}_{k_{1,1}}$ received from M_1 and sends $\{B_{1,1}\|M_2\}_{K_{1,2}}$ to M_4 and M_6, the other members of $\mathcal{G}_{1,2}$. Finally, M_2 computes his group key as: $K_{0,1} = h(B_{1,1}\|B_{1,2})$.

4   Security Analysis

The basic security property for a key establishment protocol to achieve is *implicit key authentication*, which is defined in the following context [1, 15].

Definition 3. *Let $\mathcal{G}$ be a set of parties who wish to share a common secret key by running a key establishment protocol KEP. Let K_i be the secret key computed by $M_i \in \mathcal{G}$ as a result of protocol KEP. We say that KEP provides implicit key authentication if each $M_i \in \mathcal{G}$ is assured that no party $M_q \notin \mathcal{G}$ can learn the key K_i unless helped by a dishonest $M_j \in \mathcal{G}$.*

In many real world applications, it is typical to assume that a party can establish several concurrent sessions with many different parties. Hence, the security property has to be met even when multiple instances of the protocol are run concurrently in the presence of active adversaries who may read, modify, insert, delete, replay and delay messages at their choice [3, 7, 5, 4, 12]. A protocol achieving implicit key authentication is called an authenticated key establishment protocol, and is of fundamental importance in much of modern cryptography and network security.

Unfortunately, the EGAKA-KE protocol fails to satisfy implicit key authentication, unlike the claim that it is an authenticated key establishment protocol. Our main observation is that only sender's identity concatenated with a blinded key is encrypted to be sent in the protocol. This oversight creates a vulnerability to an active attack mounted by two colluding adversaries A_1 and A_2. In our attack, the adversaries are legitimate users in the sense that they are able to set up normal protocol sessions with other users. Consider a protocol session S' to be conducted by the members of group $\mathcal{G}'$, where A_1 and A_2 are not invited to participate (i.e., $A_1, A_2 \notin \mathcal{G}'$). Without loss of generality, we assume that M_1 and M_2 serve respectively as $M_{1,1}$ and $M_{1,2}$ in session S'. We also assume that M_1 and M_2 accept the invitation by the adversaries to participate respectively as $M_{1,1}$ and $M_{1,2}$ in a new concurrent session S (the set of participants of S is denoted by $\mathcal{G}$). That is, the attack involves the following two sessions running concurrently:

$$\text{Session } S: \quad \mathcal{G} = \{M_1, M_2, A_1, A_2\},$$
$$\text{Session } S': \quad \mathcal{G}' = \{M_1, M_2, \dots, M_n\}.$$

For now, to simplify matters, we assume that the size n of group $\mathcal{G}'$ is small, say 16 or less.

Our attack leads to a serious consequence. At the end of the attack, every member in $\mathcal{G}'$ computes a group key as per protocol specification and thinks that the session is finished successfully, when, in fact, the computed key is available also to the adversaries A_1 and A_2. A bird's-eye view of the collusion attack is shown in Fig. 2 and a more detailed description is now given. Let M_i^S and $M_i^{S'}$ denote the instances of M_i participating in S and S', respectively. The adversaries' strategy is to let the two sessions proceed as specified in the protocol except for changing some message flows as follows:

1. In the first phase, the adversaries have M_1^S establish a pairwise key with $M_2^{S'}$ instead of M_2^S, and, similarly, have $M_1^{S'}$ establish a pairwise key with M_2^S instead of $M_2^{S'}$. A little thought will make it clear that no matter what key agreement protocol is selected as the underlying two-party protocol, it is always possible for an active adversary to do so without being detected.

2. In the second to last round (i.e., $d-1$th round) of each session's second phase, M_1 ($M_{1,1}$) and M_2 ($M_{1,2}$) will send to each other a ciphertext encrypted under their pairwise key. But, the adversaries redirect these ciphertexts sent in two sessions so that the ciphertext sent by M_1^S (respectively, M_2^S, $M_1^{S'}$ and $M_2^{S'}$) is delivered to $M_2^{S'}$ (respectively, $M_1^{S'}$, M_2^S and M_1^S).

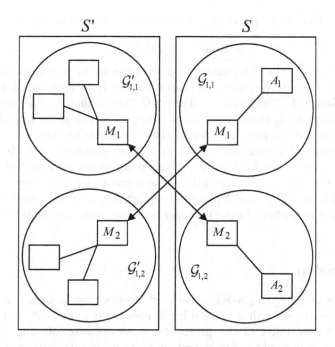

Fig. 2. A high-level description of an attack on the EGAKA-KE protocol

M_1 and M_2 cannot notice any disturbance at all since all the decryptions will be successful producing a correct sender's identity. Hence, M_1 and M_2 will proceed to finish the executions of the protocol. To be concrete, let $K'_{l,r}$ and $B'_{l,r}$ be, respectively, the secret key and the blinded key of node $N_{l,r}$ of the key tree for session S'. Then, in the last round of session S,

- M_1^S recovers $B'_{1,2}$ by decrypting the ciphertext received from $M_2^{S'}$ and sends $\{B'_{1,2}\|M_1\}_{K_{1,1}}$ to the other members of $\mathcal{G}_{1,1}$.
- M_2^S obtains $B'_{1,1}$ by decrypting the ciphertext received from $M_1^{S'}$ and sends $\{B'_{1,1}\|M_2\}_{K_{1,2}}$ to the rest of $\mathcal{G}_{1,2}$.

Similarly, in the last round of session S',

- $M_1^{S'}$ recovers $B_{1,2}$ by decrypting the ciphertext received from M_2^S and sends $\{B_{1,2}\|M_1\}_{K'_{1,1}}$ to the other members of $\mathcal{G}'_{1,1}$.
- $M_2^{S'}$ obtains $B_{1,1}$ by decrypting the ciphertext received from M_1^S and sends $\{B_{1,1}\|M_2\}_{K'_{1,2}}$ to the rest of $\mathcal{G}'_{1,2}$.

Therefore, at the end of two sessions, the members in $\mathcal{G}_{1,1}$ and $\mathcal{G}'_{1,2}$ will compute their session key as

$$K_{\text{fake1}} = h(B_{1,1}\|B'_{1,2}),$$

while the members in $\mathcal{G}'_{1,1}$ and $\mathcal{G}_{1,2}$ will compute the session key as

$$K_{\text{fake2}} = h(B'_{1,1}||B_{1,2}).$$

Through the attack, the authentication mechanism of the protocol is completely compromised. Indeed, the effect of our attack is much the same as that of a man-in-the-middle attack. The members of group $\mathcal{G}'$ believe that they have established a secure session among them, while in fact they have shared the keys K_{fake1} and K_{fake2} with the adversaries. As a result, the adversaries can not only access and relay any confidential communications among the members of $\mathcal{G}'$, but can also send arbitrary messages for their own benefit impersonating any of the group members to the others. Consequently, there seems to be little reason to expect that the EGAKA-KE protocol provides implicit key authentication, as soon as two concurrent executions of the protocol have the same members for DNs $M_{1,1}$ and $M_{1,2}$.

5   Discussion

The weakness of the EGAKA-KE protocol stems from the fact that only sender's identity concatenated with a blinded key is encrypted to be sent. This oversight creates the vulnerability of the protocol and allows two colluding adversaries to switch the ciphertexts between two concurrent sessions with a different set of participants. This implies that we can improve, somewhat, the security of the protocol by integrating all the identities of protocol participants into each message being encrypted in the protocol. This modification alone, however, does not seem to be enough to completely fix the security problem, particularly in case the underlying encryption scheme is malleable [9].

It should be also noted that the adversaries' cheating in second phases may not be successful if, unlike our assumption, the size of group $\mathcal{G}'$ is much larger than that of $\mathcal{G}$, and so the second phase of session S' takes noticeably longer than that of session S; in such a case, M_1^S and M_2^S would wait the maximum timeout period to receive a ciphertext in the second to last round, and finally abort the session when the timer expires. But, the assumption on $\mathcal{G}'$'s size can be relaxed somewhat since the adversaries can slow down the progression of session S, for example by establishing, at a deliberately lazy pace, pairwise keys with M_1^S and M_2^S in the first phase. Furthermore, this assumption may be even avoided in a scenario in which there are (empirically) at least about $\lceil n/8 \rceil$ to $\lceil n/4 \rceil$ members in group $\mathcal{G}$.

6   Conclusion

In WISA'04, Ren et al. [16] proposed a group key agreement scheme which can be built on any of secure two-party key establishment protocols. In this work we have studied the main EGAKA-KE protocol of the scheme and uncovered a critical security flaw in the protocol. The security flaw has led us to present an active attack mounted by two colluding adversaries.

References

1. G. Ateniese, M. Steiner, and G. Tsudik, "New multiparty authentication services and key agreement protocols," IEEE Journal on Selected Areas in Communications, vol. 18, no. 4, pp. 628–639, 2000.
2. K. Becker and U. Wille, "Communication complexity of group key distribution," Proceedings of the 5th ACM Conference on Computer and Communications Security (CCS 1998), pp. 1-6, 1998.
3. M. Bellare and P. Rogaway, "Entity authentication and key distribution," In Advances in Cryptology — Crypto 1993, Lecture Notes in Computer Science, vol. 773, pp. 232–249, 1994.
4. C. Boyd and J.M.G. Nieto, "Round-optimal contributory conference key agreement," In PKC 2003, Lecture Notes in Computer Science, vol. 2567, pp. 161–174, 2003.
5. E. Bresson, O. Chevassut, D. Pointcheval, and J.-J. Quisquater, "Provably authenticated group Diffie-Hellman key exchange," Proceedings of the 8th ACM Conference on Computer and Communications Security (CCS 2001), pp. 255–264, 2001.
6. M. Burmester and Y. Desmedt, "A secure and efficient conference key distribution system," In Advances in Cryptology — Eurocrypt 1994, Lecture Notes in Computer Science, vol. 950, pp. 275–286, 1995.
7. R. Canetti and H. Krawczyk, "Analysis of key-exchange protocols and their use for building secure channels," In Advances in Cryptology — Eurocrypt 2001, Lecture Notes in Computer Science, vol. 2045, pp. 453–474, 2001.
8. W. Diffie and M. E. Hellman, "New directions in cryptography," IEEE Trans. on Information Theory, vol. 22, no. 6, pp. 644–654, 1976.
9. D. Dolev, C. Dwork, and M. Naor, "Nonmalleable cryptography," SIAM Journal on Computing, vol. 30, no. 2, pp. 391–437, 2000.
10. I. Ingemarsson, D. Tang, and C. Wong, "A conference key distribution system," IEEE Trans. on Information Theory, vol. 28, no. 5, pp. 714–720, 1982.
11. M. Just and S. Vaudenay, "Authenticated multi-party key agreement," In Advances in Cryptology — Asiacrypt 1996, LNCS 1163, pp. 36–49, 1996.
12. J. Katz and M. Yung, "Scalable protocols for authenticated group key exchange," In Advances in Cryptology — Crypto 2003, Lecture Notes in Computer Science, vol. 2729, pp. 110–125, 2003.
13. Y. Kim, A. Perrig, and G. Tsudik, "Tree-based group key agreement," ACM Trans. on Information and System Security, vol. 7, no. 1, pp. 60–96, 2004.
14. J. Nam, S. Kim, and D. Won, "A weakness in the Bresson-Chevassut-Essiari-Pointcheval's group key agreement scheme for low-power mobile devices," IEEE Communications Letters, vol. 9, no. 5, pp. 429–431, 2005.
15. O. Pereira and J.-J. Quisquater, "A security analysis of the Cliques protocols suites," Proceedings of the 14th IEEE Computer Security Foundations Workshop (CSFW 2001), pp. 73–81, 2001.
16. K. Ren, H. Lee, K. Kim, and T. Yoo, "Efficient authenticated key agreement protocol for dynamic groups," In 5th International Workshop on Information Security Applications (WISA 2004), Lecture Notes in Computer Science, vol. 3325, pp. 144–159, 2004.
17. M. Steiner, G. Tsudik, and M. Waidner, "Key agreement in dynamic peer groups," IEEE Trans. on Parallel and Distributed Systems, vol. 11, no. 8, pp. 769–780, 2000.
18. F. Zhang and X. Chen, "Attack on an ID-based authenticated group key agreement scheme from PKC 2004," Information Processing Letters, vol. 91, no. 4, pp. 191–193, 2004.

Cryptanalysis of Some Group-Oriented Proxy Signature Schemes

Je Hong Park[1], Bo Gyeong Kang[2], and Sangwoo Park[1]

[1] National Security Research Institute,
161 Gajeong-dong, Yuseong-gu, Daejeon 305-350, Korea
{jhpark, psw}@etri.re.kr
[2] Department of Mathematics, Korea Advanced Institute of Science and Technology,
373-1 Guseong-dong, Yuseong-gu, Daejeon 305-701, Korea
snubogus@kaist.ac.kr

Abstract. A proxy signature scheme allows an entity to delegate its signing power to another entity. Since the notion of proxy signatures was first introduced, many proxy signature schemes and various extensions have been considered. As an example, the notion of threshold proxy signature or proxy multi-signature was introduced as a group-oriented variant. In this paper, we show that the threshold proxy signature scheme proposed by Hsu and Wu, and the proxy multi-signature schemes independently proposed by Chen *et al.* and Hsu *et al.* are all insecure against the malicious original singer(s). Our result provides a simple example that the way to put the secret parts together should be carefully considered.

1 Introduction

The concept of a proxy signature is that the signer, called the original signer, can delegate his signing capability to a designated person, called the proxy signer to sign messages on its behalf. More precisely, the original signer sends a specific message with its signature to the proxy signer, who then uses this information to construct a proxy signing key. With the proxy signing key that is constructed by the proxy signer in cooperation with the original signer, the proxy signer can generate proxy signatures by employing a specific standard signature scheme. From a proxy signature, anyone can check both the original signer's delegation and the proxy signer's digital signature.

There are two kinds of proxy signature schemes depending on whether the original signer can generate the same proxy signatures as the proxy signers do. The one is proxy-unprotected where the proxy signer generates proxy signatures only with the proxy signing key given by the original signer. So the original signer can also generate the same proxy signatures. The other is proxy-protected where the proxy signer generates proxy signatures not only with the proxy signing key given by the original signer but also with his own private key. Therefore, anyone else, including the original signer, cannot generate the same proxy signatures. This differentiation is important in practical applications, since it enables proxy

J. Song, T. Kwon, and M. Yung (Eds.): WISA 2005, LNCS 3786, pp. 10–24, 2006.

signature schemes to avoid potential disputes between the original signer and proxy signer [11].

The notion of proxy signature was introduced by Mambo, Usuda and Okamoto [8]. After that, many proxy signature schemes and various types of proxy signature schemes which combine other special signatures to add that speciality in proxy signatures have been proposed [7, 14, 13, 1, 2, 4, 5, 6, 10]. Especially, it is natural to use threshold signature or multi-signature schemes to extend the notion of proxy signature to group-oriented applications.

The notion of threshold proxy signature was introduced by Zhang [14] and Kim *et al.* [7], independently. In a (t, n) threshold proxy signature scheme, the original signer can delegate his/her signing capability to a group of n proxy signers such that t or more of them can generate proxy signatures cooperatively, but $t - 1$ or less of them cannot do the same thing. Separately, the notion of proxy multi-signature was introduced by Yi *et al.* [13]. In a proxy multi-signature scheme, a designated proxy signer can sign messages in the name of a group composed of original signers.

In this paper, we will show that group-oriented proxy signature schemes proposed in [1, 2, 5, 6] are all insecure against the malicious original signer(s). For the HW scheme [5] and the HWH scheme [6] which use the same self-certified public keys, we show that they suffer from the *cheat attack*; namely, a malicious signer can cheat the CA (Certificate Authority) into *extracting a proxy signing key*. For both schemes, a malicious original signer can cheat CA into extracting a proxy signing key of a proxy signer. For the HWH scheme, furthermore, this attack can be used by a malicious proxy signer to cheat CA into extracting a proxy signing key without the permission of the original signer. Previously, Shao [10] introduced this attack for the proxy signature scheme in [4] using the same self-certified public keys. The reason why it can be applied is that CA does not able to confirm the information a user sent in the Registration stage. Our contribution is to show that this attack can be applied to the group-oriented schemes. Independently, we show that the HWH scheme also suffers from the original signer's proxy signing key forgery attack under some restrictions. Furthermore, the CCH-1 [1] and CCH-2 [2] are also vulnerable to one original signer's and all original signers' proxy signing forgery attack, respectively. Forgery by the original signer(s) means that some malicious original signers can generate valid proxy signatures which look as if they are generated by a proxy signer [11]. For this purpose, original signer(s) generally forges a proxy signing key and uses it to make a signature forgery. Our attack may be variously interpreted according to the circumstances. If a vulnerable scheme is proxy-unprotected, then the multi-signature scheme is insecure because one original signer can forge a multi-signature in the name of the group of original signers. Else if a vulnerable scheme is claimed as proxy-protected, then it is wrong because a valid proxy signature can be generated by the original signer besides the proxy signer. Although the cheat attack for the HW and HWH schemes is caused by the flaw of the self-certified public keys they used, the original signer's proxy signing key forgery attack for the HWH, CCH-1 and CCH-2 schemes comes from the security flaw of the proxy multi-signature itself.

The rest of this paper is organized as follows. The security analysis of the HW scheme [5] is given in Section 2. In Section 3, the HWH scheme proposed by [6] is analyzed. Then, we analyze the security of the CCH scheme [1, 2] in Section 4. Finally, we conclude our paper in Section 5.

2 The HW Scheme and Its Security Analysis

The HW scheme is based on the notion of self-certified public keys [3], in which each user's public key is generated by CA satisfying computationally unforgeable property and the corresponding private key is computed by the user. So no certificate is required for verifying the authenticity. Instead, the authenticity of public keys is implicitly verified with the subsequent cryptographic applications such as signature verification. To realize this notion, the HW scheme uses the self-certified public keys proposed in [4]. This scheme consists of four stages: Registration, Proxy secret share generation, Proxy signature generation and Proxy signature verification.

Let p, q be two large primes, where $q|(p-1)$ and g be a generator of a subgroup of order q in $\mathbb{F}_p^*$, and let h be a hash function. The parameters (p, q, g) and the function h are made public. The symbol $\mathrm{ID}_i{}^1$ is defined as the identity (or identifier) associated with the user U_i. The private and public keys for CA are denoted as γ and β, respectively, where $\gamma \in \mathbb{Z}_q^*$ and $\beta = g^\gamma \bmod p$.

Registration: Each user U_i associated with the identifier ID_i randomly chooses an integer $t_i \in \mathbb{Z}_q^*$, computes

$$v_i = g^{h(t_i\|\mathrm{ID}_i)} \bmod p$$

and then sends (v_i, ID_i) to CA. After receiving (v_i, ID_i) from U_i, CA chooses $z_i \in \mathbb{Z}_q^*$, computes

$$y_i = v_i h(\mathrm{ID}_i)^{-1} g^{z_i} \bmod p, \quad e_i = z_i + h(y_i\|\mathrm{ID}_i)\gamma \bmod q, \tag{1}$$

and returns (y_i, e_i) to U_i. Then, U_i computes

$$x_i = e_i + h(t_i\|\mathrm{ID}_i) \bmod q$$

and verifies its validity by checking that

$$\beta^{h(y_i\|\mathrm{ID}_i)} h(\mathrm{ID}_i)y_i = g^{x_i} \bmod p. \tag{2}$$

If it holds, then U_i accepts (x_i, y_i) as it own private/public key pair.

---

[1] In [5], ID is regarded as an element of $\mathbb{Z}_q^*$.

Proxy secret share generation: Let U_o be the original signer with key pair (x_o, y_o), $G = \{U_1, \ldots, U_n\}$ be a group of n proxy signers, and let PID be the set of all identities associated with the members in G. The original signer U_o can delegate his signing power to the group G in such a way that at least t proxy signers can sign messages on behalf of U_o and G. For delegating the signing power, U_o performs the following steps:

Step 1: Randomly chooses an integer $k \in \mathbb{Z}_q^*$, and computes

$$K = g^k \left(\beta^{\sum_{i=1}^{n} h(y_i \| \mathrm{ID}_i)} \prod_{i=1}^{n} (h(\mathrm{ID}_i)y_i) \right)^{-1} \mod p,$$

$$\sigma = h(m_w \| K \| PID)x_o + k \mod q,$$

where m_w is the warrant consisting of the original and the proxy signers' identifiers, the delegation duration, the threshold value t and etc.

Step 2: Determines a $(t-1)$-th degree polynomial $f(x)$ with coefficients $a_i \in \mathbb{Z}_q^*$ and computes A_i's (for $i = 1, 2, \ldots, t-1$), where

$$f(x) = \sigma + a_1 x + a_2 x^2 + \cdots a_{t-1} x^{t-1} \mod q, \quad \text{and} \quad A_i = g^{a_i} \mod p.$$

Step 3: Sends the proxy secret share $\sigma_i = f(\mathrm{ID}_i)$ to each proxy signer $U_i \in G$ via a secure channel.

Upon receiving σ_i from U_o, each $U_i \in G$ checks its validity by the following equation:

$$g^{\sigma_i} = \left(\beta^{h(y_o \| \mathrm{ID}_o)} h(\mathrm{ID}_o)y_o \right)^{h(m_w \| K \| PID)} K \beta^{\sum_{j=1}^{n} h(y_j \| \mathrm{ID}_j)} \prod_{j=1}^{n} (h(\mathrm{ID}_j)y_j)$$

$$\times \prod_{j=1}^{t-1} A_j^{\mathrm{ID}_i^j} \mod p.$$

If it holds, then the proxy secret share σ_i is verified.

Proxy signature generation: Given a message m, any t or more proxy signers in G can generate a valid proxy signature on behalf of U_o in this stage. Without loss of generality, let $D = \{U_1, U_2, \ldots, U_t\}$ be the group of actual proxy signers and let $ASID$ be the collection of identities of all members in D. All members in D cooperatively signs m on behalf of U_o by performing the following steps.

Step 1: Each $U_i \in D$ chooses a random integers $k_i \in \mathbb{Z}_q^*$ and then broadcasts $r_i = g^{k_i} \mod p$.

Step 2: Upon obtaining all r_j's $(j = 1, 2, \ldots, t$ and $j \neq i)$, each $U_i \in D$ computes

$$R = (m \| h(m)) \prod_{i=1}^{t} r_i^{r_i} \mod p,$$

$$s_i = k_i r_i + L_i \sigma_i h(PID \| R \| K) + x_i h(ASID \| R \| K) \mod q,$$

where $L_i = \prod_{j=1, i \neq j}^{t} -\text{ID}_j(\text{ID}_i - \text{ID}_j)^{-1} \bmod q$. And then sends to the designated clerk.

Step 3: Upon receiving s_i, the designated clerk validates it by checking

$$
\begin{aligned}
g^{s_i} = r_i^{r_i} &\left(\beta^{h(y_i\|\text{ID}_i)} h(\text{ID}_i)y_i\right)^{h(ASID\|R\|K)} \\
&\left(\left(\beta^{h(y_o\|\text{ID}_o)} h(\text{ID}_o)y_o\right)^{h(m_w\|K\|PID)} K\beta^{\sum_{i=1}^{n} h(y_i\|\text{ID}_j)} \prod_{j=1}^{n} \left(h(\text{ID}_j)y_j\right)\right. \\
&\left.\times \prod_{j=1}^{t-1} A_j^{\text{ID}_i^j}\right)^{L_i h(PID\|R\|K)} \bmod p.
\end{aligned}
$$

If it holds, then (r_i, s_i) is the valid individual proxy signature of m with respect to U_i. If all received (r_i, s_i)'s $(i = 1, \ldots, t)$ are verified, then the clerk computes

$$
S = \sum_{i=1}^{t} s_i \bmod q
$$

and announces the proxy signature $(PID, ASID, K, m_w, (R, S))$ for the message m.

Proxy signature verification: On receiving $(PID, ASID, K, m_w, (R, S))$ as the proxy signature, the verifier recovers $m\|h(m)$ from the following equality:

$$
\begin{aligned}
m\|h(m) = Rg^{-S} &\left(\beta^{\sum_{i=1}^{t} h(y_i\|\text{ID}_i)} \prod_{i=1}^{t} \left(h(\text{ID}_i)y_i\right)\right)^{h(ASID\|R\|K)} \\
&\left(\left(\beta^{h(y_o\|\text{ID}_o)} h(\text{ID}_o)y_o\right)^{h(m_w\|K\|PID)} K\beta^{\sum_{i=1}^{n} h(y_i\|\text{ID}_i)}\right. \qquad (3) \\
&\left.\times \prod_{i=1}^{n} \left(h(\text{ID}_i)y_i\right)\right)^{h(PID\|R\|K)} \bmod p.
\end{aligned}
$$

The proxy signature $(PID, ASID, K, m_w, (R, S))$ for m is valid if the hash value of m and the recovered $h(m)$ is identical.

Now we discuss the security of this scheme. Suppose that a malicious original signer U_o with identity ID_o wants to compute a threshold proxy signature without the agreement of the proxy group $G = \{U_1, \ldots, U_n\}$. Let PID be the set of all identities associated with the members in G, and let $ASID$ be the set of all identities associated with the actual signers $\{U_1, \ldots, U_t\}$ in G whom U_o wants to be involved in the forged signature. For each $1 \leq i \leq n$, let U_i have private/public key pair (x_i, y_i) satisfying Eq. (2). For an important special message m, U_o randomly chooses integers $k \in \mathbb{Z}_q^*$ and $k_i \in \mathbb{Z}_q^*$ for each $i = 1, 2, \ldots, t$, then computes

$$r_i = g^{k_i} \bmod p, \quad K = g^k \left(\beta^{\sum_{i=1}^n h(y_i \| \mathrm{ID}_i)} \prod_{i=1}^n \left(h(\mathrm{ID}_i) y_i \right) \right)^{-1} \bmod p,$$

$$R = m \| h(m) \prod_{i=1}^t r_i^{r_i} \bmod p,$$

and sets

$$\alpha = \frac{h(ASID \| R \| K)}{h(m_w \| K \| PID) h(PID \| R \| K)}.$$

To obtain the forged signature looked as being signed by the proxy signers associated with $ASID$, U_o cheats CA during the Registration stage. It is possible because CA does not confirm the information the user sent to receive a public key. First, U_o randomly chooses an integer $t \in \mathbb{Z}_q^*$, computes

$$v = g^{h(t \| \mathrm{ID}_o)} \left(\beta^{\sum_{i=1}^t h(y_i \| \mathrm{ID}_i)} \prod_{i=1}^t \left(h(\mathrm{ID}_i) y_i \right) \right)^{-\alpha} \bmod p$$

and sends (v, ID_o) to CA. Then CA chooses $z \in \mathbb{Z}_q^*$, computes

$$y_o = v h(\mathrm{ID}_o)^{-1} g^z \bmod p, \quad e = z + h(y_o \| \mathrm{ID}_o) \gamma \bmod q$$

as Eq. (1) and returns (y_o, e) to U_o. If

$$\beta^{h(y_o \| \mathrm{ID}_o)} h(\mathrm{ID}_o) y_o \left(\beta^{\sum_{i=1}^t h(y_i \| \mathrm{ID}_i)} \prod_{i=1}^t \left(h(\mathrm{ID}_i) y_i \right) \right)^{\alpha} = g^{e + h(t \| \mathrm{ID}_o)} \bmod p$$

holds, then U_o accepts (x_o, y_o) as its own private/public key pair where $x_o = e + h(t \| \mathrm{ID}_o) \bmod q$. Now, U_o computes

$$S' = \left(\sum_{i=1}^t k_i r_i \right) + x_o h(m_w \| K \| PID) h(PID \| R \| K) + k h(PID \| R \| K) \bmod q,$$

and announces the proxy signature $(PID, ASID, m_w, K, (R, S'))$ for the message m. It can be easily checked that this forged signature satisfies Eq. (3). Hence, $(PID, ASID, m_w, K, (R, S'))$ is a valid threshold proxy signature which looks like being signed by the malicious signer U_o and the proxy signers associated with $ASID$ together. As a result, the malicious original signer U_o always can generate a valid threshold proxy signature for a message m.

Remark 1. Recently, we found that the threshold proxy signature scheme proposed by Xue and Cao [12] was also based on the same self-certified public keys. By the similar method for the HW scheme, we can show that it is vulnerable to the cheat attack by the original signer. We give a detailed account of the attack in the full version of this paper [9].

In the next section, we show that the HWH proxy multi-signature scheme is also insecure against the cheat attack. Although these signatures have a different type, the same attack can be applied due to the weakness of the self-certified public keys they used.

3   The HWH Scheme and Its Security

In [6], the authors proposed two schemes: one is proxy-unprotected and the other is proxy-protected. Even though the following attack is possibly applied to the proxy-unprotected scheme, for brevity, we only consider the proxy-protected one. This scheme consists of four stages: Registration, Proxy signing key generation, Proxy signature generation and Proxy signature verification. Although there is no notification in [6], this scheme uses the same self-certified public keys with the HW scheme and so the same system parameters. Detail descriptions of the four stages except Registration are stated as follows.

Registration: As in the Registration stage of the HW scheme, each user U with the identity ID_U obtains its own private/public key pair (x_U, y_U) according to the procedures in this stage.

Proxy signing key generation: Let $A_1, \ldots, A_n$ with the key pair (x_i, y_i) be the n original signers who jointly delegate their signing power to the proxy signer B. Each original signer A_i randomly chooses an integer $k_i \in \mathbb{Z}_q^*$, computes $K_i = g^{k_i} \bmod p$, and broadcasts K_i to other original signers. Upon getting all K_j's from A_j $(1 \leq j \leq n$ and $j \neq i)$, A_i computes $K = \prod_{i=1}^{n} K_i \bmod p$ and $\sigma_i = h(m_w \| K) x_i + k_i \bmod q$. Using a secure channel, A_i sends $(m_w, (K_i, \sigma_i))$ to B who then verifies the validity by checking that

$$g^{\sigma_i} = \left(\beta^{h(y_i \| \mathrm{ID}_i)} h(\mathrm{ID}_i) y_i \right)^{h(m_w \| K)} K_i \bmod p.$$

If all $(m_w, (K_i, \sigma_i))$'s are valid, B computes $K = \prod_{i=1}^{n} K_i \bmod p$ and its own proxy signing key as

$$\sigma = x_B + \sum_{i=1}^{n} \sigma_i \bmod q.$$

Proxy signature generation and verification: For signing m on behalf of the original signers $\{A_1, \ldots, A_n\}$, B uses σ to generate a valid proxy signature $(K, m_w, \mathrm{Sig}_\sigma(m))$, where $\mathrm{Sig}_\sigma(m)$ denotes the ordinary signature operation with the signing key σ on message m as used in [6]. For verifying the signature, verifiers first compute the public value for the original signers and the proxy signer as

$$y' = \beta^{h(y_B \| \mathrm{ID}_B)} h(\mathrm{ID}_B) y_B K \left(\beta^{\sum_{i=1}^{n} h(y_i \| \mathrm{ID}_i)} \prod_{i=1}^{n} \left(h(\mathrm{ID}_i) y_i \right) \right)^{h(m_w \| K)} \bmod p, \tag{4}$$

then verify the signature following the operation corresponding to the generation of it. It works well because y' stands for g^σ.

Remark 2. There is a minor error in the computation of Eq. (4) in [6]. The authors suggest computing the following y''

$$y'' = \left(\beta^{h(y_B \| ID_B) + \sum_{i=1}^{n} h(y_i \| \mathrm{ID}_i)} h(\mathrm{ID}_B) y_B \prod_{i=1}^{n} \left(h(\mathrm{ID}_i) y_i \right) \right)^{h(m_w \| K)} K \bmod p$$

as the public value for the original signers, even in the case of proxy-protected scheme. However, to use

$$\sigma = x_B + \sum_{i=1}^{n} \sigma_i = x_B + \sum_{i=1}^{n} (h(m_w\|K)x_i + k_i) \bmod q$$

as the proxy signing key, we should not raise $\beta^{h(y_B\|ID_B)}h(ID_B)y_B \bmod p$ to $h(m_w\|K)$ powers.

Now, we discuss the security of this scheme. We will show that a malicious proxy signer can forge the proxy signing key without the permission of the original signers, and also that a malicious original signer is able to generate the proxy signing key without the approval of the other original signers and a proxy signer in such way to register its own public key faked.

Besides the above cheat attacks, this scheme enables the original signer to generate valid proxy signatures regarded as being signed by a proxy signer when there are only one original signer involved. It means that the HWH scheme is used as a proxy signature scheme not as a proxy multi-signature scheme. This restricted scheme is proxy-protected, so our attack implies that it has a security flaw.

The Cheat Attack by a Malicious Proxy Signer. Suppose that a malicious proxy signer $\mathcal{B}$ with identity $ID_\mathcal{B}$ chooses the members of original signers, A_i for $i = 1, 2, \ldots, n$ without whose permission $\mathcal{B}$ wants to extract a proxy signing key. According to the Registration stage, A_i has private/public key pair (x_i, y_i) satisfying Eq. (2).

In order to compute a proxy signing key in the name of A_i's, $\mathcal{B}$ randomly chooses integers $k_i \in \mathbb{Z}_q^*$ for each $i = 1, 2, \ldots, n$, computes

$$K = \prod_{i=1}^{n} g^{k_i} \bmod p$$

and sets $\alpha = h(m_w\|K)$ where m_w is the forged warrant consisting of the original signers' identities and the proxy signer's identity, the delegation duration, etc. Then $\mathcal{B}$ chooses a random $t \in \mathbb{Z}_q^*$, computes

$$v = g^{h(t\|ID_\mathcal{B})} \left(\beta^{\sum_{i=1}^{n} h(y_i\|ID_i)} \prod_{i=1}^{n} y_i h(ID_i) \right)^{-\alpha} \bmod p$$

and sends $(v, ID_\mathcal{B})$ to CA. With $(v, ID_\mathcal{B})$, CA chooses $z \in \mathbb{Z}_q^*$, computes

$$y = vh(ID_\mathcal{B})^{-1}g^z \bmod p, \quad e = z + h(y\|ID_\mathcal{B})\gamma \bmod q$$

as Eq. (1) and returns (y, e) to $\mathcal{B}$. If

$$\beta^{h(y\|ID_\mathcal{B})}h(ID_\mathcal{B})y \left(\beta^{\sum_{i=1}^{n} h(y_i\|ID_i)} \prod_{i=1}^{n} h(ID_i)y_i \right)^{\alpha} = g^{e+h(y\|ID_\mathcal{B})} \bmod p$$

holds, $\mathcal{B}$ accepts (x, y) as its own private/public key pair where $x = e + h(y\|\mathrm{ID}_\mathcal{B}) \bmod q$. Using chosen k_i's in advance, $\mathcal{B}$ computes a proxy signing key σ' as follows

$$\sigma' = x + \sum_{i=1}^{n} k_i \bmod q.$$

Then $\mathcal{B}$ uses σ' to sign messages on behalf of A_i, $i = 1, \ldots, n$ if

$$g^{\sigma'} = \beta^{h(y\|\mathrm{ID}_\mathcal{B})} h(\mathrm{ID}_\mathcal{B}) y K \left(\beta^{\sum_{i=1}^{n} h(y_i\|\mathrm{ID}_i)} \prod_{i=1}^{n} (h(\mathrm{ID}_i) y_i) \right)^{h(m_w\|K)} \bmod p \quad (5)$$

satisfies. Then the public value y' computed in Eq. (4) is equal to $g^{\sigma'}$, the forged proxy signing key σ' has the same property as that of the proxy signing key generated by the cooperation between the original signers and the proxy signer.

The Cheat Attack by a Malicious Original Signer. Suppose that a malicious original signer $\mathcal{A}$ with identity $\mathrm{ID}_\mathcal{A}$ wants to compute a proxy signing key without the permission of the original signers $A_1, \cdots, A_n$ and the proxy signer B. $\mathcal{A}$ cheats CA during the Registration stage. Let each A_i and B have private/public key pairs (x_i, y_i) and (x_B, y_B) satisfying Eq. (2), respectively.

First, $\mathcal{A}$ randomly chooses an integer $t \in \mathbb{Z}_q^*$, computes

$$v = g^{h(t\|\mathrm{ID}_\mathcal{A})} \left(\beta^{\sum_{i=1}^{n} h(y_i\|\mathrm{ID}_i)} \prod_{i=1}^{n} (h(\mathrm{ID}_i) y_i) \right)^{-1} \bmod p$$

and sends $(v, \mathrm{ID}_\mathcal{A})$ to CA. Then CA chooses $z \in \mathbb{Z}_q^*$, computes

$$y = v h(\mathrm{ID}_\mathcal{A})^{-1} g^z \bmod p, \quad e = z + h(y\|\mathrm{ID}_\mathcal{A}) \gamma \bmod q$$

as Eq. (1) and returns (y, e) to $\mathcal{A}$. If

$$\beta^{h(y\|\mathrm{ID}_\mathcal{A}) + \sum_{i=1}^{n} h(y_i\|\mathrm{ID}_i)} h(\mathrm{ID}_\mathcal{A}) y \prod_{i=1}^{n} (h(\mathrm{ID}_i) y_i) = g^{e + h(t\|\mathrm{ID}_\mathcal{A})} \bmod p$$

holds, then $\mathcal{A}$ accepts (x, y) as its own private/public key pair and public key where $x = e + h(t\|\mathrm{ID}_\mathcal{A}) \bmod q$. Now, $\mathcal{A}$ randomly chooses integers $k, k_i \in \mathbb{Z}_q^*$ for each $i = 1, 2, \ldots, n$, and computes

$$K = g^k \left(\beta^{h(y_B\|\mathrm{ID}_B)} h(\mathrm{ID}_B) y_B \right)^{-1} \prod_{i=1}^{n} g^{k_i} \bmod p,$$

$$\sigma' = h(m_w\|K) x + k + \sum_{i=1}^{n} k_i \bmod q,$$

where m_w is the forged warrant consisting of the original signers' identities and the proxy signer's identity, the delegation duration, etc. If

$$g^{\sigma'} = \beta^{h(y\|ID_B)} h(\mathrm{ID}_B) y_B K$$

$$\left(\beta^{h(y\|ID_\mathcal{A}) + \sum_{i=1}^{n} h(y_i\|\mathrm{ID}_i)} h(\mathrm{ID}_\mathcal{A}) y \prod_{i=1}^{n} (h(\mathrm{ID}_i) y_i) \right)^{h(m_w\|K)} \bmod p \quad (6)$$

holds, $\mathcal{A}$ can use σ' as a proxy signing key to sign messages on behalf of itself and A_i, $i = 1, \ldots, n$ which can be verified as valid signatures generated by the proxy signer B. Then the public value y' computed in Eq. (4) is equal to $g^{\sigma'}$, so $\mathcal{A}$ is enabled to generate valid proxy multi-signatures which are considered as valid ones signed by itself, the other original signers and the proxy signer together even without any approval of others.

The Original Signer's Proxy Signing Key Forgery Attack. In the HWH scheme, a proxy signing key is just summation of proxy sub key σ_i computed by original signer A_i for each $1 \leq i \leq n$ and x_B. We assume that only one original signer is involved in the HWH scheme. Then we can see it as a proxy signature scheme with one original signer. Let (x_A, y_A) and (x_B, y_B) be the private/public key pairs of a malicious original signer $\mathcal{A}$ and a honest proxy signer B, respectively. To attack this scheme, $\mathcal{A}$ chooses a random number $k \in \mathbb{Z}_q$, sets

$$K = g^k \left(\beta^{h(y_B \| \mathrm{ID}_B)} h(\mathrm{ID}_B) y_B \right)^{-1} \bmod p$$

and computes the forged proxy signing key

$$\sigma = h(m_w \| K) x_A + k \bmod q$$

which is valid since

$$\sigma_A + x_B = h(m_w \| K) x_A + k - x_B + x_B = \sigma.$$

So the HWH scheme with one original signer does not meet the proxy-protected property.

This attack does not seem to be applied to the case that more than 2 original signers join. Since this scheme requires the random factor K which is an input element of hash function h to be $\prod_{i=1}^{n} K_i$ where K_i is a random factor chosen by A_i, one malicious user cannot omit $h(m_w \| K) x_i$ included in σ_i which can be generated by only other honest user, just by modifying K_i. In addition, our attack is not applicable to the similar proxy signature scheme in [4] due to the difference of the equation for computing proxy signature key σ. In [4], σ is computed by

$$\sigma = \sigma_A + h(m_w \| K) x_B \bmod q,$$

where $\sigma_A = h(m_w \| K) x_A + k \bmod q$ is the original signer $\mathcal{A}$'s signature for the warrant m_w. In this case, there is no way to remove the proxy signer's private key x_B which is not known to $\mathcal{A}$ at all. However, note that this modification does not help to resist the cheat attack.

4 The CCH Schemes and Its Security

In this section, we briefly recall proxy multi-signature schemes in [1, 2], and show that these schemes are all insecure against the proxy signing key forgery attack induced by either one or all of original signers.

This scheme is based on conventional PKI setting, so all schemes has three stages - Proxy signing key generation, Proxy signature generation and Proxy signature verification. Basically, they have the same system initialization that all original signers select the common elliptic curve domain parameters. Let q be a power of prime p and E be an ordinary elliptic curve over $\mathbb{F}_q$ and let h be a hash function. Assume that the order of E must be divisible by a large prime r. Then there is a base point $P = (x_P, y_P)$ which generates the largest cyclic subgroup of $E(\mathbb{F}_q)$.

For each $1 \leq i \leq n$, the original signer A_i secretly selects a random number $d_i \in \mathbb{Z}_r^*$ as its own private key, and computes the corresponding public key $Q_i = d_i P = (x_{Q_i}, y_{Q_i})$. The proxy signer also selects a random number $d_B \in \mathbb{Z}_r^*$ as its own private key, and then computes $Q_B = d_B P = (x_{Q_B}, y_{Q_B})$. Each public key Q_i ($1 \leq i \leq n$) and Q_B must be certificated by CA.

4.1   The CCH-1 Scheme and Its Security

In [1], the authors proposed two proxy multi-signature schemes: one is proxy-unprotected and the other is proxy-protected. The latter is based on the former by adding the usage of a warrant m_w. Due to the space limitation, we only consider the proxy-protected scheme, denoted by the CCH-1 scheme. Clearly, our attack is also applied to the proxy-unprotected scheme with small modifications.

Proxy signing key generation: For delegating the signing power, each A_i performs the following steps:

Step A-1: Selects a random number $k_i \in \mathbb{Z}_r^*$, and computes

$$R_i = k_i P = (x_{R_i}, y_{R_i}) \quad \text{and} \quad s_i = d_i x_{Q_i} h(m_w, R_i) - k_i \bmod r.$$

Step A-2: Sends $\sigma_i = (m_w, (R_i, s_i))$ to the proxy signer via a secure channel.

Upon receiving σ_i from A_i for each $1 \leq i \leq n$, the proxy signer B generates a proxy signing key by the following steps:

Step B-1: Computes

$$U_i = \left(x_{Q_i} h(m_w, R_i) \right) Q_i - s_i P = (x_{U_i}, y_{U_i})$$

and checks $x_{U_i} = x_{R_i} \bmod r$.

Step B-2: If all σ_i is valid, then computes the proxy signing key as follows:

$$d = d_B x_{Q_B} + \sum_{i=1}^{n} s_i \bmod r.$$

Proxy signature generation and verification: When B signs a message m on behalf of the original signers $\{A_1, \ldots, A_n\}$, B executes one ECDLP-based ordinary signing algorithm with the proxy signing key d as used in [1]. Assuming that the resulting signature is $\text{Sig}_d(m)$, then the proxy signature affixed to the m for the original signers is in the form of $(m, R_1, \ldots, R_n, \text{Sig}_d(m))$. For verifying the signature, the verifier first computes the proxy public value Q corresponding to the proxy signing key d as

$$Q = x_{Q_B}Q_B + \sum_{i=1}^{n}\left(\left(x_{Q_i}h(m_w, R_i)\right)Q_i - R_i\right) (= dP).$$

With this value, the verifier confirms the validity of $\text{Sig}_d(m)$ by validating the verification equation of the designated signature scheme.

Now we discuss the security of the CCH-1 scheme. Without loss of generality, we assume that A_1 is a malicious original signer and that easily generates the designated proxy warrant m_w negotiated by $A_1, \cdots, A_n$. To achieve A_1's forgery, A_1 operates as follows. At first, A_1 selects random numbers $k_1, \cdots, k_n \in \mathbb{Z}_r^*$, and then computes

$$R_1 = x_{Q_B}Q_B + k_1P + \sum_{i=2}^{n}\left(x_{Q_i}h(m_w, R_i)\right)Q_i = (x_{R_1}, y_{R_1}) \qquad (7)$$

where $R_i = k_iP = (x_{R_i}, y_{R_i})$ for $2 \leq i \leq n$. The forged proxy signing key d is given by

$$d = d_1x_{Q_1}h(m_w, R_1) - \sum_{i=1}^{n}k_i.$$

From Eq. (7), the proxy public value Q computed by any verifier satisfies the following equation:

$$Q = x_{Q_B}Q_B + \sum_{i=1}^{n}\left(x_{Q_i}h(m_w, R_i)\right)Q_i - \sum_{i=1}^{n}R_i$$

$$= \left(x_{Q_1}h(m_w, R_1)\right)Q_1 + \left(\sum_{i=1}^{n}k_i\right)P$$

$$= \left(d_1x_{Q_1}h(m_w, R_1) - \sum_{i=1}^{n}k_i\right)P = dP.$$

Hence any verifier can verify the validity of the proxy multi-signatures generated by using d. As a result, the malicious original signer A_1 can generate a proxy signing key d without the participation of the original signers $A_2, \cdots, A_n$ and even the proxy signer B.

4.2 The CCH-2 Scheme and Its Security

In comparison with the CCH-1 scheme, the scheme proposed in [2], denoted by the CCH-2 scheme has one more step in the Proxy signing key generation stage. In the CCH-1 scheme, each original signer sends information to the proxy signer on an individual basis. But the CCH-2 scheme requests that each original signer computes a value holding in common at first, and then generates information using it.

Proxy signing key generation: For delegating signing power, each A_i performs the following steps:

Step A-1: Selects a random number $k_i \in \mathbb{Z}_r^*$, and computes $R_i = k_i P = (x_{R_i}, y_{R_i})$.

Step A-2: If $x_{R_i} = 0$, then returns Step A-1; otherwise, broadcasts R_i to the other original signers.

Step A-3: Upon receiving R_j $(1 \leq j \leq n, i \neq j)$, computes $R = \sum_{i=1}^{n} R_i = (x_R, y_R)$.

Step A-4: Computes $s_i = d_i h(m_w, x_{Q_i}, x_{Q_B}, x_R) - k_i \bmod r$.

Step A-5: Sends $\sigma_i = (m_w, s_i)$ to the proxy signer via a public channel.

Upon receiving σ_i from A_i for each $1 \leq i \leq n$, the proxy signer B generates a proxy signing key by the following steps:

Step B-1: Computes $R_i' = (x_{R_i'}, y_{R_i'})$ as follows:

$$R_i' = h(m_w, x_{Q_i}, x_{Q_B}, x_R)Q_i - s_i P,$$

and checks $x_{R_i'} = x_{R_i} \bmod r$.

Step B-2: If all σ_i is valid, then computes the proxy signing key as follows:

$$d = d_B + \sum_{i=1}^{n} s_i \bmod r.$$

Proxy signature generation and verification: The proxy multi-signature affixed to the m is in the form of $(m, m_w, R, \mathrm{Sig}_d(m))$, where $\mathrm{Sig}_d(m)$ means the signature generated by a designated scheme using the proxy signing key d. For verifying the signature, the verifier computes the proxy public value Q corresponding to the proxy signing key d as

$$Q = Q_B + \sum_{i=1}^{n} h(m_w, x_{Q_i}, x_{Q_B}, x_R)Q_i - R.$$

With this value, the verifier confirms the validity of $\mathrm{Sig}_d(m)$ by validating the verification equation of the designated signature scheme.

Now we discuss the security of the CCH-2 scheme. As similar to the case of the CCH-1 scheme, our attack shows that this scheme is not proxy-protected. Different from above attacks, however, this attack is occurred by conspiracy of the original signers $A_1, \ldots, A_n$ to generate valid proxy multi-signatures without agreement of the proxy signer B.

The original signer A_i selects random numbers $k_i \in \mathbb{Z}_r^*$ and then computes $R_i = k_i P$ for $1 \leq i \leq n$. Furthermore, A_1 adds Q_B to R_1. Next, computes

$$R = \sum_{i=1}^{n} R_i = Q_B + \left(\sum_{i=1}^{n} k_i\right)P. \qquad (8)$$

The forged proxy signing key generated by the original signers $A_1, \ldots, A_n$ is as follows:

$$d = \sum_{i=1}^{n} \Big(d_i h(m_w, x_{Q_i}, x_{Q_B}, x_R) - k_i \Big).$$

From Eq. (8), the proxy public value Q computed by any verifier satisfies the following equation:

$$
\begin{aligned}
Q &= Q_B + \sum_{i=1}^{n} h(m_w, x_{Q_i}, x_{Q_B}, x_R) Q_i - R \\
&= Q_B + \Big(\sum_{i=1}^{n} d_i h(m_w, x_{Q_i}, x_{Q_B}, x_R) \Big) P - \Big(\sum_{i=1}^{n} k_i \Big) P - Q_B \\
&= \Big(\sum_{i=1}^{n} d_i h(m_w, x_{Q_i}, x_{Q_B}, x_R) \Big) P - \Big(\sum_{i=1}^{n} k_i \Big) P \\
&= \Big(\sum_{i=1}^{n} \big(d_i h(m_w, x_{Q_i}, x_{Q_B}, x_R) - k_i \big) \Big) P = dP.
\end{aligned}
$$

This means that the verifier will be convinced that any proxy multi-signatures signed by using the forged signing key d are generated by agreement of $A_1, \ldots, A_n$ and B. Hence this scheme does not provide proxy-protected property as claimed in [2].

5   Conclusion

In this paper, we have presented a security analysis of some group-oriented proxy signature schemes proposed in [1, 2, 5, 6], and showed that all these schemes are insecure. For the HW scheme [5] and the HWH scheme [6], we showed that they suffer from the cheat attack caused by the flaw of the self-certified public keys they used. Additionally, the HWH scheme with one original signer and CCH-1 and 2 schemes are vulnerable to the proxy signing forgery attack by one or all of original signers.

Acknowledgement

The authors of this paper would like to thank anonymous referees for valuable comments. The second author was supported by the Korea Research Foundation Grant (KRF-2004-M07-2004-000-10054-0).

References

1. T.-S. Chen, Y.-F. Chung and G.-S. Huang. Efficient proxy multi-signature schemes based on the elliptic curve cryptosystem. *Comput. Secur.*, Vol. **22**(6): 527–534 (2003).

2. T.-S. Chen, Y.-F. Chung and G.-S. Huang. A traceable proxy multi-signature scheme based on the elliptic curve cryptosystem. *Appl. Math. Comput.*, Vol. **159**(1):137–145 (2004).
3. M. Girault. Self-certified public keys. *Advances in Cryptology - EUROCRYPT'91*, Lecture Notes in Comput. Sci. **547**, Springer-Verlag, pp. 257–265, 1991.
4. C.-L. Hsu and T.-S. Wu. Efficient proxy signature schemes using self-certified public keys. *Appl. Math. Comput.*, Vol. **152**(3): 807–820 (2004).
5. C.-L. Hsu and T.-S. Wu. Self-certified threshold proxy signature schemes with message recovery, nonrepudiation, and traceability. *Appl. Math. Comput.*, Vol. **164**(1):201–225 (2005).
6. C.-L. Hsu, T.-S. Wu and W.-H. He. New proxy multi-signature scheme. *Appl. Math. Comput.*, Vol. **162**(3):1201-1206 (2005).
7. S. Kim, S. Park and D. Won. Proxy signatures, revisited. *Information and Communications Security - ICICS'97*, Lecture Notes in Comput. Sci. **1334**, Springer-Verlag, pp. 223–232, 1997.
8. M. Mambo, K. Usuda and E. Okamoto. Proxy signatures for delegating signing operation. *Proc. 3rd ACM conference on Computer and Communications Security*, ACM press, pp. 48–57, 1996.
9. J.H. Park, B.G. Kang and S. Park. Cryptanalysis of some group-oriented proxy signature schemes. Full version of this paper. Availabel at `http://crypt.kaist.ac.kr/jhpark/`.
10. Z. Shao. Improvement of efficient proxy signature schemes using self-certified public keys. *Appl. Math. Comput.*, in press (2004).
11. G. Wang, F. Bao, J. Zhou and R.H. Deng. Security analysis of some proxy signatures. *Information Security and Cryptology - ICISC 2003*, Lecture Notes in Comput. Sci. **2971**, Springer-Verlag, pp. 305–319, 2004.
12. Q. Xue and Z. Cao. A threshold proxy signature scheme using self-certified public keys. *Parallel and Distributed Processing and Applications - ISPA 2004*, Lecture Notes in Comput. Sci. **3358**, Springer-Verlag, pp. 715–724, 2004.
13. L. Yi, G. Bai and G. Xizo. Proxy multi-signature scheme: a new type of proxy signature scheme. *Electron. Lett.*, Vol. **36**(6):527–528 (2000).
14. K. Zhang. Threshold proxy signature schemes. *Information Security - ISW'97*, Lecture Notes in Comput. Sci. **1396**, Springer-Verlag, pp. 282–290, 1997.

Application of LFSRs in Time/Memory Trade-Off Cryptanalysis

Sourav Mukhopadhyay and Palash Sarkar

Cryptology Research Group,
Applied Statistics Unit,
Indian Statistical Institute,
203, B.T. Road, Kolkata 700108, India
{sourav_t, palash}@isical.ac.in

Abstract. Time/memory trade-off (TMTO) attacks require the generation of a sequence of functions which are obtained as minor modifications of a one-way function to be inverted. We carefully examine the requirements for such function generation. A counter based method is used to generate the functions for the rainbow method. We show that there are functions for which the counter method fails. This is similar to the example given by Fiat and Naor for the Hellman TMTO. Our main contribution is to suggest the use of LFSR sequences for function generation to be used in the rainbow TMTO. Properties of LFSR sequences such as long period, pseudorandomness properties and efficient forward and backward generation make such sequences useful for the intended application. One specific advantage is that it is not possible to a priori construct a Fiat-Naor type example for the LFSR based rainbow method.

Keywords: Time/memory trade-off, LFSR, rainbow table.

1 Introduction

In 1980, Hellman [5] described a time/memory trade-off (TMTO) attack for block ciphers. This is a chosen plaintext attack. Let $E_k()$ be the encryption function of the block cipher. A fixed message msg is chosen and a one-way function f is defined from keys to ciphertexts by $f(k) = E_k(\text{msg})$. Given a ciphertext cpr, produced by encrypting msg using an unknown key k, i.e., $f(k) = \text{cpr}$, the task of the cryptanalyst is to obtain k. This can be seen as inverting a one-way function f and later work has viewed TMTO as a general one-way function inverter. See [6, 2] for some recent applications and analysis.

In an offline phase, a set of tables is constructed. The tables store keys and an encryption of msg under an unknown key is received in the online phase. The goal is to find the unknown key by making use of these precomputed tables. The main idea of Hellman was to store only a part of the tables. This incurs a cost in the online phase and leads to a trade-off between the memory and online time requirements.

J. Song, T. Kwon, and M. Yung (Eds.): WISA 2005, LNCS 3786, pp. 25–37, 2006.
© Springer-Verlag Berlin Heidelberg 2006

Suppose there are r tables to be used in the Hellman method. The ith table requires the use of a function f_i which is obtained from f by a minor modification such as permuting the output bits of f. For the method to work, the tables have to be assumed to be independent collection of random points. This requires the assumption that the functions f_i's are pairwise independent random functions.

Oechslin [11], proposed rainbow tables that reduces the online runtime cost to one-half of Hellman's method. The idea is to replace the collection of "small" tables by a (few) large table(s) and to use "rainbow chains" as rows of the table. As in the case of the Hellman method, assume that $f_0, \ldots, f_{t-1}$ are pairwise independent random functions obtained by modifying the one-way function f to be inverted. A rainbow chain is a sequence of points $x_0, \ldots, x_t$, where x_0 is randomly chosen and for $i \geq 0$, $x_{i+1} = f_i(x_i)$.

A crucial point in both the above constructions is to obtain the different functions f_i such that they can be assumed to be pairwise independent. In fact, Fiat and Naor [4] showed that there exists functions which are polynomial time indistinguishable from a random function and for which Hellman attack fails (if bit permutation is used to obtain the f_i's). They also proposed a method which provably succeeds for all functions but the time and memory requirement of their method is inferior to that of Hellman.

In case of rainbow tables, a counter based method is used to generate the rainbow chains. The function $f_i(x)$ is defined as $f(x) \oplus i$. If several rainbow tables are used, then the counter method is used in the following manner: if table one uses index 1 to 1000 (say), then table two uses functions 1001 to 2000, and so on.

We carefully examine the different requirements for defining the functions f_i. We show that the counter method does not ensure uniform modification of the output and an adaptation of Fiat-Naor [4] counterexample for Hellman method also works for rainbow with counter method .

This leads us to the question of obtaining a method to define the f_i's such that the output modification is uniform. Our main contribution is to show that sequences produced by linear feedback shift registers (LFSRs) are a natural choice for such an application. LFSR sequences are very efficient to generate in the forward and backward directions; they satisfy certain nice pseudorandomness properties; it is quite easy to generate very long non-repeating sequences of bit vectors. All these properties make LFSR sequences very suitable for defining the functions required in rainbow chains for one or more tables. One advantage of using LFSRs is that it is not possible to a priori construct a Fiat-Naor type example for the LFSR based rainbow method.

Details of an LFSR based multiple table rainbow method is presented and analysed. It turns out that for the same pre-computation time, the success probability of multiple table rainbow method is higher than that of Hellman method or the single table rainbow method. On the other hand, the runtime of the multiple table method is slightly higher. We show that a Kim-Matsumoto style parametrization is possible for the rainbow method and yield a higher success probability than the single table rainbow method without changing the runtime or the memory requirement.

2   Time/Memory Trade-Off Methodology

Let $f : \{0,1\}^n \to \{0,1\}^m$ be the one-way function to be inverted. As mentioned in the Introduction, this function maybe obtained from a block cipher by considering the map from the keyspace to the cipherspace for a fixed message. In general, the time/memory trade-off (TMTO) methodology attempts to invert an arbitrary one-way function and we will follow this approach.

The value of m maybe less than, equal to, or greater than n. The last case occurs in Hellman's original TMTO where f is obtained from DES and maps 56-bit keys to 64-bit ciphertexts. The first case can occur in obtaining f from AES, where 256-bit keys can be mapped to 128-bit ciphertexts. However, the TMTO methodology requires f to be applied iteratively and for this we must have $m = n$. The solution suggested by Hellman in [5] for the case $m > n$ is to use a so-called "reduction function", which maps a 64-bit string to a 56-bit string. Hellman further suggested that the reduction can be as simple as dropping the first eight bits. A dual strategy for expansion can be used in the case where $m < n$. Assuming these to have taken place, TMTO methodology considers the domain and range of f to be the same and hence f can be iteratively applied. We will follow this approach and in the rest of the paper we will assume f is a map from $f : \{0,1\}^n \to \{0,1\}^n$. Thus, our problem will be that given a string y, we will have to find a string x such that $f(x) = y$. We will denote $N = 2^n$.

In the following by $(f \circ g)(x)$ we will mean $f(g(x))$ and similarly for the composition of more than two functions.

2.1   The Hellman Method

Hellman's attack consists of two phases: precomputing the tables in an offline phase and searching the tables in an online phase. In a precomputed table, chains of length t are generated from a start point x_0 as,

$$x_0 \xrightarrow{f} x_1 \xrightarrow{f} x_2 \to \cdots \to x_{t-2} \xrightarrow{f} x_{t-1} \xrightarrow{f} x_t.$$

For an $m \times t$ table, m chains of length t are generated. The start points and the end points of the table are stored, sorted in the increasing order of end points. The intermediate points are not stored.

Using the birthday paradox [1], m and t have to satisfy $mt^2 = N$. So one table can cover only a fraction $\frac{mt}{N} = \frac{1}{t}$ of the N points. Hence, t different (unrelated) tables are needed to cover all N keys. These are created as follows. For the t tables, t different functions $f_1, \ldots, f_t$ are used, where each f_i is a simple output modification of the function f, i.e. $f_i(x) = \psi_i(f(x))$, where ψ_i is the ith output modification function. The total memory requirement is $m \times t$ many start-point/end-point pairs.

In the online phase, given y, it is required to find x such that $y = f(x)$. The t tables are searched one after the other. The search for x in the ith is as follows. We repeatedly apply f_i to $\psi_i(y)$ at most t times and after each application we check whether the output of f_i is in the set of end points of the ith table. The number of table lookups for this is at most t. If the output is an end point, then we come to the corresponding start point and repeatedly apply the function f_i until it reaches $\psi_i(y)$. The previous value it visited is x. The total runtime for searching in all the tables is $= t^2 + t \approx t^2$ invocations of f and t^2 table look-ups.

2.2   Rainbow Method

Rainbow table has been proposed by Oechslin [11] to reduce the runtime cost to one-half of Hellman's method. Rainbow chains are used in rainbow tables. To construct a rainbow chain of size t we choose t functions $f_0, f_1, \ldots, f_{t-1}$, which are again simple output modifications of f. Taking a start point x_0, a rainbow chain is generated as follows,

$$x_0 \xrightarrow{f_0} x_1 \xrightarrow{f_1} x_2 \rightarrow \cdots \rightarrow x_{t-1} \xrightarrow{f_{t-1}} x_t.$$

To construct a rainbow table of size $mt \times t$, we randomly choose mt keys from the key space and generate these many rainbow chains. The start and end points of the table are again stored in the increasing order of end points. The memory required is mt start-point/end-point pairs.

In the online phase, we will be given a y and we have to find an x such that $f(x) = y$. Suppose the functions $f_0, \ldots, f_{t-1}$ are used to define the rainbow chains, where $f_i(x) = \psi_i(f(x))$. For $0 \le j \le t-1$, we apply ψ_j to y and compute $y_0 = f_{t-1}(f_{t-2}(\ldots (f_{j+1}(\psi_j(y)) \ldots)$. If y_0 is in the last column of the table, then let x_0 be the corresponding start point. This gives us the equations:

$$\left. \begin{aligned} y_0 &= f_{t-1}(f_{t-2}(\ldots (f_{j+1}(\psi_j(y)) \ldots) \\ &= f_{t-1}(f_{t-2}(\ldots (f_1(f_0(x_0)) \ldots) \\ &= f_{t-1}(f_{t-2}(\ldots (f_{j+1}(f_j(x)) \ldots) \\ &= f_{t-1}(f_{t-2}(\ldots (f_{j+1}(\psi_j(f(x))) \ldots) \end{aligned} \right\} \tag{1}$$

where $x = f_{j-1}(f_{j-2}(\ldots (f_1(f_0(x_0)) \ldots)$. The first equality follows by the online search condition and the second equality follows from the table construction. From the first and last row of (1) we would like to infer that $y = f(x)$, i.e., x is a pre-image of y. Note that this might not always hold, leading to a false alarm. During the actual attack, this needs to be verified. The total runtime $= \frac{t(t-1)+2t}{2} \approx \frac{t^2}{2}$ invocations of f.

The same technique can be applied to multiple rainbow tables, even though this is not explicitly mentioned in the paper [11] but appears in the implementation [13]. If r tables are used, then the runtime increases to $rt^2/2$ and hence for practical implementation, r will be a small constant.

2.3   Time/Memory Trade-Off Curve

The online runtime T and memory requirement M of the Hellman method satisfy a so-called TMTO curve: $TM^2 = N^2$ and an important point on this curve is $M = T = N^{2/3}$ leading to $m = t = N^{1/3}$. The asymptotic behaviour of the rainbow method is same as that of the Hellman method and in an asymptotic sense the TMTO curves are the same. This is perhaps the reason, why the TMTO curve for the rainbow method is not explicitly given in [11]. For rainbow method, $M = N^{2/3}$ and $T = N^{2/3}/2$.

2.4   Success Probability

The success probability for any TMTO method is the probability that the key is present in the tables. The total size of all the tables is rmt, where r is the number of tables and each table has m rows and t columns. (Note that only rm pairs of keys are stored.) Thus, the repetition of the values in the tables reduces the success probability of the method. If we set $rmt = N$, then the success probability of both Hellman and rainbow method is known to be around 60%. Thus, to increase the success probability, it has been advocated [7, 13] to take $rmt = \lambda N$ for small λ. In fact, [7] has shown that it is possible to take $\lambda > 1$ in the Hellman method to increase the success probability but without increasing the online runtime or the memory.

3   Function Generation

In this section, we first consider the requirements on the functions f_i's. The definition of f_i has been suggested by Hellman to be $f_i(x) = \psi_i(f(x))$. We will call this to be the output modification approach. One can similarly consider $f_i(x) = f(\psi_i(x))$, or the input modification approach.

We first consider the case of input modification and argue that this is actually the same as output modification. Consider the rainbow method and suppose $f_i(x)$ is defined as $f_i(x) = f(\psi_i(x))$. Consider the rainbow chain

$$(f_{t-1} \circ f_{t-2} \circ \cdots \circ f_1 \circ f_0)(x_0)$$

where x_0 is a start point and $x_i = f_{i-1}(x_{i-1})$ for $i \geq 1$. Expanding the above sequence, we can write

$$(f \circ \psi_{t-1} \circ f \circ \psi_{t-2} \circ \cdots \circ f \circ \psi_1 \circ f \circ \psi_0)(x_0).$$

Now, for $1 \leq i \leq t - 1$, if we define $g_i(x) = \psi_i(f(x))$, then we get the rainbow chain $x_0', \ldots, x_{t-1}'$, where $x_0' = \psi_0(x_0)$ and $x_i' = g_i(x_{i-1}')$. This gives a rainbow chain of output modified form of length one less than the original chain. Also, note that x_0 is chosen to be a random point and hence it does not matter whether we start from x_0 or from $\psi_0(x_0)$. This shows that we can convert a chain of input modified form into a chain of output modified form. A similar conversion will also convert a chain of output modified form into a chain of input modified form. Further, the technique also works for the original Hellman method.

The literature considers only output modification. To the best of our knowledge, the above argument regarding input modification does not appear in the literature. In view of this argument, like previous papers, we will consider only output modification.

3.1   Invertibility

Consider the search technique of the rainbow method. From (1), we assume $f_j(x) = \psi_j(y)$ and infer that $f(x) = y$. If ψ_j is invertible, then using $f_j(x) = \psi_j(f(x)) = \psi_j(y)$, we have $f(x) = y$ and x is a pre-image of y. If ψ_j is not invertible, then the relation might not give a pre-image of y, leading to a false alarm. The condition ψ_j being invertible ensures that there are no false alarms due to the use of ψ_j. (Note that there may be false alarms due to f itself or due to the modification to f to make the domain and range same.) A similar argument shows that ψ_j's used in the Hellman method should also be invertible.

3.2   Efficient Function Generation

To apply the function f_i we need to apply f and the function ψ_i. For this we need a description of the function ψ_i. One approach is to store the description of all the t functions $\psi_0, \ldots, \psi_{t-1}$. This requires an additional storage space of order t. Since $t = N^{1/3}$ in both Hellman and rainbow method, this storage amount can be substantial. One way to avoid this storage is to generate the functions "on the fly". Thus, we need an efficient on the fly method to generate the functions ψ_i's.

3.3   Long Period

Consider the on-the-fly method discussed above. This means that we should actually be capable of generating a sequence of bit vectors and use these to define the functions ψ_i's. Since we do not want repetition of the functions, the sequence must consist of distinct bit vectors. In other words, it must be possible to generate a sequence of bit vectors with period long enough to ensure that all the ψ_i's are distinct.

3.4   Uniform Modification of Output

One simple way to achieve the above requirements is to use the so-called counter method. In this section, we discuss this method and its problem.

For both Hellman and rainbow method to work, the functions f_i's need to be pairwise unrelated. For the Hellman method, this requirement was carefully examined by Fiat and Naor [4]. They show that there exists functions, which are polynomial time indistinguishable from a truly random function and for which the Hellman attack fails with overwhelming probability. The following construction is given in [4]: consider a function f with the property that a certain set of $N^{1-\delta}$ domain points ($\delta < 1/3$) map to the same image. One can design a cryptographic scheme so that only $N - N^{1-\delta}$ of the keys induce a permutation and the other keys map all ciphertext values to zero. Hellman attack fails for such an f.

Rainbow method uses a sequence $f_0, f_1, \ldots, f_{t-1}$ of functions. These are generated using a counter. We argue that the counter method also suffers from a problem similar to the one described by Fiat and Naor for the Hellman method. Given a function f, rainbow method constructs the modification functions f_i by defining $f_i(x) = f(x) \oplus i$. Since $i \leq t$, this modifies at most the $\log t$ least significant bits of $f(x)$. Now one can construct a function f as follows: $f : \{0,1\}^n \to \{0,1\}^n$ with the property that for any $x \in \{0,1\}^n$, if $\mathsf{First}_{n_1}(x) = (0,0,\ldots,0)$ (n_1 bits) then $f(x) = (0,0,\ldots,0)$ (n bits). Let S_1 be the set of all n-bit vectors whose most significant n_1 bits are zero. Then the size of S_1 is $N_1 = 2^{n-n_1}$. We choose $n - \log t = n_1 < \frac{n}{3}$. Considering such a function, we may construct a cryptographic scheme so that $N - N_1$ of the keys induce a permutation and other keys map all ciphertext values to zero. For a rainbow chain

$$x_0 \xrightarrow{f_0} x_1 \xrightarrow{f_1} x_2 \to \ldots \to x_{t-1} \xrightarrow{f_{t-1}} x_t,$$

if any x_i is in S_1, then $x_{i+1}, x_{i+2}, \ldots$ up to x_{N_1} (if $N_1 \leq t$) are zeros. This will generate a huge number of zeros inside a rainbow table, resulting in the failure of rainbow method in this case.

For multiple rainbow tables, Oechslin [11, 12, 13] uses counter method to get rainbow tables as follows: the second rainbow table use a different set of reduction functions, i.e., if table one uses index 1 to 1000 (say), then table two uses functions 1001 to 2000. This method also suffers from the above mentioned problem and we may get a huge number of zeros inside the tables.

3.5   Pseudorandomness

One way to avoid the above problem is to define $f_i(x) = f(x) \oplus X_i$, where $X_0, X_2, \ldots, X_{t-1}$ is a pseudo-random sequence of n-bit vectors. This ensures that all output bits are uniformly modified unlike the counter method where only some least significant bits are modified. Further, the pseudorandom sequence $X_0, X_2, \ldots, X_{t-1}$ should be efficient to generate "on-the-fly". The cost of generating the next element of the sequence should be negligible compared to the cost of one invocation of f.

Choices like $f_i(x) = f(x) * i$ in $GF(2^n)$ or $f_i(x) = f(x) + f(i)$ can also provide uniform modification of the output. However, these are quite expensive operations, the first one involves a polynomial multiplication and the second one involves an extra invocation of f. *We would like to define f_i such that the cost of one invocation of f_i is almost the same as that of f.*

4   Introducing LFSRs as Function Generators

A linear feedback shift register (LFSR) [8, 9] of length l consists of l stages $0, 1, 2, \ldots, l - 1$, each capable of storing one bit. An l-bit LFSR is denoted by $(l, p(x))$, where $p(x) = 1 \oplus c_1 x \oplus \cdots \oplus c_{l-1} x^{l-1} \oplus x^l$ is called the connection polynomial [9]. LFSRs can produce sequences having large periods. If the initial content of stage i is $a_i \in \{0,1\}$, for $0 \leq i \leq l - 1$, then $(a_{l-1}, a_{l-2}, \ldots, a_0)$ is called the initial internal state of the LFSR. Let at time $t \geq 0$ the content of the stage i be $a_i^t \in \{0,1\}$, for $0 \leq i \leq l - 1$, then the internal state of the LFSR at time t is $(a_{l-1}^t, a_{l-2}^t, \ldots, a_0^t)$. Let $X_t = (a_{l-1}^t, \ldots, a_1^t, a_0^t)$ for $t \geq 0$, be a sequence of l-bit vectors, with t^{th} term as X_t. If $p(x)$ is a primitive polynomial, then each of the $2^l - 1$ non-zero initial states of the LFSR $(l, p(x))$ produces an output sequence with maximum possible period $2^l - 1$.

Let us consider the kth and $(k+1)^{th}$ terms of the sequence, i.e., $X_k = (a_{l-1}^k, \ldots, a_1^k, a_0^k)$ and $X_{k+1} = (a_{l-1}^{k+1}, \ldots, a_1^{k+1}, a_0^{k+1})$ respectively where,

$$\left. \begin{array}{l} a_{l-1}^{k+1} = c_{l-1} a_{l-1}^k \oplus c_{l-2} a_{l-2}^k \oplus \cdots \oplus c_1 a_1^k \oplus a_0^k; \\ a_{l-2}^{k+1} = a_{l-1}^k; a_{l-3}^{k+1} = a_{l-2}^k; \ldots; a_0^{k+1} = a_1^k. \end{array} \right\} \tag{2}$$

From (2), we get,

$$\left. \begin{array}{l} a_0^k = a_{l-1}^{k+1} \oplus c_{l-1} a_{l-2}^{k+1} \oplus c_{l-2} a_{l-3}^{k+1} \oplus \cdots \oplus c_1 a_0^{k+1}; \\ a_1^k = a_0^{k+1}; a_2^k = a_1^{k+1}; \ldots; a_{l-1}^k = a_{l-2}^{k+1}. \end{array} \right\} \tag{3}$$

Equations (2) and (3) show that forward and backward generation of LFSR sequences requires at most l XOR operations on bits and can be done very fast in hardware and software (see for example [3]).

In this paper, we consider binary LFSRs. We note, however, that the technique described in this paper also holds for LFSRs over larger alphabets and for other linear sequence generators like cellular automata.

In Hellman method, we can use an LFSR to generate the random variations of f as follows. For t Hellman tables we generate a sequence $X_1, X_2, \cdots, X_t$ of n-bit vectors using an LFSR $(n, p(x))$ (say). Then we construct f_i's as follows: $f_i(x) = f(x) \oplus X_i$ for $i = 1, 2, \ldots t$. We require the X_i's to be distinct. Choosing $l = n$ (recall that $f : \{0,1\}^n \to \{0,1\}^n$) and $p(x)$ to be a primitive polynomial will ensure this. Since the LFSR connection polynomial and the initial condition are chosen randomly *after* f is given, it is not possible to a priori construct a Fiat-Naor type example for the LFSR based Hellman method.

We now consider the application of LFSR sequences to the generation of functions for use in (multiple) rainbow tables. Suppose there are r tables each having t columns. We choose an LFSR of length $l = n$ having a primitive connection polynomial. Each bit vector in the sequence is of length n. Let the sequence be $X_0, \ldots, X_{rt-1}$.

Define $\psi_i(x) = x \oplus X_i$ and $f_i(x) = \psi_i(f(x)) = f(x) \oplus X_i$. The first table uses the functions $f_0, \ldots, f_{t-1}$; the second table uses the functions $f_t, \ldots, f_{2t-1}$; and so on. The functions ψ_i defined using the LFSR sequence satisfy the desirable properties discussed above. We mention some details.

Invertible: Each ψ_i is clearly invertible.

Efficient Generation: The function ψ_i is defined from X_i. Since the sequence $X_0, \ldots, X_{rt-1}$ is efficiently generable in both forward and backward directions, the corresponding functions are also efficiently generable.

Hardware Versus Software Implementation: A hardware implementation of the rainbow method is explored in [10] using FPGA platform, where a counter based method is used for function generation. However, a counter is slower than an LFSR in hardware. Counter method is fast in software implementation but slow in hardware implementation whereas LFSR based method is very fast in hardware implemetaion.

Long Period: For all the ψ_i's to be distinct, we need to have the X_i's to be distinct. The period of the sequence is $2^n - 1$. For the rainbow method, r is a small constant and $t = N^{1/3} = 2^{n/3}$. Thus, we have $2^n - 1 > rt$ and hence all the X_i's are distinct as required.

Pseudorandomness: LFSR sequences satisfy some nice pseudorandomness properties [8]. Using the ψ functions in the rainbow method means that at each stage the output of f is being XORed with a bit vector from the pseudorandom sequence $X_0, \ldots, X_{t-1}$. This, unlike the counter method, ensures a uniform modification of all the bits of the output of f.

Avoiding Fiat-Naor: An advantage of using LFSR based method is that the primitive connection polynomial and the intial condition can be chosen randomly *after* the function f is specified. This ensures that it is not possible to a priori construct a Fiat-Naor type example for the LFSR based rainbow method. On the other hand, it is not clear that the use of LFSR method can provably invert any one-way function. This is an open question.

5   LFSR Based Rainbow Method

In this section, we provide the details of the LFSR based implementation of the rainbow method. As before, let $f : \{0,1\}^n \to \{0,1\}^n$ be the one-way function to be inverted.

Suppose r tables each of size $m \times t$ are to be constructed in the precomputation phase. Let $p(x)$ be a primitive polynomial over $GF(2)$ of degree n and $0 \neq X_0, \ldots, X_{rt-1}$ be a sequence of n-bit vectors produced with an LFSR having connection polynomial $p(x)$ and initial condition X_0. We define $\psi_{i,j}(x) = x \oplus X_{(i-1)*t+j}$ and $f_{i,j}(x) = \psi_{i,j}(f(x))$, where $i = 0, \ldots, r-1$ and $j = 0, \ldots, t-1$.

Let $S_0, \ldots, S_{r-1}$ be r sets each containing m many randomly chosen n-bit strings. We write $S_i = \{x_i^0, \ldots, x_i^{m-1}\}$. For $0 \leq i \leq r-1$ and $0 \leq j \leq m-1$, we define strings y_i^j's in the following manner.

$$y_i^j = (f_{i,t-1} \circ f_{i,t-2} \circ \cdots \circ f_{i,0})(x_i^j).$$

Let $T_0, \ldots, T_{r-1}$ be tables where T_i stores the set of pairs $(x_i^0, y_i^0), \ldots, (x_i^{m-1}, y_i^{m-1})$ sorted on the second component. For $0 \leq i \leq r$, define $Y_i^0 = X_{(i-1)*t}$ and $Y_i^1 = X_{(i-1)*t+(t-1)}$. With the ith table, we associate the pair (Y_i^0, Y_i^1). These two values mark the start and end of the LFSR sequence required to generate the $f_{i,j}$'s used in table T_i. This completes the description of the table preparation, which requires rmt invocations of the function f.

Next we describe the online search technique. We will be given a y and have to find an x such that $f(x) = y$. Since there are r tables, we successively search in each of the tables. Hence, it is sufficient to describe the search method in the ith table T_i.

Algorithm. Search in table T_i
Input: An n-bit string y.
Output: An n-bit string x such that $f(x) = y$, else failure.
1. $Z = Y_i^1$;
2. for $j = t - 1$ downto 0 do
3.   set $z = y \oplus Z$; $W = Z$;
4.   for $k = j + 1$ to $t - 1$ do
5. $z = f(z) \oplus W$; $W = L(W)$;
6.   end do;
7.   search for z in the second component of table T_i;
8.   if found,
9.   let $(x_s, y_s) \in T_i$ such that $z = y_s$;
10.   set $W = Y_i^0$; $w = x_s$;
11.   for $k = 0$ to $j - 1$ do
12. $w = f(w) \oplus W$; $W = L(W)$;
13.   end do;
14.   if $f(w) = y$, then return w;
15.   end if;
16. $Z = L^{-1}(Z)$;
17. end do;
18. return "failure";
end Search

The algorithm implements Equation (1). If in Line 14, we have equality, then w is a pre-image of y, otherwise we have a false alarm. The total number of invocations of f made per table is the same as the rainbow method and is $\approx t^2/2$. The total number of invocations of f is $\approx rt^2/2$. The memory requirement is rm many pairs of n-bit strings. Additionally, it is required to store (Y_i^0, Y_i^1) for $i = 0, \ldots, r-1$. Since for practical implementation, r will be a constant, this storage requirement is negligible compared to the storage requirement for the tables.

6   Further Analysis

We consider the success probability of the method. The success probability of any TMTO method is the probability that the required key is covered by the tables. Let $\mathsf{P}_{\mathsf{succ}}$ be the success probability of any such time/memory trade-off method. As before, consider that we have r tables of size $m \times t$ each and let $\mathsf{PS}_{\mathsf{single}}$ and PS_r be the success probability for a single table and r tables respectively. Let E_i be the event that the key is not in the ith table for $i = 1, 2, \ldots, r$. So, $\mathrm{Prob}(E_i) = 1 - \mathsf{PS}_{\mathsf{single}}$ for all $i = 1, 2, \ldots, r$. The probability of success for r tables,

$$\mathsf{PS}_r = 1 - \mathrm{Prob}(E_1 \cap E_2 \cap \ldots \cap E_r)$$
$$= 1 - \prod_{i=1}^{r} \mathrm{Prob}(E_i)$$
$$= 1 - (1 - \mathsf{PS}_{\mathsf{single}})^r.$$

In [5], Hellman has given the following lower bound for $\mathsf{PS_{single}}$ (assuming that the encryption function is a random function.),

$$\mathsf{PS^H}_{single} \geq \frac{1}{N} \sum_{i=1}^{m} \sum_{j=0}^{t-1} \left(1 - \frac{it}{N}\right)^{j+1}.$$

In Hellman method, $r = t$, and $\mathsf{PS^H}_t \geq 1 - \left(1 - \frac{1}{N} \sum_{i=1}^{m} \sum_{j=0}^{t-1} (1 - \frac{it}{N})^{j+1}\right)^t = \mathsf{PS^H}(m,t)(say)$.

Let $\mathsf{PRB}(m,t)$ be the success probability for a single rainbow table of size $m \times t$. In [11], Oechslin has given an approximate expression for $\mathsf{PRB}(m,t)$ as follows:

$$\mathsf{PRB}(m,t) = 1 - \prod_{i=1}^{t} \left(1 - \frac{m_i}{N}\right)$$

where $m_1 = m$ and $m_{i+1} = N \times \left(1 - e^{-\frac{m_i}{N}}\right)$. Then the success probability for r rainbow tables is: $\mathsf{PRB}_r(m,t) = 1 - (1 - \mathsf{PRB}(m,t))^r$.

Consider the tuple (# tables, # rows, # columns, $\mathsf{P_{succ}}$, memory, runtime). We have computed this tuple for each method with different values of N. Success probability for multiple rainbow tables is seen to be better than Hellman or the single rainbow method. On the other hand, the runtime for the multiple rainbow method is slightly higher. In Table 1, we have taken the search space to be equal

Table 1. (# tables, # rows, # columns, $\mathsf{P_{succ}}$, memory, runtime) with different N and $\lambda = 1$

N	Hellman	single rainbow	multiple rainbow
2^{56}	$(2^{19}, 2^{19}, 2^{18}, 0.59, 2^{39}, 2^{36})$	$(1, 2^{37}, 2^{19}, 0.59, 2^{39}, 2^{35})$	$(8, 2^{35}, 2^{18}, 0.94, 2^{39}, 2^{38})$
2^{64}	$(2^{22}, 2^{21}, 2^{21}, 0.59, 2^{44}, 2^{42})$	$(1, 2^{43}, 2^{21}, 0.59, 2^{44}, 2^{41})$	$(4, 2^{41}, 2^{21}, 0.90, 2^{44}, 2^{43})$
2^{72}	$(2^{24}, 2^{24}, 2^{24}, 0.55, 2^{49}, 2^{48})$	$(1, 2^{48}, 2^{24}, 0.56, 2^{49}, 2^{47})$	$(8, 2^{46}, 2^{23}, 0.91, 2^{49}, 2^{49})$

to N. In this case, the success probability for Hellman (and rainbow method) is around 0.6. This fact is also observed in [7]. Further, [7] considers the case where the total coverage is equal to $\lambda \times N$ for $\lambda \geq 1$ and present simulation results to indicate that the success probability of Hellman method can be higher than 0.9 for $\lambda > 2$. As shown in Table 1, using multiple rainbow tables, it is possible to achieve success probability of 0.9 even with search space N.

To achieve higher success probability with the same runtime and memory requirement of rainbow method we can choose the parameters in a way similar to [7] as follows: we choose three constants a, b and λ such that

- the memory required $rm = \frac{N}{a}$,
- the runtime $\frac{rt^2}{2} = \frac{N}{b}$ and the
- size of the search space $rmt = \lambda \times N$.

Solving the three equations we get

$$r = \frac{2N}{\lambda^2 a^2 b}, \quad m = \frac{\lambda^2 ab}{2} \text{ and } t = \lambda a.$$

For $N = 2^{64}$ and 2^{72}, taking $\lambda = 0.8$ and fixing the memory and runtime to be equal to that of the rainbow method in Table 1 we get success probability of around 73% with $r = 2$. While this is lower than 90%, it is still higher than 60% achievable with a single rainbow table.

7   Conclusion

In this paper, we have studied the function generation problem for TMTO attacks. We have pointed out a Fiat-Naor type problem with the counter method employed for implementing rainbow tables. Our study of the required properties of the function generation leads us to suggest LFSR sequences as natural candidates for such application. One advantage of using LFSRs is that it is not possible to a priori construct a Fiat-Naor type example for LFSR based rainbow method. Finally, we describe an LFSR based multiple table rainbow method for TMTO attack. The time, memory and success probability of the multiple-table rainbow method is analysed in greater details than has been previously done.

Acknowledgments

We thank Prof. Harald Niederreiter, Prof. Willi Meier, Prof. Vincent Rijmen and Prof. Amr Youssef for carefully reading an initial draft of the paper.

References

[1] A. Biryukov and A. Shamir. Cyptanalytic Time/Memory/Data Tradeoffs for Stream Ciphers, in the proceedings of ASIACRYPT 2000, LNCS, vol 1976, pp 1-13, 2000.

[2] Alex Biryukov, Sourav Mukhopadhyay and Palash Sarkar. Improved Time-Memory Trade-offs with Multiple Data, in the proceedings of SAC 2005, LNCS, to appear.

[3] S. Burman and P. Sarkar. An Efficient Algorithm for Software Generation of Linear Binary Recurrences. *Applicable Algebra in Engineering, Communication and Computing*, Volume 15, Issue 3/4, December 2004.

[4] A. Fiat and M. Naor. Rigorous time/space tradeoffs for inverting functions, In STOC 1991, pp 534-541, 1991.

[5] M. Hellman. A cryptanalytic Time-Memory Trade-off, IEEE Transactions on Information Theory, vol 26, pp 401-406, 1980.

[6] J. Hong and P. Sarkar. Rediscovery of Time Memory Tradeoffs. Cryptology eprint archive. http://eprint.iacr.org/2005/090.

[7] I.J. Kim and T. Matsumoto Achieving Higher Success Probability in Time-Memory Trade-Off Cryptanalysis without Increasing Memory Size, TIEICE: IE-ICE Transactions on Communications/Electronics/Information and Syaytem, pp 123-129, 1999.

[8] R. Lidl and H. Niederreiter. Introduction to Finite Fields and their applications, Cambridge University Press, Cambridge, pp 189-249, 1994 (revised edition).

[9] A.J. Menezes, P.C. van Oorschot and S.A. Vanstone. Handbook of Applied Cryptography, pp 195-201. CRC, Boca Raton, 2001.

[10] N. Mentens, L. Batina, B. Preneel, and I. Verbauwhede. Cracking Unix passwords using FPGA platforms, Presented at SHARCS'05, 2005 in submission.

[11] P. Oechslin. Making a faster Cryptanalytic Time-Memory Trade-Off, in the proceedings of CRYPTO 2003, LNCS, vol 2729, pp 617-630, 2003.

[12] P. Oechslin, Les compromis temps-memoire et leur utilisation pour casser les mots de passe Windows (in French), Symposium sur la Securite des Technologies de l'information et de la Communication SSTIC, Rennes, June 2004.

[13] RAINBOWCRACK: General propose implementation of rainbow method, http://www.antsight.com/zsl/rainbowcrack/.

[14] J.J. Quisquater and J.P. Delescaille. How easy is collision search? Application to DES, in the proceedings of EUROCRYPT'89, LNCS, vol 434, pp 429-434, 1990.

[15] F.X. Standaert, G. Rouvroy, J.J. Quisquater and J.D. Legat. A Time-Memory Tradeoffs using Distinquished Points: New Analysis and FPGA Results, in the proceedings of CHES 2002, LNCS, vol 2523, pp 593-609, 2002.

[16] P.C. van Oorschot and M.J. Wiener. Parallel collision search with cryptanalytic applications, Journal of Cryptology, 12(1), pp 1-28, Winter 1999.

An Alert Data Mining Framework for Network-Based Intrusion Detection System

Moon Sun Shin[1] and Kyeong Ja Jeong[2]

[1] Dept. of Computer Science, KonKuk University,
Danwol-Dong, Chungju-Si, Chungbuk 380-701, Korea
msshin@kku.ac.kr
[2] ChungCheong University, Korea
kjeong@ok.ac.kr

Abstract. Intrusion detection techniques have been developed to protect computer and network systems against malicious attacks. However, there are no perfect intrusion detection systems or mechanisms, because it is impossible for the intrusion detection systems to get all the packets in the network system. Current intrusion detection systems cannot fully detect novel attacks or variations of known attacks without generation of a large amount of false alerts. In addition, all the current intrusion detection systems focus on low-level attacks or anomalies. Consequently, the intrusion detection systems usually generate a large amount of alerts. And actual alerts may be mixed with false alerts and unmanageable. As a result, it is difficult for users or intrusion response systems to understand the intrusion behind the alerts and take appropriate actions. The standard format of alert messages is not yet defined. Alerts from heterogeneous sensors have different types although they are actually same. Also false alarms and frequent alarms can be used as Denial of Service attack as alarm messages by themselves and cause alert flooding. So we need to minimize false alarm rate and prevent alert flooding through analyzing and merging of alarm data. In this paper, we propose a data mining framework for the management of alerts in order to improve the performance of the intrusion detection systems. The proposed alert data mining framework performs alert correlation analysis by using mining tasks such as axis-based association rule, axis-based frequent episodes and order-based clustering. It also provides the capability of classifying false alarms in order to reduce false alarms from intrusion detection system. The final rules that were generated by alert data mining framework can be used to the real time response of the intrusion detection system and to the reduction of the volume of alerts.

1 Introduction

Recently, due to the open architecture of the internet and wide spread of the internet users, the cyber terror threatening to the weak point of network tends to grow[1,2]. Until now the information security solutions have been passive on security host and particular security system.

As the network-based computer systems play the vital roles increasingly these days, they have become the targets of the intrusions. Because of the large traffic volume, IDS often needs to be extended and be updated frequently and timely.

J. Song, T. Kwon, and M. Yung (Eds.): WISA 2005, LNCS 3786, pp. 38–53, 2006.
© Springer-Verlag Berlin Heidelberg 2006

Intrusion detection systems collect the information from various advantages within network, and analyze the information. There are no perfect intrusion detection systems or mechanisms, because it is impossible for the intrusion detection systems to get all the packets in the network system. Especially, the unknown attacks can hardly be found. Currently building the effective IDS is an enormous knowledge engineering task. Recent data mining algorithms have been designed for the application domains involved with the several types of objects stored in the relational databases. All IDSs require a component that produces basic alerts as a result of comparing the properties of an input element to the values defined by their rules. Most of systems perform the detection of basic alarms by each input event to all rules sequentially, and IDSs raise the alarm when possible intrusion happens. Consequently, IDSs usually generate a large amount of alerts that can be unmanageable and also be mixed with false alerts. Sometimes the volume of alerts is large and the percentile of the false alarms is very high. So it is necessary to manage alerts for the correct intrusion detection. As a result, nearly all IDSs have the problem of managing alerts, especially false alarms, which cause seriously to impact performance of the IDSs. A general solution to this problem is needed. We describe an approach that decreases the rate of false alarms. However, many researches have been performed to apply the data mining techniques to the intrusion detection systems. The data mining techniques is to discover useful information from huge databases. It is used to analyze large audit data in the intrusion detection system efficiently and just select features for constructing intrusion detection models.

This paper provides an introduction to apply the data mining techniques for the management of the alerts from the intrusion detection system. We propose an alert data mining framework for IDSs. We also implement the mining system that analyzes the alert data efficiently and supports the high-level analyzer for the security policy server. The rest of this paper is organized as follows. Section 2 describes the framework for the policy-based network security management and the data mining for IDS as related works. In section 3 we propose an alert data mining framework. Section 4 and 5 presents the implementation of the alert data mining framework and the experiments of our system. In the last section, we will summarize our works.

Our approach is useful to improve the detection rate of network-based intrusion detection systems and to reduce the sheer volume of alerts.

2 Related Works

2.1 Policy-Based Network Security Management

The policy-based network management is the network management based on policy. A policy is defined as an aggregation of the policy rules. Each policy rule consists of a set of conditions and a corresponding set of actions. The condition should be described when the policy rule is applicable. If a policy rule is activated, one or more actions contained by that policy rule may be executed. So, we can use the policy for the modification of system behavior. The policy-based network management for the network security is the concept and technology that uses the policy-based Network Management for the network security.

Figure 1 shows the policy-based network architecture and the relationships among the components. The architecture of the policy-based network management for the network security has hierarchical structure, and there are at least two levels.

One is a management layer that includes the security policy server system, and the other is the enforcement layer that executes the intrusion detection to perceive and prepare the hacking traffic between the connection points.

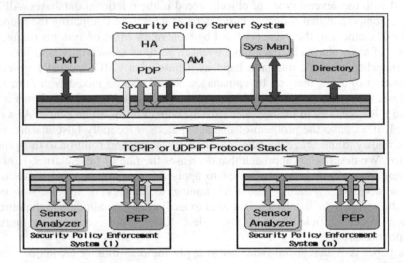

Fig. 1. Framework of Policy-based Network Management for Network Security

The security policy enforcement system consists of two blocks. One is Sensor/Analyzer block that provides the detection and the analysis for the input packet between the network connection points, the other is the PEP block that provides an enforcement function for the security policy.

2.2 Data Mining for Intrusion Detection System

Some of the recent researches have started to apply the data mining techniques to the IDSs[3]. Because of the sheer volume of audit data, the efficient and intelligent data analysis tools are required to discover the behavior of the system activities. Data mining generally refers to the process of extracting useful information from large stores of data. The current intrusion detection systems do not offer grouping the related alerts logically. Also the existing intrusion detection systems are likely to generate false alerts, either false positive or false negative. To solve these critical problems, the intrusion detection community is actively developing standards for the content of the alert messages and some researches are on going about the alert correlation.

In [8] they introduced probabilistic approach for the coupled sensors to reduce the false alarm. An aggregation and correlation algorithm is presented in [7] for acquiring the alerts and relating them. The algorithm could explain more condensed view of the security issues raised by the intrusion detection systems.

Some of the recent researches have started to apply the data mining techniques to the IDSs[7]. Because of the sheer volume of audit data, the efficient and intelligent data analysis tools are required to discover the behavior of the system activities. Data mining generally refers to the process of extracting useful information from large stores of data. The aim of our research is to develop mining system for the analysis of the alert data. The recent rapid development in data mining has made a wide variety of algorithms available, drawn from the fields of statistics, the pattern recognition, machine learning and databases. Some algorithms are particularly useful for the mining audit data. In the other cases of the alert data, these algorithms are also useful. Follows are the several data mining areas that support IDS:

Classification: maps data item into one of the several predefined categories. An ideal application in the intrusion detection will be to gather sufficient the "normal" and the "abnormal" audit data for a user or a program.

Association rules: determines the relationships between the fields in the database records.

Frequent episodes: models the sequential patterns. These algorithms can discover what time-based sequence of audit events and frequent episodes are.

Clustering: gathers similar patterns to the same group. These algorithms can measure the similarity of sequence.

2.3 Alert Correlation

In the response to the attacks and potential attacks against networks, administrators are increasingly deploying IDSs. IDSs products have become widely available in recent years. But the intrusion detection techniques are still far from being perfect. These systems monitor hosts, networks and critical files and these systems deal with a potentially large number of alerts. These systems should report all alerts to the security policy server or operator. So the security policy server has to manage the reporting alerts in order to build the new security policy rule. But current intrusion detection systems do not make it easy for operators to logically group the related alerts. Also the existing intrusion detection systems are likely to generate false alerts, be it false positive or false negative. To solve these critical problems, the intrusion detection community is actively developing standards for the content of the alert messages and some researches is on going about the alert correlation. In [8] they introduced probabilistic approach for the coupled sensors to reduce the false alarm. An aggregation and correlation algorithm is presented in [9] for acquiring the alerts and relating them. The algorithm could explain more condensed view of the security issues raised by the intrusion detection systems.

The current intrusion detection systems usually focus on detecting the low-level attacks and/or the anomalies. None of them can capture the logical steps or attack strategies behind these attacks. Consequently, the IDSs usually generate a large amount of alerts. Whereas actual alerts can be mixed with false alerts and also the amount of alerts will also become unmanageable. As a result, it is difficult for the human users or intrusion response systems to understand the intrusions behind the alerts and take the appropriate actions. In [10] they propose the intrusion alert correlator based on the prerequisites of intrusions.

3   An Alert Data Mining Framework

In this chapter, we describe the outline of an alert data mining framework for IDS. The proposed alert data mining framework consists of four components such as the association rule miner, the frequent episode miner, the clustering miner and false alarm classification miner. In order to perform alert correlation analysis the three formers are proposed and the latter is for reducing false alarms. The association rule miner can find the correlation among the attributes in the record, although the frequent episode miner searches event patterns in records. In addition, the clustering miner discovers the similar attack patterns by grouping the alert data with similarity among the alert data. The clustering analysis provides the data abstraction from the underlying structure. And it groups the data objects into the clusters so that the objects belonging to the same cluster are similar, while those belonging to the different cluster are dissimilar. Because we consider the characteristics of the alert data, we improve the existing data mining algorithms to create the candidate item sets that include the only interesting attributes.

3.1   Axis Based Association Rule Miner

The existing association rule mining algorithms search for interesting relationships in the transaction database. However, we expanded the Apriori algorithm without grouping the items by T_id because of the characteristics of the alert data.

The alert data is different from that of the general transaction database. In addition, the rules can be generated only with attributes of interest. The process of the expanded algorithm is composed of three steps. The steps of the process of the association rule miner are as follows.

Step 1) Find all frequent item sets:
   In this step, the candidate item sets are generated for the items composed of the attributes of interest in the selected tables, and then a set of frequent itemsets is generated for each candidate itemset which satisfies the minimum support (minsupp) in the entire records (D). Here, items that do not satisfy the minimum support are removed in the pruning step

Step 2) Generating the strong association rules from the frequent item sets:
   In this step, the association rules are generated for the frequent itemsets after pruning, which satisfy the minimum support. Here, the minimum confidence(minconf) is calculated using the minimum support among frequent items to generate the association rules. The minimum confidence refers to the probability that forecasts how much items satisfying the minimum support

Step 3) Generating the final rules:
   In this step, the final rules that satisfy the minimum confidence, namely, Conf(R)$\geq$ minimum confidence, are generated to be stored in the final rule table.

3.2   Axis Based Frequent Episodes Miner

The frequent episodes mining is to search a series of event sequences for the frequently occurring episodes. An episode is defined by a sequence of the specific events that occurs frequently. The events composed of a sequence are closely related with one another. Here, exploring is to find all the frequent episodes within the rate of time windows when the episodes occur in a set of time windows that defined by user satisfies the minimum frequency. A sequence pattern and an episode are similar in that they explore patterns in the sequence. However, they are different in that a sequence pattern explores a whole database, while an episode explores while using windows. Using episodes, an infiltration detection system can detect the frequently repeated patterns, and apply them to the rule or use them as the guidelines for the service refusal attacks.

When the existing algorithms are used to apply the data mining to a search for the useful patterns from the alert data, the correlations among the attributes must be considered. The alert data comprise the various attributes, and each of these attributes has many values. Because all of these data cannot be converted into a binary database, we propose an expanded algorithm using axis-attribute. In addition, as the standard attributes are applied, only the items including the standard attributes have to be considered in generating the candidate items. This reduces the number of the unnecessary episodes in generating the rules. Frequent episode mining is carried out through the following 3 steps.

Step 1) Generating candidate episodes:
   In this step, the tuples composed of the attributes of interest are arranged by given time window units. Time within a window must be included in the time span of the window. That is, win = Te - Ts + width (w) , win_start time <= time < win_end time. A set of candidate episodes is generated from the table arranged in window unit.

Step 2) Generating frequent episodes:
   In this step, a set of frequent episodes, which satisfy the minimum frequency, are extracted from the set of the candidate episode.

Step 3) Generating final episodes:
   Frequent episodes, which satisfy the minimum confidence, are generated from the set of frequent episodes.

3.3 Order Based Clustering Miner

Clustering analysis is the technique to find the distribution or the patterns of given data by classifying the data into groups based on similarity [11]. Such a clustering analysis technique improves the efficiency of the analysis of the alert data, and abstracts high-level meanings through grouping data. This technique is a process of grouping the sets. Here, individuals belonging to the same cluster are homogenous, and individuals belonging to different clusters are heterogeneous.

There are several methods of measuring the similarity between the entities but mainly the concept of distance is used. The cluster miner implemented in this paper used Euclidean distance function in order to define the similarity between the entities. It is based the assumption if the data entities have the same values then they may be similar. Considering the characteristics of the alert data, we implemented the modified CURE algorithm, which can cluster the datasets with the multi-dimensional attributes. The implemented clustering miner has four steps of process.

Step 1) Data preprocessing
Step 2) Clustering alert data
Step 3) Analyzing the result of clusters
Step 4) Classify new alert data

In Step 1, the input data are preprocessed so that the dataset is suitable for the clustering. This process is largely composed of two tasks. One is to select appropriate attributes for efficient clustering and the other is to add extended attributes if necessary. The domain knowledge is required in this step. The purpose of clustering the alert data is grouping the input data to abstract the meaning of sequence among the groups. In Step 2, the input data preprocessed in Step 1 are clustered. The CURE algorithm was used in generating clusters from the given dataset [11]. Step 3 is to abstract the relationships among clusters generated in Step 2 by analyzing the causes of generation. To abstract the relationships among clusters, we used the distribution of the alerts previous to the alerts included in the generated clusters. The previous alert of an alert is the most recently occurred one among those that have the same source address and the destination address as that of the alert.

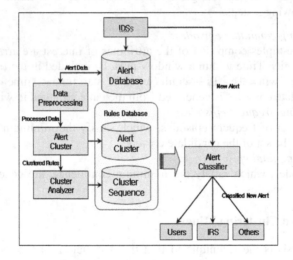

Fig. 2. Alert Data Clustering System

It is possible to search the alerts frequently occurring prior to the alerts included in the cluster by analyzing the distribution of the alerts previous to the alert data included in a specific cluster. In Step 4, when the new alert data occur, the data are automatically clustered and the possible next alerts are forecasted using the data cluster model and the cluster sequences generated previous steps.

A clustering mining system that analyzes the similarity of the alert data is composed of Data Processor, Alert Cluster, Cluster Analyzer and Alert Classifier. The architecture of clustering miner system is shown in Figure 2. Data Preprocessor preprocesses the input dataset so that the dataset can be clustered by Alert Cluster. Here, extended attributes based on domain knowledge are added for efficient and accurate clustering, and selected attributes are normalized. Alert Cluster clusters the data preprocessed by Data Preprocessor. The final output of this module is a set of grouped data. The output is stored in the rule database, and is used in the automatic classification of the new alerts and the analysis of the relationships among generated clusters. Cluster Analyzer analyzes the causes of generation of clusters. The output of the module is represented by the sequence of clusters. The output is used in analyzing the relationships among clusters, and in predicting a set of possible alerts for a specific alert. Alert Classifier classifies new alerts into appropriate clusters using the cluster model generated by Alert Cluster, and abstracts possible alerts to occur next by using the sequence generated by Cluster Analyzer.

3.4 Building False Alarm Classification Model

The idea of false alarm classification model is to filter the false alarms from intrusion detection system and minimize the false alarm rate by matching the alarms compared to the false alarm classification rules. Then we can expect the higher detection rate of intrusion detection system at the same time. For that purpose, we applied data mining techniques for the classification. The data mining techniques can be generally used in data reduction and data clustering. Classification is to build a model(called classifier) to predict future data objects for which the class label is unknown. Decision tree, rule learning, naive-Bayes classification and statistical approaches can be used. In general, given a training data set, the task of classification is to build a classifier from the data set such that it can be used to predict class labels of unknown objects with high accuracy. So we extend the basic decision tree algorithm C4.5[4] to the association based classification for the feature construction.

Network-based IDS outputs the sheer volume of alerts that can be mixed with false alerts. The false alarm is the alarm classified as attack while in fact it is not. Actually a large volume of false alarms makes it impossible for IDS to respond immediately and prevents IDS from correct detection. So we propose false alarm classifier to improve intrusion detection rate of IDS.

Here is the framework of our approach that has two parts: First is feature construction and second is classification part as shown in figure 3. From the sensor, we preprocess the alert data and store them into database. And then we construct the false alarm classification model by learning false positive alarm pattern from false alarm decision tree using training dataset.

Building accurate and efficient classifiers for large databases depends on training dataset. We used association rule-based feature construction. We built our false alarm classification model by using decision tree especially C4.5[4] algorithm because this algorithm is very efficient in memory and performance.

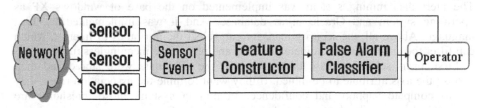

Fig. 3. Framework of False Alarm Classifier

The whole process consists of four phases: feature construction, rule generation, rule analysis and classification. In the first phase, feature construction, the preprocessor computes the high correlated attributes based on associative feature construction in order to decide the nodes for decision tree. Association rule mining searches for interesting relationships among the given data set under the assumption in terms of confidence and support. Large itemsets of training dataset were extracted as the feature from the alert_DB and stored in attribute_list table. We sent Darpa Tcpdump data through the Snort and counted all the false positives for the generation of training dataset. The training data set was stored in alert_DB w.r.t. each protocol after preprocessing task because they were raw network data. In the second phase, rule generation, the decision tree builder computed the complete set of rules in the form of R: P->c, where P is the pattern in the training data set, and c is a class label such that *sup(R)* and *conf(R)* pass the given support and confidence thresholds, respectively. Furthermore, following task prunes some rules and only selects a subset of high quality rules for classification. Before the tree construction, information gain of each attribute must be computed. The attribute which had the highest value of information gain can be used as root node. The expression of (1) is the information value for each attributes and (2) is the entropy of each attribute.

$$Information = -log_2 p \quad (p = number\ of\ attributes)\ \dots\dots\dots (1)$$
$$Entropy(S) = -p_{FP}\ log_2\ p_{FP} - p_{TP}\ log_2\ p_{TP} \quad\quad \dots\dots\dots (2)$$

Using the values of (1) and (2), we can compute the information gain value of each attributes as shown in (3) where S is the class labels of nodes, S_v is the class labels of branches. Then decision tree builder can make root node and repeat the process of computing (1)-(3) and decide root node of subtree again. The recursive process will be finished when there is no split. Then final rule sets are generated after pruning.

$$Gain(S, A) = Entropy - \sum |S_v| / |S| * Entropy(S_v) \quad \dots\dots\dots (3)$$

The pruning process was performed to remove outliers. Final rules were generated as the form of <IF><THEN>. These rules were stored in the rule table, too.

In the third phase, rule analysis, the validation task was performed about constructed decision tree using test data. If needed, the tree must be overfitted and pruned.

In the last phase, the classification model classifies new data by pattern matching with rule and gives the class for each new data.

4 Implementation

The alert data mining system was implemented on the base of windows XP as operating system and Oracle 8i as database. And it was implemented by Java language. Above all, the security manager can select the attributes of interest, which can filter the unnecessary candidate item sets and reduce the meaningless rules.

First, users select database table in which the alert data were stored and then choose the axis attribute to be mined. If they want to mine the association rules, they try to compute support and confidence. In mining system, those thresholds are essential, because the knowledge from the result of mining process was some confidence information.

4.1 Examples

As described above, when we used the axis attributes, we deducted a great many candidate itemsets and useless rules. The final association rules were stored in the rule tables. We tested the implemented mining system using the virtual alert data. The alert data used in test were obtained by simulation programs. Table 1 presented an example of the final rules after mining task. Here we found out the correlations among the alert data inter-records or intra-records.

Table 1(a) showed the example rule of the results after the association rule mining. These rules had some confidence information. For example, the first rule meant that there was close correlation between "attack id" 50 and "destination port" 21. That also implied the strong relation between the attributes "attack id" and "destination port". Therefore we were able to extract the relationships between the attributes using the association rule miner. The final rules of the frequent episode mining were shown in Table 1(b). We were able to find sequential pattern of the events as results. In the example, we might guess the fact that attack 5001 brings about attack 5007.

It was a simple test, yet the alert data used in our experiments were just simulated data. In addition, we should verify the implemented mining engine. By the way, we assured that our mining engine for the alert analyzer should provide the confidence information to the security policy server.

The prototype of false alarm classifier consists of four components such as Data Preprocessor, Feature Constructor, Decision Tree Builder and Data Classifier. Data Preproceesor transformed binary raw data and stored them into database table. Feature Constructor selects attributes using association rule-based or probabilistic correlation method. Decision Tree Builder constructs classification model based on training data and Data Classifier actually classifies test data.

Final rules were also stored in the relational database and they were used by security administrator or intrusion detection system.

Table 1. Example of Final Rules

(a) Association Rule

Association Rule	Meaning
50<=>21 (supp:49, conf:100%)	Attribute 50(Atid) correlated with attribute 21(dsc_port)
21<=>tcp (supp:49, conf:100%)	Attribute 21(dsc_port) correlated with attribute tcp(protocol)
...	...

(b) Frequent Episodes Rule

Frequent Episode Rule	Meaning
5001:210.155.167.10:21:tcp => 5007:210.155.167.10.21 :tcp (fre:10, conf:100%, time:10sec)	If 5001(Ftp Buffer Ovrflow) occur, then 5007(Anonymous FTP) occur together.
...	...

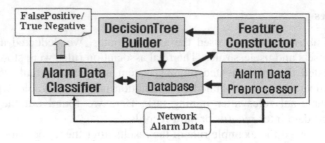

Fig. 4. Architecture of False Alarm Classifier

Figure 4 shows the architecture of the false alarm classifier and the relationships among the components. The false alarm classifier was implemented by Java and Oracle 8i as database. For evaluation, we used Snort-1.8.7 as sample IDS. The implemented prototype had three levels such as user interface, data repository and main program that were composed of database connection, decision tree builder and data classifier. Decision tree builder class constructs the decision tree of false positive with the training data set. Data classifier class classifies the test data by using the rules of the decision tree. All the rules and dataset were stored in the relational database. C4.5 algorithm as the extension of association rule based-classification for the decision tree of false alarm classification. The C4.5 algorithm has the advantage of memory and performance comparing to other decision tree algorithms.

5   Experiments and Evaluation

In this section, we describe the experimental study conducted in order to evaluate our mining system. Our experiments were performed with the factors like minimum support and window width of the frequent episodes. We evaluated 32,000 records of the simulated alert data. The experiments were designed for two objectives. First, how can we decide the minimum support for the alert data. And second, we estimated of window width which could make the frequent episodes miner keep higher performance. Figure 5 showed the time of each minimum support value. In the association rule miner, if the value of minimum support was smaller than the performance is higher. In the frequent episodes miner, the support depended on window width. Therefore time was less related with minimum support. In Figure 5, we could see a little change in the case of the frequent episodes. Figure 6 showed the performance of the frequent episodes miner as the window width changes. We experimented the time as the window width was increased. The frequent episode miner required time window value, frequency and confidence. The results of the frequent episode miner were affected by time variables. Like the association rules, the frequent episodes rules were stored in the final rule table, too. Then these rules were used in the security policy server to construct the active policy rule.

For the clustering miner, two experiments were carried out. The first experiment was to test the performance of clustering of the implemented system. This experiment evaluated the accuracy of each cluster generated by the clustering miner.

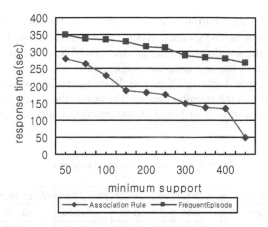

Fig. 5. The results of performance evaluation as the value of minimum support

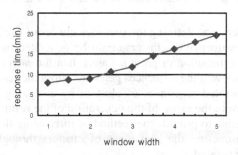

Fig. 6. The performance of frequent episodes mineras the window width

The second experiment was to define the cluster previous to each cluster generated, and to determine if the sequence of clusters could be generated based on the sequence. The training data of DARPA 1998 were TCP Dump data composed of network traffic for 7 weeks. The dataset contained approximately 5,000,000 data instances including various types of infiltrations that could occur in network environments. In addition, the test dataset contained approximately 2,000,000 data instances, which were based on network traffic for two weeks.

Table 2. Test data distribution and Results of clustering test

Attack type	Distribution rate	Results:Clustering accuracy
DOS	73.90%	98.34%
R2L	5.20%	47.52%
U2R	0.07%	51.37%
Probing	1.34%	83.84%

Table 2 showed the distribution rate of the test data for each attack type. Large amount of the test data is DOS attack type. Table 2 also showed the result of an experiment applying the test dataset to the model created from the training dataset.

As shown in Table 2, the test data were assigned to clusters with relatively high accuracy for attack types such as DOS and Probing, which were distributed in a relatively large amount in the training dataset. However, the attack types such as R2L and U2R, which were rarely distributed in the training dataset, were clustered less accurately.

Table 3. Results of clustering analysis

ClsuterID	Alert_PRE1	Alert_PRE2	Alert_PRE3	Alert_PRE4
Clsuter1	0 %	0 %	50 %	50 %
Clsuter2	95 %	0 %	0 %	0 %
Clsuter3	0 %	0 %	50 %	50 %
Clsuter4	0 %	0 %	0 %	90 %

The second experiment was defining the previous cluster of each generated cluster, and determining if the sequence of clusters could be generated based on the defined previous clusters. The distribution of previous alert data for each cluster generated is as in Table 3. Figure 7 showed the sequences generated from the results shown in Table 3. This experiment generated sequences of clusters by analyzing the distribution of previous alerts, which were the cause of the generation of the resulting sequences, and showed that it was possible to provide the method of forecasting the future type of the alerts occurring by abstracting the sequences of clusters through integrating each sequences of clusters generated.

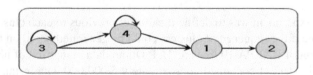

Fig. 7. Generated cluster sequence base on table 3

Here, we can find out potential alert sequences, which might mean attack scenario or strategies behind attack. It provides for the intrusion detection system to capture the high-level detection.

We examine the experimental results of our false alarm classifier. Two experiments were performed. For the experiments, we placed the implemented system in front of Snort-1.8.6[5]. And we sent the Darpa tcpdump data through the Snort that obtained the false alarm classifier. Our performance results are compared to those of only Snort alone. Other experiments were preformed to handle the processing of an input element at nodes of decision tree efficiently. The ability of false classification depended on feature construction. We proposed association rule-based classification.

So the features for nodes of decision tree were selected by association rule-based approach. Also we tried to evaluate statistical based correlation analysis for the feature construction. The mixed method of those approaches was evaluated for the best feature construction. Experimental data were Darpa 1998 raw packet data of DOS attack. We could find out the different nodes of the each method for feature construction, the correctness of false alarm classifier and the performance of the detection rate of Snort. The training data set for the classification model was the tcpdump data for 7 weeks. We only chose the DOS attack labeled data among the various types of attack data. The ratio of normal and intrusive was same.

We used 1-4 weeks data as training dataset and 5-7 weeks data as test data. For utilizing the decision tree, we had to remove the improper attributes and select appropriate attributes. For the feature construction, we proposed association rule-based feature selection. However, we tried to do statistics approach too.

■   *The correctness of false alarm classification model*

From the first experiment, the nodes of decision tree were made and two decision trees were constructed. One is the statistical correlation based decision tree. And the other was constructed by the feature construction based on association rule based approach. We evaluated these decision trees correctly.

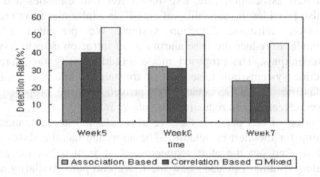

Fig. 8. Detection rate of Normal Packet for Each Decision Tree

Figure 8 shows the results of detection rate of normal packets. The experiments were performed with three methods like association based, statistical correlation based and the mix of both above methods. Figure 10 shows that association rule-based decision tree marked higher performance than statistical correlation based decision tree. And among the three approaches, the mixed method was the most efficient in detection rate of normal packet.

■   *The performance of the IDS with false classifier*

The last experiment was performed for the evaluation of false positive rate of IDS in both cases: with false alarm classifier and without false alarm decision tree. For this experiment, we used Snort-1.8.6 open source[5] and Darpa data that were already used in previous experiments. As shown in figure 9, the mixed method and association rule based decision tree were more effective. But in the case of week 5 data, it showed especially high value.

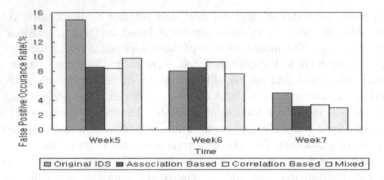

Fig. 9. Results of False Positive Rate of Each Decision Tree

6 Conclusion

In this paper we propose a data mining framework for the management of alerts in order to improve the performance of the intrusion detection systems. The proposed alert data mining framework performs alert correlation analysis by using mining tasks such as axis-based association rule, axis-based frequent episodes and order-based clustering. It also provides the capability of classifying false alarms in order to reduce false alarms from intrusion detection system. We presented a false alarm classification model to reduce the false alarm rate of intrusion detection systems using data mining techniques. The proposed model could classify the alarms from the intrusion detection systems into false alert or true attack. We also implemented the false alarm classifier of DDOS attack. We proved that the proposed false alarm classifier worked effectively in reducing false alarm rate.

The contribution of this paper is that we have adapted and extended the notions from data mining for the alert correlation. The approach has the ability to aggregate the alerts and to find out the alert sequences. And it also has the advantages in reduction of alert volume. For each new alert, we compute similarity and enter the alert to similar cluster. And then for each cluster, we compute the pre-cluster and post-cluster so that we can discover the alert sequences. We can predict possible attack sequences in the intrusion detection domain. But we have to improve the efficiency of speed.

References

1. D. Schnackenberg, K. Djahandari, and D. Sterne, "Infrastructure for Intrusion Detection and Response", Proceedings of the DARPA ISCE, Hilton Head, SC, Jan. 2000
2. M.J. Lee, M.S. Shin, H. S. Moon, K. H. Ryu "Design and Implementation of Alert Analyzer with Data Mining Engine", in Proc. IDEAL'03, HongKong, March. 2003
3. W. Lee, S. J. Stolfo, K. W. Mok "A Data Mining Framework for Building Intrusion Detection Models in Proc. The 2nd International Symposium on Recent Advances in Intrusion Detection (RAID 1999).
4. J. Ross Quinlan, C4.5: Programs for and Neural Networks, Machine Learning, Morgan Kaufman publishers, 1993

5. Snort. Open-source Network Intrusion Detection System. http://www.snort.org.
6. E.H. Spafford and D. Zamboni., "Intrusion detection using autonomous agents", Computer Networks, pp. 34:547–570, 2000.
7. H. Debar and A.Wespi, "Aggregation and correlation of intrusion-detection alerts", In Recent Advances in Intrusion Detection, in Lecture Notes in Computer Science, pp. 85 – 103, 2001.
8. A. Valdes and K. Skinner, "Probabilistic alert correlation", in Proc. The 4th International Symposium on Recent Advances in Intrusion Detection (RAID 2001), pp. 54–68, 2001.
9. Tcpdump/Libpcap, Network Packet Capture Program, http://www.tcpdump.org, 2003
10. P. Ning and Y. Cui., "An intrusion alert correlator based on prerequisites of intrusions", Technical Report TR-2002-01, Department of Computer Science, North Carolina State University

Key Factors Influencing Worm Infection
in Enterprise Networks

Urupoj Kanlayasiri[1] and Surasak Sanguanpong[2]

[1] Office of Computer Services, Kasetsart University,
Chatuchak, Bangkok 10900, Thailand
urupoj.k@ku.ac.th
[2] Department of Computer Engineering, Kasetsart University,
Chatuchak, Bangkok 10900, Thailand
surasak.s@ku.ac.th

Abstract. Worms are a key vector of computer attacks that produce great damage of enterprise networks. Little is known about either the effect of host and network configuration factors influencing worm infection or the approach to predict the number of infected hosts. In this paper we present the results of real worm attacks to determine the factors influencing worm infection, and to propose the prediction model of worm damage. Significant factors are extracted from host and network configuration: openness, homogeneity, and trust. Based on these different factors, fuzzy decision is used to produce the accurate prediction of worm damage. The contribution of this work is to understand the effect of factors and the risk level of infection for preparing the protection, responsiveness, and containment to lessen the damage that may occur. Experimental results show that the selected parameters are strongly correlated with actual infection, and the proposed model produces accurate estimates.

1 Introduction

A self-propagating program or worm was released into the Internet and infected a lot of vulnerable hosts. A dramatic increase in worm outbreaks occurred in the last few years, including Code Red [1], Code Red II [1-3], Nimda [5], and Slammer [4]. Code Red infected hosts running Microsoft Internet Information Server by exploiting an .ida vulnerability. Code Red II is even more dangerous than the original: rebooting of an infected machine did not halt the worm. Nimda used multiple mechanisms for infection: email, open network shares, and browsing of compromised web sites. Slammer rapidly spreads across the Internet by exploiting a buffer overflow vulnerability in Microsoft's SQL Server or Microsoft SQL Server Desktop Engine.

All above worms exploited holes in optional component of servers (except Nimda – targets both server and client). Recent worms such as Blaster [6] and Sasser infect vast number of desktop computers in enterprise networks by exploiting vulnerabilities in the default configuration of desktop operating systems. The trend of worm today is to attack the desktop computers that comprise the majority of hosts in most organizations. Since the prevention, treatment [10-12], and containment [3, 13, 14] are still not effective and rapid enough for handling worm propagation. Therefore, to understand the effect of factors

J. Song, T. Kwon, and M. Yung (Eds.): WISA 2005, LNCS 3786, pp. 54–67, 2006.

influencing worm infection, and to predict the worm damage are important for preparing the protection planning, incident responsiveness, user awareness, and policy enforcement.

This paper addresses two basic questions: (1) *What are the factors influencing worm infection in networks?* and (2) *What is the model to predict the worm damage?* From the first question, the worm infection depends upon several factors. However, there is no exact answer to the question of which factors are influential for infection significantly. We study host and network configuration factors to answer this question. From the second question, the model will predict the worm damage before the attack occurs. Our basic idea is to develop the measurements of different factors, and to predict the worm damage by obtaining and fusing the values from these different measurements. There are many ways for information fusion, but in this problem, fuzzy decision must be better than other methods, because the measures are uncertain and imprecise, and human experts can have some intuition or knowledge on the characteristics of measures that relate to worm behavior [7].

The remainder of this paper is organized as follows. In Section 2, we give related work. Section 3 presents the factors influencing worm infection and their measurements. We propose the prediction model of worm damage in Section 4. The experimental results are described in Section 5. Finally, Section 6 gives the conclusion.

2   Related Work

In studying the factors influencing worm infection, Wang et al. [22], discuss factors that influence infection of computer viruses. These factors are system topology, node immunity, temporal effects, propagation selection, multiple infections, and stochastic effects. The simulation study considered hierarchical and cluster topologies with the selective immunizations of hosts. Both topologies support critical infrastructure that contrasts with the fully connected, open nature of the Internet. Ellis [18] describes the analytical framework for worm infection in relational description and attack expression. Four conditions for infection are targeting, vulnerability, visibility, and infectability, which are used to calculate the set of infectable hosts.

There are several approaches to model the spread of worms in networks, principally the Epidemiological model [15], the two-factor worm model [16], and the Analytical Active Worm Propagation (AAWP) model [17]. The Epidemiological model is a simple model that explains the spread of computer viruses by employing biological epidemiology. The number of infected hosts depends on vulnerability density and scanning rate. In this model, the infection initially grows exponentially until the majority of hosts are infected, then the incidence slows toward a zero infection rate.

The two-factor worm model describes the behavior of worm based on two factors: the dynamic countermeasure by ISPs and users, and a slowed down worm infection rate. This model explains observed data for Code Red and the decrease in scanning attempts during the last several hours before it ceased propagation. The AAWP model extends the model of worms that employ random scanning to cover local subnet scanning worms. Parameters in this model include the number of vulnerable machines, size of hitlists, scanning rate, death rate, and patching rate. AAWP better models the behavior of Code Red II than the previous models.

Unlike all above models, our model does not require observing variables during attacks. Therefore, it can be used to predict worm damage before the attack occurs. The model does not rely on attack type and configuration of worm program. Such factors are: (1) scanning rate in the Epidemiological and the AAWP models and (2) size of hitlists in the AAWP model. In addition, our model does not depend on human factors that are hard to simulate in the real world: (1) patching rate in the AAWP model and (2) dynamic countermeasure by ISPs and users in the two-factor worm model.

The worm damage depends on several factors. However, there is no exact answer to the question of which factors are optimal for damage prediction. In this paper, we analyze factors extracted from host and network configuration: openness, homogeneity, and trust. Fuzzy decision will combine them to find the prediction result. The important task of fuzzy decision that is often difficult and time consuming is the determination of membership functions. Traditionally it can be performed by experts but it is not always the most suitable method. In this paper, we use inductive reasoning method to define membership functions.

Several techniques, such as inductive reasoning, neural networks, and genetic algorithms, have been used to generate membership functions and production rules. In inductive reasoning, as long as the data is not dynamic the method will produce good results [8]. Inductive reasoning method uses the entire data to formulate membership functions and, if the data is not large, this method is computationally inexpensive. Compared to neural networks and genetic algorithms, inductive reasoning has an advantage in the fact that the method may not require a convergence analysis, which in the case of neuron networks and genetic algorithms is computationally very expensive.

3   Factors Influencing Worm Infection

We initially study an *enterprise* network and *scanning* worms. The enterprise network N is a set of hosts $\{N_1, N_2, ..., N_n\}$ partitioned into two mutually exclusive sets, the set of vulnerable hosts S and immune hosts I, with sizes $n(S)$ and $n(I)$, respectively. The total population is $n(S) + n(I) = n$. The scanning worm assumption is that worms target to exploit vulnerability of desktop computers that comprise the majority of hosts in an enterprise network. The scanning worms require no user intervention for their executions. We define the *worm damage* as the number of infected hosts in the network.

The general behavior of worms [18-21] includes three processes: scanning, attacking, and propagation. We study and define parameters that relate to these three processes: openness, homogeneity, and trust. Openness describes the quantity of hosts that can be scanned; homogeneity defines the area of infection – the more hosts with the same vulnerability, the more number of infected hosts. Finally, trust determines relations among hosts that worms use for propagation. Three factors are extracted from the host and network configuration: openness (O), homogeneity (H), and trust (T). The worm damage (D) can be given as a function of these factors:

$$D = \Gamma(O,H,T) \tag{1}$$

3.1   Openness

Openness describes the vulnerability of enterprise networks to scanning by worms. Typically, machines that are hidden from scanning by worms are safer than visible ones. The visibility can be configured by Network Address Translation (NAT) or firewall technology. Openness (O) can be measured by the ratio of the number of hosts that can be scanned by any host to the total number of hosts by

$$O = \frac{\sum_j |\xi_s(e_j)|}{n} \qquad (2)$$

where e_j is the collection of hosts on subnetwork j, ξ_s is a function that selects hosts in e_j that can be connected to via TCP, UDP or ICMP from outside the network j, and n is total number of hosts on the network. For example the network E shown in Figure 1, if the gateway $G1$ configures NAT for the network $E3$ then the enterprise network E has $O = 0.66$.

3.2 Homogeneity

Homogeneity measures the density of hosts that can be attacked by a worm. When a worm attacks a host, it will exploit other hosts through the same vulnerability. In this study, we assume that the operating system, rather than application software, represents the mode of vulnerability. Therefore, the homogeneity (H) is defined as the homogeneity of operating system by hosts on the network:

$$H = \frac{1}{n} \max_{k \in K} n(k) \qquad (3)$$

where K is a set of operating system types on the network, $n(k)$ is the number of hosts running operating system k, and n is total number of hosts on the network. For the example network E shown in Figure 1, b operating system has the maximum number of hosts, $H = 0.53$.

3.3 Trust

Trust is a relationship between a trustor and a trustee. The trustor allows the trustee to use, manipulate its resources, or influence the trustor's decision to use resources or services provided by the trustee. The trust relationship can be represented by a directed graph. We use a nondeterministic finite-state automaton M to describe the trust relationship of desktop computers in the enterprise network, where $M = (Q, P, f, q_o, F)$ consists of a set Q of states, an input alphabet P, a transition function f between states Q which depends on the input, a starting state q_o, and a subset F of Q consisting of the final states. The set of states Q is a group of machines in enterprise network. The function f represents the propagation of a worm. q_o is the starting node that the worm first exploits and F contains a set of possible attacked nodes. The input for function f is assumed to be a constant. Then, T can be calculated by:

$$T = \frac{\sum_{i=1}^{n} [n(F \mid q_o = i) - 1]}{n(n-1)} \qquad (4)$$

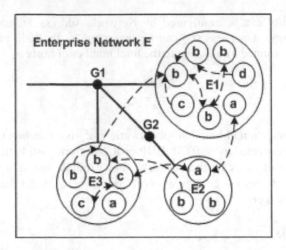

Fig. 1. Extracted factors of enterprise network

where $n(F \mid q_{Bo}B = i)$ and n are the number of elements in the set F with the starting node i and the number of elements in the set Q, respectively. In Figure 1, the directed graph of nodes illustrates the example of trust relationship. Using equation (4), T = 0.17.

4 Fuzzy Prediction Model

The model uses fuzzy decision for the prediction. Three steps are performed; fuzzification, inference, and defuzzification. The fuzzy sets for inputs and output are as follows.

- Input: evaluation factors (O, H, T)
  Fuzzy set: {Low, Middle, High}
- Output: worm damage (D)
  Fuzzy set: {Normal, Critical}

The exact partitioning of input and output spaces depends upon membership functions. Triangular shapes specify the membership functions of inputs by inductive reasoning. The *damage threshold*, which is defined by an organization, divides the output into two classes. Expert experiences are used to generate production rules. For fuzzy inference, we use the minimum correlation method, which truncates the consequent fuzzy region at the truth of the premise. The centroid defuzzification method is adopted to yield the expected value of the solution fuzzy region.

4.1 Fuzzification

Membership functions can be accommodated by using the essential characteristic of inductive reasoning. The induction is performed by the entropy minimization principle [9]. A key goal of entropy minimization analysis is to determine the quantity of information in a given data set. The entropy of a probability distribution is a measure of the uncertainty of the distribution. To employ the entropy minimization for generating membership functions of inputs, it is based on a partitioning or analog screening. It draws a threshold line between two classes of sample data as in Figure 2. This classifies the samples while minimizing the entropy for an optimum partitioning. We select a threshold value x in the range between x_1 and x_2. This divides the range into two regions, $[x_1, x]$ and $[x, x_2]$ or p and q, respectively.

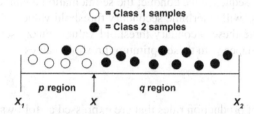

Fig. 2. Basic concept of entropy minimization

The entropy for a given value of x is

$$S(x) = p(x)S_p(x) + q(x)S_q(x) \tag{5}$$

where

$$S_p(x) = -[p_1(x)\ln p_1(x) + p_2(x)\ln p_2(x)] \tag{6}$$

$$S_q(x) = -[q_1(x)\ln q_1(x) + q_2(x)\ln q_2(x)] \tag{7}$$

and where

$p_k(x)$ and $q_k(x)$ are the conditional probabilities that the class k sample is in the region $[x_1, x_1+x]$ and $[x_1+x, x_2]$, respectively.

$p(x)$ and $q(x)$ are probabilities that all samples are in the region $[x_1, x_1+x]$ and $[x_1+x, x_2]$, respectively.

$$p(x) + q(x) = 1$$

We calculate entropy estimates of $p_k(x)$, $q_k(x)$, $p(x)$, and $q(x)$, as follows:

$$p_k(x) = \frac{n_k(x)+1}{n(x)+1} \tag{8}$$

$$q_k(x) = \frac{N_k(x)+1}{N(x)+1} \tag{9}$$

$$p(x) = \frac{n(x)}{n} \tag{10}$$

$$q(x) = 1 - p(x) \tag{11}$$

where
$n_k(x)$ is the number of class k samples in $[x_1, x_1+x]$
$n(x)$ is the total number of samples in $[x_1, x_1+x]$
$N_k(x)$ is the number of class k samples in $[x_1+x, x_2]$
$N(x)$ is the total number of samples in $[x_1+x, x_2]$
n is the total number of samples in $[x_1, x_2]$

The value of x in the interval $[x_1, x_2]$ that gives the minimum entropy is chosen as the optimum threshold value. This x divides the interval $[x_1, x_2]$ into two sub-intervals. In the next sequence we conduct the segmentation again, on each of the sub-intervals; this process will determine secondary threshold values. The same procedure is applied to calculate these secondary threshold values. Fuzzy sets of inputs are defined by triangular shapes with these optimum threshold values.

4.2 Inference

A rule base is a set of production rules that are expressed as follows.

- Rule 1: If $(x_1$ is $A^1{}_1)$ and $(x_2$ is $A^1{}_2)$ and ... and $(x_w$ is $A^1{}_w)$, then y is B^1
- Rule 2: If $(x_1$ is $A^2{}_1)$ and $(x_2$ is $A^2{}_2)$ and ... and $(x_w$ is $A^2{}_w)$, then y is B^2 ...
- Rule z: If $(x_1$ is $A^z{}_1)$ and $(x_2$ is $A^z{}_2)$ and ... and $(x_w$ is $A^z{}_w)$, then y is B^z

Here, x_j $(1 \leq j \leq w)$ are input variables, y is an output variable, and $A^i{}_j$ and B^i $(1 \leq i \leq z)$ are fuzzy sets that are characterized by membership functions. The numbers of input and output variables are three and one, respectively. Total 27 production rules are generated by expert experiences. The example of rule set is described in table 1.

Table 1. The example of rule set

O	H	T	D
Low	Low	Low	Normal
Low	Low	Medium	Normal
Low	Low	High	Normal
High	Medium	High	Critical

4.3 Defuzzification

Fuzzy decision estimates worm damage in the fuzzy set {Normal, Critical}. In addition, these are defuzzified to numerical values (the number of infected hosts) as shown in Figure 3. In these graphs, the Z-axis values are the fraction of infected hosts. The values on X-axis and Y-axis represent (1) H and T in Figure 3(a), (2) O and T in Figure 3(b), and (3) O and H in Figure 3(c). Comparison of the three graphs for a given the maximum value (1.0) of O, H, and T shows the effect on worm damage. These surfaces show that the factors have different effects on the fraction of infected hosts over a broad range of values.

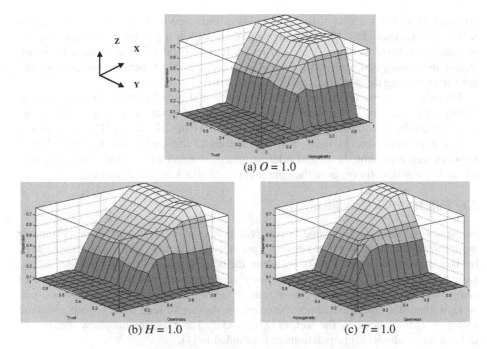

(a) $O = 1.0$

(b) $H = 1.0$ (c) $T = 1.0$

Fig. 3. The surfaces of worm damages

5 Experiments

The test environment consists of a class C heterogeneous IP network subdivided into three wired subnets and one wireless subnet. There are 200 hosts of desktop computers and laptops, running a mixture of Windows NT, Windows 2000, Windows XP, Solaris, and Linux operating systems. In this network, a router connects the four subnets with 6 Ethernet switches and 2 IEEE 802.11b wireless access points. The bandwidth of the core network is 100 Mbps.

The experiments aim to study the full infection condition, to investigate the usefulness of factors, and to evaluate the ability of the model to predict the worm damage. Blaster and Sasser, which attack the default configuration of desktop computers in enterprise networks and require no user intervention, are selected. Code Red and Slammer are not chosen because they target server application and attack the optional component of application. Nimda was not selected since it requires user intervention for some modes of infection, hence its behavior is difficult to simulate.

Two variants of Blaster and two variants of Sasser randomly attack the test network. The infection was performed for 192 different test configurations that are the combination of different values of three factors: O, H, and T. The openness value is varied by NAT for computers in subnets. The homogeneity is the density of hosts running Windows family. Finally, the configuration of file transfer and file sharing service is used to represent trust conditions.

During worm execution, the number of infected computers is calculated at the average time of full infection condition (as described in the Section 5.1) for each test configuration. The fraction of infected nodes is translated into two classes: Normal (D < 0.3) and Critical ($D \geq 0.3$). The damage threshold is the condition defined by the organization; here, we use 0.3 for our test network. Total 1,728 data have been collected and among 864 are used for generating membership functions and another 864 are for evaluating the performance of the prediction.

There are two main reasons that we perform real attacks rather than simulation. Firstly, the real attack can provide the conditions of practical configuration setup, effect of environmental factors, and stochastic behaviors of attacks. The other reason is that it is reasonable to setup host populations in the real networks. One class C network can represent the actual address space of small or medium enterprise network. We can directly observe the consequence of attack in a real manner.

5.1 Full Infection Condition

We study the full infection condition of real attacks in enterprise networks. From our assumption, computers in the networks are not all infected. We assume that partial hosts are protected from attacks by some factors. To prove this assumption, worms were released in two networks of 200 hosts: *real network* and *ideal network*. The first setup is a network with the configuration of factors O, H, and T. The later is a network without the configuration of these factors. As can be seen from Figure 4, the full infection is influenced by the factors O, H, and T. The experiments show that worms did not infect almost all populations as concluded in [1].

Again, from Figure 4, we can imply that the number of infected hosts can be calculated at the time of zero increase of infection. The time values are different in each test case. For example, we can report the number of infected hosts of the real network at the time of 19. In this paper, the experiments use this concept to define time values for calculating the number of infected hosts.

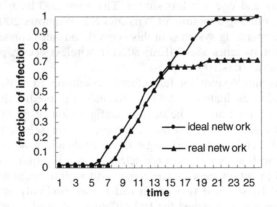

Fig. 4. Full infection condition

5.2 Usefulness of Factors

In general, there is no exact answer to the question of which factors are optimal for damage prediction. It is believed that the factors that influence the worm infection significantly can be used to predict the worm damage. To observe the effect of single variable to the infection, Figure 5 shows the number of infected hosts (Y-axis) as a function of one variable when the other two are held fixed. As can be seen, the number of infected hosts increases as the factor values increases. This means that the proposed factors effect to the number of infected hosts significantly and therefore can be used to predict the worm damage.

We also consider the factors that are useful to classify the worm damage into two classes. Actually, we investigate Receiver Operating Characteristics (ROC) curve that presents the variation of true positives (Y-axis) according to the change of false positives (X-axis). Figure 6 shows the ROC curves with respect to the different damage threshold of classification. Several thresholds are considers: 0.3, 0.4, 0.5, and 0.6.

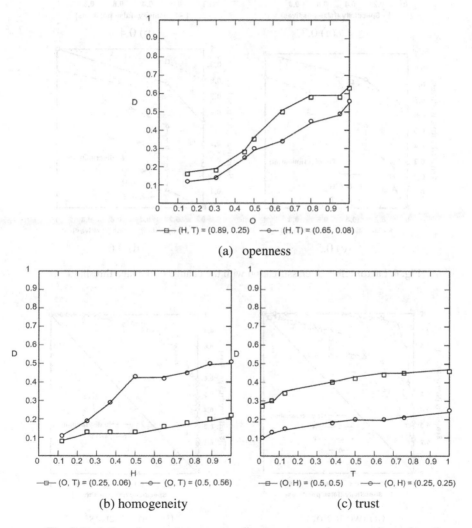

(a) openness

(b) homogeneity

(c) trust

Fig. 5. Variation of worm damage according to openness, homogeneity, and trust

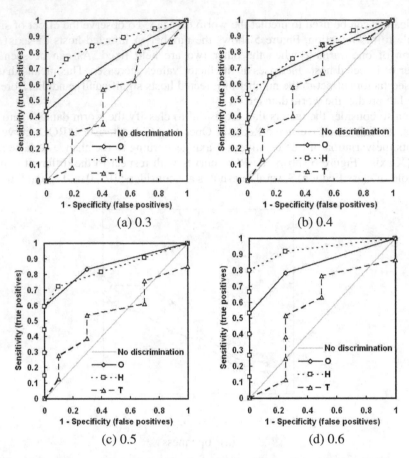

Fig. 6. Factor effect of classification with the change of damage threshold

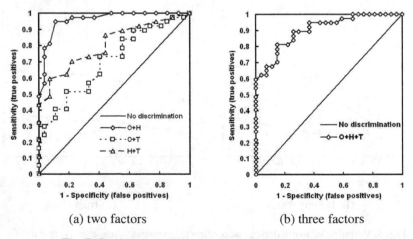

(a) two factors   (b) three factors

Fig. 7. Combination of factors with the damage threshold 0.3

The ROC curve determines that the factor is effective if its curve draws above the no discrimination line. In addition, we can compare the significance of factors for binary classification by comparing the area under ROC curve. The greater area the more effective factor for classification. As can be seen in Figure 6, most factors are above the no discrimination line. Homogeneity is likely the most significant factor in classification for all damage thresholds in this study.

Figure 7 shows ROC curves of combination of factors with the damage threshold 0.3. Figure 7(a) shows ROC curves of combination $O+H$, $O+T$, and $H+T$. Figure 7(b) shows ROC curve of combination $O+H+T$. As can be seen, combination of factors produces more effective in classification than the single factor as shown in Figure 6. Here, $O+H$ and $O+H+T$ are the effective combinations of factors for classification in this study.

5.3 Performance of Prediction

The experiments are conducted with different population sizes and damage thresholds. Table 2 shows the prediction rate (true-positive rate) and false-positive error rate for 200 hosts of heterogeneous networks with the damage thresholds of 0.3, 0.4, 0.5, and 0.6. The outputs of prediction are Normal and Critical. As can be seen, the prediction rate is 100% for all threshold cases. The greater threshold does not guarantee the low false-positive error rate because it can be worse than the smaller threshold.

Table 2. The prediction rate and false-positive error rate with test data

Damage Threshold	0.3	0.4	0.5	0.6
Prediction rate	100%	100%	100%	100%
False-positive error rate	4.68%	3.12%	1.56%	3.12%

Table 3. Prediction accuracy for different network sizes measured by RMSE (MAE)

Number of nodes	100	150	200
Wired networks	0.101 (0.087)	0.100 (0.083)	0.097 (0.083)
Wireless networks	0.095 (0.084)	0.098 (0.084)	0.107 (0.089)
Heterogeneous networks	0.106 (0.088)	0.097 (0.081)	0.106 (0.089)

From the outputs of prediction (Normal and Critical), the model translates the output to the number of infected hosts. Therefore, we can analyze the performance of prediction by comparing the number of infected hosts from prediction to the real infection. The prediction accuracy of the model is measured by the root mean squared error (RMSE) and the mean absolute error (MAE).

RMSE is the most commonly used measure of accuracy of prediction. If this number is significantly greater than MAE, it means that there are test cases in which the prediction error is significantly greater than the average error. MAE is the average of the difference between predicted and actual value in all test cases; it is the average prediction error. Table 3 shows that there is no significant difference in the prediction accuracy for the three network architectures with the damage threshold 0.3. The RMSE in all cases is about 0.1. We can observe that the network size does not have much effect on prediction accuracy, for the range of networks used in this study.

6 Concluding Remarks

This paper analyzes the key factors that influence the worm damage and propose a new model to estimating the worm damage utilizing these key factors. By employing fuzzy decision, the model uses inductive reasoning in determining membership functions. Experiments using real worms on a variety of test configurations were used to compare predicted and test results. The experimental results show that the selected parameters are strongly correlated with actual infection rates, and the proposed model produces accurate estimates. These results suggest that this model represents a viable approach for damage prediction of the worm class that targets desktop computers in organization. Future work will be aimed at finding more sophisticated techniques of integrating soft computing and hard computing to predict worm damage, as well as evaluate the system with larger data sets and by simulation.

Acknowledgement

The authors would like to thank Yuen Poovarawan, James Brucker, Pirawat Watanapongse, Yodyium Tipsuwan, and anonymous referees for valuable comments to improve the quality of the paper.

References

1. Staniford, S., Paxon, V., Weaver, N.: How to Own the Internet in Your Spare Time. Proceedings of the 11th USENIX Security Symposium (2002) 149-167
2. Moore, D., Shannon, C.: Code-Red: a Case Study on the Spread and Victims of an Internet Worm. Proceedings of the ACM SICGOMM Internet Measurement Workshop (2002) 273-284
3. Moore, D., Shannon, C., Voelker, G., Savage, S.: Internet Quarantine: Requirements for Containing Self-Propagating Code. Proceedings of the IEEE INFOCOM Conference (2003) 1901-1910
4. Moore, D., Paxon, V., Savage, S., Shannon, C., Staniford, S., Weaver, N.: The Spread of the Sapphire/Slammer Worm. CAIDA (2003)
5. CERT/CC Advisory: Nimda worm. CA-2001-26, CERT (2001)
6. CERT/CC Advisory: W32/Blaster worm. CA-2003-20, CERT (2003)
7. Jang, J. R.: Neuro-Fuzzy and Soft Computing. Prentice-Hall, NJ (1997)
8. Timothy, J. R.: Fuzzy Logic With Engineering Applications. McGRAW-HILL, Singapore (1997)
9. Kim, C. J.: An Algorithmic Approach for Fuzzy Inference. IEEE Transaction on Fuzzy Systems 5(4) (1997) 585-598
10. Toth, T., Kruegel, C.: Connection-history Based Anomaly Detection. Proceedings of the IEEE Work shop on Information Assurance and Security (2002) 30-35
11. Williamson, M.: Throttling Viruses: Restricting Propagation to Defeat Malicious Mobile Code. HP Laboratories Bristol, Report No. HPL-2002-172 (2002)
12. Cheung, S., Crawford, R., Dilger, M., Frank, J., Hoagland, J., Levitt, K., Rowe, J., Staniford Chen, S., Yip, R., Zerkle, D.: The Design of GrIDS: A Graph-Based Intrusion Detection System. Computer Science Dept., UC Davis, Report No.CSE-99-2 (1999)

13. Kephart, J. O., White, R. S.: Measuring and Modeling Computer Virus Prevalence. Proceedings of the IEEE Symposium on Security and Privacy (1993) 2-14
14. Eustice, K., Kleinrock, L., Markstrum, S., Popek, G., Ramakrishna, V., Reiher, P.: Securing Nomads: The Case for Quarantine, Examination and Decontamination. Proceedings of the ACM New Security Paradigms Workshop (2004) 123-128
15. Kephart, J. O., White, R. S.: Directed-graph Epidemiological Models of Computer Virus Prevalence. Proceedings of the IEEE Symposium on Security and Privacy (1993) 343-359
16. Zou, C. C., Gong, W., Towsley, D.: Code Red Worm Propagation Modeling and Analysis. Proceedings of the ACM CCS'02 (2002) 138-147
17. Chen, Z., Gao, L., Kwiat, K.: Modeling the Spread of Active Worms. Proceedings of the IEEE Symposium on Security and Privacy (2003) 1890-1900
18. Ellis, D.: Worm Anatomy and Model. Proceedings of the ACM Worm'03 (2003) 42-50
19. Kenzle, D. M., Elder, M. C.: Recent Worms: A Survey and Trends. Proceedings of the ACM Worm'03 (2003) 1-10
20. Wegner, A., Dubendorfer, T., Plattner, B., Hiestand, R.: Experiences with Worm Propagation Simulations. Proceedings of the ACM Worm'03 (2003) 34-41
21. Weaver, N., Paxson, V., Staniford, S., Cunningham, R.: A Taxonomy of Computer Worms. Proceedings of the ACM Worm'03 (2003) 11-18
22. Wang, C., Knight, J., Elder, M.: On computer viral infection and the effect of immunization. Proceedings of the 16th Annual Computer Security Applications Conference (2000) 246-256

Evaluation of the Unified Modeling Language for Security Requirements Analysis*

Marife G. Ontua and Susan Pancho-Festin

Department of Computer Science, University of the Philippines,
Diliman, Quezon City 1101, Philippines
marife.ontua@up.edu.ph, susan.pancho@up.edu.ph

Abstract. Security protocols can be difficult to specify and analyze. These difficulties motivate the need for models that will support the development of secure systems from the design to the implementation stages. We used the Unified Modeling Language (UML), an industry standard in object-oriented systems modeling, to express security requirements. We also developed an application, the *UML Analyzer*, to help identify possible vulnerabilities in the modeled protocol. This was achieved by checking the XML Meta-data Interchange (XMI) files generated from the UML diagrams. When compared with other analyses of IKE, our results indicate that UML diagrams and XMI files offer promising possibilities in the modeling and analysis of security protocols.

1 Introduction

Security protocols can be difficult to specify and analyze, particularly for developers with very little background on formal methods. These difficulties motivate the need for approaches that will support the development of secure systems from the design to the implementation stages without being inaccessible to system developers. We investigate the use of the Unified Modeling Language (UML) to describe and analyze security protocols. We chose UML for its accessibility to system developers. We used a free UML tool [1] which offers the facility of generating XML Meta-data Interchange (XMI) files from the UML protocol diagrams. These XMI files were utilized in the analysis of the security protocol modeled. We chose to model the Internet Key Exchange (IKE) [2] due to the availability of other analyses for this protocol with which we can compare our findings. Our aim was to investigate UML's capacity for expressing security protocol features.

The paper is organized as follows. Section 2 outlines related work, while Section 3 describes how we have utilized UML and XMI in the description and analysis of IKE. In Section 4, we discuss our findings and compare them with previous analyses of IKE. Section 5 summarizes our results and outlines our recommendations for future work.

---

* Support for this research was provided by the University of the Philippines and the University of the Philippines Engineering Research and Development Foundation Inc.

J. Song, T. Kwon, and M. Yung (Eds.): WISA 2005, LNCS 3786, pp. 68–80, 2006.

2   Related Work

We propose to utilize the Unified Modeling Language (UML) [3] in the expression and analysis of the Internet Key Exchange (IKE) [2] protocol. We briefly describe UML and the diagrams available within the modeling language. We also describe IKE and the modes available within the protocol. Previous work has applied UML for protocol specification and/or analysis (e.g., [4, 5, 6, 7]) but we have yet to find work which compares results of a UML-based specification and analysis with results from other methods.

2.1   Unified Modeling Language (UML)

The Unified Modeling Language (UML) [3] defines a meta-model and provides a standard for visual models. It has four views of the software development process and UML diagrams are grouped into these views. However, UML does not prescribe the use of any specific modeling process in the application of these diagrams.

1. **Use Case View.** The Use case view has one diagram, the Use Case diagram. It describes the relationship between actors and use cases, which is a set of situations describing an interaction between a user and a system.
2. **Logical View.** Logical view models every aspect of the software solution. It has six diagrams namely *Class, Object, Activity, Statechart, Sequence,* and *Collaboration* diagrams.
   - The **Class Diagram** models class structure and contents.
   - The **Object Diagram** models objects and their attributes. It complements class diagrams.
   - The **Activity Diagram** illustrate the work flow behavior of the system. It allows modeling of concurrent and synchronized processes or activities.
   - The **Statechart Diagram** describes the life of an object by viewing it in terms of state changes, which are triggered by events.
   - The **Sequence Diagram** models interaction between objects. It is composed of objects and messages that are mapped into timelines.
   - The **Collaboration Diagram** is an alternative form of interaction diagram.
3. **Component View.** The Component Diagram models the physical implementation of the software. It defines software modules and their relationships, which are referred to as dependencies.
4. **Deployment View.** The Deployment Diagram describes the physical relationship between software and hardware. It provides a static view of the implementation environment.

2.2   UML and Computer Security

Devanbu and Stubblebine suggest unifying security with software engineering [8]. Several efforts have applied UML to security. In [9], the authors present SecureUML to model role-based access control. In a different application, Jürgens

[10] developed UMLsec and showed how UML can be used to express security requirements such as confidentiality and integrity. In this paper, we focus on the UMLsec approach.

UML Diagrams. Jürgens [10] showed how four UML diagrams can be used to reflect security requirements. The first diagram is the Class diagram, which is a set of classes and a set of dependencies. The second diagram is the Statechart diagram where an object is said to preserve security if an output with low level security does not depend on an input value with a high level security or when leak of information is prevented. The third diagram is the Sequence diagram, which describes the interaction of objects via message exchange. Finally, to define the physical architecture of the design, Deployment diagrams can be used to ensure that the physical layer meets security requirements on communication links between different components.

In [6], two additional UML diagrams were used to express security requirements. One was the Use Case diagram, which describes typical interactions between different components of a computer system and the other diagram was the Activity diagram . A security requirement specified in the Use Case diagram is said to be achieved if processes included in the Activity diagram show that it has been satisfied when the final state has been reached.

UMLsec. To further support the use of UML as a tool in developing secure systems, UMLsec, an extension of UML was developed. In [7], *stereotypes, tagged values* and *constraints*, which are UML extension mechanisms, were used to represent common security requirements. Some of these requirements were *fair exchange, secrecy or confidentiality* and *secure information flow*.

Other work which used UML to express security requirements are:

- **UMLsec and CEPS.** In [4], UMLsec was used to model and investigate a security-critical part of the Common Electronic Purse Specification (CEPS).
- **UML and Java Security.** In [5], UML was was used to specify access control mechanisms provided by Java.
- **UML and CORBA.** UML was also used to model Common Object Request Broker Architecture (CORBA) Security [11].

2.3   Internet Key Exchange (IKE)

The Internet Key Exchange (IKE) [2] is a hybrid protocol that allows for the establishment of security associations. It is a key management protocol used in conjunction with IPSec [2]. IKE has two methods used in establishing an authenticated key exchange and these are: *Main Mode and Aggressive Mode*. In *Main mode*, the first two messages negotiate the policy, the next two exchange Diffie-Hellman public values and ancillary data such as nonces, and the last two messages authenticate the Diffie-Hellman exchange. On the other hand, in the *Aggressive mode*, the first two messages negotiate the policy, exchange Diffie-Hellman public values and ancillary data. Authentication of the responder also takes place in the second message and the third message authenticates the initiator and provides a proof of participation in the exchange [2].

Main mode and aggressive mode operate in one of the two phases in IKE. Phase I is where two ISAKMP [12] peers establish a secure authenticated channel to communicate while Phase 2 is where security associations are negotiated on behalf of security services that need key material or parameter negotiation.

Four different authentication methods are allowed. These are:

1. Pre-Shared Key
2. Public Key Signature/Digital Signatures
3. Public Key Encryption
4. Revised Public Key Encryption

3   Methodology

We used UML to model the IKE protocol, considering the different modes possible. Resulting models were saved in XMI format and were later converted to XML files that were analyzed by our application to identify possible vulnerabilities in the protocol.

3.1   Modeling with Poseidon for UML

IKE [2] was modeled using Gentleware's Poseidon for UML tool [1]. Sequence diagrams were used since they best describe the interaction between principals in a protocol by specifying the messages passed between them. To model IKE using Poseidon, the object and stimuli diagram elements were used.

Objects. Objects are elements responsible for sending and receiving messages. In protocols, these are the principals involved. To identify the principals, one will simply enter a name under the properties of an object. For example,

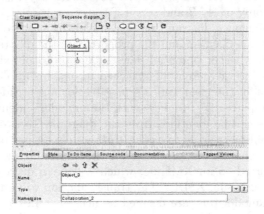

Fig. 1. The Object Diagram Element

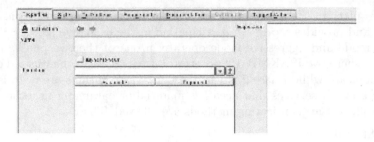

Fig. 2. The CallAction Properties

in (Figure 1), specifying `Object_2` under the name property would identify the object as `object_2`.

Stimuli. In Poseidon's sequence diagram, messages are referred to as stimuli and it can either be a *call, send* or *return* stimuli. *Call* stimuli represent synchronous messages while *send* stimuli demonstrate asynchronous messages. On the other hand, *return* stimuli correspond to return statements of *Call* stimuli.

A stimulus can be connected with any operation or method provided by the receiving object. This can be done by connecting the stimulus with an action (DispatchAction) that will call the operation (CallAction). In the diagram, this can be achieved by opening the DispatchAction property of the stimulus and provide the formula of the operation in the Expression property of the CallAction (Figure 2). A CallAction's name can also be provided.

3.2   Analyzing the UML Diagram

Suppose we have a simplified protocol wherein the principals involved are A, B and a trusted server S that will be responsible for generating a session key. The aim of the protocol is for A and B to know the session key K_{ab}. The session key should be known only to A, B and server S.

Using UML's sequence diagram, we can model the protocol above as shown in Figure 3. With this diagram and the properties of the diagram elements, one can visually check whether potential flaws in the protocol exist. For instance, notice that Msg 1 has no stereotype attached to it. This implies that Stimulus A,B has been sent in the clear and it's possible for an intruder to manipulate the message, i.e. replace "B" in *(A,B)* with the intruder's identity.

Other problems can be identified from the diagram. To assist the analyst, a program, which will be referred to as the *UML Analyzer*, has been developed to determine possible threats in a protocol. For the UML diagram to be processed, it has to be exported to an XMI file, which will be transformed by the program to an XML file using XSLT.[1] The transformation will only consider parts of the UML metamodel that are deemed as necessary in checking the model.

---

[1] XSLT [13] is a language used to transform XML documents into other XML documents.

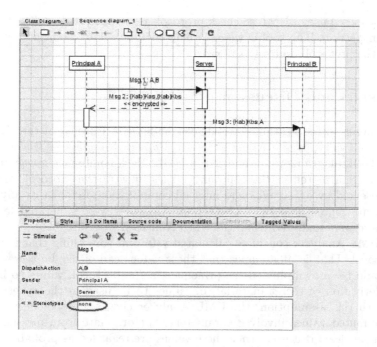

Fig. 3. Simple Protocol Model

The resulting XML file will then be used by the application to detect potential vulnerabilities in the protocol being modeled.

With Document Object Modeling (DOM) as the parser, information on the elements and its attributes are stored in hash tables and linked lists. After parsing the XML file, the *UML Analyzer* will check the parameters of the called operations (*CallAction*). That is, it will identify whether values used in the calculation of the *CallAction* originate from messages (*Stimuli*) that were sent in clear. If the message's stereotype is *encrypted* then confidentiality and integrity of information exchanged between principals is assumed to exist. That is, unauthorized leak of information and unauthorized modification of information is prevented.

When no stereotype has been defined for a *Stimulus*, and a *CallAction* has parameters coming from this message, then the latter is considered as a source of threat in the protocol and the *Stimulus* from which the parameter originated will be considered as the reason why the *CallAction* is considered a threat.

On the other hand, if at least one of the *CallAction's* parameters, as defined in its expression property in the diagram, comes from a stimulus, or from another *CallAction* that is considered as suspect then the *CallAction* is also considered as suspect. If its arguments are not found in any of the stimuli and other *CallActions*, its state cannot be determined. Just like the *Stimulus*, a list of possible reasons why it became suspect will be generated.

The proposed use of UML to check protocols is not intended to dispense with human inspection. The tool is there to help the analyst by pointing out where flaws in the protocol are likely to exist.

4   Results and Discussion

Four different authentication methods can be used in Phase 1 of the IKE protocol. With two types of exchanges namely *Main and Aggressive Modes*, a total of eight UML diagrams were modeled in UML. Each combination was modeled in one diagram to reflect the continuity in the flow of the protocol. Messages are represented by a *Stimulus* and internal computation of values or any secret material are represented by a *CallAction*. XMI files were generated for these models and were analyzed using the UML Analyzer program.

The UML Analyzer considers calculated values as something that is vital in the protocol. That is, it assumes that these values can either be secret values that should be known only to the principals in the protocol, values to be used in the derivation of secret materials or values to be used in the generation of keys. With this assumption, the UML Analyzer checks whether derivation of these computed values involves parameters that originate from messages that were sent in clear. If it does, then these values are regarded as probable sources of problems in the protocol. Messages that were sent in clear and containing some of the computed value's parameters are considered as sources of threat for that computed value.

4.1   Sample Result – IKE Using PreShared Key

As an example, for the main mode of the IKE protocol, the result indicates that eight calculated values may cause problems in the protocol. These values and their possible sources of threat are as follows:

1. SKEYID = prf(pre-shared key, Ni | Nr)
   - Sources
     - Source 1 = Message : HDR,g^xr,Nr
     - Source 2 = Message : HDR,g^xi,Ni
     - Source 3 = Message : HDR*, HASH1, SA, Ni, (g^xi), (IDui, IDur)
2. HASH_I = prf(SKEYID, g^xi | g^xr | CKY-I | CKY-R | SA | IDii)
   HASH_R = prf(SKEYID, g^xr | g^xi | CKY-R | CKY-I | SA | IDir)
   - Sources
     - Source 1 = Message : HDR,g^xr,Nr
     - Source 2 = Message : HDR,SA
     - Source 3 = Message : HDR,g^xi,Ni
     - Source 4 = Message : HDR*, HASH1, sA, Ni, (g^xi), (IDui, IDur)
     - Source 5 = Computed Value : SKEYID = prf(pre-shared key, Ni | Nr)

3. SKEYID_d = prf(SKEYID, g^xy |CKY-I | CKY-R | 0)
   SKEYID_a = prf(SKEYID, SKEYID_d, g^xy |CKY-I | CKY-R | 1)
   SKEYID_e = prf(SKEYID, SKEYID_a, g^xy |CKY-I | CKY-R | 2)
   − Sources
     • Source 1 = Computed value: SKEYID = prf(pre-shared key, Ni | Nr)

4. HASH1 = prf(SKEYID_a, M-ID | SA | Ni [g^xi] [| IDui | IDur])
   − Sources
     • Source 1= Message : HDR,SA
     • Source 2= Message : HDR,g^xi,Ni
     • Source 3= Message : HDR*, HASH1, SA, Ni, (g^xi), (IDui, IDur)
     • Source 4= Computed Value : SKEYID = prf(pre-shared key, Ni | Nr)

5. HASH2 = prf(SKEYID_a, M-ID | Ni | SA | Nr [g^xr] [| IDui | IDur])
   − Sources
     • Source 1= Message : HDR,g^xr,Nr
     • Source 2= Message : HDR,SA
     • Source 3= Message : HDR,g^xi,Ni
     • Source 4= Message : HDR*, HASH1, SA, Ni, (g^xi), (IDui, IDur)
     • Source 5= Computed Value : SKEYID = prf(pre-shared key, Ni | Nr)

The first value that is considered to cause a problem in the protocol is SKEYID. In its derivation, it made use of a pre-shared key and nonces from the initiator and responder. Two messages containing the nonces were sent unencrypted before the calculation of SKEYID took place. This means, that it is possible for a third party to modify the values of the nonces before sending it to the desired party. The intruder may not be able to compute for SKEYID due to the absence of the pre-shared key. However, the initiator and responder may have different values for SKEYID. Source 3 of SKEYID is not a valid source of threat since this message was sent after the calculation of SKEYID took place.

Problems encountered with SKEYID have a cascading effect since it was used in the derivation of other values in the protocol. These values include:

1. HASH_I
2. HASH_R
3. SKEYID_d
4. SKEYID_e
5. SKEYID_a

HASH_I and HASH_R are used for authenticating the initiator and responder. If both parties have arrived at different values for SKEYID, then authentication will fail and denial of service may occur; moreover, the succeeding exchange of messages will not occur. Source 4 for both values is deemed invalid since the message was sent after HASH_I (HASH_R) was computed .

Values of SKEYID_d, SKEYID_e and SKEYID_a keying materials may also be compromised if the value for SKEYID is doubtful. However, since the computation of these keys involves g^xy, which is a Diffie-Hellman shared secret, then it would be difficult for a third party to identify the values for these keys. If authentication has been successful, then the exchange of messages between the initiator and responder can continue without being compromised.

It was also noted that, in the computation for HASH1 and HASH2, the message *HDR, SA* was flagged as a potential vulnerability source. This means that HASH1 (HASH2) relies on a value *(SA)* that is sent in clear and is easily modifiable by an attacker.

Finally, HASH1 and HASH2 may be compromised since most of the values used in its derivation came from messages that were sent in clear or unencrypted. But since it is difficult for a third party to identify the value of SKEYID_a then it is also difficult to identify the values of HASH1 and HASH2.

4.2   False Positives

The current implementation of the program produces many false positives since it does not yet use the details regarding the sequencing of messages. For example, in the given sample result, SKEYID was flagged to be a potential threat since two parameters used in deriving it (Ni and Nr) were detected to have been sent in the clear in several messages. These messages were enumerated as:

 − Source 1 = Message : HDR,g^xr,Nr
 − Source 2 = Message : HDR,g^xi,Ni
 − Source 3 = Message : HDR*, HASH1, SA, Ni, (g^xi), (IDui, IDur)

Of these three flagged sources, only the first two may be considered as valid threat sources since these messages were sent prior to the computation of SKEYID. The last source is a false positive since this message was sent after SKEYID has already been computed.

4.3   Summary of Flaws Identified by the Analyzer

The UML Analyzer generated eight files one for each mode *(Main, Aggressive)* and authentication method pair, namely:

1. Pre-Shared Key, Main Mode
2. Pre-Shared Key, Aggressive Mode
3. Public Key Signature, Main Mode
4. Public Key Signature, Aggressive Mode
5. Public Key Encryption, Main Mode
6. Public Key Encryption, Aggressive Mode
7. Revised Public Key Encryption, Main Mode
8. Revised Public Key Encryption, Aggressive Mode

The potential vulnerabilities identified in IKE can be summarized as follows:

1. Man-in-the-middle attack leading to modification of messages. This may include messages containing parameters used in the subsequent derivation of secret values or any keying material.
2. Possibility for an intruder to dictate what security association will be used. This was detected in all result files since the security association (SA) was flagged to have been sent in clear.
3. Denial of service attack. The potential for denial of service stems from the ability of an attacker to subvert attempts to either authenticate or establish a security association by modifying parameters sent in messages.

4.4 Comparison of Analyses

Two other analyses of IKE, namely that of Meadows [14] and Zhou [15] were consulted after analyzing IKE with the use of UML diagrams. The results of the analysis results were compared to measure UML's capability in specifying security requirements. Consultation of the other two analyses was performed after the UML Analyzer was developed and applied to avoid bias in the generation of the results.

In Meadow's analysis, the NRL Protocol Analyzer, which is a special purpose formal methods tool, was used to evaluate IKE. On the other hand, no tool was involved in Zhou's analysis. The flaw was discovered when the protocol was inspected by the author.

Three main problems were also identified by Meadows [14] and these were:

1. **Ambiguous specification of identities resulting to a man-in-the-middle attack.** In Phase I of the protocol, before the identities are exchanged, only the IP addresses can be used to identify the peers involved. With this, it is possible for an intruder to replace the IP address of say peer B with its own address and convince peer A that peer B is linked to the modified IP address.
2. **Penultimate authentication failure** leading to a fail-stop situation in a protocol or inability of the protocol to proceed.
3. **Denial of service without the knowledge of the principal that such attack has occurred.** In Phase II of the protocol, inclusion of identification information in the exchange of messages is optional. With this, receiver B of the message can use the IP address of sender A of the message as index to the encryption key. In this situation, B cannot distinguish messages coming from A or B. Therefore, an intruder can substitute A's IP address for B's, ending with B sharing a key with itself. B has been denied sharing a key with A without knowing it.

Items one and two are from the analysis of IKE's phase one while item three is from phase II of IKE. On the other hand, the flaw that was detected in [15] was on the possibility for an intruder to dictate what Security Association (SA) will be used. This will occur when an intruder will intercept the SA negotiation between the initiator and responder.

Due to some limitations, analysis of IKE using the NRL Protocol Analyzer was conducted in phases, with some adjustments to the tool [14]. Part of the motivation for the NRL study was to determine NRL's applicability in the analysis of a protocol such as IKE. With the UML Analyzer, each possible mode and authentication method pair was depicted with a UML sequence diagram. From these diagrams, it identified that a man-in-the-middle attack is possible for some messages that were sent in clear. This leads to modification of some the parameters used later for computed values. Nevertheless, unlike the NRL Protocol Analyzer that had identified ambiguous specification of identities as source of the attack, the UML Analyzer only indicated what messages were sent in clear that could have contributed to the attack.

The second problem identified by the UML Analyzer is the penultimate authentication failure identified in [14]. Penultimate authentication in the context of IKE requires that if B accepts a SA to have originated from A, then A must have also accepted the security association. Failure of this type of authentication was identified by the UML Analyzer. It indicated that it is possible for a third party to modify the contents of the initiator's SA proposal without the initiator and responder's knowledge. With this, a responder might choose (and accept) a proposal that was never part of the initiator's offer.

Finally, a likely denial of service scenario was identified by the UML Analyzer. This generally stems from the use of $SKEYID$, utilized in the derivation of the keys eventually used in authentication. When the value of $SKEYID$ is compromised, the values of the authentication keys are also compromised. The UML Analyzer identifies parameters that an attacker can deliberately modify; these are the parameters subsequently used in the derivation of $SKEYID$. An authentication failure can occur since both the initiator and responder may end up computing different values for $SKEYID$. Meadow's analysis stated that at the time of the research, it was impossible to model denial of service directly in the NRL Analyzer.

5   Conclusion and Recommendations

Based on the analysis of IKE using UML and the comparison of our results with the two other analyses, it can be said that UML can be used as a tool in analyzing security requirements. The tool's sequence diagrams made it easier to see the exchanges of messages between the principals involved in the protocol including the calculations that were done internally by the principals. Normally, one would only assume that these calculations took place. UML's feature in providing XMI files for the diagrams paved the way for creating an application that would aid the analyst in identifying potential flaws in a security design.

5.1   Future Research

In this research, Gentleware's Poseidon UML sequence diagram was used to model a protocol and a Java-based application (UML Analyzer) was created to analyze the diagrams generated. The UML Analyzer works on the premise that a calculated value plays an important role in attaining the goals of confidentiality and integrity in a protocol. That is, these values have the potential to be either used in the derivation of keys and other secret values that have to be shared among principals of the protocol. With this, the UML Analyzer considers a calculated value to be a possible source of problem in the protocol if at least one of its parameters originate from messages that were sent in clear. In the following list, enhancements on the functionalities of the UML Analyzer and the use of UML will be highlighted to be able to maximize the capability of using UML to model security specifications.

1. **Encryption of Messages.** Stereotypes are used in UML diagrams to indicate the encryption of messages. Currently, the research considers encryption of the whole message. However, it is possible that only certain parts of the messages are encrypted. For it to handle encryption of certain parts of the message, other features of the UML that would be able to support this can be looked into.

2. **Consider Other Stereotypes.** Aside from *encrypted*, other terminologies like *high* can be used to indicate the message's security level. When this is done, it should be added in the program that stereotypes declared as such will be treated like how the analyzer currently treats messages tagged as *encrypted*.

3. **Improve Pattern Matching.** As mentioned, the program checks for parameters of the computed values that were sent in clear. To be able to do this, the analyzer made use of Java's *Regex* class to identify the existence of the parameters in the messages. However, use of *Regex* would mean special handling of symbols that are used in protocols or other security design. *Regex* might have its own way of interpreting these symbols that might result in the inability of the UML Analyzer to identify existence of patterns. A better pattern matching facility can also be developed.

4. **Consider Other UML Diagrams.** This research only considered the sequence diagram. Other UML diagrams can be used as well to specify security requirements. These diagrams have to be considered since it is possible that the sequence diagram is not the best UML diagram that can reflect a security protocol.

5. **False Positives.** The UML Analyzer currently errs on the side of caution and has erroneously identified some items to be flaws in the protocol being studied. Further study is needed to lessen the false positive rate.

6. **Improve the GUI interface.** For the application to be easier to use and understand, it would be better to improve the GUI interface of the application. It would also be best to have the output that contains the possible sources of threats to be presented in the GUI itself. This way, the user can right away see the result of the analysis.

References

1. Gentleware: Poseidon for UML, Community Edition version 3.1. http://www.gentleware.com (2005)
2. Harkins, D., Carrel, D.: The Internet Key Exchange (RFC 2409). http://www.ietf.org/rfc/rfc2409.txt (1998)
3. Unified modeling language 2.0 draft specifications. http://www.omg.org/uml/ (2003)
4. Jürjens, J.: Developing secure systems with UMLsec - from business processes to implementation. In: Proceedings of VIS 2001, Kiel, Germany. (2001)
5. Jürjens, J.: Modelling audit security for smart-card payment schemes with UMLsec. In: Proceedings of IFIP/SEC 2001 - 16th International Conference on Information Security, Paris, France. (2001)
6. Jürjens, J.: Secure Java development with UML. In: Proceedings of I-NetSec 01 - First International IFIP TC-11 WG 11.4 Working Conference on Network Security, Leuven,Belgium. (2001)
7. Jürjens, J.: UMLsec: Extending UML for secure systems development. In: Proceedings of UML 2002 Dresden. (2002)
8. Devanbu, P., Stubblebine, S.: Software engineering for security: a roadmap. In: The Future of Software Engineering. (2000) Special volume published in conjunction with International Conference on Software Engineering, Limerick, Ireland.
9. Lodderstedt, T., Basin, D., Doser, J.: SecureUML: A UML-based modeling language for model-driven security. In Jezequel, J., Hussmann, H., Cook, S., eds.: Proceedings of the UML 2002 - 5th International Conference. Number 2460 in Lecture Notes in Computer Science, Springer (2002)
10. Jürjens, J.: Towards development of secure systems using UMLsec. In Hußmann, H., ed.: Fundamental Approaches to Software Engineering (FASE, 4th International Conference, Part of ETAPS). Volume 2029 of Lecture Notes in Computer Science., Springer Verlag (2001) 187–200
11. Pachl, J.: UML model for CORBA security. www.omg.org/docs/security (1999)
12. Maughhan, D., Schertler, M., Schneider, M., Turner, J.: Internet Security Association and Key Management Protocol (RFC 2408). http://www.ietf.org/rfc/rfc2408.txt (1998)
13. Consortium, W.W.W.:   XSL   transformations   (XSLT)   version   1.0. http://www.w3.org/TR/1999/REC-xslt-19991116.html (1999)
14. Meadows, C.: Analysis of the Internet key exchange protocol using the NRL protocol analyzer. In: Proceedings of the 1999 IEEE Symposium on Security and Privacy. (1999) 216–231
15. Zhou, J.: Fixing a security flaw in IKE protocols. Electronics Letters **35** (1999) 1072–1073

A Simple and Efficient Conference Scheme
for Mobile Communications

Wen-Shenq Juang

Department of Information Management, Shih Hsin University,
No. 1, Lane 17, Sec. 1, Muja Rd., Wenshan Chiu,
Taipei, Taiwan 116, R.O.C.
wsjuang@cc.shu.edu.tw

Abstract. By using wireless communications, conferees can join a
teleconference at any time and any place. In order to hold a secure teleconference, they must share a conference key before holding the conference.
Up to date, public key cryptosystems are used in all proposed conference
key distribution schemes for protecting the privacy of conferees' locations
during the conference. The computation cost and communication cost
of these schemes is still high. In this paper, we propose a simple and
efficient conference scheme for mobile communications. The main merits
of our scheme include: (1) conferees can share a common conference key
to hold a secure teleconference over a public channel; (2) the location of a
particular conferee is protected to prevent a tracking attack; (3) it allows
a user to join or quit a mobile teleconference dynamically; (4) only secure
one-way hash functions and symmetric key cryptosystems are used, and
the computation and communication cost is very low; (5) there needs no
passwords or shared keys table in the network center.

Keywords: Mobile communications, Conference keys, Network security,
Symmetric cryptosystems, One-way hash functions.

1   Introduction

In mobile communications, subscribers can communicate quickly and conveniently with others at any time and any place. To date, mobile communications
have become one of the major mediums for transmitting information. It makes
subscribers possible to use various network services, e.g. shopping, payment,
teleconference , etc., conveniently [6, 8, 9, 20]. By using wireless communications,
conferees can join a teleconference at any place. All conferees can use their mobile
units at remote locations for cooperating a board meeting, a group discussion,
or a virtual classroom. Via the nearest base station, all conferees can transmit
their messages to a mobile switching center called a network center or conference
bridge. The network center receives messages from conferees, performs proper
processing, and then sends the result to base stations. The base station then
broadcasts the result to conferees.

In order to hold a secure conference in networks, all conferees must share
a common secret key named the conference key before holding the conference.

J. Song, T. Kwon, and M. Yung (Eds.): WISA 2005, LNCS 3786, pp. 81–95, 2006.

Since the concept of conference key establishment was first introduced in [4], some schemes [5, 11] about conference key distribution have been proposed. These schemes are not suitable for implementation on mobile devices with low computation and communication power and small amount of flash memory. To solve this problem, Hwang and Yang proposed a conference key distribution schemes [8] based on RSA and congruence mechanism for mobile communications. This scheme was improved by Hwang in [9] to allow a participant to join or quit a conference dynamically. In [20], Yi *et al.* used the modular square root technique [17, 19] to design a user efficient conference scheme for limited computing power mobile devices.

In consideration of the feasibility of holding a conference in mobile communication environments, the following two major criteria are important [8, 9, 20].

C1: Low computation and communication cost: Due to the computation power constraint and small flash memory of mobile units, they could not provide a high bandwidth and powerful computation ability.

C2: Dynamic participation: A participant can join or quit a conference dynamically.

Also, wireless communications transmit messages via radio. They are more easy to unauthorized access and eavesdropping than wireline communications. Generally, there are three major threats in mobile communications [3, 8, 9, 20].

T1: Impersonation: An impersonator disguises himself as a legitimate mobile subscriber and uses the permitted services for this subscriber.

T2: Eavesdropping: An eavesdropper intercepts mobile users' conversation or identities information.

T3: Tracking: A tracker locates the current location of an individual mobile user.

As mentioned in [8, 9, 20], for preventing these threats in mobile communication environments, the following security criteria are important for a conference scheme.

S1: Content privacy: Preserve the privacy of the conversation contents during the conference.

S2: Location privacy: Preserve the privacy of conferees' locations during the conference.

S3: Authenticity: Prevent the fraud by ensuing that the mobile units are authentic.

S4: Prevention of the replaying attack: The intruders can not get sensitive data by replaying a previously intercepted message.

To satisfy the S2 security requirement, all proposed conference schemes [8, 9, 20] in mobile communication environments are based on public-key cryptosystems. These approaches still need a large or medium computation and communication cost for establishing a conference.

In this paper, we propose a novel conference scheme for mobile communications. Our proposed scheme can not only satisfy the above two major criteria but also satisfy the four security criteria. By using a new concept named one-time random indicators for preserving location privacy, no public-key cryptosystem is used in our proposed scheme. This approach can dramatically improve the efficiency for conference key distribution in mobile communications.

The remainder of this paper is organized as follows: In Section 2, a brief review of related conference schemes for mobile communications is given. In Section 3, we present our conference scheme for mobile communications. In Section 4, we analyze the security of our scheme. In Section 5, the performance considerations are given. Finally, a concluding remark is given in Section 6.

2   Review

Yi *et al.* proposed a conference scheme for mobile communications based on modular square root technique [20]. The major contribution of their scheme compared with Hwang's scheme [9] is to decrease the computation cost of the mobile user's portable device because the mobile device only needs to perform two modular multiplication operations and some secret-key encryption and decryption operations. Since *Yi et al.*'s scheme is also based on public-key cryptosystems to ensure the location privacy, the computation and communication cost of this scheme is still medium for establishing a teleconference. In this section, we will brief review Yi *et al.*'s scheme. A typical session of the scheme involves m conferees, the certificate authority and the conference bridge. The certificate authority is a trusted third party for issuing certificates to users. The conference bridge is a trusted central authority for conference key distribution and updating. The scheme consists of four subschemes: the secret key certificate issuing scheme, the secret key establishing scheme, the conference key distribution scheme, and the conference key updating scheme. The proposed scheme is as following.

2.1   Secret Key Certificate Issuing Scheme

The certificate authority randomly selects two distinct large primes p_{ca} and q_{ca} where $p_{ca} \equiv q_{ca} \equiv 3 \pmod 4$, computes $n_{ca} = p_{ca} * q_{ca}$, publishes n_{ca} to all participants and keeps p_{ca} and q_{ca} secret. Let ID_a be the unique identification of the participant A. The certificate authority issues a secret certificate (ID_a, i_a, s_a) to A, where (i_a, s_a) is the output of the following procedure.

1. $i_a = 0$.
2. Compute $a = h(ID_a, i_a)$, where h is a one-way function [15, 18].
3. Check if $a^{\frac{p-1}{2}} = 1 \pmod{p_{ca}}$ and $a^{\frac{q-1}{2}} = 1 \pmod{q_{ca}}$. If not, $i = i_a + 1$ and go back to step 2.
4. Compute four modular square roots of $x^2 = a \pmod{n_{ca}}$ and choose the smallest square root as s_a.
5. Output (i_a, s_a).

The certificate authority then issues a smart card, e.g., the subscriber identity module (SIM) containing the secret certificate (ID_a, i_a, s_a) to A.

2.2   Secret Key Establishing Scheme

The aim of this scheme is to generate a shared secret key between the conference bridge B and each conferee $C_i, 1 \leq i \leq m$. Initially, the trusted conference bridge selects two distinct large primes p_b and q_b where $p_b \equiv q_b \equiv 3 \pmod 4$, computes $n_b = p_b * q_b$, publishes n_b to all participants and keeps p_b and p_b secret. Let $R = 2^l$ and $2^{l-1} < n_b < 2^l$. The chairperson (C_1) can initialize a conference as follows.

Step 1: C_1 chooses a random integer r_1, where $\sqrt{n_b} < r_1 < (n_b/2)$ and computes

$$R_1 = r_1^2 * R^{-1} (\text{mod } n_b)$$
$$k_1 = g(h(r_1))$$
$$U_1 = E_{k_1}(ID_B)$$
$$V_1 = E_{k_1}(t_1 || (ID_1, i_1, s_1) || A_1 || ID_2 || \cdots || ID_m)$$

where
h one-way hash fuction;
g trivial map to the key space of a secret key cryptosystems;
E_{k_1} encryption of a secret key cryptosystem with key k_1;
ID_B identification information of the conference bridge B;
ID_j identification information of the conferee C_j (j=1,2,...,m);
t_1 time when the chairperson C_1 sends the request to the bridge B;
A_1 alias of C_1;
$||$ string concatenation operator.
C_1 then sends (R_1, U_1, V_1) to B and keeps k_1 secret.

Step 2: Upon receiving (R_1, U_1, V_1), B extracts k_1 and authenticates C_1 by the following way.

1. Compute four square roots r_1, r_2, r_3 and r_4 of $x^2 = R_1 * R (\text{mod } n_b)$, where $R = 2^l$.
2. Compute four secret key candidates $x_i = g(h(r_i))$, where $1 \leq i \leq 4$.
3. Determine which secret key candidate satisfies $D_{x_i}(U_1) = ID_B$. The matched one is k_1.
4. Decrypt V_1 with k_1 to obtain t_1, $(ID_1, i_1, s_1), A_1, ID_2, ..., ID_m$, check the validity of timestamp t_1, and verify whether

$$s_1^2 = h(ID_1, i_1) (\text{mod } n_{ca}).$$

If yes, C_1 is authenticated. Finally, B and C_1 establish a secret key k_1 for protecting communications between them. B then calls all other conferees $C_j, 2 \leq j \leq m$, respectively.

Step 3: Each conferee $C_j, 2 \leq j \leq m$, randomly chooses an integer r_j, where $\sqrt{n_b} < r_j < (n_b/2)$ and computes

$$R_j = r_j^2 * R^{-1} (\bmod n_b)$$
$$k_j = g(h(r_j))$$
$$U_j = E_{k_j}(ID_B)$$
$$V_j = E_{k_j}(t_j \| (ID_j, i_j, s_j) \| A_j)$$

where A_j is the alias of C_j. C_j then sends (R_j, U_j, V_j) to B.

Upon receiving (R_j, U_j, V_j), B extracts k_j and authenticates C_j by the same way as Step 2. Finally, the secret key k_j known only to B and C_j is established.

2.3   Conference Key Distributing Scheme

The bridge B chooses a random number k as a conference key and encrypts it with the key $k_j, 1 \leq j \leq m$, respectively.

B broadcasts to all conferees $C_j, 1 \leq j \leq m$, the information $(I_1 = E_k(ID_B)$, $I_2 = E_k(t \| L)$, $I_3 = [(A_1, E_{k_1}(k) \| (A_2, E_{k_2}(k)) \| \cdots \| (A_m, E_{k_m}(k))])$, where t is the timestamp and L is the lifetime of the conference key k.

Upon receiving (I_1, I_2, I_3), conferee $C_j, 1 \leq j \leq m$, looks up his alias A_j and extracts $E_{k_j}(k)$ from I_3. He decrypts $E_{k_j}(k)$ with key k_j to get k, decrypt I_2 with key k to obtain t, checks the validity of the timestamp t, and verifies if $D_k(I_1) = ID_B$. If yes, k is an authenticated conference key.

When a person C_{m+1} wants to join the conference, he needs to get the conference key k as follows.

1. C_{m+1} obtains the permission to join the conference from the chairperson C_1.
2. C_1 sends to the bridge B the information $J = E_{k_1}(t' \| ID_{m+1} \| JOIN)$, where t' is the timestamp and ID_{m+1} is the identification information of C_{m+1}.
3. B decrypts J with key k_1 to obtain t' and ID_{m+1} and checks the validity of the timestamp t'. If the timestamp is valid, B calls C_{m+1}.
4. C_{m+1} and B establish a common secret key k_{m+1} with the secret key establishing scheme.
5. B sends C_{m+1} the message $(I_1 = E_k(ID_B)$, $I_2 = E_k(t'' \| L)$, $I_3 = (A_{m+1}, E_{k_{m+1}}(k)))$, where t'' is the timestamp and A_{m+1} is the alias of C_{m+1}.
6. C_{m+1} extracts key k from I_3, checks the validity as the other conferees do, and joins the conference.

2.4   Conference Key Updating Scheme

When a conferee (not the chairperson) quits the conference, the conference key needs to be updated. Without loss of generality, assume that conferee C_m has quitted the conference. The conference key is updated as follows.

1. C_1 sends to the bridge B the information $(Q = E_{k_1}(t' \| ID_m \| QUIT))$, where t' is the timestamp.

2. B chooses another random number k^* as the new conference key and broadcasts to all remaining conferees the information $(I_1 = E_{k^*}(ID_B), I_2 = E_{k^*}(t^*||L^*), I_3 = [(A_1, E_{k_1}(k^*)||(A_2, E_{k_2}(k^*))|| \cdots ||(A_{m-1}, E_{k_{m-1}}(k^*))])$, where t^* is the timestamp and L^* is the lifetime of the updated conference key k^*.
3. $C_j, 1 \le j \le m - 1$, extracts k^* from I_3 and checks authenticity according the conference key distribution scheme.

3   Simple and Secure Conference Scheme

3.1   Notation

We first define the notation used in this section.

NC The network center.

C_i Conferee i.

$NCID$ The unique identification of NC.

CID_i The unique identification of C_i.

α, β $NC's$ master secret keys, where α is for generating all shared secret keys between NC and C_i, and β is for generating all one-time secret keys used for encrypting conferees' identifications.

$E_k[M]$ Encryption of M using a symmetric encryption scheme [1, 16] with a shared key K.

$h(M)$ A secure one-way hash function [14, 15] applied to M.

γ_i The secret key, shared between C_i and NC, can only be computed by NC, and stored in $C_i's$ smart card after registered at NC, where $\gamma_i = h(\alpha||CID_i)$.

$r_{i,j}$ The one-time random number chosen by NC as an indicator for generating the one-time secret key $\delta_{i,j}$, stored in $C_i's$ smart card after jth authentication of C_i with NC, and used during the $(j+1)th$ authetication as $C_i's$ alias.

$\delta_{i,j}$ The one-time secret key, computed by NC, stored in $C_i's$ smart card after jth authentication of C_i with NC, and used for encrypting $C_i's$ identification CID_i for preserving location privacy, where $\delta_{i,j} = h(\beta||r_{i,j})$.

CA The conference acknowledgement message.

CR The conference requesting message.

CQ The conference quitting message.

CU The conference updating message.

k The conference key.

k' The updated conference key.

L The life time of the conference key k.

L' The updated life time of the conference key k'.

$||$ The conventional string concatenation operator.

3.2   The Proposed Scheme

In this section, we propose an efficient conference scheme for mobile communications. A typical session of the scheme involves conferees and the network center. We assume that the network center is a trusted central authority for conferees registration, and conference key distribution. The proposed scheme is as following.

Registration Phase: Assume C_i submits his identity CID_i to NC for registration. If NC accepts this request, he will perform the following steps:

Step 1: Choose a one-time random number $r_{i,0}$ as an indicator for the one-time secret key $\delta_{i,0}$ and compute $C_i's$ secret information $\gamma_i = h(\alpha||CID_i)$, $\delta_{i,0} = h(\beta||r_{i,0})$.

Step 2: Store CID_i, γ_i, $r_{i,0}$ and $\delta_{i,0}$ to the memory of a smart card and issue this smart card, e. g., the subscriber identity module (SIM), to C_i.

Conference Key Distribution Phase: After getting the smart card from NC, C_i can use it in secure conferences. Without loss of generality, we assume there are $m \geq 3$ conferees, $C_i, 1 \leq i \leq m$, willing to join the conference and C_1 is the chairperson to initialize the conference, and at this moment, $r_{i,t}$ and $\delta_{i,t}$ are stored in $C_i's$ smart card since C_i has used his smartcard t times. The conference key distribution is as follows.

Step 1: C_1 sends NC the message $(r_{1,t}, E_{\delta_{1,t}}[CID_1], E_{\gamma_1}[t_1, CR, (CID_i, 2 \leq i \leq m), h(t_1||CR||(CID_i, 2 \leq i \leq m))])$, where $r_{1,t}$ is the one-time random indicator stored in $C_1's$ smart card and t_1 is the timestamp.

Step 2: Upon receiving the message $(r_{1,t}, E_{\delta_{1,t}}[CID_1], E_{\gamma_1}[t_1, CR, (CID_i, 2 \leq i \leq m), h(t_1||CR||(CID_i, 2 \leq i \leq m))])$, NC first computes $\delta_{1,t} = h(\beta||r_{1,t})$ and then decrypts the message $E_{\delta_{1,t}}[CID_1]$ and records $r_{1,t}$ is the alias of CID_1. He then computes $\gamma_1 = h(\alpha||CID_1)$, decrypts the message $E_{\gamma_1}[t_1, CR, (CID_i, 2 \leq i \leq m), h(t_1||CR||(CID_i, 2 \leq i \leq m))]$, and then checks the validity of the timestamp t_1 and the authentication tag $h(t_1||CR||(CID_i, 2 \leq i \leq m))$. If yes, C_1 is authentic. He then calls all other conferees $C_i, 2 \leq i \leq m$, respectively.

Step 3: Each $C_i, 2 \leq i \leq m$, sends NC the message $(r_{i,t}, E_{\delta_{i,t}}[CID_i], E_{\gamma_i}[t_i, CA, h(t_i||CA)])$, where $r_{i,t}$ is the one-time random indicator stored in $C_i's$ smart card and t_i is the timestamp.

Step 4: Upon receiving the messages $(r_{i,t}, E_{\delta_{i,t}}[CID_i], E_{\gamma_i}[t_i, CA, h(t_i||CA)])$, $2 \leq i \leq m$, NC first computes $\delta_{i,t} = h(\beta||r_{i,t})$, $2 \leq i \leq m$, and then decrypts the messages $E_{\delta_{i,t}}[CID_i]$, $2 \leq i \leq m$, and records $r_{i,t}, 2 \leq i \leq m$, as the one-time aliases of $CID_i, 2 \leq i \leq m$, respectively. He then computes $\gamma_i = h(\alpha||CID_i)$, $2 \leq i \leq m$, decrypts the messages $E_{\gamma_i}[t_i, CA, h(t_i||CA)]$, $2 \leq i \leq m$, and then checks the validity of the timestamps t_i, $2 \leq i \leq m$, and the authentication tags $h(t_i||CA)$, $2 \leq i \leq m$. If the timestamp t_i and the authentication tag $h(t_i||CA)$ are both valid, C_i is authentic. If C_i, $2 \leq i \leq m$, are all authentic, NC broadcasts the message $(E_k[t_{nc}, L, h(t_{nc}||CA||L)], (r_{i,t}, E_{\gamma_i}[r_{i,t+1}, \delta_{i,t+1}, k], 1 \leq i \leq m))$, to all conferees $C_i, 1 \leq i \leq m$, where t_{nc} is the timestamp, k is the randomly generated number as the conference key, L is the life time of the conference key k, $r_{i,t+1}$ is a one-time random number chosen by NC as an indicator for one-time secret key generation, and $\delta_{i,t+1} = h(\beta||r_{i,t+1})$.

Step 5: After each C_i, $1 \leq i \leq m$, sieving the message $(E_k[t_{nc}, L, h(t_{nc}||CA||L)],$ $(r_{i,t}, E_{\gamma_i}[r_{i,t+1}, \delta_{i,t+1}, k]))$ from the downlink channel, each C_i, $1 \leq i \leq m$, decrypts the message $E_{\gamma_i}[r_{i,t+1}, \delta_{i,t+1}, k]$, and then decrypts $E_k[t_{nc}, L,$ $h(t_{nc}||CA||L)]$ using the conference key k. He then checks the validity of the timestamp t_{nc} and the authentication tag $h(t_{nc}||CA||L)$. If yes, he then replaces $r_{i,t}$ and $\delta_{i,t}$ with $r_{i,t+1}$ and $\delta_{i,t+1}$ in his smart card.

Now a common conference key k has been established among all conferees and the network center. The messages of the conference conversation can be protected by any secure symmetric cryptosystem using this conference key k.

During holding the conference, if another user C_{m+1} wants to join this conference, he must do the following.

Step 1': C_{m+1} requests the permission of C_1 to join the conference.

Step 2': C_1 sends NC the message $(r_{1,t}, E_{\gamma_1}[t'_1, CJ, CID_{m+1}, h(t'_1||CJ||$ $CID_{m+1})])$, where t'_1 is a timestamp

Step 3': Upon receiving the message $(r_{1,t}, E_{\gamma_1}[t'_1, CJ, CID_{m+1}, h(t'_1||CJ||$ $CID_{m+1})])$, NC first finds the real identification CID_1 by using the one-time alias $r_{1,t}$, computes $\gamma_1 = h(\alpha||CID_1)$, decrypts the message $E_{\gamma_1}[t'_1, CJ,$ $CID_{m+1}, h(t'_1||CJ ||CID_{m+1})]$, and then checks the validity of timestamp t'_1 and the authentication tag $h(t'_1||CJ||CID_{m+1})$. NC rejects this request if the tag is not valid. If the tag and timestamp are both valid, he calls C_{m+1}.

Step 4': C_{m+1} sends NC the message $(r_{m+1,t}, E_{\delta_{m+1,t}}[CID_{m+1}], E_{\gamma_{m+1}}[t_{m+1},$ $CA, h(t_{m+1}||CA)])$, where t_{m+1} is the timestamp, $r_{m+1,t}$ is the one-time random indicator stored in $C'_{m+1}s$ smart card.

Step 5': Upon receiving the message $(r_{m+1,t}, E_{\delta_{m+1,t}}[CID_{m+1}], E_{\gamma_{m+1}}[t_{m+1}, CA,$ $h(t_{m+1}||CA)])$, NC first computes $\delta_{m+1,t} = h(\beta||r_{m+1,t})$, and then decrypts the message $E_{\delta_{m+1,t}}[CID_{m+1}]$ and records $r_{m+1,t}$ is the one-time alias of CID_{m+1}. He then computes $\gamma_{m+1} = h(\alpha||CID_{m+1})$, decrypts the message $E_{\gamma_{m+1}}[t_{m+1}, CA, h(t_{m+1}||CA)]$, and then checks the validity of the timestamp t_{m+1}, and the authentication tag $h(t_{m+1}||CA)$. NC rejects $C'_{m+1}s$ request if his tag is not valid. If the tag and timestamp are both valid, NC sends C_{m+1} the message $(r_{m+1,t}, E_{\gamma_{m+1}}[r_{m+1,t+1}, \delta_{m+1,t+1}, k], E_k[t'_{nc}, L, h(t'_{nc}||CA||L)])$, where t'_{nc} is a timestamp, $r_{m+1,t+1}$ is a one-time random number chosen by NC as an indicator for one-time secret key generation, and $\delta_{m+1,t+1} = h(\beta||r_{m+1,t+1})$.

Step 6': After C_{m+1} sieving the message $(r_{m+1,t}, E_{\gamma_{m+1}}[r_{m+1,t+1}, \delta_{m+1,t+1}, k],$ $E_k[t'_{nc}, L, h(t'_{nc}||CA||L)])$ from the downlink channel, C_{m+1} decrypts the message $E_{\gamma_{m+1}}[r_{m+1,t+1}, \delta_{m+1,t+1}, k]$ and then decrypts the message $E_k[t'_{nc}, L,$ $h(t'_{nc}||CA ||L)]$ using the conference key k. He then checks the validity of the timestamp t'_{nc} and the authentication tag $h(t'_{nc}||CA||L)$. If yes, he then replaces $r_{m+1,t}$ and $\delta_{m+1,t}$ with $r_{m+1,t+1}$ and $\delta_{m+1,t+1}$ in his smart card. He then can use k as the conference key to join the conference.

Conference Key Updating Phase: When a conferee wants to quit the conference, the conference key k must be updated. Without loss of generality, we assume that C_m is willing to quit the conference. The conference key is updated as follows.

Step 1: C_1 sends NC the message $(r_{1,t}, E_{\gamma_1}[t''_1, CQ, CID_m, h(t''_1||CQ||CID_m)])$, where t''_1 is the timestamp.

Step 2: Upon receiving the message $(r_{1,t}, E_{\gamma_1}[t''_1, CQ, CID_m, h(t''_1||CQ||CID_m)])$, NC first finds the real identification CID_1 by using the one-time alias $r_{1,t}$, computes $\gamma_1 = h(\alpha||CID_1)$, decrypts the message $E_{\gamma_1}[t''_1, CQ, CID_m, h(t''_1||CQ|| CID_m)]$ and then checks the validity of the authentication tag $h(t''_1||CQ||CID_m)$ and the timestamp t''_1. If yes, he broadcasts the remaining conferees C_i, $1 \leq i \leq (m - 1)$, the message $((r_{i,t}, E_{\gamma_i}[k'], 1 \leq i \leq (m - 1)), E_{k'}[t''_{nc}, CU, L', h(t''_{nc}||CU||L')])$, where t''_{nc} is the timestamp, k' is a random number chosen by NC as the new conference key, L' is the new lifetime.

Step 3: After each C_i, $1 \leq i \leq (m-1)$, sieving the message $((r_{i,t}, E_{\gamma_i}[k']), E_{k'}[t''_{nc}, CU, L', h(t''_{nc}||CU||L')])$, each C_i, $1 \leq i \leq (m - 1)$, decrypts the message $E_{\gamma_i}[k']$, and then decrypts the message $E_{k'}[t''_{nc}, CU, L', h(t''_{nc}||CU||L')]$ using the updated conference key k'. He then checks the validity of the timestamp t''_{nc} and the authentication tag $h(t''_{nc}||CU||L')$. If yes, he updates the new conference key k' and the new lifetime L'. He then can use the new conference key k' to join the conference.

4   Security Analysis

1. In our conference scheme, the privacy of the conversation content during the conference is preserved since the conference conversation content is encrypted by a symmetric key cryptosystem with the conference key k. If C_i has quitted the conference, he cannot get the new conference conversation content without the updated conference key k'.

2. The privacy of conferees' locations during the conference is preserved since each $CID_i, 1 \leq i \leq m$, is encrypted by a one-time random secret key $\delta_{i,t} = h(\beta||r_{i,t})$ which can only be computed by NC using the one-time random indicator (alias) $r_{i,t}$ and his master secret key β. The one-time random indicator $r_{i,t}$ can only be used in a single conference and will be replaced by another one-time random indicator $r_{i,t+1}$ when C_i gets the conference key k. In the conference, C_i uses $r_{i,t}$ as his alias to use the medium. It is hard to derive NC's master secret key β from the one-time random secret key $\delta_{i,t}$ and the one-time random indicator (alias) $r_{i,t}$ since NC's master secret key β is protected by the public secure one-way hash function $h()$[14, 15].

3. Differently from that the alias A_i of conferee C_i is chosen by each conferee C_i in Yi et al.'s scheme [20], the one-time alias (indicator) $r_{i,t}$ of conferee C_i is randomly generated by the network center (conference bridge) in our proposed scheme. Our approach is more practical since the network center can generate a unique alias for each conferee in every conference. In Yi et al.'s scheme [20], two conferees C_i and C_j may choose two same aliases A_i

and A_j in a distributed environment. It will cause more effort to handle this situation.

4. After step 2 and 4 in the conference key distribution phase, each identification of $C_i, 1 \leq i \leq m$, is authenticated by NC. When C_i wants to join the conference, he must use his $r_{i,t}$ as the alias and the conference k to encrypt all conversations.

5. The replay attack of the conference key distribution phase is prevented by the timestamps t_i and t_{nc} since in step 2 and 4, NC will check the validity of $t_i, 1 \leq i \leq m$, and in step 5, each C_i will check the validity of t_{nc}.

6. The replay attack of the conference key updating phase is prevented by the timestamps t_1'' and t_{nc}'' since in step 2, NC will check the validity of t_1'' and in step 3 each C_i will check the validity of t_{nc}''.

7. In our scheme, NC only needs to protect two master secret keys α and β. All shared keys $\gamma_i = h(\alpha \| CID_i)$ and one-time shared keys $\delta_{i,j} = h(\beta \| r_{i,j})$ can be computed from these two master secret keys α and β. No passwords or shared keys table is needed in NC. The security of these two secret keys α and β is protected by the secure one-way hashing function $h()$ [14, 15].

8. If the conference chairperson C_1 wants to quit the conference, a simple method to solve this situation is to select a new chairperson and restart the conference. Another approach is to elect a new chairperson from conferees and redistribute a new conference key k' to all participants.

9. In our proposed scheme and Yi et al.'s scheme [20], when a person C_{m+1} wants to join the conference, he needs to get the conference key k. If C_{m+1} wiretaped the secret conversation of the conference before joining this conference, he can derive the passed content of the conference. For solving this problem, a new conference key k' can be redistributed when C_{m+1} joins the conference. But this approach will increase the computation and communication cost of all participants.

10. In practical implementation, the smart cards used in our scheme are issued by the trusted network center and assumed to be tamperproof devices. For protecting $C_i's$ smart card from being used by an illegal user, a weak password can be chosen and used to protect it. Its role is like the personal identification number (PIN) used in the banking system. If some illegal user tries to use the smart card by wrong passwords exceeding some fixed times, the operating system of the smart card will lock the login function.

11. In our scheme, for improving the repairability mentioned in [10, 12], the secret value $\gamma_i = h(\alpha \| CID_i)$ stored in each C_i's smart card can be replaced with the new formula $\gamma_i = h(\alpha \| CID_i \| j)$, where j is the number of times that C_i has revoked his used secret key γ_i [12].

12. Some security weaknesses in schemes [7, 9] were proposed in [2]. Both our proposed scheme and Yi et al.'s scheme [20] can prevent the attacks proposed in [2] since the conference key is protected by the shared key between each conferee and the network center but not embedded in a number combined with each conferee's secret using least common multiple (LCM).

13. In our proposed scheme and Yi et al.'s scheme [20], when the chairperson C_1 is authenticated by the network center, the network center needs to call all

other conferees. For hiding the identification information of all other conferees, the concept of random indicators can be used. But in this approach, the conferee must register his random number indicator for notifying the network center his position. The calling message then can be encrypted using the corresponding one-time random secret key.

5 Performance Consideration

Due to the fast progress of integrated circuit technology, using the factoring method proposed in [13], factoring a 512-bit moduli can be done in less than ten minutes on a US$10K device and factoring a 1024-bit moduli can be done in a year on a US$10M device in 2003. Differently from the schemes [8, 9, 20] using public-key cryptosystems, only symmetric cryptosystems and one-way hashing functions are used in our proposed scheme for improving the efficiency. Our approach provides another alternative for better efficiency and no need to base on any assumed hard number theoretical problem, e.g., factoring or discrete logarithm.

We assume that there are m conferees in the conference; the identifications are represented with 64 bits; the block size and key size of secure symmetric cryptosystems [1, 16] and the output size of secure one-way hashing functions [14, 15] all are 128 bits; the timestamps, the conference commands CA, CR, CQ, CU and the lifetime of a conference key are of 32 bits. The modulus n_b and n_{ca} in the scheme [20] are of 1024 bits in order to make the factoring problem infeasible [13]. Communication cost for our scheme and the related scheme is listed in Table 1.

In step 1 of our proposed scheme in the conference key distribution phase, C_1 needs to sends NC the message $(r_{1,t}, E_{\delta_{1,t}}[CID_1], E_{\gamma_1}[t_1, CR, (CID_i, 2 \leq i \leq m), h(t_1||CR||(CID_i, 2 < i \leq m))])$, which is of $128 + \lceil (m+2)/2 \rceil * 128 = 128 + \lceil (m+2)/2 \rceil * 128$ bits since the output size of an encryption message must be the multiple of the block size and only cryptographic values are counted for comparing with Yi et al.'s scheme [20]. In step 3, each $C_i, 2 \leq i \leq m$, needs to send NC the message $(r_{i,t}, E_{\delta_{i,t}}[CID_i], E_{\gamma_i}[t_i, CA, h(t_i||CA)])$, which is of $128 + \lceil 3/2 \rceil * 128 = 384$ bits. In step 4, NC needs to broadcasts the message $(E_k[t_{nc}, L, h(t_{nc}||CA||L)], (r_{i,t}, E_{\gamma_i}[r_{i,t+1}, \delta_{i,t+1}, k]), 1 \leq i \leq m)$, which is of $(\lceil (32 + 32 + 128)/128 \rceil * 128 + (\lceil (64 + 128 + 128)/128 \rceil * 128) * m = 256 + 384 * m$

Table 1. Communication cost (bits) for our scheme and other related schemes for conference key distribution ($m = 100$)

Participant	Communication type	Our scheme	Yi et al.'s scheme [20]
Bridge (NC)	Send	≈38656	≈13056
Bridge (NC)	Receive	≈44672	≈249472
Chairperson	Send	≈6656	≈8704
Chairperson	Receive	≈640	≈384
Other conferee	Send	≈384	≈2432
Other conferee	Receive	≈640	≈384

bits and each $C_i, 1 \leq i \leq m$, must sieve the message $(E_k[t_{nc}, L, h(t_{nc}||CA)], (r_{i,t},$ $E_{\gamma_i}[r_{i,t+1}, \delta_{i,t+1}, k]$)), which is of 640 bits. When $m = 100$, NC needs to send $256 + 384*100 = 38656$ bits and receive $128 + \lceil(100 + 2)/2\rceil*128 + 99*384 = 44672$ bits, the chairperson C_1 needs to send $128 + \lceil(100 + 2)/2\rceil * 128 = 6656$ bits and receive 640 bits, and the other conferee needs to send 384 bits and receive 640 bits.

In step 1 of Yi *et al.*'s scheme [20] in the secret key certificate issuing scheme, C_1 needs to sends B the message (R_1, U_1, V_1), which is of $1024 + 128 + \lceil(1152 + 64 * m)/128\rceil * 128 = 2304 + \lceil(64 * m)/128\rceil * 128$ bits. In step 3, each C_i, $2 \leq i \leq m$, needs to sends B the message (R_i, U_i, V_i), which is of $1024 + 128 + \lceil(32 + 64 + 32 + 1024 + 64)/128\rceil * 128 = 2432$ bits. In the conference key distribution scheme of Yi *et al.*'s scheme [20], B broadcasts the message $(E_k(ID_B), E_k(t||L), (A_i, E_{k_i} (k)), 1 \leq i \leq m)$, which is of $128 + 128 + 128*m = 256 + 128*m$ bits, to all conferees and each $C_i, 1 \leq i \leq m$, must sieve the message $(E_k(ID_B), E_k(t||L), (A_i, E_{k_i}(k)))$, which is of 384 bits. When $m = 100$, B needs to send $256 + 128 * 100 = 13056$ bits and receive $2304 + \lceil(64 * 100)/128\rceil*128 + 2432*99 = 249472$ bits, the chairperson C_1 needs to send $2304 + \lceil(64 * 100)/128\rceil * 128 = 8704$ bits and receive 384 bits, and the other conferee needs to send 2432 bits and receive 384 bits.

In Yi *et al.*'s scheme [20], the conference bridge must compute the 4 modular square roots of a quadratic residue modulo n_b in registration of each conferee. Using the method suggested in [20], 2 modulo exponentiations and 3 modular multiplications are required to compute 4 modular square roots. Computational cost for our scheme and Yi *et al.*'s scheme [20] is listed in Table 2 when $m = 100$.

In the registration phase, our scheme only needs 2 hash operations. In the conference key distribution phase for establishing a common conference key among 100 conferees, NC must perform 651 symmetric encryption or decryption operations and 301 hashing operations. The chairperson C_1 must perform 57 symmetric encryption or decryption operations and 2 hashing operations. Each other conferee must perform 8 symmetric encryption or decryption operations and 2 hashing operations.

In Yi *et al.*'s scheme [20], for becoming an eligible conferee, the secret key certificate issuing scheme must be executed in advance. The certificate authority must perform 4 exponential operations, 4 multiplication operations and 1 hashing operation for each conferee. For establishing a common conference key among 100 conferees, the secret key establishing scheme and the conference key dis-

Table 2. Computational cost for our scheme and other related schemes for conference key distribution ($m = 100$)

	Our scheme			Yi *et al.*'s scheme [20]		
	NC	C_1	C_i	B (or CA)	C_1	C_i
Registration	2H	0	0	4E+4M+1H	0	0
Conference key distribution	651S+ 301H	57S+ 2H	8S+ 2H	200E+400M+ 1650S+401H	1I+2M+ 62S+1H	1I+2M+ 13S+1H

E: Exponential operation I: Inverse operation M: Multiplication operation
S: Symmetric encryption or decryption H: Hashing operation

tributing scheme must both be executed. The conference bridge B must perform 200 exponential operations, 400 multiplication operations, 401 hashing operations and 1650 symmetric encryption or decryption operations. The chairperson C_1 must perform 2 multiplication operations, 1 inverse operation, 62 symmetric encryption or decryption operations and 1 hashing operation. Each other conferee must perform 2 multiplication operations, 1 inverse operation, 13 symmetric encryption or decryption operations and 1 hashing operation. The inverse operation for C_1 and other conferee can be performed in advance.

We summarize the complexity and functionality of related schemes and our scheme in Table 3. In our scheme, only one-way hash functions and symmetric key encryptions (decryptions) are required for each participant. In practical considerations, one-way hash functions can be constructed by symmetric cryptosystems [14]. This method can reduce the needed memory in smart cards for storing cryptographic programs. The computation cost of our scheme is extremely low compared to that of the scheme in [20] based on public key cryptosystems. In our scheme, NC only has to protect his master keys α and β. No shared keys table is needed. In Yi et al.'s scheme [20], after the secret key establishing scheme is executed, the secret key k_i is shared between C_i and the conference bridge. The conference bridge must keep a shared keys table for later use. After the registration phase, CID_i, γ_i, $r_{i,0}$ and $\delta_{i,0}$ are stored in the memory of C_i' smart card in our scheme. The needed memory in a smart card for our scheme is of $(64 + 128 + 64 + 128) = 384$ bits. The values (ID_a, i_a, s_a) are stored in the memory of $A's$ smart card after the secret key certificate issuing scheme of Yi et al.'s scheme [20]. The needed memory in a smart card for Yi et al.'s scheme [20] is of $(64 + 32 + 1024) = 1120$ bits. For preserving location privacy, the identification and secret certificate (ID_i, i_i, s_i) of C_i in the secret key establishing scheme of Yi et al.'s scheme [20] must be encrypted by the secret key k_i, which is randomly

Table 3. Comparisons between our proposed scheme and other related schemes

	Our scheme	Yi et al.'s scheme [20]
C1	Very low	Medium
C2	Yes	Yes
C3	Yes	No
C4	384 bits	1120 bits
S1	Yes	Yes
S2	Yes	Yes
S3	Yes	Yes
S4	Yes	Yes

C1: Computation cost
C2: Dynamic participation
C3: No shared keys or password table in the server
C4: Needed memory in a smart card
S1: Content privacy
S2: Location privacy
S3: Authenticity
S4: Prevention of the replaying attack

chosen by C_i and protected by the Rabin's public key cryptosystem [17, 19]. In our scheme, for preserving location privacy the identification CID_i is encrypted by the one-time secret key $\delta_{i,t} = h(\beta||r_{i,t})$, which can only be computed by NC using the one-time random indicator $r_{i,t}$ and the secret key β. When NC derives the identification CID_i, he then can compute the shared key $\gamma_i = h(\alpha||CID_i)$ between NC and C_i using the secret key α, and verify the authentication tags.

6 Conclusion

In this paper, we have proposed a simple and efficient conference scheme for mobile communications. By using one-time random indicators for preserving location privacy, only symmetric cryptosystems and one-way hashing functions are used in our proposed scheme. This approach can significantly improve the efficiency and provide much functionality for conference key distribution in mobile communications.

Acknowledgment. This work was supported in part by the National Science Council of the Republic of China under contract NSC-93-2213-E-128-005. The reviewers' insightful comments helped us to improve the paper significantly.

References

1. "Data encryption standard," in National Bureau of Standards. Washington, DC: U.S. Dept. of Commerce, 1977.
2. B. Feng, "Analysis of a conference scheme under active and passive attacks", In H. Wang et al. (ed.), ACISP 2004, LNCS 3108, pp. 157-163, Springer, New York, 2004.
3. Y. Frankel, A. Herzberg, P. Karger, H. Krawczyk, C. Kunzinger and M. Yung, "Security issues in a CDPD wireless network," IEEE Personal Communi., Vol. 2, pp. 16-27, 1995.
4. I. Ingemarsson, D. Tang and C. Wong, "A conference key distribution system," IEEE Trans. on Inform. Theory, Vol. IT-28, pp. 714-720, 1982.
5. S. Hirose and K. Ikeda, "A conference key distribution system for the star configuration based on the discrete logarithm problem," Inform. Processing Lett., Vol. 62, pp. 189-192, 1997.
6. G. Horn, K. Martin and C. Mitchell, "Authentication protocols for mobile network environment value-added services," IEEE Trans. on Vehicular Technology, Vol. 51, No. 2, pp. 383-392, 2002.
7. K. Hwang and C. Chang, "A self-encryption mechanism for authentication of roaming and teleconference service," IEEE Trans. on Wireless Communications, Vol. 2, No. 2, pp. 400-407, 2003.
8. M. Hwang and W. Yang, "Conference key distribution schemes for secure digital mobile communications," IEEE J. Select Areas Communi., Vol. 13, pp. 416-420, 1995.
9. M. Hwang, "Dynamic participation in a secure conference scheme for mobile communications," IEEE Trans. on Vehicular Technology, Vol. 48, No. 5, pp. 1469-1474, 1999.

10. T. Hwang and W. Ku, "Repairable key distribution protocols for internet environ-ments," IEEE Trans. on Communications, Vol. 43, No. 5, pp. 1947-1950, 1995.
11. K. Koyama and K. Ohta, "Identity-based conference key distribution scheme," Advances in Cryptology-Crypt'87, pp. 175-184, Springer, New York, 1987.
12. W. Ku and S. Chen, "Weaknesses and improvements of an efficient password based remote user authentication scheme using smart cards," IEEE Trans on Consumer Electronics, Vol. 50, No. 1, pp. 204-207, 2004.
13. A. Lenstra, E. Tromer, A. Shamir, W. Kortsmit, B. Dodson, J. Hughes and P. Leyland, "Factoring estimates for a 1024-bit RSA modulus," In Laih, C. (ed.), Advances in Cryptology-AsiaCrypt'03, Lecture Notes in Computer Science, 2894, pp. 55-74, Springer, New York, 2003.
14. R. Merkle, "One way hash functions and DES," In Brassard, G. (ed.), Advances in Cryptology-Crypt'89, Lecture Notes in Computer Science, 435, pp. 428-446, Springer, New York, 1989.
15. NIST FIPS PUB 180-2, "Secure Hash Standard," National Institute of Standards and Technology, U. S. Department of Commerce, 2004.
16. NIST FIPS PUB 197, "Announcing the Advanced Encryption Standard(AES)," National Institute of Standards and Technology, U. S. Department of Commerce, 2001.
17. M. Rabin, "Digitalized signatures and public key functions as intractable as fac-torization," MIT Lab. Computer Sci., TR 212, Jan. 1979.
18. R. L. Rivest, "The MD5 message-digest algorithm," RFC 1321, Internet Activities Board, Internet Privacy Task Force, 1992.
19. H. Williams, "A Modification of RSA public-key encryption," IEEE Trans. on Inform. Theory, Vol. IT-26, No. 6, pp. 726-729, 1980.
20. X. Yi, C. Siew and C. Tan, "A secure and efficient conference scheme for mobile communications," IEEE Trans. on Vehicular Technology, Vol. 52, No. 4, pp. 784-793, 2003.

A Hash-Chain Based Authentication Scheme for Fast Handover in Wireless Network*

Kihun Hong[1], Souhwan Jung[1,**], and S. Felix Wu[2]

[1] School of Electronic Engineering, Soongsil University, 1-1, Sangdo-dong,
Dongjak-ku, Seoul 156-743, Korea
Kihun@cns.ssu.ac.kr, souhwanj@ssu.ac.kr
[2] Department of Computer Science, University of California, Davis, CA 95616, USA
wu@cs.ucdavis.edu

Abstract. This paper proposes a hash-chain based authentication scheme for fast handover in wireless network (HAS). The full authentication procedure described in IEEE 802.11 is inappropriate to be applied to a handover, since it has heavy operation and delay time during handover. Though various methods were proposed to solve the problem, the existing schemes degrade the security of authentication or impose the entire administrative burden of the authentication on the authentication server. The main focus of this paper is on reducing the administrative burden of the authentication server and enhances the security strength of the fast handover authentication. The proposed scheme in this paper is robust to the attack by a compromised AP by using hash key chain between a mobile station and the authentication server. The scheme also decentralizes the administrative burden of the authentication server to other network entities.

1 Introduction

For the upcoming mobile environment on the Internet, much of research focuses on the mobile access and seamless connection when user moves. Currently, IEEE 802.11 standard [1,2,3,4] includes not only wireless connection of a station with one access point (AP), but also the station's mobility via several APs. The handover of the mobile station (STA) from the serving AP to the other AP incurs delay time due to probe, decision, re-authentication, and re-association. On the other hand, with increasing multimedia applications, Internet traffic stream has changed from text and picture-based data to video and audio-based data, and these multimedia traffics are unable to endure the delay time during the handover. This paper addresses reducing the latency of the authentication incurred by the handover of the station. In the bootstrapping procedure, the full authentication described in IEEE 802.11 consists of EAP/TLS [5] which

---

* This work was supported by the Korea Research Foundation Grant (M07-2004-000-10295-0). This research is supported by the ubiquitous Autonomic Computing and Network Project, the Ministry of Information and Communication (MIC) 21st Century Frontier R&D Program in Korea.
** Corresponding author.

J. Song, T. Kwon, and M. Yung (Eds.): WISA 2005, LNCS 3786, pp. 96–107, 2006.
© Springer-Verlag Berlin Heidelberg 2006

requires over one second for authentication process with the authentication server (AS). Therefore, it is difficult to apply the full authentication procedure, including RADIUS, to the handover due to its heavy operations and long delay time. In solving the latency problem, two solutions based on pre-authentication are considered: security context transfer method and proactive key distribution method. The schemes based on pre-authentication have a similar delay time in the handover since they perform re-authentication before the mobile station's handover. First, the security context transfer or proactive caching methods [8] securely transfer hashed security credentials from a current AP to neighboring APs using IAPP (Inter-Access Point Protocol). But these kinds of solutions weaken security of the authentication process since the old AP still knows about security credentials of new AP after the handover of the mobile station. As an alternative method, proactive key distribution scheme uses neighbor graph to deliver new pairwise master key (PMK) to neighboring APs in the manner of one-hop ahead of the mobile station. The scheme, however, imposes the entire administrative burden of the re-authentication like neighbor graph, key generation, and delivery on the authentication server. For that reason, our main focus in this paper is on reducing the administrative burden of the authentication server and enhancing the security strength of the fast handover authentication.

The main idea of HAS (a hash-chain based authentication scheme for fast handover in wireless network), as proposed in this paper, is based on key sharing between the AS and the STA using the hash chain without an additional message. The authentication key generated in the AS is delivered to each neighboring AP and each AP makes new PMK from this key and hashed old PMK delivered from an old AP. Since the mobile station having the same initial value of the authentication key also can generate the hash key chain, it consecutively shares the authentication key with the AP without an additional message. This key derived from hash-chain enhances the security strength of the security context transfer method and reduces the administrative burden of the authentication server of the proactive key distribution method. The proposed scheme in this paper is robust to the attack by a compromised AP using the hash key chain between the mobile station and the authentication server, and it decentralizes the administrative burden of the authentication server to other network entities.

The paper is structured as follows: 1) Section 2 introduces an environment of the wireless network and problem statement and reviews related works; 2) Section 3 describes an initial full authentication procedure and a pre-authentication procedure of the proposed scheme; 3) Section 4 explains a security analysis of the HAS and compares the performance of some authentication schemes based on computation and communication overhead in section 5; 4) Finally, the concluding remarks are presented in Section 6.

2 Motivation and Related Works

2.1 Motivation

In this section, the wireless network entities for the authentication and problems of the existing schemes for the fast handover authentication are introduced. The wireless network consists of a mobile station, access point, access router (AR), and authentication server. Users having the mobile station are usually moving to any place and use the Internet through the access point. And the correspondent access point requests authentication information to the mobile station to verify access permission on the wireless network. When the mobile station first accesses the network, the mobile station performs an initial full authentication with the authentication server. However, since the full authentication is a heavy procedure consisting of EAP (Extensible Authentication Protocol)/TLS (Transport Layer Security) and AAA (Authorization, Authentication and Accounting) protocol like RADIUS or Diameter, and spends a lot of the network resources and delay time, the full authentication is not suitable for the handover of the mobile station. Hence, a novel and optimal authentication scheme is required for the fast handover. To reduce the latency, various schemes were proposed.

Now, the pros and cons of the existing schemes for the recently proposed fast-handover authentication will be discussed. There are two approaches in fast handover authentication schemes in wireless network: an authentication method during handover and a pre-authentication method. In the initial study, though a number of the studies focus on the authentication method during a handover, they got more delay time in comparison to the pre-authentication method. Therefore, the current study mostly focuses on the pre-authentication method for fast handover.

Pack *et al.* have proposed the predictive authentication scheme using FHR(Frequent Handoff Region) selection in [6]. First, this method finds the FHR which is a set of neighboring APs and is determined by the users' movement pattern and the APs' locations. The mobile station requests the authentication process to the AS and the AS responds to all APs belonging to the FHR using multiple authentication messages containing a key. This method, however, does not support consecutive handover to other area without the full authentication and incurs the attack by disclosed key of a compromised AP because APs share the authentication key information among them.

Mishra *et al.* suggested proactive key distribution method for fast handover in [7]. To reduce the delay time of the authentication procedure, proactive key distribution method is based on pre-distribution of the authentication key one hop ahead of the mobile station. AS can know a set of neighboring APs using a neighbor graph and constructs new PMK for neighboring APs from old PMK and MAC addresses of the neighbor AP and the mobile station. These new PMKs are sent to each neighboring AP in the neighbor graph. It is an efficient authentication scheme for reducing the authentication latency of the handover. However, this scheme adds an administrative burden to the AS such as the computation of the neighbor graph, an encryption of the key delivery message, and pseudo-random function for generating PMK, since AS performs the most of the authentication operation. In particular, in case that user and user's mobility increases, AS may get the serious burden of the authentication. Another problem is that this scheme has no method to perform a fast re-authentication from the station or AP when AS loses trace of the station due to any reason since the authentication procedure is only initiated by the AS.

Wang *et al.* proposed an authentication scheme using an exchange of random number in [9]. The current AP sends exclusive ORed key with random number to a mobile station and a target AP. Then the two nodes exchange nonces and construct the new PMK from nonces and the key received from the current AP. It is a simple authentication method without communication with AS. But since an attacker, having exclusive ORed key from a compromised AP, may also get the nonces in plaintext, he could easily make the new PMK. In case of a simple context transfer method using IAPP, the same security problem occurs.

We review the problems of existing schemes such that predictive authentication scheme and the authentication scheme, using an exchange of random number, require strengthening security between APs, or the proactive key distribution method demands high computation overheads and neighbor graph in AS. It may not be appropriate to authenticate a fast moving node using the existing schemes.

2.2 Trust Relationship

The entities in the wireless network have a trust relationship between them and use it for authentication and protection of the communication channel. Figure 1 shows the trust relationship among the mobile station, the access point, and the authentication server. AP keeps the trust relationship with the neighboring APs, and this kind of the relationship supports the security of the IAPP. The inter-access point protocol is a communication protocol between APs to manage various local events occurred in network. It also includes RADIUS infrastructure to provide mapping the ID of the AP to IP address and key distribution between APs for the protection of the channel. IAPP supports the managements of service set and the mobility of STA. IAPP includes the proactive caching method to support fast handover by caching the context of the station in the candidate set of APs and can dynamically find its neighboring APs. AP also has the trust relationship with AS for protecting authentication messages. The mobile station trusts AS with each other via EAP-TLS established through the full authentication procedure and uses it for protecting the path between them. These trust relationships will be used to design our hash-chain based authentication scheme for fast handover.

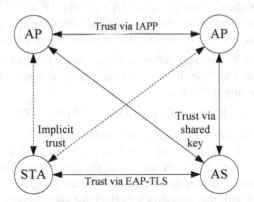

Fig. 1. The trust relationship between network entities

3 A Hash-Chain Based Authentication Scheme for Fast Handover

This section describe an initial full authentication procedure and a pre-authentication procedure applying hash key chain for network access authentication that is named a hash-chain based authentication scheme for fast handover in wireless network (HAS).

The underlying idea is that the current access point and a local authentication server send authentication keys to neighboring APs before the mobile station moves from the current AP to any neighboring AP. To reduce the computation burden of the authentication server, the current AP sends its hashed pairwise master key to the neighboring APs in this scheme.

3.1 Initial Full Authentication Procedure

When the mobile station is booting, since the AP requests that the mobile station must be authenticated by a home authentication server to access the network, the mobile station performs the initial full authentication procedure with the AP, the local authentication server, and the home authentication server. Through this procedure, the mobile station and AP share an initial PMK defined in 802.11i and calculate PMK_0 used for protecting the channel between the mobile station and the current AP as follows:

$$PMK_0 = prf(PMK_{initial} \mid AP\_MAC \mid STA\_MAC)$$

For device authentication, PMK_0 is calculated from initial PMK, AP's MAC (Medium Access Control) address, and STA's MAC address using prf (pseudo-random function). The mobile station and AP make data encryption key and data MIC (Message Integrity Check) key from this PMK_0. In this procedure, the mobile station and AP decide cryptography algorithms for encryption and message integrity check. In particular, the mobile station and the local authentication server except AP also share initial authentication key (IAK) which will be used to authenticate the mobile station.

3.2 Pre-authentication Procedure

After the initial full authentication procedure, the current AP and neighboring APs perform a pre-authentication procedure for reducing authentication delay time during handover of the mobile station before the mobile station moves to one of neighboring APs.

- **cAP → nAPs:** The current AP securely transfers handover key (HOK) to the neighboring APs using IAPP. In the first, the current AP respectively makes handover keys for each neighboring AP as follows:

$$HOK_i = prf(PMK_{i-1} \mid NEIGHBOR\_AP\_MAC \mid STA\_MAC)$$

An index of HOK means the sequence of handover of the STA from 1 to n against each handover of it. The current AP can find neighbors using IAPP or neighbor graphs introduced in [4, 8] and keep the list of the neighboring APs and their MAC addresses. HOK_i provides mutual layer 2 authentication using AP's MAC address and STA's MAC address and also supports a perfect forward secrecy to the current AP using pseudo-random function because neighboring APs or the attacker cannot make the current PMK between the current AP and STA from the HOK_i. Figure 2 shows the current AP sending the handover key to each AP in the one-hop neighbors circle, which consists of APs in one hop distance from the current AP. The mobile station served by the current AP can move to the only one AP in the one-hop neighbors circle. G is the group of the entire neighboring APs and describes as follows:

$$G = \{ AP1, AP2, AP3, AP4, AP5 \}$$

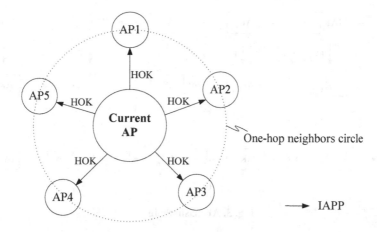

Fig. 2. Handover key distribution

IAPP provides context delivery service for fast handover between APs. IAPP message is protected by the trust relationship between APs and includes STA ID, sender ID, and security context containing the handover key, AK index information, and cryptography algorithms for encryption and message authentication code used in the current AP.

After the current AP sends the HOK_i, the authentication server has to deliver another authentication key to the neighboring APs so that each AP may construct PMK as the complete authentication key. However, for an isolation of the authentication key before and after the handover, the authentication server must generate a sub-series of the IAK (Initial Authentication Key) shared from the initial full authentication procedure. For the sub-key generation of the IAK, two kinds of method are proposed. The mobile station and the authentication server already share initial AK in the initial full authentication procedure and compute using the same method on each side. The first method is used for real-time generation of the AK at the handover of STA. IAK_0 is the same value as the initial AK, as depicted in figure 3(a). F and F' are two different pseudo-random functions. An index of AK means the sequence of handover of the mobile station and AS consecutively uses the same index from 1 to n against each handover of it. In the pre-authentication procedure, the mobile station and the authentication server individually compute IAK_i and AK_i at each side. The authentication server uses AK_i as authentication key for the handover of STA and sends it to the neighboring APs. Though this method may not include additional operations in the initial full authentication time, it has little computation burden at each pre-authentication phase.

The second one is used for pre-generation of AK chain, and the key chain as shown in figure 3(b) will be stored in the mobile station and the authentication server. This pre-generation is completely performed just after the initial full authentication procedure. In this method, IAK_n is the same value with initial AK as depicted in figure 3(b). After the initial full authentication procedure, the mobile station and the authentication server individually compute the hash key chain from IAK_n and AK_1 at each side. The authentication server uses AK_1 as AK for the first handover of the mobile station and sends it to the neighboring APs. It has the computation burden of the initial full authentication procedure. From now on, the first method in the description of the scheme will be used.

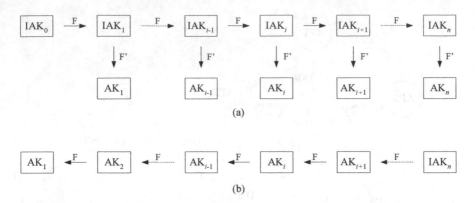

(a)

(b)

Fig. 3. AK hash-chain

- **nAPs → AS:** After exchanging the IAPP messages, the neighbor AP (nAP), who received the security context immediately, requests the authentication key to the authentication server using Authentication Key Request message including ID of the current AP (cAP), its ID and AK index information as shown in figure 4.
- **AS → nAPs:** Since AS already has the IAK shared with the mobile station in the initial full authentication procedure, after computing AK_i, AS simply transfers Authentication Key Response message with AK_i to the AP.

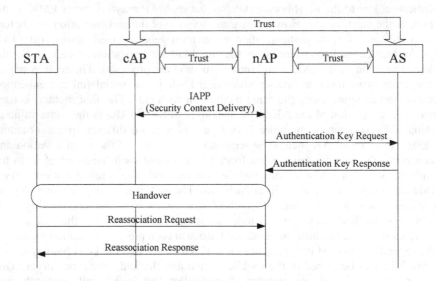

Fig. 4. Pre-authentication message exchange

In case of AK pre-generation method, the AS sends AK_i in the storage. The type of AK depends on AK generation method mentioned above. It must be noted that the AS in this procedure must transfer AK_i to the neighbors except the current AP, because the current AP may make new PMK between STA and new AP if it has handover key and AK_i. The information of the current AP can be sent by the mobile station. After exchanging authentication key messages, each neighboring AP ultimately calculates PMK_i for the mobile station and itself using the handover key and AK_i with pseudo-random function as follows:

$$PMK_i = prf(\ HOK_i \mid AK_i\ )$$

The AP maintains this key in the soft state for a specific time. If the handover event of the mobile station does not occur in time, the key information in the soft state is dropped by the AP. When the mobile station moves to nAP, it constructs PMK_i without additional messages with other network entities and may send a re-association request message for access to new AP after handover.

After the pre-authentication, the mobile station can move to any neighboring AP. It performs four-way handshake with new AP after the exchange of re-association message. It is used to confirm the freshness of shared key and the liveness of the station and the AP. Using the exchange of the index information of the keys in this procedure, the station and AS confirm the synchronization of the sub keys of the AK and PMK.

3.3 Re-authentication Without HOK

It can happen that the station moves fast to new AP before the arrival of the handover key through IAPP or reconnects to a new AP which is not neighboring AP after loss of its connection due to any reason. In this case, since the AP doesn't have the handover key, it cannot compute PMK with the station. Therefore, the PMK computation method without handover key is also recommended. When the AP, not having handover key, receives re-association message from any station, it can make PMK as follows:

$$PMK_i = prf(\ AK_i \mid AP\_MAC \mid STA\_MAC\ )$$

However, since the station doesn't know about the situation of the AP, AP can notify parameters of PMK computation to the station using a four-way handshake as mentioned before. The cipher suite between AP and STA can be also exchanged in this handshake.

4 Security Analysis

One of the main goals is to enhance the security strength of the fast handover authentication. The HAS strengthens the weakness of the security context from the old AP using AK. As mentioned before, since the old AP in security context transfer scheme still holds security credentials after handover of the mobile station, security context transfer scheme using IAPP does not support perfect forward secrecy (PFS). Wang's authentication scheme using random number also has the similar security problem. In this scheme, even if the mobile station and nAP exchange nonces, the attacker, cooperated with the compromised old AP, easily captures the nonces in the plaintext. However, the HAS brings AK of the AS into security context transfer scheme and solves the security problem of the existing schemes.

AP is usually located in the public area and any attacker can easily access the AP and get secret in the memory. However, HAS guarantees perfect forward secrecy using the authentication server. If the old AP was compromised with an attacker, then the attacker can easily obtain the old pairwise master key used between the old AP and the mobile station. Even if the attacker has the old PMK, he cannot generate a new PMK without AK from the local authentication server because the local AS only transfers AK to APs having trust relationship with him except the old AP. The HAS also supports perfect backward secrecy (PBS) using pseudo-random function. Even if the attacker obtains HOK and AK of the new AP, he is unable to create the old PMK from HOK according to the cryptographic character of the pseudo-random function. The attacker also cannot compute AK_{i-1} or AK_{i+1} from AK_i, since each AK with index i was isolated by F'.

5 Performance Evaluation

When the mobile station moves to the new AP, the pre-authentication methods obviously have smaller delay time than the general authentication methods during handover since the neighboring APs in pre-authentication schemes already performed the authentication of the mobile station before handover. After the handover, they just do key freshness and key derivation. For that reason, the general authentication methods during handover are not suitable to compare performance with HAS. Pack's predictive authentication scheme [6] and Wang's authentication scheme [9] have similar security problem by the compromised AP. In Pack's model, the compromised AP can obtain the key of the mobile station due to the multiple authentication messages containing the key. Old AP in Wang's scheme is also able to make new PMK from old PMK with random numbers in the plain text message. Due to these weaknesses of security, Pack and Wang's schemes have been excluded from the performance comparison. Hence, in this section, only the HAS with the proactive key distribution method has been compared.

The latency of the pre-authentication is not an important problem in a viewpoint of performance since it doesn't have an effect on the handover delay time. The important point in the pre-authentication schemes is the computation and communication burden

Table 1. Comparison of handover authentication schemes. (m is the average number of neighboring APs. The numbers in computation overhead are the number of pseudo-random function and the number of encryption or decryption in order.)

		Proactive key distribution	HAS with real-time key generation	HAS with key pre-generation
Neighbor discovery		AS	APs	APs
Computation overhead [prf, enc. and dec.]	AS	$m, 3m$	$2, 2m$	$0, 2m$
	cAP	$0, 0$	$m, 0$	$m, 0$
	nAP	$0, 3m$	$1, 2m$	$1, 2m$
	STA	$1, 0$	$4, 0$	$2, 0$
Communication overhead between AS and AP		$3m$	$2m$	$2m$

of the network entities. In particular, these overheads must not be centralized in only one node. However, in case of the proactive key distribution scheme, AS performs all authentication operations as neighbor discovery, PMK computation for each candidates and key delivery. This scheme also requires additional processes for updating the topology of the APs and confirming the mobility of the station, because AS doesn't know a change of the APs' topology and the actual destination AP of the station after handover. Though these processes increase more the computation and communication overhead of the AS, since the details of these additional processes were not described in the paper [7], the overhead of the PMK computation and the communication between AS and AP have been compared. This comparison of the handover authentication schemes is described in table 1. Since the inter-access point protocol is basically used to support fast roaming by caching the context of the STA in the candidate set of APs, the general overhead related with IAPP, except the computation of the handover key, is not included in the table 1. Although, in case of HAS, the total computation overhead of the pseudo-random function of the network entities is a little increased than the proactive key distribution scheme, the computation and communication burden of the AS are decreased. The neighbor discovery in HAS is also performed by APs.

The computation cost of the AS for two handover authentication schemes has also been compared, proactive key distribution and HAS using a simulation. The real-time generation method is used to generate AK for the HAS. To show the difference of the computation cost due to variation of the number of the station, simulation is performed individually with 100 stations and 1000 stations. It is assumed that the mobile station can move in four directions in a building or street, and each user having the station randomly moves six times for one hour. The descriptions of parameters for simulation are given in table 2.

Table 2. Simulation Parameters for Figure 5

Parameters	Description
m	the average number of neighboring APs $m = 4$.
p	the handover number per hour $p = 6$
computation cost	the number of the pseudo-random function computed in AS

Figure 5 shows the difference of the computation overhead of the AS in two authentication schemes. The number of the pseudo-random function in AS must be counted every 10 minutes as the computation cost. For 100 stations, the difference between the proactive key distribution scheme presented by the asterisk markers and HAS presented by the dot markers is small. On the other hand, the difference between the proactive key distribution scheme presented by the triangle markers and HAS presented by the circle markers is large for 1000 stations. As a result, the authentication processes of the station are increased by the addition of users, and AS has a less computation burden in HAS.

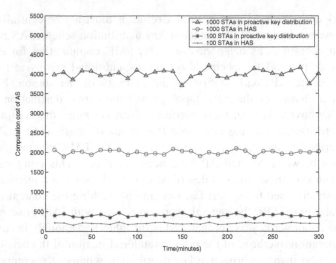

Fig. 5. Comparison of the computation cost of the AS

6 Conclusions

In this study, a hash-chain based authentication scheme for fast handover in wireless network has been proposed. The pros and cons of the existing schemes have been investigated and their problems have been described. The main problem is heavy operations and delay time during the handover of the full authentication procedure described in IEEE 802.11. In particular, to solve the security problem and the administrative burden of the authentication server, this paper introduced the hashed key chain and handover key concept. In solving the security problem, the authentication key is brought into the authentication scheme based on the context transfer of IAPP. The administrative burden of the authentication server is reduced by combining the security context transfer with hash key chain. The authentication server in the HAS responds only to the AK request message. This method can be used for a seamless service on the mobile system such as VoIP, multicast broadcasting, online movies, and so on. This scheme can be extended to a fast-handover authentication scheme for inter-domain movements.

References

1. IEEE standard, "Part 11: Wireless LAN Medium Access Control (MAC) and Physical Layer (PHY) Specifications," IEEE 802.11, 1999.
2. IEEE standard, "Part 11: Wireless LAN Medium Access Control (MAC) and Physical Layer (PHY) specifications Amendment 6: Medium Access Control (MAC) Security Enhancements," IEEE 802.11i, 2004.
3. IEEE standard, "Port-Based Network Access Control," IEEE 802.1x, 2001.
4. IEEE standard, "IEEE Trial-Use Recommended Practice for Multi-Vendor Access Point Interoperability via an Inter-Access Point Protocol Across Distribution Systems," IEEE 802.11f, 2003.

5. B. Aboba, D. Simon, "PPP EAP TLS Authentication Protocol," IETF RFC 2716, October 1999.
6. S. Pack, Y. Choi, "Fast handoff scheme based on mobility prediction in public wireless LAN systems," Communications, IEE Proceedings Volume 151, Issue 5, 24 Oct. 2004 Page(s):489 – 495
7. Arunesh Mishra, Min Ho Shin, Nick L. Petroni, Jr., T. Charles Clancy, William A. Arbauch, "Proactive key distribution using neighbor graphs," IEEE Wireless Communications, Volume 11, Issue 1, 26 – 36., 2004.
8. Arunesh Mishra, Min Ho Shin, William A. Arbauch, "Context Caching using Neighbour Graphs for Fast Handoffs in a Wireless Network," in Proc of IEEE INFOCOM, Hong Kong, Mar. 2004.
9. Hu Wang, Anand R. Prasad, "Fast Authentication for Inter-domain Handover," ICT 2004, LNCS 3124, pp. 973-982, 2004.
10. M.S. Bargh, R.J. Hulsebosch, E.H. Eertink, A. Prasad, H. Wang, P. Schoo, "Fast Authentication Methods for Handovers between IEEE 802.11 Wireless LANs," WMASH'04, October 1, 2004.

Efficient Multicast Stream Authentication for the Fully Adversarial Network Model*

Christophe Tartary** and Huaxiong Wang

Division of ICS, Department of Computing,
Macquarie University, NSW 2109, Australia
{ctartary, hwang}@ics.mq.edu.au

Abstract. We consider the stream authentication problem when an adversary has the ability to drop, reorder or inject data packets in the network. We propose a coding approach for multicast stream authentication using the list-decoding property of Reed-Solomon codes. We divide the data to be authenticated into a stream of packets and associate a single signature for every λn packets where λ and n are predesignated parameters. Our scheme, which is also joinable at the boundary of any n-packet block, can be viewed as an extension of Lysyanskaya, Tamassia and Triandopoulos's technique in which $\lambda = 1$. We show that by choosing λ and n appropriately, our scheme outperforms theirs in both signature and verification time.

Our approach relies on signature dispersion as SAIDA and eSAIDA. Assuming that we use RSA for signing and MD5 for hashing, we give an approximation of the proportion of extra packets per block which could be processed via our technique with respect to the previous scheme. As example when we process $\lambda = 1000$ blocks of 20000 64-byte-packets, the gain of our scheme with respect to Lysyanskaya et al.'s is about 30%.

Keywords: Stream authentication, signature dispersion, Reed-Solomon codes.

1 Introduction

Broadcast communication enables a sender to distribute data to many receivers via a public communication channel such as the Internet. Their applications cover a large scope of areas such as software updates, sensor networks, GPS signals, pay-TV, stock quotes and military defense systems for instance. Nevertheless existing IP protocols in the Internet only provide a best-effort delivery process and the large number of receivers prevents lost content from being redistributed. In addition malicious users having access to the network can perform harmful actions on the data stream. Thus the security relies on two aspects: the network properties and opponents' computational power. In this paper we will consider the computationally secure model for broadcast authentication. That is, the opponents have bounded computational abilities.

---

* This work was supported by the Australian Research Council under ARC Discovery Project DP0344444.
** The author's work was funded by a iMURS scholarship provided by Macquarie University.

J. Song, T. Kwon, and M. Yung (Eds.): WISA 2005, LNCS 3786, pp. 108–125, 2006.

Many techniques have been designed to deal with multicast stream authentication [3]. Examples as pay-TV and stock quotes involve that data stream can be infinite and must be consumed as soon as they reach the receivers (or within a short delay). The most basic idea of signing each packet[1] is inappropriate, as digital signatures are typically time expensive. The available transmission bandwidth does not allow the use of one-time or k-time signatures [5, 21] either because of their large size whereas the construction of Boneh et al.'s short signatures [2] is too restrictive to be used in our case. Since signing each packet is prohibitive, other techniques rely on signature amortization. This means that one signature is produced and its cost (both in time and overhead) is amortized over several packets (due to hash functions for instance).

In [23], Wong and Lam built a Merkle-hash tree [10] to distribute hashes. Their scheme is tolerant against any kind of packet loss. Nevertheless the tag[2] size is logarithmic in the number of packets per block.

In [5], Gennaro and Rohatgi proposed to sign the first stream packet and link the hash of each packet into the next one's tag. This approach needs the entire stream to be known in advance and if a single packet is lost then the whole process fails.

To deal with packet loss, Perrig et al. designed EMSS [17, 18] and MESS [18] by appending the hash of each packet to a fixed number of followers according to a specific pattern. One packet is signed from time to time to ensure non-repudiation and is always assumed to be received. They modeled the network loss pattern by a k-state Markov chain (see [16, 24]) and provided bounds on the packet verifiability. Considering the diversity of computational abilities within the set of receivers, Challal et al. [4] used different layers for hash distribution. Their H_2A protocol gave good practical improvements with respect to MESS. Golle and Modadugu [6] and Miner and Staddon [11] proved other bounds based on augmented chains. The main drawback of all these schemes is that they rely on the signature reception reliability (except Wong and Lam's one [23]). To overcome this problem, one possibility is to split the signature into k smaller parts where only ℓ of them $(\ell < k)$ are enough for recovery.

The Information Dispersal Algorithm [20] has been used by Park et al. [13, 14] and Park and Cho [15] to design two similar schemes SAIDA and eSAIDA (the later having a better packet verification probability). Al-Ibrahim and Pieprzyk [1] used linear equations and polynomial interpolation whereas Pannetrat and Molva [12] proposed some erasure codes to achieve signature dispersion. Nevertheless these four schemes share a commun drawback: they do not tolerate a single packet injection.

Using an error-correcting code approach, Lysyanskaya et al. [8] designed a scheme resistant to packet loss and injections (provided some assumptions on the network delivery reliability). As the five previous schemes above, a single signature is created per block and amortized over several packets. These techniques extended the notion of packet signature to block signature. The scheme developed in [5] generates a single signature for the whole stream but does not tolerate a single packet loss.

In order to decrease time spent for signature generation and verification, our approach is to generate one signature for every family of λ blocks where each of them

---

[1] Since the data stream is large it is divided into fixed-size entities called *packets*.

[2] We call *authentication tag* the extra information appended to a packet to provide its authenticity.

consists of n packets. The value of the parameter λ has to be chosen carefully by the sender since he will have to memorize λn packets at a time. Nevertheless, as in [8], data are sent and can be authenticated by receivers per block. This regulates the traffic in the network avoiding too irregular throughput variations which could create a bottleneck. The family signature is spread within each block which enables a receiver to join the communication group at any block boundary. The minimal value, Λ, of λ from which our protocol is faster than Lysyanskaya et al.'s one remains very small. For instance we have $\Lambda = 2$ up to $n = 30000$ when using RSA and MD5 for 64-byte packets. This value for n is much larger than the one used by Perrig et al. to implement EMSS ($n = 1000$). The profit of our approach is significant. For instance we have a benefit of at least 50% more packets per block with respect to Lysyanskaya et al.'s technique and linear equations' approach (up to $n = 11500$) and to SAIDA and eSAIDA (up to $n = 13300$). If $n = 1000$ (as for EMSS) then our technique provides a benefit larger than 90% more packets per block than Lysyanskaya et al.'s scheme.

The paper is organized as follows. In the following section, we describe the scheme developed in [8]. In Sect. 3 we will introduce our modifications and prove the security of this new scheme under similar assumptions to those made in [8]. In Sect. 4 we will compare our extended scheme to some above ones to get an idea of the gain it provides towards them. In Sect. 5 we will improve the signature verification complexity. The last section will summarize our contribution to the multicast stream authentication problem.

2 Preliminaries

Definition 1. *An* $[N, K]_q$ *systematic Reed-Solomon (SRS) code over the finite field* $\mathbb{F}_q$ $(q > N)$ *is a function:*

$$\mathcal{C}: \quad (\mathbb{F}_q \times \mathbb{F}_q)^K \quad \rightarrow \quad (\mathbb{F}_q \times \mathbb{F}_q)^N$$
$$\{(i, y_i)\}_{i \in \{1, \ldots, K\}} \mapsto \{(i, p(i))\}_{i \in \{1, \ldots, N\}}$$

such that p is an element of $\mathbb{F}_q[X]$ *of degree at most K with* $\forall i \in \{1, \ldots, K\}$ $p(i) = y_i$. *The rational* $\frac{K}{N}$ (< 1) *is called the rate of the code.*

The code is called *systematic* since the first K symbols of any codeword are its corresponding message [9]. Given the K points $\{(i, y_i)\}_{i \in \{1, \ldots, K\}}$, the polynomial p defined above is unique. In order to deal with the attack of packet injections, we will list-decode this SRS code using the Guruswami-Sudan decoder (GS-Decoder) developed in [7]. It is based on the polynomial reconstruction problem, takes as input integers K, t, and M couples of field elements $\{(\tilde{x}_i, \tilde{y}_i)\}_{i \in \{1, \ldots, M\}}$, and outputs the list of all univariate polynomials $\tilde{p}$ of degree at most K such that $\tilde{y}_i = \tilde{p}(\tilde{x}_i)$ for at least t values of $i \in \{1, \ldots, M\}$. It is shown in [7] that if $t > \sqrt{K M}$ then the polynomial reconstruction problem could be solved in polynomial time. Then it has been deduced that any $[N, K]_q$ Reed-Solomon code (systematic or not) with an error at most $N - t$ could be list-decoded using $O(N^2)$ field operations producing a list of $O(1)$ candidates.

We consider the scenario where the sender has much larger computational memory storage (to buffer a piece of the data stream) and computational abilities than the receivers. This illustrates most cases since, in general, the sender is a server delivering data to personal computers.

In the fully adversarial model, the adversary $\mathcal{A}$ can introduce packets into the channel, drop and rearrange some chosen original ones. Thus reliable transmission of the signature is not possible since $\mathcal{A}$ would only need to drop the signature packet to make the authentication scheme fail. Since the authentication problem is our major concern, we assume that a reasonnable number of original packets reaches the receivers. Indeed if too many packets are discarded or modified by $\mathcal{A}$ then the main problem becomes data transmission since the small number of packets reaching the receivers would be useless for their original purposes even authenticated. On the other hand if too many packets are received then prevention against denial-of-service attacks becomes the main concern. We split the stream into blocks of n packets and define two parameters:

- α $(0 < \alpha \leq 1)$: the *survival rate*. At least αn original packets are received
- β $(\beta \geq 1)$: the *flood rate*. A maximum of βn packets reaches each receiver

We now breafly describe the scheme defined by Lysyanskaya et al. [8]. Let ρ be the rate of the SRS code we will use. Since $\frac{\alpha^2}{\beta} \in (0,1]$ there exists $\epsilon > 0$ such that: $\rho = \frac{\alpha^2}{(1+\epsilon)\beta}$. ϵ is called the *tolerance parameter* of the decoder. The choice of ρ will be explained later. We use a signature scheme [22] (the key generator of which is $Keygen$) and a collision-resitant hash function [19]. Each block of n packets has an identification tag BID (representing its position within the whole stream). The authenticator $Auth$ first hashes each packet and signs the concatenation of BID together with the n hashes. Then we form the authentication stream S which is the concatenation of the n hashes and the signature. S is split into $\rho n + 1$ field elements over $\mathbb{F}_q$ where $q = 2^{\lceil \frac{|S|}{\rho n + 1} \rceil}$ (after padding if necessary). S is encoded using the $\mathrm{SRS}[n, \rho n]_q$ code giving n pieces of signature. Each authenticated packet is the concatenation of BID, the packet position within the block, the packet itself and the corresponding piece of signature.

From [7], we must have $t > \sqrt{KM}$ to ensure the success of GS-Decoder. In our case we have $t = \alpha n$ (minimum number of original packets arrived at the receiver end), $K = \rho n$ and $M = m$ (number of received packets ($\alpha n \leq m \leq \beta n$)). Thus from the inequality $t > \sqrt{KM}$ we have $\beta n > \frac{m}{1+\epsilon}$. So GS-Decoder can be run successfully for our choice of ρ. Since ϵ has an impact on the success of that decoder we denote it: GS-Decoder$_\epsilon$. To fit the fact that our code is systematic we need to modify GS-Decoder$_\epsilon$ before using it for authenticating packets.

MGS-Decoder$_\epsilon$
Input: The number of packets per block n, the network characteristics α, β and m elements $\{(x_i, y_i), 1 \leq i \leq m\}$.

1. **If** $m > \beta n$ **or** we have less than αn distinct values of x_i **then** the algorithm rejects the input.

2. Run GS-Decoder$_\epsilon$ on the m elements to get a list L of polynomials. Evaluate each $Q_i(X)$ at $1, \ldots, \rho n + 1$ and concatenate these values to form c_i.

Output: $\{c_1, \ldots, c_{|L|}\}$: list of candidates.

We notice that since α, β and ϵ are known, ρ can be easily computed. Thus there is no need to consider it as an input. Now we describe the decoding algorithm $Decoder_\epsilon$ used in [8]. After verifying that the number of packets with suitable BID and packet numbering is between $\alpha\, n$ and $\beta\, n$, MGS-Decoder$_\epsilon$ is run to obtain a list of candidates for signature verification. The list is processed until the signature is checked or the whole list is exhausted. If the MGS-Decoder$_\epsilon$ rejects the input or the list is processed in vain then the family of received packets is dropped. Otherwise (i.e. the signature has been verified successfully) the good candidate is split as above (as the concatenation of the BID and n hashes). Then each of the received packets is processed and we check whether its hash matches one of the n ones. If so the corresponding packet is output as authentic. We now describe the improvements we made on Lysyanskaya et al.'s scheme.

3 Our Protocol

Our work is an extension of the scheme described in Sect. 2 [8]. Since signatures are time expensive to generate and verify, our idea is to compute one signature for a family of λ blocks where each block consists of n packets. We assume that the sender can buffer $\lambda\, n$ packets. Nevertheless our scheme works in such a way that a receiver only needs to get enough packets from a block before verifying it (he does not have to wait for the whole sequence). As the previous scheme, it will be joinable at any block boundary. We need a collision-resistant hash function h as well as a signature scheme ($KeyGen, sign, verify$) where KeyGen generates the private key SK and its corresponding public key PK. We denote $\cdot\|\cdot$ the concatenation of two elements. Figure 1 gives a description of the sender's work for the sequence of blocks $\{B_1, \ldots, B_\lambda\}$.

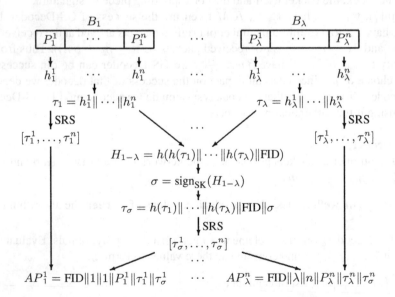

Fig. 1. Authentication process of the extended scheme

We keep the same definitions for n, α, β, ρ and ϵ as before. Each family $\{P_1^1, \ldots, P_\lambda^n\}$ of λn packets of the stream has an identification tag FID representing its position within the whole stream. Each one of its blocks of n packets also has a tag BID. Thus a packet is now identified within the stream by its position i within a block BID belonging to the family FID, i.e. its *identification number* is (FID, BID, i). We now describe the family authenticator $AuthFamily$ which outputs the packets per block of n elements.

AuthFamily

Input: The private key SK, the network characteristics α, β, a family $\{P_1^1, \ldots, P_\lambda^n\}$, its FID and λ.

1. Within each block b we hash the n packets and concatenate them to form the block tag τ_b. It is then encoded using the SRS code and we get $(\tau_b^1, \ldots, \tau_b^n)$.

2. Hash the λ block tags and concatenate them together with FID. This concatenation is hashed to get $H_{1-\lambda}$ which is signed to form σ using SK. The resulting signature is encoded using the SRS code and we get $(\tau_\sigma^1, \ldots, \tau_\sigma^n)$.

3. The λn authenticated packets are defined as $AP_b^p = \text{FID}\|b\|p\|P_b^p\|\tau_b^p\|\tau_\sigma^p$. As soon as the n packets of a block are processed then the whole block is sent immediately.

Output: $\{AP_1^1, \ldots, AP_\lambda^n\}$: set of authenticated packets sent per block of n packets.

In order to use the same SRS code, τ_σ and the τ_b's ($1 \leq b \leq \lambda$) must be padded appropriately. If we denote $\mathcal{H}$ the size of a hash, s the signature size and $|\cdot|$ the mapping giving the size of an element then $|\tau_b| = n\mathcal{H}$ and $|\tau_\sigma| = \lambda\mathcal{H} + s + |\text{FID}|$. In our work we can assume that $\lambda < n$. Otherwise our scheme requires the sender to buffer too many packets to preserve the live diffusion of data. We can also assume that $|\text{FID}|$ does not exceed the size of a hash. Thus we can assume that $|\tau_b| < n\mathcal{H} + s$ and $|\tau_b| < n\mathcal{H} + s$. So we will use in both cases the $\text{SRS}[n, \rho n]_q$ code where q is the same integer as in Sect. 2. Thus our extension does not increase the size of the field we work with. τ_σ and τ_i's are padded according to that finite field.

If we do not take into account the identification number then any packet's tag is $\tau_{\text{BID}}^i\|\tau_\sigma^i$ which is the concatenation of 2 field elements. Once a generator of the extension $\mathbb{F}_q/\mathbb{F}_2$ is chosen then any element of $\mathbb{F}_q$ requires $\log_2(q)$ bits. So our tag is as large as $2\log_2(q)$ bits which is approximately $\frac{2}{\rho}\mathcal{H}$ bits. Since $\rho < 1$, the tag is sligthly larger than two hashes produced by h.

Since each block carries the signature, it is sufficient to run the signature verification process for family FID until one of its blocks makes the authentication process successful. Therefore when a new block of packets is received, the receiver must react differently whether the family signature has already been verified or not. We first design the signature verification routine $VerifySignatureFamily$.

VerifySignatureFamily

Input: The public key PK, the network characteristics α, β, a set of pairs of field elements $\{(x_i, y_i), 1 \leq i \leq m\}$, the family FID and λ.

1. Run MGS-Decoder$_\epsilon$ on $\{(x_i, y_i), 1 \leq i \leq m\}$ to get a list L of candidates for the family signature verification. If MGS-Decoder$_\epsilon$ rejects this input then the algorithm stops.

2. While the signature has not been verified and the list L has not been exhausted, we pick a new candidate $\tilde{h}(\tau_1)\| \cdots \|\tilde{h}(\tau_\lambda)\|\tilde{\sigma}$. If verify$_{PK}(h(\tilde{h}(\tau_1)\| \cdots \|\tilde{h}(\tau_\lambda)\|FID), \tilde{\sigma})$ = TRUE then $\tilde{\sigma}$ is considered as the authentic family signature σ and the $h(\tau_i)$'s are memorized within the table $HashBlock$ as the authentic hash blocks $h(\tau_i)$'s. 3. If the signature has not been verified then our algorithm stops.

Output: (σ, HashBlock): family signature and hashes of the λ blocks.

Now we describe our block decoder $DecoderBlock_\epsilon$. The definition of the boolean $TestSignature$ is necessary because our scheme only checks the family signature until it is verified by one block within the family FID. Once it has been done block hashes are stored into HashBlock and only block authentications are performed. Let $RP = \{R_1, \ldots, R_m\}$ be the set of received packets.

DecoderBlock$_\epsilon$
Input: The public key PK, the network caracteristics α, β, n, FID, BID, λ, a boolean TestSignature, a table HashBlock and the set of received packets RP.

1. Write the packets as $FID_i\|BID_i\|j_i\|P_{BID_i}^{j_i}\|\tau_{BID_i}^{j_i}\|\tau_\sigma^{j_i}$ and discard those having $FID_i \neq FID$, $BID_i \neq BID$ or $j_i \notin \{1, \ldots, n\}$. Denote m' the number of remaining packets. If $m' < \alpha n$ or $m' > \beta n$ then the algorithm stops.
2. If (TestSignature = TRUE) then go to step 3. Otherwise run VerifySignatureFamily on the m' remaining points. If it rejects the input then the algorithm stops. Otherwise set TestSignature = TRUE
3. Run MGS-Decoder$_\epsilon$ on the set $\{(j_i, \tau_\sigma^{j_i}), 1 \leq i \leq m'\}$ and get a list L of candidates for block tag verification. If MGS-Decoder$_\epsilon$ rejects that set then the algorithm stops.
4. While the block BID has not been verified and the list L has not been exhausted, we pick a new candidate $\tilde{c} := \tilde{h}_{BID}^1\| \cdots \|\tilde{h}_{BID}^n$. If $(h(\tilde{c}) = HashBlock(BID))$ then the tag of block BID is verified and we set $h_{BID}^j = \tilde{h}_{BID}^j$ for $j \in \{1, \ldots, n\}$. If L is exhausted without a successful block tag verification then the algorithm stops.
5. For $i \in \{1, \ldots, n\}$, set $P'^i_{BID} = \emptyset$. For each packet of RP (written as $R_{BID}^i = FID\|BID\|j\|P_{BID}^j\|\tau_{BID}^j\|\tau_\sigma^j$ where $j \in \{1, \ldots, n\}$) if $h(P_{BID}^j) = h_{BID}^j$ then $P'^j_{BID} = P_{BID}^j$.

Output: $\{P'^1_{BID}, \ldots, P'^n_{BID}\}$: set of identified packets.

After step 1 the remaining m' packets are renumbered as $\{R_{BID}^1, \ldots, R_{BID}^{m'}\}$ where $R_{BID}^i = FID\|BID\|j_i\|P_{BID}^{j_i}\|\tau_{BID}^{j_i}\|\tau_\sigma^{j_i}$. When we enter step 4 the table HashBlock is full since the family signature has been verified.

Since a single signature is created per family of λ blocks, one might think that our scheme is only joinable at a family boundary. Nevertheless $[\tau_\sigma^1, \ldots, \tau_\sigma^n]$ is present within each bock of n packets the sender emits. Thus any receiver can join the communication group at any block boundary as in [8].

Since the families of λ blocks are independant from each other, the security of our scheme relies on the security of a family of λ blocks. Similar to [8], we give the following definition.

Definition 2. $(KeyGenerator, Authenticator, Decoder)$ *is a secure and* (α, β)-*correct multicast authentication scheme if no probabilistic polynomial-time adversary* $\mathcal{A}$ *can win with a non-negligible probability to the following game:*

i) *A key pair* $(\mathrm{SK}, \mathrm{PK})$ *is generated by* $KeyGenerator$.

ii) $\mathcal{A}$ *is given:* (a) *The public key* PK *and* (b) *Oracle access to* $Authenticator$ (*but* $\mathcal{A}$ *can only issue at most one query with the same family identification tag* FID).

iii) $\mathcal{A}$ *outputs* $(\mathrm{FID}, n, \alpha, \beta, RP)$.

$\mathcal{A}$ *wins if one of the following happens:*

a) *(violation of the correctness property) The adversary succeeds to output* RP *such that even if it contains* $\alpha_i \, n_i$ *packets of some authenticated packet set* AP_i *for family identification tag* $\mathrm{FID}_i = \mathrm{FID}$ *and block identification tag* $\mathrm{BID}_i = \mathrm{BID}$, *the decoder still fails at authenticating some of the correct packets.*

b) *(violation of the security property) The adversary succeeds to output* RP *such that the decoder outputs* $\{P'^{1}_{\mathrm{BID}}, \ldots, P'^{n}_{\mathrm{BID}}\}$ *(for some* BID*) that were never authenticated by* $Authenticator$ *(as a part of a family of* λ *blocks) for the family tag* FID.

Lysyanskaya et al. [8] showed that their scheme $(\mathrm{Keygen}, \mathrm{Auth}, \mathrm{Decoder}_\epsilon)$ was secure and (α, β)-correct. Following their arguments, we obtain the following result for our scheme.

Theorem 1. *The authentication scheme* $(\mathrm{KeyGen}, \mathrm{AuthFamily}, \mathrm{DecoderBlock}_\epsilon)$ *is secure and* (α, β)-*correct.*

Proof. Suppose that our scheme is neither secure nor (α, β)-correct. By definition an adversary $\mathcal{A}$ can break the scheme with a non-negligible probability $\mathcal{P}(k)$. We have:

$$\mathcal{P}(k) = p(\{\text{the scheme is not } (\alpha, \beta)\text{-correct or unsecure}\})$$
$$= p(\{\text{the scheme is not } (\alpha, \beta)\text{-correct}\} \cup \{\text{the scheme is unsecure}\})$$

Since p is a measure, we deduce that one of the following two cases is true:

$$p(\{\text{the scheme is not } (\alpha, \beta)\text{-correct}\}) \geq \frac{\mathcal{P}(k)}{2} \tag{1}$$

$$p(\{\text{the scheme is unsecure}\}) \geq \frac{\mathcal{P}(k)}{2} \tag{2}$$

Point (1). If a polynomial-time adversary $\mathcal{A}$ breaks the (α, β)-correctness of the scheme then the digital signature scheme can be forged. This will be proved by turning an attack breaking the (α, β)-correctness into an attack against the signature scheme. For this attack, $\mathcal{A}$ has access to the signing algorithm $\mathrm{sign}_{\mathrm{SK}}$ (but not SK itself), can use the public signature key PK and the cryptographic hash function h. He is also able to run the authentication scheme AuthFamily. The queries made to it are written as $(\mathrm{FID}_i, \lambda_i, n_i, \alpha_i, \beta_i, DP_i)$ where DP_i is the set of $\lambda_i \, n_i$ data packets to be authenti–

cated. In order to get the corresponding output, the signature is obtained by querying sign_{SK} within the authenticator. Following this process, $\mathcal{A}$ is able to break the scheme correctness since he got values FID, $\lambda, n, \alpha, \beta$ and a set of received packets RP_{BID} (for some BID $\in \{1, \ldots, \lambda\}$) such that:

- $\exists i \, / \, (\text{FID}, \lambda, n, \alpha, \beta) = (\text{FID}_i, \lambda_i, n_i, \alpha_i, \beta_i)$.

Denote $DP = \{P_1^1, \ldots, P_\lambda^n\} (= DP_i)$ the data packets associated with this query and AP the response given to $\mathcal{A}$. In particular we denote $\sigma = \text{sign}_{\text{SK}}(H_{1-\lambda})$ where $H_{1-\lambda} = h(h(\tau_1) \| \ldots \| h(\tau_\lambda) \| \text{FID})$ with $\forall j \in \{1, \ldots, \lambda\} \, \tau_j = h(P_j^1) \| \ldots \| h(P_j^n)$.

- $|RP_{\text{BID}} \cap AP| \geq n\alpha$ and $|RP_{\text{BID}}| \leq \beta n$.
- $(P'^1_{\text{BID}}, \ldots, P'^n_{\text{BID}}) = \text{DecoderBlock}_\epsilon(\text{PK}, \text{FID}, \text{BID}, n, \alpha, \beta, \text{TestSignature}, \text{Hash-Block}, RP_{\text{BID}})$ where for some j such that $R^j_{\text{BID}} \in RP$ we have $P^j_{\text{BID}} \neq P'^j_{\text{BID}}$ with: $R^j_{\text{BID}} = \text{FID} \| \text{BID} \| j \| P'^j_{\text{BID}} \| \tau^j_{\text{BID}} \| \tau^j_\sigma$.

Since $\text{DecoderBlock}_\epsilon$ first checks the family signature and second outputs packets, TestSignature can take two different values (each of them involves a specific value of HashBlock). Thus $\mathcal{A}$ must be able to succeed in both following cases:

A. The set RP_{BID} is used to verify the signature
B. The signature of the family has already been checked

Case B illustrates the event when the receiver has already verified the family signature when he receives fake packets introduced by $\mathcal{A}$.

Case A. Since the set RP_{BID} verifies the signature, the query 3 above gives us a candidate $c' = h'_1 \| \ldots \| h'_\lambda \| \sigma'$ with $\text{verify}_{\text{PK}}(h(h'_1 \| \ldots \| h'_\lambda \| \text{FID}), \sigma') = \text{TRUE}$. We have to prove that sign_{SK} was not run on the input $h(h'_1 \| \ldots \| h'_\lambda \| \text{FID})$. This is proved in [8]. Here we have a slight difference. That is, we have $h(h'_1 \| \ldots \| h'_\lambda \| \text{FID})$ whereas [8] deals with $h'_1 \| \ldots \| h'_\lambda \| \text{FID}$. As h is collision resistant, this difference is not a problem.

Case B. Now we consider that the signature has previously been verified. That is the receiver has buffered $h'_1, \ldots, h'_\lambda$ and σ' such that $\text{verify}_{\text{PK}}(h(h'_1 \| \ldots \| h'_\lambda \| \text{FID}), \sigma') = \text{TRUE}$. We have two possibilities: $P'^j_{\text{BID}} \neq \emptyset$ or $P'^j_{\text{BID}} = \emptyset$.

- Sub-case B1: $P'^j_{\text{BID}} \neq \emptyset$. Since h is collision-resistant, we have $h(P'^j_{\text{BID}}) \neq h(P^j_{\text{BID}})$. Since P'^j_{BID} is a non-empty part of a received packet, the decoding algorithm $\text{DecoderBlock}_\epsilon$ outputs a candidate $c'_{\text{BID}} = h'^1_{\text{BID}} \| \ldots \| h'^n_{\text{BID}}$ such that $h'_{\text{BID}} = h(h'^1_{\text{BID}} \| \ldots \| h'^n_{\text{BID}})$. Moreover $\text{DecoderBlock}_\epsilon$ includes P'^j_{BID} into the output packets if and only if $h(P'^j_{\text{BID}}) = h'^j_{\text{BID}}$. Remember that $h(P'^j_{\text{BID}}) \neq h(P^j_{\text{BID}})$. We get: $h(P'^1_{\text{BID}}) \| \ldots \| h(P'^j_{\text{BID}}) \| \ldots \| h(P'^n_{\text{BID}}) \neq h(P^1_{\text{BID}}) \| \ldots \| h(P^j_{\text{BID}}) \| \ldots \| h(P^n_{\text{BID}})$.

Since h is a collision-resistant we get: $h'_{\text{BID}} \neq h_{\text{BID}}$ and for the same reason: $h(h(P'^1_{\text{BID}}) \| \ldots \| h(P'^j_{\text{BID}}) \| \ldots \| h(P'^n_{\text{BID}})) \neq h(h(P^1_{\text{BID}}) \| \ldots \| h(P^j_{\text{BID}}) \| \ldots \| h(P^n_{\text{BID}}))$ Thus the digital signature is not secure.

- Sub-case B2: $P'^j_{\text{BID}} = \emptyset$. Due to the consistency of $\text{MGS-Decoder}_\epsilon$ (see [8]), $\text{DecoderBlock}_\epsilon$ will include the candidate value $c = h^1_{\text{BID}} \| \ldots \| h^n_{\text{BID}}$. By definition $h(c) = h_{\text{BID}}$, so the decoder cannot provide $(h'^1_{\text{BID}}, \ldots, h'^n_{\text{BID}}) = (\emptyset, \ldots, \emptyset)$. If $(h'^1_{\text{BID}}, \ldots, h'^n_{\text{BID}}) = (h^1_{\text{BID}}, \ldots, h^n_{\text{BID}})$ then the design of $\text{DecoderBlock}_\epsilon$ involves that $P'^{j}_{\text{BID}} = P^{j}_{\text{BID}}$ be non-empty and R^{j}_{BID} is a received packet. In order to avoid this contraction, we must have $(h'^{1}_{\text{BID}}, \ldots, h'^{n}_{\text{BID}}) \neq (h^{1}_{\text{BID}}, \ldots, h^{n}_{\text{BID}})$. Nevertheless $h(h'^{1}_{\text{BID}} \| \ldots \| h'^{n}_{\text{BID}}) = h_{\text{BID}}$ which is impossible since h is collision-resistant. Thus we get a contradiction.

Point (2). If a polynomial-time adversary $\mathcal{A}$ breaks the security property of the scheme than the underlying signature scheme is not secure. We consider the same kind of scheme as in point (1). $\mathcal{A}$ will succeed if one of the following will hold:

A. AuthFamily was never queried on input $FID, \lambda, n, \alpha, \beta, DP$ and the decoding algorithm $\text{DecoderBlock}_{\epsilon}$ does not reject it, i.e. $OP_{\text{BID}} \neq \emptyset$ where $OP_{\text{BID}} = \text{DecoderBlock}_{\epsilon}(\text{PK}, \text{FID}, \text{BID}, n, \alpha, \beta, RP_{\text{BID}})$ with $\text{BID} \in \{1, \ldots, \lambda\}$.
B. AuthFamily was queried on input $FID, \lambda, n, \alpha, \beta, DP$. However some non-empty output packet P'^{j}_{BID} is different from P^{j}_{BID} where $OP_{\text{BID}} = \{P'^{1}_{\text{BID}}, \ldots, P'^{n}_{\text{BID}}\}$ and $DP = \{P^{1}_{1}, \ldots, P^{n}_{\lambda}\}$ for some $\text{BID} \in \{1, \ldots, \lambda\}$.

Case A. Due to the design of $\text{DecoderBlock}_{\epsilon}$, the only possibilities to output non-empty packets were either (exhibiting a valid signature and valid hashes for block BID) or (valid hashes for block BID which are consistant with the signature and block hashes already buffered)

• Sub-case A1: Because we exhibit a valid signature, the MGS-Decoder$_{\epsilon}$ has output an element $c' = h'(\tau_{1}) \| \ldots \| h'(\tau_{\lambda}) \| \sigma'$ such that $\text{verify}_{\text{PK}}(h(h'(\tau_{1}) \| \ldots \| h'(\tau_{\lambda}) \| \text{FID}), \sigma') = \text{TRUE}$. Since AuthFamily was never queried with FID, neither does $\text{verify}_{\text{PK}}$. Thus σ' is a successful forgery, that is the signature scheme is not secure.
• Sub-case A2: Denote σ and $h(\tau_{1}), \ldots, h(\tau_{\lambda})$ the valid signature and its corresponding tags of blocks. Since $P'^{j}_{\text{BID}} \neq P^{j}_{\text{BID}}$ we deduce: $h(P'^{j}_{\text{BID}}) \neq h(P^{j}_{\text{BID}})$ because h is collision-resistant. For the same reason $h(\tau'_{\text{BID}}) \neq h(\tau_{\text{BID}})$. We get a contradiction since outputing packets involves $h(\tau'_{\text{BID}}) = h(\tau_{\text{BID}})$. We notice that even if we do not know all P'^{j}_{BID}'s (some can be empty), the hash $h(\tau'_{\text{BID}})$ is known thanks to VerifySignatureFamily.

Case B. Here we have the same situation as point (1) case A and sub-case B2. We get a contradiction with the security of the signature scheme. □

Thus our modifications do not weaken either the security or the correctness of the technique developed in [8]. In order to compare our protocol to those relying on the same principle, namely signature dispersion, we need to compute its cost.

AuthFamily requires $\lambda (n + 1) + 1$ hashes, 1 signature generation and, based on the analysis of Lysyanskaya et al.'s scheme, $O(\lambda n \log n)$ field operations over $\mathbb{F}_{q}$.

$\text{DecoderBlock}_{\epsilon}$ is more complex to analyze since its complexity depends on the block used to successfully verify the family signature. First we compute the cost generated by one block, say $b (1 \leq b \leq \lambda)$, assuming that we received k packets where $k \leq \beta n$ and at least αn with right numbering. In the following the field is the one used for the SRS code. We have two cases:

1. *The signature of the family has not been verified yet.* MGS-Decoder$_{\epsilon}$ is run in $O(n^{2})$ field operations and outputs a list of $O(1)$ signature candidates. We compute one hash and one signature verification for each of them until the signature be verified. So there

is a total of $O(n^2)$ field operations, $O(1)$ hashes and $O(1)$ signature verification.
2. *The signature of the family has already been verified.* MGS-Decoder$_\epsilon$ is run as above. Each element of the list is hashed. Then $O(k)$ hashes are computed to authenticate the packets. Since $k \leq \beta n$ and β is constant we have $k = O(n)$. So there is a total of $O(n^2)$ field operations and $O(n)$ hashes.

Consider the whole family of λ blocks. We notice that block authentications are only processed after a successful signature verification. Denote $\mathcal{B}$ the block which verifies the family signature. From block 1 to $\mathcal{B} - 1$ only unsuccessful signature verifications are performed (case 1). For block $\mathcal{B}$ one successful verification and one block authentication are performed (both cases). For block $\mathcal{B} + 1$ to λ only block authentications are performed (case 2). We deduce the cost of the group of λ blocks:

$O((\mathcal{B} - 1) n^2 + n^2 + (\lambda - (\mathcal{B} + 1) + 1) n^2)$ field operations
$O(\mathcal{B} - 1 + n + 1 + (\lambda - (\mathcal{B} + 1) + 1) n)$ hashes
$O(\mathcal{B} - 1 + 1)$ signature verifications

So we have $O(\lambda n^2)$ field operations, $O(\mathcal{B} + (\lambda - \mathcal{B}) n)$ hashes and $O(\mathcal{B})$ signature verifications. We notice that the field operations complexity does not depend on the block $\mathcal{B}$. We also have $\mathcal{B} \leq \lambda$, so $\mathcal{B} = O(\lambda)$. Therefore we have $O(\lambda n)$ hashes and $O(\lambda)$ signature verifications. Nevertheless this kind of approximation is not relevant since the number of hashes depends on the signature verifications performed. Assuming $\mathcal{B} = O(\lambda)$, we lose this dependance and therefore get two "upper bounds" which are not reached at the same time.

4   Comparison of Signature Dispersion-Based Schemes

Complexity Comparison. Our scheme relies on signature dispersion so we will compare it to SAIDA, eSAIDA, linear equations scheme and the Lysyanskaya et al.'s one. We will not consider erasure codes from [12] since they do not specify a particular class of codes. Thus we cannot evaluate the complexity of this technique. The results of Table 1 are built based on the definitions found in [13, 14, 15, 1, 8] where SAIDA, e-SAIDA, linear equations scheme and Lysyanskaya et al.'s scheme are iterated λ times.

We notice that the approach of [8] is much more efficient than the other three schemes on every category but signature verification. Nevertheless this is where its strength against packet loss is. So we can say that it is the most efficient technique using sig-

Table 1. Cost for signature dispersion-based schemes

	Sender			Receiver		
	Field Op.	Hash	Signature	Field Op.	Hash	Sign. Verif.
SAIDA	$O(\lambda n^2)$	$\lambda(n+1)$	λ	$O(\lambda n^2)$	$O(\lambda n)$	λ
e-SAIDA	$O(\lambda n^2)$	$\lambda(\frac{3n}{2}+1)$	λ	$O(\lambda n^2)$	$O(\lambda n)$	λ
Linear Equations	$O(\lambda n^3)$	$\lambda(n+1)$	λ	$O(\lambda n^2)$	$O(\lambda n)$	λ
Lysyanskaya et al.'s Scheme	$O(\lambda n \log n)$	λn	λ	$O(\lambda n^2)$	$O(\lambda n)$	$O(\lambda)$
Our Scheme	$O(\lambda n \log n)$	$\lambda n + \lambda + 1$	1	$O(\lambda n^2)$	$O(\lambda n)$	$O(\lambda)$

nature dispersion (amongst those quoted above). So our focus is to compare it (when iterated λ times) to our technique. At the receiver the complexities of both schemes seem to be equivalent but bounds (for our work) concerning hashes and signature verifications are linked together and their exact values are smaller (see Sect. 3). So the complexity at the receiver is slightly better for our scheme. In Sect. 5 we will define a property for the rates α and β allowing $O(1)$ for signature verification. At the sender we experiment the same field operations complexity but our technique computes a single signature whereas the other scheme generates λ of them. This is at the cost of $\lambda + 1$ more hashes computations. As said before generating a digital signature is more time expensive than computing a hash. Since a hash function takes inputs of any length, the time spent hashing the extra quantity generated by our scheme will be more relevant than the number of extra hashes itself to get an approximation of the gain provided.

Threshold Values. Denote $\mathcal{H}$ the size of a hash (in bytes), t_h is time needed to hash one byte and t_s the time needed to produce one signature (both t_h and t_s must be expressed in the same unity). The extra $(\lambda + 1)$ hashes are $h(\tau_1), \ldots, h(\tau_\lambda)$ and $H_{1-\lambda}$. We have: $\forall i \in \{1, \ldots, \lambda\} |\tau_i| = n\mathcal{H}$ and $|h(\tau_1)\| \cdots \|h(\tau_\lambda)\|\text{FID}| = \lambda\mathcal{H} + |\text{FID}|$. If we assume that $|\text{FID}|$ is negligible with respect to $\mathcal{H}$ then the size of the extra quantity to be hashed is $(n + 1)\lambda\mathcal{H}$. Since our scheme experiences $(\lambda - 1)$ less signatures we deduce that it is the faster one if and only if:

$$(n + 1)\,\lambda\,\mathcal{H}\,t_h < (\lambda - 1)\,t_s \iff \left(1 - (n + 1)\,\mathcal{H}\,\frac{t_h}{t_s}\right)\lambda > 1 \qquad (3)$$

Denote $\mathcal{K} := 1 - (n + 1)\,\mathcal{H}\,\frac{t_h}{t_s}$. If $\mathcal{K} < 0$ then $\lambda < 1/\mathcal{K}$. This upper bound is logical. Indeed $\mathcal{K} < 0$ means $t_s < (n + 1)\,\mathcal{H}\,t_h$. Since t_h is small (in comparison to t_s) and $\mathcal{H}$ not too large, this configuration happens when n is large enough. In that case we have a lot more hashes per block. Thus if λ is too large then it is faster to compute one signature per block than all the extra hashes plus the family signature. We are interested in the case where n is reasonable and so $\mathcal{K} > 0$. Since $\lambda > \frac{1}{\mathcal{K}}$ we define $\Lambda := \lceil\frac{1}{\mathcal{K}}\rceil$ (which depends on n). We implemented the mapping $n \mapsto \Lambda(n)$ with different hash functions (MD5, SHA-1, SHA-256, RIPEMD-160 and Panama Hash (little and big endian)) and signature schemes (RSA, DSA (both produce a 1024-bit signature) and ESIGN (1023 bits)). The graphs are depicted as Fig. 2.

When Perrig et al. implemented EMSS [17, 18], one signature packets was sent every 1000 ones. Park and Cho [15] used $n = 200$ and $n = 512$ to implement both SAIDA and eSAIDA. Figure 2 shows that $\Lambda = 2$ when n is up to 1000 for our choice of hash functions and signature schemes.

Once Λ has been chosen as on Fig. 2 we determine the gain in term of proportion of extra packets per block our scheme provides. That is, once $\lambda \geq \Lambda$ and n are fixed ((3) being checked) we determine $\frac{n - \tilde{n}}{n}$ where n is defined such that proccessing a family of $\lambda\tilde{n}$ packets with our technique is as time consuming as λ consecutive iterations of Lysyanskaya et al.'s one with n packets per block. We also want to compute the gain of our model with respect to the schemes previously quoted. As before we need to determine the time spent at the sender for both schemes ($|\text{FID}|$ will be considered as negligible). We denote $\mathcal{P}$ the size of a packet (in bytes). Results are shown in Table 2.

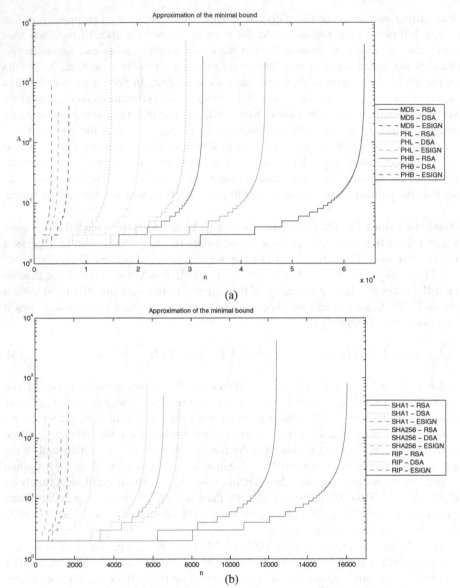

Fig. 2. computations of Λ for our different signature schemes and hash functions

Table 2. Time at the sender

Our Extension	Lysyanskaya et al.'s Scheme (λ times)	Linear Equations (λ times)	SAIDA (λ times)	e-SAIDA (λ times)
$\lambda[n(\mathcal{P}+\mathcal{H})+\mathcal{H}]t_h + t_s$	$\lambda(n\mathcal{P}t_h + t_s)$		$\lambda[n(\mathcal{P}+\mathcal{H})t_h + t_s]$	

Thus it is sufficient to study Lysyanskaya et al.'s scheme and SAIDA. Denote $T_{\text{EX}}^{\lambda,n}, T_{\text{LY}}^{\lambda,n}, T_{\text{SAIDA}}^{\lambda,n}$ the time spent at the sender for our protocol, Lysyanskaya et al.'s technique and SAIDA respectively with λ blocks of n packets each. We want to determine the minimal integers $\mathcal{N}_{\text{LY}}$ and $\mathcal{N}_{\text{SAIDA}}$ such that:

$$\forall \mathcal{N} \geq \mathcal{N}_{\text{LY}} \quad T_{\text{EX}}^{\lambda,\mathcal{N}} > T_{\text{LY}}^{\lambda,n} \quad \text{and} \quad \forall \mathcal{N} \geq \mathcal{N}_{\text{SAIDA}} \quad T_{\text{EX}}^{\lambda,\mathcal{N}} > T_{\text{SAIDA}}^{\lambda,n}$$

This is equivalent to:

$$\mathcal{N}_{\text{LY}} = \left\lceil \frac{\mathcal{P}}{\mathcal{P}+\mathcal{H}} n + \frac{(1-\frac{1}{\lambda})\frac{t_s}{t_h} - \mathcal{H}}{\mathcal{P}+\mathcal{H}} \right\rceil \quad \text{and} \quad \mathcal{N}_{\text{SAIDA}} = \left\lceil n + \frac{(1-\frac{1}{\lambda})\frac{t_s}{t_h} - \mathcal{H}}{\mathcal{P}+\mathcal{H}} \right\rceil$$

Nevertheless (3) must be checked. It can be proved that if the above two numbers do not check that equation then none does (the proof relies on the minimality of these integers). So we define the following two integers and then the gain for each scheme:

$$n_{\text{LY}} = \begin{cases} \left\lceil \frac{\mathcal{P}}{\mathcal{P}+\mathcal{H}} n + \frac{(1-\frac{1}{\lambda})\frac{t_s}{t_h} - \mathcal{H}}{\mathcal{P}+\mathcal{H}} \right\rceil & \text{if (3) is checked} \\ \text{is not defined} & \text{otherwise} \end{cases}$$

$$n_{\text{SAIDA}} = \begin{cases} \left\lceil n + \frac{(1-\frac{1}{\lambda})\frac{t_s}{t_h} - \mathcal{H}}{\mathcal{P}+\mathcal{H}} \right\rceil & \text{if (3) is checked} \\ \text{is not defined} & \text{otherwise} \end{cases}$$

The gains are defined as:

$$G_{\text{LY}} = 1 - \frac{n}{n_{\text{LY}}} \quad \text{and} \quad G_{\text{SAIDA}} = 1 - \frac{n}{n_{\text{SAIDA}}}$$

Perrig et al. [17] and Pannetrat and Molva [12] attempted to solve two particular cases. They had two different packet sizes: 64 and 512 bytes. We chose the same ones and used MD5 (as hash function) and RSA (as signature scheme). Our results indicate that when λ is fixed, increasing the number of packet per block n makes the benefit decrease in all cases. This observation is consistant with what we noticed in Sect. 4. Table 3 gives us an approximation of the gain provided by our scheme for $\mathcal{P} = 64$. The value of λ is not precised since it appeared not to have an important impact on the gain.

Our results also showed that when n was small then the gains were close to 1. Remember that λ is fixed (so that (3) is checked). When n becomes small (i.e. the block size decreases) Lysyanskaya et al.'s technique and SAIDA "tends to" be similar to the sign-each approach scheme (where each packet carries its own signature) whereas our scheme "tends to" be similar a block signature scheme (with λ packets). This justifies the important gain we earn for these values of n. Our observations also indicated that when λ and n were fixed then increasing the packet size $\mathcal{P}$ (from 64 to 512 bytes) made the gain provided by our scheme decrease.

Table 3. Approximation of threshold values about n for G_{LY} and G_{SAIDA} when $\mathcal{P} = 64$

	10%	25%	50%	75%	90%
G_{LY}	45700	25700	11500	2800	1400
G_{SAIDA}	×	40000	13300	4700	1900

5 Improvements on the Signature Verification Complexity

Accuracy of the Parameters. The signature verification complexity is $O(\lambda)$ for our scheme which is the same as Lysyanskaya et al.'s (when their technique is iterated λ times). We present a modification of our approach which allows to have $O(1)$ instead under some assumptions. We need to introduce the following definition.

Definition 3. *We say that a couple (A, B) of survival and flood rates is accurate to the network for a flow of N symbols if: (1) data are sent per block of N elements through the network and (2) for any block of N elements $\{E_1, \cdots, E_N\}$ emitted by the sender, if we denote $\{\tilde{E}_1, \ldots, \tilde{E}_\mu\}$ the set of received packets then $\mu \leq BN$ and at least AN elements of $\{E_1, \cdots, E_N\}$ belong to $\{\tilde{E}_1, \ldots, \tilde{E}_\mu\}$. Condition (2) must be true for each receiver belonging to the communication group.*

<u>Remark:</u> We notice that, when N is fixed, (A, B) is not unique. Indeed any $(\tilde{A}, \tilde{B})$ with $\tilde{B} \geq B$ and $0 < \tilde{A} \leq A$ is also accurate for the same flow N.

In our case, we have $N = n$ (see step 3 of AuthFamily). We have the following proposition:

Proposition 1. *If (α, β) is accurate then any set of received packet verifies the family signature using $O(1)$ signature verifications.*

Proof. Denote FID the family number. Assume that we receive a set RP of packets for some block number BID where BID $\in \{1, \ldots, \lambda\}$. Since (α, β) is accurate, we have $|\text{RP}| \leq \beta n$ and at least αn packets of RP come from the sender. Denote S_{RP} that subset of RP and C_{RP} the subset of RP consisting of elements having correct numbering (FID, BID, ψ) where $\psi \in \{1, \ldots, n\}$. We have: $S_{\text{RP}} \subset C_{\text{RP}} \subset \text{RP}$ so: $\alpha n \leq |S_{\text{RP}}| \leq |C_{\text{RP}}| \leq |\text{RP}| \leq \beta n$.

We will prove that RP verifies the signature by running VerifySignatureFamily with C_{RP} as input. In step 1, a request to run MGS-Decoder$_\epsilon$ on C_{RP} is executed. The above inequalities prove that C_{RP} is not rejected and a list of size $O(1)$ is output by MGS-Decoder$_\epsilon$. Due to its consistency (see [8]), $h(\tau_1)\| \cdots \|h(\tau_\lambda)\|\sigma$ must belong to that list where σ is the signature and $h(\tau_i)$ the hash of the ith original block created by the sender for the family FID. Therefore step 2 of VerifySignatureFamily will be successful after at most $O(1)$ signature verifications (step 3 is not executed). Thus RP verifies the family signature. □

We deduce the following theorem:

Theorem 2. *If (α, β) is accurate then the complexity of signature verification is $O(1)$.*

Proof. Denote FID the family number. Assume that we receive a set RP of packets for some block number BID (BID $\in \{1, \ldots, \lambda\}$). We run Decoder$_\epsilon$ on RP. Its design indicates that once the family signature has been verified for some set $\widehat{\text{RP}}$, no more signature verifications are performed for FID. Since (α, β) is accurate, we can apply Proposition 1. Therefore signature verifications for FID are only computed for the first received set $\widehat{\text{RP}}$ for this value FID. Thus if $RP = \widehat{\text{RP}}$ then $O(1)$ signature verifications are performed, else no signature verifications are computed. This involves that only $O(1)$ signature verifications are performed for FID. Since no specific values have been assigned to FID, we get our result. □

Limitations. In practical applications, it is difficult to find a couple (α, β) which is accurate and realistic due to the large number of receivers (potentially several tens of thousands). Using the remark following Definition 3, we can say that if α is "close to" 0 and β "large enough" then (α, β) is accurate for a flow of n. The drawback is that the length of the tag $\tau^i_{\text{BID}} \| \tau^i_\sigma$ appended to each packet is approximately $\frac{2}{\rho} \mathcal{H}$ (see Sect. 3) where $\rho = \frac{\alpha^2}{(1+\epsilon)\beta}$. That is, this tag is around $\frac{\beta}{\alpha^2} (2(1+\epsilon)\mathcal{H})$ large. If the sender chooses unrealistic values as $\alpha = \frac{1}{10}$ and $\beta = 5$ then we get: $\frac{\beta}{\alpha^2} = 500$. So the tag is larger than 1000 hashes produced by h (since $\epsilon > 0$). This creates too large an overhead per packet for distribution in the network. The previous values were called "unrealistic" because this choice of (α, β) means that at least 10% of the original packets and a total of no more than $5n$ packets are received. If these values were really accurate then it would mean that the opponent would have a very huge control over the network and the few packets the receivers would authenticate would be probably useless.

If the number of receivers is relatively small then each of them can send back a report of the transmission consisting of his own (α_i, β_i). Thus the sender can adjust (α, β) which will be accurate for further transmission as $\alpha = \min_i \alpha_i$ and $\beta = \max_i \beta_i$. Nevertheless this approach is impracticable when the size of the communication group increases. In this case the sender has to choose a couple $(\tilde{\alpha}, \tilde{\beta})$ which seems suitable for a large proportion of receivers (for instance 95%) but which is not guaranteed to be accurate for all of them. Therefore 95% of the receivers will have $O(1)$ as signature verification complexity whereas the other ones will experience $O(\lambda)$ due to potential rejects of received packets by Decoder$_\epsilon$.

6   Conclusion

In [8], Reed-Solomon codes were used to solve the multicast authentication problem in the fully adversarial network. Extending this approach, we designed a scheme where a single signature is computed for every family of λ blocks of n packets. Our technique still allows any receiver to join the communication group at any block boundary. The complexity at the receiver (in term of signature verifications and hash computations) is better than the complexity of λ iterations of Lysyanskaya et al.'s protocol. In particular, when the sender has knowledge of an accurate couple (α, β) for most receivers, the complexity of signature verification for a family of λ blocks becomes $O(1)$ (for these participants) which is the complexity of Lysyanskaya et al.'s technique for 1 block only.

The minimal value, Λ, of λ such that our extension is the faster one at the sender remains small. For instance $\Lambda = 2$ up to $n = 30000$ for RSA and MD5. Thus the extra requirements consisting of buffering λn packets is quickly amortized. Since packets are sent and authenticated per block, the throughput of data within the network does not vary too much. Our technique also allows joinability at any block boundary since the family signature is spread into every block. Therefore the size of the communication group can grow even after the beginning of data transmission. The gain provided by our technique is larger than 50% of extra packets per block with respect to SAIDA, eSAIDA, Lysyanskaya et al.'s and linear equations protocols up to $n = 11500$. This large value of n should be sufficient for most live applications.

What remains to design is a technique allowing a single signature to be computed for the whole stream respecting the property of joinability. Indeed in our work, Reed-Solomon codes are used to deal with opponent's malicious actions but we still need to compute one signature every λ blocks to achieve the non-repudiation and joinability property. If such a process exists then it will also be faced with the fully adversarial network model where the opponent can drop a certain amount of chosen data packets.

References

[1] M. Al-Ibrahim and J. Pieprzyk. Authenticating multicast streams in lossy channels using threshold techniques. In *ICN 2001*, LNCS 2094. Springer - Verlag, July 2001.

[2] D. Boneh, B. Lynn, and H. Shacham. Short signatures from the Weil pairing. In *Asiacrypt 2001*. Springer-Verlag, December 2001.

[3] Y. Challal, H. Bettahar, and A. Bouabdallah. A taxonomy of multicast data origin authentication: Issues and solutions. In *IEEE Communications Surveys and Tutorials*, volume 6, October 2004.

[4] Y. Challal, A. Bouabdallah, and H. Bettahar. H_2A: Hybrid hash-chaining scheme for adaptive multicast source authentication of media-streaming. In *Computer & Security*, volume 24, February 2005.

[5] R. Gennaro and P. Rohatgi. How to sign digital streams. In *Proceedings of the 17th Annual International Cryptology*. Springer-Verlag, August 1997.

[6] P. Golle and N. Modadugu. Authenticating streamed data in the presence of random packet loss. In *NDSS 2001*. Internet Society, February 2001.

[7] V. Guruswami and M. Sudan. Improved decoding of Reed-Solomon and algebraic-geometric codes. In *IEEE Trans. Info. Theory*, May 1999.

[8] A. Lysyanskaya, R. Tamassia, and N. Triandopoulos. Multicast authentication in fully adversarial networks. In *IEEE Symposium on Security and Privacy*, November 2003.

[9] F. J. MacWilliams and N. J. A. Sloane. *The Theory of Error-Correcting Codes*. North-Holland, 1977.

[10] R. Merkle. A certified digital signature. In *Crypto'89*. Springer - Verlag, 1989.

[11] S. Miner and J. Staddon. Graph-based authentication of digital streams. In *IEEE Symposium on Security and Privacy*, May 2001.

[12] A. Pannetrat and R. Molva. Authenticating real time packet streams and multicasts, July 2002.

[13] J. M. Park, E. K. P. Chong, and H. J. Siegel. Efficient multicast packet authentication using signature amortization. In *IEEE Symposium on Security and Privacy*, May 2002.

[14] J. M. Park, E. K. P. Chong, and H. J. Siegel. Efficient multicast stream authentication using erasure codes. In *ACM - TISSEC*, volume 6, May 2003.

[15] Y. Park and Y. Cho. The eSAIDA stream authentication scheme. In *ICCSA*, April 2004.

[16] V. Paxson. End-to-end Internet packet dynamics. In *IEEE/ACM Transactions on Networking*, June 1999.

[17] A. Perrig, R. Canetti, J. Tygar, and D. Song. Efficient authentication and signing of multicast streams over lossy channels. In *IEEE Symposium on Security and Privacy*, May 2000.

[18] A. Perrig and J. D. Tygar. *Secure Broadcast Communication in Wired and Wireless Networks*. Kluwer Academic Publishers, 2003.

[19] J. Pieprzyk, T. Hardjono, and J. Seberry. *Fundamentals of Computer Security*. Springer, 2003.

[20] M. O. Rabin. Efficient dispersal of information for security, load balancing, and fault tolerance. In *Journal of the Association for Computing machinery*, volume 36, April 1989.

[21] P. Rohatgi. A compact and fast hybrid signature scheme for multicast packet authentication. In *CCS'99*, 1999.

[22] D. R. Stinson. *Cryptography: Theory and Practice*. CRC Press, 1995.

[23] C. K. Wong and S. S. Lam. Digital signatures for flows and multicasts. In *IEEE/ACM Transactions on Networking*, volume 7, August 1999.

[24] M. Yajnik, S. Moon, J. Kurose, and D. Towsley. Measurement and modeling of the temporal dependence in packet loss. In *IEEE Infocom*. IEEE Press, 1999.

Elastic Security QoS Provisioning for Telematics Applications*

Minsoo Lee, Sehyun Park**, and Ohyoung Song

School of Electrical and Electronics Engineering, Chung-Ang University,
221, Heukseok-dong, Dongjak-gu, Seoul 156-756, Korea
lemins@wm.cau.ac.kr, {shpark, song}@cau.ac.kr

Abstract. In the vision of 4G networks there is a strong demand for universal wireless access and ubiquitous computing through consistent personal and terminal mobility supports. The ability to provide seamless and adaptive QoS guarantees is key to the success of 4G systems. This paper proposes the novel concept of the elastic security QoS provisioning and the autonomous context transfer scheme in the future wireless networks, taking into account the specific requirements for highly dynamic vehicular users. We designed Mobile Manager that can make the autonomous and user transparent decision for the context-aware secure handover. To demonstrate the effectiveness of the proposed security mechanism, we also analyze the performance of our handover scheme by using the multi-class queuing network model. Our scheme can obtain the performance improvement of seamless security services and can be used as an intelligent add-on model to existing networking systems like mobile networks for telematics applications and home networks for efficient mobility-aware applications.

Keywords: 4G, context transfer, home networks, mobility management, security, telematics, ubiquitous computing.

1 Introduction

In recent years there has been increasing demands for intelligent and autonomous services in universal wireless access and ubiquitous computing through seamless personal and terminal mobility. The most popular communication service for moving vehicles is currently provided by cellular networks at relatively low data rate. In the vision of 4G networks the demand for telematics applications in vehicles will rise steeply over the next few years with navigation services, emergency call, telephone, and becoming increasingly popular choices among motorists. Seamless security, mobility, QoS management are required for mobile users of-

---

* This research was supported by the MIC(Ministry of Information and Communication), Korea, under the Chung-Ang University HNRC(Home Network Research Center)-ITRC support program supervised by the IITA(Institute of Information Technology Assessment).

** The corresponding author.

ten equipped with several wireless network technologies, for example, wireless local area networks (WLANs), 3G cellular networks and wireless metropolitan area networks (WMANs).

In order to provide secure telematics applications over the heterogeneous networks, it is necessary to create a secure vertical handover protocol: a secure handover protocol for users that move between different types of networks[1]. Traditional operations for handover detection policies, decision metrics, and radio link transfer are not able to adapt to dynamic handover criteria or react to user inputs and changing network availabilities. Nor are they able to deliver context-aware services or ensure network interoperability.

The success of telematics applications in 4G systems may strongly depend on the ability to provide seamless security QoS. There has been a considerable amount of QoS research recently. However, the main part of this research has been in the context of individual architectural components, and much less progress has been made in addressing the issue of an overall QoS architecture for the mobile Internet[2]. The seamless communication environments require a variety of context such as user identity, current physical location, time of day, date or season, and whether the user is driving or walking.

However, the context information is difficult to manage, because the amount of context information can be enormous and location dependent. This context information can be either dynamic or static. The context information should be distributed in both networks and mobile terminals. Sometimes, wireless link may be the bottle neck for the context exchange. For these reasons, mobility management in heterogeneous wireless networks requires more adaptive and autonomous techniques.

When the handover occurs, the Mobile Node (MN) and the Access Router (AR) need to exchange keys and authenticate each other. This process is time-consuming and creates a significant amount of signaling. To minimize the need to signal over the wireless link, context transfer mechanism could be one solution[3][4]. In the absence of the context transfer, multiple message exchanges are required between these entities before the MN is authorized to access the network. This delay could be very large, especially if the AAA server resides far away from the new access networks[5][6].

In this paper, we propose an efficient context transfer mechanism between Mobile Managers, minimizing the signaling overhead after the handover event at layer 2. Our mechanism provides the appropriate and necessary context for seamless secure vertical handovers. We also designed the detailed context transfer procedure for secure telematics applications. We analyzed the handover performance of our context-aware secure roaming with context transfer in mobile networks by using a multi-class queuing network model.

The rest of this paper is organized as follows. Section 2 describes the fast handover with mobility prediction and context transfer in mobile networks. Section 3 suggests our context transfer framework for telematics applications. Section 4 describes performance analysis of our context-aware handover through a closed queuing network model. Section 5 concludes this paper.

2   Fast Handover with Context Transfer in Mobile Networks

In the 4G networks, the mobile users will be seamlessly served with tracking and navigation services, emergency call, telephone and multimedia services. However, the highly dynamic mobility of the vehicles brings about new research challenges because of the heterogeneities of access technologies, network architectures, protocols and various service demands of mobile users. The seamless secure mobility and QoS management should be considered to fulfill the promising future telematics applications.

For adaptive QoS management, the location information will play a vital role in defining context-awareness. Intuitively, it is clear that successful mobility prediction can lead to fully automated activation of handovers.The mobility prediction is possible by validating location history[7], by trajectory[8], by road topology[9], by the handover statistics[10] of other vehicles, by the profiles[17], by the direction to the destination of a vehicle, by the map of mobile networks (network coverage, handover region).

Primary motivation of our context transfer protocol with mobility prediction is to quickly re-establish context transfer candidate services without requiring the MN to explicitly perform all protocol flows for seamless security services.

If mobile users can get location information without margin of error and handover area (y) is fixed, an optimal point of time (t_f) to forward indication for setting the next context transfer zones is equal to average context transfer time (T_p) from the MN to new AR through a Location Manager. In this case,

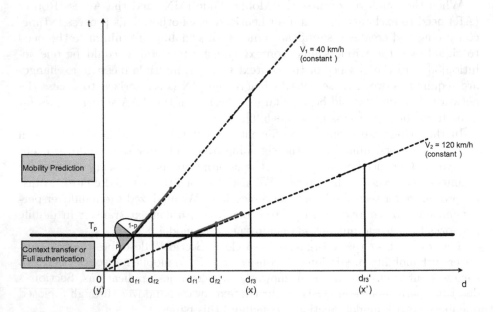

Fig. 1. Setting security context transfer zones in consideration of margin of error

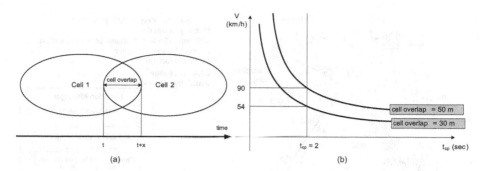

Fig. 2. Relationship among cell overlap, context transfer time and speed (a) cell overlap region and context transfer time (b) maximum velocity according to the context transfer time and cell overlap regions ($t_{cp} = 2$)

when a MN moves at a constant speed of 40 km/h as shown in Figure 1, setting for the next context transfer zones begins at $d_f \simeq vT_p$. For example, if T_p is 2 sec and MN's speed (v) is 40 km/h, the MN begins setting up the next context transfer zones $22.2m$ ahead from the handover area.

However, current GPS based location data has margin of error, the range is about $\pm 20m$. In this case, when the MN moves at 40 km/h and the MN sets up the next context transfer zones after position d_f, the fast context-aware handover is not possible as the probability of the location error (p). When the MN determines the optimal point of time to transmit signal for the next context transfer zones, these facts should be taken into account in the design considerations.

If a MN moves using context transfer protocol, whether context transfer is successful or not depends on the cell overlap ratio and MN's speed within cell overlap region, and the Round-Trip-Times (RTT) of the message exchange between the previous AR and the new AR during the handover[11][12]. If the cell overlap ratio is too high, the MN experiences radio interference and performance degradation of the wireless link. On the other hand, when its overlap ratio is too low, the MN may not get sufficient time to complete the handover using the context transfer. As shown in Figure 2(a), the layer 2 scan triggers the handover anticipation at time t. At time $t + x$, the MN loses the connection to Cell 1. So the context transfer must be terminated within time x. If the overlap region is $30m$ and the average context transfer handover time (t_{cp}) is about $2sec$, the MN may not perform the handover with context transfer when it moves above $v = 54[km/h]$ as shown in Figure 2(b).

3   A Mobility-Aware Security Context Management Framework for Seamless Vehicular Services

Aiming to make the creation of context-aware seamless vehicular services easier and more efficient, we designed the mobility-aware security management framework. Figure 3 shows our handover scheme for vehicular users in mobile networks.

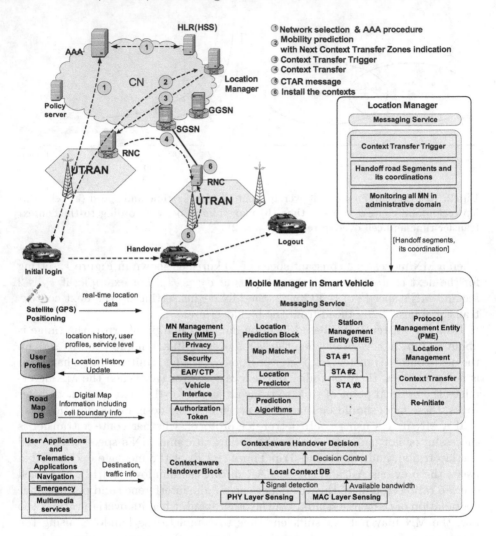

Fig. 3. The Mobility-aware Context Management Framework for Telematics

The MN performs full authentication for initial login in core network (CN) where stores registration data for users after network selection procedure. At the initial login, the mobile user may configure the user specific information such as destination, user applications and downloaded telematics services.

After the login process, AAA context including the cipher key is installed in current AR and the MN gets GPS-based real-time location information and receives handover road segments and its coordination periodically from Location Manager. The MN predicts next cell(s) through Mobile Manager inside the vehicle or within the mobile terminal, and transmits the next Context Transfer Zones Indication (CTZI) to Location Manager at the appropriate time as described in section 2[13]. Location Manager which received CTZI from MN sends a Context

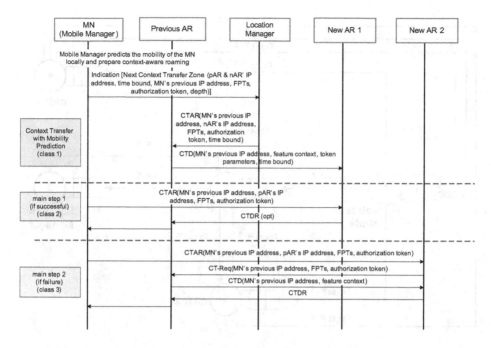

Fig. 4. Protocol design and job classes for the context-aware handover

Transfer Activate Request (CTAR) message as a context transfer triggering that causes the current AR to transfer AAA context. New AR installs AAA context and waits for the MN's CTAR message within time bound. If the MN transfers CTAR message to new AR with authorization token during handover, New AR sends success message to the MN if token verification is successful. This protocol flow is depicted in Figure 4.

Mobile Manager may be built inside a vehicle typically. It predicts next cell(s) using real-time location data and mobility prediction application, and determines the next context transfer zones at appropriate time. Location Manager plays a key role of context transfer trigger in the proposed architecture. It also monitors all MN's movements and maintains handover road segments and their coordination in its local DB. While a Location Manager interoperates all MNs in an administrative domain, it mediates AAA context transfer among ARs.

Figure 4 shows the protocol flow from the point of time transferring MN's CTZI to Location Manager. If the mobility prediction is correct, MN performs secure context-aware handover procedure. However, when it is failure, the MN can complete the handover using general context transfer in our scheme.

4   Performance Analysis

The performance of the proposed secure context-aware handover scheme with mobility prediction and secure context transfer is evaluated by the simulation

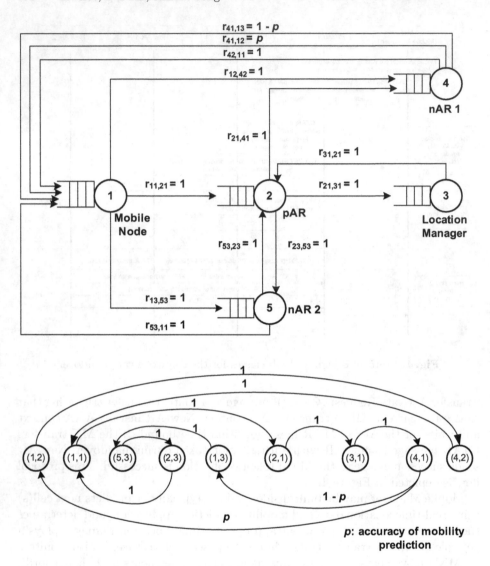

Fig. 5. Multiple Queuing Network Model and State Transition Diagram for the Proposed Secure Context-aware Handover Protocol

environment as shown in Figure 5. We assumed that each router guarantees compatibilities for the context transfer and the context transfer between two routers is possible only if the receiving router supports the same context transfer-candidate services as the sending router.

In the scenario of Figure 4, the context-aware handover procedure has three job classes; the context transfer zone setup step and two main steps according as it is success or failure. If the mobility prediction is successful, the MN performs the secure context-aware handover procedure. However, when the mobility prediction is wrong, it is possible to use general context transfer protocol.

Table 1. The Process for the Job Classes in the Queuing Network Model

Class	Context Transfer Zone Setup step (class 1)	Context-aware authentication step (class 2)	Context-transfer step (class 3)
Mobile node (node 1)	1 mobility prediction indication	1 CTAR	1 CTAR
pAR (node 2)	2 forwarding (indication, context)	0	1 token verification 1 forwarding (context)
Location Manager (node 3)	1 forwarding (CT Trigger)	0	0
nAR 1 (node 4)	1 install context	1 token verification	0
nAR 2 (node 5)	0	0	1 CT-Req forwarding 1 install context

We have modeled and tried to solve our architecture as a closed queuing system for the proposed protocol as in Figure 5 and Table 1. We analyzed the performance of our scheme by approximate Mean Value Analysis (MVA) as described in [14][15]. $r_{im,jn}$ means the probability that a class m job at node i moves to class n at node j after completing the services. p represents the probability of the mobility prediction accuracy.

We analyzed our scheme according to following steps of class switching closed queuing system.

Step1: Calculate the number of visits in original network by using (1)

$$e_{ir} = \sum_{j=1}^{K} \sum_{s=1}^{C} e_{js} r_{js,ir} \tag{1}$$

where K = total number of queues, C = total number of classes.
Step 2: Transform the queuing system to chain.
Step 3: Calculate the number of visits e_{iq}^* for each chain by using (2)

$$e_{iq}^* = \frac{\sum_{r\in\pi_q} e_{ir}}{\sum_{r\in\pi_q} e_{1r}} \tag{2}$$

where r= queue number in chain q, π_q = total queue number
Step 4: Calculate the scale factor α_{ir} and service times s_{iq} by using (3) with (1).

$$s_{iq} = \sum_{r\in\pi_q}^{s_{ir}\alpha_{ir}}, \quad \alpha_{ir} = \frac{e_{ir}}{\sum_{s\in\pi_q} e_{is}} \tag{3}$$

Step 5: Calculate the performance parameters for each chain using MVA.

Table 2. The Measured Parameters for the Queuing Network Model

Entity	Operation in scenario	Performance
	Setting Context Transfer Zones	
Mobile Node	Context Transfer Zone Indication with authorization token	30.34 ms
Location Manager	context transfer trigger with authorization token	27.4 ms
pAR	context transfer with token parameter	30 ms
nAR 1	Compute authorization token using parameter(RSA encrypt on 512 bit keys)	31.201 KB/s
nAR 1	install AAA context	200 ms
	Context-aware handover	
Mobile Node	CTAR with authorization token	30 ms
nAR 1	Token Verification (3DES Symmetric key decryption)	1.090 MB/sec
	Context transfer handover	
Mobile Node	CTAR with authorization token	30 ms
nAR 2	CT-Req with authorization token	27.4 ms
pAR	context transfer	30 ms
nAR 2	install AAA context	200 ms

Table 2 summarizes the basic parameter settings underlying the performance experiments. Location Manager and ARs used Solaris 8 machine with Pentium III 933 MHz, 512 MB RAM. MN used Pentium III 800 MHz, 256MB RAM, Windows XP operating system with Lucent Orinoco IEEE 802.11b wireless LAN

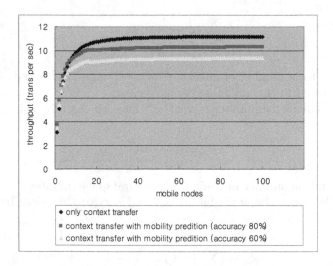

Fig. 6. Throughputs of Secure Context-aware Handover with Various Mobility Prediction Accuracies

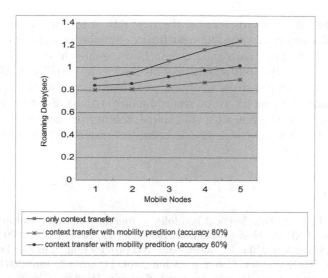

Fig. 7. Authentication Delays of Secure Context-aware Handover with Various Mobility Prediction Accuracies

card. The cryptographic library was Openssl 0.9.7c [16], and data size was 1KB in token verification and 10 KB in context transfer.

Figure 6 shows the average throughput for the security context transfer with the mobility prediction when the prediction accuracy p varies. The overall overhead increases because the proposed method completes setting up context in advance. However, when the accuracy of the mobility prediction is higher, it shows that differences between the general context transfer method and our context transfer method with mobility prediction is smaller.

Figure 7 describes the authentication latency for each case after the handover events at layer 2. Our method sets up AAA context in advance before the handover events and only performs token verification if the mobility prediction is successful. Therefore, the MN experiences low latency relatively when it uses our secure context-aware handover protocol with high mobility prediction accuracy.

5   Conclusions

With the proliferation of wireless networks and telematics applications there is a tremendous pressure to provide seamless and secure services. In this work we suggest a mobility-aware handover to optimize the handover management in the future mobile networks. We designed Mobile Manager and Location Manager to effectively provide the seamless mobile services with the context transfer and the mobility prediction for fast re-authentication. To reduce the signaling overhead after the handover events at layer 2, we propose an efficient context transfer mechanism between Mobile Manager and the Location Manager, providing the context is available in the right place at right time. Previous AR forwards the pre-established AAA information to the new AR of the predicted wireless cell where the MN might move in the near future. Simulations of our conext-aware handover performance gave a good insight into the current excitation. The analytical results show that our scheme can be used as an intelligent add-on model to existing networking systems to obtain performance and service improvement.

Additionally, the context-aware secure handover must also take into account the fast recovery methods against the failure mobility prediction of vehicles. The proposed mobility-aware mechanism is being integrated with the new interworking systems [18][19].

References

1. McNair, J., Fang Zhu: Vertical handoffs in fourth-generation multinetwork environments. IEEE Wireless Communications, vol. 11, issue 3, June 2004 pp:8-15.
2. Xio Gao, Gang Wu, Miki, T.: End-to-end QoS provisioning in mobile heterogeneous networks. IEEE Wireless Communications, vol. 11, issue 3, June 2004 pp.24-34.
3. J. Loughney: Context Transfer Protocol. Seamoby Working Group, Internet Engineering Task Force, draft-ietf-seamoby-ctp-11.txt
4. Christos Politis, Kar Ann Chew, Nadeem Akhtar, Michael Georgiades and Rahim Tafazolli: Hybrid Multilayer mobility management with AAA context transfer capabilities for All-IP networks. IEEE Wireless Communications, Aug 2004
5. J.Kempf: Problem Description: Reasons For Performing Context Transfers Between Nodes in an IP Access Network. RFC 3374, Internet Engineering Task Force.
6. Abhishek Roi, Sajal K. Das: Exploiting Information Theory for adaptive mobility and Resource Management in future cellular networks. IEEE Wireless Communications, Aug 2004.
7. G. Liu and G. Maguire Jr., A Class of Mobile Motion Prediction Algorithms for Wireless Mobile Computing and Communications, *ACM/Baltzer MONET*, vol. 1, no. 2, Oct. 1996, pp. 113-121.
8. T. Liu, P Bahl, and I. Chlamtac, Mobility Modeling, Location Tracking and Trajectory Prediction in Wireless ATM Networks, IEEE Selected Areas in Communications, vol. 16, no. 16, Aug. 1998, pp. 922-936.
9. Wee-Seng Soh and Hyong S. Kim, Dynamic Bandwidth Reservation in Cellular Networks Using Road Topology Based Mobility Predictions, *Proc. IEEE INFOCOM 2004*, Mar. 2004.
10. Kam-Yiu Lam et al., On Using Handoff Statistics and Velocity for Location Management in Cellular Wireless Networks. Computer Journal, January 2005, vol. 48, no. 1, pp.84-100.
11. Tim Ruckforth, Jan Linder: AAA Context Transfer for Fast Authenticated Interdomain Handover. Swisscom SA, Mar 2004
12. Juan M. Oyoqui, J. Antonio Garcia-Macias: Context transfer for seamless micromobility. IEEE ENC' 03, 2003
13. Hubaux, J.P. et. al: The security and privacy of smart vehicles. IEEE Security & Privacy Magazine, vol 02, issue 3, May-June 2004. pp.49-55.
14. Boudewijn R. Haverkort John: Performance of Computer Communication Systems: A Model-Based Approach' , Wiley & Sons, October 1999.
15. Gunter Bolch, Stefan Greiner, Kishor Trevedi: A Generalized Analysis technique for queueing networks with mixed priority strategy and class switching. Technical Report TR-I4-95-08, Oct. 1995.

16. OpenSSL, http://www.openssl.org
17. V. Bhargavan and M. Jayanth: Profile-based Next-cell Prediction in Indoor Wireless LAN. in Proc. IEEE SICON'97, Apr. 1997.
18. Minsoo Lee, Jintaek Kim, Sehyun Park, Ohyoung Song and Sungik Jun, A Location-Aware Secure Interworking Architecture Between 3GPP and WLAN Systems, Lecture Notes in Computer Science, vol. 3506, May 2005, pp. 394-406.
19. Minsoo Lee, Gwanyeon Kim, and Sehyun Park: Seamless and Secure Mobility Management with Location Aware Service (LAS) Broker for Future Mobile Interworking Networks, JOURNAL of COMMUNICATIONS and NETWORKS, vol. 7, no. 2, JUNE 2005, pp. 207-221.

An Improved Algorithm to Watermark
Numeric Relational Data[*]

Fei Guo[1], Jianmin Wang[1], Zhihao Zhang[1], Xiaojun Ye[1], and Deyi Li[1,2]

[1] School of Software, Tsinghua University, Beijing 100084, China
f-guo03@mails.tsinghua.edu.cn
jimwang@tsinghua.edu.cn
[2] China Constitute of Electronic System Engineering,
Beijing 100039, China

Abstract. This paper studies an improved algorithm to watermark numeric attributes in relational databases for copyright protection. It reviews related researches and presents an improved insertion algorithm, a detection algorithm and a recover algorithm. We introduce a varied-size grouping method in our insertion algorithm to insert a meaningful watermark. We also introduce a new mechanism to insert watermarks using the mark itself to decide marked positions. This insertion mechanism can be validated in our detection algorithm to decide whether a watermark exists or not. A badly destroyed marked relation or only a small part of it could still be detected successfully. Our recover algorithm introduces a competing mechanism to help recover the exact meaningful watermark after the detection result confirms the existence of the watermark. The experiments show it's robust to various attacks.

1 Introduction

Data has become merchandise in this information age. Since valuable data could be copied and distributed throughout networks easily, it faces the same problem of rights protection as digital multimedia products [6]. Digital watermarking technology is a good solution too. Watermarking technology aims to protect digital rights by introducing small errors into the original content without affecting the usability for intended purpose.

1.1 Related Work

Watermarking relational databases has become an important topic in both fields of database and information hiding. As far as we know, related work published recently includes:

- *M1*. Bit-resetting method [1]
- *M2*. Distribution preserving method [3]
- *M3*. Cloud watermarking method [7]
- *M4*. Classifying bit-resetting method [4]

---

[*] This research is supported by the National Basic Research Program under Grant No. 2002CB312000 and by National Natural Science Foundation of China under Project No. 60473077.

J. Song, T. Kwon, and M. Yung (Eds.): WISA 2005, LNCS 3786, pp. 138–149, 2006.

For M1 and M3, both use a secret key to answer the question "whether a watermark exists or not", in other words, the embedded information is only one bit. For M2 and M4, watermarks with real meanings could be inserted, e.g. specific names or pictures of the owner. But it has trouble to argue ownership if the watermark has been badly destroyed and only fragmentary parts of the watermark could be recovered. Because it can't tell whether the "unlike" watermark is a result of an attack or because no certain watermarks exist at all, i.e., it might be a similar relation belonging to others. Furthermore, both methods have to record extra classifying information [3], which has almost the same size of the watermark itself or even more. It means not a total blind system (R3 in Section 2).

1.2 Our Contributions

In this paper, we study an improved algorithm to watermark numeric attributes in relational databases. We use groups of tuples to represent each bit of the meaningful watermark. To maintain the same classifying result for successful recovering, we introduce a varied-size classifying method. A value of "remainder" of each tuple is calculated to identify which group it should belong to. Only the length of the watermark is needed while recovering the watermark, thus we achieve a total blind system.

We also introduce a new mechanism to insert a watermark that could be detected in despite of the exact content of the meaningful watermark. For example, if we have inserted a picture of the owner as a watermark, the detection result could prove the existence of this picture, i.e. prove the ownership, even when the picture can not be recovered totally for any reason. Thus we divide the traditional "extraction" step into two phases: the "detection phase" to judge whether a watermark exists and the "recover phase" to recover the entire watermark.

In the detection phase, we use the secret key to find enough proof to claim the ownership based on statistics. A badly destroyed watermark could still be detected successfully. So the owner is capable of proving ownership at least and could start further investigation reasonably. It's also an efficient way to distinguish unauthorized use of the owner's relations from legal use of similar ones that belong to others. That's because we only need to detect a relatively small part of large relations with millions of tuples or more.

In the recover phase, the entire watermark will be recovered. If the content of the watermark is some information to identify data users, it can be used to trace the source of an illegal copy among those users. The recover algorithm only need to be applied to the suspect relations selected in the detection phase. Since we know a watermark has been inserted with adequate confidence, we can use looser qualifications to decide each mark bit is actually "1" or "0". A competing mechanism simply decides either is more likely by detecting more matches. An original mark is expected to match 100%. Since an attack may reduce both matches that indicate "1" or "0", we can recover the mark bit successfully if the real marked bit still wins over the other. This makes our watermark more robust.

Our algorithm also has incremental updateability (R4 in Section 2). It's very useful when the algorithm is applied in a practical database which will be inserted or updated frequently. Because our insertion algorithm can be applied to each tuple independently, we can preserve the watermark simply by applying our insertion algorithm to those involved tuples without affecting other original ones.

1.3 Organization

The rest of the paper is organized as follows: Section 2 describes the requirements for a watermark and specific challenges for watermarking relational data. Section 3 provides our insertion algorithm, detection algorithm and recover algorithm. Section 4 gives the implementation of our watermarking algorithms on real data and a test for robustness and some analysis. Section 5 gives conclusions and directions for future work.

2   Challenges for Watermarking Relational Databases

The requirements for watermarking relational data are mostly in common with digital watermarks:

- *R1. Imperceptibility*: The embedding process should not introduce any perceptible artifacts into the host data [10].
- *R2. Robustness*: Immunity against data distortions introduced through standard data processing and attacks [10].
- *R3. Blind system*: Watermark detection should neither require the knowledge of the original database nor the watermark [1].
- *R4. Incremental Updatability*: The watermark values should only be recomputed for the added or modified tuples [1].

There are some special challenges for relational data too. It's hard to preserve the order of a meaningful watermark in a relational database. The error induced should be within the usability bounds of the original data. Since a relational database may often face operations including insertion, selection and update, the watermark should be query-preserving [9] for those benign updates and also be robust to corresponding malicious attacks below:

- *A1. Subset selection*: randomly take a subset of the tuples of a marked relation.
- *A2. Subset addition*: mix tuples from other sources to the original marked relation or a part of it, also called mix-and-match attack [2].
- *A3. Subset Alteration*: modify some tuples in a marked relation to erase the watermark. Either reset each attacked bit to the opposite or reset each attacked bit randomly.

3   Algorithms

Now we provide our insertion, detection and recover algorithm. Table 1 shows the notations used in this paper.

3.1 Conditions

Obviously, a watermark needs to modify the original data. Watermarking relational databases doesn't make any exception. Some small errors must be acceptable for rights protection in return. Since any changes to a number will finally induce some changes in one bit or some bits, bit is the smallest unit of distortion to numeric data. Our algorithm

Table 1. Notations

η	Number of tuples in the relation
1/γ	Target fraction of tuples marked
ε	Number of candidate bits to be modified
ω	Number of tuples actually marked
k	The secret key
α	Significance level for detecting a watermark
PK	The primary key in a relation

is able to be applied to one single attribute with only one candidate bit available to be changed. So we only ask the smallest available bandwidth [3] for watermarking.

A primary key is asked. We use the primary key for the identification of each tuple. It's really important for classifying and recovering. But sometimes most significant bits (MSBs) could substitute the primary key (Section 3.5) in a relation without a primary key.

In the relation to be marked, the probabilities of a randomly selected bit to be either 1 or 0 are both 1/2. This assumption will help form a binominal distribution with p = 1/2 used in Section 3.3 and is always satisfied in real databases.

3.2 Insertion Algorithm

First we transform a meaningful watermark in any form into a bit flow. The candidate attributes and candidate bits to be modified for watermarking are predefined based on practical data properties and intended using purposes. We only mark in one attribute in the following for simplicity.

It's well-accepted in academic research that if the watermarking algorithm is open, the security of the algorithm lies in one or several secret and cryptographically secure keys used in the embedding and extraction process [5] [10]. We use a one-way hash function result decided by the primary key PK and the secret key k to choose where to mark and what to mark. An attacker can't guess all of these for the secret key and other parameters are private to the owner. We can use $γ$ to choose the insertion granularity effectively. Since the hash result is expected to be uniform distributed, we can divide the relation into groups of varied but similar sizes.

We use the hash result of PK concatenated with k to calculate the remainder i for each tuple, then collect tuples with same values of i into the same group. Thus we have mark_length (the number of bits of the watermark) groups. The ith bit of the watermark will be inserted into the ith group. The ascending order of i ranging from 0 to mark_length-1 naturally preserves the order of the watermark. The mark value to be embedded will affect the inserting positions. Let's see how a bit of mark is actually inserted in each group. For example, we want to insert the bit of "1". We use the hash result of "1" concatenated with PK and k to select tuples to be marked (line 5 of insertion algorithm), the hash result of PK concatenated with k and "1" to select the bit positions to be modified out of candidate bits in the predefined attribute (line 6), then set the selected bit to "1" in each selected tuple. To insert "0" is alike simply by changing "1" into "0" during the process above. Within each tuple, we use different concatenation order to expect different hash results to decide which tuple to mark, what to mark and which bit position to mark. The purpose of doing this is to avoid any correlations which may potentially make the watermark easier to be found and attacked. We can see that one tuple is marked independently of the other tuples during the insertion process, so it achieves incremental updatability.

Finally we check the usability with respect to the intended use of the data. If not acceptable, we simply give up watermarking this tuple and roll back. This kind of tuples is very limited based on our conditions in Section 3.1.

Insertion algorithm: Only the owner of the relational data knows the secret key k. R is the relation to be marked.

```
1)   mark[] = bit(watermark)
2)   record mark_length
3)   for each tuple τ∈R do
4)      i = Hash(PK ∘ k) mod mark_length
5)      if(Hash(mark[i] ∘ PK ∘ k) mod γ == 0) then
6)         j = Hash(PK ∘ k ∘ mark[i]) mod ε
7)         set the jᵗʰ bit to mark[i]
8)      if(not within_usability(new_data))
9)         rollback
10)     else commit
```

3.3 Detection Algorithm

Let's see the mechanism to prove ownership in our detection phase. If a pattern with rather small probability is likely to happen following a certain predefined routines decided by a secret key, we can conclude that the owner of the watermarked relation is the one who has the secret key once the pattern is detected. We use α, also called the significance level, to represent this small probability. The parameter α is decided by the detector freely. The smaller α is, the more reliable each suspect of piracy is. The larger α is, the more suspects are expected.

For detecting a watermark, we identify a candidate set of tuples first. The candidate set is formed by two subsets. The conditions for each tuple to be selected in "subset_1" or "subset_0" are quite the same as the conditions to select marked tuples in the insertion algorithm except replacing mark[i] with "1" and "0" respectively. The two selections are independent. If a tuple is selected in both subsets, it's simply treated as two tuples, i.e., the tuple will count once in "subset_1" and once more in "subset_0". Total_count is used to count the size of this candidate set. Almost ω tuples will be selected in "subset_1" and another ω tuples in "subset_0". So total_count will be 2ω approximately. Tuples selected in the candidate set are for further detection. For each tuple in the candidate set, we follow the same condition to choose a bit position (jᵗʰ bit of candidate bits) as in the insertion algorithm except replacing mark[i] with "1" or "0" accordingly. We say a match happens when either the jᵗʰ bit of candidate bits is "1" in a tuple belongs to "subset_1" or "0" in a tuple belongs to "subset_0". We use the parameter match_count to count the number of matches.

Detection algorithm: k, γ and ε have the same values used in watermark insertion. α is the significance level for detecting a watermark. S is the relation to detect.

```
1)    total_count = match_count = 0
2)    for each tuple τ∈S do
3)       if(Hash(1 o PK o k) mod γ == 0) then   //subset_1
4)          total_count = total_count + 1
5)          j = Hash(PK o k o 1) mod ε
6)          if(the jth candidate bit == 1)
7)             match_count = match_count + 1
8)       if(Hash(0 o PK o k) mod γ == 0) then   //subset_0
9)          total_count = total_count + 1
10)         j = Hash(PK o k o 0) mod
11)         if(the jth candidate bit == 0)
12)            match_count = match_count + 1
13)   least_matches = threshold(total_count,  )
14)   if(match_count > least_matches) then
15)      suspect piracy
```

The selecting process above can be modeled as a Bernoulli trial, thus the number of matches is a random variable that meets a binominal distribution with parameters total_count and 1/2, see (1).

$$\text{MATCH\_COUNT} \sim b(\text{total\_count}, 1/2) \tag{1}$$

For a non-marked relation, the number of matches is expected to be around ω. But for a marked relation, all of the marked tuples have been selected into the candidate set and each will contribute a match if we use the same PK and k. That's because the detection algorithm ensures us to find all marked bit positions and the insertion algorithm ensures that all marked positions are matched ones. Among about 2ω tuples in the candidate set totally, the ω marked tuples will match and half of the rest may match randomly, so we expect to see roughly 1.5ω matches, which is distinctly bigger than ω matches if not marked.

Given total_count and α, we can calculate the least_matches, which is the smallest number of matches to satisfy (2) below based on statistics theory. (2) means the probability to detect least_matches for a certain total_count is smaller than α in any non-marked relations.

$$P\{ \text{MATCH\_COUNT} > \text{least\_matches} \mid \text{total\_count} \} < \alpha \tag{2}$$

Figure 1 shows the results of least_matches when α is 0.01. We can see that if total_count is big enough (more than 30), match_count of a relation marked by our insertion algorithm is larger than least_matches and meanwhile the match_count of a non-marked relation is smaller than least_matches. So we suspect piracy at the confidence level $(1-\alpha)$ once match_count is found larger than least_matches. Besides, our watermarking algorithm is likely to meet a higher significance level of α with the increase of total_count. Given a fixed significance level, it provides a potential ability to resist attacks when total_count is bigger. In reality, total_count is always big enough.

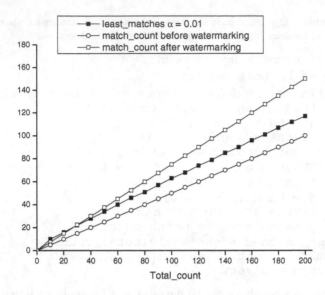

Fig. 1. The relationship between least_mathes and the expected match numbers before and after watermarking when $\alpha = 0.01$. It's effective to use least_matches to detect watermarked or not when total_count is big enough.

Situations are almost the same when $\alpha = 0.001$, except that the least_matches is just a little bigger than the least_matches when $\alpha = 0.01$ (see Table 2). A smaller significance level will be easily achieved by our insertion algorithm when total_count is bigger. We usually set $\alpha = 0.01$.

Table 2. Least_matches when $\alpha = 0.01$ and $\alpha = 0.001$

totalcount($\approx 2\omega$)	10	20	30	40	50	60	70	80	90	100	...
least_matches(α=0.01)	10	16	22	28	34	40	46	51	57	63	...
least_matches(α=0.001)	10	18	24	31	37	43	49	55	61	66	...

3.4 Recover Algorithm

We will apply our recover algorithm to a suspect relation after the detection result confirms a watermark does exist. To recover the entire watermark, the order of the mark is needed which we pay no attention to in the detection phase. In our detection algorithm, we can form exactly the same groups as in the insertion algorithm if *PK*, *k* and mark_length are all the same, so the original order of the watermark is preserved. What we have to decide next is what has been inserted into each group. There are only two choices, either "1" or "0". Suppose it's "1", we follow exactly the same routes while inserting "1" to find all marked positions, and then count matches similar as we do in the detection algorithm. We also count matches supposing "0" has been inserted.

Then we compare the two results of matches and judge either has more matches. Since we believe each group must have been inserted a bit with adequate confidence, we use very loose qualifications to recover a bit of the watermark in spite of match_count should equal total_count in an original marked group. The whole watermark's reliability has already been proved to meet the significance level α in the detection phase.

We can also use the significance level similar as in the detection algorithm in each group, so each bit of the watermark is reliable at a certain confidence level, but some bits may fail to recover. Thus we can make it an independent extraction algorithm that doesn't need the detection phase like M2 and M4.

Recover algorithm: k, γ, ε and mark_length have the same values used in watermark insertion, S is a marked relation selected by the detection algorithm.

```
1)   for each tuple τ∈S do
2)      i = Hash(PK o k) mod mark_length
3)      subset ← tuple
4)   for(i = 0; i < mark_length; i + +)
5)      recover(subset_i)
6)   return mark[]


7)      recover(subset_i)    //recover a bit from each subset
8)      total_count_0 = match_count_0 = 0
        total_count_1 = match_count_1 = 0
9)      for each tuple in subset_i do
10)        if(Hash(1 o PK o k) mod γ == 0) then
11)           total_count_1 = total_count_1 + 1
12)           j = Hash(PK o k o 1) mod ε
13)           if(the j^th candidate bit == 1)
14)              match_count_1 = match_count_1 + 1
15)        if(Hash(0 o PK o k) mod γ == 0) then
16)           total_count_0 = total_count_0 + 1
17)           j = Hash(PK o k o 0) mod ε
18)           if(the j^th candidate bit == 1)
19)              match_count_0 = match_count_0 + 1
20)        if(match_count_0 / total_count_0 >
              match_count_1 / total_count_1)
21)           mark[i]= 0
22)        else mark[i]= 1
23)        return mark[i]
```

3.5 Extensions

Our algorithm only marks a single attribute for simplicity. We can also extend our algorithm to more candidate attributes in two different ways. One is to simply propagate it to other attributes available to be marked, thus the same mark is inserted to different attributes repeatedly. The other is to add a similar step to select an attribute to be marked in each tuple right before line 6 in the insertion algorithm, thus we can disperse one watermark into several candidate attributes.

If a primary key doesn't exist in the relation, we expect to use most significant bits (MSBs) for they are hardly changed since a distortion in MSBs will reduce the usability badly. However, in situations when the MSBs have many duplicates, to use them as the primary key may induce many identical marks, which are easier to be found and attacked.

4 Implementation and Experiments

We ran experiments in Windows 2003 with 2.0 GHz CPU and 512MB RAM. Algorithms are written in Visual C++ 6.0 using ODBC connectivity to access Microsoft Office Access 2003. We applied our algorithms to Wisconsin Diagnostic Breast Cancer (WDBC) dataset, available at the UCI Machine Learning Repository (http://www.ics.uci.edu/~mlearn/databases/breast-cancer-wisconsin/wdbc.data). There are 569 tuples in this dataset, each with 32 attributes. The first attribute which is the ID number of each patient is used as the primary key. The sixth attribute which is the area of the cell nucleus is used as the candidate attribute to be marked. The area values are ranging from 143.5 to 2501. The candidate bit positions to be modified are the first 3 bits right before the radix point. The watermark to be inserted is an 8-bit flow "01100001" which is the ASCII code for letter "a". Target fraction of tuples marked is set to 1/8 and 1/5 respectively.

When $\gamma = 8$, before watermarking the detection result is 69 match_count out of 143 total_count which means the relation doesn't contain a watermark because least_matches is 86 out of 143 total_count when the significance level is 0.01. For inserting a watermark, we only need to modify 34 tuples by changing one bit in each tuple and total marked tuples are 67, i.e., $\omega = 67$. After watermarking, it's 100 match_count out of 143 total_count (larger than the least_matches) which confirms the existence of a watermark. The average value of the candidate attribute to be marked is 654.8891 before watermarking and 654.8821 after watermarking; the

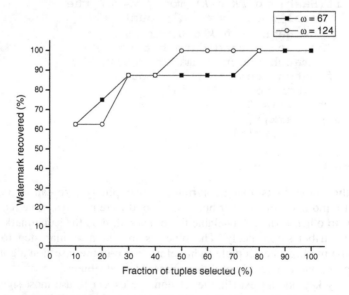

Fig. 2. Watermark recovered in subset selection attack (α=0.01)

variance is about 352 both before and after watermarking. So we can say the distortion resulted by watermarking is small enough to maintain the usability of the original relation. When $\gamma = 5$, it's almost the same except $\omega = 124$.

4.1 Subset Selection Attack

The attacker attempts to omit parts of the watermark by selecting a subset of tuples that are still valuable from the original marked relation. We can see in Figure 2 that when $\omega = 67$, it has no effect at all to our watermark by selecting 80% of the watermarked relation. Even when 10% of the data is selected, only 62.5% of the watermark can be successfully recovered, it still meets the significance level 0.01 to prove ownership, i.e. 14 match_count out of 15 total_count, which is larger than least_matches 13. In most cases, more bits of the watermark can be successfully recovered when $\omega = 124$ compared with $\omega = 67$. We can see that even a small part of the marked relation is enough for a successful detection. This is especially meaningful when detecting large size relations.

4.2 Subset Addition Attack (Mix-and-Match Attack)

In this part, the attacker randomly selects out part of the watermarked relation and mixes them with similar tuples probably without watermarks to form a new relation of approximately the same size of the original one. Figure 3 shows the result. When $\omega = 67$, 100% of the watermark can be recovered when we randomly select 70% tuples from the watermarked relation and mix them with 30% tuples from the original unmarked relation. But when we select 50% or less of the watermarked relation, we fail to detect the watermark based on statistics at the significance level of 0.01 which means no

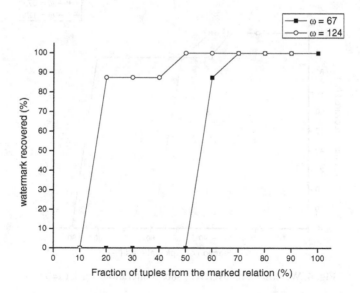

Fig. 3. Watermark recovered in subset addition attack (α=0.01)

watermark, although in fact we can still apply our recover algorithm and recover "00100001" which is only 1 bit error from the original watermark. The reason is the limited number of marked tuples, 67 is relatively small. The bigger ω is, the more robust the watermark is, i.e., more likely to detect and recover. When we enlarge ω to 124 by increasing the insertion rate from 1/8 to 1/5, we get better results. Even when we only select 20% of the marked relation and mix them with 80% of the original unmarked relation, we can detect the watermark successfully for the 139 match_count out of 237 total_count is larger than the least_matches 137, and meanwhile recover 87.5% of the watermark. However, a bigger ω means more distortion to the original data, so there is a tradeoff between usability and robustness. We can usually get a much bigger ω when watermarking a bigger relation without enlarging the insertion rate. For example ω is expected to be 1000 when we mark only 1% of a relation with 100,000 tuples.

4.3 Subset Alteration Attack

Since we can modify some tuples a little to insert a watermark, the attacker is also able to modify the watermarked relation a little to destroy our watermark. Suppose the attacker is lucky enough to discover accidentally what the three candidate bits are which could make the attack more effective. We randomly altered a portion of watermarked tuples by resetting one bit oppositely among the 3 candidate bits in each tuple, i.e., change the value 0 of a bit into 1 and value 1 into 0. When ω = 67, we can see in Figure 4 that we can successfully recover the entire watermark when we altered 40% or less tuples. But fail to detect the watermark when 60% or more tuples are attacked. It's a same problem we met in 4.2 and could be solved when ω is larger. When ω = 124, we can detect the watermark and recover 87.5% of it even when 80% of tuples have been changed.

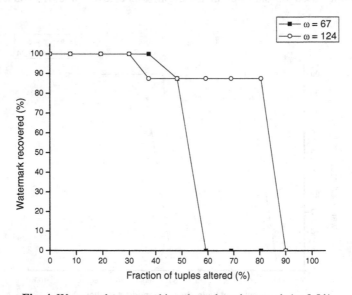

Fig. 4. Watermark recovered in subset alteration attack (α=0.01)

5 Summary

In this paper, we studied an improved watermarking algorithm for numeric relational data, which makes it possible to judge "whether a watermark has been inserted" first, and find "what has been inserted" afterwards. The detection phase can give the reliability of the watermark recovered in the next recover phase quantitatively. It's meaningful when serious attacks happen. A badly destroyed watermark still can be detected successfully to prove ownership. It also provides a simple way to judge whether a relation has been watermarked or not for large relations. We provided three algorithms for insertion, detection and recovering separately. The algorithm proved to have immunity to popular attacks to relational data and ask the smallest available bandwidth. It also achieved incremental updatability in relational databases and a total blind system. In the future, we'd like to add watermarking function using our algorithms to an open-sourced DBMS like PostgreSQL, making it a "Watermarking DBMS" system.

References

1. Rakesh Agrawal and Jerry Kiernan.: Watermarking relational databases. Proceedings of the 28th International Conference on Very Large Databases VLDB. (2002).
2. Rakesh Agrawal, Peter J. Haas, Jerry Kiernan.: Watermarking Relational Data: Framework, Algorithms and Analysis. VLDB Journal. (2003).
3. Radu Sion, Mikhail Atallah, Sunil Prabhakar.: Rights Protection for Relational Data. Proceedings of ACM SIGMOD. (2003) 98–109.
4. Min Huang, Jiaheng Cao, Zhiyong Peng, Ying Fang.: A New Watermark Mechanism for Relational Data. The Fourth International Conference on Computer and Information Technology (CIT'04). (2004) 946–950.
5. Bingxi Wang, Qi Chen, Fengsen Deng.: Technology of Digital Watermarking. Xidian University Press, Xi'an. (2003).
6. Voyatzis G, Pitas I.: The Use of Watermarks in The Protection of Digital Multimedia Products. Proceedings of IEEE. (1999)1197–1207.
7. Zhang Yong, Zhao Dong-ning, Li De-yi.: Digital Watermarking for Relational Databases. Computer Engineering and Application. (2003)193–195.
8. Ingemar J. Cox, Matt L. Miller and Jeffrey A. Bloom.: Watermarking Applications and Their Properties. International Conference on Information Technology'2000. (2000)6–10.
9. David Gross-Amblard.: Query-preserving Watermarking of Relational Databases and XML Documents, PODS 2003, San Diego CA. (2003)191–201.
10. F. Hartung and M. Kutter.: Multimedia Watermarking Techniques, Proceedings of the IEEE, Special Issue on Identification and Protection of Multimedia Information 87. (1999).

Video Fingerprinting System Using Wavelet and Error Correcting Code

Hyunho Kang[1], Brian Kurkoski[2], Youngran Park[3], Hyejoo Lee[4], Sanguk Shin[3], Kazuhiko Yamaguchi[2], and Kingo Kobayashi[2]

[1] Graduate School of Information Systems, University of Electro-Communications,
1-5-1, Chofugaoka, Chofu-shi, Tokyo 182-8585, Japan
[2] Dept. of Inf. and Communications Eng., University of Electro-Communications,
1-5-1, Chofugaoka, Chofu-shi, Tokyo 182-8585, Japan
{kang, kurkoski, yama, kingo}@ice.uec.ac.jp
[3] Department of Information Security, Pukyong National University,
599-1 Daeyeon-3Dong, Nam-Gu, Busan 608-737, Republic of Korea
Podosongei@hanmail.net, shinsu@pknu.ac.kr
[4] Department of Computer Science, Kyungsung University, 324-79 Daeyeon-3Dong,
Nam-Gu, Busan 608-736, Republic of Korea
iamhj@paran.com

Abstract. In this paper, we present a video fingerprinting system to identify the source of illegal copies. Content is distributed along a specified tree, with the seller as the root of the tree, the legitimate users as the leaves, and the internal nodes as content buyer or seller. Because there is a limited number of user areas available in each tree, we propose to build sub-trees, where each sub-tree has a distinctive logo. In this paper, we will use logos which are bit mapped images of the tree number. The extracted logo shows better performance visually using ECC. The fingerprinting step is achieved by the insertion of a unique information in the video wavelet coefficients by temporal wavelet transform. Our fingerprinting system is able to detect unique fingerprinting information in video content even if it has been distorted. In addition, our method does not need original video frame for extraction step.

1 Introduction

The rapid development of the Internet and digital technologies in the past years have increased the availability of multimedia content. One of the great advantages of digital data is that it can be reproduced without loss of quality. However, it can also be modified easily. The question then arises about copyright protection.

Watermarking can be used for copyright protection or for identification of the receiver. Copyright protection watermarks embed some information in the data to identify the copyright holder or content provider, while receiver-identifying watermarking, commonly referred to as fingerprinting, embeds information to identify the receiver of that copy of the content. Thus, if an unauthorized copy of the content is recovered, extracting the fingerprint will show who the initial receiver was [1]. Namely, fingerprinting is a method of embedding a unique, inconspicuous serial

J. Song, T. Kwon, and M. Yung (Eds.): WISA 2005, LNCS 3786, pp. 150–164, 2006.
© Springer-Verlag Berlin Heidelberg 2006

number (fingerprint) into every copy of digital data that would be legally sold. The buyer of a legal copy is discouraged from distributing illegal copies, which can be traced back to the last legitimate owner via the fingerprint. In this sense, fingerprinting is a passive form of security, meaning that it is effective after an attack has been applied, as opposed to active forms of security, such as encryption, which is effective from the point it is applied to when decryption takes place[2].

Although a large number of studies have been made on cryptographic point of view [3-10], little is known about practical application. The purpose of this paper is to address the problem of implementation of video fingerprinting. In this paper, we use a tree as in Ref. [11] to distribute video content and wavelet transform as in Ref. [12-15] to embed data in video content and make it robust to attack.

Content is distributed along a specified tree, with the seller as the root of the tree, the legitimate users as the leaves, and the internal nodes as content buyer or seller according to circumstances. Because there are a limited number of user areas available in each tree, we propose to build sub-trees, where each sub-tree has a distinctive logo(Fig. 1). In this paper, we will use logos which are bit mapped images of the tree number. The extracted logo shows better performance visually using ECC(Error Correcting Code). We have used the technique in Ref. [16] to insert a logo in a fast and straightforward manner.

Our fingerprinting system is able to detect unique fingerprinting information of video content even if it has been distorted by an attack. In addition, our method does not need the original video content for fingerprint extraction. Experimental results are presented to demonstrate the ability of our system to trace unauthorized distribution of video content, and to show its robustness to various collusion attack operations and MPEG2 compression.

This paper is outlined as follows. In Section 2 we propose an embedding and detecting process that is based on temporal wavelet transforms. Section 3 presents analysis and simulation results. Section 4 shows experimental results for important attacks that are often considered in video fingerprinting. Finally, Section 5 gives the conclusion.

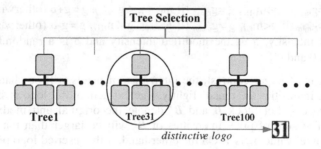

Fig. 1. Tree Selection – We can select the type of content distribution tree before sending to fingerprinting channel. If we are select the Tree 31, then 31 logo image will be embed into all video frames.

2 Proposed Method

Our system consists of four phases—embedding logo(Sect. 2.1), making content distribution tree(Sect. 2.2), embedding of fingerprinting information(Sect. 2.3), and extracting of fingerprinting information(Sect. 2.4).

2.1 Embedding Logo

The logo is a bit-mapped image of the tree number(we use 31 as an example). We have used the technique in Ref. [16] to insert a logo and briefly describe the method. With the logo embedding technique, a large number of logos, and thus a large number of end users can be supported with this proposed system.

After the binary logo image is permuted, the scrambled data sequence is then inserted into the frames in the spatial domain. Before insertion, the host video frame is first decomposed into blocks of size $k \times k$(we use 4×4 as an example). Let B be a selected block, the logo insertion method is described as follows:

Step 1. Sort the pixels in block B in an ascending order of pixel intensities.

Step 2. Compute the average intensity g_{mean}, maximal intensity g_{max}, and minimal intensity g_{min} of the block.

$$g_{mean} = \frac{1}{n^2} \sum_{i=0}^{n-1} \sum_{j=0}^{n-1} b_{ij} , \; g_{max} = \max(b_{ij}, 0 \le i,j < n), \text{ and } g_{min} = \min(b_{ij}, 0 \le i,j < n)$$

where b_{ij} represents the intensity of the (i,j)-th pixel in block B.

Step 3. Classify every pixel in B according to:

$b_{ij} \in Z_H$ if $b_{ij} > g_{mean}$, $b_{ij} \in Z_L$ if $b_{ij} \le g_{mean}$, where Z_H and Z_L represent high-intensity category and low-intensity category, respectively.

Step 4. Compute the mean values, m_H and m_L, of Z_H and Z_L.

Step 5. Define the contrast value of block B as $C_B = \max(C_{min}, \alpha(g_{max} - g_{min}))$, where α is a constant, and C_{min} is a constant value which determines the minimal value for pixel modification.

Step 6. Let $b_w \in \{0,1\}$ be the embedded value. Modify the pixel values in block B according to the following rules:

If $b_w = 1$: $g' = g_{max}$ (if $g > m_H$), $g' = g_{mean}$ (if $m_L \le g < g_{mean}$), $g' = g + \delta$ (otherwise)

If $b_w = 0$: $g' = g_{min}$ (if $g < m_L$), $g' = g_{mean}$ (if $g_{mean} \le g < m_H$), $g' = g - \delta$ (otherwise), where g is the original intensity, g' is the modified intensity and δ is a randomly generated value between 0 and C_B.

If the block is of larger contrast, the intensities of pixels will be changed greatly. Otherwise, the intensities are tuned slightly. The extraction of a logo is similar to the embedding process. Let block B and B' denote the original and modified blocks, respectively. The sum of pixel intensities of B' will be larger than that of B if the inserted logo pixel value b_w is 1. On the other hand, if the inserted logo pixel value b_w is 0, the sum of pixel intensities of B' will be smaller than that of B.

In our method, ECC is integrated into Ref. [16] watermarking system. The convolutional error correcting code is easy to implement and fast, so we use this encoder to correct errors in the logo, which were introduced by attacks and compression. The resulting system is evaluated under our fingerprinting system channel with collusion attacks and MPEG compression.

To sum up(Fig. 2), first, tree number is encoded by the convolutional code. The encoded information is then embedded into each video frame using Ref. [16] watermarking system. Next, the resulting frames are fingerprinted according to the

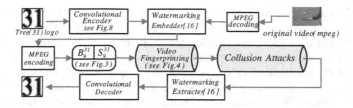

Fig. 2. The overall diagram

content distribution tree. In the experimental section, we show that the convolutional code enhances the robustness of Ref. [16] watermarking system.

2.2 Content Distribution Tree

Remark 1. Let γ ($\in Z+$) be the unique ID for seller S, let k be the key expansion obtained from the seed ID γ, where k is a vector of real number from -1 to 1 of dimension $h{\times}v$ (as a video frame size).

Remark 2. Let δ ($\in Z+$) be the unique ID for buyer B, let p be the pseudo-random number of the seed ID δ, where p is a vector of length $h{\times}v$ (as a video frame size).

The buyer(B) transmits pseudo-random number(p) to the seller(S). The seller then inserts fingerprinting information $I = p(k)$ into the appropriate user area of the wavelet transform.

When video content is distributed, fingerprinting information, I is inserted to each user's area of video content as described by the tree (31). Fig. 3 tells us each path has a unique fingerprint. There exists a unique path between the seller and buyer, and the unique fingerprint can be extracted to distinguish between the paths.

For example, when node-S_0 and node-B_1 engage in a transaction, fingerprinting information(I_1)—generated by the buyer and seller exchanging keys—is inserted into

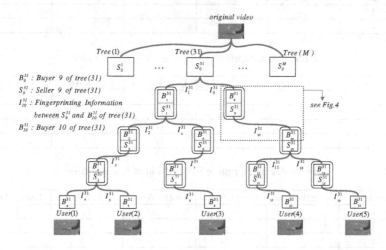

Fig. 3. Content Distribution Tree. Pay attention number of tree was omitted in the text. If we have M sub-trees(with M logos) and N users per sub-tree, then we can support M×N users.

user1, user2 and user3 area of the transmitted video. Because user1, user2 and user3 are the end users of the video in this transaction. The fingerprint is inserted into the frame by wavelet transform, and is described in Section 2.3. When node-S_1 and node-B_2 engage in a transaction, fingerprinting information(I_2) is inserted into user1 and user2 area of the transmitted video. When node-S_2 and node-B_3 engage in a transaction, fingerprinting information(I_3) is inserted into user1 and user2 area of the transmitted video. Finally, When node-S_3 and node-B_4 engage in a transaction, fingerprinting information(I_4) is inserted into user1 area of the end user1 video only.

Therefore, whenever a seller distributes content to a buyer, different fingerprinting information is inserted. Lastly, four different fingerprints are embedded into user1's video, placed in user1, user2 and user3 area. The fingerprinting information in user1's video are presented in Table 1. If it can detect the existence or nonexistence of fingerprinting information of illegal distributions, 70 correlation computations are required in Tree 31(See Fig. 3).

A 2-level temporal wavelet transform was performed on 32 frames of video, resulting in 4 types of frames(LL, LH, HL, HH where L and H stand for low and high

Table 1. Fingerprinting information of User1 video

Tree level	User1 Area	User2 Area	User3 Area	User4 Area	User5 Area
1	I_1	I_1	I_1		
2	I_2	I_2			
3	I_3	I_3			
4	I_4				

Table 2. Fingerprinting information of User2 video

Tree level	User1 Area	User2 Area	User3 Area	User4 Area	User5 Area
1	I_1	I_1	I_1		
2	I_2	I_2			
3	I_3	I_3			
4		I_5			

Table 3. Fingerprinting information of User3 video

Tree level	User1 Area	User2 Area	User3 Area	User4 Area	User5 Area
1	I_1	I_1	I_1		
2			I_6		
3			I_7		
4			I_8		

Table 4. Fingerprinting information of User4 video

Tree level	User1 Area	User2 Area	User3 Area	User4 Area	User5 Area
1				I_9	I_9
2				I_{10}	I_{10}
3				I_{11}	
4				I_{12}	

Table 5. Fingerprinting information of User5 video

Tree level	User1 Area	User2 Area	User3 Area	User4 Area	User5 Area
1				I_9	I_9
2				I_{10}	I_{10}
3					I_{13}
4					I_{14}

frequency respectively)[17]. In the experiment, user's areas were 5 sequential frequency frames among 8 frames of LH(low-high) areas. The LH means kind of intermediate frequency area(see Fig. 6). The LH region was selected because it was found to have the best detectability while not interfering with image quality.

Below is a series of five tables illustrating the information that is inserted in video content having five end users.

2.3 Embedding of Fingerprinting Information

Fig. 4 shows the embedding process using temporal wavelet transform, selection of the end user's area and insertion of fingerprinting information. The fingerprint is composed of information from seller and buyer. The seller information is a random sequence (-1~1) of h×v real numbers from a pseudo-random number generation, with a seed acting as an ID.

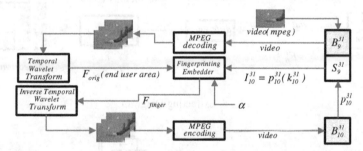

Fig. 4. Embedding Diagram (when node-S_9 and node-B_{10} engage in a transaction) (See Fig. 3)

Apply Eq. (1) to get fingerprinted video frames. In Fig. 3, when the content are distributed from the seller node-S to the buyer node-B, Eq. (1) is used once. The parameter α is the insertion strength; in this experiments, we choose α=0.5.

$$F_{finger} = F_{orig} + \alpha \cdot F_{orig} \cdot I_j \tag{1}$$

F_{finger} : *Fingerprinted video*
F_{orig} : *Original video, LH frames which are the user areas*
α : *Insertion strength*
I_j : *Fingerprinting Information (j: buyer's path index)*

2.4 Extracting of Fingerprinting Information

In the extraction step, we can extract the embedded information with Eq. (2). Note that the original video frames are not needed for extraction step.

$$I_{extract} = F_{finger} - F_{\beta}^{any}$$

(2)

$I_{extract}$: *Extracted fingerprinting information, an estimate of fingerprint*
F_{finger} : *Fingerprinted frames*
F_{β}^{any} : *any one frame among F_{β}*
F_{β} : *frames except $F_{finger[LL]},\ F_{finger[LH[User1, User2, User3, User4, User5]]}$* (see Fig. 6)

Linear correlation is calculated by Eq. (3). The linear correlation is known to be an optimal method of detecting signals in the presence of additive, white Gaussian noise[18]. In our experiments, collusion attacks and MPEG compression appear to have AWGN characteristics. Therefore, linear correlation is suitable.

$$Cor = \frac{1}{N} \sum I_{original} \cdot I_{extract}$$

(3)

N : video frame size ($h \times v$)

In Figure 6, we show each user's area and F_{β} frames that are used in extracting fingerprinting information.

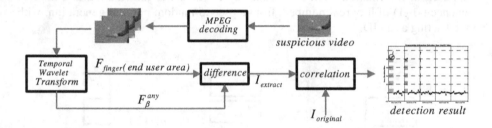

Fig. 5. Extracting Diagram

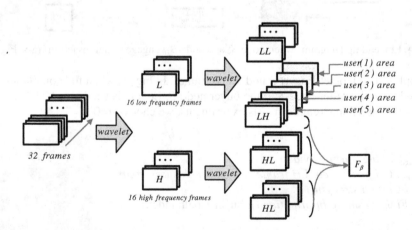

Fig. 6. User areas and F_{β} areas after temporal wavelet transform

3 Simulation Result

We have used the video sequence "table-tennis" with a frame size of 240×360 pixels and a total of 32 frames. We use convolutional codes to correct errors introduced by attacks and MPEG compression. A block diagram of the binary rate $R \cong 1/2$ nonsystematic feedforward convolutional encoder with memory order m=2 is shown in Figure 7(far right).

Fig. 7. (left) test video, (middle) bit mapped tree number logo(51*52), (right) convolutional encoder

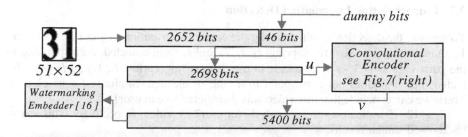

Fig. 8. Detailed model of tree number embedding part of Fig. 2. We used a convolutional error correcting code which is easy to implement and fast.

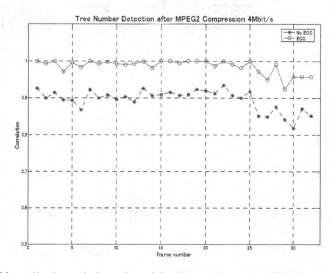

Fig. 9. Normalized correlation value of the detected logo after MPEG2 compression

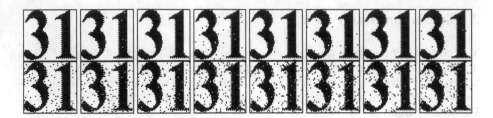

Fig. 10. Extracted tree number logo after MPEG2 compression, (above) with ECC, (below) without ECC. The 8 pairs show 8 of the 32 frames.

3.1 Tree Number

In this experiment, we show that the addition of ECC improves the correlation value of the system. As Figure 9 indicates, our system has good performance under MPEG2 compression.

3.2 Fingerprinting Information Detection

To analyze the detection result, consider the content distribution tree in Fig. 3. As Fig. 11 indicates, we see that fingerprints I_1, I_2, I_3 and I_4 were detected, corresponding to the path $1 \rightarrow 2 \rightarrow 3 \rightarrow 4$ for user1. In user2 area, fingerprints I_1, I_2 and I_3 were detected, but, this does not correspond to a path in the tree. Similarly for user3 area. Thus, we can conclude that this video was distributed to end user1.

Figs. 12~15 indicate a similar analysis for user2~5 video, respectively. This analysis showed similar results.

As Fig. 12 indicates, we see that fingerprints I_1, I_2, I_3 and I_5 were detected, corresponding to the path $1 \rightarrow 2 \rightarrow 3 \rightarrow 5$ for user2. In user1 area, fingerprints I_1, I_2 and I_3

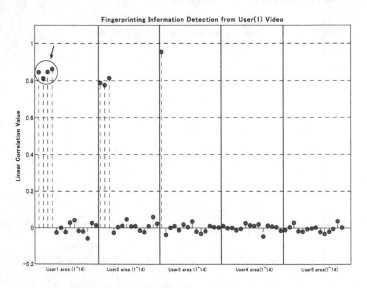

Fig. 11. Detection Result from User(1) Video

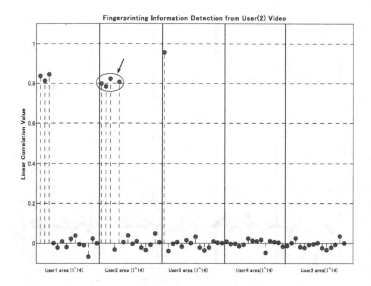

Fig. 12. Detection Result from User(2) Video

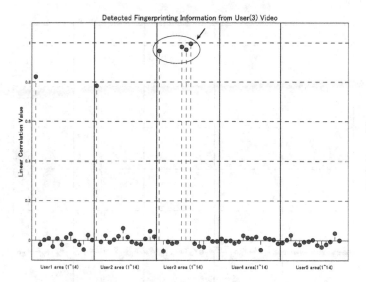

Fig. 13. Detection Result from User(3) Video

were detected, but, this does not correspond to a path in the tree. Similarly for user3 area. Thus, we can conclude that this video was distributed to end user2.

As Fig. 13 indicates, we see that fingerprints I_1, I_6, I_7 and I_8 were detected, corresponding to the path $1 \rightarrow 6 \rightarrow 7 \rightarrow 8$ for user3. In user1 area, fingerprints I_1 was detected, but, this does not correspond to a path in the tree. Similarly for user2 area. Thus, we can conclude that this video was distributed to end user3.

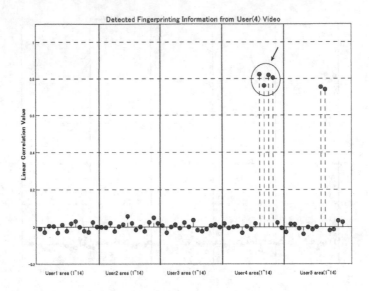

Fig. 14. Detection Result from User(4) Video

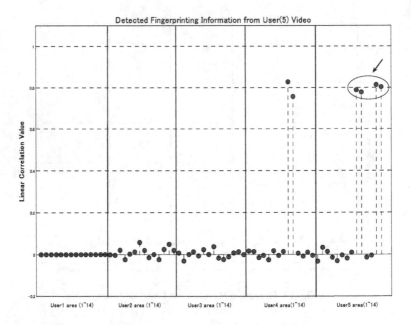

Fig. 15. Detection Result from User(5) Video

As Fig. 14 indicates, we see that fingerprints I_9, I_{10}, I_{11} and I_{12} were detected, corresponding to the path $9 \to 10 \to 11 \to 12$ for user4. In user5 area, fingerprints I_9 and I_{10} were detected, but, this does not correspond to a path in the tree. Thus, we can conclude that this video was distributed to end user4.

As Fig. 15 indicates, we see that fingerprints I_9, I_{10}, I_{13} and I_{14} were detected, corresponding to the path $9 \rightarrow 10 \rightarrow 13 \rightarrow 14$ for user5. In user4 area, fingerprints I_9 and I_{10} were detected, but, this does not correspond to a path in the tree. Thus, we can conclude that this video was distributed to end user5.

4 Attacks

A powerful attack against digital fingerprinting is the collusion attack. The results of our experiment show that the algorithm has some built-in resilience to collusion attacks, since the algorithm uses a long, uniformly distributed random number as fingerprinting information. In this attack, the following results were obtained.

4.1 Collusion Attack

(1) Averaging Collusion Attack
The averaging collusion attack was introduced by Cox, et al. [19]. The attacked video is created by averaging four fingerprinted videos such as user1, user2, user3 and user4's video. Fig. 16(left) shows the results of user1 colluding with user2, user3 and user4.

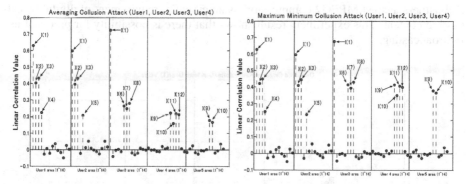

Fig. 16. Detection Result after Averaging Collusion(left), Maximum-Minimum Collusion Attack(right)

(2) Maximum-Minimum Collusion Attack
A more powerful collusion attack is the maximum-minimum collusion attack proposed by Stone [20]. The attacked video is created by taking the average of the maximum and minimum values across the components of the fingerprinted video. Fig. 16(right) shows the results of user1 colluding with user2, user3 and user4.

(3) Negative-Correlation Collusion Attack
This attack is drives the correlation coefficient to a negative value[20]. However, we can know that user1 colluded with user2, user3 and user4 in Fig. 17(left).

(4) Zero-Correlation Collusion Attack
This attack[21] is a modification method from Stone's collusion attack. This attack select a fingerprinted video from a number of available fingerprinted videos(user3

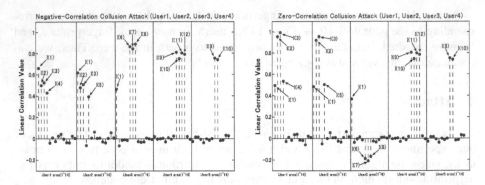

Fig. 17. Detection Result after Negative-Correlation Collusion(left), Zero-Correlation Collusion Attack(right)

(selected as an example). In user3 area, the correlation value has decreased perceptibly. However, we consider the case of user1 colluding with user2, user3 and user4 in Fig. 17(right).

4.2 Robustness to MPEG2 Compression

Robustness against MPEG2 compression, is an essential requirement of digital broadcasting content. This experiment result shows that there is possibility for practical use in broadcasting.

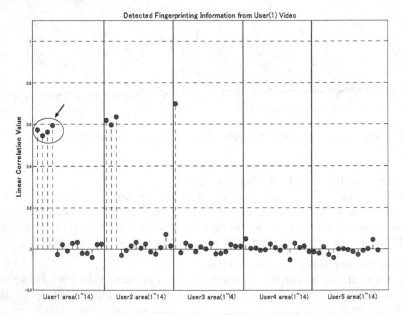

Fig. 18. Detection Result after MPEG2 Compression 4Mbit/s (User1)

In user1's video(Fig. 18), we can clearly see the points in distribution path $1 \rightarrow 2$ $\rightarrow 3 \rightarrow 4$ in user1 area, path $1 \rightarrow 2 \rightarrow 3$ in user2 area, and path 1 in user3 area in 4Mbits/s video quality. That is, the end buyer is identified as user1 because this agrees with the content distribution path of user1 in Figure 3.

5 Conclusion

We have presented here an approach for video fingerprinting implementation using a watermarking technique. The embedding method in video frames is robust to various attacks because of the use of the temporal wavelet transform. We showed robustness of tree number insertion using ECC, which permits support of a large number of users in the proposed fingerprinting scheme. Future research will include improvement applying with cryptographic algorithm technique.

References

1. Judge, P., Ammar, M.: Security Issues and Solutions in Multicast Content Distribution: A Survey. IEEE Network, Vol. 17. (2003) 30–36
2. Furht, B., Kirovski, B.: Multimedia Security Handbook. CRC Press (2005)
3. Pfitzmann, B., Schunter, M.: Asymmetric Fingerprinting. EUROCRYPTO'96, Lecture Notes in Computer Science, Vol. 1070, Springer-Verlag, (1996) 84-95
4. Pfitzmann, B., Waidner, M.: Anonymous Fingerprinting EUROCRYPTO'97, Lecture Notes in Computer Science, Vol. 1233, Springer-Verlag, (1997) 88-102
5. Domingo-Ferrer, J.: Anonymous Fingerprinting Based on Committed Oblivious Transfer. PKC'99, Lecture Notes in Computer Science, Vol. 1560, Springer-Verlag, (1999) 43-52
6. Wang, Y., Lu, S., Liu, Z.: A Simple Anonymous Fingerprinting Scheme Based on Blind Signature. Information and Communications Security, Lecture Notes in Computer Science, Vol. 2836, Springer-Verlag, (2003) 260-268
7. Kuribayashi, M., Tanaka, H.: A Watermarking Scheme Applicable for Fingerprinting Protocol. IWDW'03, Lecture Notes in Computer Science, Vol. 2939, Springer-Verlag, (2004) 532-543
8. Ahmet, M.E.: Multimedia Security in Group Communication: Recent Progress in Key Management, Authentication, and Watermarking. Multimedia Systems, Vol. 9, No. 3, Springer-Verlag, (2003) 239-248
9. Emmanuel, S., Kankanhalli, M.S.: A Digital Rights Management Scheme for Broadcast Video. Multimedia Systems, Vol. 8, No. 6, Springer-Verlag, (2003)
10. Kundur, D., Karthik, K.: Video Fingerprinting and Encryption Principles for Digital Rights Management. Proceedings of the IEEE, Vol. 92, No. 6, (2004) 918-932
11. Wang, Y., Doherty, J., Dyck, R.V.: A Watermarking Algorithm for Fingerprinting Intelligence Images. Conference on Information Sciences and Systems, (2001)
12. Swanson, M.D., Zhu, B., Tewfik, A.H.: Multiresolution Scene-based Video Watermarking using Perceptual Models. IEEE Journal on Selected Areas in Comm., Vol. 16, No. 4, (1998) 540-550
13. Sagetong, P., Zhou, W.: Dynamic Wavelet Feature-based Watermarking for Copyright Tracking in digital Movie Distribution Systems. IEEE International Conference of Imaging Processing. Sep. (2002)

14. Yang, J., Lee, M.H, Liu, Q., Tan, G.Z., Wan, X.: Robust 3D Wavelet Video Watermarking. IEEE International Conference on Consumer Electronics. June. (2003)
15. Li, Y., Gao, X., Ji, H.: A 3D Wavelet Based Spatial-Temporal Approach for Video Watermarking. International Conference on Computational Intelligence and Multimedia Applications. Sept. (2003)
16. Lee, C.H., Lee, Y.K.: An Adaptive Digital Image Watermarking Technique For Copyright Protection. IEEE Trans. On Consumer Electronics, Vol. 45, No. 4, (1999) 1005-1015
17. Burrus, C.S., Gopinath, R.A., Guo, H.: Introduction to Wavelets and Wavelet Transforms. Prentice Hall (1997)
18. Cox, I.J., Miller, M.L., Bloom, J.A.: Digital Watermarking. Morgan Kaufmann, Academic Press (2002)
19. Cox, I.J., Kilian, J., Leighton, T., Shanmoon, T.: Secure Spread Spectrum Watermarking for Multimedia. IEEE Trans. On Image Processing, Vol. 6, No. 12, (1997) 1673-1687
20. Stone, H.: Analysis of Attacks on Image Watermarks with Randomized Coefficients. NEC Technical Report. (1996)
21. Wahadaniah, V., Guan, Y.L., Chua, H.C.: A New Collusion Attack and Its Performance Evaluation. IWDW'02, Lecture Notes in Computer Science, Vol. 2613, Springer-Verlag, (2003) 64-80

Secure Asymmetric Watermark Detection
Without Secret of Modified Pixels

Mitsuo Okada and Hiroaki Kikuchi

Graduate School of Engineering, Tokai University,
1117 Kitakaname, Hiratsuka Kanagawa, Japan
{mitsuookada, kikn}@ep.u-tokai.ac.jp

Abstract. A new method of secure digital watermarking detection protocol is proposed in this paper. Our methodology applies to the protection of the digital contents against illegal use. Based upon the principle of our methodological induction, an improvement of protecting copyright contents has been achieved by means of allowing watermark verifier to detect the embedded information with no secret information exposed in extraction process. We set force our method by applying such a combination of patchwork watermark and public-key encryption protocol. Furukawa proposed a secure watermark detection scheme [4] in 2004 using Paillier encryption, but its drawback is the heavy overhead in processing time. We replace the cryptosystem with El Gamal encryption to improve performance, and clarify improvement in processing time and robustness against attacks based on experimental results.

1 Introduction

A new method of digital contents security for copyright protection is proposed in this paper by hybridizing digital watermarking and public-key encryption protocol. The protocol has successfully set off a downside of the watermark, a symmetric property in embedding and extracting process.

The demand for contents security is increasing due to severe crime augmentation accompanying rapid development of information technology. All kinds of contents have become available in digital form, which might accelerate making of perfect copies of digital video, image, and music data. Despite the fact that an enormous number of those contents might be pirated for an illegal use, the copyright law had been the only enforceable protection against the crime till the technical protection mechanism such as information hiding was introduced. One of the major information hiding technique is a digital watermarking that makes copyright notice or some secret data concealed in the contents. The hidden information is used for claiming copyright, detecting tamper, communicating confidentially, and so forth.

The ideal form of digital watermark is the one in which hidden information should not be removed by any contents manipulations, the embedded contents should not be spoiled by embedding information, and hiding should not perceptually appear. However, the most critical issue of watermarking is its symmetric

J. Song, T. Kwon, and M. Yung (Eds.): WISA 2005, LNCS 3786, pp. 165–178, 2006.

property, that is, exactly the same secret key is used for hiding, and extracting a message. In almost all of watermarking algorithms, the secret key of modified pixels is exposed in extraction process. The author embeds information into the image by using a secret key, and extracts the watermark by using the same key. Hence, the risk in extraction process is not avoidable.

Furukawa proposed a method [4] to overcome the problem by combining public-key algorithm and patchwork watermarking algorithm [1]. Patchwork watermark is one of the statistical digital watermarking schemers which may be one of the most robust methods because it embeds information in the skew of statistics. His scheme allows an authorized verifier to detect the hidden message without revealing the secret information, the indexes of modified pixels. In the scheme, unique public-key algorithm, Paillier encryption [6], is used to conceal the indexes. However, the drawback is the heavy overhead of Paillier encryption, which makes the scheme inefficient. To address the issue, we propose a new scheme based on [4], which employs El Gamal encryption instead of Paillier encryption.

In this paper, after reviewing patchwork watermark and Furukawa's scheme, we present a new watermarking scheme which allows secure detection of hidden message and improves the efficiency. We evaluate the performance of the proposed scheme with our testbed implementation, which qualifies the scheme for secure watermark detection.

2 Preliminarily

2.1 Statistical Watermarking

Patchwork watermarking, proposed in 1995 by Bender et al., embeds information in statistical value of contents. In this method, embedding key is a seed of pseudo-random process which chooses a large number of pairs of pixels. The first pixel value of a pair is made slightly brighter and the second one of the pair is made slightly darker. This process is iterated for all pairs. Conceptually, the contrast between pixels of the pairs encodes some secret information.

The extraction is carried out by finding the same pairs of the pixels chosen in the embedding process and analyzing the difference of their brightness values for all pairs. This provides invisible watermarks that have a higher degree of robustness against attacks and image manipulations.

We describe an embedding process of patchwork watermark. First, we choose a large number of pairs from original image I, and then obtain difference in each pair. Let a, b be the first and second pixel of a pair, and S_n be the sum of $(a_i - b_i)$ for n pairs, i.e.,

$$S_n = \sum_{i=1}^{n}(a_i - b_i).$$

Let $\bar{S}_n$ be an expected value defined by $\bar{S}_n = S_n/n$. Note that $\bar{S}_n$ approaches 0 as n increases,

$$\lim_{n \to \infty} \bar{S}_n \to 0. \tag{1}$$

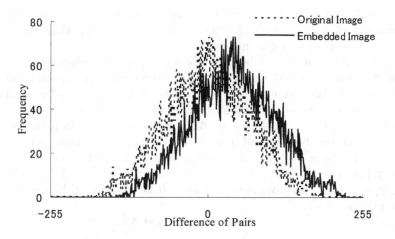

Fig. 1. Distributions of Differences $(a_i - b_i)$ and $(a'_i - b'_i)$

Fig. 1 labeled as "Original Image" shows a distribution of differences in Lena $(256 \times 256$ pixels, 256 gray scale level), with $n = 10000$. At this experiment, we obtained $\bar{S}_n = 0.0121$, that satisfies the condition (1).

We describe an embedding process, how to hide secret message ω into I. We choose a seed of pseudo-random sequence to assign two pixels (a_i, b_i) for n pairs. Next, to generate embedded image I', we modify the assigned pixels as, $a'_i = a_i + \delta$, and $b'_i = b_i - \delta$, for $i = 1, \ldots, n$, where δ is a constant that governs robustness of the watermark. Note that the expected value $\bar{S}_n{}'$, an average of sum of the difference of the embedded image I', approaches 2δ as

$$\bar{S}_n{}' = \frac{1}{n} \sum_{i=1}^{n} (a_i + \delta) - (b_i - \delta) = \frac{1}{n} \sum_{i=1}^{n} (a_i - b_i) + 2\delta = 2\delta. \tag{2}$$

With the parameter, $\delta = 20$, the distribution of $(a'_i - b'_i)$ is shifted 40 to right as illustrated in Fig. 1. Hence, as δ goes larger, accuracy of detection increases, and as δ goes smaller, the risk of a false detection increases.

To extract hidden message ω, we choose a'_i, and b'_i according to the random numbers, and then determine,

$$\omega = \begin{cases} 0 & \bar{S}_n{}' < \tau, \\ 1 & \bar{S}_n{}' \geq \tau, \end{cases}$$

where τ is a threshold. The optimal threshold is given as $\tau = \delta$ to equalize the false positive and false negative. In the sample image Lena, we have $\bar{S}_n{}' = 40.0158$, which satisfies the condition of $\bar{S}_n \geq \tau = \delta = 20$.

2.2 Cryptosystems

In this section, we review two cryptosystems, El Gamal encryption, and Paillier encryption.

El Gamal encryption, a public key encryption algorithm is used with patchwork watermark for our method. The security of the encryption relies on the difficulty of the discreet logarithm problem.

Let p be a secure prime number and g be a generator of multiplicative group of order q. A public key y is defined by $y = g^x \bmod p$ where $x \in Z_q$ is a private key. A ciphertext of plaintext m, $E(m) = (c, d)$, is defined by $c = g^m y^r \bmod p$ and $d = g^r$. The decrypted ciphertext is obtained by $g^m = D(c, d) = c/d^x \bmod p$.

Paillier encryption is proposed in [6]. For the key generation phase, generate large prime numbers p, and q, and pick $g \in Z_{N^2}$ such that $\gcd(L(g^\lambda \bmod N^2), N) = 1$, where $N = pq$, $\lambda = \mathrm{lcm}(p - 1, q - 1)$. Note that public key is (g, N) and private key is p, q. For the encryption phase, let m be a plaintext to be encrypted, r be a random number chosen from Z_N, and E be an encryption function defined by

$$e = E(m) = g^m r^N \bmod N^2. \tag{3}$$

For decryption phase, the decrypted ciphertext m' is obtained by

$$m' = D(e) = \frac{L(e^\lambda \bmod N^2)}{L(g^\lambda \bmod N^2)} \bmod n, \tag{4}$$

where $L(t) = (t - 1)/N$.

2.3   Asymmetric Watermark Detection [2]

Minematsu proposed an asymmetric watermark scheme [2] in 2000. His scheme applies patchwork watermark detection by using homomorphic public-key encryption in order to detect watermark with exposing no secret information used in embedding process. A verifier possesses an embedded image and sends the image to a key authority for watermark verification either watermark exists or not. As homomorphic encryption algorithm, he uses Okamoto-Uchiyama encryption [3].

2.4   Secure Watermark Detection [4]

Furukawa proposed a secure patchwork watermark detection protocol by adopting Paillier encryption. The primal idea of this method is nearly same as [2]. However, the detection scheme is modified so that verifier can prove validity of results without revealing secret information. With proof of validity, the scheme prevents dishonest users from cheating a key authority.

In this protocol, detection is carried out by verifying a ciphertext which contains the indexes of the modified pixels. Due to its unique property of Paillier encryption, the watermark information is encoded as exponents of the ciphertext. In other words, the indexes of the modified pixels are never exposed to a verifier even after the extraction process is carried out.

An author defines threshold τ, and number of pixels l, and chooses random subsets $A, B \subset \{1, \ldots, l\}$. He also generates a pair of public key and private key of Paillier encryption. He then generates ciphertext $(e_1, \ldots, e_l)$ such that

$$e_i = \begin{cases} E[1] & \text{if } i \in A, \\ E[-1] & \text{if } i \in B, \\ E[0] & \text{otherwise.} \end{cases}$$

In watermark extraction scheme, a verifier who posses the embedded image $I' = (z_1, \ldots, z_l)$ computes $e = \prod_{i=1}^{l} e_i^{z_i}$, and sends e to a trusted key authority. In watermark detection process, the verifier identifies watermark message ω as

$$\omega = \begin{cases} 0 & \text{if} \quad D(e) < \tau, \\ 1 & \text{if} \quad D(e) \geq \tau. \end{cases}$$

For more detail, refer [4].

3 Proposed Scheme

3.1 Outline

To resolve the problem of the symmetric property of watermark system, our approach employs a concept of public-key encryption protocol to conceal the indexes of the modified pixels against the verifier. In order to assure a trust between an author and verifier, extraction process requires cooperation of a third party, who holds a private key of El Gamal encryption.

A drawback of [4] is the heavy overhead of Paillier encryption, which is replaced by El Gamal encryption in our scheme. Since patchwork watermark only needs to determine the sum of differences to be close to either 0 or $2n\delta$, it is possible to examine all possible messages, i.e., g^0, or $g^{2n\delta}$. Note that we examine $2n\delta$ (not 2δ as shown in equation 2) in our scheme, because of cryptographical reason. Moreover, El Gamal encryption is a lighter process, and thus more efficient than Paillier encryption.

3.2 Model

In this section, we describe a model of our scheme using three entities, Alice, Bob, and Kevin, representing an author, a verifier, and a key authority.

Assume, Alice embeds information into the contents, Bob verifies the watermark, and Kevin generates a secret key sk and public key pk for El Gamal encryption. Not only does interposal of the third party enhance the reliability of verification, but also prevent the author from cheating a verifier, and vise versa. Note that Kevin needs not to be trustworthy. He does not know the embedding key, the indexes of modified pixels specified by Alice.

Let $I = (x_1, \ldots, x_l)$ be an original image, $I' = (z_1, \ldots, z_l)$ be an embedded image, and l be number of pixels in image I and I'. We illustrate our model in Fig. 2.

3.3 The Proposed Protocol

Kevin generates an El Gamal public key, $y = g^x \bmod p$, where secret key is x. Let EXT be conversion function in second step, and $IDENTIFY$ be a function to obtain ω at the final step, respectively.

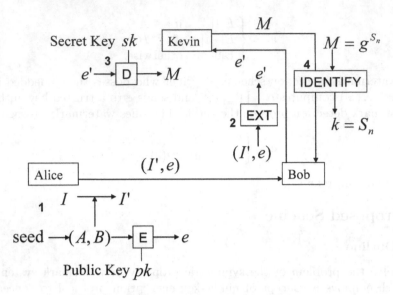

Fig. 2. The Model of the Proposed Scheme

STEP 1: (Embedding). Alice generates random numbers by giving a seed to pseudo-random generator, and obtains subsets A and B of set of indexes $\{1, 2, \ldots, l\}$ such that $A \cap B = \phi$ and $|A| = |B| = n$. She chooses δ and modifies pixels according to (A, B) in the image I to generate I' as

$$z_i = \begin{cases} x_i + \delta & \text{if } i \in A, \\ x_i - \delta & \text{if } i \in B, \\ x_i & \text{otherwise,} \end{cases}$$

for $i = 1, \ldots, l$. Alice computes e, a ciphertext of (A, B) as $e = (c_1, \ldots, c_l, d_1, \ldots, d_l)$, where $c_i = g^{m_i} y^{r_i}$, $d_i = g^{r_i} \bmod p$,

$$m_i = \begin{cases} 1 & \text{if } i \in A, \\ -1 & \text{if } i \in B, \\ 0 & \text{otherwise,} \end{cases}$$

and r_i is random number of Z_q, for $i = 1, \ldots, l$. Finally, Alice sends $I' = (z_1, \ldots, z_l)$ to Bob in conjunction with encrypted indexes $e = (c_1, \ldots, c_l, d_1, \ldots, d_l)$.

STEP 2: (Extracting). Bob computes ciphertext $e' = EXT(I', e) = (C, D)$ as follow;

$$C = c_1^{z_1} c_2^{z_2} \cdots c_l^{z_l} = \prod_{i=1}^{l} g^{m_i z_i} y^{r_i z_i} = g^{\sum^l m_i z_i} y^{\sum^l r_i z_i} = g^{S_n} y^R,$$

$$D = d_1^{z_1} d_2^{z_2} \cdots d_l^{z_l} = \prod_{i=1}^{l} g^{r_i z_i} = g^R,$$

where $R = \sum_{i=1}^{l} r_i z_i \bmod q$, and S_n is the sum of difference in patchwork watermark scheme, i.e., $S_n = 2n\delta$, and then sends e' to Kevin.

STEP 3: (Decrypting). Kevin uses his private key x to decrypt $e' = (C, D)$ as $M = D(e') = C/D^x = g^{S_n}$, and then sends back the decrypted text M to Bob.

STEP4: (Identifying). Bob identifies exponent k of M as $IDENTIFY(M)$ such that $M = g^k$ by testing for all possible $k = 1, 2, \ldots, q$. He obtains the hidden message ω by

$$\omega = \begin{cases} 0 & \text{if } k < \tau, \\ 1 & \text{if } k \geq \tau, \end{cases}$$

where τ is the threshold.

4 Evaluation

4.1 Security

Security of patchwork watermark relies on the following facts. First, the embedding key A and B, the indexes of the modified pixels are uniformly distributed over $\{1, \ldots, l\}$. The distribution of (A, B) is illustrated in Fig. 3(b), where white dots represent (A, B). Hence, it is almost impossible to attack to determine (A, B) in I' without the knowledge of the embedding key. Second, the property that the original image is not required in extraction process improves security against watermark removal due to a leakage of the original image. Third, since the brightness of some of the pixels has slightly changed, the difference is hardly perceptible. Fig. 3(a) illustrates an example of a single-bit information being embedded into Lena (256×256 pixels, 256 gray scale level) with the parameters of $n = 2053$, and $\delta = 3$. The SNR for Fig. 3(a) is 50.6[dB] which is considered to be acceptable. Therefore, we can conclude that it is hard to retrieve the hidden message from given image I' as well as ordinary patchwork algorithm.

We discuss security of El Gamal encryption and robustness against manipulation attacks. From given image I' and ciphertext e, Bob learns nothing about embedding key A and B, under the assumption of difficulty of discrete logarithm problem. From given ciphertext (C, D) sent from Bob, Kevin knows neither the image I' nor (A, B), which has been accumulated into the ciphertext.

4.2 Optimal Parameter

In this section, we discuss an optimal parameter δ in the sense that the least number of δ with an accuracy of 95% succeeds in detection.

Let σ' be standard deviation of n samples of $(a_i - b_i)$, and σ be standard deviation of the average value $\bar{S}_i$. Noting the well-known relation of variances, $\sigma = \sigma'/n$, we can predict true σ from the sampled σ'. Hence, variance of average S_n decreases as n increases. In other words, an accuracy of S_n increases along with the increment of n. In order to achieve 95% confidence for detection, under an assumption of normal distribution, the embedded image should be shifted by at least 2σ which is identical to δ.

(a) Embedded Image   (b) Distribution of A and B

Fig. 3. Embedded Image and Distribution of A and B

Table 1. Parameters for δ Determination

n	μ	σ'	σ	δ
4613	0.8847	67.4449	0.4769	2
2053	1.9206	67.9670	1.5000	3
1165	-0.4335	68.2865	2.0007	4
757	-1.3805	68.8136	2.5011	5
539	-2.0260	69.7601	3.0048	6

The parameters, average of S_n, μ, standard deviation σ, and optimal δ with respects to n are demonstrated on Table 1, and the optimal δ given n is obtained from Fig. 4. Note that the false positive of 5% with the following δ is not sufficient to practical use. In order to make an image more robust, δ could be increased taking consideration of subjective evaluation.

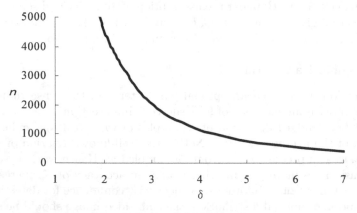

Fig. 4. Optimal δ Distribution

For the sake of determination of δ, we study the relation between number of modified pairs of pixels n and quality of image, which is estimated by means of Signal to Noise Ratio defined by,

$$\text{SNR} = 10 \cdot \log_{10} \frac{255^2}{\text{MSE}^2} = 10 \cdot \log_{10} \frac{255 \cdot 255}{1/l \sum (x_i - z_i)^2},$$

where MSE is the mean-square error between I and I'. Lena of 256×256 pixels is used for this test with the parameters in Table 1. Fig. 4 indicates no significant difference between $n = 2053$ and $n = 4613$. This implies the parameter of $n > 2053$, which is $\delta = 3$, is the optimal choice to prevent the embedded image from being spoiled, under the condition that SNR is almost the same.

4.3 Implementation System

In order to estimate a total performance of the proposed scheme, we implemented watermark embedding and extracting process for gray scale images in C. Cryptographic computations are implemented in Java. Environment specifications are described in Table 2.

Table 2. Implementation Environment

Detail	Specification
CPU	Xeon 2.3GHz
OS	Redhat 9.0, Linux 2.4.20
Memory	1GB
Encryption Algorithms	1024-bit El Gamal, 1024-bit Paillier
Programming Languages	J2SDK 1.4.2, gcc 3.3.3

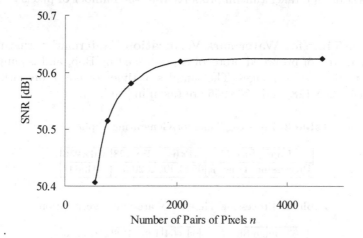

Fig. 5. The Relation between Number of Modified Pairs of Pixels n and SNR

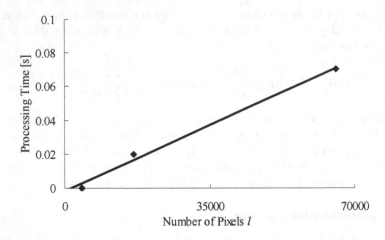

Fig. 6. Processing Time for Embedding

4.4   Performance

We use Lena as a host image I in three different sizes; l =64×64, 128×128, and 256×256 pixels to perform embedding, encrypting, decrypting, and extracting processes.

Watermark Embedding Scheme. Embedding processing time for image size l is illustrated in Fig. 6, which is performed in C. Time consumption increases proportionally to image size l.

Ciphertext e Generation in El Gamal Encryption. A single 1024-bit El Gamal encryption and decryption time are 0.104 [s], and 0.077 [s], respectively. The generation of e takes time in proportion to the number of pixels l, shown in Table 3.

Processing Time for Watermark Verification. Watermark verification process, second step of proposed protocol is preformed by Bob, and is supposed to be linear to the size of images. The samples of time consumption with respect to l, 64×64, 128×128, and 256×256 are taken in Table. 4.

Table 3. Prcessing Time for Generating Ciphertext e

Image Size l	64×64	128×128	256×256
Processing Time [s]	654.840	2620.57	10496.0

Table 4. Processing Time for Watermark Verification

Image Size l	64×64	128×128	256×256
Processing Time [s]	5.68	22.07	88.52

Table 5. Total Verification Processing Time

Image Size l	$64{\times}64$	$128{\times}128$	$256{\times}256$
Average Processing Time [s]	11.562	26.875	93.876
standard deviation	0.8277	0.8356	0.7750

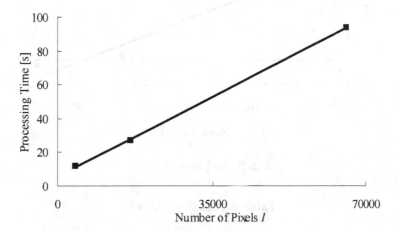

Fig. 7. Processing Time for Total Watermark Verification

Processing Time for Total Watermark Verification. Bob needs to send ciphertext to Kevin and requests him to perform decryption, which is independent from the size of image. Total time required for the whole verification process including identification process with respect to the number of n pairs is shown in Table 5, and Fig. 7.

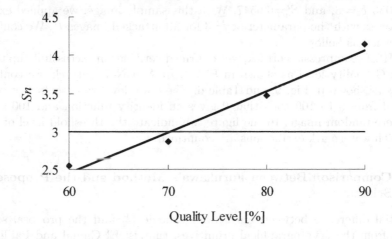

Fig. 8. JPEG Compression Attack

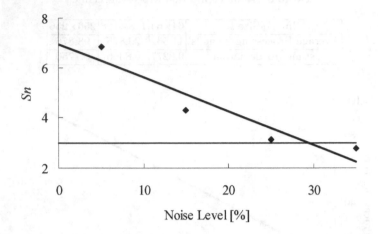

Fig. 9. Add Noise Attack

Table 6. Add Noise Attack

Noise Level[%]	5	15	25	35
S_n	6.8378	4.3064	3.1173	2.7681

4.5   Robustness Against Image Manipulation Attack Using StirMark

We evaluate the robustness of patchwork watermarking against attack of "Add Noise", and "JPEG Compression" using StirMark [7] [8]. We have used I' originated from Lena (256×256 pixels, 256 gray scale level), with the parameters of $n = 2053, \delta = 3$, and $\bar{S}'_n$=6.9547. With this sample image, we applied extracting process with the parameter of τ=3 for all attacked images I'. We confirmed verification as bellow.

In JPEG compression attack, we confirmed verification successfully up to 80% of JPEG quality level as shown in Fig. 8. In Add Noise attack, we confirmed success as shown in Fig. 9, and Table 6. The noise level represents that of normalized from 0 to 100 such that 0 gives an identity function and 100 gives a complete random image. In the figure, we indicate the threshold level of $\tau = 3$ by which watermark extractions are confirmed.

4.6   Comparison Between Furukawa's Method and the Proposed Scheme

Essential difference between Furukawa's scheme [4] and the proposal scheme comes from the cryptographical primitives, that is, El Gamal and Paillier encryption. Fig. 10 shows the processing time of extracting phase in El Gamal and

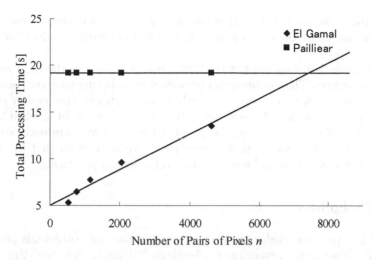

Fig. 10. Processing Time of Proposed Scheme and that of [4]

Table 7. Processing Time in Watermark Detecting

n	539	757	1165	2053	4613
Proposed Scheme (El Gamal)	5.279	6.475	7.697	9.590	13.47
[4] (Paillier)	19.11	19.11	19.11	19.11	19.11

Paillier encryptions. We examine processing time for all cases in Table 1. Each of cases is provided average of ten samples of different seeds. The values used to plot in Fig. 10 are shown in Table 7.

For El Gamal encryption, the processing time includes decrypting and identifying process, whereas Paillier encryption includes only decrypting process. The processing time of El Gamal increases proportionally to n, while processing time of Paillier encryption remains the same since we only needs to perform exact one decryption to extract watermark.

Supposing the processing time follows linearly to n as illustrated in Fig. 10, Paillier processing time would crosse over that of El Gamal at n^*=7403, where El Gamal processing time is estimated by $y = 0.0019x + 5.0446$. From the result, we can say that our scheme is superior to Furukawa's method [4] with the condition when n is less than or equal to n^*.

5   Conclusions

We have proposed secure watermark detection scheme by hybridizing patchwork watermarking and asymmetric cryptography protocol. The experiment proves that our method has fulfilled the primal requirement that reduces the risk in an extraction process by concealing the secret information. Experimental results also show that detection processes take time proportional by the size of images, with the size of 256×256, which takes approximately 93 second for detection.

From the above, we can conclude that our proposed scheme is more efficient than Furukawa's one [4] for the case when a number of the modified pairs of pixels is $n < 7403$.

We will proceed to enhance our method. First, we consider the improvement of success detection. This problem can be solved by applying an error correction coding technology. Second, we try to reduce the high communication cost of e sent from Alice to Bob. For example, the size of e for k bit embedding in an image ($l = 256 \times 256$) using the proposed method will approximately be $|e| = 1024 \times 2 \times l \times k$, which should be smaller. We are certain that by solving the issues, our scheme would be made more reliable and practical.

Acknowledgement

We would like to acknowledge the precious suggestion and corrections provided Dr.Yasuhiko Matsuda, an emeritus professor in Yokohama National University, and Mr.Junji Nakazato, a Ph.D. candidate in Tokai University, as well as anonymous referees for their support.

References

1. W. Bender, D. Gruhl, N. Morimoto "Technique for Data Hiding", SPIE, vol.2020, pp. 2420-2440, 1995.
2. K. Minematsu, "On a Secure Digital Watermark Detection Protocol Using Patchwork Watermarking", ISITA 2000, pp. 673-676, 2000.
3. T. Okamoto and S. Uchiyama, "A New Public-key Cryptosystem as Secure as Factoring", Enrocrypt' 98, LNCS 1403, pp. 308-318, 1998.
4. J. Furukawa, "Secure Detection of Watermarks", IEICE Trans., vol. E87-A, no. 1, pp. 212-220, 2004.
5. T. El Gamal, "A Public Key Cryptosystem and a Signature Scheme Based on Discrete Logarithms", IEEE Trans., IT-31, 4, pp. 649-472, 1985.
6. P. Paillier, "Public-key Cryptosystems based on Composite Degree Residuosity Classes", Proc. of Eurocrypt'99, LNCS 1525, pp. 223-238, 1999.
7. Fabin A. P. Petitcolas, Ross. J. Anderson, and Markus. G. Kuhn. "Attacks on Copyright Marking Systems", Information Hiding, Second International Workshop IH'98, LNCS 1525, pp. 219-239, 1998.
8. Fabin A. P. Petitcolas, "Watermarking Schemes Evaluation", IEEE Signal Processing, vol.17, no. 5, pp. 58-64, 2000.

Kimchi: A Binary Rewriting Defense Against Format String Attacks

Jin Ho You[1], Seong Chae Seo[1], Young Dae Kim[1], Jun Yong Choi[2],
Sang Jun Lee[3], and Byung Ki Kim[1]

[1] Department of Computer Science, Chonnam National University,
300 Yongbong-dong, Buk-gu, Gwangju 500-757, Korea
{jhyou, scseo, utan, bgkim}@chonnam.ac.kr
[2] School of Electrical Engineering and Computer Science,
Kyungpook National University, Daegu 702-701, Korea
jychoi@ee.knu.ac.kr
[3] Department of Internet Information Communication, Shingyeong University,
1485 Namyang-dong, Hwaseong-si, Gyeonggi-do 445-852, Korea
aura88@empal.com

Abstract. We propose a binary rewriting system called Kimchi that
modifies binary programs to protect them from format string attacks in
runtime. Kimchi replaces the machine code calling conventional `printf`
with code calling a safer version of `printf`, `safe_printf`, that prevents its
format string from accessing arguments exceeding the stack frame of the
parent function. With the proposed static analysis and binary rewriting
method, it can protect binary programs even if they do not use the frame
pointer register or link the `printf` code statically. In addition, it reduces
the performance overhead of the patched program by not modifying the
calls to `printf` with the format string argument located in the read-only
memory segment, which are not vulnerable to the format string attack.

1 Introduction

Since the format string vulnerability was discovered in 1999 [1], 30~40 format
string vulnerabilities have been reported every year [2], causing serious software
security problems [3, 4, 5].

Format string vulnerability occurs when a format string argument of the
`printf` family function in the standard C library includes a user input string
which can be manipulated by an attacker; the attacker can execute arbitrary
malicious code by modifying the program's critical memory using this vulnerability [5, 6, 7, 8, 9].

Previous research into the detection of and defense against format string vulnerability has led to the following recommended safe guards:

- Type qualifiers [10]: detect format string vulnerabilities in C source code by
  the *taint* propagation analysis using type qualifiers before compile time;
- FormatGuard [5]: automatically replaces `printf` function calls in the source
  program with calls to a protected version of `printf` at compile time;

J. Song, T. Kwon, and M. Yung (Eds.): WISA 2005, LNCS 3786, pp. 179–193, 2006.

- libformat [11], libsafe [12]: link to the protected version of `printf` instead of the original in the standard library at program loading time;
- TaintCheck [13]: traces a process's running code and checks whether an external user input is included in the format string at program execution time.

Though the static analysis of binary programs is more difficult compared with source programs, the security protection provided by rewriting the binary program is expedient when we can neither rebuild it from the patched source code nor obtain the patched binary program from the vendor in a timely manner [14]; or when a malicious developer might introduce security holes deliberately in the binary program.

There are limitations to the previous binary program level protection tools. Libformat and libsafe can treat only the binary programs to which the shared C library libc.so is dynamically linked, and libsafe requires the program to be compiled to use a frame pointer register. TaintCheck slows the traced program execution by a factor 1.5 to 40 [13]. Because it runs a binary program in *traced mode* similar to a debugger monitoring all running binary code while tracing the propagation paths of user input data—incurring a significant amount of overhead.

We propose a tool called Kimchi for the UNIX/IA32 platform that modifies binary programs—even if they are statically linked to the libc library, or they do not use a frame pointer register—to prevent format string attacks at runtime. Kimchi inserts an additional binary code block including a protected version of `printf` into the binary program, and replaces the original `printf` calls with those to the protected version. The protected `printf` inhibits the attack by preventing the format string from accessing memory beyond the stack frame address of its parent function. Kimchi can protect any binary program that does not use a frame pointer register by the static analysis of run-time change in stack frame depth. In addition, it reduces the performance overhead of the patched program by leaving unchanged the calls to `printf` with the format string argument located in the read-only memory segment, which are not vulnerable to the format string attack.

The rest of the paper is organized as follows. Section 2 explains format string vulnerability. Section 3 describes the runtime defense against format string attacks in the rewritten binary program. Section 4 describes the structure of Kimchi and its binary rewriting processes. Section 5 shows the results of performance overhead testing. Finally, Section 6 presents our conclusion and future work.

2   Format String Attack

The given example C program, myecho.c, in Fig. 1, which simply echoes its first command argument string, has a `printf` function call code at line 4 with a vulnerable format string.

As shown in Fig. 2, the second execution of myecho with the command argument "%x %x %x %9$d %12$d %62$s" displays a strange result; the printf call

```
1: int main(int argc, char *argv[])
2: {
3:     if (argc > 1)
4:         printf(argv[1]);
5:     printf("\n");
6: }
```

Fig. 1. A format string vulnerable C program, myecho.c

```
$ ./myecho 'hello, world'
hello, world

$ ./myecho '%x %x %x %9$d %12$d %62$s'
0 bfe04cb8 80483d6 10 2 USER=hacker
```

Fig. 2. An execution of myecho.c

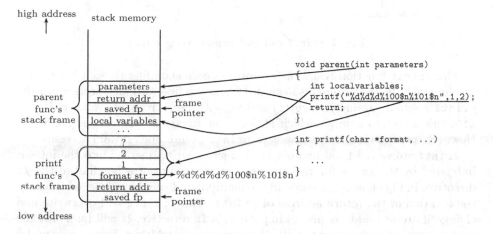

Fig. 3. A stack frame for a running function

at line 4 is `printf("%x %x %x %9$d %12$d %62$s")`, which does not have any arguments corresponding to the format control characters. The vulnerable code must be changed to `printf("%s", argv[1])`.

The previous `printf` implementations do not verify whether the accesses to the arguments corresponding to each % directive in a format string are valid [5]. It permits a malicious user to put % directives into the user provided input that will be inserted into the `printf` format string—leading the format string vulnerability.

Figure 3 shows the stack which a stack frame is being created while a function is running. A running function creates a stack frame where stores arguments, a return address, a saved frame pointer, and local variables. Figure 3 shows the stack memory layout while `printf("%d%d%d%100$n%101$n", 1, 2)` is running; the function arguments are pushed onto the stack.

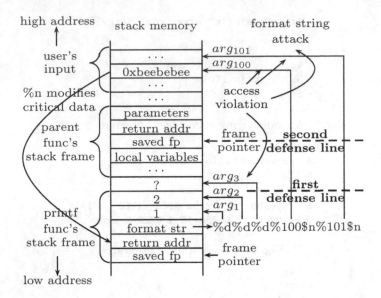

Fig. 4. `printf` call and format string attack

The `printf` function reads the arguments corresponding to each % directive on the stack. In the example shown in Fig. 4, the first two %ds' accesses to the `printf`'s actual parameters $arg_1(1)$ and $arg_2(2)$ respectively are valid; while the %100\$n's access to arg_{100}—which is not a parameter of `printf`—is not valid. However, previous implementations of `printf` permit such invalid accesses.

`Printf` stores the total number of characters written so far into the integer indicated by the `int *` (or variant) pointer argument corresponding to the %n directive. In Fig. 4, arg_{100} located in the manipulated user input has 0xbeebebee, the location of the return address of `printf`. Thus, `printf` will overwrite and change its return address processing the %100\$n directive. It will interrupt the control flow of the program; the attacker can execute arbitrary binary code under the program's privilege. There are many ways to change the program's control flow by overwriting critical memory [7, 8, 9].

There are two types of functions related to the format string in the standard C library: the printf family and the vprintf family. Functions in the printf family in the GNU glibc library are as follows:

```
#include <stdio.h>

int printf(const char *format, ...);
int fprintf(FILE *stream, const char *format, ...);
int sprintf(char *str, const char *format, ...);
int snprintf(char *str, size_t size, const char *format, ...);

#include <syslog.h>

void syslog(int priority, const char *format, ...);
```

```
#include <err.h>

void err(int eval, const char *fmt, ...);
void errx(int eval, const char *fmt, ...);
void warn(const char *fmt, ...);
void warnx(const char *fmt, ...);
```

Functions in the vprintf family in the GNU glibc library are as follows:

```
#include <stdarg.h>

int vprintf(const char *format, va_list ap);
int vfprintf(FILE *stream, const char *format, va_list ap);
int vsprintf(char *str, const char *format, va_list ap);
int vsnprintf(char *str, size_t size, const char *format, va_list ap);
void vsyslog(int priority, const char *format, va_list ap);


#include <stdarg.h>

void verr(int eval, const char *fmt, va_list args);
void verrx(int eval, const char *fmt, va_list args);

void vwarn(const char *fmt, va_list args);
void vwarnx(const char *fmt, va_list args);
```

In the case of the printf family, the argument values corresponding to the format directives are passed as parameters and stored in the stack frame. On the other hand, in the case of the vprintf family, a pointer to the argument vector is passed as a parameter; the arguments can be located at stack or other places. Thus, the protection method of the vprintf family is different from the printf family. Format string vulnerabilities can arise in both families; Kimchi, however, can treat only the printf family currently.

The following shows two real-world examples of the format string vulnerability reported in the current literature:

- proftpd-1.2.0pre6 FTP server's source code
  at line 782 in proftpd-1.2.0pre6/src/main.c in 1999 [1]
      snprintf(Argv[0], maxlen, statbuf);
  instead of
      snprintf(Argv[0], maxlen, "%s", statbuf);
- bind-4.9.5 DNS server's source code
  at line 353 in bind-4.9.5/named/ns_forw.c(CVE-2001-0013) [4]
      syslog(LOG_INFO, buf);
  instead of
      syslog(LOG_INFO, "%s", buf);

3 Runtime Defense Against Format String Attacks

Kimchi rewrites a binary program to redirect printf calls to safe_printf, the protected version of printf. We explain, in this section, how our safe_printf defends against format string attacks in runtime.

3.1   The Detection of Format String Attacks

The defense against format string attacks is to prevent % directives from accessing arguments which are not real parameters passed to printf. An adequate solution is to modify printf so that it counts arguments and checks the range of argument accesses of the directives for preventing access beyond "the first defense line" as shown in Fig. 4.

However, it is not easy to analyze the types of stack memory usage of the optimized or human written binary code [15, 16]. Kimchi protects from accessing arguments beyond "the second defense line"—i.e. the stack frame address of the parent function of printf: it is a weaker protection method than the one to protect from accessing arguments beyond "the first defense line".

The improved version of printf, safe_printf checks the existence of the argument access violation of % directives while parsing the format string. And then, if all of them are safe, safe_printf calls the real printf, otherwise, regards the access violation as a format string attack and runs the reaction procedure of attack detection.

The reaction procedure optionally logs the attack detection information through syslog, and terminates the process completely or returns −1 immediately without calling the real printf. The reaction of just terminating the process can be used as another DoS attack; ignoring the printf call might be much safer unless its side effect is not dangerous.

This same defense method is applied to other functions in the printf family: fprintf, sprintf, snprintf, syslog, warn, and err.

3.2   The Analysis of Change of Stack Frame Depth

Our detection method needs to know the stack frame address of the parent function of safe_printf; its relative distance to the stack frame address of safe_printf is passed to safe_printf.

If the parent function uses a frame pointer register storing the base address of the stack frame, safe_printf can get the parent's stack frame address easily by reading the frame pointer register; otherwise, the relative stack frame address of the parent function is previously calculated by static analysis of the change in the stack pointer at the parent function during Kimchi's binary rewriting stage.

We can determine whether a function uses the stack frame pointer register by checking the presence of prologue code which sets up the frame pointer register %ebp as shown in Fig. 5.

3.3   An Algorithm for Stack Frame Depth Calculation

The stack frame depth at any given node of the machine code control flow graph is defined as the sum of changes in the stack pointer at each node on the execution path reachable from function entry.

The static analysis calculates the stack frame depth at the node calling printf, and determines whether this value is constant over all reachable execution paths to the node. The problem is a kind of data flow analysis of *constant propagation* [17, 18]; we use Kildall's algorithm giving the *maximal fixed*

```
foo:
    pushl %ebp                      ;save old frame address
    movl %esp, %ebp                 ;setup frame pointer
    subl $256, %esp                 ;reserve local area
    ...
    movl -16(%ebp), %eax            ;frame relative address
    ...
    leave                           ;restore old frame address
    ret
```

Fig. 5. A typical function code pattern using frame pointer register

$point$(MFP) solution. For a given *basic block* B in the *control flow graph* CFG of a function, we define $IN(B)$ and $OUT(B)$ as the stack frame depth at the entry and the exit of B:

$$OUT(B) = \begin{cases} -addrsz & \text{if } B \text{ is a function epilogue} \\ IN(B) \oplus \delta_B & \text{otherwise,} \end{cases} \tag{1}$$

where δ_B is the increment amount of the stack pointer by B and the operation $x \oplus y$ is defined as following:

$$
\begin{array}{c|ccc}
\hspace{0.5em}^{\displaystyle y}\!\!\diagdown & \top & m & \bot \\
x & & & \\
\hline
\top & \top & m & \bot \\
n & n & n+m & \bot \\
\bot & \bot & \bot & \bot \\
\end{array}
$$

where m and n are integers;

$$IN(B) = \begin{cases} 0 & \text{if } B \text{ is entry} \\ \bigwedge\{OUT(B')|B' \text{ is a predecessor of } B\} & \text{otherwise,} \end{cases} \tag{2}$$

where $\wedge$ is the *meet* operator over *the flat lattice of integers*:

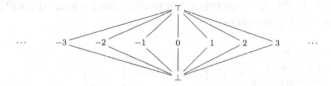

Algorithm 1 calculates the stack depth of each basic block. The value $\bot$ of $IN(B)$ means that the stack frame depth is not *constant* at B and $\top$ means *undefined*.

If the stack frame depth is not constant, Kimchi will not modify the **printf** call, and just reports a warning. In general, typical binary code automatically generated by a C compiler does not have such variable stack frame depth at the same location of the function call instruction: the compiler itself also analyzes changes in stack frame depth by static analysis.

Algorithm 1. The stack depth calculation algorithm

```
 1 forall B in CFG do
 2 │   IN(B) ← ⊤;
 3 │   OUT(B) ← ⊤;
 4 end
 5 IN(B_entry) ← 0;
 6 Q ← {B_entry};
 7 while Q is not empty do
 8 │   B ← delete from Q;
 9 │   calculate IN(B);
10 │   OUT(B)_old ← OUT(B);
11 │   calculate OUT(B);
12 │   if OUT(B) ≠ OUT(B)_old then
13 │   │   add successors of B to Q ;
14 │
15 end
```

4   Binary Rewriting Defense Against Format String Attacks

In this section, we describe how Kimchi modifies binary programs so that previous calls to `printf` are redirected to the safe version, `safe_printf`.

4.1   The Structure of Kimchi

Figure 6 describes the structure of Kimchi. The binary rewriting process consists of six subprocesses: (1) the disassembly of binary code, (2) the search of `printf` calls, (3) the construction of the control flow graph(CFG), (4) the analysis of stack frame depth, (5) the construction of patch information, and (6) the creation of the patched binary program.

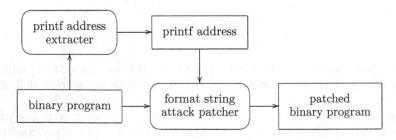

Fig. 6. The structure of Kimchi

```
.FMT: .string "%d%d%d%100$n"
foo:
  pushl %ebp
  movl  %esp, %ebp
  subl  $24, %esp
  subl  $4, %esp
  pushl $2
  pushl $1
  pushl $.FMT
  call  safe_printf_fp
  addl  $16, %esp
  leave
  ret
safe_printf_fp:         ;INSERTED CODES
  movl  %ebp, %eax
  subl  %esp, %eax
  subl  $8, %eax
  pushl %eax            ;call
  call  safe_printf     ;safe_printf(%eax,
  addl  $4, %esp        ;retaddr,format,...)
  ret
safe_printf:
  ...
```

```
.FMT: .string "%d%d%d%100$n"
foo:
  pushl %ebp      ; setup frame pointer
  movl  %esp, %ebp ;
  subl  $24, %esp ; alloc local var mem
  subl  $4, %esp  ; typical pattern of
  pushl $2        ; function call
  pushl $1        ;
  pushl $.FMT     ; printf(.L0,1,2);
  call  printf    ;
  addl  $16, %esp ;
  leave           ; reset frame pointer
  ret             ; return
```

(a) The original code   (b) The rewritten code

Fig. 7. An example of the modification of a call to printf in a function using the frame pointer register

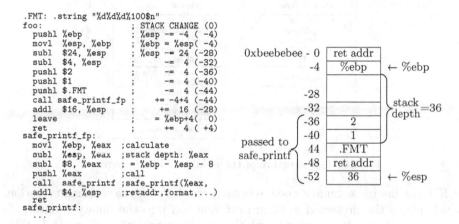

```
.FMT: .string "%d%d%d%100$n"
foo:                 ; STACK CHANGE (0)
  pushl %ebp         ; %esp -= -4 ( -4)
  movl  %esp, %ebp   ; %ebp = %esp( -4)
  subl  $24, %esp    ; %esp -= 24 (-28)
  subl  $4, %esp     ;     -= 4 (-32)
  pushl $2           ;     -= 4 (-36)
  pushl $1           ;     -= 4 (-40)
  pushl $.FMT        ;     -= 4 (-44)
  call  safe_printf_fp ;  += -4+4 (-44)
  addl  $16, %esp    ;     += 16 (-28)
  leave              ;   = %ebp+4( 0)
  ret                ;     += 4 ( +4)
safe_printf_fp:
  movl  %ebp, %eax   ;calculate
  subl  %esp, %eax   ;stack depth: %eax
  subl  $8, %eax     ; = %ebp - %esp - 8
  pushl %eax         ;call
  call  safe_printf  ;safe_printf(%eax,
  addl  $4, %esp     ;retaddr,format,...)
  ret
safe_printf:
  ...
```

Fig. 8. An example of the stack change and the arguments passed to safe_printf in a function using the frame pointer register

4.2 Rewriting the Binary Program

In the proposed binary rewriting method of Kimchi, `printf` calls in the function using the stack frame pointer are replaced with calls to `safe_printf_fp` as in the example shown in Fig. 7; otherwise, for functions not using the stack frame pointer, `printf` calls are replaced with calls to `safe_printf_n` as shown in Fig. 9, where n is the stack frame depth of the current function at the time it calls `printf`: this value is calculated by static analysis in Sect. 3.3.

Figure 8 shows how `safe_printf_fp` calculates the parent's stack frame depth, pushes it onto the stack, and calls `safe_printf`.

```
.FMT: .string "%d%d%d%100$n"
foo:                          ; STACK CHANGE (  0)
  subl  $12, %esp       ;          %esp = -12
  subl  $4, %esp        ;               = -16
  pushl $2              ;               = -20
  pushl $1              ; stack depth = -24
  pushl $.FMT
  call  printf
  addl  $16, %esp
  addl  $12, %esp
  ret
safe_printf_sp_24:      ; INSERTED CODES
  pushl $24             ; stack depth = 24
  call  safe_printf
  addl  $4, %esp
  ret
safe_printf:
  ...
```

```
.FMT: .string "%d%d%d%100$n"
foo:
  subl  $12, %esp
  subl  $4, %esp
  pushl $2
  pushl $1
  pushl $.FMT
  call  printf
  addl  $16, %esp
  addl  $12, %esp
  ret
```

(a) The original binary code   (b) The rewritten binary code

Fig. 9. An example of the modification of a call to printf in a function not using the frame pointer register

Before translation

```
ELF header
other sections...
.text section
  ...call printf ...
  ...call printf ...
  ...call printf ...
  ...call printf ...
other sections...
```

After translation

```
ELF header
other sections...
.text section
  ...call safe_printf_fp ...
  ...call safe_printf_32 ...
  ...call safe_printf_64 ...
  ...call safe_printf_fp ...
.text.safe_format section
  safe_printf_fp: ...
  safe_printf_32: ...
  safe_printf_64: ...
  safe_printf: ...
other sections...
```

Fig. 10. The structure of the modified binary program

Kimchi inserts a binary code section named .text.safe_format section, which places the protected safe_printf function into the binary program; it replaces previous calls to printf with those to safe_printf as shown in Fig. 10. The inserted code section is placed at an address location lower than and not used by any other code sections so as not to corrupt the program's behaviour.

The inserted binary code forms like the one shown in Fig. 11.

4.3   Read-Only Format String

A printf call with a constant format string argument located in a read-only memory region is not affected by format string attacks, because the attack is possible only when it is modifiable. Therefore, printf calls with constant format strings do not need to be protected. Kimchi skips the printf calling codes of pattern: a pushl $*address* instruction directly followed by call printf, where the *address* is located in a read-only memory region, as shown in Fig. 12. We can get read-only memory regions from the section attribute information of the binary program file as shown in Fig. 12 [19].

```
        .section .text.safe_format:
    safe_printf_48:
        pushl $48
        jmp call_safe_printf
    safe_printf_56:
        pushl $56
        jmp call_safe_printf
                .
                .
                .
    safe_printf_fp:
        movl %ebp, %eax
        subl %esp, %eax
        push %eax
        jmp call_safe_printf

    call_safe_printf:
        call safe_printf
        addl $4, %esp
        ret

    void safe_printf(int parameter_range,
            int return_address, char *format, ...)
    {
        if (format is safe) {
            va_start(ap, format);
            vprintf(format, ap);
            va_end(ap);
        } else {
            /* format string attack detected! */
            ...
        }
    }
```

Fig. 11. The .text.safe_format section

printf call with Constant Format String

```
    C code: printf("%d %d %d %100$n", 1, 2);
Binary code:
  804836e: 83 ec 04       sub  $0x4,%esp
  8048371: 6a 02          push $0x2
  8048373: 6a 01          push $0x1
  8048375: 68 88 84 04 08 push $0x8048488
  804837a: e8 31 ff ff ff call 80482b0 <printf>
  804837f: 83 c4 10       add  $0x10,%esp
```

ELF binary file information

```
foo:      file format elf32-i386

Sections:
Idx Name       Size      VMA       LMA       File off  Algn
 13 .rodata    00000015  08048480  08048480  00000480  2**2
                CONTENTS, ALLOC, LOAD, READONLY, DATA

Contents of section .rodata:
 8048480: 03000000 01000200 25642564 25642531  ........%d%d%d%1
 8048490: 3030246e 00                           00$n.
```

Fig. 12. An example of a read-only constant string

4.4   Searching the printf Function Address

In case libc library is dynamically linked to the binary program, Kimchi can get the address of the printf function from the dynamic relocation symbol table in the binary program, as shown in Fig. 13. Otherwise, Kimchi searches the address of the printf code block in the binary program by a pattern matching method using the signature of binary codes as shown in Fig. 14 [20, 21].

```
foo:     file format elf32-i386

DYNAMIC RELOCATION RECORDS
OFFSET    TYPE                VALUE
08049578  R_386_GLOB_DAT      __gmon_start__
08049588  R_386_JUMP_SLOT     __libc_start_main
0804958c  R_386_JUMP_SLOT     printf
```

Fig. 13. An example of a dynamic relocation records in ELF binary program

```
the signature of _IO_vfprintf in glibc-2.3.4/Linux i686

5589e557 565381ec bc050000 c78558fb ffff0000 0000e8XX XXXXXX8b 108b4d08
89953cfb ffff8b51 5c85d2c7 8538fbff ff000000 00750cc7 415cffff ffffbaff
ffffff42 b9ffffff ff752e8b 75088b16
```

Fig. 14. An example of a signature of binary codes

5   Performance Testing

We implemented a draft version of proposed tool Kimchi, which is still under development. Figure 15 shows a screen shot where this tool modifies the binary program myecho in Fig. 1. Figure 16 shows a screen shot where the re-written version of myecho detects the format string attack and reports the related information. Later the detection report is sent to syslog server.

We measured the marginal overhead of Kimchi protection on printf calls with a tight loop as shown in Fig. 17. The experiment was done under single-user mode in Linux/x86 with kernel-2.6.8, Intel Pentium III 1GHz CPU and 256MB RAM.

Experiments shows that safe_sprintf and safe_fprintf have more 29.5 % marginal overhead than the original sprintf and fprintf. Safe_printf has more 2.2 % marginal overhead than printf due to its heavy cost of terminal I/O operation.

The overall performance overhead of the patched program is much smaller, because general programs have just a few printf calls with non-constant format strings.

Kimchi increases the size of binary programs by the sum of the following: memories for safe_printf code, safe_printf_fp code, and safe_printf_n codes of the number of printf call patches in the function not using the frame pointer register.

Fig. 15. The Kimchi's binary rewriting of the program *myecho* in Fig. 1

Fig. 16. The detection of the format string attack to the program *myecho* in Fig. 1

```
int main(void) {
    int i;
    for (i = 0; i < 10000000; i++)
        printf("%s %s %s\n", "a", "b", "c");
    printf("%d\n", i);
    exit(0);
}
```

Fig. 17. Micro-benchmark

6 Conclusion

We proposed a mechanism that protects binary programs that are vulnerable to format string attacks by static binary translation. The proposed Kimchi can treat the binary programs not using the frame pointer register as well as the ones statically linked to the standard C library; moreover, the patched program has a very small amount of performance overhead. We are currently researching static analysis of the range of `printf` call's parameters and a format string defense mechanism applicable to the `vprintf` family functions.

References

1. Twillman, T.: Exploit for proftpd 1.2.0pre6 (1999) http://www.securityfocus.com/archive/1/28143/1999-09-16/1999-09-22/0.
2. The MITRE Corporation: CVE dictionary (2004) http://www.cve.mitre.org/cgi-bin/cvekey.cgi?keyword=format+string.
3. tf8: Wu-Ftpd remote format string stack overwrite vulnerability (2000) http://www.securityfocus.com/bid/1387.
4. Osborne, A., McDonald, J.: Isc bind 4 nslookupcomplain() format string vulnerability (2001) http://www.securityfocus.com/bid/2309.
5. Cowan, C., Barringer, M., Beattie, S., Kroah-Hartman, G., Frantzen, M., Lokier, J.: FormatGuard: Automatic protection from printf format string vulnerabilities. In: the 10th USENIX Security Symposium, Washington, DC (2001) 191–200
6. scut / team teso: Exploiting format string vulnerabilities (2001) http://www.cs.ucsb.edu/~jzhou/security/formats-teso.html.
7. Lhee, K.S., Chapin, S.J.: Buffer overflow and format string overflow vulnerabilities. Software: Practice and Experience **33** (2003) 423–460
8. gera, riq: Advances in format string exploitation (2002) http://www.phrack.org/phrack/59/p59-0x07.txt.
9. Core Security Team: Vulnerabilities in your code - format strings (2002) http://www.core-sec.com/examples/core_format_strings.pdf.
10. Shankar, U., Talwar, K., Foster, J.S., Wagner, D.: Detecting format string vulnerabilities with type qualifiers. In: Procdings of the 10th USENIX Security Symposium (SECURITY-01), Berkeley, CA, USENIX Association (2001) 201–220
11. Robbins, T.J.: libformat (2000) http://www.securityfocus.com/data/tools/libformat-1.0pre5.tar.gz.
12. Singh, N., Tsai, T.: Libsafe 2.0: Detection of format string vulnerability exploits (2001) http://www.research.avayalabs.com/project/libsafe/doc/whitepaper-20.ps.
13. Newsome, J., Song, D.: Dynamic taint analysis for automatic detection, analysis, and signature gerneration of exploits on commodity software. In: Proceedings of the 12th Annual Network and Distributed System Security Symposium (NDSS '05). (2005)
14. Prasad, M., Chiueh, T.C.: A binary rewriting defense against stack-based buffer overflow attacks. In: the Proceedings of USENIX 2003 Annual Technical Conference (2003) 211–224
15. Landi, W.: Undecidability of static analysis. ACM Letters on Programming Languages and Systems **1** (1992) 323–337
16. Ramalingam, G.: The undecidability of aliasing. ACM Transactions on Programming Languages and Systems **16** (1994) 1467–1471
17. Kildall, G.A.: A unified approach to global program optimization. In ACM Symposium on Principles of Programming Languages (1973) 194–206
18. Aho, A.V., Sethi, R., Ullman, J.D.: Compilers Principles, Techniques, and Tools. Addison Wesley (1986)

19. Tool Interface Standard (TIS) Committee: Executable and linking format (ELF) specification, version 1.2 (1995)
20. Emmerik, M.V.: Signatures for library functions in executable files. Technical Report FIT-TR-1994-02 (1994)
21. Guilfanov, I., DataRescue: Fast library identification and recognition technology (1997)

Software Protection Through Dynamic Code Mutation

Matias Madou[1], Bertrand Anckaert[1], Patrick Moseley[2], Saumya Debray[2], Bjorn De Sutter[1], and Koen De Bosschere[1]

[1] Department of Electronics and Information Systems,
Ghent University, B-9000 Ghent, Belgium
{mmadou, banckaer, brdsutte, kdb}@elis.UGent.be
[2] Department of Computer Science,
University of Arizona, Tucson, AZ 85721, U.S.A.
{moseley, debray}@cs.arizona.edu

Abstract. Reverse engineering of executable programs, by disassembling them and then using program analyses to recover high level semantic information, plays an important role in attacks against software systems, and can facilitate software piracy. This paper introduces a novel technique to complicate reverse engineering. The idea is to change the program code repeatedly as it executes, thereby thwarting correct disassembly. The technique can be made as secure as the least secure component of opaque variables and pseudorandom number generators.

1 Introduction

To reverse-engineer software systems, i.e., to obtain an (at least partial) understanding of the higher-level structure of an executable program, a malicious attacker can subvert many recent advantages in program analysis technology and software engineering tools. Thus, the existing technology can help an attacker to discover software vulnerabilities, to make unauthorized modifications such as bypassing password protection or identifying and deleting copyright notices or watermarks within the program, or to steal intellectual property.

One way to address this problem is to maintain the software in encrypted form and decrypt it is as needed during execution, using software decryption [1], or specialized hardware [18]. Such approaches have the disadvantages of high performance overhead or loss of flexibility, because software can no longer be run on stock hardware.

To avoid these disadvantages, this paper instead focuses on an alternative approach using code obfuscation techniques to enhance software security. The goal is to deter attackers by making the cost of reverse engineering programs prohibitively high.

The seminal paper on decompilation and reverse engineering [4] considers two major difficulties in the process of reverse engineering programs. The first problem is that data and code are indistinguishable, as code on a Von Neumann

J. Song, T. Kwon, and M. Yung (Eds.): WISA 2005, LNCS 3786, pp. 194–206, 2006.
© Springer-Verlag Berlin Heidelberg 2006

computer is nothing more than a specific type of (binary) data. The second problem relates to self-modifying code, which does not follow the convention of static code that there is a one-to-one mapping between instructions and memory addresses.

In this paper, we propose a novel technique to automatically aggravate and/or introduce these problems in existing programs. The basic idea is to mutate a program as it executes, so that a region of memory is occupied by many different code sequences during the course of execution. We show how this technique undermines assumptions made by existing analyses for reverse engineering. Furthermore, we claim that our technique can be made as secure as the least secure component of opaque variables [5] and pseudorandom number generators [24].

The goal of this research is to deter "ordinary attackers" by making it substantially more difficult to reverse engineer the obfuscated code; it is consistent with the prior work on code obfuscation, which aims primarily to raise the bar against reverse engineering high enough so as to deter all but the most determined of attackers.

The remainder of this paper is structured as follows: Section 2 discusses related work. Our technique is introduced in Section 3. The security of this technique is the topic of Section 4. An evaluation of the impact on the size and execution time of the program is discussed in Section 5. Finally, conclusions are drawn in Section 6.

2   Related Work

The only other paper we are aware of that proposes dynamic code modifications for obfuscation purposes is that of Kanzaki *et al.* [16], which describes a straightforward scheme for dynamically modifying executable code. The central idea is to scramble a selected number of instructions in the program at obfuscation time, and to restore the scrambled instructions into the original instructions at run time. This restoration process is done through modifier instructions that are put along every possible execution path leading to the scrambled instructions. Once the restored instructions are executed, they are scrambled again. It is however not clear how the modifier instructions pose problems for a static analysis targeted at restoring the original program.

There is a considerable body of work on code obfuscation that focuses on making it harder for an attacker to decompile a program and extract high level semantic information from it [6, 7, 21, 25]. Typically, these authors rely on the use of computationally difficult static analysis problems, e.g., involving complex Boolean expressions, pointers, or indirect control flow, to make it harder to understand the statically disassembled program. Our work is complementary to these proposals: we aim to make a program harder to disassemble correctly to begin with, let alone recover high level information. If a program has already been obfuscated using any of these higher level obfuscation techniques, our techniques add an additional layer of protection that makes it even harder to decipher the actual structure of the program.

Researchers have looked into run-time code generation and modification, including high-level languages and APIs for specifying dynamic code generation [3, 12, 13] and its application to run-time code specialization and optimization [2, 17, 20]. Because that work focuses primarily on improving or extending a program's performance or functionality, rather than hindering reverse engineering, the developed transformations and techniques are considerably different from those described in this paper.

A run-time code generation techniques that to some extent resembles the technique proposed in this paper was proposed by Debray and Evans [11] for applying profile-guided code compression. To reduce the memory footprint of applications, infrequently executed code is stored in compressed format, and decompressed when it needs to be executed. At any point, only a small fraction of the infrequently executed code is in decompressed form. Because of the large decompression overhead however, the frequently executed code is always available in decompressed, i.e., the original, form. Hence this compression technique does not hide the frequently executed portions of a program, which are generally also likely to contain the code one might wish to protect.

3   Dynamic Software Mutation

This section discusses the introduction of dynamic software mutation into a program. We consider two types of mutation: one-pass mutation, where a procedure is generated once just before its first execution, and cluster-based mutations, where the same region of memory is shared by a cluster of "similar" procedures, and where we will reconstruct procedures (and thus overwrite other procedures) as required during the execution. We first discuss our novel approach to run-time code editing (Sec. 3.1). This will enable us to treat the one-pass mutations (Sec. 3.2). Next, we look at how "similar" procedures are selected (Sec. 3.3) and clustered (Sec. 3.4). Finally, we propose a protection method for the edit scripts against attacks (Sec. 3.5) and discuss our technique's applicability (Sec. 3.6).

3.1   The Run-Time Edit Process

Our approach is built on top of two basic components: an editing engine and edit scripts. When some procedure, say f, is to be generated at run-time, it is statically replaced by a template: a copy of the procedure in which some instructions have been replaced by random, nonsensical, or deliberately misleading instructions. All references to the procedure are replaced by references to a stub that will invoke the editing engine, passing it the location of the edit script and the entry point of the procedure. Based upon the information in the edit script, the editing engine will reconstruct the required procedure and jump to its entry point.

Edit Script. The edit script must contain all the necessary information to convert the instructions in the template to the instructions of the original procedure.

This information includes the location of the template and a specification of the bytes that need to be changed and to what value. The format we used to encode this information is the following:

```
editscript = address <editblock>1 <editblock>2 ...<editblock>l $
editblock  = m <edit>1 <edit>2 ...<edit>m
edit       = offset n byte1 byte2 ...byten
```

An edit script starts with the address of the template, i.e., the code address where the editing should start. It is followed by a variable sequence of edit blocks, each of which specifies the number of edits it holds and the sequence thereof, and is terminated by the stop symbol $. An edit specifies an offset, i.e., a number of bytes that can be skipped without editing, followed by the number of bytes that should be written and the bytes to write. As all the values in the edit script, except the address, are bytes, this allows us to specify the modifications compactly, while still maintaining enough generality to specify every possible modification.

Editing Engine. The editing engine will be passed the address of the edit script by the stub. It will save appropriate program state, such as the register contents, interpret the edit script, flush the instruction cache if necessary, restore the saved program state and finally branch to the entry point of the procedure, passed as the second argument. Note that the necessity of flushing the instruction cache depends on the architecture: on some architectures, such as the Intel IA-32 architecture used for our current implementation, an explicit cache flush is not necessary.

Our approach to dynamic code editing modifies the template code *in situ*. This is an important departure from classical sequence alignment and editing algorithms [9], which scan a read-only source sequence, copying it over to a new area of memory and applying modifications along the way where dictated by the edit script. With *in situ* modifications this copying can be avoided, thereby increasing performance. Insertion operations are however still expensive, as they require moving the remainder of the source. Consequently, we do not support insertion operations in our edit scripts. Instead only substitution operations are supported. Deletion operations may be implemented by overwriting instructions with no-op instructions, but as this introduces inefficiencies, we will avoid this as much as possible.

3.2 One-Pass Mutations

We are now ready to discuss one-pass modifications. With this technique, we scramble procedures separately, meaning that each procedure will have its own template. Consequently, different procedures are not mapped to the same memory location. The idea at obfuscation time is to alter portions of a procedure in the program. At run-time, these alterations are undone via a single round of editing, just before the procedure is executed for the first time. To achieve this, we place the stub at the entry point of the procedure. At the first invocation of the editing engine, this stub will be overwritten with the original code of the procedure. This way, the call to the editor will be bypassed on subsequent calls to the procedure.

3.3   Cluster-Based Mutations

The general idea behind clustering is to group procedures of which the instruction sequences are sufficiently similar to enable the reconstruction of the code of each of them from a single template without requiring too many edits. The procedures in a cluster will then be mapped to the same memory area, the cluster template. Each call to a clustered procedure is replaced by a stub that invokes the editing engine with appropriate arguments to guide the edit process, as illustrated in Figure 1.

To avoid reconstructing a procedure that is already present, the editing engine will rewrite the stub of a constructed procedure in such a way that it branches directly to that procedure instead of calling the editing engine. The stub of the procedure that has been overwritten, will be updated to call the editing engine the next time it needs to be executed.

Clustering. Clustering is performed through a node-merging algorithm on a fully-connected undirected weighted graph in which each vertex is a cluster of procedures and the weight of an edge (A, B) represents (an estimate of) the additional run-time overhead (i.e., the cost of the edits) required when clusters A and B are merged.

The number of run-time edits required by a cluster, i.e., the number of control flow transfers between two members of that cluster, is estimated based on profiling information drawn from a set of training inputs.

As usual, the clustering process has to deal with a performance trade-off. On the one hand, we would like every procedure to be in an as large as possible cluster. The larger we make individual clusters –and therefore, the fewer clusters we have overall– the greater the degree of obfuscation we will achieve, since more different instructions will map to the same addresses, thus moving further away from the conventional one-to-one mapping of instructions and memory addresses.

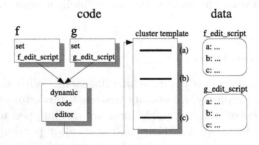

Fig. 1. Run-time code mutation with clustered procedures

On the other hand, the larger a cluster, the more differences there will likely be between cluster members, resulting in a larger set of edit locations, and hence a greater run-time overhead. Furthermore, this will result in an increasing number of transitions between members within a cluster. With transition, we mean the execution of one member of a cluster after the execution of another member. Clearly, each transition requires editing the next procedure to be executed. Both these factors increase the total run-time cost of the dynamic modification.

When our greedy clustering algorithm starts, each cluster consists of a single procedure. The user needs to specify a run-time overhead "budget" (specified as a fraction ϕ of the number of procedure calls n that can be preceded by a call to the editing engine, i.e, budget=$n \times \phi$). As we want all procedures to be in an as large as possible cluster, we proceed as follows. First we try to create two-procedure clusters by only considering single-procedure clusters for merging. The greedy selection heuristic chooses the edge with the lowest weight and this weight is subtracted from the budget. We then recompute edge weights by summing their respective weights to account for the merge. When no more two-procedure clusters can be created, we try to create three-procedure clusters, using the same heuristic, and so on.

Merging clusters is implemented as node coalescing. This sets an upper bound to the actual cost and hence is conservative with regard to our budget. This is repeated until no further merging is possible. A low value for the threshold ϕ produces smaller clusters and less run-time overhead, while a high value results in larger clusters and greater obfuscation at the cost of higher overhead. It is important to note that two procedures that can be active together should not be clustered. Otherwise, their common template would need to be converted into two different procedures at the same time, which obviously is not possible.

These concepts are illustrated in Figure 2. The call graph is shown in Figure 2(a). It is transformed into a fully connected new graph, where the initial

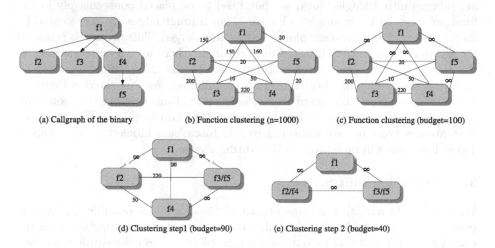

(a) Callgraph of the binary   (b) Function clustering (n=1000)   (c) Function clustering (budget=100)

(d) Clustering step1 (budget=90)   (e) Clustering step 2 (budget=40)

Fig. 2. The creation of clusters, ϕ=0.1

nodes are clusters consisting of exactly one procedure. The weight given to the other edges between two clusters is the number of transitions between the respective procedures in those clusters, i.e., the number of calls to the editor that would result from merging these two procedures. These values are collected from a set of training inputs. The resulting graph is shown in Figure 2(b). We furthermore assume that $\phi=0.1$ and as the maximum number of procedure calls to the editing engine n is 1000 $(10+3*20+50+2*150+160+200+220)$, a budget of 100 calls is passed to the clustering algorithm. To avoid clustering procedures that can be active at the same time, the edges between such procedures are assigned the value infinity, as illustrated in Figure 2(c).

As our clustering algorithm starts with clusters consisting of a single procedure, the algorithm looks for the edge with the smallest value, which is $(f3, f5)$. The weights of the edges of the merged cluster to the other clusters are updated accordingly. Our graph now consists of three clusters consisting of single procedure ($f1$, $f2$, and $f4$) and one cluster consisting of two procedures (Figure 2(d)). As it is still possible to make clusters of two procedures, the edge with the smallest weight between the three clusters consisting of a single procedure will be chosen (if its weight is smaller than our budget). This way, procedure $f2$ and $f4$ are clustered (Figure 2(e)). As we can no longer make clusters of two procedures, the algorithm now tries to make clusters of size three. This is impossible, however, and so the algorithm terminates.

3.4   Minimizing the Edit Cost

In this section, we will discuss how the template for a cluster is generated. This is done in such a way that the number of edits required to construct a procedure in the cluster from the template is limited.

This is achieved through a layout algorithm which maximizes the overlap between two procedures. First of all, basic blocks connected by fall-through edges are merged into a single block, as they need to be placed consecutively in the final program. In the example of Figure 3, fall-through edges are represented by dashed lines. Therefore, basic blocks 1 and 2 are merged. This process is repeated for all procedures in the cluster. In our example, there are three procedures in the cluster and the procedures each have two blocks. These blocks are placed such that the number of edits at run-time is minimized, as illustrated in Figure 3. The cluster template consists of sequences of instructions that are common to all the procedures and locations that are not constant for the cluster. The locations that are not constant are indicated by the black bars labeled a, b, c, and d. These locations will be edited by the editing engine.

3.5   Protecting Edit Scripts

With the code mutation scheme described thus far, it is possible, at least in principle, for an attacker to statically analyze an edit script, together with the code for the editor, to figure out the changes effected when the editor is invoked with that edit script. To overcome this problem, we will use a pseudorandom

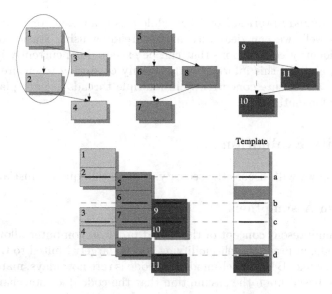

Fig. 3

number generator seeded with an opaque variable [5]. A variable is opaque at point p in a program, if it has a property at p which is known at obfuscation time, but which is computationally difficult to determine analytically.

The basic idea is to combine the values statically present in the edit script with a value generated by the pseudorandom number generator. As we know the value of the seed (opaque variable) at obfuscation time, we can predict the values that will be generated by the pseudorandom number generator. Therefore, it is possible to write values in the edit script which will produce the needed values when combined with the pseudorandom numbers. Every byte in the edit script is then xor'ed with a byte created by the pseudorandom number generator before it is passed to the editing engine.

3.6 Applicability

Dynamic code mutation relies fundamentally on statically constructing edit scripts that can be used to carry out run-time code mutation. This presumes that a program's code is statically available for analysis and edit script construction. Because of this, the technique is not applicable to code that is already self-modifying. Dynamic code mutation also causes instruction opcodes and displacements to change. New instructions are inserted in procedure stubs, and displacements in branch and call instructions may change as a result of code movement. This precludes the application of dynamic code mutation to programs that rely on the actual binary values of code locations (as opposed to simply their instruction semantics), e.g., programs that compute a hash value of their instructions for tamper-proofing.

Finally, the contents of the code locations change as dynamically mutating code executes. This means that the technique cannot be applied to reentrant code such as shared libraries. Note that while this is an issue for multi-threaded programs as well, we can deal with multi-threading using static concurrency analyses to identify code regions that can be executed concurrently in multiple threads [19], and use this information to modify clustering to ensure that code regions that can execute concurrently in multiple threads are not placed in the same cluster for mutation.

4   Security Evaluation

In this section we will discuss the security of our technique against attacks.

4.1   Broken Assumptions

While the omnipresent concept of the stored program computer allows for self-modifying code, in practice, self-modifying code is largely limited to the realm of viruses and the like. Because self-modifying code is rare nowadays, many analyses and tools are based upon the assumption that the code does not change during the execution.

Static disassemblers, e.g., examine the contents of the code sections of an executable, decoding successive instructions one after another until no further disassembly is possible [22]. Clearly these approaches fail if the instructions are not present in the static image of the program.

Dynamic disassemblers by contrast, examine a program as it executes. Dynamic disassemblers are more accurate than static disassemblers for the code that is actually executed. However, they do not give disassemblies for any code that is not executed on the particular input(s) used.

In order to reduce the runtime overheads incurred, dynamic disassembly and analysis tools commonly "cache" information about code regions that have already been processed. This reduces the runtime overhead of repeatedly disassembling the same code. However, it assumes that the intervening code does not change during execution.

Many other tools for program analysis and reverse engineering cannot deal with dynamically mutating code either. For example, a large number of analyses, such as constant propagation or liveness analysis require a conservative control flow graph of the program. It is not yet fully understood how this control flow graph can be constructed for dynamically mutating code without being overly conservative. Through the use of self-modifying code, we cripple the attacker by making his tools insufficient.

4.2   Inherent Security

While undermining assumptions made by existing analyses and tools adds a level of protection to the program and will slow down reverse engineering, its security is ad-hoc. However, no matter how good reverse engineering tools will become, a certain level of security will remain. As long as the opaque variable or the pseudorandom number generator are not broken, an attacker cannot deduce any other information than guessing from the edit script. Assuming that the opaque variable and pseudorandom number generator are secure, it corresponds to a one-time pad.

Depending on the class of expressions considered, the complexity of statically determining whether an opaque variable always takes on a particular value can range from NP-complete or co-NP-complete[8], through PSPACE-complete[23], to EXPTIME-complete[14].

A lot of research has gone into the creation of secure pseudorandom number generators. For our purposes, we need a fast pseudorandom number generator. ISAAC [15] for example meets this requirement and, in practice, the results are uniformly distributed, unbiased and unpredictable unless the seed is known.

5 Experimental Results

We built a prototype of our dynamic software mutation technique using Diablo, a retargetable link-time binary rewriting framework[10]. We evaluated our system using the 11 C benchmarks from the SPECint-2000 benchmark suite. All our experiments were conducted on a 2.80GHz Pentium 4 system with 1 GiB of main memory running RedHat Fedora Core 2. The programs were compiled with gcc version 3.3.2 at optimization level -O3 and obfuscated using profiles obtained using the SPEC training inputs. The effects of obfuscation on performance were evaluated using the (significantly different) SPEC reference inputs.

The prototype obfuscator is implemented on top of the tool Diablo, which only handles statically linked programs. In real-life however, most programs are dynamically linked. To mimic this in our experiments, and obtain realistic results, our prototype obfuscator does not obfuscate library procedures.

Table 1. Number of procedures that can be protected

	bzip2	crafty	gap	gcc	gzip	mcf	parser	perlbmk	twolf	vortex	vpr	**Mean**
Nr of functions	31	105	848	1272	56	16	176	891	165	655	91	
No protection	3.23%	5.71%	6.01%	20.68%	17.86%	0.00%	5.68%	11.78%	3.03%	1.22%	13.19%	8.04%
One-pass protection	6.45%	6.67%	75.12%	46.15%	46.43%	25.00%	6.82%	80.13%	4.85%	41.07%	14.29%	32.09%
Cluster protection	90.32%	87.62%	18.87%	33.18%	35.71%	75.00%	87.50%	8.08%	92.12%	57.71%	72.53%	59.88%
total protected	96.77%	94.29%	93.99%	79.32%	82.14%	100.00%	94.32%	88.22%	96.97%	98.78%	86.81%	91.96%

Table 1 shows the number of procedures that are scrambled by applying our new obfuscation technique. The value of ϕ was set to 0.0005. Procedures containing escaping edges[1] can't be made self-modifying in our prototype, as it is impossible to make sure that the targeted procedure of the escaping edge is present in memory. On all other procedures, we first applied the clustering mutation. After this first pass, we scrambled the remaining procedures with the

---

[1] Escaping edges are edges where control jumps from one procedure into another without using the normal call/return mechanism for interprocedural control transfers. They are rare in compiler generated code, and can most often be avoided by disabling tail-call optimization.

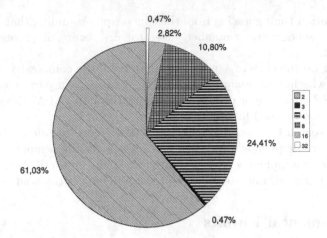

Fig. 4. Number of procedures per cluster

one-pass mutation. On average this combined application of the two mutation technique is capable of protecting 92% of all (non-library) procedures in the programs.

In Figure 4 the distribution of the number of procedures per cluster is shown. The value of ϕ was set to 0.0005. On average, there are 3.61 procedures per cluster.

Table 2. Relative execution time, $\phi=0.0005$

	bzip2	crafty	gap	gcc	gzip	mcf	parser	perlbmk	twolf	vortex	vpr	geo. mean
Original (T_0)	89.140	159.303	128.227	36.623	42.757	429.057	305.060	1.423	611.513	87.820	90.369	
Obfuscated(T_1)	88.037	229.567	150.853	39.697	43.753	429.583	317.573	1.183	618.850	168.170	173.340	
Slowdown (T_1/T_0)	0.988	1.441	1.176	1.084	1.023	1.001	1.041	0.831	1.012	1.915	1.918	1.177

Table 2 shows the run-time effects of our transformations. On average, our benchmarks experience a slowdown of 17.7%; the effects on individual benchmarks range between slight speedups (for gzip and vpr), to an almost 2x slowdown (for vortex). This slight speedup experience is due to cache effects. In general, frequently executed procedures, and especially frequently executed procedures that form hot call chains, will be put in separate clusters. Hence these procedures will be mapped to different memory regions. If the combined size of the templates of all clusters becomes smaller than the instruction cache size, the result is that all hot call chains consist of procedures at different locations in the cache. Hence few or none hot procedures will throw each other out of the instruction cache. For gzip and vpr, the resulting gain in cache behavior more than compensates for the, already small, overhead of executing the edit scripts.

Figure 5 summarizes the run-time overhead of our transformations for different ϕ's. On average benchmarks are 31.1% slower with a $\phi=0.005$ and 5.9% slower with $\phi=0.00005$.

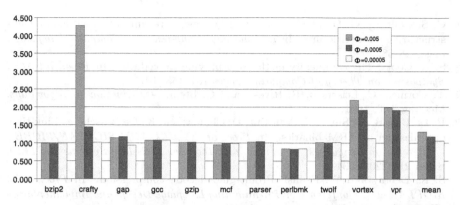

Fig. 5. Execution time slowdown for different values of ϕ

6 Conclusion

This paper introduces an approach to dynamic software protection, where the code for the program changes repeatedly as it executes. As a result, a number of assumptions made by existing tools and analyses for reverse engineering are undermined. We have further argued that the technique is secure as long as the opaque variables or random number generator have not been broken.

Acknowledgments

The authors would like to thank the Flemish Institute for the Promotion of Scientific-Technological Research in the Industry (IWT), the Fund for Scientific Research - Belgium - Flanders (FWO) and Ghent University for their financial support. The work of Debray and Moseley was supported in part by NSF Grants EIA-0080123, CCR-0113633, and CNS-0410918.

References

1. D. Aucsmith. Tamper resistant software: an implementation. *Information Hiding, Lecture Notes in Computer Science*, 1174:317–333, 1996.
2. V. Bala, E. Duesterwald, and S. Banerjia. Dynamo: a transparent dynamic optimization system. In *Proc. SIGPLAN '00 Conference on Programming Language Design and Implementation*, pages 1–12, 2000.
3. B. Buck and J. Hollingsworth. An API for runtime code patching. *The International Journal of High Performance Computing Applications*, 14(4):317–329, 2000.
4. C. Cifuentes and K. J. Gough. Decompilation of binary programs. *Software - Practice & Experience*, pages 811–829, July 1995.
5. C. Collberg, C. Thomborson, and D. Low. Manufacturing cheap, resilient, and stealthy opaque constructs. In *Principles of Programming Languages 1998, POPL'98*, pages 184–196, 1998.
6. C. S. Collberg and C. Thomborson. Watermarking, tamper-proofing, and obfuscation - tools for software protection. In *IEEE Transactions on Software Engineering*, volume 28, pages 735–746, Aug. 2002.

7. C. S. Collberg, C. D. Thomborson, and D. Low. Breaking abstractions and unstructuring data structures. In *International Conference on Computer Languages*, pages 28–38, 1998.

8. S. A. Cook. The complexity of theorem-proving procedures. In *Proc. 3rd ACM Symposium on Theory of Computing*, pages 151–158, 1971.

9. T. Cormen, C. Leiserson, R. Rivest, and C. Stein. *Introduction to Algorithms*. McGraw Hill, 1991.

10. B. De Bus, B. De Sutter, L. Van Put, D. Chanet, and K. De Bosschere. Link-time optimization of ARM binaries. In *Proc. of the 2004 ACM SIGPLAN/SIGBED Conference on Languages, Compilers, and Tools for Embedded Systems (LCTES)*, pages 211–220, 2004.

11. S. K. Debray and W. Evans. Profile-guided code compression. In *Proc. ACM SIGPLAN 2002 Conference on Programming Language Design and Implementation (PLDI-02)*, pages 95–105, June 2002.

12. D. Engler, W. Hsieh, and F. Kaashoek. 'c: A language for high-level, efficient, and machine-independent dynamic code generation. In *Symposium on Principles of Programming Languages*, pages 131–144, 1996.

13. M. Hicks, J. Moore, and S. Nettles. Dynamic software updating. In *Proc. SIGPLAN Conference on Programming Language Design and Implementation*, pages 13–23, 2001.

14. P. Hudak and J. Young. Higher-order strictness analysis in the untyped lambda calculus. In *Proc. 13th ACM Symposium on Principles of Programming Languages*, pages 97–109, Jan. 1986.

15. R. Jenkins. Isaac. In *Fast Software Encryption*, pages 41–49, 1996.

16. Y. Kanzaki, A. Monden, M. Nakamura, and K. ichi Matsumoto. Exploiting self-modification mechanism for program protection. In *Proc. of the 27th Annual International Computer Software and Applications Conference*.

17. M. Leone and P. Lee. A Declarative Approach to Run-Time Code Generation. In *Workshop on Compiler Support for System Software (WCSSS)*, 1996.

18. D. Lie *et al.* Architectural support for copy and tamper resistant software. In *Proc. 9th International Conference on Architectural Support for Programming Languages and Operating Systems (ASPLOS-IX)*, pages 168–177, 2000.

19. S. Masticola and B. Ryder. Non-concurrency analysis. In *PPOPP '93: Proceedings of the fourth ACM SIGPLAN symposium on Principles and practice of parallel programming*, pages 129–138. ACM Press, 1993.

20. F. Noel, L. Hornof, C. Consel, and J. L. Lawall. Automatic, template-based runtime specialization: Implementation and experimental study. In *Proceedings of the 1998 International Conference on Computer Languages*, pages 132–142, 1998.

21. T. Ogiso, Y. Sakabe, M. Soshi, and A. Miyaji. Software obfuscation on a theoretical basis and its implementation. In *IEICE Transactions on Fundamentals*, pages 176–186, 2003.

22. B. Schwarz, S. Debray, and G. Andrews. Disassembly of executable code revisited. In *WCRE '02: Proceedings of the Ninth Working Conference on Reverse Engineering (WCRE'02)*, pages 45–54. IEEE Computer Society, 2002.

23. L. J. Stockmeyer and A. R. Meyer. Word problems requiring exponential time. In *Proc. 5th ACM Symposium on Theory of Computing*, pages 1–9, 1973.

24. J. Viega. Practical random number generation in software. In *Proc. 19th Annual Computer Security Applications Conference*, pages 129–141, 2003.

25. C. Wang, J. Davidson, J. Hill, and J. Knight. Protection of software-based survivability mechanisms. In *International Conference of Dependable Systems and Networks*, Goteborg, Sweden, July 2001.

Efficient Hardware Implementation of Elliptic Curve Cryptography over $GF(p^m)$

Mun-Kyu Lee[1], Keon Tae Kim[2,*], Howon Kim[3],
and Dong Kyue Kim[2,**]

[1] School of Computer Science and Engineering,
Inha University, Incheon 402-751, Korea
mklee@inha.ac.kr
[2] Department of Computer Engineering,
Pusan National University, Busan 609-735, Korea
{ktkim, dkkim}@islab.ce.pusan.ac.kr, dkkim1@pusan.ac.kr
[3] Electronics and Telecommunications Research Institute,
161 Gajeong-dong, Yuseong-gu, Daejeon 305-350, Korea
khw@etri.re.kr

Abstract. Elliptic curve cryptography (ECC) was discovered by Koblitz and Miller, and there has been a vast amount of research on its secure and efficient implementation. To implement ECC, three kinds of finite fields are being widely used, i.e. prime field $GF(p)$, binary field $GF(2^m)$ and optimal extension field $GF(p^m)$. There is an extensive literature on hardware implementation of prime fields and binary fields, but almost nothing is known about hardware implementation of OEFs. At a first glance, this may seem natural because OEF has been devised originally for efficient software implementation of ECC. However, we still need its hardware implementation for the environments where heterogeneous processors are communicating with each other using a single cryptographic protocol. Since the ECC software implementation over the weaker processor may not guarantee reasonable performance, a customized ECC coprocessor would be a good solution.

In this paper, we propose an ECC coprocessor over $GF(p^m)$ on an FPGA. Since the most resource-consuming operation is inversion, we focus on the efficient design of inversion modules. First we provide four different implementations for inversion operation, i.e. three variants of Extended Euclidian Algorithm and inversion using the iterative Frobenius map. We use them as the building blocks of our ECC coprocessor over OEF. According to our analysis, inversion using the iterative Frobenius map shows the best performance among the four choices, from the viewpoints of speed and area.

Keywords: Elliptic Curve Coprocessor, Finite Field, Optimal Extension Field, FPGA.

---

* This work was supported by the Regional Research Centers Program (Research Center for Logistics Information Technology), granted by the Korean Ministry of Education & Human Resources Development.
** Corresponding author.

J. Song, T. Kwon, and M. Yung (Eds.): WISA 2005, LNCS 3786, pp. 207–217, 2006.

1   Introduction

Elliptic curve cryptography (ECC) was discovered by Koblitz [1] and Miller [2], and there has been a vast amount of research on its secure and efficient implementation. In elliptic curve systems, a desired security level can be attained with significantly smaller keys than is possible with other public key systems such as RSA.[1] This means faster implementation as well as more efficient use of power, bandwidth and storage. Hence ECC is attracting more and more attention nowadays, especially in the area of mobile and embedded systems where resource-constrained devices are used, and many standards organizations have recently been adopting ECC in their public key cryptography standards [4, 5, 6, 7, 8].

To implement ECC, the underlying finite field should be supported properly. Generally, three kinds of elliptic curves are used for ECC, i.e. prime field $GF(p)$, binary field $GF(2^m)$ and optimal extension field (OEF) $GF(p^m)$ [9, 10] .

While there is an extensive literature on hardware implementation of prime fields and binary fields, almost nothing is known about hardware implementation of OEFs. At a first glance, this may seem natural because OEF has originally been devised for software optimization of ECC.[2] But in fact, the hardware implementation of OEF is necessary in the following sense: consider, for example, an environment where a 32-bit general purpose CPU generates an ECDSA signature over $GF(p^m)$ with $p \approx 2^{32}$ and a weaker CPU verifies the signature (and vice versa). Since all the participants in the protocol should use the same parameters according to a given standard,[3] the weaker CPU would suffer from its poor performance, especially if its word size is smaller than 32 bits. The problem is easily solved by installing a customized $GF(p^m)$ ECC coprocessor in the weaker system, which is our motivation for the study of hardware implementation of ECC over OEF.

In this paper, we propose an ECC coprocessor over $GF(p^m)$ with $p = 2^{31} - 1$ and $m = 7$ on an FPGA. The most important part of our work is the efficient design of the field inversion module, since inversion is much more time-consuming than other finite field operations such as multiplication and addition. We provide four different implementations for the inversion module, i.e. three variants of the Extended Euclidian Algorithm (Algorithms IE, IP and IM [12]) and inversion using the Frobenius map [10] which we call Algorithm IFM in this paper, as well as other basic modules including an adder and a multiplier. These modules are used to design an ECC coprocessor which is capable of EC point addition and EC point doubling. According to our analysis, Algorithm IFM is more efficient

---

[1] For example, it is generally accepted that a 160-bit elliptic curve key provides the same level of security as a 1024-bit RSA key [3].

[2] Actually, p in OEF $GF(p^m)$ is selected to fit into a word of the target CPU so that built-in arithmetic operations of that CPU may be fully used. A precise comparison of software implementations of ECC shows that OEFs are more efficient than prime fields and binary fields under the same level of security [11].

[3] Some recently established standards (e.g. [8]) have already included OEF as the underlying field for ECC.

than the other alternatives: its throughput is 1.8 times higher than the best of the other three methods, and moreover, it uses much less area. As a result, the ECC coprocessor using Algorithm IFM as its inversion module shows the best performance from the viewpoints of throughput and area.

2 Preliminaries

2.1 Optimal Extension Field

Finite fields are denoted by $GF(p^m)$, where p is a prime and m is a positive integer. An OEF is a finite field $GF(p^m)$ that satisfies the following [9, 10]:

1. $p = 2^n - c$, where $\log_2 |c| \leq n/2$.
2. An irreducible binomial $f(x) = x^m - w$ $(w \in GF(p))$ exists.

An element $A(x)$ in an OEF is represented as $A(x) = \sum_{i=0}^{m-1} a_i x^i$ using the polynomial basis representation, where $a_i \in GF(p)$.

All arithmetic operations in OEF are performed modulo $f(x)$ [10]:

- Addition and subtraction of two field elements is implemented in a straight-forward manner by adding or subtracting the coefficients of their polynomial representation and, if necessary, performing a modular reduction by subtracting or adding p once from the intermediate result. Note that the costs for these operations are negligible compared to multiplication and inversion.
- Multiplication is done in two stages.
  - In the first stage, we perform an ordinary polynomial multiplication of two field elements $A(x)$ and $B(x)$, resulting in an intermediate product $C'(x)$ of degree less than or equal to $2m - 2$, i.e., $C'(x) = \sum_{i=0}^{2m-2} c_i' x^i$. The schoolbook method to calculate the intermediate coefficients c_i', $i = 0, 1, \ldots, 2m - 2$, requires m^2 multiplications and $(m - 1)^2$ additions in the subfield $GF(p)$. Note that squaring can be considered a special case of multiplication. The only difference is that the number of coefficient multiplications can be reduced to $m(m + 1)/2$.
  - The second stage is the reduction stage where $C'(x) \bmod f(x)$ is calculated to get $C(x) = A(x) \cdot B(x) \bmod f(x)$. Because the field polynomial $f(x) = x^m - w$ is a binomial, the reduction can be done as

    $$C(x) = c_{m-1}' x^{m-1} + (wc_{2m-2}' + c_{m-2}' \bmod p) + \cdots + (wc_m' + c_0' \bmod p).$$

    As an optimization, when possible we choose those fields with $f(x) = x^m - 2$, i.e., $w = 2$, in order to implement the multiplications as shifts. OEFs that offer this optimization are known as Type II OEFs.

- The most interesting operation is inversion, which is to find $B(x) \in GF(p^m)$ such that $A(x) \cdot B(x) \equiv 1 \bmod f(x)$, when $A(x) \in GF(p^m)$ is given. We will give a brief survey of this operation in the next section.

2.2   Inversion in Optimal Extension Fields

Since inversion is the most time-consuming part among the finite field operations, it is very important to design this operation efficiently for the implementation of ECC. Although the Extended Euclidean Algorithm (EEA) is a good choice for inversion in every finite field, there are various algorithms optimized for specific fields as follows:

- For prime field $GF(p)$, the Binary EEA is known as the best choice [13]. In this algorithm, divisions of the original EEA are replaced with shift operations and subtractions.
- For binary field $GF(2^m)$, the Almost Inverse Algorithm [14] and its modified version [15] are used as well as the EEA.
- For OEF, we have four choices, i.e., three variants of the EEA [12] and inversion using efficient powering [10, 16]. According to [12], Algorithm IM, which is one of the variants of the EEA, shows the best performance in software implementation of OEF. We assume that this observation cannot be applied directly to the hardware implementation, and decide to implement all of the four possible choices. Hence most of our work in this paper is dedicated to the implementation of inversion modules and also to the task of investigating what is the best choice for hardware implementation of OEF.

2.3   Elliptic Curve Operations

An elliptic curve over $GF(p^m)$ is given by

$$E : Y^2 = X^3 + AX + B, \tag{1}$$

where $A, B \in GF(p^m)$ and $4A^3 + 27B^2 \neq 0$. It is well known that E forms an additive group under point addition operation. For cryptographic applications, an elliptic curve is chosen so that its group order may be divisible by a sufficiently large prime, i.e., order $= hr$ for a large prime r and a small integer h [7, 8].

In (1), a point on an elliptic curve is represented in the form (X, Y), which is called affine coordinates. There is also an alternative form, i.e., projective coordinates (X, Y, Z). The motivation of using projective coordinates is that we can change one inversion, which is contained in point addition or point doubling, into several multiplications (and squarings). Therefore, if the ratio of (inversion cost)/(multiplication cost), which we call the I/M ratio, is large, projective coordinates would be a better choice. It is known that for binary fields $GF(2^m)$ and prime fields $GF(p)$, the I/M ratio is quite large, and ECC implementations using projective coordinates are much more efficient than those using affine coordinates [13, 15].

For an OEF, we should be more careful with the choice of the coordinate system, since the I/M ratio varies according to the change of p and m. The I/M ratio at the break-even point between affine and projective representations lies between 3.6 and 7.6 for various choices of p and m [12]. If the measured I/M ratio for a specific $GF(p^m)$ is greater than the break-even point value for that field, then the projective coordinates should be used. In our case, the I/M ratio is about 3.4 (See Table 1.), which is below the break-even point. Moreover, the number of required gates for projective coordinates are much larger than those of affine coordinates. Hence we use affine coordinates in this paper.

When two points $P = (X_1, Y_1)$ and $Q = (X_2, Y_2)$ on the curve (1) are given, we can define point operation $P + Q = (X_3, Y_3)$ as

$$X_3 = \lambda^2 - (X_1 + X_2), Y_3 = \lambda(X_1 - X_3) - Y_1, \tag{2}$$

where $\lambda = (X_2 - X_1)^{-1}(Y_2 - Y_1)$ if $X_1 \neq X_2$ (point addition) and $\lambda = (2Y_1)^{-1}$ $(3X_1^2 + A)$ if $X_1 = X_2$ (point doubling).

3   Design of Hardware Inversion Modules

To implement an ECC coprocessor, we should support the underlying field operations. Now we focus on the presentation of inversion modules, since the implementation of other field operations such as an addition and a multiplication is straightforward. In this section, we show four different implementations for the inversion module, i.e. three variants of the Extended Euclidian Algorithm (Algorithms IE, IP and IM [12]) and inversion using the Frobenius map [10] which we call Algorithm IFM in this paper.

3.1   Variants of the Extended Euclidian Algorithm

Assuming that we are given $A(x) \in GF(p^m)$, we want to find $B(x) \in GF(p^m)$ such that $A(x) \cdot B(x) \equiv 1 \mod f(x)$. The inversion using the Extended Euclidian Algorithm is to maintain the following relationships throughout its internal processing [12]:

$$A(x)B(x) + U(x)f(x) = F(x), \quad A(x)C(x) + V(x)f(x) = G(x).$$

Bearing this in mind, we begin with $B(x) \leftarrow 0, U(x) \leftarrow 1, F(x) \leftarrow f(x), C(x) \leftarrow 1, V(x) \leftarrow 0$ and $G(x) \leftarrow A(x)$. Then we try to reduce the degrees of $F(x)$ and $G(x)$ until one of them becomes 1, which means that $A(x)B(x) \equiv 1 \mod f(x)$ or $A(x)C(x) \equiv 1 \mod f(x)$.

In [12], three methods are given to reduce the degrees of $F(x)$ and $G(x)$, which are called Algorithm IE, Algorithm IP and Algorithm IM, respectively. We have implemented each of these three algorithms, and have found out that Algorithm IM gives the most efficient hardware implementation. Fig. 1 shows the block diagram of the IM module. The control logic issues appropriate control signals according to the IM algorithm, and there are several sub-modules for addition, subtraction and multiplication. There are four registers to store the intermediate results of $B(x), C(x), F(x)$ and $G(x)$, and also two additional registers to store the degrees of $F(x)$ and $G(x)$. Note that we do not store $U(x)$ and $V(x)$ because they are not required for our computation.

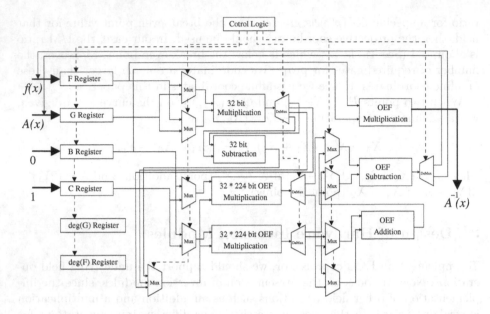

Fig. 1. Inversion module using Algorithm IM

3.2   Fast Inversion Algorithm Using the Frobenius Map (IFM)

In this section, we first show an interesting property of the Frobenius map over OEFs, and then explain Bailey and Paar's inversion algorithm using this property.

Let $A(x) = \sum_{j=0}^{m-1} a_j x^j \in GF(p^m)$. The Frobenius map is an automorphism defined by $A(x) \to A^p(x)$. Then the i-th iterate of the Frobenius map $A(x) \to A^{p^i}(x)$ is also an automorphism and it can be represented as $a_0 + \sum_{j=1}^{m-1} a_j x^{jp^i}$ since $a_j^p = a_j$ in $GF(p)$. By $x^m \equiv w \mod f(x)$, we get

$$x^{jp^i} \equiv x^{(jp^i \bmod m)} w^{\lfloor jp^i/m \rfloor} \mod f(x)$$

for $1 \le j \le m-1$, and

$$A^{p^i}(x) = a_0 + \sum_{j=1}^{m-1} a_j w^{\lfloor jp^i/m \rfloor} x^{(jp^i \bmod m)}. \tag{3}$$

After reordering terms in the above equation, we can obtain a polynomial basis representation of $A^{p^i}(x)$. Note that we can pre-compute $w^{\lfloor jp^i/m \rfloor}$, since p, m, and w are independent of $A(x)$. Hence, (3) can be computed by only $m-1$ on-line multiplications in $GF(p)$. Note that the costs to reorder terms are negligible.[4]

---

[4] In the original paper of Bailey and Paar [10], (3) is computed as $A^{p^i}(x) = a_0 + \sum_{j=1}^{m-1} a_j w^{\lfloor jp^i/m \rfloor} x^j$, i.e. without any reordering. As Baktir and Sunar [17] have pointed out, however, this simplification is faulty.

Bailey and Paar's inversion algorithm for OEFs [10] is based on the observation that Itoh and Tsujii's inversion algorithm [16] over $GF(2^m)$ may be efficiently used in the context of OEFs. Note that for any element $A(x) \in GF(p^m)$, $A^r(x)$ will be in $GF(p)$, where $r = (p^m - 1)/(p - 1)$. The following is a high-level description of Bailey and Paar's inversion algorithm.

Algorithm. OEF inversion [10]
Input. $A(x) \in GF(p^m)$.
Output. $B(x) \in GF(p^m)$ s.t. $A(x) \cdot B(x) \equiv 1 \bmod f(x)$.
Step 1. $B(x) \leftarrow A^{r-1}(x)$.
Step 2. $c_0 \leftarrow B(x) \cdot A(x)$.
Step 3. $c \leftarrow c_0^{-1} \bmod p$.
Step 4. $B(x) \leftarrow B(x) \cdot c$.

The core of the algorithm is the first step. Since the exponent $r - 1 = p^{m-1} + p^{m-2} + \cdots + p$ will be fixed for a given field, we know the p-adic representation of $r - 1$ in advance, i.e., $r - 1 = (11 \ldots 10)_p$. Hence we can compute A^{r-1} by an addition chain for $(11 \ldots 10)_p$. In our coprocessor, where $m = 7$ is used, A^{r-1} will be computed as follows:

$$B \leftarrow A^p = A^{(10)}; \qquad B_0 \leftarrow BA = A^{(11)};$$
$$B \leftarrow B_0^{p^2} = A^{(1100)}; \qquad B \leftarrow BB_0 = A^{(1111)};$$
$$B \leftarrow B^{p^2} = A^{(111100)}; \qquad B \leftarrow BB_0 = A^{(111111)};$$
$$B \leftarrow B^p = A^{(1111110)}.$$

Note that a p-th power and a p^2-th power over $GF(p^m)$ can be computed efficiently using (3). Therefore the only significant operation for Step 1 is several multiplications over $GF(p^m)$.

Now we consider the other steps. Since $c_0 = A^r(x)$ is always an element in $GF(p)$, we use the Extended Euclidian Algorithm over $GF(p)$ for Step 3. Steps 2 and 4 are one multiplication over $GF(p^m)$ and one multiplication by a constant in $GF(p)$, respectively.

3.3   Design of the IFM Module

In this section, we design the IFM module, i.e. a fast inversion module using the iterative Frobenius maps. First, the parameters that we have used are as follows.

1. Finite field: OEF $GF(p^m)$ with $p = 2^{31} - 1$, $m = 7$
2. Field polynomial: $f(x) = x^7 - 3$
3. Basis: polynomial basis

Fig. 2 shows the block diagram of the IFM module. The control logic issues appropriate control signals according to the inversion algorithm described in the previous section. The register A stores the input data of the inversion module, and register B stores the result. The register B0 and register C0 are used to store the intermediate results. There are other arithmetic units for addition and

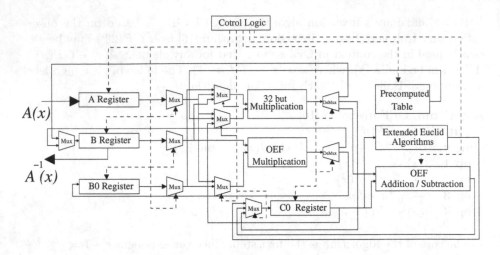

Fig. 2. Fast inversion module using the Frobenius map (IFM module)

multiplication, a single-precision EEA module to compute $c = c_0^{-1} \mod p$, and a precomputed table to store twelve values of $x^{jp^i} = w^{\lfloor jp^i/m \rfloor} x^{(jp^i \mod m)}$ for $i = 1, 2$ and $j = 1, \ldots, 6$ as follows:

$$x^p \mod f(x) \equiv 1752599774x \qquad x^{p^2} \mod f(x) \equiv 1600955193x$$
$$x^{2p} \mod f(x) \equiv 1600955193x^2 \qquad x^{2p^2} \mod f(x) \equiv 894255406x^2$$
$$x^{3p} \mod f(x) \equiv 1537170743x^3 \qquad x^{3p^2} \mod f(x) \equiv 1205362885x^3$$
$$x^{4p} \mod f(x) \equiv 894255406x^4 \qquad x^{4p^2} \mod f(x) \equiv 1752599774x^4$$
$$x^{5p} \mod f(x) \equiv 1599590586x^5 \qquad x^{5p^2} \mod f(x) \equiv 1537170743x^5$$
$$x^{6p} \mod f(x) \equiv 1205362885x^6 \qquad x^{6p^2} \mod f(x) \equiv 1599590586x^6$$

4   Design of ECC Coprocessor

In this section, we propose an ECC coprocessor over $GF(p^m)$ using the modules given in the previous sections. We use the following elliptic curve parameters, which are selected from curve ECP31M07K in [8].

1. Finite field: OEF $GF(p^m)$ with $p = 2^{31} - 1$, $m = 7$ and binomial $f(x) = x^7 - 3$.
2. Elliptic curve: $Y^2 = X^3 + 2147483644X + 270$ (We use affine coordinates.)
3. Base point: (x_G, y_G), where

$$x_G = \text{0x 006C41AD F9756CDD 5A59E058 9F63D27F}$$
$$\qquad \text{0AA730D4 72AA5D63 8511A3A5,}$$
$$y_G = \text{0x 006527DB 66D7A794 F1424E42 1CF86FE1}$$
$$\qquad \text{75F96FDD 649F576F 172F5E4C}$$

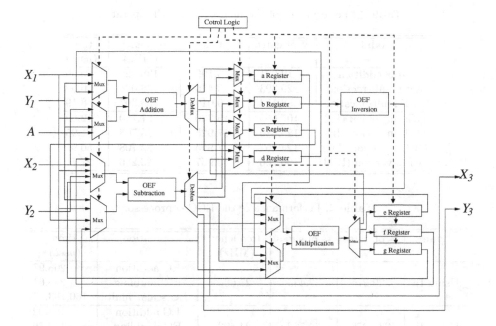

Fig. 3. ECC Coprocessor over $GF(p^m)$

Fig. 3 shows the block diagram of our ECC coprocessor, which uses the formula defined as (2). The control logic is responsible for deciding which operation to do, i.e. EC point addition or EC point doubling. The inputs are given as X_1, Y_1, X_2 and Y_2 for point addition, and X_1, Y_1 and A for point doubling. Then the result of the point operations are returned as X_3 and Y_3. Registers a through g are used to store the intermediate results. The inversion module can be implemented using one of the four algorithms given in Sections 3.1 and 3.3. Therefore we have four different implementations of the ECC coprocessor.

5   Implementation Results and Performance Analysis

In this section, we investigate the performance of the implemented modules and the resulting ECC coprocessor, which are modeled using VHDL and ModelSim 5.8, and then implemented with FPGA Xilinx Virtex-E XCV2000E-6-BG560.

Table 1 shows the performance of our modules for OEF operation. We can see that the performance of inversion operation is critical for the efficient implementation of the ECC coprocessor. We also see that among the four types of inversion modules, the IFM module consumes the smallest number of gates. While the maximum frequency of the IE module is slightly higher than that of the IFM module, the throughput of the IFM module is significantly higher than those of the others, i.e. the IFM module is about 1.8–11.3 times faster than the other inversion modules.

Table 1. Performance of the modules for OEF operation

module	# of gates	# of slices	frequency (MHz)	time (μsec)
OEF addition	19,091	3,199	138.026	0.09
OEF subtraction	20,393	3,416	138.026	0.09
OEF multiplication	58,153	9,019	39.307	8.19
OEF inversion (IE)	107,695	15,730	27.780	312.89
OEF inversion (IP)	125,386	17,925	23.708	201.95
OEF inversion (IM)	124,267	17,905	23.708	50.91
OEF inversion (IFM)	106,166	14,957	26.286	27.77

Table 2. Performance of the ECC coprocessor

type	# of gates	# of slices	frequency (MHz)	operation	time (μsec)
Using IE	229,276	32,433	27.666	EC addition	268.97
				EC doubling	248.67
				EC scalar mult.	160,183.97
Using IP	236,276	34,722	24.492	EC addition	188.02
				EC doubling	163.76
				EC scalar mult.	50,806.17
Using IM	243,955	34,330	23.542	EC addition	70.77
				EC doubling	76.83
				EC scalar mult.	18,338.08
Using IFM	228,597	31,607	26.183	EC addition	33.20
				EC doubling	43.94
				EC scalar mult.	11,294.85

Table 2 presents a summary of the characteristics of the four types of ECC coprocessors implemented using these OEF modules. In a scalar multiplication kP, we used $k \approx 2^{186}$. In this table, we first see that the coprocessor using the IFM module takes the smallest area. We also see that the speed of EC scalar multiplication of the coprocessor using the IFM module is faster than the other types of coprocessors by 1.6–14.2 times.

6   Conclusions

We have proposed an ECC coprocessor over $GF(p^m)$ on an FPGA. Specifically, we have implemented four different types of inversion modules for the coprocessor, i.e. three variants of Extended Euclidian Algorithm and inversion using the Frobenius map. From our implementation results, we can get the following facts:

- Among the various OEF operations, inversion is the dominant one.
- The performance of ECC coprocessor over OEF is closely related to the performance of an inversion module. The performance gain obtained by the

optimization of an inversion module is directly reflected in that of the co-processor as almost the same ratio.
- For a hardware implementation of OEF, inversion using the Frobenius map outperforms variants of the Extended Euclidian Algorithm.

References

1. Koblitz, N.: Elliptic curve cryptosystems. Mathematics of Computation **48** (1987) 203–209
2. Miller, V.: Use of elliptic curves in cryptography. In: Advances in Cryptology-CRYPTO 85. Volume 218 of LNCS., Springer (1986) 417–428
3. Hankerson, D., Menezes, A., Vanstone, S.: Guide to Elliptic Curve Cryptography. Springer, New York (2004)
4. ISO/IEC 14888-3: Information Technology–Security Techniques–Digital Signatures with Appendix–Part 3: Certificate Based-Mechanisms. (1998)
5. ANSI X9.62: Public Key Cryptography for the Financial Services Industry: The Elliptic Curve Digital Signature Algorithm (ECDSA). (1999)
6. National Institute of Standards and Technology: Digital Signature Standard, FIPS Publication 186-2. (2000)
7. IEEE P1363-2000: IEEE Standard Specifications for Public-Key Cryptography. (2000)
8. TTAS.KO-12.0015: Digital Signature Mechanism with Appendix– Part 3: Korean Certificate-based Digital Signature Algorithm using Elliptic Curves. (2001)
9. Bailey, D.V., Paar, C.: Optimal extension fields for fast arithmetic in public-key algorithms. In: CRYPTO '98. Volume 1462 of LNCS., Springer (1998) 472–485
10. Bailey, D.V., Paar, C.: Efficient arithmetic in finite field extensions with application in elliptic curve cryptography. Journal of Cryptology **14** (2001) 153–176
11. Smart, N.P.: A comparison of different finite fields for elliptic curve cryptosystems. Computers and Mathematics with Applications **42** (2001) 91–100
12. Lim, C., Hwang, H.: Fast implementation of elliptic curve arithmetic in $GF(p^n)$. In: Public Key Cryptography-PKC 2000. Volume 1751 of LNCS., Springer (2000) 405–421
13. Brown, M., Hankerson, D., López, J., Menezes, A.: Software implementation of the NIST elliptic curves over prime fields. In: CT-RSA 2001. Volume 2020 of LNCS., Springer (2001) 250–265
14. Schroeppel, R., Orman, H., O'Malley, S., Spatscheck, O.: Fast key exchange with elliptic curve systems. In: Advances in Cryptology-CRYPTO 95. Volume 963 of LNCS., Springer (1995) 43–56
15. Hankerson, D., Hernandez, J.L., Menezes, A.: Software implementation of elliptic curve cryptography over binary fields. In: Cryptographic Hardware and Embedded Systems (CHES 2000). Volume 1965 of LNCS., Springer (2000) 1–24
16. Itoh, T., Tsujii, S.: A fast algorithm for computing multiplicative inverses in $GF(2^m)$ using normal bases. Information and Computation **78** (1988) 171–177
17. Baktir, S., Sunar, B.: Optimal tower fields. IEEE Transactions on Computers **53** (2004) 1231–1243

Developing and Implementing IHPM on IXP 425 Network Processor Platforms*

Bo-Chao Cheng[1], Ching-Fu Huang[1], Wei-Chi Chang[1],
and Cheng-Shong Wu[2]

[1] Institute of Communications Engineering,
National Chung Cheng University, Chia-yi, Taiwan
bcheng@ccu.edu.tw,
{hellojared, fatcat}@insa.comm.ccu.edu.tw
http://insa.comm.ccu.edu.tw
[2] Department of Electrical Engineering,
National Chung Cheng University, Chia-yi, Taiwan
ieecsw@ccu.edu.tw

Abstract. This paper describes a technique for tracing attacks back toward the attackers somewhere in the Internet. There are many solutions existing for IP traceback problem, such as packet marking and algebraic approach. Many of them are not efficient and work under some unreasonable assumptions. The "Island Hopping Packet Marking (IHPM)" algorithm, truly incorporating the combination of the best features of the edge/node sampling and the cut vertex, is able to counter those disputed assumptions and provides great performance to reconstruct attacking paths with fewer collected packets under multiple attacks. The assessing of IHPM performance on IXP425 network processor shows the practical feasibility in routers implementations. Such a technique can provide a key answer required for advancing the state-of-the-art in DDoS mitigation and defenses in a realistic environment.

1 Introduction

Distributed Denial-of-Service (DDoS) attacks have increasingly become an annoying unfriendly behavior in the current Internet. When suffering a DDoS attack, the victim can almost do nothing but tolerate it. The best solution should be to find out the attackers and stop the attack at the origin. But as for those tricky attackers, they usually use spoofed IP as their source IP address so that it is difficult to find out where they really are. Therefore, we need some countermeasures to know the actually path the packets traveled to against the DDoS attacks.

The Internet protocol has a serious fault that the source host can fill itself in the IP source host field at each outgoing IP datagram that is forwarded by intermediate gateways by looking the destination address in the IP header. The gateways don't check the source address field to see if the datagram is really from this address. Therefore, the source host can fill random, arbitrary IP address in the IP source field, resulting IP spoofing. A large number of attackers exploited this IP spoofing technique and many attack tools are available in the Internet.

---

* This work was sponsored by NSC grant 93-2219-E-194-006 and Intel Taiwan.

J. Song, T. Kwon, and M. Yung (Eds.): WISA 2005, LNCS 3786, pp. 218–231, 2006.

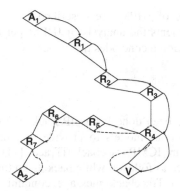

Fig. 1. IP spoofed problem. An attack path is indicated by solid line while a dotted line is a path that ended at a spoofed source.

As opposed to other types of attacks, attackers launch DDoS attacks, which involving IP spoofing with changing the source IP address of a host, to exhaust the remote host resources, such as bandwidth, socket spaces to limit legitimate users accessing a machine or services. Using the source IP address inside the IP header to trace back is not an intelligent behavior because the source IP address is spoofed. Consider the scenario shown in **Fig. 1.** Attacker A_1 starts the DoS attack to victim V, declaring that he is with the source address of A_2. According to topology showing, packets traverse the path R_1, R_2, R_3, and R_4 to victim (indicated by solid line). While victim is aware of low performance of services, he investigates the traffic and recognizes that a large number traffic is coming from A_2. Then, his failure in the traceback problem results an erroneous path R_4, R_5, R_6, and R_7 sequentially (indicated by dotted line) and cannot stop the noise traffic. Consequently, there should be a mechanism against the IP spoofed to traceback to the right origin of the attacks.

Filtering at router may be a possible solution to validate source address. A router drops an egress packet whose source address is from outside domain, and discards an ingress packet whose source address is the same as inside domain. Unfortunately, Internet is asymmetric routing network. Asymmetric route means that there is more than one way to reach the destination (e.g., redundant connections to the network) [5]. That means if a path is blocked because of filtering, there would be another redundant path to that destination. Further, packet filtering is not deployed everywhere. So far, it's still possible for hackers to send malicious packets with source address manipulation.

The trace back problem involves constructing an attack graph G that contains the attack path(s) and the associated attack source(s) for each victim [6]. IP protocol is vulnerability and it cannot provide a solution to the traceback problem. Clearly, a supplementary or complementary mechanism to provide traceback information to identify the source of the attack rapidly is required.

In this paper, we propose Island Hopping Packet Marking algorithm, carry it out on the network processor platform and assess its performance. The rest of this paper is organized as follows: Section 2 overviews a number of well-known published packet tracing techniques, their assumptions and the motive to propose this paper. Some prerequisites and theorems of IHPM are described in section 3. We provide the feasibility study that documents the analysis of IHPM performance data on IXP425 network processor, and section 6 concludes this paper.

2   Background

Some previous works have been done in the IP Packet Traceback problem domain. There are two kinds of famous models to provide the fundamental on a range of different researches. They are ICMP traceback (iTrace) [11] and marking packets [2]. The basic idea behind iTrace as follows: while packets go through, routers can, with a low probability, generate a Traceback message containing information about the adjacent routers and sent along to the destination. Upon receiving enough Traceback messages from various routers along the path, the victim of an attack can identify traffic source and determine attack path. In probabilistic marking packet approaches, three different solutions are provided: router stamping [3], algebraic approach [12] and Network support for IP traceback [2].

Edge sampling [2], the pioneer in the IP Traceback problem domain, reserves three fields in each packet for two addresses and the distance. Based on the edge sampling algorithm, routers mark packets with a probability p. Two adjoining routers are sampled as an edge and the *distance* represents the distance of the sampled edge from the victim. Savage and colleagues described assumptions that constrain the design of the marking algorithms. Many of these assumptions may be under dispute. We address these argued assumptions following.

- The route within attacker and victim is general stable: This assumption assumes that the route is general stable during attack and/or before/after attack. Actually, the routing is not static and stable on real Internet. Even with the same source and destination, the route changes dynamically. Their primitive design is only good under the static routing environment.
- Attackers must send enough packets to reconstruct paths: While speaking to DoS/DDoS attack, it stuffs the bandwidth with a huge number of packets. To mitigate the effect of DoS/DDoS attack is the main purpose of why we doing such an effort. It is not tolerable since the attack sends numerous packets to cause bandwidth consumption or system resource starvation. The solution to mitigate the influence on our network is to reduce the packets needed at the construction phase and locate the source as soon as possible.
- Attackers may work together: Before launching a DDoS attack, the attackers first compromise a lot number of machines as their zombies. Therefore, the source of a DDoS attack may come from not only one zombie. The capacity of detecting multiple sources is the basic requirement. Their archaic design can not detect multi-attacks under DDoS scenarios.

This paper is motivated by these unrealistic assumptions. We regard that the time needed to locate the source is as more significant than wasting time to draw a detail path. For this reason, we propose Island Hopping Packet Marking (IHPM) algorithm to improve the drawbacks of Savage's work and provide an efficient way to mitigate intrusion impacts.

3 Island Hopping Packet Marking Algorithms

Inspired by the idea that node and edge sampling techniques [2] might be a primitive solution for intrusion source identification and IP traceback problem, we propose a more efficient and flexible solution, Island Hopping Packet Marking (IHPM) algorithm. This combination of the best features of the node/edge sampling with the best characteristics of cut vertex sounds great in theory and dissolves in practice.

First, we introduce the key theorem that forms the fundamental of IHPM path reconstruction procedure. If v is a vertex in $G = (V, E)$, the graph obtained from G by deleting vertex v as well as the edges incident to the vertex v is denoted by $G - v$. A vertex v of a graph $G = (V, E)$ is a cut-vertex of G if the graph $G - v$ contains at least two components. On the other words, $G - v$ is not connected [1]. The removal of the cut-vertex from the connected graph results in the separation of two sub-graphs. The property of the cut-vertex can be adapted to the network IP traceback problem. A cut-vertex router works like a bridge between two networks. For example, a cut-vertex router can be a connector between ISP X and ISP Y. It implies that packets from a network to another one should have to travel through the cut-vertex router. Just like an entranceway to another domain, efforts must be made at the cut-vertex router to ensure security. Let us denote a path between v_0 and v_k as P $(v_0, v_k) = \{(v_0, v_1), (v_1, v_2), \ldots, (v_{k-1}, v_k)\}$ and a *X-Path* as *XP* $(cv_0, cv_k) = \{(cv_0, cv_1), (cv_1, cv_2), \ldots, (cv_{k-1}, cv_k)\}$ where $cv_0, cv_1, \ldots, cv_{k-1}, cv_k$ are cut-vertex routers.

Theorem 1
Let G be a connected graph, there are two path P (v_a, v_z) and P (v_b, v_y) both from domain I to another domain J where v_a, $v_b \in$ domain I and v_y, $v_z \in$ domain J, then XP_1 (v_a, v_z) is identical to XP_2 (v_b, v_y)[4].

We categorize routers into two classes: normal router and cut-vertex router. Normal routers reside in either the same *domain* or a different *domain* (e.g., v, x, y and z in **Fig. 2.**) and do the similar procedure what routers have done in edge sampling [2]. The cut-vertex routers (e.g., cv_1, cv_2 and cv_3) should perform the edge sampling procedure plus the node marking procedure. We will describe those procedures more detail in following section. The reason that we name this algorithm toward modernization an "island-hopping strategy" is because *X-Path* is hopping between the cut-vertex routers.

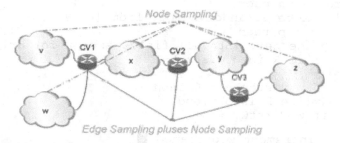

Fig. 2. Island Hopping Packet Marking scheme. Node append algorithm is implemented at each cut-vertex routers, while other routers enforce the edge sampling algorithm.

3.1 The Description of Each Fields Required in IHPM

Let us denote tuple M_ω = (*start, end, distance, OriginCV, FirstCV, NextCV*) representing these fields of each packet marked at node ω. The definition of each field is given below.

1. *start*: When router decides to mark the packet, it writes its IP address to this field. The *start* field represents the head of an edge.
2. *end*: While the start field is not empty and the value of the distance is zero, router writes its address into end field. This field represents the end of an edge.
3. *distance*: While a packet travels through, router increases this field by one. The *distance* represents the distance from the sampled edge to the closest downstream cut-vertex router.
4. *OriginCV*: This field is written by the original cut-vertex router while packet travels through and it is non-volatile. It represents the original and closest downstream cut-vertex router to the source of attack traffic.
5. *FirstCV*: It is also written by cut-vertex router, but it is volatile and can be re-written by downstream cut-vertex router. The value of this field characterizes the first downstream cut-vertex of the sampled edge.
6. *NextCV*: This field represents the next downstream cut-vertex router of the *FirstCV*. It is also re-writable.

3.2 Normal Router Marking Algorithm

A modification of the marking procedure from the edge sampling algorithm [2] is applied to each normal router that marks the packet with a probability p. When deciding to mark the packet, the normal router resets all fields to zero except for *OriginCV* and writes its address into the *start* field. Otherwise, if the normal router finds that the *distance* field is equal to zero, then it writes its address into the *end* field. Finally, it increases the *distance* by one until the packet arriving the closest downstream cut-vertex router. The marking procedure of normal router is illustrated in **Fig. 3**.

There are two differences from edge sampling: (1). IHPM takes care *OriginCV, FirstCV, NextCV*; (2). This modified edge sampling algorithm is executed only on the routers, named normal routers, between two neighbor cut-vertex routers.

```
Marking procedure at normal router R:
  for each packet w
  let x be a random number from [0..1)
  if x < p then
    place zero into all fields except for OriginCV
    write R into w.start
  else
    if w.distance = 0 then
     write R into w.end
    if w.FirstCV = 0

      increment w.distance ■
```

Fig. 3. Modified edge sampling algorithm executed by normal routers

3.3 Cut-Vertex Router Marking Algorithm

Cut-vertex router is deployed at the critical places of the Internet and acts like gateway to transmit the traffic from one *domain* to anther *domain*. Three fields, *OriginCV*, *FirstCV* and *NextCV* will be used by cut-vertex routers that write their addresses into. We describe this algorithm in **Fig. 4**.

The cut-vertex routers perform a procedure as easy as you look. If a packet goes through the first cut-vertex, the cut-vertex router stuff the *OriginCV* field with its address and no one can re-write this field with its address anymore. Otherwise, if the *OriginCV* has been written but the *FirstCV* is empty, then the cut-vertex router writes its address into the *FirstCV* field. Finally, if the *NextCV* field is empty, the router stuffs it with its address. This procedure is very similar to node appending but only three node space used.

```
Marking procedure at cut-vertex router R:
   for each packet w
   performs our modified edge sampling
   if w.OriginCV = 0 then
      write R into w.OriginCV
   if w.FirstCV = 0 then
      write R into w.FirstCV
      break
   if w.NextCV = 0 then
      write R into w.NextCV

   break ■
```

Fig. 4. The marking procedure executed by cut-vertex routers

3.4 Victim Path Reconstructing Algorithm

Under IHPM marking technique scheme, routers execute the specified marking algorithms to append necessary information (such as its address, and the distance) to routed packets. At the mean time, the victim will perform the path reconstructing algorithm based on collecting those marked packets. The reconstructing path procedure for IHPM consists two parts: skeleton path and fishbone path. Just like X-raying, *X-Path* (denoted as *XP*) is able to show the skeleton path consists of a sequence of traversal cut vertex routers. On the other hand, the fishbone path shows the detailed path about traversal routers within a *domain*.

In the path reconstruction procedure (see **Fig. 5.**, there are two basic functions: *findLeaf* and *findParent*. The process of *findLeaf* is to find out a leaf packet that contains a zero value at the *NextCV* field and return *FirstCV* value that resides in the same packet. The *findParent* function searches the ancestor for the input node, i.e., returns the *FirstCV* value where its *NextCV* field has the same value as the input parameter. The IHPM path reconstruction procedure begins by partitioning each packet *w* into different group based on the different of *OriginCV* field. For each partitioned groups, *findLeaf* is used to find out the leaf packet and the corresponding *FirstCV* value associated with the leaf packet is pushed into stack and passed to *findParent* function. The function *findParent* traces out the remainder cut-vertex hop-by-hop until it can not find any cut-vertex left. The *X-Path* of an attack is obtained from pushing out all elements in the stack. If more accurate and fine path is required for each *domain j* (constrained by two cut vertices: $C_{i,j}$ and $C_{j,k}$), the path reconstruction algorithm in edge sampling [2] is applied.

```
Path reconstructing procedure at victim V:
   for each packet w from attacker
   w was grouped by its OriginCV field;
   for each group {
     x=findLeaf();
     push x into stack;
     while ( (y=findparent(x)) !=null) {
       push y into stack;
       x=y;
     }
     extract X-path by pop all elements in stack;
   };
   For each domain {
     obtain fishbone path;

   };  ■
```

Fig. 5. Path reconstructing algorithm

3.5 A Example of Marking Algorithms

The below example illustrates the details of the marking procedures for IHPM. A scenario network topology is shown in **Fig. 6**; a packet is marked at router *a,* and remarked again at router *d*. Each field value at different traversal nodes are shown in the Table 1. For example, if node *a* decides to mark a packet, the tuple M_a of the packet should be (a, 0, 0, 0, 0, 0) while it leaving node *a*; The M_d = (d, 0, 0, I, 0, 0) means that the packet is marked at node *d*.

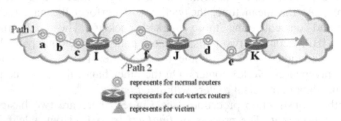

Fig. 6. A scenario network topology consists of three cut-vertex routers, a lot of normal routers, and two attack paths

Suppose there is another attack that takes through the Internet along the path 2 to the same victim as in path 1, and node *d* will mark the packets of both attacks. The victim will receive two marked packet tuples as follows: (d, e, 2, I, K, 0) and (d, e, 2, J, K, 0). Utilizing the tuple of (start, end, distance) = (d, e, 2), the edge sampling algorithm is not equipped with the ability to detect multiple attacks because all packets come from different attacks are marked on an equal basis. IHPM can easily detect multiple attacks by employing the *OriginCV* field (i.e., path 1 has *OriginCV = I* and path 2 has *OriginCV = J*). Thus, IHPM offers a unique feature resolve multiple attacks from different *domains*.

Table 1. The tuple's evolvement of a packet. This table shows the tuple's evolvement of a packet while leaving a node.

Fields	Routers							
	a	b	c	I	J	d	e	K
Start	a	a	a	a	a	d	d	d
End	0	b	b	b	b	0	e	e
Distance	0	1	2	3	3	0	1	2
OriginCV	0	0	0	I	I	I	I	I
FirstCV	0	0	0	I	I	0	0	K
NextCV	0	0	0	0	J	0	0	0

3.6 IP Options Brief

In Probabilistic Packet Marking algorithms, some storage space in each packet is required for path information. However, there is no enough room in the IP header to accumulate all path information. IP option may be the only solution to accumulate these 24 bytes information. This section describes how the path information is stuffed into IP options.

IHPM utilizes five fully IP addresses — *start*, *end*, *OriginCV*, *FirstCV*, and *NextCV* and 16 bits *distance* fields, that are too big to IP header accommodating the path information even encoding is used. Further, utilizing encoding technique (e.g., exclusive-or operator) will pay penalty for router performance and more packets needed to calculate the attack path. That is why we decide doing nothing to reduce the required space in order to gain a faster convergence time. This tradeoff problem makes it extremely challenging to consider the space requirements and the convergence time.

Based on RFC791 [9], IHPM uses the IP option space to carry the information of $M_\omega = $ (*start, end, distance, OriginCV, FirstCV, NextCV*) as shown in **Fig. 7**. It starts with the "type" octet containing three fields: one bit for copy flag, two bits for option class and five bits for option number. The IHPM "type" octet is (11011001_2) which includes copied bit enabled, debugging and measurement class, and the option number is defined as 25 (11001_2).

– The copy bit is asserted for fragmentation and avoidance of security vulnerability.
– The class bits are set to 2 (10_2) for debugging and measurement purpose.
– The number field is filled with 25 (11001_2) which is an undefined number space in RFC 791 [9] to represent the Island Hopping Packet Marking.

The second byte of option is the length octet that is used to indicate the entire length of the packet option. The length field is set to 0x18 implying that IP option

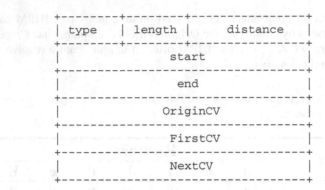

Fig. 7. IP option format for IHPM algorithms

totally has 24 bytes. The following bytes include the actual data of option. There two octets to present the distance field followed by five fully IP addresses. The End-of-Option-List packet option could be superfluous if the end of the option list is aligned at a 32-bit boundary [7].

4 The Advantages of IHPM Algorithm

This section evaluates the IHPM algorithms. The analysis can be done by going through three items: convergence time analysis, multiple attacks, single packet defense and DDoS mitigation, and the *X-Path* reuse.

4.1 Convergence Time Analysis

Probability problem plays an important role in packet marking approach for traceback problem. Routers mark received packet depending on the pre-defined probability value p. Victim constructs the path according to the information embedded in the IP header of each packet. How many packets should be received by victim to construct the path? If each router has an identical probability value p, the probability of receiving a marked packet from a router N hops away from the victim is

$$p\,(1-p)^{N-1} \tag{1}$$

So that, victim can nearly not get a marked packet from a router N hops away while N is greater than fifteen and the marking probability is 0.3. In IHPM algorithm, a few number of cut-vertex routers are deployed in the network. According to coupon collector problem [12], its smaller quantity will reduce the convergence time. That is, we can construct the skeleton path which is made up of a sequence of traversal cut vertex routers with a few numbers of packets.

4.2 Multiple Attacks, Single Packet Defense and DDoS Mitigation

We demonstrated the capability of IHPM to capture multi-attack from different *domains* in section 3.5. *OriginCV* field helps victim grouping different attacks because each attacking *domain* has its own signature in *OriginCV* field.

The fault diagnosis problem in circuit systems can be taken as a model in order to stop or isolate the DDoS/DoS traffic. Kim stated that some components can be equipped with alarms for the fault detection or the faulty components identifications [6]. We consider that the cut-vertex routers should be a good choice to deploy IDS or ACL control mechanism. Upon receiving a single packet from the attacking domain, the victim is able to finds out the cut-vertex router closest to attacking source based on *OriginCV* field. This provides a quick way to mitigate DDoS attacks and contains damages in the hacker's domain.

4.3 The *X-Path* Reuse

Consider a scenario that one attack occurring travels along almost the same route with another attack happened before. Do we need to waste time to construct the path again? By theorem 1 in section 3, it states that two paths have an identical *X-Path* if they are from and to the same *domain*. Therefore, we can reuse the *X-Path* if we have already constructed an *X-Path* that has a same *OriginCV* value with the occurring attacks.

5   Implement and Experiment Results

Every network system is unique and has special capabilities. With a programmable advantage over ASIC-based solutions and providing *m*W/MIPS performance and wide line speeds over software-based solutions, network processor becomes a cost-effective core technology to implement network systems. As you think about network systems design and implementation, it is important to plan how to make the dream come true. Network processor delivers all the flavors with programmability, flexibility and performability as well as with the added benefits of low cost such that it helps network engineers intelligently and efficiently designing and implementing their network systems. To match up the trend of industry development and eliminate the practice gap between academic and industry, we choose ADI's Coyote Gateway Reference Design board, based on Intel IXP425 network processor [8], as our implementation platform. This section describes the implementation of marking algorithms of IHPM on the IXP 425 network processor reference platform and presents the experiment results.

5.1 IXP 425 Network Processor Description

Intel IXP 425 network processor is chosen to be the platform of IHPM packet marking algorithms because of its high-performance and fully programmable architecture. Intel network processor provides an ease-of-use and flexibility solution to accelerate time-to-market. Its wire-speed packet processing power originates from the combination of a high performance Intel XScale core with additional Network Processor Engines (NPEs). It also combines integration with support for multiple WAN and LAN technologies in a common architecture designed providing wired-speed performance. Two 10/100 Ethernet MACs are included in its feature set that can used to simulate the interfaces of a route.

Intel IXP400 Software, coming with the IXP42X production line processors, is used to enable the processor's hardware in a way which gives the maximum flexibility. IXP Software is composed of four main components [10]: NPE microcode, Acccess Layer, Codelets, and Operating System Abstraction Layer (OSAL). We explain each of them briefly:

- The NPE microcode contains a lot of loadable and executable NPE instruction files that implement the NPE functionality. The NPEs are RISC co-processors embedded in the main processor providing specific hardware services such as Ethernet processing and MAC interfaces.
- The Access Layer is an entry which allows customized code accessing the underlying abilities of the IXP42X. This layer is made up of a set of software access-layer components while clients can use it to configure, control and communicate with the hardware.
- The Operating System Abstraction Layer (OSAL) is defined as a portable interface between operating system services and the access-layer components and the codelets.
- The Codelets are example applications that demonstrate how to use functions provided by the Intel XScale core library and the underlying hardware. Codelets are sorted by hardware port type and typically exercise some Layer-2 functionality on that port. To short the develop period, the IHPM marking algorithms are implemented based on the ethAcc codelets.

5.2 Testbed Environment and Experiment Results

The testbed environment includes a target board, SmartBits 2000 device, and SmartWindow 8.50.120. The target board is Coyote Gateway Reference Design from ADI and runs with MontaVista Linux Professional Edition version 3.1. The codelets (Intel IXP400 software v1.5 releases) provide us a good starting point to implement two marking algorithms, normal router marking algorithm and cut-vertex router marking algorithm. In order to assess and measure the algorithms performance, we establish a performance baseline: a regular route receives, looks for routing table and forwards packets without any packet marking procedures. The normal router marking algorithm and cut-vertex router marking algorithm associated with the baseline router behavior are implemented respectively, i.e., both targets have the tasks of receiving packets, probabilistic packet marking packets, looking for routing table and eventually routing packets. Let RR represent the regular router implementation, NR stand for the normal router marking implementation and CVR denote cut-vertex router marking implementation. Suppose that there are five routing table entries which are needed to look up in our performance testing. To get the worst case of performance scenarios, the marking probability value is set to 1. Finally, we collect performance data from the testbed environment to analyze how IHPM marking algorithm performance varies from the baseline in terms of the throughput and latency.

Fig. 8 shows how throughput depends on the different frame size. This picture gives us an impression that the difference in throughput between normal router and cut-vertex router almost tends to zero. Table 2 shows that all routers have wire-speed throughput while the frame size is greater than 900 bytes.

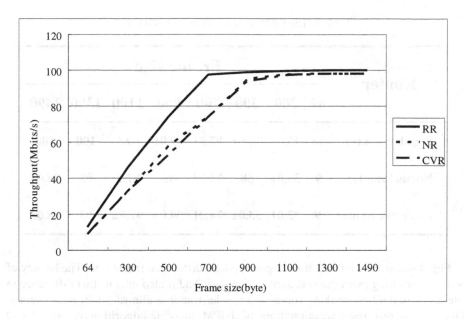

Fig. 8. The throughput of three different routers

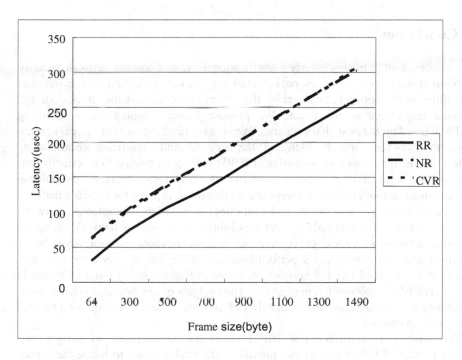

Fig. 9. Latency analysis via difference frame size

Table 2. The value representation of throughput

Router	Frame size							
	64	300	500	700	900	1100	1300	1490
Regular Router	13	46.02	74.01	97.51	99.01	99.5	100	100
Normal Router	9	33.01	58	74.03	95	97.5	98	98.03
Cut-Vertex Router	9	33.01	53.01	74.01	94.05	97.02	98	98.03

Fig. 9 shows how latency time depends on the difference frame size. The latency of both two marking procedures is almost identical. And it also tells us that difference in latency between two marking router and regular router is almost 30-40 microsecond. That means that the execution time of IHPM marking algorithm is only 30-40 microsecond on Xscale processor.

6   Conclusion

The challenge of intrusion source identification is a well-known network security problem domain -- it involves packet marking, packet collection and correlation algorithms to the network, and enables the victim to reconstruct the attack path and pinpoint the source of the attack. We propose Island Hopping Packet Marking (IHPM), based on the best characteristics from packet marking and cut vertex, to track down the attacking source. Many of the credible and significant contributions underlying the theorems and properties of IHPM have been proved to be effective in: reducing the number of packets to construct skeleton paths; resisting to multiple attacks simultaneously; relaxing unrealistic assumptions; reusing the skeleton path.

Network Processor is a nature and cost-effective solution to implement network systems in term of performability and flexibility. As a core of network appliance systems, network processor provides programmable advantages over ASIC-based solutions and offers $mW/MIPS$ performance and wide line speeds over software-based solutions. Intel IXP425 network processor evaluation board (ADI's Coyote) is chosen as IHPM implementation platform. The analysis of performance criteria (such as latency and throughput) shows that IHPM is feasible and desirable for practical router implementations.

This study has confirmed that IHPM meets the requirements to mitigate the growing threat of DDoS attacks and provide a practical solution to locate the source of intrusion.

References

1. K. Thulasiraman, M. N. S. Swamy: Graphs: Theory and algorithms. Wiley-Interscience, 1992
2. S. Savage, D. Wetherall, A. Karlin and T. Anderson: Network Support for IP Traceback. In: ACM/IEEE Transactions on Networking, 9(3), June 2001.
3. Thomas W. Doeppner, Philip N. Klein and Andrew Koyfman: Using Router Stamping to Identify the Source of IP Packets. In: Proc. of 7th ACM Conference on Computer and Communications Security, Nov. 2000.
4. Bo-Chao Cheng, Ching-Fu Huang and Er-Kai Tsao: IHPM: A Fast Pathfinder and Intrusion Source Identifier for DDoS Attacks, submitted to European Symposium on Research in Computer Security (ESORICS 2005)
5. Rik Farrow: Spoofing source addresses, http://www.spirit.com/Network/net0300.html
6. Jonghyun Kim, Sridhar Radhakrishnan, Sudarshan K. Dhall: On Intrusion Source Identification. In: 2nd IASTED International Conference on Communications, Internet and Information Technology, November 17-19, 2003
7. Klaus Wehrle, Frank Pählke, Hartmut Ritter, Daniel Müller, Marc Bechler: The Linux® Networking Architecture: Design and Implementation of Network Protocols in the Linux Kernel. First edition. Prentice Hall, Upper Saddle River, New Jersey (2004)
8. Intel IXP 425 Network Processor, http://developer.intel.com/design/network/products/npfamily/ixp425.htm
9. RFC 791 Internet Protocol, http://www.ietf.org/rfc/rfc0791.txt
10. Intel® IXP400 Software Programmer's Guide 1.5 edn, ftp://download.intel.com/design/network/manuals/252539_v1_5.pdf
11. Steven M. Bellovin: ICMP Traceback Messages, Internet Draft: draft-bellovin-itrace-00.txt, submitted Mar. 2000, expiration date Sep. 2000,http://www.research.att.com/~smb/papers/draft-bellovin-itrace-00.txt
12. Drew Dean, Matt Franklin and Adam Stubblefield: An Algebraic Approach to IP Traceback. In proceedings of NDSS'01, February 2001.
13. Kai Lai Chung: Elementary Probability Theory with Stochastic Processes, third edition. Springer-Verlag New York Inc., 1979, chap. 6, pp. 159.

Analysis on the Clockwise Transposition Routing for Dedicated Factoring Devices*

Tetsuya Izu[1], Noboru Kunihiro[2], Kazuo Ohta[2], and Takeshi Shimoyama[1]

[1] Fujitsu Limited, 4-1-1, Kamikodanaka, Nakahara-ku,
Kawasaki 211-8588, Japan
{izu, shimo-shimo}@jp.fujitsu.com
[2] The University of Electro-Communications,
1-5-1, Chofugaoka, Chofu 182-8585, Japan
{kunihiro, ota}@ice.uec.ac.jp

Abstract. Recently, dedicated factoring devices have attracted much attention since they might be a threat for a current RSA-based cryptosystems. In some devices, the clockwise transposition routing is used as a key technique, however, because of the lack of theoretic proof of the termination, some additional circuits are required. In this paper, we analyze the packet exchanging rule for the clockwise transposition and propose some possible alternatives with keeping the "farthest-first" property. Although we have no theoretic proof of the termination, experimental results show practical availability in the clockwise transposition. We also propose an improvement on the routing algorithm for the relation finding step in the number field sieve method of factorization, which establishes two times speed-up.

Keywords: Integer factoring, clockwise transposition, routing.

1 Introduction

The integer factoring problem is one of the most fundamental topics in the area of cryptology since the hardness of this problem assures the security of some public-key cryptosystems such as the famous RSA. The number field sieve method (NFS) [LLP+90] is the best algorithm for this problem. In fact, a 663-bit integer was factored by NFS recently, which is a current record of the factorization [RSA200]. NFS has 4 major steps, the polynomial selection step, the Relation Finding (RF) step or the sieving step, the Linear Algebra (LA) step, and the final step. Among them, RF and LA steps are theoretically and experimentally dominant steps. Because of these steps, factoring 1024-bit integers is considered infeasible in next 10 years (by similar approaches).

In order to overcome the difficulty, ASIC-based dedicated factoring devices have been studied actively. In 2001, Bernstein employed a sorting algorithm

---

* A part of this work is financially supported by a consignment research from the National Institute of Information and Communications Technology (NICT), Japan.

J. Song, T. Kwon, and M. Yung (Eds.): WISA 2005, LNCS 3786, pp. 232–242, 2006.

for LA step with standard ASIC architectures [Ber01]. Then Lenstra-Shamir-Tomlinson-Tromer enhanced the device by using a routing algorithm [LST+02]. Furthermore, the design is substantially improved by Geiselmann-Steinwandt [GS03b]. On the other hand, Geiselmann-Steinwandt applied these algorithms to RF step, and proposed two designs DSH [GS03a] and YASD [GS04]. Shamir-Tromer improved an optical sieving device TWINKLE [Sha99] into a novel ASIC-based device TWIRL [ST03]. Both YASD and TWIRL handle RF step corresponding to 768-bit integers, properties are quite different: the speed of TWIRL is about 6.3 times faster than YASD, but required circuit area of YASD is smaller than that of TWIRL. Recently, Franke-Kleinjung-Parr-Pelzl-Priplata-Stahlke proposed a challenging device SHARK for RF step based on the lattice sieving [FKP+05]. From these contributions, it is expected that the linear algebra step is easily proceeded compared to the relation finding step in factoring large integers.

A purpose of this paper is to analyze the routing algorithm used in some devices [LST+02, GS04], since Geiselmann-Köpfer-Steinwandt-Tromer constructed a "livelock" example in which the routing algorithm falls into an infinite loop [GKS+05]. We show possible alternatives for packet exchanging rules in the routing. Although we have no theoretic proof of the termination, experimental results show the availability of these alternatives. Especially, some of our proposed alternatives terminate for the livelock examples. We also propose an improvement on the routing algorithm for RF step, namely YASD [GS04], to use a sub-torus structure, which possibly establishes two times speed-up.

This paper is organized as follows: in section 2, we briefly introduce the clockwise transposition routing, and analyze the packet exchanging rules in section 3. Section 4 shows our experimental results. We also propose an improvement on YASD in section 5.

2   Preliminaries

In some factoring devices for both the relation finding step and the linear algebra step in NFS, the clockwise transposition routing algorithm on a mesh is used as a key technique. This section briefly introduces the clockwise transposition routing [LST+02, GKS+05].

2.1   Clockwise Transposition Routing

A *mesh* is a set of $m \times m$ processors (called *nodes*) in a two-dimensional network. Each node is connected to its upper, right, lower, and left nodes (if exist) and is able to hold a *packet*, a pairwise data of a value and a target node (to be routed) or NIL, and exchanges packets to its one of the neighbors. When a packet is reached its target node, the data value is took into the node and the packet is updated to NIL. For a given mesh filled with packets, a purpose of the routing is to deliver all packets to their target nodes. Since we are interested in the behavior of packets, we omit describing data values in the packets. Moreover, for simplicity, we identify a node in the i-th row and the j-th column as (i, j) ($0 \le i, j < m$).

Table 1. Clockwise transposition routing

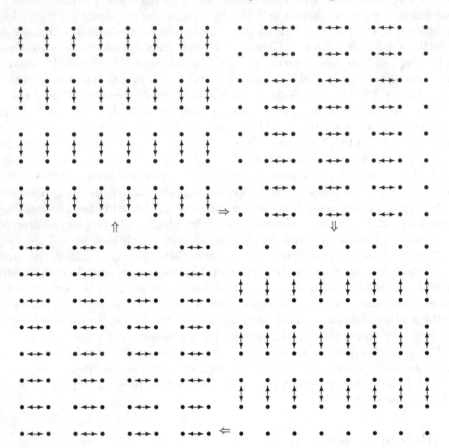

The clockwise transposition [LST+02] routes packets in a mesh. The algorithm is proceeded by a repetition of the following 4 steps until all packets are delivered to their target nodes (also see Table 1), where t denotes the time:

$t \equiv 0$ **(mod 4)** For every column j and odd row i, a node (i, j) compares and exchanges packets to its upper node $(i - 1, j)$ (if exist).

$t \equiv 1$ **(mod 4)** For every row i and odd column j, a node (i, j) compares and exchanges packets to its right node $(i, j + 1)$ (if exist).

$t \equiv 2$ **(mod 4)** For every column j and odd row i, a node (i, j) compares and exchanges packets to its lower node $(i + 1, j)$ (if exist).

$t \equiv 3$ **(mod 4)** For every row i and odd column j, a node (i, j) compares and exchanges packets to its left node $(i, j - 1)$ (if exist).

Compared directions changes in a "clockwise" manner for nodes in odd rows and odd columns. Here, the packet exchanging is ruled by the "farthest-first exchange" [LST+02]. Details of the rules are discussed in the following sections.

It is claimed that the algorithm terminates in $2m$ steps with high probability [LST+02]. However, there is no theoretic proof whether the clockwise transposition terminates in finite steps or not. In fact, Geiselmann et al. constructed a concrete "livelock" example in which the algorithm falls into an infinite loop with a period $4m$ [GKS+05]. However, such exceptional cases are very rare in factoring so that we can expect the termination of the algorithm in practice.

2.2 Torus

In [GS04], Geiselmann-Steinwandt added a torus structure into the mesh for RF step: the leftmost nodes are connected to the rightmost nodes and the uppermost nodes are connected to the lowermost nodes. In this structure, since the maximum distance from a node to its target becomes half, the clockwise transposition only requires reduced steps. This structure is also applicable to LA step [GKS+05]. In the followings, a mesh with this torus structure is described as a torus. Strongly note that the wiring problem for realizing the torus structure is not serious in practice [GS04, GKS+05].

3 Packet Exchange

This section analyzes packet exchanging rules for the clockwise transposition routing. The rule is very naive in terms of that the termination of the algorithm depends on many factors including the exchanging rule and initial data of packets. In addition, the beginning step also has an effect on the termination. We denote a target node of a node (i, j) as $p(i, j)$ in the followings.

3.1 Farthest-First Rule

The packet exchanging rule for the clockwise transposition routing is described as follows [GKS+05]: suppose we are comparing two nodes (i, j) and $(i, j + 1)$ horizontally. We exchange packets when

- $p(i, j) = \text{NIL}$ and $j + 1 > j_1$
- $p(i, j + 1) = \text{NIL}$ and $j_0 > j$
- $p(i, j), p(i, j + 1) \neq \text{NIL}$ and $j_0 \geq j_1$

where $p(i, j) = (i_0, j_0)$, $p(i, j + 1) = (i_1, j_1)$ if they are not NIL. The 3rd rule is described as the "farthest-first along the direction" rule [GKS+05]. For vertical cases, the similar rule is easily established. Note that in the original rule [LST+02], the 3rd condition was given as "$j_0 > j_1$". However, this condition does not work well for the livelock and the pathology examples described in the next section.

3.2 Livelock and Pathology Examples

Geiselmann et al. constructed a livelock in which the routing algorithm fails into an finite loop with a period $4m$, and a pathology for which the routing algorithm requires more than $2m$ steps on an $m \times m$ mesh [GKS+05]. The livelock and

Table 2. The livelock and the pathology example [GKS+05]

Livelock ($m = 4$)				Pathology ($m = 4$)			
0	1	2	3	0	1	2	3
0 (3,0) (2,0) (1,0) (0,0)				0 (0,0) (1,0) (2,0) (3,0)			
1 (3,1) (2,1) (1,1) (0,1)				1 (0,1) (1,1) (2,1) (3,1)			
2 (3,2) (2,2) (1,2) (0,2)				2 (0,2) (1,2) (2,2) (3,2)			
3 (3,3) (2,3) (1,3) (0,3)				3 (0,3) (1,3) (2,3) (3,3)			

the pathology for $m = 4$ are in Table 2. In fact, the routing actually falls into a $4m$-step loop for the livelock.

As we have mentioned, the clockwise transposition is naive: for the livelock example, the algorithm terminates if we change the first step from 'upper' procedure to other procedures.

Treatments for such livelock cases differs in RF step and LA step. In RF step, packets in an infinite loop can be omitted since the step does not require all packets [GS04]. However, on the other hand, in LA step, any omission is not permitted. Thus Geiselmann et al. proposed additional circuits to treat such cases [GKS+05].

3.3   Exchanging Rule in Torus

In order to apply the clockwise transposition in the torus, the exchanging rule should be modified. Geiselmann et al. proposed the following algorithm [GKS+05]: before the routing, search the shortest paths of all packets to their target nodes. If the path crosses the borders (i.e. wires between the leftmost and the rightmost nodes, or the uppermost and the lowermost nodes) add (subtract) m to (from) corresponding addresses of target nodes. Then apply the same exchanging rule as before. However, this modification does not solve the termination problem either theoretically nor experimentally. Thus we would like to explore other possible rules with keeping the "farthest-first" property.

3.4   Rephrasing Exchanging Rule

In order to use the clockwise transposition routing in the factoring devices, exchanging rules without any livelocks are required. Thus we start from rephrasing the previous "farthest-first rule" by a 1-dimensional ℓ_0 distance function.

Suppose we are comparing two nodes (i, j) and $(i, j + 1)$ with their target nodes being non-NIL, namely $p(i, j) = (i_0, j_0)$, $p(i, j + 1) = (i_1, j_1)$. Intuitively, the farthest-first rule along rows should be described as

1. $|j_1 - (j + 1)| > |j_0 - j|$ and $|j_1 - (j + 1)| \geq |j_1 - j|$, or
2. $|j_0 - j| > |j_1 - (j + 1)|$ and $|j_0 - j| \geq |j_0 - (j + 1)|$.

However, and interestingly, these conditions are not equivalent to the 3rd condition $j_0 \geq j_1$. In fact, we have the following proposition, which is a beginning of our discussion. All proofs of the following propositions are omitted, since they are obtained by elementary arithmetics.

Proposition 1. *Suppose a node (i, j) has a packet with its target node (i_0, j_0) and a node $(i, j+1)$ has a packet with its target node (i_1, j_1). Then the following "farthest-first along the compared direction" rule*

1. $|j_1 - (j+1)| > |j_0 - j|$ and $|j_1 - (j+1)| \geq |j_1 - j|$, or
2. $|j_0 - j| > |j_1 - (j+1)|$ and $|j_0 - j| \geq |j_0 - (j+1)|$,

is equivalent to $j_0 \geq j_1$ and $j_0 + j_1 \neq 2j+1$. Especially, the rule is not equivalent to the condition $j_0 \geq j_1$.

On the other hand, the following very similar conditions are not equivalent to the 3rd condition $j_0 \geq j_1$ either.

Proposition 2. *In the same assumption to Proposition 1, conditions*

1. $|j_1 - (j+1)| \geq |j_0 - j|$ and $|j_1 - (j+1)| \geq |j_1 - j|$, or
2. $|j_0 - j| \geq |j_1 - (j+1)|$ and $|j_0 - j| \geq |j_0 - (j+1)|$,

are equivalent to $j_0 + 1 \geq j_1$. Especially, the rule is not equivalent to the condition $j_0 \geq j_1$.

In proposition 1, 2, distances between nodes are measured by the ℓ_0-distance, namely absolute values of the difference of coordinate values. By changing the distance function, we have other possible alternatives for the "farthest-first" rule as follows:

(a) 1. $d((i, j+1), p(i, j+1)) > d((i, j), p(i, j))$ and $d((i, j+1), p(i, j+1)) \geq d((i, j), p(i, j+1))$, or
     2. $d((i, j), p(i, j)) > d((i, j+1), p(i, j+1))$ and $d((i, j), p(i, j)) \geq d((i, j+1), p(i, j))$,
(a') 1. $d((i, j+1), p(i, j+1)) \geq d((i, j), p(i, j))$ and $d((i, j+1), p(i, j+1)) \geq d((i, j), p(i, j+1))$, or
     2. $d((i, j), p(i, j)) \geq d((i, j+1), p(i, j+1))$ and $d((i, j), p(i, j)) \geq d((i, j+1), p(i, j))$.

By a definition $d((i, j), \text{NIL}) = 0$, the above rules include NIL cases. Thus we can describe the exchanging rule mathematically. Moreover, by applying other distance functions $d(\cdot, \cdot)$, other exchanging rules can be obtained. In the followings, we use 4 distance functions on an $m \times m$ mesh or torus:

- 1-dimensional distance in a mesh: $d_1^m((i, j), (i', j')) = |i - i'|$ or $|j - j'|$
- 1-dimensional distance in a mesh: $d_1^t((i, j), (i', j')) = \min(|i - i'|, m - |i - i'|)$ or $\min(|j - j'|, m - |j - j'|)$
- 2-dimensional distance in a mesh: $d_2^m((i, j), (i', j')) = |i - i'| + |j - j'|$
- 2-dimensional distance in a mesh: $d_2^t((i, j), (i', j')) = \min(|i - i'|, m - |i - i'|) + \min(|j - j'|, m - |j - j'|)$

Note that $0 \leq d_1^m(\cdot, \cdot) < m$, $0 \leq d_1^t(\cdot, \cdot) < m/2$, $0 \leq d_2^m(\cdot, \cdot) < 2m$, and $0 \leq d_2^t(\cdot, \cdot) < m$.

Let us consider other possible way to rephrase the 3rd condition $j_0 \geq j_1$. In Proposition 1 and 2, the additional conditions $j_0 + j_1 = 2j + 1$ and $j_1 = j_0 + 1$ imply $d^{\text{before}} = d^{\text{after}}$, where $d^{\text{before}} = d((i,j), p(i,j)) + d((i,j+1), p(i,j+1)) = d((i,j)$, $d^{\text{after}} = d((i,j), p(i,j+1)) + d((i,j+1), p(i,j))$. By treating this case separately, we have the following satisfactory rule equivalent to $j_0 \geq j_1$ for $d = d_1^{\text{m}}$.

(b) 1. $d^{\text{before}} > d^{\text{after}}$, or
     2. $d^{\text{before}} = d^{\text{after}}$ and $d((i,j+1), p(i,j+1)) > d((i,j), p(i,j))$ and $d((i,j+1), p(i,j+1)) \geq d((i,j), p(i,j+1))$, or
     3. $d^{\text{before}} = d^{\text{after}}$ and $d((i,j), p(i,j)) > d((i,j+1), p(i,j+1))$ and $d((i,j), p(i,j)) \geq d((i,j+1), p(i,j))$.

We also have the following similar conditions:

(b') 1. $d^{\text{before}} > d^{\text{after}}$, or
      2. $d^{\text{before}} = d^{\text{after}}$ and $d((i,j+1), p(i,j+1)) \geq d((i,j), p(i,j))$ and $d((i,j+1), p(i,j+1)) \geq d((i,j), p(i,j+1))$, or
      3. $d^{\text{before}} = d^{\text{after}}$ and $d((i,j), p(i,j)) \geq d((i,j+1), p(i,j+1))$ and $d((i,j), p(i,j)), \geq d((i,j+1), p(i,j))$.

Consequently, we obtain 4 mathematical descriptions of the "farthest-first" rule and 4 distance functions, namely 16 possible exchanging rules. Since we have no theoretic proofs, terminations are not assured. However, experimental results and practical availability will be shown in the next section.

4 Experimental Results

This section shows experimental results of some packet exchanging rules. In the previous section, we established 4 alternative exchanging rules and 4 distance functions, namely 16 rules. With these rules plus the original 2 rules, we compute required steps in some cases.

Firstly, we routined the livelock example under these exchanging rules and with changing the initial step. Numerical results are summarized in Table 3 ($m = 4$) and Table 4 ($m = 8$), where 'u', 'r', 'lo', and 'le' stands for upper, right, lower, and left step as an initial step, respectively, and 'NT' stands for non-termination. As described in [GKS+05], the naiveness of the algorithm can be observed. For example, changing an initial step has an effect of the termination. Interestingly, beginning from 'u' inclines to fall into 'NT'. Compared to these results, the number of NT seems more in Table 3. But this may be because of the smallness of m and does not show any algorithmic defects.

Next, we routined a mesh filled with m^2 non-NIL packets with $m = 8$ (Table 5), and m^2 non-NIL packets with $m = 8$. Of course, although these are just examples, we can observe some properties. First, the original rule with d_1^{m} works well in a sense that it does not fall into 'NT'. Second, rules (a), (a') work worse than (b), (b'). Moreover, an effect of the torus structure is observed. In these examples, rules (b), (b') combined with distance functions d_1^{t}, d_2^{t} work better than other cases. However, changing initial step seems to have less effect here.

Table 3. Required steps for the livelock example ($m = 4$)

Distance Function	Original				(a)				(a')				(b)				(b')			
	u	r	lo	le	u	r	lo	le	u	r	lo	le	u	r	lo	le	u	r	lo	le
d_1^m	NT	15	14	19	NT	15	14	19	NT	23	22	21	NT	15	14	19	NT	15	14	21
d_2^m		—			NT	NT	NT	NT	21	16	20	18	38	NT	NT	NT	17	12	19	15
d_1^t	NT	NT	NT	NT	NT	12	11	14	NT	23	7	25	NT	15	7	17	NT	16	7	18
d_2^t		—			NT	NT	NT	NT	NT	11	7	13	NT	NT	NT	NT	NT	16	7	18

Table 4. Required steps for the livelock example ($m = 8$)

Distance Function	Original				(a)				(a')				(b)				(b')			
	u	r	lo	le	u	r	lo	le	u	r	lo	le	u	r	lo	le	u	r	lo	le
d_1^m	NT	42	36	38	NT	NT	NT	58	NT	NT	NT	NT	NT	42	37	41	NT	40	41	44
d_2^m		—			NT	NT	NT	NT	41	44	39	46	93	NT	NT	NT	43	44	39	43
d_1^t	NT	NT	NT	NT	NT	NT	35	NT	NT	60	NT	NT	NT	28	26	32	NT	34	26	37
d_2^t		—			62	NT	77	NT	33	32	33	37	40	NT	31	NT	25	31	21	26

Table 5. Required steps for a mesh with m^2 non-NIL packets ($m = 8$)

Distance Function	Original				(a)				(a')				(b)				(b')			
	u	r	lo	le	u	r	lo	le	u	r	lo	le	u	r	lo	le	u	r	lo	le
d_1^m	24	22	21	20	45	40	NT	NT	NT	NT	43	NT	22	22	25	22	31	24	22	26
d_2^m		—			NT	NT	NT	NT	30	44	33	30	39	38	28	34	31	28	28	27
d_1^t	NT	NT	NT	NT	NT	36	39	NT	NT	NT	NT	NT	19	23	18	21	20	22	21	23
d_2^t		—			NT	NT	NT	NT	25	34	29	27	23	41	30	19	21	22	22	20

Table 6. Required steps for a mesh with $m^2/8$ non-NIL packets ($m = 8$)

Distance Function	Original				(a)				(a')				(b)				(b')			
	u	r	lo	le	u	r	lo	le	u	r	lo	le	u	r	lo	le	u	r	lo	le
d_1^m	16	17	17	16	NT	18	19	20	NT	NT	NT	NT	16	17	17	16	16	17	17	16
d_2^m		—			NT	18	19	15	16	20	19	20	16	17	17	16	16	17	17	16
d_1^t	NT	NT	NT	NT	NT	NT	17	11	NT	NT	35	NT	11	10	10	12	11	12	10	12
d_2^t		—			NT	NT	17	13	11	10	12	12	11	11	10	12	11	12	11	12

5   Improvements

The clockwise transposition is used for both RF and LA steps [LST+02, GS04]. However, the efficiency of RF step case, YASD, is not compatible to TWIRL: YASD is 6.3 times slower than TWIRL without considering the frequency and 3.2 times with considering the frequency. This section proposes an improvement on YASD, which establishes two times speed-up.

5.1   Structure of YASD

First, we describe procedures in RF step. Suppose we are going to find relations (a, b) from a given interval $[a_0, a_0 + S - 1]$ and a fixed value b (here we assume

a_0 being even without loss of generality), where a pair (a, b) is called a relation if it satisfies three conditions (i) $\gcd(a, b) = 1$, (ii) $F_r(a, b)$ is B_r-smooth for a given multivariable polynomial $F_r(x, y)$ and an integer B_r, and (iii) $F_a(a, b)$ is B_a-smooth for a given multivariable polynomial $F_a(x, y)$ and an integer B_a. An integer x is described as B-smooth if x is a product of prime integers smaller than B. Since $\log x \approx \sum_{p < B, \; p|x} \log p$, the sieving method for RF step proceeds as follows: first, we prepare S registers $s[a_i]$ $(a_i \in [a_0, a_0 + S - 1])$. For each prime $p < B$, find the smallest integer $\bar{a} \in [a_0, a_0 + S - 1]$ such that $F(\bar{a}, b) = 0$ (mod p), here $F(x, y) = F_r(x, y)$ or $F_a(x, y)$, and $B = B_r$ or B_a. Since the polynomial $F(x, y)$ has a property that

$$F(a, b) = 0 \quad (\text{mod } p) \quad \Rightarrow \quad F(a + p, b) = 0 \quad (\text{mod } p),$$

we set $s[\bar{a}] \leftarrow s[\bar{a}] + \log p$, $s[\bar{a} + p] \leftarrow s[\bar{a} + p] + \log p, \ldots$. Finally, pick up a's such that $s[a] \approx \log F(a, b)$, which can be treated as candidates as the relations.

YASD is a dedicated factoring device for RF step by using the clockwise transposition [GS04]. Each node has three parts, the main part, the mesh part, and the memory part. The main part generates pairs (a, p) such that $F(a, b) = 0$ (mod p) as packets and these packets are sent to the mesh part. The mesh part proceeds the clockwise routing as in the previous sections. When a packet reaches the target node, it is delivered to the memory part which consists of u registers $s[a_1], \ldots, s[a_1 + u - 1]$ and the log value $\log p$ is accumulated to the corresponding register $s[a]$. Note that there is no need to hold all primes in all nodes: In fact it is sufficient to hold at least 1 node for large primes.

5.2   Use of Sub-torus

This section proposes to use sub-tori for RF step similar to for LA step proposed in [GKS+05]. For an $m \times m$ mesh, we divide nodes into 4 sets $T^{o,o}$, $T^{o,e}$, $T^{e,o}$, $T^{e,e}$, nodes in odd-rows and odd-columns, nodes in odd-rows and even-columns, nodes in even-rows and odd-columns, and nodes in even-rows and even-columns, respectively. Then, we give the torus structure to these sets. Thus we have 4 sub-tori in the mesh. Since the size of sub-tori is halved, efficient routings on these sub-tori are expected. But a problem arises: how to generate packets in which a packet with its target node being odd-odd, for example, is sent to an odd-odd node from a main part. One idea is to let 1 main part to hold 4 nodes (odd-odd, odd-even, even-odd, and even-even). Then all packets can be easily sent to the proper sub-torus. However the frequency is reduced to $1/4$. So, we do not want to change the number of main parts and nodes.

For this problem, we have an algorithmic and hardware-oriented solutions. In YASD, each prime is held by at least 1 node. We increase the frequency of each prime 4 times so that all primes can be sent to all types of sub-tori. As a drawback we require 4 times larger memory for main parts (to hold primes).

The other solution is to put a cyclic permutation buffer device between 4 main parts and 4 nodes. Let us explain in detail. First, we change the memory part so that $T^{o,o}$ has registers corresponding to $a \in [a_0, a_0 + S - 1]$ such that $a \equiv 0 \bmod 4$.

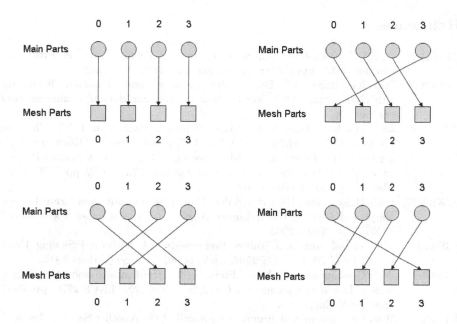

Fig. 1. Cyclic wiring between main parts and mesh parts

Similarly, $T^{o,e}$, $T^{e,o}$, $T^{e,e}$ correspond to $a \equiv 1, 2, 3 \bmod 4$. Next, we divide primes (except 2) into two sets $P_1 = \{\, p \mid p \equiv 1 \bmod 4 \,\}$ and $P_3 = \{\, p \mid p \equiv 3 \bmod 4 \,\}$. Moreover, we divide these sets into 8 sets $P_1^{(i)} = \{\, p \in P_1 \mid p \equiv i \bmod 4 \,\}$, $P_3^{(i)} = \{\, p \in P_3 \mid p \equiv i \bmod 4 \,\}$ $(i = 0, 1, 2, 3)$. The numbers of primes in these sets $P_j^{(i)}$ will be almost same. Then, suppose a main part generates packets for a prime $p \in P_1^0$ and we have $\bar{a} \in [a_0, a_0 + S - 1]$ such that $F(\bar{a}, b) = 0 \pmod{p}$ and $\bar{a} \equiv 0 \pmod{4}$, Namely the target node of this packet belongs to $T^{o,o}$. Then, since the next packet corresponds to $\bar{a} + p$, the target node of this packet belongs to $T^{o,e}$. Thus the target node of this main part will be changed in a cyclic way: $T^{o,o}$, $T^{o,e}$, $T^{e,o}$, $T^{e,e}$, $T^{o,o}, \ldots$ Moreover, 4 main parts can generate packets in this way in simultaneously (see Fig. 1). Here the cyclic permutation device can be easily implemented so that a drawback of this solution is rather small. By this improvement. we can establish the reduction about $1/2$.

6   Concluding Remarks

This paper analyzed the dedicated hardware device based on the clockwise transposition routing. First, we discussed possible alternatives for packet exchanging. Although we have no theoretic proof of the termination, experimental results show actual availability of some exchanging rules in the clockwise transposition for integer factoring. We also proposed an improvement on the routing algorithm for the relation finding step, which establishes two times speed-up.

References

[Ber01]   Daniel J. Bernstein, "Circuits for Integer Factorization: A Proposal", preprint, 2001. http://cr.yp.to/papers/nfscircuit.pdf

[RSA200]   Friedrich Bahr, M. Böhm, Jens Franke, and Thorsten Kleinjung, "RSA200", May 2005. http://www.crypto-world.com/announcements/rsa200.txt

[FKP+05]   Jens Franke, Thorsten Kleinjung, Christof Paar, Jan Pelzl, Christine Priplata, Colin Stahlke, "SHARK: A Realizable Special Hardware Sieving Device for Factoring 1024-bit Integers", *Workshop on Special Purpose hardware for Attacking Cryptographic Systems (SHARCS)*, pp.27-37, 2005. Also, to appear at *CHES 2005*.

[GKS+05]   Willi Geiselmann, Hubert Köpfer, Rainer Steinwandt, and Eran Tromer, "Improved Routing-based Linear Algebra for the Number Field Sieve", *IEEE ITCC 2005*, 2005.

[GS03a]   Willi Geiselmann and Rainer Steinwandt, "A Dedicated Sieving Hardware", *PKC 2003*, LNCS 2567, pp.254-266, Springer-Verlag, 2003.

[GS03b]   Willi Geiselmann and Rainer Steinwandt, "Hardware to Solve Sparse Systems of Linear Equations over GF(2)", *CHES 2003*, LNCS 2779, pp.51-61, Springer-Verlag, 2003.

[GS04]   Willi Geiselmann and Rainer Steinwandt, "Yet Another Sieveing Device", *CT-RSA 2004*, LNCS 2964, pp.278–291, Springer-Verlag, 2004.

[LL93]   Arjen K. Lenstra and Hendrik W. Lenstra, editors. The development of the number field sieve, Vol. 1554 of Lecture Notes in Mathematics (LNM), Springer-Verlag, 1993.

[LLP+90]   Arjen K. Lenstra, Hendrik W. Lenstra, M.S. Manasse and John M. Pollard, "The Number Field Sieve", *STOC 1990*, pp.564-572, 1990.

[LST+02]   Arjen K. Lenstra, Adi Shamir, Jim Tomlinson, and Eran Tromer, "Analysis of Bernstein's Circuit", *ASIACRYPT 2002*, LNCS 2501, pp.1–26, Springer-Verlag, 2002.

[Sha99]   Adi Shamir, "Factoring Large Numbers with the TWINKLE Device (extended abstract)", *CHES 1999*, LNCS 1717, pp.2-12, Springer-Verlag, 1999.

[ST03]   Adi Shamir and Eran Tromer, "Factoring Large Numbers with the TWIRL Device", *CRYPTO 2003*, LNCS 2729, pp.1–26, Springer-Verlag, 2003.

mCrypton – A Lightweight Block Cipher for Security of Low-Cost RFID Tags and Sensors

Chae Hoon Lim and Tymur Korkishko

Dept. of Internet Engineering, Sejong University, Korea
Samsung Advanced Institute of Technology (SAIT), Korea
chlim@sejong.ac.kr, k.tymur@samsung.com

Abstract. This paper presents a new 64-bit block cipher **mCrypton** with three key size options (64 bits, 96 bits and 128 bits), specifically designed for use in resource-constrained tiny devices, such as low-cost RFID tags and sensors. It's designed by following the overall architecture of Crypton but with redesign and simplification of each component function to enable much compact implementation in both hardware and software. A simple hardware implementation of mCrypton is also presented to demonstrate its suitability to our target applications. Our prototype implementation based on the straightforward 1 cycle/round architecture just requires about 3500 to 4100 gates for both encryption and decryption, and about 2400 to 3000 gates for encryption only (under 0.13μm CMOS technology). The result shows that the hardware complexity of mCrypton is quite well within an economic range of low-cost RFID tags and sensors. A more compact implementation under development promises that further size reduction around 30% could be achievable using the 5 cycles/round architecture.

1 Background

The ubiquitous computing paradigm pursues true elimination of time and space barriers by embedding wirelessly networked processors in everyday objects and thereby making a variety of services available to users all the time everywhere. The ubiquitous computing vision however could bring a great deal of security risks due to the ubiquity of tiny interconnected devices embedded into everyday environments [2, 11]. In particular, much research attention has been recently paid to the security and privacy issues of RFID and sensor networks [4, 9].

Traditionally, block ciphers have been used as a basic security building block for most resource-constrained applications, such as smart cards and security tokens. The same and even more compelling reasoning can apply to tiny ubiquitous devices such as low-cost RFID tags and sensors. In such resource-constrained devices it is undesirable or even impossible to implement multiple security primitives for cost reason. So a compact, hardware- and software-efficient block cipher could be the most promising candidate for security in such applications.

Design Constraints. Typical ubiquitous computing devices however impose new constraints in block cipher design due to their size and shape [11]. First of all, the chip area required for hardware implementation of a block cipher should

J. Song, T. Kwon, and M. Yung (Eds.): WISA 2005, LNCS 3786, pp. 243–258, 2006.

be small enough not to much increase the cost of ubiquitous devices due to the added security feature. For example, in the case of low-cost RFID tags, one of the most resource-scarce ubiquitous computing devices, it is estimated that security resources available to a 5 cent design may be limited to hundreds of bits of storage, roughly 500-5,000 gates [12]. Note that low-cost RFID tags only have a simple logic for data processing even without CPU, so the only way to implement a crypto algorithm would be its hardware integration into tag chips.

Another and more critical issue in tiny ubiquitous devices is the limited amount of power available. Only a small, finite amount of energy may be available through a miniature battery to the tiny processors embedded in ubiquitous computing devices such as mote-class sensors. Even more cheap devices, such as passive RFID tags, cannot be self-powered and thus should obtain energy from larger communicating devices through electromagnetic coupling. This limited power availability places a bound on the total amount of computation such devices can perform, rather than on the speed. Therefore, the most relevant performance figure here might be bits per joule rather than the traditional bits per second. In this respect, most widely-used block ciphers such as AES may not be much attractive for use in such limited computing environments.

Design Objectives and Choices. The block cipher mCrypton is designed with above new constraints in low-cost ubiquitous computing devices in mind. The goal is to design a block cipher with extreme efficiency in resource usage and power consumption, so that they can be hardware integrated or software implemented in tiny processors embedded in inexpensive everyday commodities. The design of mCrypton is based on the overall architecture of Crypton [7] (mCrypton actually stands for a miniature of Crypton and can be thought of as a 64-bit variant of Crypton with variable key sizes). The basic building blocks were redesigned to fit the block/key sizes and the overall architecture was a little bit simplified for better implementation efficiency. The key scheduling algorithm was also completely redesigned.

The main objective of designing mCrypton is to come up with a block cipher optimized for resource-constrained applications, so we decided to use the parameters of 64-bit block length and variable key lengths of 64 bits, 96 bits and 128 bits. Note that a large volume of bulk data encryption is unnecessary or even impossible in most tiny ubiquitous computing devices. Therefore, there will be no security concern with small block size and it will be a natural choice for new design of a block cipher with specific application to extremely resource-constrained devices. We also decided to provide three key size options (for minimal, moderate and standard security, respectively) for better flexibility of cost-security trade-offs. Note that production cost may be one of most critical factors in practice for large scale deployment of tiny devices such as low-cost RFID tags.

Minimizing power consumption certainly should be one of most important considerations in software/hardware design for tiny ubiquitous devices. In general, a block cipher will be more power-efficient in hardware/software implementations if it can be implemented using less amount of computing resources. So one obvious goal in designing a block cipher should be to achieve low complexity in hardware and software while providing sufficient security. Furthermore, power consumption in CMOS hardware largely depends on signal transition frequency during the processing. For example, branched signal paths may cause dynamic hazards (multiple signal transitions before being stable) due to different arrival times at a logic gate, which consumes extra power. So, from the standpoint of algorithm design, it would be preferable to make signal paths as uniform as possible and to reduce signal transition probability as possible as one can. These considerations would provide good reasons of basing our design on the overall structure of Crypton: It has a regular and quite uniform structure with its component functions efficiently implementable in both hardware and software.

Related Work. There is no published literature recognized by the authors for new design of block ciphers targeted to tiny ubiquitous devices. As a related work to RFID security, Bono et al. reported successful reverse engineering and key cracking for the secret algorithm (with only 40-bit key size) embedded in the currently circulating TI RFID tags [1]. Their work once again signifies the importance of using well-scrutinized open crypto algorithm for wide deployment of security products. As a related work to efficient implementation on RFID tags, Feldhofer et al. presented an 8-bit architecture, encryption-only mode implementation of AES for RFID authentication, which consumes about 3,600 gates and requires about 1,000 clock cycles at 100KHz for one block encryption [3].

On the other hand, the TinySec implementation experience provides valuable information on feasibility of software implementation of a block cipher in low-cost sensor nodes [5]. Implementation experiments in Mica2 mote (8 MHz 8-bit Atmel ATMEGA128L MCU with 4KB of RAM, 128 KB of flash (program space) and 4KB of EEPROM, Chipcon radio module of up to 19.2 Kbps bandwidth) showed that there was almost no performance degradation even with software implementation of RC5 in Mica2 sensor nodes. Of course, the situation may be different for sensor nodes with faster radio, such as Telos (8 MHz 16-bit TI MSP430 MCU with 4KB of RAM, 60KB of flash and 16KB of EEPROM) whose IEEE 802.15.4 radio can transmit at a much faster data rate of 250 Kbps [10].

General rule of thumb on the performance of security primitives required for sensor nodes is that one block processing should be completed in under a few byte times to avoid performance degradation due to the added cryptographic operation, where byte time refers to the time required to transmit a single byte over the radio [5]. Interestingly, Law et al. reported bench-marking data for various block ciphers on TI MSP430 MCU adopted by the Telos mote [6]. Their performance result (on speed-optimized counter mode) shows that RC5 requires $85\mu sec$ (at 8MHz) per block encryption using 5.2Kbytes of code memory, while AES requires $27\mu sec$ using 13.3Kbytes of memory. Since the byte time of Telos mote is $32\mu sec$, we can see that software implementation of cryptographic operations may be acceptable even for low-end sensor nodes. This also shows that software efficiency (in particular on low-end 8-bit and 16-bit microprocessors) should be an important consideration in designing a block cipher for ubiquitous computing security.

Notation. The following notation will be used throughout this paper:

- A 4-bit string is denoted by nibble and one byte of data is represented by two 4-bit nibbles numbered from left to right (i.e., $b = b_0\|b_1$). Similarly, one word of data consists of two bytes numbered from left to right.
- An 8-byte data consisting of 16 nibbles $\{a_0, a_1, \cdots, a_{15}\}$ is internally represented as a 4×4 nibble array as follows:

$$A = \begin{pmatrix} a_0 & a_1 & a_2 & a_3 \\ a_4 & a_5 & a_6 & a_7 \\ a_8 & a_9 & a_{10} & a_{11} \\ a_{12} & a_{13} & a_{14} & a_{15} \end{pmatrix} = \begin{pmatrix} A_r[0] \\ A_r[1] \\ A_r[2] \\ A_r[3] \end{pmatrix} = (A_c[0]A_c[1]A_c[2]A_c[3]),$$

where $A_r[i]$ and $A_c[i]$ denote the i-th row and column of A, respectively.

- For an array A, A^t denotes transposition of A.
- $X^{\ll k}$: left rotation of a 16-bit word X by k-bit positions.
- $f \circ g$: composition of functions f and g, i.e., $(f \circ g)(x) = f(g(x))$.
- $\bullet, \oplus$: bit-wise logical operations for AND and XOR, respectively.

2   Algorithm Specifications

mCrypton processes an 8-byte data block by representing it into a 4×4 nibble array as in Crypton [7]. The round transformation consists of four steps: nibble-wise substitution, column-wise bit permutation, column-to-row transposition, and then key addition. The encryption process involves 12 repetitions of the same round transformation. The decryption process can be made almost identical to the encryption process with a different key schedule.

2.1   Basic Building Blocks

Nonlinear Substitution γ. The nonlinear transformation γ consists of nibble-wise substitutions on a 4×4 nibble array using four 4-bit S-boxes, S_i ($0 \leq i \leq 3$), such that $S_2 = S_0^{-1}$ and $S_3 = S_1^{-1}$ (see Section 3.2 for details). Each component substitution function γ_i operates on the 4-nibble vector of the i-th row (or column). That is, for a 4-nibble word $a = (a_0, a_1, a_2, a_3)$

$$\gamma_i(a) = (S_i(a_0), S_{i+1}(a_1), S_{i+2}(a_2), S_{i+3}(a_3)),$$

where indices are taken modulo 4 (see Fig.1).

a_0	a_1	a_2	a_3		$S_0(a_0)$	$S_1(a_1)$	$S_2(a_2)$	$S_3(a_3)$
a_4	a_5	a_6	a_7	$\longrightarrow$	$S_1(a_4)$	$S_2(a_5)$	$S_3(a_6)$	$S_0(a_7)$
a_8	a_9	a_{10}	a_{11}		$S_2(a_8)$	$S_3(a_9)$	$S_0(a_{10})$	$S_1(a_{11})$
a_{12}	a_{13}	a_{14}	a_{15}		$S_3(a_{12})$	$S_0(a_{13})$	$S_1(a_{14})$	$S_2(a_{15})$

Fig. 1. The nibble-wise substitution γ

The transformation γ and γ^{-1} can thus be defined for 4×4 data array A by

$$\gamma(A) = (\gamma_0(A_c[0])\ \gamma_1(A_c[1])\ \gamma_2(A_c[2])\ \gamma_3(A_c[3]))$$
$$= (\gamma_0(A_r[0])\ \gamma_1(A_r[1])\ \gamma_2(A_r[2])\ \gamma_3(A_r[3]))^t$$
$$\gamma^{-1}(A) = (\gamma_2(A_c[0])\ \gamma_3(A_c[1])\ \gamma_0(A_c[2])\ \gamma_1(A_c[3]))$$
$$= (\gamma_2(A_r[0])\ \gamma_3(A_r[1])\ \gamma_0(A_r[2])\ \gamma_1(A_r[3]))^t.$$

Note that the symmetry in S-box arrangement ensures that γ/γ^{-1} and τ commute, i.e., $\tau \circ \gamma = \gamma \circ \tau$ and $\tau \circ \gamma^{-1} = \gamma^{-1} \circ \tau$ (see below the definition for τ). Obviously, we have $\gamma_i(a) = \gamma_0(a^{\lll 16-4i})^{\lll 4i}$.

Bit Permutation π. The bit permutation π bit-wise mixes each column of 4×4 array A using column permutation π_i for each column i ($0 \le i \le 3$) (Fig.2):

$$\pi(A) = (\pi_0(A_c[0])\ \pi_1(A_c[1])\ \pi_2(A_c[2])\ \pi_3(A_c[3]))$$

Each component column permutation π_i is defined for nibble columns $a = (a_0, a_1, a_2, a_3)^t$ and $b = (b_0, b_1, b_2, b_3)^t$ by

$$b = \pi_i(a) \iff b_j = \oplus_{k=0}^3 (m_{i+j+k \bmod 4} \bullet a_k),$$

where four masking nibbles m_i's are given by

$$m_0 = 1110_2,\ m_1 = 1101_2,\ m_2 = 1011_2,\ m_3 = 0111_2.$$

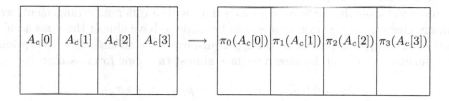

Fig. 2. The column-wise bit permutation π

Note that the π transformation is involution (i.e. $\pi = \pi^{-1}$) and satisfies the shift property: $\pi_i(a) = \pi_0(a)^{\lll 4i}$. and $\pi_i(a^{\lll 4k}) = \pi_i(a)^{\lll 16-4k}$, where cyclic shift on a column vector should be interpreted aover its row-transformed equivalent.

Column-to-Row Transposition τ. It simply moves the nibble at the (i, j)-th position to the (j, i)-th position, i.e., $B = \tau(A) \iff b_{ij} = a_{ji}$. Obviously, $\tau^{-1} = \tau$.

Key Addition σ. For a round key $K = (K[0], K[1], K[2], K[3])$, $B = \sigma_K(A)$ is defined by $B_r[i] = A_r[i] \oplus K[i]$ ($0 \le i \le 3$).

2.2 Encryption and Decryption

The encryption round transformation ρ of mCrypton consists of applying γ, π, τ and σ in sequence to the 4×4 data array. More specifically, the round functions for encryption and decryption are defined (for round key K) by

$$\rho_K = \sigma_K \circ \tau \circ \pi \circ \gamma,$$
$$\rho_K^{-1} = \gamma^{-1} \circ \pi \circ \tau \circ \sigma_K$$

For 4×4 data array A and round key K, we can express $B = \rho_K(A)$ using the component functions γ_i's and π_i's as

$$B_c[i] = \pi_i(\gamma_i(A_c[i]))^t \oplus K[i] = \pi_0(\gamma_0(A_c[i]^{\lll 16-4i}))^t \oplus K[i] \quad (0 \le i \le 3).$$

Let us define ρ_K' as $\rho_K' = \sigma_K \circ \tau \circ \pi \circ \gamma^{-1}$, i.e., the round transformation obtained by replacing γ by γ^{-1} in ρ_K, which will be used as a decryption round transformation below. Then $\rho_K'(A)$ can be similarly expressed as:

$$B_c[i] = \pi_i(\gamma_{i+2}(A_c[i]))^t \oplus K[i] = \pi_i((\gamma_i(A_c[i]^{\lll 8})^{\lll 8}))^t \oplus K[i] \quad (0 \le i \le 3)$$

Let K_e^i be the i-th encryption round key consisting of 4 words, derived from a user-supplied key K using the encryption key schedule. The encryption transformation E_K of mCrypton under key K consists of an initial key addition and 12 times repetitions of ρ and then a final output transformation. More specifically, E_K can be described as

$$E_K = \phi \circ \rho_{K_e^{12}} \circ \rho_{K_e^{11}} \circ \cdots \circ \rho_{K_e^2} \circ \rho_{K_e^1} \circ \sigma_{K_e^0},$$

where ϕ is defined by $\phi = \tau \circ \pi \circ \tau$.

Since γ^{-1} uses the same S-boxes as γ only with a different arrangement, we can imagine that decryption process can be made to have almost the same architecture as encryption process by using ϕ-transformed round keys. The decryption transformation D_K can be shown to have almost the same form as E_K:

$$D_K = \phi \circ \rho_{K_d^{12}}' \circ \rho_{K_d^{11}}' \circ \cdots \circ \rho_{K_d^2}' \circ \rho_{K_d^1}' \circ \sigma_{K_d^0},$$

where the decryption round keys are defined by

$$K_d^{r-i} = \phi(K_e^i) \quad \text{for} \ \ 0 \le i \le 12.$$

Note that the output transformation ϕ can be incorporated into the final round as $\phi \circ \rho_{K_e^{12}} = \tau \circ \pi \circ \tau \circ (\sigma_{K_e^{12}} \circ \tau \circ \pi \circ \gamma) = \sigma_{K_d^0} \circ \tau \circ \gamma$.

2.3 Key Scheduling

mCrypton supports three key sizes: 64 bits, 96 bits and 128 bits. The 64-bit key size may certainly be not enough for adequate security in general computing environments, but it may provide still good security in resource-constrained, cost-driven applications such as low-cost RFID tags. On the other hand, with

96-bit keys we will be able to achieve moderate security in most applications. In general, however, it would be more desirable to use the current standard key size of 128 bits in any application if there is no severe restriction on available resources.

The key scheduling algorithm for mCrypton consist of two stages: round key generation through nonlinear S-box transformation and then key variables update through simple rotations (word-wise rotation and bitwise rotation within word). The simple linear key variables update makes it easy to carry out backward processing for decryption key schedule and the nonlinear round key generation together with linear update of key variables in each round provides the basis for the security against various attacks on key scheduling algorithms.

Let $K = \{K[i]\}_{i=0}^{t-1} = (K[0], K[1] \cdots K[t-1])$ be the user key ($t = 4, 6, 8$ for key sizes of 64, 96, 128 bits, respectively), where $K[i]$ represents the i-th 16-bit key word in K. Let $C[i]$ be the round constant for round i (we will regard the initial key addition as round 0 for notational purpose). Each round constant $C[i]$ consists of four identical nibbles, i.e., $C[i] = 0\mathtt{x}c_i c_i c_i c_i$, where c_i is generated by x^i in $\mathrm{GF}(2^4)$ defined by the irreducible polynomial $f(x) = x^4 + x + 1$ (That is, $c_0 = 1, c_1 = 2, \cdots, c_4 = 3, c_5 = 6, \cdots$, etc.).

Specific key schedules for each key size are now presented in the following. Here $U = \{U[i]\}_{i=0}^{t-1}$ and $V = \{V[i]\}_{i=0}^{t-1}$ will be used as key registers for state update in encryption and decryption key schedules, respectively. Note that $\phi_i = \tau \circ \pi_i \circ \tau$ ($0 \leq i \leq 3$). The S-box operation on a word in the key schedule is performed in nibble-wise with the same S-box S_0, i.e., for $a = (a_0, a_1, a_2, a_3)$, $S(a) = (S_0(a_0), S_0(a_1), S_0(a_2), S_0(a_3))$. We also use four masking words M_i to take the i-th nibble from word, i.e., $M_0 = 0\mathtt{xf000}$, $M_1 = 0\mathtt{x0f00}$, $M_2 = 0\mathtt{x00f0}$, $M_3 = 0\mathtt{x000f}$.

Key Schedule for 64-Bit Keys

– Encryption round keys: The key register U is first initialized with K and then encryption round keys are computed for round $r = 0, 1, \cdots, 12$ as:

$$T \leftarrow S(U[0]) \oplus C[r], \quad T_i \leftarrow T \bullet M_i \ (0 \leq i \leq 3),$$
$$K_e^r \leftarrow (U[1] \oplus T_0, U[2] \oplus T_1, U[3] \oplus T_2, U[0] \oplus T_3)$$
$$U \leftarrow (U[1], U[2], U[3], U[0]^{\lll 3})$$

– Decryption round keys: The key register V is first initialized as

$$V \leftarrow (K[0]^{\lll 9}, K[1]^{\lll 9}, K[2]^{\lll 9}, K[3]^{\lll 9}).$$

Then decryption round keys are successively computed as follows: for round $r = 0, 1, \cdots, 12$,

$$T \leftarrow S(V[0]) \oplus C[12 - r], \quad T_i \leftarrow T \bullet M_i \ (0 \leq i \leq 3),$$
$$K_d^r \leftarrow (\phi_0(V[1] \oplus T_0), \phi_1(V[2] \oplus T_1), \phi_2(V[3] \oplus T_2), \phi_3(V[0] \oplus T_3))$$
$$V \leftarrow (V[3]^{\lll 13}, V[0], V[1], V[2])$$

Key Schedule for 96-Bit Keys

-   Encryption round keys: The key register U is first initialized with the user key K and encryption round keys are successively computed as follows: for round $r = 0, 1, \cdots, 12$,

$$T \leftarrow S(U[0]) \oplus C[r], \quad T_i \leftarrow T \bullet M_i \ (0 \le i \le 3),$$
$$K_e^r \leftarrow (U[1] \oplus T_0, U[2] \oplus T_1, U[3] \oplus T_2, U[4] \oplus T_3)$$
$$U \leftarrow (U[5], U[0]^{\lll 3}, U[1], U[2], U[3]^{\lll 8}, U[4])$$

-   Decryption round keys: The key register V is first initialized as

$$V \leftarrow (K[0]^{\lll 6}, K[1]^{\lll 6}, K[2]^{\lll 6}, K[3]^{\lll 6}, K[4]^{\lll 6}, K[5]^{\lll 6}),$$

and decryption round keys are successively computed as follows: for round $r = 0, 1, \cdots, 12$,

$$T \leftarrow S(V[0]) \oplus C[12 - r], \quad T_i \leftarrow T \bullet M_i \ (0 \le i \le 3),$$
$$K_d^r \leftarrow (\phi_0(V[1] \oplus T_0), \phi_1(V[2] \oplus T_1), \phi_2(V[3] \oplus T_2), \phi_3(V[4] \oplus T_3))$$
$$V \leftarrow (V[1]^{\lll 13}, V[2], V[3], V[4]^{\lll 8}, V[5], V[0])$$

Key Schedule for 128-Bit Keys

-   Encryption round keys: The key register U is first initialized with the user key K and encryption round keys are successively computed as follows: for round $r = 0, 1, \cdots, 12$,

$$T \leftarrow S(U[0]) \oplus C[r], \quad T_i \leftarrow T \bullet M_i \ (0 \le i \le 3),$$
$$K_e^r \leftarrow (U[1] \oplus T_0, U[2] \oplus T_1, U[3] \oplus T_2, U[4] \oplus T_3)$$
$$U \leftarrow (U[5], U[6], U[7], U[0]^{\lll 3}, U[1], U[2], U[3], U[4]^{\lll 8})$$

-   Decryption round keys: The key register V is first initialized as

$$(V[0], V[1], \cdots, V[7]) \leftarrow (K[4]^{\lll 3}, K[5]^{\lll 14}, K[6]^{\lll 3}, K[7]^{\lll 14},$$
$$K[0]^{\lll 14}, K[1]^{\lll 3}, K[2]^{\lll 14}, K[3]^{\lll 3}),$$

and decryption round keys are successively computed as follows: for round $r = 0, 1, \cdots, 12$,

$$T \leftarrow S(V[0]) \oplus C[12 - r], \quad T_i \leftarrow T \bullet M_i \ (0 \le i \le 3),$$
$$K_d^r \leftarrow (\phi_0(V[1] \oplus T_0), \phi_1(V[2] \oplus T_1), \phi_2(V[3] \oplus T_2), \phi_3(V[4] \oplus T_3))$$
$$V \leftarrow (V[3]^{\lll 13}, V[4], V[5], V[6], V[7]^{\lll 8}, V[0], V[1], V[2]).$$

3   Security Analysis

3.1   Diffusion Property of Linear Transformation

First note that it suffices to consider any one component transformation π_i of π to examine the diffusion property of π, since π acts on each column independently. It is also easy to see that any column vector with n ($n < 4$) nonzero nibbles is transformed by π_i into a column vector with at least $4 - n$ nonzero nibbles (this number 4 is called as the diffusion order of π_i). This is due to the operation of exclusive-or sum in π. More important is that such input vectors giving minimum diffusion take only a very small fraction of all possible inputs due to the masked bit permutation.

Let us examine in more detail the set of 16-bit numbers giving minimal diffusion. For this, we define two sets of 4-bit values, Ω_x and Ω_y, as

$$\Omega_x = \{0x1, 0x2, 0x4, 0x8\}, \quad \Omega_y = \{0x5, 0xa\} \cup \Omega_x.$$

Let I_j be a set of input vectors with j nonzero nibbles which are transformed by π_i into output vectors with $4 - j$ nonzero nibbles. Then all possible 16-bit values with minimum diffusion can be obtained as:

$$I_1 = \{(x,0,0,0)^t, (0,x,0,0)^t, (0,0,x,0)^t, (0,0,0,x)^t \mid x \in \Omega_x\},$$
$$I_2 = \{(x,x,0,0)^t, (0,x,x,0)^t, (0,0,x,x)^t, (x,0,0,x)^t \mid x \in \Omega_x\},$$
$$I_2^* = \{(y,0,y,0)^t, (0,y,0,y)^t \mid y \in \Omega_y\},$$
$$I_3 = \{(0,x,x,x)^t, (x,0,x,x)^t, (x,x,0,x)^t, (x,x,x,0)^t \mid x \in \Omega_x\}.$$

Then, it is easy to see that an element in I_j is transformed by π_i into some element in I_{4-j} depending on the nonzero value x. The set I_2^*, containing two separated nonzero nibbles, is somewhat special: it has 12 elements and is closed under π_i. In summary,

$$a \in I_j \Rightarrow \pi_i(a) \in I_{4-j} \text{ for } j = 1,2,3,$$
$$a \in I_2^* \Rightarrow \pi_i(a) \in I_2^*.$$

Type-1	Type-2	Type-3	Type-4
x 0 0 0 0 0 0 0 0 0 0 0 0 0 0 0	x 0 0 0 x 0 0 0 0 0 0 0 0 0 0 0	x 0 0 0 0 0 0 0 x 0 0 0 0 0 0 0	x 0 x 0 0 0 0 0 x 0 x 0 0 0 0 0
⇓	⇓	⇓	⇓
x x x 0 0 0 0 0 0 0 0 0 0 0 0 0	x 0 0 x 0 0 0 0 0 0 0 0 0 0 0 0	x 0 x 0 0 0 0 0 0 0 0 0 0 0 0 0	x 0 x 0 0 0 0 0 x 0 x 0 0 0 0 0
⇓	⇓	⇓	⇓
x 0 x x x 0 x x x 0 x x 0 0 0 0	0 x x x 0 0 0 0 0 0 0 0 0 x x x	x 0 x x 0 0 0 0 x 0 x x 0 0 0 0	0 x 0 x 0 0 0 0 0 x 0 x 0 0 0 0
⇓	⇓	⇓	⇓
x 0 0 0 0 0 0 0 x 0 0 0 x 0 0 0	0 0 0 0 0 x x 0 0 x x 0 0 x x 0	0 x 0 x 0 0 0 0 0 x 0 x 0 x 0 x	0 0 0 0 x 0 x 0 0 0 0 0 x 0 x 0

Fig. 3. Examples of active nibble propagation in each diffusion type (x : active nibble)

Since $|I_1| = |I_2| = |I_3| = 16$ and $|I_2^*| = 12$, we can see that there are only 60 vectors with minimum diffusion. Observe that the nonzero nibbles in each input vector should have the same value to achieve minimum diffusion. Also note that the two values in $\Omega_y - \Omega_x$ can only occur in the set I_2^*.

Now let us examine the diffusion effect of $\tau \circ \pi$ through consecutive rounds by assuming that in each round the S-box output can take any desired value, irrespective of the input value. This assumption is to maximally take into account the probabilistic nature of S-box transformation without details of the S-box characteristics. Since it suffices to consider worst-case propagations, we only examine inputs with 1, 2, or 3 nonzero nibbles in any one column vector of a 4×4 nibble array, say the first column. The result is depicted in Fig.3. The sum of the number of nonzero nibbles throughout the evolution is of great importance to ensure resistance against differential and linear cryptanalysis(DC/LC). It is easy to see that the number of nonzero nibbles per round is repeated with period 4 and their sum up to round 8 is at least 32.

3.2 S-Boxes Construction and Their Property

The maximum characteristic and linear approximation probabilities for an $n \times n$ S-box S (δ_S and λ_S for short) can be defined as follows. Let X and Y be the set of all possible 2^n inputs/outputs of S, respectively. Then δ_S and λ_S are defined by

$$\delta_S \stackrel{def}{=} \max_{\Delta x \neq 0, \Delta y} \frac{\#\{x \in X | S(x) \oplus S(x \oplus \Delta x) = \Delta y\}}{2^n},$$

$$\lambda_S \stackrel{def}{=} \max_{\Gamma x, \Gamma y \neq 0} \left(\frac{|\#\{x \in X | x \bullet \Gamma x = S(x) \bullet \Gamma y\} - 2^{n-1}|}{2^{n-1}} \right)^2.$$

The nonlinear transformation adopted in mCrypton is substitution using four 4×4 S-boxes, S_i ($i = 0, 1, 2, 3$) such that $S_0^{-1} = S_2$ and $S_1^{-1} = S_3$. These 4-bit S-boxes were searched for over some limited space of good 4-bit permutations produced by field inversion and affine transformation in $GF(2^4)$ (actually in $GF((2^2)^2)$, i.e., $x \rightarrow ax^{-1} + b$, $a, b \in GF((2^2)^2)$. The main selection criteria is that the number of high-probability difference pairs (selection patterns, resp.) in the resulting S-boxes should be as small as possible when the input is restricted to the minimal diffusion set Ω_y. This is to ensure that high-probability differences/selection patterns should be more rapidly diffused by linear transformations and that it should be more difficult to form a chain of high-probability

Table 1. The selected 4×4 S-boxes

	0	1	2	3	4	5	6	7	8	9	10	11	12	13	14	15
S_0	4	15	3	8	13	10	12	0	11	5	7	14	2	6	1	9
S_1	1	12	7	10	6	13	5	3	15	11	2	0	8	4	9	14
S_2	7	14	12	2	0	9	13	10	3	15	5	8	6	4	11	1
S_3	11	0	10	7	13	6	4	2	12	14	3	9	1	5	15	8

S-box characteristics/linear approximations through consecutive rounds. Table 1 shows the four 4-bit S-boxes selected.

The inversion function in $GF(2^4)$ is well-known to be differentially 4-uniform and have the nonlinearity of 2^{-1}, so the characteristic/linear probabilities of the S-boxes are limited to at most $\delta_{S_i} = \frac{4}{16} = 2^{-2}$ and $\lambda_{S_i} = (\frac{4}{8})^2 = 2^{-2}$. More importantly, if the input is restricted to the minimum diffusion set Ω_y, the maximum entry value in DC/LC tables is at most 2. So, for the best-case analysis of DC and LC, we define these probabilities as

$$p_d \stackrel{\text{def}}{=} \delta_{S_i}^{\Omega_y} = \frac{2}{16} = 2^{-3}, \quad p_l \stackrel{\text{def}}{=} \lambda_{S_i}^{\Omega_y} = (\frac{2}{8})^2 = 2^{-4}.$$

3.3 Differential/Linear Cryptanalysis

The complexity of DC and LC is completely determined by the number of active S-boxes involved and their characteristic/linear approximation probabilities. Since the number of active S-boxes involved in any 8-round characteristic/linear approximation is at least 32, we can obtain the most rough upper bound for the best 8-round characteristic/linear approximation probability as $(2^{-2})^{32} = 2^{-64}$ without details of the S-box characteristic/nonlinear properties.

However, the minimum number of active S-boxes can be obtained only for the difference pairs/selection patterns in the minimum diffusion set and the best S-box characteristic/linear approximation probabilities that can be achieved for the values in the minimum diffusion set in our selected S-boxes are at most $p_d = 2^{-3}$ and $p_l = 2^{-4}$. Since it is reasonable to assume that a characteristic/linear approximation involving a smaller number of active S-boxes with smaller S-box characteristic/linear approximation probabilities should give better overall probability than a characteristic/linear approximation involving a larger number of active S-boxes with larger probabilities. Therefore, we can obtain a tighter bound for the 8-round characteristic/linear approximation probabilities as

$$p_{C8} \leq (p_d)^{32} = 2^{-96}, \quad p_{L8} \leq (p_l)^{32} = 2^{-128}.$$

Actually we can find such characteristics (no linear approximation, however) by careful examination of DC/LC tables together with minimum diffusion patterns. Note however that the probability of 2^{-64} is the threshold for applicability of DC/LC since the number of all possible difference pairs/selection patterns cannot exceed 2^{64} in 64-bit block ciphers. There also exist a number of variants or generalizations of differential and linear cryptanalysis, but theses attacks are unlikely to much reduce the attack complexity. We thus strongly believe that 12-round mCrypton is far secure against differential/linear cryptanalysis.

We should also consider a variety of other cryptanalysis techniques for the security of mCrypton, such as algebraic attacks, related key attacks and key schedule cryptanalysis, etc. We believe that these attacks are equally unlikely for 12-round mCrypton as in the case of Crypton (see [7] for further discussion on the applicability of these attacks to mCrypton).

4   Implementation Efficiency

4.1   Software Efficiency

The overall structure of mCrypton allows a very high degree of parallelism. This results in high efficiency and flexibility in both software and hardware implementations. The encryption round of mCrypton can be efficiently implemented using lookup tables by precomputing and storing 4 tables, each containing sixteen 16-bit words, such that for $0 \leq j \leq 16$,

$$SS_0[j] = S_0[j] \wedge m_0 \parallel S_0[j] \wedge m_1 \parallel S_0[j] \wedge m_2 \parallel S_0[j] \wedge m_3,$$
$$SS_1[j] = S_1[j] \wedge m_1 \parallel S_1[j] \wedge m_2 \parallel S_1[j] \wedge m_3 \parallel S_1[j] \wedge m_0,$$
$$SS_2[j] = S_2[j] \wedge m_2 \parallel S_2[j] \wedge m_3 \parallel S_2[j] \wedge m_0 \parallel S_2[j] \wedge m_1,$$
$$SS_3[j] = S_3[j] \wedge m_3 \parallel S_3[j] \wedge m_0 \parallel S_3[j] \wedge m_1 \parallel S_3[j] \wedge m_2,$$

where $\parallel$ denotes concatenation of bit strings. These four extended S-boxes altogether take a storage of only 128 bytes, small enough to be used even in very limited computing environments such as mote-class sensor nodes. With these lookup tables, we can implement one round of mCrypton only using 20 table lookups (16 to SS tables and 4 to round key tables).

Note that for decryption we need 8-bit rotated versions of the above extended SS-boxes and we also need the original S-boxes for key scheduling. This will not be any problem in most computing environments since the storage requirement is still at most 320 bytes altogether. Further, there may be no need of storing rotated versions of SS tables in more resource-constrained 8-bit processors, since the same SS tables can be used for decryption as well by referring to the second byte of the table entry first. The four S-boxes may also be stored more compactly only using 32 bytes of storage if desirable. So in this minimal setting we only need 160 bytes of storage for four SS-boxes and four S-boxes.

We also need to consider the key scheduling overhead in software implementations. Real-time computation of round keys for every block of encryption/decryption should be the last choice even in the resource-constrained devices since its computational overhead is never negligible. mCrypton requires two set of 52 round keys of 16 bits for both encryption and decryption, corresponding to a storage of 208 bytes. This amount of temporary storage (RAM) will not be much overhead even in typical sensor nodes such as Mica2 motes. Therefore, we can see that mCrypton can be very efficiently implemented even in the very restricted 8-bit computing environments. Furthermore, mCrypton will be particularly efficient on 16-bit platforms such as Telos motes, since most operations are performed over 16-bit words.

4.2   Hardware Efficiency

Efficiency in low-cost hardware implementation is one of main design objectives of mCrypton. Each component function is carefully designed with hardware implementations in mind. To check the hardware complexity of mCrypton, a simple, straightforward hardware was designed and simulated. The processor is based

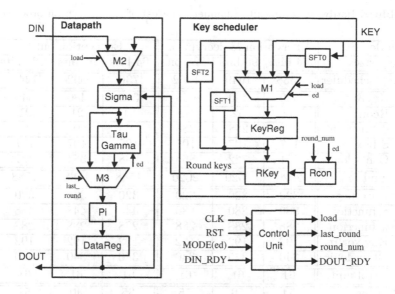

Fig. 4. Hardware architecture of mCrypton processor

on the implementation of a single round per clock cycle and transforms input data in 13 clocks as depicted in Fig.4.

The circuit can start processing as soon as key and data are available on their input pins (loaded in parallel), and execute both encryption and decryption in 13 rounds, where each round consists of $\pi \circ \gamma \circ \tau \circ \sigma$, except for the last round, which corresponds to $\pi \circ \sigma$. Here note that for simplicity we process data and key internally in column basis, instead of in row basis described in the specification. Encryption and decryption rounds share the same datapath logic. Note that encryption and decryption rounds make use of just different arrangement of the same S-boxes. Therefore, γ and γ^{-1} can be implemented using a single set of 16 S-boxes and a pair of appropriate selectors (multiplexers). This is actually achieved in the γ transformation in Fig.4.

Key scheduler logic generates round keys from a given user key (64, 96, or 128 bits) and supplies them to the datapath for both encryption and decryption. The initial secret key for encryption (decryption, resp.) is first loaded into the key register KeyReg from which round keys are generated by the RKey component, where round constants $C[r]$'s are generated by the Rcon component. The key register is then updated for next round key generation through specified rotations SFT1 (SFT2 for decryption, resp.).

The architecture shown in Fig.4 has been implemented for each key size using $0.13\mu m$ CMOS technology. The encryption-only mode is also implemented as well as the full (encryption and decryption) mode, since encryption capability is often sufficient for security in more resource-constrained low-cost RFID tags. The resulting gate counts (1 gate = 2-input NAND gate-equivalent) are summarized in Table 2. As can be seen from the table, elimination of decryption components

Table 2. Hardware complexity (number of gates) of the mCrypton processor

Mode	Encryption & decryption			Encryption-only		
Key size	64 bits	96 bits	128 bits	64 bits	96 bits	128 bits
Key scheduler	1338	1649	1952	736	992	1249
KeyReg	320	480	640	320	480	640
Rcon	52	52	52	21	21	21
ϕ function	288	288	288	0	0	0
S-box	107	107	107	107	107	107
Other logic	571	722	865	288	384	481
Round func.	2020	2020	2020	1588	1588	1588
DataReg	320	320	320	320	320	320
γ function	880	880	880	448	448	488
π function	288	288	288	288	288	288
Key xor(σ)	192	192	192	192	192	192
Other logic	340	340	340	340	340	340
Control unit	61	61	61	61	61	61
Routing	54	59	75	35	40	51
Total	3473	3789	4108	2420	2681	2949

greatly (more than 25%) reduces the overall complexity. We can see that the full
mode consumes about 3.5K to 4.1Kgates while the encryption-only mode about
2.4K to 3.0Kgates, depending on key sizes. The gate count for encryption-only
modes appears to be well within an economic range of 5-cent RFID tags.

The critical path delay (CPL) of our implemented architecture can be relatively long, since it traverses from round key generation to round function evaluation. However, it turned out that the maximum CPL was still less than 9 ns
(allowing frequency over 100MHz) even for the full mode of 128-bit key version.
We did not much concentrate on speed issues during our implementation, since
operating frequencies in our target applications are extremely low: Most modern
UHF RFID chips use on-board oscillators with frequencies over 1MHz and most
mote-class sensor nodes operate at frequencies below 10MHz. Nevertheless, if

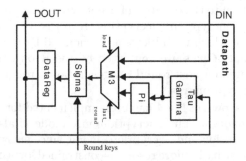

Fig. 5. Alternative datapath architecture for shorter delay

higher performances are preferred, the architecture may be modified as shown in Fig.5. This architecture may reduce the CPL to almost a half of the original but may somewhat increase the gate count in the case of encryption-only mode, mainly due to the added complexity of the last round key conversion.

To further reduce the hardware complexity, we may adopt multiple clock cycles/round architectures. At the minimum we may process input data in column-by-column basis, based on the 5 cycles/round architecture. In this case the core datapath logic can only implement four S-boxes, one π_i transformation and 16 XORs. We are now developing such an architecture for more compact implementation. Our preliminary analysis based on the this architecture promises that the overall hardware complexity can be considerably reduced (by about 30%). For example, the encryption-only mode with 128-bit keys may be implemented with about 2000 gates and the full mode with about 2500 gates.

Finally, we note that we did not consider any specific power consumption minimization during the implementation. Clearly we would have to sacrifice the circuit size more or less to apply power consumption minimization strategies (e.g., see [8]). One way to reduce power consumption in the present architecture would be to reduce the operating frequency (say, far below 100KHz), as far as it satisfies the minimum response time required by standards such as EPC Gen2 and ISO/IEC 18000-6 (e.g., see [3]).

5   Conclusion

We presented a 64-bit block cipher mCrypton specifically designed for security in resource-constrained applications, such as low-cost RFID tags and sensors, and analyzed its security and efficiency. mCrypton is based on the proven architecture of Crypton with some improvements in hardware and software efficiency under restricted environments. It also incorporates a flexible key schedule with key sizes of 64 bits, 96 bits and 128 bits, which may provide greater flexibility in cost-security tradeoffs often encountered in cost-driven applications such as low-cost RFID tags. Our preliminary security analysis shows that mCrypton is far secure against well-known attacks on block ciphers such as differential and linear cryptanalysis. We also demonstrated through hardware simulation that mCrypton is well-suited for our target applications. Our simple hardware design shows that it can be implemented with the complexity of about 2.4K to 4.1K gates, depending on key sizes and capabilities (encryption-only, encryption and decryption). Furthermore, we expect that a more compact 5 cycles/round architecture under development could considerably reduce the complexity (by about 30%). As another possible future work, we could perform validation of software efficiency on the 8/16-bit processors used in typical sensor nodes.

References

1. S.Bono, M.Green, A. Stubblefield, A.Juels, A.Rubin and M.Szydlo, Security analysis of a cryptographically-enabled RFID device, In *14th USENIX Security Symposium*, Baltimore, Maryland, July-August 2005.

2. R.Campbell, J.A.-Muhtadi, P.Naldurg, G.Sampemane1 and M.D.Mickunas, Towards Security and Privacy for Pervasive Computing, In *Software Security - Theories and Systems*, LNCS 2609, Springer-Verlag, 2003, p.1-15.
3. M.Feldhofer, S.Dominikus and J.Wolkerstorfer, Strong authentication for RFID systems using the AES algorithm, In *Cryptographic Hardware and Embedded Systems - CHES 2004*, LNCS 3156, Springer-Verlag, 2004, pp.357-370.
4. S.L.Garfinkel, A.Jeuls and R.Pappu, RFID privacy: An overview of problems and proposed solutions, *IEEE Security & Privacy*, May/June 2005, pp.34-43.
5. C.Karlof, N.Sastary and D.Wagner, TinySec: A link layer security architecture for wireless sensor networks, In *ACM SenSys 2004*, Nov. 3-5, 2004.
6. Y.W.Law and J.M.Doumen and P.H.Hartel, Benchmarking block ciphers for wireless sensor networks (Extended abstract), In *1st IEEE Int. Conf. on Mobile Ad-hoc and Sensor Systems(MASS)*, Fort Lauderdale, Florida, Oct. 2004.
7. C.H.Lim, A revised version of CRYPTON: CRYPTON v1.0, In *Fast Software Encryption-FSE'99*, LNCS 1636, Spinger-Verlag, 1999, pp.31-45
8. S.Morioka and A.Satoh, An Optimized S-Box Circuit Architecture for Low Power AES Design, In *Cryptographic Hardware and Embedded Systems - CHES 2002*, LNCS 2523, Springer-Verlag, 2003, pp.172-186.
9. A.Perrig, J.Stankovic and D.Wagner, Security in wireless sensor networks, *Commun. of ACM*, 47(5), June 2004, pp.53-57.
10. J.Polastre, R.Szewczyk and D.Culler, Telos: enabling ultra-low power wireless research, In *Proceedings of the 4th Int. Conf. on Information Processing in Sensor Networks: Special track on Platform Tools and Design Methods for Network Embedded Sensors (IPSN/SPOTS)*, April 25-27, 2005.
11. F.Stajano and R.Anderson, The Resurrecting Duckling: Security Issues for Ubiquitous Computing, *IEEE Security & Privacy*, April 2002, pp.22-26.
12. S.A.Weis, S.E.Sarma, R.L.Rivest and D.W.Engels, Security and privacy aspects of low-cost radio frequency identification systems, *Int. Conference on Security in Pervasive Computing - SPC 2003*, LNCS 2802, Springer-Verlag, 2003, pp.454-469.

Practical Modifications of Leadbitter et al.'s Repeated-Bits Side-Channel Analysis on (EC)DSA

Katsuyuki Takashima

Information Technology R&D Center,
Mitsubishi Electric Corporation,
5-1-1, Ofuna, Kamakura, Kanagawa 247-8501, Japan
takasima@iss.isl.melco.co.jp

Abstract. In this paper, we will report practical modifications of the side-channel analysis to (EC)DSA [1, 2, 4, 31] that Leadbitter et al. have proposed in [12]. To apply the analyses, we assume that the window method is used in the exponentiation (EC scalar multiplication) calculation and the side-channel information described in Section 2 can be collected. So far, the method in [12] haven't been effective when q is 160 bit long and the window size $w < 9$. We show that the modified method we propose in this paper is effective even when q is 160 bit long and $w = 4$, that is, in the case of frequent implementation. First, we estimate the window size w necessary for the proposed analyses (attacks) to succeed. Then by experiment of the new method, we show that private keys of (EC)DSA can be obtained under the above assumptions, in practical time and with sufficient success rate. The result raises the necessity of countermeasures against the analyses (attacks) in the window method based implementation of (EC)DSA.

Keywords: (EC)DSA, Side-channel analysis (attack), Window method, Lattice basis reduction algorithm.

1 Introduction

Presently, it becomes more important to do countermeasures to various side-channel analyses (SCA, side-channel attacks) [10, 11], and to study such analysis methods arouses much interest. In this paper, we will propose practical modifications of SCA of Leadbitter et al. [12]. In addition, we will also describe countermeasures against that attack.

In [12], the authors have proposed a SCA to the window method used in the exponentiation (elliptic curve scalar multiplication) calculation in (EC)DSA signatures. DSA and ECDSA are specified in several specification documents [1, 2, 4, 31]. First in their method, they searched repetitions of window values several times using side-channel information such as power consumption etc. Then they constructed a lattice based on the side-channel information, and applied a practical lattice basis reduction algorithm to it to obtain secret information.

J. Song, T. Kwon, and M. Yung (Eds.): WISA 2005, LNCS 3786, pp. 259–270, 2006.

Their method is similar to SCA methods in [8, 27, 20, 21, 19] etc. In the scenario in [8, 27, 20, 21, 19], by knowing some part of secret information k, they applied lattice basis reduction algorithm. The situation in these papers is different from that in [12] and this paper (See Section 2 and 5). The lattices used are also different. We should note that the real fault attack on smart card using lattice reduction has been succeeded in [19] recently. The result makes further investigations of the method in [12] more important also.

The method in [12] isn't effective when q is 160 bit long and the window size $w < 9$, in particular in the frequent case that $w = 4$ (See Section 6.1). In this paper, we propose two practical modifications of their method. Then we will show that the methods are effective when q is 160 bit long and $w = 4$. Using the heuristic estimate similar to that of [12], we predict that the success rate of the proposed method is very high. In addition, by experiments using random signature values, we verified that the proposed method succeeded with sufficiently high success rate in several minutes. This result suggests that some countermeasure is necessary when side-channel information in Section 2 can be collected.

As described in [12], by modifying lattices appropriately, our method in Section 5.1 can also be applied to (EC)DLP-based signatures other than (EC)DSA (For example, to signatures in [5]). In addition, our attack strategy seems to be applicable to a variety of window-based implementations, e.g., sliding window method, width-w (T)NAF method, fractional window method etc. (See [7, 18, 25], for example). Also, it can be applied to both of "Right-to-Left" and "Left-to-Right" exponentiations and EC scalar multiplications (See Section 5.1 also).

In [24], another attack on window-based method has been proposed. However, the method is different from our methods in the respect that their method uses statistical processing.

In this paper, we won't discuss the collection phase of side-channel information further than that in Section 2.

This paper is organized as follows. In Section 2, we describe side-channel information used in lattice based SCA in [12] and this paper. Collection methods of them are also described there. Next, in Section 3, we briefly review the target signature algorithms DSA and ECDSA. In Section 4, lattice basis reduction algorithms (LLL and BKZ) used in experiments in this paper are briefly reviewed. In Section 5, we describe analysis method in [12] and our proposed two methods. In Section 6, we show the effectiveness of the proposed methods by experimentation. Finally, in Section 7, countermeasures against the proposed methods are described.

2   Side Channel Information Used in Lattice Based SCA

In [12] and this paper, by detecting a repeated reading of some window values, we use the corresponding repetition of bit patterns (See Section 5). For example, as described in [12], such continuous readings can be detected by the following two methods:

The first one is that by detecting reuses of data on cache memory using timing information etc. This methodology was already pointed out in [10]. Such a method can be used when reading values from a precomputation table. In [32] etc., the method has been applied to real implementations. Recently, in [26], a cache-based attack on RSA was applied to processors with simultaneous multithreading.

The second one is that by collecting side-channel information such as power consumption data etc. for address-bit accesses. In [9], by processing such data statistically, a method to deduce some secret information (ADPA : Address-bit DPA) was described. Countermeasures against such attacks were also described.

For countermeasures against the above attacks, see Section 7. In addition, it seems interesting to investigate to make use of fault analysis effectively as in [19].

3   DSA (ECDSA)

In this section, we will briefly review signature algorithms DSA and ECDSA. First, we will describe a map f called projection in [5].

For DSA, primes p and q are set s.t. $q|p-1$, and g ($\in \mathbb{F}_p^*$) is an element of order q in $\mathbb{F}_p^*$. For G ($:= \langle g \rangle \subset \mathbb{F}_p^*$), a map $f : G \to \mathbb{F}_q$ is defined by $h \mapsto h \bmod q$.

For ECDSA, we need a cyclic subgroup G ($\subset E(\mathbb{F}_p)$) s.t. $q := \sharp G$ is a large prime. For such G, a map $f : G \to \mathbb{F}_q$ is defined by $P \mapsto x_P \bmod q$ (where x_P is the x-coordinate of P).[1]

In the following, DSA is explained using the above f. ECDSA is defined similarly. Let H be a hash function. A signature (r, s) for a message m using a private key α is defined as follows using an ephemeral key k.

$$r = f(g^k), \quad s = (H(m) + r\alpha)/k \bmod q \tag{1}$$

Here, we note that when we know k, private key α can be easily calculated by using the second equation in (1) and publicly known informations. By that, in the following analysis, our aim is to obtain (at least one) k from several pairs of a message and a signature.

4   Lattice Basis Reduction Algorithm

In this section, we will explain the LLL algorithm [13] and the block Korkine-Zolotareff (BKZ) algorithm [28] briefly. In the following sections, they are used for an approximation algorithm of the shortest vector in a lattice L.

In this paper, we consider only a lattice $L(\subset \mathbb{R}^d)$ of maximal rank. For a lattice L, $L = L(M)$ means that a matrix M consists of column vectors representing its

---

[1] Here, to avoid notational confusion, we described it for prime-field elliptic curves. Of course, the results in this paper are also effective when using composite-field elliptic curves in ECDSA.

basis. Additionally, $||\cdot||$ means the Euclidean norm, and $\lambda_1(L)$ is $\min_{b(\neq 0)\in L} ||b||$. For a $L = L(M)$, $\Delta(L) := |\det(M)|$.

The LLL algorithm has a time-accuracy trade-off parameter δ ($1/4 < \delta < 1$). For the definition, see [15] p.33, for example. It is known that for an obtained basis $(b_1, \ldots, b_d)$ by the LLL algorithm,

$$||b_1|| \leq (2/\sqrt{4\delta - 1})^{d-1}\Delta(L)^{1/d} . \tag{2}$$

This gives a theoretical upper bound for $||b_1||$. In fact, it is known that we can obtain a shorter vector than that expected by the equation (2).

By using the BKZ algorithm [28], we can obtain a shorter vector that can not be obtained by the LLL algorithm. The BKZ algorithm is parametrized by a block-size parameter κ ($2 \leq \kappa \leq d$), and when $\kappa = 2$, it equals to the LLL algorithm. As a corresponding estimate to the inequality (2), the following (3) is known for a BKZ basis $(b_1, \ldots, b_d)$ defined in [28, 29].

$$||b_1|| \leq \gamma_\kappa^{\frac{d-1}{\kappa-1}}\lambda_1(L) \leq \gamma_\kappa^{\frac{d-1}{\kappa-1}}\sqrt{\gamma_d}\Delta(L)^{1/d} . \tag{3}$$

Here, γ_d(and γ_κ) is called Hermite constant, and has a property that $\frac{1}{2\pi e} \leq \liminf_{d\to\infty} \frac{\gamma_d}{d} \leq \limsup_{d\to\infty} \frac{\gamma_d}{d} \leq \frac{1}{\pi e}$. However, the real BKZ algorithm has a parameter δ similar to the LLL algorithm, so output an "approximate" BKZ basis. Therefore, in general, the outputted basis doesn't have to satisfy the inequality (3). As the block-size κ get larger, we can obtain a "shorter" vector compared to that by the LLL algorithm as is seen from the estimation (3), however, the computation time gets longer.

5   SCA Under Repeated Bits Assumption

In this section, we will describe methods to get private key information efficiently when side-channel information in Section 2 is available. First, in Section 5.1, a method in [12] is described, and two proposed methods, that are generalizations of that in [12], are given in Section 5.2 and 5.3. By applying an estimate method to them, we show that they can be applied to DSA (or ECDSA) of the practical parameter size.

5.1   SCA of Leadbitter et al. [12]

Let l be the bitlength of the modulus q, and w be the window size. By using side-channel information in Section 2, we collect the following form $k = k_i$ ($i = 0, \ldots, n$) where $n \geq 30$. For some t (≥ 0), k_i has a form $x_i||y_i||y_i||v_i$ ($v_i < 2^t$, $x_i < 2^{l-t-2w}$, $y_i < 2^w$). Using these k_i and corresponding r_i, s_i etc., we construct some lattice L. For that lattice, search for a short vector leads to disclosure of all the k_i. In fact, for the sake of simplicity, the case that $t = 0$ ($v_i = \emptyset$) is only considered in [12]. Also for the argument in this paper, considering that case is sufficient. Therefore, we consider only

$$k_i = x_i 2^{2w} + y_i(1 + 2^w) \quad (x_i < 2^{l-2w}, y_i < 2^w) \,.^2 \tag{4}$$

In the following, we assume that the exponentiation (or scalar multiplication) is executed as Right-to-Left. Then we use repetitions of bit patterns in the LSB part as above. Also for the Left-to-Right execution, if we can detect repetitions, the following arguments can be applied by modifying the lattice appropriately.

According to the experiment in [12], when $w \geq 10$, the analysis is suceeded in high rate by collecting k_i of the form (4) more than or equal to 40 (See Table 1 in [12]).

Even for the case that $w = 10$ and $n \approx 100$, $2^w * 100$ ($< 2^{17}$) exponentiations (or scalar multiplications) are enough on average to obtain n k_i's satisfying the pattern (4) under the assumption of uniform appearance of bits in k.

The following equations are deduced from simultaneous equations $s_i = (H(m_i) + r_i \alpha)k_i^{-1} \bmod q$ $(i = 0, \ldots, n)$.

$$r_0 s_i k_i - r_i s_0 k_0 = r_0 H(m_i) - r_i H(m_0) \bmod q \quad i = 1, \ldots, n. \tag{5}$$

These equations are rewritten as $y_i = a_i + b_i x_0 + c_i x_i + d_i y_0 + \lambda_i q$ $(i = 1, \ldots, n)$ for $W := (2^w + 1)^{-1} \bmod q$, $N := 2^{2w}$,

$$
\begin{aligned}
a_i &:= W s_i^{-1}(H(m_i) - H(m_0)r_i r_0^{-1}) \bmod q \,, \\
b_i &:= NW s_i^{-1} s_0 r_i r_0^{-1} \bmod q \,, \\
c &:= -NW \bmod q \,, \\
d_i &:= s_i^{-1} s_0 r_i r_0^{-1} \bmod q \,,
\end{aligned}
\tag{6}
$$

and some λ_i. In general, the solution (x_i, y_i) in formulas (4) is small compared to coefficients a_i, b_i, c, d_i $(i = 1, \ldots, n)$. That is why we can reveal (x_i, y_i) by using a lattice basis reduction algorithm.

The following matrix M is defined using a_i, b_i, c, d_i $(i = 1, \ldots, n)$ in formulas (6). L $(:= L(M))$ is a d $(:= 2n + 3)$-dimensional lattice generated by column vectors of M.

$$
M = \begin{pmatrix}
\beta & 0 & 0 & & 0 & 0 & & \\
0 & \varepsilon & 0 & & 0 & 0 & & \\
0 & 0 & \varepsilon & & 0 & 0 & & \\
\vdots & \vdots & & \ddots & \vdots & & 0 & \\
0 & 0 & 0 & & \varepsilon & 0 & & \\
0 & 0 & 0 & & 0 & \theta & 0 & & 0 \\
\theta a_1 & \theta b_1 & \theta c & & 0 & \theta d_1 & \theta q & & 0 \\
\vdots & \vdots & & \ddots & & \vdots & & \ddots & \\
\theta a_n & \theta b_n & 0 & & \theta c & \theta d_n & 0 & & \theta q
\end{pmatrix}
\tag{7}
$$

---

[2] In [12], 2^{2w} in the formula (4) is written as 2^{l-2w}. However, it seems a mistake in writing. Also, elements θa_i, θb_i, θc, θd_i $(i = 1, \ldots, n)$ in lower n rows of the matrix (7) are a_i, b_i, c, d_i $(i = 1, \ldots, n)$ in [12], respectively. The description seems also a mistake because the vector z is not in L described in [12].

Here, integers β, ε, and θ are set so that $\varepsilon \approx 2^{2w-l}\beta$ and $\theta \approx 2^{-w}\beta$ for a lattice basis reduction algorithm to run effectively (See Section 4 of [12]).[3]

For $x = {}^t(1, x_0, x_1, \ldots, x_n, y_0, \lambda_1, \ldots, \lambda_n)$, the following point $z = M \cdot x$ is in L.[2]

$$z = {}^t(\beta, \varepsilon x_0, \varepsilon x_1, \ldots, \varepsilon x_n, \theta y_0, \theta y_1, \ldots, \theta y_n) . \tag{8}$$

The ratio of $\Delta(L)^{1/d}$ and $||z||$ is used as follows for an estimate of success of the analysis in [12] (See the formulas (2) and (3)). They consider if

$$||z|| \leq \Delta(L)^{1/d} , \tag{9}$$

the success rate that the solution z can be obtained is high. We call this heuristic condition used in [12] "condition A," and is used also in this paper in Section 5.2 and 5.3.

In [12], it is deduced that when $n \approx 100$,

$$w \geq 9.28 \tag{10}$$

is a sufficient condition for satisfying the condition A (9). See Section 6.1 for the validity of the condition (10) also.

5.2   SCA Using General Window Value Repetition Frequency u

We consider the following method using general repetition number u (i.e. $u \geq 2$) to succeed in the case that q is 160 bit long and window-size w is 4. The target k_i is given by

$$x_i || \underbrace{y_i || \cdots || y_i}_{u \text{ times}} \ (x_i < 2^{l-uw}, y_i < 2^w) . \tag{11}$$

That is, $k_i = x_i 2^{uw} + y_i \sum_{j=0}^{u-1} 2^{wj}$. In the case that $u = 2$, it is the pattern in Section 5.1.

Similar to Section 5.1, under the assumption of uniform distribution of bits of k, we require about $2^{(u-1)w}n$ exponentiations (or scalar multiplications) to collect n k_i's such as the formula (11) on average. The number is $2^8 * 100 \ (< 2^{15})$ in the case that $w = 4$, $n \approx 100$, and $u = 3$. Therefore, we can collect the necessary data in practical time.

For this SCA using general u, we modify the lattice L in Section 5.1 replacing $N := 2^{uw}$, $W := (\sum_{j=0}^{u-1} 2^{wj})^{-1} \mod q$ instead of N, W in the formulas (6). Parameters β, ε, and θ are chosen so that $\varepsilon = \varepsilon_u = 2^{uw-l}\beta$, $\theta = 2^{-w}\beta$.

We also estimate the successful w for the proposed method using the condition A (9). First, $\Delta(L)^2$ and $||z||^2$ are evaluated as follows, respectively.

---

[3] We use a different notation from that in [12]. ε and θ in this paper are written as γ and δ in [12], respectively, to avoid confusion with notations in Section 4 and 6.

$$\Delta(L)^2 = \beta \varepsilon^{n+1} \theta^{n+1} q^n$$
$$\approx \beta^{2n+3} 2^{(n+1)(uw-l-w)} 2^{ln} \tag{12}$$
$$= \beta^{2n+3} 2^{(u-1)(n+1)w-l} \ ,$$

$$||z||^2 = \beta^2 + \sum_{i=0}^{n} (\varepsilon^2 x_i^2 + \theta^2 y_i^2)$$
$$\leq \beta^2 (2n+3) \ .$$

From these estimates, we can see that the next condition (13) is sufficient for the condition A (9).

$$\sqrt{2n+3} \leq 2^{((u-1)(n+1)w-l)/(2n+3)} \ . \tag{13}$$

When $n \approx 100$, considering the formula (13) as an inequality in $(u-1)w$, we get

$$w \geq 9.28/(u-1) \ . \tag{14}$$

Thus, for $u = 3$, we obtain an inequality

$$w \geq 9.28/2 = 4.64 \ .$$

That is, we show the applicability of the proposed method to the practical case that q is 160 bit long and w is 4. For the corresponding experimentation result, see Section 6.2. Also, for $u = 4$, the inequality (14) implies the applicability to the case that $w = 3$ (when q is 160 bit long).

5.3   SCA Using Multiple u's

When we detect n u-time repetitions of the same window value as the formula (11), $n/2^w$ samples are $(u+1)$-time repetitions on average. Using these data effectively, we can construct a lattice L so that the norm $||z||$ is smaller than that for the previous lattice compared to $\Delta(L)$.

We set that k_0 in the equations (5) has the largest u_0 among all collected data. In addition, let n_u be the number of u-time repetitions (i.e. $n = \sum_u n_u$). Then the constants $\varepsilon(= \varepsilon_u)$'s for several u's are different from each other. Therefore, the equation (12) is modified to

$$\Delta(L)^2 \approx \beta \theta^{n+1} q^n \varepsilon_{u_0}^{n_{u_0}+1} \prod_{u \neq u_0} \varepsilon_u^{n_u}$$
$$= \beta^{2n+3} 2^{-(n+1)w+(u_0 w-l)(n_{u_0}+1)} \prod_{u \neq u_0} 2^{(uw-l)n_u} 2^{ln} \tag{15}$$
$$= \beta^{2n+3} 2^{-(n+1)w+(u_0 w-l)(n_{u_0}+1)+\sum_{u \neq u_0}((uw-l)n_u)+ln} \ .$$

For example, we consider the case that $n_3 \approx 15n/16 = 93.75$, $n_4 \approx n/16 = 6.25$, and other n_u's are 0 (i.e. $u_0 = 4$, $n = 100$, and $n = n_3 + n_4$). Thus the formula (15) is evaluated as

$$\Delta(L)^2 = \beta^{2n+3} 2^{-(n+1)w+(4w-l)(n_4+1)+(3w-l)n_3+ln}$$
$$\approx \beta^{2n+3} 2^{n(-w+1/16(4w-l)+15/16(3w-l)+l)+3w-l} \ .$$

Consequently, we get the following condition as a sufficient condition for the condition A (9) similar to the case in the previous subsection.

$$\sqrt{2n + 3} \leq$$
$$2^{(n(-w+1/16(4w-l)+15/16(3w-l)+l)+3w-l)/(2n+3)}$$
$$= 2^{((837/4)w-160)/203} .$$

From this, we obtain $w \geq 4.482...$ We see that the effective window size for the method in this subsection is smaller than that in the previous subsection.

6   Experimentation Results

After mentioning the experimentation results in [12] in Section 6.1, we will describe our experimentation results for the method proposed in Section 5.2 in Section 6.2.

6.1   Experimentation Results of Leadbitter et al. [12]

Leadbitter et al. implemented their method (in Section 5.1) using 50 Linux workstations (2 GHz Pentium 4, 512 MB RAM for each). Then they have verified the validity of the estimate (the formula (10)) of effective window size for 160 bit q for their method based on the condition A (9).

The result was summarized in Table 1 in [12]. The success rates were tabulated through 100 experimentations for each n and w.

Average times (minutes) for one execution were also given. Although there was no detailed description for the way of the experimentation, it seems the same as the way in Section 6.2 we adopted.

They used the floating-point arithmetic Schnorr-Euchner algorithm [30] (with the "deep insertion" method) as a first lattice basis reduction algorithm. To obtain shorter vectors, after executing the Schnorr-Euchner algorithm, they applied the so-called integral LLL algorithm (de Weger method [34]).

6.2   Experimentation Results for the Method in Section 5.2

We executed the similar experimentation to that in [12] for the method in Section 5.2 ($u = 3$). On a PC (1.3 GHz Pentium M, 0.98 GB RAM, Windows XP), we verified the effectivity of our proposed method using NTL [23] implementation (See Table 2).

We describe the experimentation method in the following. First, we generate random r_i, $h_i(= H(m_i))$, x_i and y_i s.t. $x_i < 2^{l-uw}$ and $y_i < 2^w$ ($i = 0, \ldots, n$).

Table 1. Options for NTL lattice basis reduction algorithm

main algorithm	BKZ
flag of floating-point arithmetic	QP
δ	0.99
diagonalization	(classical) Gram-Schmidt

Table 2. Experimentation results for the method in Sec. 5.2 ($w = 4, l = 160, u = 3, \varepsilon = 1000$)

$n(\approx \sharp$ of sig.)	block size κ	$\sharp$ of suc.	suc. rate	ave. time (m.)	total time (m.)
	10	5	8.3%	0.41	24.50
30	20	28	46.7%	0.60	36.06
	30	54	90.0%	3.35	201.14
	10	26	43.3%	0.85	51.22
40	20	55	91.6%	1.06	63.54
	30	60	100.0%	2.66	159.68
50	10	60	100.0%	1.67	99.96
	20	60	100.0%	1.89	113.59
60	10	60	100.0%	3.04	182.29
	20	60	100.0%	3.94	236.57

Using the second equation of (1), s_i are calculated. Based on (6), a_i, b_i, c, and d_i are calculated, and the corresponding lattice $L(M)$ is constructed. Finally, we run a lattice basis reduction algorithm with the specification (or parameters) as in Table 1.

Here, parameters δ (in Table 1) and κ (in Table 2) were explained in Section 4. See the NTL manual for the details of "flag of floating-point arithmetic" and "diagonalization."

As is seen in Table 1 in [12], the execution time of basis reduction in [12] takes 106 minutes even when $n = 40$. Therefore, we don't adopt the time-consuming integral LLL algorithm. As the use of the BKZ algorithm is recommended in the NTL manual instead of the use of "deep insertion," we follow it as in Table 1. For the size of numbers in this experimentation, the BKZ function in NTL library execute the ordinary LLL algorithm at first, and for appropriately small matrix entries obtained, the BKZ algorithm is executed.

By the expression (8), the desired z can be calculated using known x_i, y_i (and β, ε, θ) in the experimentation. Therefore, we count the case that there exists an index j s.t. b_j or $-b_j$ obtained by the basis reduction and z are equal as a success, and tabulate the success rates in Table 2.

For parameters $w = 4, l = 160, u = 3, \varepsilon = 1000$ ($\beta = 2^{l-nw}\varepsilon, \theta = 2^{l-(n+1)w}\varepsilon$), we repeat the experimentation 60 times. Hence, the success rates are "$\sharp$ of success" / 60 *100%. In the "total time" column, the total times of the 60 trials are described. Data in "average time" are "total time" / 60.

By the results in Table 2, we can see the effectiveness and practical running time for the method in Section 5.2 for the widely-used parameters q and w.

7   Countermeasures

In this section, we give 3 (possible) countermeasures against the proposed analysis methods. The method in Section 7.1 is suitable for a group of points on an elliptic curve (EC) because projective (Jacobian) coordinates are available. Also, that in Section 7.2 is suitable for EC because the inverse calculation of points on EC is easy. Both methods are effective for the proposed analyses in this paper. However, the countermeasure in Section 7.3 can not be applied directly. Therefore, we should modify the method appropriately.

7.1   Table Randomization Renewal

This is a standard countermeasure adopted in [16, 24] etc. For each reading of an element in a precomputed table, the value is randomized so that the reuse of the values on cache-memory is prevented.

7.2   Möller's Scalar Multiplication

Using the countermeasure in Section 7.1, the computational amount increases as randomizations are done for each reading to a precomputed table. Hence, to avoid such increases, Möller implemented a modification of Yao's exponentiation calculation (scalar multiplication) method [33] in [17]. That realizes "uniform calculation process" and "randomization of data" (For the details, see [17]. For the Yao's method, see [3, 14] also.).

For 160 and 256 bit EC cases, Möller has shown in [17] that his method is superior than the method in Section 7.1 when $w \leq 4$ w.r.t. comparison of time complexity.

7.3   Address-Bit Randomization

This is the method to mask address-bits by some random values so that repetitions of reading the same value get difficult to be detected. However, as is already noticed in [12], direct application of that in [9] doesn't make meaningful effects because we must deal with the correlations of address-bits in one exponentiation (scalar multiplication) execution.

8   Conclusions

In this paper, we proposed generalizations of the side-channel analysis method to (EC)DSA in [12]. They assumed collections of side-channel informations for repetitions of window values. Then we have shown our proposed method is effective for the practical situations (e.g. 160 bit q and $w = 4$). For such situations, the previous method in [12] is not effective. The effectiveness is shown by the heuristic estimates used in [12] and by simulation experiments using random signature values. In the experimentation, a private key has been revealed in practical time.

By this, the necessity of implementing countermeasures as in Section 7 get higher when the window method is used in (EC)DSA.

Acknowledgement. We thank the anonymous refrees for their useful comments.

References

1. ANSI X 9.30 : 1, "*American National Standard for Financial Services - Public Key Cryptography for the Financial Services Industry : Part 1 : The Digital Signature Algorithm (DSA)*," American National Standard Institute, 1997.
2. ANSI X 9.62, "*American National Standard for Financial Services - Public Key Cryptography for the Financial Services Industry : The Elliptic Curve Digital Signature Algorithm (ECDSA)*," American National Standard Institute, 1998.
3. E.F. Brickell, D.M. Gordon, K.S. McCurley, and D.B. Wilson, "Fast exponentiation with precomputation," *Eurocrypt '92*, LNCS 658, 200–207, Springer Verlag, 1993.
4. FIPS 186-2, "*Digital Signature Standard (DSS)*," Federal Information Processing Standards Publication 186-2, U.S. Department of Commerce/ N.I.S.T., January 27 2000.
5. L. Granboulan, "PECDSA : How to build a DL-based digital signature scheme with the best proven security," *NESSIE Report*, available at https://www.cosic.esat.kuleuven.ac.be/nessie/reports/.
6. P.M. Gruber and C.G. Lekkerkerker, *Geometry of numbers*, North-Holland, 1987.
7. D. Hankerson, A. Menezes, and S. Vanstone, *Guide to Elliptic Curve Cryptography*, Springer Verlag, 2004.
8. N. Howgrave-Graham and N.P. Smart, "Lattice attacks on digital signature schemes," *Designs, Codes and Cryptography*, **23**, 283–290, 2001.
9. K. Itoh, T. Izu, and M. Takenaka, "A practical countermeasure against address-bit differential power analysis," *CHES 2003*, LNCS 2779, 382–396, Springer Verlag, 2003.
10. P.C. Kocher, "Timing attacks on implementations of Diffie-Hellman, RSA, DSS, and other systems," *CRYPTO '96*, LNCS 1109, 104–113, Springer Verlag, 1996.
11. P.C. Kocher, J. Jaffe, and B. Jun, "Differential power analysis," *CRYPTO '99*, LNCS 1666, 388–397, Springer Verlag, 1999.
12. P.J. Leadbitter, D. Page, and N. Smart, "Attacking DSA under a repeated bits assumption," *CHES 2004*, LNCS 3156, 428–440, Springer Verlag, 2004.
13. A.K. Lenstra, H.W. Lenstra, and L. Lovász, "Factoring polynomials with rational coefficients," *Math. Ann.*, **261**, 515–534, 1982.
14. A. Menezes, P. van Oorschot, and S. Vanstone, *Handbook of Applied Cryptography*, CRC Press, 1996.
15. D. Micciancio and S. Goldwasser, *Complexity of lattice problems : A cryptographic perspectives*, Kluwer Academic Publishers, 2002.
16. B. Möller, "Securing elliptic curve point multiplication against side-channel attacks," *ISC 2001*, LNCS 2200, 324–334, Springer Verlag, 2001. "addendum: Efficiency improvement," available at http://bmoeller.de/.
17. B. Möller, "Parallelizable elliptic curve point multiplication method with resistance against side-channel attacks," *ISC 2002*, LNCS 2433, 402–413, Springer Verlag, 2002.
18. B. Möller, "Improved techniques for fast exponentiation," *ICISC 2002*, LNCS 2587, 298–312, Springer Verlag, 2003.
19. D. Naccache, P.Q. Nguyen, M. Tunstall, and C. Whelan, "Experimenting with faults, lattices and the DSA," *PKC '05*, LNCS 3386, 16–28, Springer Verlag, 2005.
20. P.Q. Nguyen and I.E. Shparlinski, "The insecurity of the digital signature algorithm with partially known nonces," *J. Cryptology*, **15**, 151–176, 2002.
21. P.Q. Nguyen and I.E. Shparlinski, "The insecurity of the elliptic curve digital signature algorithm with partially known nonces," *Design, Codes and Cryptology*, **30** (2), 201–217, 2003.

22. P.Q. Nguyen and J. Stern, "The two faces of lattices in cryptology," *CaLC 01*, LNCS 2146, 146–180, Springer Verlag, 2001.
23. NTL, available at `http://shoup.net/ntl/`.
24. K. Okeya and K. Sakurai, "A second-order DPA attack breaks a window-method based countermeasure against side channel attacks," *ISC 2002*, LNCS 2433, 389–401, Springer Verlag, 2002.
25. K. Okeya and T. Takagi, "SCA-resistant and fast elliptic scalar multiplication based on wNAF," *IEICE Trans. Fundamental*, E87-A, No.1, 2004.
26. C. Percival, "Cache missing for fun and profit," BSDCan 2005, Ottawa, 2005. available at `http://www.daemonology.net/hyperthreading-considered-harmful/`.
27. T. Römer and J.-P. Seifert, "Information leakage attacks against smart card implementations of the elliptic curve digital signature algorithm," *E-smart 2001*, LNCS 2140, 211–219, Springer Verlag, 2001.
28. C.-P. Schnorr, "A hierarchy of polynomial time lattice basis reduction algorithms," *Theor. Comput. Sci.*, **53**, No.2-3, 201–224, 1987.
29. C.-P. Schnorr, "Block Korkin-Zolotarev bases and successive minima," *Combinatorics, Probability and Computing*, **3**, 507–533, 1994.
30. C.-P. Schnorr and M. Euchner "Lattice basis reduction : Improved practical algorithms and solving subset sum problems," *Proc. Fundamentals of Computation Theory*, LNCS 529, 68–85, Springer Verlag, 1991.
31. Standards for Efficient Cryptography, *"SEC1 : Elliptic Curve Cryptography,"* version 1.0, 20 September 2000.
32. Y. Tsunoo, T. Saito, T. Suzaki, M. Shigeri, and H. Miyauchi, "Cryptanalysis of DES implemented on computers with cache," *CHES 2003*, LNCS 2779, 62–76, Springer Verlag, 2003.
33. A.C.-C. Yao, "On the evaluation of powers," *SIAM J. Comput.*, **5**, 100–103, 1976.
34. B.M.M. de Weger, "Solving exponential diophantine equations using lattice basis reduction algorithms," *J. Number Theory*, **26**, 325–367, 1987.

A DPA Countermeasure by Randomized Frobenius Decomposition

Tae-Jun Park[1], Mun-Kyu Lee[2], Dowon Hong[1], and Kyoil Chung[1]

[1] Electronics and Telecommunications Research Institute,
161 Gajeong-dong, Yuseong-gu, Daejeon 305-350, Korea
{papswann, dwhong, kyoil}@etri.re.kr
[2] School of Computer Science and Engineering,
Inha University, Incheon 402-751, Korea
mklee@inha.ac.kr

Abstract. There have been various methods to prevent DPA (Differential Power Analysis) on elliptic curve cryptosystems. As for the curves with efficient endomorphisms, Hasan suggested several countermeasures on anomalous binary curves, and Ciet, Quisquater and Sica proposed a countermeasure on GLV curves. Ciet et al.'s method is based on random decomposition of a scalar, and it is a two-dimensional generalization of Coron's method. Hasan's and Ciet et al.'s countermeasures are applied only to a small class of elliptic curves.

In this paper, we enlarge the class of DPA-resistant curves by proposing a DPA countermeasure applicable to any curve where the Frobenius expansion method can be used. Our analysis shows that our countermeasure can produce a probability of collision around $\mathcal{O}(2^{-20})$ with only 15.4–34.0% extra computation for scalar multiplications on various practical settings.

Keywords: Elliptic curve, scalar multiplication, Frobenius expansion, GLV decomposition, DPA.

1 Introduction

Since Koblitz [1] and Miller [2] proposed the use of elliptic curves in cryptography, an extensive research has been done on the efficiency and security of elliptic curve cryptosystems.

The most time-consuming operation in elliptic curve cryptosystems is a scalar multiplication of an elliptic curve point. One of the well-known techniques to speed up the scalar multiplication is to use Frobenius expansions. Koblitz [3] suggested the use of Frobenius expansions and anomalous elliptic curves. Müller [4] and Cheon et al. [5] extended this idea to give the Frobenius expansion over small fields of characteristic two. Smart [6] generalized Müller's idea to elliptic curves over fields with small odd characteristic. Gallant, Lambert and Vanstone (GLV) [7] suggested that efficiently computable endomorphisms other than Frobenius endomorphisms can be used for fast scalar multiplications. Further research on the improvement of their methods has been done by Y.-H. Park

J. Song, T. Kwon, and M. Yung (Eds.): WISA 2005, LNCS 3786, pp. 271–282, 2006.

et al. [8] and Ciet et al. [9, 10]. Recently, T.J. Park et al. [11, 12] presented alternative Frobenius expansion algorithms combined with other efficient maps such as the GLV endomorphisms.

Power analysis attack, first introduced by Kocher et al. [13], is a powerful technique allowing the recover of the secret information by monitoring power signals. There are two kinds of power analysis attacks; SPA (simple power analysis) and DPA (differential power analysis), where DPA is believed to be more effective than SPA. Various research has been done to prevent SPA and DPA. Substantially, the countermeasures against SPA are to make the power consumption of unit operations independent of the secret key bits, and the countermeasures against DPA are to randomize computation so that the same operations produce different power signals.

As for the power analysis attacks on elliptic curves, Coron [14] first showed that the naive implementations of ECC are also highly vulnerable to SPA and DPA. Various methods [14, 15, 16, 17, 18, 19, 20] have been proposed to prevent this attack on elliptic curves. Especially, Hasan [19] suggested several countermeasures against SPA and DPA on Koblitz curves (a.k.a. anomalous binary curves), and Ciet et al. [20] proposed randomizing the GLV decomposition method to prevent DPA on GLV curves. Ciet et al.'s method can be viewed as a two dimensional generalization of Coron's [14]. Note that Hasan's method is applied only to anomalous binary curves, and Ciet et al.'s method is applied only to GLV curves.

In this paper we propose a new countermeasure against DPA, which is applicable to any curve where the Frobenius expansion method can be used. Our countermeasure is based on random decomposition of a scalar, which is inspired by the randomized GLV decomposition in [20]. We also analyze the relation between immunity to DPA and computational overheads. According to our analysis, the new countermeasure can produce a collision probability around 2^{-20} with only 15.4–34.0% extra computation for scalar multiplications on curves over various fields.

2   Preliminaries

2.1   Ordinary Frobenius Expansion Methods

In this section, we briefly explain the previous Frobenius expansion methods. Let q be a prime power. If q is of the form 2^m or 3^m, then an nonsupersingular elliptic curve over $\mathbb{F}_q$ is given by an equation of the form

$$E : y^2 + xy = x^3 + a_2 x^2 + a_6,$$

where a_2, $a_6 \in \mathbb{F}_q$ and $a_6 \neq 0$. Otherwise, an elliptic curve over $\mathbb{F}_q$ is given by an equation of the form

$$E : y^2 = x^3 + ax + b,$$

where a, $b \in \mathbb{F}_q$.

The Frobenius endomorphism of E is given by

$$\phi : E(\bar{\mathbb{F}}_q) \longrightarrow E(\bar{\mathbb{F}}_q)$$
$$(x, y) \longmapsto (x^q, y^q).$$

where $\bar{\mathbb{F}}_q$ is the algebraic closure of $\mathbb{F}_q$. The Frobenius endomorphism satisfies the following minimal polynomial,

$$\phi^2 - \tau\phi + q = 0 \tag{1}$$

where $|\tau| \leq 2\sqrt{q}$. Note that even if we consider $\mathbb{F}_{q^n}$-rational points on E, i.e., $E(\mathbb{F}_{q^n})$, the properties of the Frobenius endomorphism on $E(\mathbb{F}_q)$ holds.

To avoid the MOV attack [21], we have to use nonsupersingular elliptic curves. The endomorphism ring of a nonsupersingular elliptic curve E is an order in the imaginary quadratic field $\mathbb{Q}(\sqrt{\tau^2 - 4q})$. Obviously, the ring $\mathbb{Z}[\phi] = \{a + b\phi \mid a, \ b \in \mathbb{Z}\}$ is a subring of the endomorphism ring of E.

Müller [4] proposed a Frobenius expansion method by iterating divisions for fast scalar multiplication on elliptic curves over small fields of characteristic two. Smart [6] proposed a similar method on small fields of odd characteristic. The following lemma proves the existence of a division by ϕ with remainder in the ring $\mathbb{Z}[\phi]$. We give a proof which is a little bit different from the original ones.

Lemma 1. *[4, 6] Suppose that q be even (respectively, odd) prime power. Let $s \in \mathbb{Z}[\phi]$. There exists an integer $r \in \mathbb{Z}$, $-q/2 \leq r \leq q/2$ (respectively, $-(q+1)/2 \leq r \leq (q+1)/2$), and an element $t \in \mathbb{Z}[\phi]$ such that*

$$s = t \cdot \phi + r.$$

Proof. Let $s = s_1 + s_2\phi$ with $s_1, \ s_2 \in \mathbb{Z}$. We will choose integers $t_1, \ t_2, \ r \in \mathbb{Z}$, such that

$$s_1 + s_2\phi = (t_1 + t_2\phi) \cdot \phi + r.$$

Using (1), we transform the right-hand side of this equation into

$$(t_1 + t_2\phi) \cdot \phi + r = t_1\phi + t_2(\tau\phi - q) + r$$
$$= (-t_2 q + r) + (t_1 + \tau t_2) \cdot \phi.$$

Comparing coefficients, we get $s_1 = -t_2 q + r$. Let $t_2 = -\lfloor s_1/q \rceil$, where $\lfloor x \rceil$ is the nearest integer to x. We can compute $t_1 = s_2 - \tau t_2$ and $r = s_1 + t_2 q$.

By iterating the process of divisions by ϕ with remainder, one can expand

$$s = \sum_{j=0}^{l} r_j \cdot \phi^j,$$

where $r_j \in \{-q/2, \ldots, q/2\}$ ($r_j \in \{-(q+1)/2, \ldots, (q+1)/2\}$) with $l = \lceil 2\log_q \|s\| \rceil + 3$ ($l = \lceil 2\log_q 2\|s\| \rceil + 3$) and $\|s\|$ is the Euclidean length of s.

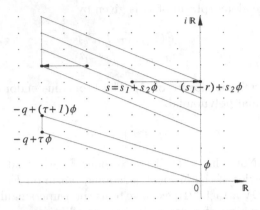

Fig. 1. Choosing smaller integer r in L_1

From a different point of view, the proof of Lemma 1 can be reconstructed as follows. We remark that its main idea comes from [11, 12]. Let L be the lattice generated by 1 and ϕ. Let's consider the elements in L which can be divided by ϕ. Such an element is of the form $\phi \cdot (l + m\phi)$ and

$$\phi \cdot (l + m\phi) = l\phi + m\phi^2$$
$$= l\phi + m(-q + \tau\phi)$$

by (1). Thus, the set of all elements which can be divided by ϕ is the lattice generated by ϕ and $\phi^2 = -q + \tau\phi$. We denote this lattice by $L_1 = [\phi, -q + \tau\phi]$.

We want to divide $s = s_1 + s_2\phi \in L$ by ϕ with remainder. If $s_1 + s_2\phi$ is in L_1, then $s_1 + s_2\phi$ is divided by ϕ, i.e. $s_1 + s_2\phi = (t_1 + t_2\phi) \cdot \phi$. If $s_1 + s_2\phi$ is not in L_1, then we move $s_1 + s_2\phi$ horizontally left or right to $s_1 - r + s_2\phi \in L_1$ by choosing smaller $r \in \mathbb{Z}$. See Fig. 1. Since $s_1 - r + s_2\phi$ is in L_1,

$$s_1 - r + s_2\phi = (t_1 + t_2\phi) \cdot \phi,$$
$$s_1 + s_2\phi = (t_1 + t_2\phi) \cdot \phi + r.$$

2.2   DPA Against Scalar Multiplication

In this section, we explain Coron's DPA attack [14] against ECC scalar multiplication. DPA (differential power analysis) uses the correlation between power consumption and specific key-dependent bits which appear at known steps of a certain computation. Now we briefly describe how Coron's attack [14] uses this idea to recover the secret k from h scalar multiplications kP_i $(1 \le i \le h)$ that involve the fixed k and distinct points P_i. Let $k = \sum_{j=0}^{l} k_j 2^j$ $(k_j \in \{0, 1\})$, and assume $k_l = 1$ without loss of generality.

First, consider the case that the scalar multiplications are done using the conventional left-to-right double-and-add algorithm. Then the computation sequence of kP_i will be

$$P_i \to 2P_i \to 3P_i \to 6P_i \to \cdots \quad \text{if } k_{l-1} = 1,$$

or

$$P_i \to 2P_i \to 4P_i \to \cdots \quad \text{if } k_{l-1} = 0.$$

Hence, if $k_{l-1} = 0$, $4P_i$ is computed in the above sequence, and power consumption is correlated with any specific bit s_i in the binary representation of point $4P_i$. In other words, the correlation function

$$g(t) = \sum_{i=1,\ldots,h \mid s_i=1} C_i(t) - \sum_{i=1,\ldots,h \mid s_i=0} C_i(t),$$

where $C_i(t)$ is the power consumption of kP_i at time t, has a non-negligible value at some point $t = t'$. (t' is the moment when s_i is being dealt.) On the other hand, if $k_{l-1} = 1$, $g(t)$ should have negligible values at any t since kP_i and $4P_i$ have no relation. Thus an attacker can distinguish between $k_{l-1} = 0$ and $k_{l-1} = 1$ by computing the correlation function from many scalar multiplications with a fixed k. After recovering k_{l-1} using the above procedure, the remaining bits of k can be recursively recovered in the same way.

It is easy to see that the above attack can be extended to any scalar multiplication algorithm that uses a fixed addition-subtraction chain

$$P \to a_1 P \to a_2 P \to \cdots \to kP,$$

for a fixed k, regardless of P. The attacker can recover k by successively guessing a_i. At step $i \geq 1$, he constructs the set A_i of all possible a_i, and for each $a_i' \in A_i$ computes the correlation function between the point $a_i'P$ and power consumption. Note that the Frobenius expansion-based scalar multiplications, which we are interested in, are vulnerable to this kind of attack.

We remark that the vulnerability results from the fact that the same k is used many times. Therefore, an obvious solution is to use different k' such that $k'P = kP$, instead of k. Most of the countermeasures against DPA have adopted this approach, and our countermeasure is also based on this idea.

3 DPA Countermeasure by Randomized Frobenius Decomposition

In this section we propose a random decomposition method and show how it can be used for a countermeasure against DPA on any curve where the Frobenius expansion is used. Actually, our work is inspired by the countermeasure in [20] which randomizes the GLV decomposition.

3.1 Randomized GLV Method

Now, we briefly review the GLV decomposition method (see [7, 10]). Let E be an elliptic curve over a prime field $\mathbb{F}_q$. Assume that there exists an efficiently computable endomorphism Ψ on E whose minimal polynomial is $X^2 + rX + s = 0$.

For $P \in E(\mathbb{F}_q)$ of prime order n, $\Psi(P) = \lambda P$ for some $\lambda \in [1, n-1]$ where λ is a root of $X^2 + rX + s \equiv 0 \bmod n$. The GLV method decomposes a scalar k as $k \equiv k_1 + k_2\lambda \pmod{n}$ where $k_1, k_2 = \mathcal{O}(\sqrt{n})$.

In order to find such a decomposition $k \equiv k_1 + k_2\lambda \pmod{n}$, Gallant et al. [7] introduced a way to use two linearly independent small vectors v_1, v_2 in the kernel of the homomorphism $f : \mathbb{Z} \times \mathbb{Z} \to \mathbb{Z}/n$ defined by $f(i,j) = i + j\lambda \pmod{n}$. Let V be a lattice generated by v_1, v_2. The lattice V consists of the kernel of the homomorphism f. The goal is to find the nearest lattice point of V to k. We can decompose $(k,0) = av_1 + bv_2$ for $a, b \in \mathbb{Q}$, then $(k,0) = \lfloor a \rceil v_1 + \lfloor b \rceil v_2 + (k_1, k_2)$. Since $f(v_1) = f(v_2) = 0$, $kP = (k_1 + k_2\lambda)P$.

We show DPA countermeasure for GLV method in [20]. Let $A = \begin{pmatrix} a & b \\ c & d \end{pmatrix}$ be a random 2×2 matrix and $ad - bc \neq 0$. The domain $\mathbb{Z} \times \mathbb{Z}$ of the GLV homomorphism f can be regarded as a lattice with the basis $\{1, \Psi\}$ and $\mathcal{L} = A(\mathbb{Z} \times \mathbb{Z})$ is obviously a random sublattice of $\mathbb{Z} \times \mathbb{Z}$ with the basis $\{\Psi_0, \Psi_1\}$ where $\Psi_0 = a + c\Psi$ and $\Psi_1 = b + d\Psi$.

We need to compute two linearly independent small vectors v_1', v_2' in the kernel of homomorphism $f|_{\mathcal{L}} : A(\mathbb{Z} \times \mathbb{Z}) \to \mathbb{Z}/n$ as the usual GLV method. Using the same strategy as in the original GLV method, Ciet et al. introduced a way to find two linearly independent small vectors v_1' and v_2' as follows;

$$v_1' = \hat{A}v_1 \tag{2}$$
$$v_2' = \hat{A}v_2 \tag{3}$$

where $\hat{A} = \begin{pmatrix} d & -c \\ -b & a \end{pmatrix}$ is the adjoint matrix of A. To decompose $kP = k_1'\Psi_0(P) + k_2'\Psi_1(P)$ for some $k_1', k_2' = \mathcal{O}(\sqrt{n})$, they proceed as in the GLV method with v_1' and v_2'.

3.2   Frobenius Expansion Using Random Decomposition

Now, we propose a new decomposition method analogous to the GLV method. We transform $L = [1, \phi]$ in Section 2 to another lattice L' by the 2×2 random matrix $A = \begin{pmatrix} a & b \\ c & d \end{pmatrix}$, $ad - bc \neq 0$, where

$$\begin{aligned} A : L &\longrightarrow L' \\ 1 &\longmapsto a + c\phi \\ \phi &\longmapsto b + d\phi. \end{aligned}$$

Obviously, $L' = [a + c\phi, b + d\phi]$ is a sublattice of L. While the lattice in GLV method is the kernel of the homomorphism f, the lattice L is a subring of the endomorphism ring of E.

Our goal is to decompose $s = s_1 + s_2\phi \in L$ with the basis of the lattice L'.

Lemma 2. *For any $s = s_1 + s_2\phi \in \mathbb{Z}[\phi]$, we can find k_1, k_2, r_1, and $r_2 \in \mathbb{Z}$ such that*

$$
\begin{aligned}
s &= k_1(a + c\phi) + k_2(b + d\phi) + r_1 + r_2\phi \\
&= k_1 a + k_2 b + (k_1 c + k_2 d)\phi + r_1 + r_2\phi,
\end{aligned}
$$

where the Euclidean length of $r = r_1 + r_2\phi$ is bounded by

$$
\max\left\{ \frac{\sqrt{(a-b)^2 + (c-d)^2}}{2}, \frac{\sqrt{(a+b)^2 + (c+d)^2}}{2} \right\} \tag{4}
$$

Proof. There exist $x_1, x_2 \in \mathbb{Q}$ such that

$$
\begin{pmatrix} s_1 \\ s_2 \end{pmatrix} = \begin{pmatrix} a & b \\ c & d \end{pmatrix} \begin{pmatrix} x_1 \\ x_2 \end{pmatrix}.
$$

We can compute $x_1, x_2 \in \mathbb{Q}$ by

$$
\begin{pmatrix} x_1 \\ x_2 \end{pmatrix} = \frac{1}{(ad - bc)} \begin{pmatrix} d & -b \\ -c & a \end{pmatrix} \begin{pmatrix} s_1 \\ s_2 \end{pmatrix}.
$$

To obtain $k_1, k_2 \in \mathbb{Z}$ from x_1, x_2, set

$$
\begin{pmatrix} k_1 \\ k_2 \end{pmatrix} = \begin{pmatrix} \lfloor x_1 \rceil \\ \lfloor x_2 \rceil \end{pmatrix}.
$$

Then

$$
\begin{pmatrix} r_1 \\ r_2 \end{pmatrix} = \begin{pmatrix} s_1 \\ s_2 \end{pmatrix} - \begin{pmatrix} a & b \\ c & d \end{pmatrix} \begin{pmatrix} k_1 \\ k_2 \end{pmatrix}. \tag{5}
$$

See Fig. 2.

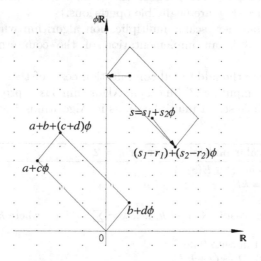

Fig. 2. Choosing $r = r_1 + r_2\phi$ in L'

Note that since a scalar k is in $\mathbb{Z}[\phi]$, k can be expanded as $k = k_1 a + k_2 b + (k_1 c + k_2 d)\phi + r_1 + r_2\phi$ using the above lemma. Also, we can get $k_1 a + k_2 b + (k_1 c + k_2 d)\phi = \sum_{i=0}^{l} k_i' \phi^i$ by iterating the division algorithm in Lemma 1. Hence, a scalar multiplication kP can be done as follows:

$$kP = (\sum_{i=0}^{l} k_i' \phi^i P) + (r_1 + r_2\phi)P,$$

where $l \approx 2n$ when we use the original expansion algorithms in [4, 6], and $l = n$ when we use optimized ones [22, 23, 24, 25]. Since we have chosen a, b, c and d randomly, the computation sequence of kP is randomized. Hence this algorithm can be used as a DPA countermeasure.

4   Efficiency and Security

In this section we describe our scalar multiplication algorithms secure against DPA. Then we analyze the immunity to DPA and the extra computation costs of the new countermeasures.

We begin by describing two well-known scalar multiplication algorithms using the Frobenius expansion. Algorithm 1 [22, 23] is for the fields with $q = 2$, and Algorithm 2 [24, 25] is for the fields with $q \gg 2$. Originally, the length of the expansion in line 1 of each algorithm is approximately $2n$. However, we can reduce it to n by reducing k to $k \bmod (\phi^n - 1)$ before the expansion, since $\phi^n(P) = P$ for any P. In Algorithm 2, k_i^j means the j-th digit of k_i, where the 0-th digit is regarded as the least significant digit.

The approximate numbers of elliptic curve point operations are $n/3$ additions for Algorithm 1, and $(n \log_2 q)/3$ additions and $\log_2 q$ doublings for Algorithm 2 on the average. (We do not consider the costs for ϕ expansions and ϕ-map computations, since they are negligible operations.)

Next we give our new scalar multiplication algorithm which is immune to DPA. Algorithm 3 is an implementation of the countermeasure given in Section 3.

Now we estimate the additional computation costs of these algorithms. Note that the cost for computing P' (line 2) in Algorithm 3 is approximately the same as those of the whole scalar multiplications in Algorithms 1 and 2. Hence other

---

Algorithm 1. Scalar multiplication for $q = 2$

Input: scalar k, point $P \in E(\mathbb{F}_{2^n})$
Output: point $Q = kP$
   begin
      1. Compute the ϕ-adic NAF of k, i.e., $k = \sum_{i=0}^{n-1} k_i \phi^i$, where $k_i \in \{0, 1, -1\}$.
      2. $Q \leftarrow O$.
      3. for $i = n - 1$ downto 0 do
         $Q \leftarrow \phi(Q); Q \leftarrow Q + k_i P.$
   end

Algorithm 2. Scalar multiplication for $q \gg 2$

Input: scalar k, point $P \in E(\mathbb{F}_{q^n})$
Output: point $Q = kP$
  begin
  1. Compute the ϕ-expansion of k, i.e., $k = \sum_{i=0}^{n-1} k_i \phi^i$,
     where each k_i is represented as NAF,
     and $k_i \in \{-q/2, \ldots, q/2\}$ for even q, $k_i \in \{-(q+1)/2, \ldots, (q+1)/2\}$ for odd q.
  2. for $i = 0$ to $n-1$ do
     $P_i \leftarrow \phi^i(P)$.
  3. $Q \leftarrow O$.
  4. for $j = \lceil \log_2 q \rceil$ downto 0 do
     $Q \leftarrow 2Q; \ Q \leftarrow Q + \sum_{i=0}^{n-1} k_i^j P_i$.
  end

Algorithm 3. Randomized scalar multiplication ($q = 2$ or $q \gg 2$)

Input: scalar k, point $P \in E(\mathbb{F}_{q^n})$
Output: point $Q = kP$
  begin
  1. Compute the randomized expansion of k, i.e., $k = \left(\sum_{i=0}^{n-1} k_i \phi^i \right) + (r_1 + r_2 \phi)$,
     where r_1, r_2 are represented as NAF.
  2. Compute $P' = \sum_{i=0}^{n-1} k_i \phi^i(P)$.
     (Use Algorithm 1 for $q = 2$ and Algorithm 2 for $q \gg 2$.)
  3. $P_0 = P; \ P_1 = \phi(P)$.
     // Now we compute $P' + r_1 P_0 + r_2 P_1$.
  4. $Q \leftarrow O$.
  5. for $j =$(max digit index of r_1, r_2) downto 0 do
     $Q \leftarrow 2Q; \ Q \leftarrow Q + r_1^j P_0 + r_2^j P_1$.
  6. $Q \leftarrow Q + P'$.
  end

---

operations are computational overheads for DPA countermeasures, and it is easy to see that the overhead for Algorithm 3 is $(\log_2 \|r_1\| + \log_2 \|r_2\|)/3 + 1$ additions and $\max(\log_2 \|r_1\|, \log_2 \|r_2\|)$ doublings. These values become approximately $(2 \log \|a\| + 1)/3 + 1$ and $\log_2 \|a\|$, respectively, if we set $\|a\| \approx \|b\| \approx \|c\| \approx \|d\|$ in (4) for the worst case.

For the security estimate, we have to compute the probability of collision. If we choose randomly a, b, c and d where $\|a\|, \|b\|, \|c\|, \|d\| \leq 2^{10}$ as in [20], by lemma 2 the lengths of $r = r_1 + r_2 \phi$ are bounded by $\mathcal{O}(2^{10})$. The number of such $r's$ is about $\pi \cdot 2^{20}$ since the area of a circle with its radius r is πr^2. Therefore, the probability of collision is about $\frac{\pi \cdot 2^{20}}{2^{40}}$, that is $\mathcal{O}(2^{-20})$, since the total number of matrices is around 2^{40}.

Table 1 shows the computational overhead of the countermeasure for various q and n. If we assume the complexities of an addition and a doubling are approximately the same, the computational overhead is 15.4–34.0% according to the table. We also see that it decreases as q increases for a fixed q^n value, since the overhead is fixed regardless of q or n while the total cost increases as q increases.

Table 1. Number of point operations (A: addition, D: doubling)

q	n	Algorithms 1 and 2	overhead for Algorithm 3
	160	53A+0D	8A+10D (34.0%)
2	192	64A+0D	8A+10D (28.1%)
	256	85A+0D	8A+10D (21.2%)
	20	53A+8D	8A+10D (29.5%)
$\approx 2^8$	24	64A+8D	8A+10D (25.0%)
	32	85A+8D	8A+10D (19.4%)
	10	53A+16D	8A+10D (26.1%)
$\approx 2^{16}$	12	64A+16D	8A+10D (22.5%)
	16	85A+16D	8A+10D (17.8%)
	5	53A+32D	8A+10D (21.2%)
$\approx 2^{32}$	6	64A+32D	8A+10D (18.8%)
	8	85A+32D	8A+10D (15.4%)

5   Conclusions

In this paper we have proposed a new countermeasure against DPA. Our countermeasure is based on random decomposition of a scalar and it is applicable to any curve where the Frobenius expansion is possible. According to our analysis, the new countermeasure can produce a probability of collision around $\mathcal{O}(2^{-20})$ with only 15.4–34.0% extra computation for scalar multiplications on curves over various fields.

We remark that the random decomposition technique used in our countermeasure is related to the expansion methods given in [11, 12]. Hence the hyperelliptic curve analog [26] of [11, 12] can be used to develop a DPA countermeasure over hyperelliptic curves.

Note that not only our technique is used independently, but also it can be used in conjunction with other countermeasures such as Coron's method [14] and Hasan's method [19]. Note also that instead of the NAF-based simultaneous scalar multiplication algorithms in Algorithms 2 and 3, we can use further optimized methods such as Straus-Shamir method of Solinas [27]. However, the overhead ratio is almost not changed since the original computation and the overhead are equally optimized.

References

1. Koblitz, N.: Elliptic curve cryptosystems. Mathematics of Computation **48** (1987) 203–209
2. Miller, V.: Use of elliptic curves in cryptography. In: Advances in Cryptology-CRYPTO 85. Volume 218 of LNCS., Springer-Verlag (1986) 417–428
3. Koblitz, N.: CM-curves with good cryptographic properties. In: Advances in Cryptology-CRYPTO 91. Volume 576 of LNCS., Springer-Verlag (1991) 279–287
4. Müller, V.: Fast multiplication on elliptic curves over small fields of characteristic two. Journal of Cryptology **11** (1998) 219–234

5. Cheon, J., Park, S., Park, S., Kim, D.: Two efficient algorithms for arithmetic of elliptic curves using Frobenius map. In: Public Key Cryptography 98. Volume 1431 of LNCS., Springer-Verlag (1998) 195–202
6. Smart, N.: Elliptic curve cryptosystems over small fields of odd characteristic. Journal of Cryptology **12** (1999) 141–151
7. Gallant, R., Lambert, R., Vanstone, S.: Faster point multiplication on elliptic curves with efficient endomorphisms. In: Advances in Cryptology-CRYPTO 2001. Volume 2139 of LNCS., Springer-Verlag (2001) 190–200
8. Park, Y.H., Jeong, S., Kim, C., Lim, J.: An alternate decomposition of an integer for faster point multiplication on certain elliptic curves. In: Public Key Cryptography 2002. Volume 2274 of LNCS., Springer-Verlag (2002) 323–334
9. Sica, F., Ciet, M., Quisquater, J.J.: Analysis of the Gallant-Lambert-Vanstone Method Based on Efficient Endomorphisms: Elliptic and Hyperelliptic Curves. In: SAC 2002. Volume 2595 of LNCS., Springer-Verlag (2002) 21–36
10. Ciet, M., Lange, T., Sica, F., Quisquater, J.J.: Improved algorithms for efficient arithmetic on elliptic curves using fast endomorphisms. In: Advances in Cryptology-EUROCRYPT 2003. Volume 2656 of LNCS., Springer-Verlag (2003) 388–400
11. Park, T.J., Lee, M.K., Park, K.: New frobenius expansions for elliptic curves with efficient endomorphisms. In: ICISC 2002. Volume 2587 of LNCS., Springer-Verlag (2003) 264–282
12. Park, T.J., Lee, M.K., Kim, E., Park, K.: A general expansion method using efficient endomorphisms. In: ICISC 2003. Volume 2971 of LNCS., Springer-Verlag (2004) 112–126
13. Kocher, P., Jaffe, J., Jun, B.: Differential power analysis. In: Advances in Cryptology-CRYPTO 99. Volume 1666 of LNCS., Springer-Verlag (1999) 388–397
14. Coron, J.S.: Resistance against differential power analysis for elliptic curve cryptosystems. In: CHES 99. Volume 1717 of LNCS., Springer-Verlag (1999) 292–302
15. Joye, M., Quisquater, J.J.: Hessian elliptic curves and side-channel attacks. In: CHES 2001. Volume 2162 of LNCS., Springer-Verlag (2001) 402–410
16. Joye, M., Tymen, C.: Protections against differential analysis for elliptic curve cryptography-an algebraic approach. In: CHES 2001. Volume 2162 of LNCS., Springer-Verlag (2001) 377–390
17. Liardet, P.Y., Smart, N.: Preventing SPA/DPA in ECC systems using the Jacobi form. In: CHES 2001. Volume 2162 of LNCS., Springer-Verlag (2001) 391–401
18. Möller, B.: Securing elliptic curve point multiplication against Side-Channel Attacks. In: Advances in Cryptology-ISC 2001. Volume 2200 of LNCS., Springer-Verlag (2001) 324–334
19. Hasan, M.: Power analysis attacks and algorithmic approaches to their countermeasures for Koblitz curve cryptosystems. IEEE Transactions on Computers **50** (2001) 1071–1083 A preliminary version was presented at CHES 2000, pp.94–109.
20. Ciet, M., Quisquater, J.J., Sica, F.: Preventing differential analysis in GLV elliptic curve scalar multiplication. In: CHES 2002. Volume 2523 of LNCS., Springer-Verlag (2003) 540–550
21. Menezes, A., Okamoto, T., Vanstone, S.: Reducing elliptic curve logarithms to a finite field. IEEE Trans. Inform. Theory **39** (1993) 1639–1646
22. Solinas, J.: An improved algorithm for arithmetic on a family of elliptic curves. In: Advances in Cryptology-CRYPTO 97. Volume 1294 of LNCS., Springer-Verlag (1997) 357–371
23. Solinas, J.: Efficient arithmetic on Koblitz curves. Designs, Codes and Cryptography **19** (2000) 195–249

24. Kobayashi, T., Morita, H., Kobayashi, K., Hoshino, F.: Fast elliptic curve algorithm combining Frobenius map and table reference to adapt to higher characteristic. In: Advances in Cryptology-EUROCRYPT 99. Volume 1592 of LNCS., Springer-Verlag (1999) 176–189
25. Kobayashi, T.: Base-ϕ method for elliptic curves over OEF. IEICE Trans. Fundamentals **E83-A** (2000) 679–686
26. Park, T.J., Lee, M.K., Park, K., Chung, K.: Speeding up scalar multiplication in genus 2 hyperelliptic curves with efficient endomorphisms. (2005) To appear in ETRI Journal vol. 27, no. 5.
27. Solinas, J.: Low-weight binary representations for pairs of integers (2001) Technical Report CORR 2001-41, CACR, Available at `http://www.cacr.math.uwaterloo.ca/techreports/2001/corr2001-41.ps`.

DPA Attack on the Improved Ha-Moon Algorithm*

Jong Hoon Shin, Dong Jin Park, and Pil Joong Lee

Information Security Laboratory,
Dept. of EEE, Postech, Pohang, Korea
{jhshin, djpark}@oberon.postech.ac.kr, pjl@postech.ac.kr

Abstract. The Ha-Moon algorithm [4] is a countermeasure against power analysis using a randomized addition chain. It has two drawbacks in that it requires an inversion and has a right-to-left approach. Recently, Yen *et al.* improved the algorithm by removing these drawbacks [11]. Their new algorithm is inversion-free, has a left-to-right approach, and employs a window method. They insisted that their algorithm leads to a more secure countermeasure in computing modular exponentiation against side-channel attacks. This algorithm, however, still has a similar weakness observed in [2, 10]. This paper shows that the improved Ha-Moon algorithm is vulnerable to differential power analysis even if we employ their method in selecting s_i.

Keywords: Ha-Moon algorithm, randomized exponentiation algorithm, side-channel attack.

1 Introduction

Recent progress in side channel attacks on the embedded cryptosystem indicates a need for a secure implementation of cryptographic primitives. These attacks are so practical that attackers can obtain secret information, such as secret exponent, even if the implemented cryptosystem is mathematically secure. Therefore, developers should implement cryptographic primitives securely as well as efficiently. This principle is essential for exponentiation or elliptic curve scalar multiplication, which is a major process in many cryptosystems.

Side channel attacks include power analysis attacks [6], timing attacks [5], fault-based attacks [1], and EM attacks [3]. The most practical attacks are power analysis attacks, which are widely studied. They exploit correlation between an exponent and sampled power traces. According to the techniques employed, power analysis is called *simple power analysis* (SPA) or *differential power analysis* (DPA). SPA is based on the common belief that different group operations have different power trace shapes. If one implements the elliptic curve cryptosystem (ECC), an SPA attacker can discover the secret exponent using the

---

* This research was supported by University IT Research Center Project, the Brain Korea 21 Project.

J. Song, T. Kwon, and M. Yung (Eds.): WISA 2005, LNCS 3786, pp. 283–291, 2006.

difference between addition and doubling. On the other hand, DPA is based on the same underlying principle of SPA, but uses statistical techniques to extract subtle differences in power traces. Classic DPA entails averaging and subtraction. After measuring a sufficient number of power traces, DPA divides them into two groups by a selection function. The power traces of each group are averaged, and then subtracted. A correct estimation of the secret key provides a peak in a subtracted trace. Because averaging can improve the signal-to-noise (SNR), DPA is sensitive to smaller differences below the noise level.

In 2002, Ha and Moon proposed an algorithm that prevents power analysis [4] using a randomized addition chain. That is, the Ha-Moon algorithm randomizes a secret exponent into a signed binary representation. Many researchers are interested in this algorithm because of its simplicity and efficiency. Two drawbacks of the Ha-Moon algorithm are that it requires an inversion of a group element and recodes an exponent into a randomized representation from LSB to MSB (i.e. right-to-left).

Recently, Yen *et al.* improved these drawbacks of the Ha-Moon algorithm [11]; their new algorithm, *the improved Ha-Moon algorithm*, has a left-to-right approach and does not require an inversion of a group element. Thus, their algorithm can be applied in computing modular exponentiations, such as RSA and DSA. They insisted that their algorithm leads to a more secure countermeasure implementing exponentiation against side-channel attacks. However, this paper shows that the improved Ha-Moon algorithm is still vulnerable to differential power analysis (DPA) [6, 7]. Thus, the improved Ha-Moon algorithm should not be implemented in low-powered devices for which it was originally designed.

The remainder of this paper organized as follows: In Section 2, we briefly review the improved Ha-Moon algorithm. In Section 3, we propose an attack method that shows the improved Ha-Moon algorithm is still vulnerable to DPA. Finally, in Section 5, we conclude this paper.

2   Improved Ha-Moon Algorithm

The improved Ha-Moon algorithm has three improvements compared with the original Ha-Moon algorithm. This algorithm uses a left-to-right approach, a non-inversion technique, and a window method. In this section, we summarizes the improved Ha-Moon Algorithm. See [11] for details.

2.1   Notations

Suppose that K is the n-bit private exponent and $(k_{n-1}k_{n-2}\ldots k_1k_0)_2$ denotes K's binary representation. Let $D = (d_n d_{n-1} \cdots d_1 d_0)_{SD2}$ be one of K's possible signed-digit representations. K_i denotes the bit string from $(n-1)$th to ith bits of K, and D_i denotes the signed-digit bit string from nth to ith bits of D. The subscripts $()_2$ and $()_{SD2}$ mean that the numbers in the bracket are binary (0 or 1) and signed-digit binary (-1, 0, or 1) represented, respectively.

$$K = (k_{n-1}k_{n-2} \cdots k_1 k_0)_2, K_i = (k_{n-1} \cdots k_i)_2$$
$$D = (d_n d_{n-1} \cdots d_1 d_0)_{SD2}, D_i = (d_n \cdots d_i)_{SD2}.$$

2.2   Left-to-Right Recoding

The improved Ha-Moon algorithm randomly recodes a binary exponent into a signed-digit exponent from MSB toward LSB. In this method, the original exponent $K = (k_{n-1}k_{n-2} \dots k_1 k_0)_2$ is randomly recoded into a signed-digit exponent $D = (d_n d_{n-1} \cdots d_1 d_0)_{SD2}$ by the following equations:

$$c_i - d_i = 2c_{i+1} - k_i,$$
$$(k_{n-1}k_{n-2} \dots k_{i+1}k_i)_2 + c_i = (d_n d_{n-1} \cdots d_{i+1} d_i)_{SD2},$$

where c_i is the carry bit, and c_{n+1} is initialized to be 0.

2.3   Non-inversion Technique

When $d_i = -1$, an inversion occurs. To prevent an inversion, they modified a recoding method in order not to generate a negative integer. The basic idea of them is to reserve a small value b_i (called the *pre-borrow*) from the higher priority digit to the lower priority digit. Using the following equations, a randomized exponent D can be changed to an inversion-free exponent D':

$$D_i = 2D_{i+1} + d_i,$$
$$D_i' = D_i + b_i = 2(D_{i+1} + b_{i+1}) + (b_i - 2b_{i+1} + d_i)$$
$$= 2D_{i+1}' + d_i',$$
$$d_i' - b_i = d_i - 2b_{i+1}.$$

For example, if $d_i = -1$ and $b_{i+1} = -1$ (i.e., a pre-borrow of one from its higher priority digit), then the expected value at digit i becomes $d_i - b_{i+1} \times 2 = 1$ and we have the re-recoded $d_i' = 1$.

The proposed exponentiation without division is given in Algorithm 1, where the variable b is initially set to $-(d_n d_{n-1})_{SD2}$ and $\mathcal{F}(\cdot)$ calculates pre-borrow and the re-recoded digit. For the details, see Section 3.3 in [11].

Algorithm 1. Exponentiation without division (Fig. 2 in [11])

INPUT: $g, D = (d_n, \cdots, d_0)_{SD2}$ where $2^{n-1} \le D \le 2^n - 1$
OUTPUT: g^D
1. Precomputation: all values of $g^{d_i'}$
2. $R = 1$
3. $b = -(d_n d_{n-1})_{SD2}$
4. for i from $n - 2$ downto 0 do
    4.1 $(b, d') = \mathcal{F}(b, d_i)$
    4.2 $R = R^2$
    4.3 $R = R \times g^{d'}$
5. $R = R \times g^{-b}$
6. output R

2.4 The Windowing Technique

The non-inversion technique can be combined with the windowing method to improve the performance. Necessary mathematical relationships with window size of two are provided in the following equations:

$$D_i = 4D_{i+2} + (d_{i+1}d_i)_{SD2},$$
$$D'_i = D_i + b_i = 4(D_{i+2} + b_{i+2}) + (b_i - 4b_{i+2} + (d_{i+1}d_i)_{SD2})$$
$$= 4D'_{i+2} + d'_i,$$
$$d'_i - b_i = (d_{i+1}di)_{SD2} - 4b_{i+2},$$
$$g^{D'_i} = (g^{D'_{i+2}})^4 \times g^{d'_i}.$$

For every two bits of the exponent, the windowing technique requires two squarings and one multiplication (if $d'_i \neq 0$).

2.5 Randomized Exponentiation Without Inversion

Using these techniques, Yen *et al.* proposed the randomized exponentiation without inversion. As a result, a randomized exponent d'_i is recoded from the following equation:

$$d'_i - s_i = (k_{i+1}k_i)_2 - 4s_{i+2}$$

where $(k_{i+1}k_i)_2$ is a secret exponent to be recoded and $s_i \in_R \{-1, -2, -3\}$ introduces randomness in the representation. Since d'_i becomes a positive integer for all i, there is no inversion operation in Algorithm 2. In Algorithm 2, there are always two squarings and multiplication sequences, which are not dummy operations. Thus, the improved algorithm can resist SPA-like attacks, such as Okeya *et al.*' attack [9], and the safe-error attack [12]. Also, the improved Ha-Moon algorithm may resist Fouque *et al.*' attack [2], because the probability of each state transitions seems to be equal.

Algorithm 2. Improved Ha-Moon algorithm with 2-bit window (Fig. 3 in [11])

INPUT: $g, K = (k_{n-1}, \cdots, k_0)_2$ where n is even and $(k_{n-1}k_{n-2})_2 = (01)_2, (10)_2,$ or $(11)_2$
OUTPUT: g^K

1. $R[0] = 1; R[1] = g$
2. Precomputation: $R[2] = g^2, \cdots, R[14] = g^{14}$
3. $s = -(k_{n-1}k_{n-2})_2$
4. for i from $n - 4$ downto 0 step -2 do
    4.1 $d = -4s$
    4.2 $s =$ RandomInteger$(-1, -3)$
    4.3 $R[0] = R[0]^4$
    4.4 $R[0] = R[0] \times R[d + s + (k_{i+1}k_i)_2]$
5. $R[0] = R[0] \times R[-s]$
6. output $R[0]$

2.6 DPA Countermeasure

However, Algorithm 2 has a weakness similar to the original Ha-Moon algorithm in that there are only a few possible intermediate values [2, 10]. After processing $(k_{i+1}k_i)_2$ in Step 4.4 of Algorithm 2, $R[0]$ becomes one of $g^{(k_{n-1}\cdots k_i)_2-1}$, $g^{(k_{n-1}\cdots k_i)_2-2}$, and $g^{(k_{n-1}\cdots k_i)_2-3}$. In other words, there are only three possible intermediate values in any iteration.

Table 1. Intermediate values, $g^{4(k_{n-1}\cdots k_{i+2})_2+x_i}$, after processing $(k_{i+1}k_i)_2$ (without DPA countermeasure)

$(k_{i+1}k_i)_2$	x_i					
	-3	-2	-1	0	1	2
0	◯	◯	◯			
1		◯	◯	◯		
2			◯	◯	◯	
3				◯	◯	◯

Table 1 shows different pattern of intermediate values according to $(k_{i+1}k_i)_2$. Given $(k_{n-1}\cdots k_{i+2})_2$, each occurrence of $g^{4(k_{n-1}\cdots k_{i+2})_2+x_i}$ can be checked by DPA, such as ZEMD attack [7]. For example, $(k_{i+1}k_i)_2 = 0$ results peaks in $x_i = -3, -2,$ and -1 and $(k_{i+1}k_i)_2 = 1$ in $x_i = -2, -1,$ and 0. Thus, given $(k_{n-1}\cdots k_{i+2})_2$, we can find a correct $(k_{i+1}k_i)_2$.

Note that, in this attack, a third of the samples are meaningful and the others are treated as noise, because the possible distribution of intermediate values is three.

Therefore, Yen et al. suggested a method to prevent this attack. Their method is selecting $s_i = -1$ or -2 when $(k_{i+1}k_i)_2 = 0$ or 2 as well as selecting $s_i = -2$ or -3 when $(k_{i+1}k_i)_2 = 1$ or 3. The allowed parameters are summarized in Table 2.

Table 2. Parameters with the Yen et al.'s method

s_{i+2}	$(k_{i+1}k_i)_2$	(s_i, d_i')
-1	0	$(-2, 2)$ or $(-1, 3)$
-1	1	$(-3, 2)$ or $(-2, 3)$
-1	2	$(-2, 4)$ or $(-1, 5)$
-1	3	$(-3, 4)$ or $(-2, 5)$
-2	0	$(-2, 6)$ or $(-1, 7)$
-2	1	$(-3, 6)$ or $(-2, 7)$
-2	2	$(-2, 8)$ or $(-1, 9)$
-2	3	$(-3, 8)$ or $(-2, 9)$
-3	0	$(-2, 10)$ or $(-1, 11)$
-3	1	$(-3, 10)$ or $(-2, 11)$
-3	2	$(-2, 12)$ or $(-1, 13)$
-3	3	$(-3, 12)$ or $(-2, 13)$

Table 3. Intermediate values, $g^{4(k_{n-1}\cdots k_{i+2})_2+x_i}$, after processing $(k_{i+1}k_i)_2$ (with DPA countermeasure)

			x_i			
$(k_{i+1}k_i)_2$	-3	-2	-1	0	1	2
0		◯	◯			
1		◯	◯			
2				◯	◯	
3				◯	◯	

Their method can make $(k_{i+1}k_i)_2 = 0$ and $1(2$ and $3)$ indistinguishable. For this reason, they insisted that this attack can be avoided. Table 3 shows different pattern of intermediate values according to $(k_{i+1}k_i)_2$, when their method (DPA countermeasure) is applied.

3   Proposed Attack

Yen *et al.* wanted to increase a randomness by adding random integer s in each iteration. Unfortunately, their method does not provide additional randomness in the intermediate values. The indistinguishability after processing $(k_{i+1}k_i)_2$ can be removed in the successive iteration. After processing $(k_{i-1}k_{i-2})_2$ in Step 4.4 of Algorithm 2, $R[0]$ becomes

$$g^{16(k_{n-1}\cdots k_{i+2})_2+4(k_{i+1}k_i)_2+(k_{i-1}k_{i-2})_2+s_{i-2}}$$

where $s_{i-2} \in \{-1, -2, -3\}$.

Table 4 shows possible values of $R[0]$ after processing $(k_{i-1}k_{i-2})_2$. If $(k_{n-1}\cdots k_{i+2})_2$ is known, we can determine $(k_{i+1}k_i)_2$ and classify $(k_{i-1}k_{i-2})_2$ into a group A (0 or 1) or a group B (2 or 3). For example, if a peak is recorded in Step 1.1.3 of Algorithm 3 when $x = 6$ and 7, then we can find that $(k_{i+1}k_i)_2$ is 2 and $(k_{i-1}k_{i-2})_2$ is classified into a group A. Thus, we can determine a secret exponent K except $(k_1k_0)_2$, of which we can classify the group, A or B; the size of the search space from the remaining ambiguity in $(k_1k_0)_2$ is only two. In addition, our attack does not assume anything beyond ZEMD attack.

Table 4. Intermediate values, $g^{16(k_{n-1}\cdots k_{i+2})_2+x_{i-2}}$, after processing $(k_{i-1}k_{i-2})_2$

							x_{i-2}									
$(k_{i+1}k_i)_2$	-2	-1	0	1	2	3	4	5	6	7	8	9	10	11	12	13
0	A	A	B	B												
1					A	A	B	B								
2									A	A	B	B				
3													A	A	B	B

A means $(k_{i-1}k_{i-2})_2 = 0$ or 1, and
B means $(k_{i-1}k_{i-2})_2 = 2$ or 3.

Algorithm 3. ZEMD-like attack on the improved Ha-Moon algorithm

---

INPUT: sufficiently many power trace samples of g_w^K for different g_w's
OUTPUT: K

1. for i from $n-2$ downto 2 step -2 do
   1.1 for x from -2 to 13 step 1 do
      1.1.1 divide the samples into two sets $S1$ and $S2$ according to a decision function, such as the Hamming weight of $g_w^{16(k_{n-1}\cdots k_{i+2})_2+x}$
      1.1.2 get the bias signal as $D = \mathrm{avg}(S1) - \mathrm{avg}(S2)$
      1.1.3 record an appearance of a peak in D
   1.2 determine $(k_{i+1}k_i)_2$ and classify $(k_{i-1}k_{i-2})_2$ into a group A or B according to records in Step 1.1.3
2. guess $(k_1k_0)_2$
3. output K

Therefore, the improved Ha-Moon algorithm is vulnerable to the proposed attack. Yen *et al.*'s method does not prevent DPA, it rather helps DPA to break the improved Ha-Moon algorithm by increasing the rate of the meaningful power traces from a third to a half, because their method makes the possible distribution of intermediate values be two. Even enlarging the range of the intermediate values will not increase the complexity of DPA significantly, but only decrease the rate in inverse proportion to the range.

4   Improvements of Proposed Attack

4.1   Reducing Test Space of DPA

After we classify $(k_{i-1}k_{i-2})_2$ in Step 1.2 of Algorithm 3, it is not necessary to test for all x from -2 to 13 in the next iteration. For example, if $(k_{i-1}k_{i-2})_2$ is classified as group A, then $(k_{i-1}k_{i-2})_2$ is 0 or 1. Therefore we can find a peak in tests for x from -2 to 5 and there is no peak in tests for x from 6 to 13 in the next iteration. That is, a half of tests for x is not necessary in Step 1.1 of Algorithm 3. This can be applied in each iteration and doubles the efficiency of the Algorithm 3.

4.2   Analysis of Power Traces

In Algorithm 3, a peak is appeared twice in the successive iteration for x and each bias signal D is independently analyzed. If two bias signals in two successive iterations are analyzed at the same time, then a peak is found more easily. For example, if we analyze the addition of two bias signal by using a peak detection algorithm, such as mean square, then peak is detectable more easily compared with Algorithm 3.

4.3   Appliance of Two Improvements

By applying two things mentioned Section 4.1 and 4.2, we modify Algorithm 3 to Algorithm 4.

Algorithm 4. Modified ZEMD-like attack on the improved Ha-Moon algorithm

---

INPUT: sufficiently many power trace samples of g_w^K for different g_w's
OUTPUT: K

1. for x from -2 to 12 step 2 do
   1.1 divide the samples into two sets $S1$ and $S2$ according to the Hamming weight of g_w^x
   1.2 divide the samples into two sets $S3$ and $S4$ according to the Hamming weight of g_w^{x+1}
   1.3 get the bias signal as $D = \mathrm{avg}(S1) - \mathrm{avg}(S2) + \mathrm{avg}(S3) - \mathrm{avg}(S4)$
   1.4 record an appearance of peak in D
2. determine $(k_{n-1}k_{n-2})_2$ and classify $(k_{n-3}k_{n-4})_2$ into a group A or B
3. for i from $n-4$ downto 2 step -2 do
   3.1 if $(k_{i+1}k_i)_2$ is classified A, then $start = -2$, else $start = 6$
   3.2 for x from $start$ to $(start + 6)$ step 2 do
      3.2.1 divide the samples into two sets $S1$ and $S2$ according to the Hamming weight of $g_w^{16(k_{n-1}\cdots k_{i+2})_2+x}$
      3.2.2 divide the samples into two sets $S3$ and $S4$ according to the Hamming weight of $g_w^{16(k_{n-1}\cdots k_{i+2})_2+x+1}$
      3.2.3 get the bias signal as $D = \mathrm{avg}(S1) - \mathrm{avg}(S2) + \mathrm{avg}(S3) - \mathrm{avg}(S4)$
      3.2.4 record an appearance of peak in D
   3.3 determine $(k_{i+1}k_i)_2$ and classify $(k_{i-1}k_{i-2})_2$ into a group A or B
4. guess $(k_1k_0)_2$
5. output K

---

5   Conclusion

In this paper, we reviewed the improved Ha-Moon algorithm and analyzed it with respect to DPA. The improved Ha-Moon algorithm introduced interesting properties, such as a left-to-right approach, an inversion-free, and a window method. However, the improved Ha-Moon algorithm does not resolve one critical property of the Ha-Moon algorithm: its vulnerability to DPA. Therefore, the improved Ha-Moon algorithm should be used with another DPA countermeasure.

Acknowledgements

The authors would like to thank an anonymous referee for many valuable comments.

References

1. D. Boneh, R. A. DeMillo, and R. J. Lipton, "On the importance of checking cyprto-graphic protocols for faults," *EUROCRYPT 1997*, LNCS 1233, pp. 37–51, Springer-Verlag, 1997.
2. P.-A. Fouque, F. Muller, G. Poupard, and F. Valette, "Defeating countermeasures based on randomized BSD representation," *CHES 2004*, LNCS 3156, pp. 312–327, Springer-Verlag, 2004.

3. K. Gandolfi, C. Mourtel, and F. Olivier, "Electromagnetic analysis: Concrete results," *CHES 2001*, LNCS 2162, pp. 255–265, Springer-Verlag, 2001.
4. J. C. Ha, and S. J. Moon, "Randomized signed-scalar multiplication of ECC to resist power attacks," *CHES 2002*, LNCS 2523, pp. 551–563, Springer-Verlag, 2002.
5. P. Kocher, "Timing attack on implementations of Diffie-Hellman, RSA, DSS and other systems, "*CRYPTO 1996*, LNCS 1109, pp. 104–113, Springer-Verlag, 1996.
6. P. Kocher, J. Jaffe, and B. Jun, "Differential power analysis," *CRYPTO 1999*, LNCS 1666, pp. 388–397, Springer-Verlag, 1999.
7. T. S. Messerges, E. A. Dabbish, and R. H. Sloan, "Power analysis attacks of modular exponentiation in smartcards," *CHES 1999*, LNCS 1717, pp. 144–157, Springer-Verlag, 1999.
8. K. Okeya, and T. Takagi, "A more flexible countermeasure against side channel attacks using window method." *CHES 2003*, LNCS 2779, pp. 397–410, Springer-Verlag, 2003.
9. K. Okeya, and D.-G. Han, "Side channel attack on Ha-Moon's countermeasure of randomized signed scalar multiplication," *INDOCRYPT 2003*, LNCS 2904, pp. 334–348, Springer-Verlag, 2003.
10. S. G. Sim, D. J. Park, and P. J. Lee, "New power analyses on the Ha-Moon algorithm and the MIST algorithm," *ICICS 2004*, LNCS 3269, pp. 291–304, Springer-Verlag, 2004.
11. S.-M. Yen, C.-N. Chen, S. Moon and J. Ha, "Improvement on Ha-Moon randomized exponentiation algorithm," *ICISC 2004*, to appear in LNCS, Springer-Verlag, 2004.
12. S.-M. Yen, S. Kim, S. Lim, and S. Moon, "A countermeasure against one physical cryptanalysis may benefit another attack," *ICISC 2001*, LNCS 2288, pp. 414–427, Springer-Verlag, 2004.

An Efficient Masking Scheme
for AES Software Implementations*

Elisabeth Oswald[1] and Kai Schramm[2]

[1] Institute for Applied Information Processing and Communciations (IAIK),
TU Graz, Inffeldgasse 16a, A–8010 Graz, Austria
[2] Horst Görtz Institute for IT Security (HGI), Universitätsstr. 150,
Ruhr University Bochum, Germany, 44780 Bochum, Germany
elisabeth.oswald@iaik.tugraz.at,
schramm@crypto.ruhr-uni-bochum.de

Abstract. The development of masking schemes to secure AES implementations against power-analysis attacks is a topic of ongoing research. The most challenging part in masking an AES implementation is the SubBytes operation because it is a non-linear operation. The current solutions are expensive to implement especially on small 8-bit processors; they either need many large tables or require a large amount of operations. In this article, we present a masking scheme that requires considerably less tables and considerably less operations than the previously presented schemes. We give a theoretical proof of security for our scheme and confirm it with actually performed DPA attacks.

1 Introduction

The *Advanced Encryption Standard* (short: AES) [Nat01] is the worldwide de-facto standard for symmetric encryption. It succeeds the older *Data Encryption Standard* (short: DES) [Nat99]. Therefore, it will be used in manifold services ranging from high-performance applications such as web services to low-cost (low memory, low power consumption) implementations on smart cards. Especially in the case of software implementations for smart cards limited memory (ROM, RAM, XRAM) poses a challenging constraint for implementors. Even worse, implementation attacks such as differential power analysis attacks (short: DPA attacks) [KJJ99] require considerable effort from the implementor's side to come up with implementations that do not succumb to such attacks.

During the past years, a lot of effort has been devoted to the research in DPA attacks. It has become clear that smart cards without built in countermeasures are highly susceptible to all kinds of DPA attacks. Hence, researchers have proposed all kinds of schemes to secure implementations of different kinds of cryptographic algorithms. The AES algorithm has received the largest attention amongst symmetric schemes because of its expected widespread use.

---

* The work described in this paper has been supported in part by the European Commission through the IST Programme under Contract IST-2002-507932 ECRYPT.

J. Song, T. Kwon, and M. Yung (Eds.): WISA 2005, LNCS 3786, pp. 292–305, 2006.

In this article, we focus on the scenario where AES is implemented in software on 8-bit platforms such as commonly available smart cards. We propose a masking scheme for this scenario which requires less tables, *i.e.*, less memory, and less operations than comparable schemes in the same scenario.

The remainder of this article is organized as follows. In Sect. 2, we give a brief overview of AES. In Sect. 3, we review the problem of masked AES implementations on restricted platforms and we survey related work. In Sect. 4, we introduce our new scheme and provide a theoretical analysis of its security against DPA attacks. In Sect. 5, we describe our implementation of our new scheme on an 8-bit smart card. In Sect. 6, we report on the results of practical DPA attacks that we have performed on our implementation. We conclude this article in Sect. 7.

2 Advanced Encryption Standard

The AES is a symmetric cipher which encrypts/decrypts data with a block size of 128 bits using a key of size 128, 192 or 256 bits. In the following we will briefly decribe the encryption scheme of AES. The decryption scheme is equivalent but uses the inverse transformations. The 16-byte plaintext $p_0 p_1 ... p_{15}$ is arranged in four-by-four byte matrix, called *state*. All transformations in AES operate on the state.

p_0	p_4	p_8	p_{12}
p_1	p_5	p_9	p_{13}
p_2	p_6	p_{10}	p_{14}
p_3	p_7	p_{11}	p_{15}

The following transformations are used in the AES cipher:

1. **AddRoundKey:** A round key is added to the state matrix using the XOR operation. The round keys are derived from the key with the *Key Expansion* algorithm.
2. **ShiftRows:** The second row of the state matrix is cyclically shifted by one byte to the left, the third row by two bytes and the fourth row by three bytes. The first row remains unchanged. The ShiftRows transformation increases the *diffusion* properties of AES.
3. **SubBytes:** Each byte of the state matrix is substituted using a bijective substitution box (short: S-box). The S-box is based on the non-linear inversion in the finite field $GF(2^8)$ and a bitwise affine transformation. The S-box step increases the *confusion* properties of AES.
4. **MixColumns:** The MixColumns step is a linear transformation, which increases the *diffusion* properties of AES. Each column is mixed using the following matrix multiplication:

$$\begin{pmatrix} c_0 \\ c_1 \\ c_2 \\ c_3 \end{pmatrix} = \begin{pmatrix} 02 & 03 & 01 & 01 \\ 01 & 02 & 03 & 01 \\ 01 & 01 & 02 & 03 \\ 03 & 01 & 01 & 02 \end{pmatrix} \begin{pmatrix} b_0 \\ b_1 \\ b_2 \\ b_3 \end{pmatrix}$$

where b_i are the bytes of the input column, c_i are the bytes of the output column, and matrix elements $\{03\}$, $\{02\}$ and $\{01\}$ correspond to the polynomials $x + 1$, x and 1.

5. **Key Expansion:** The key expansion derives the round keys from the cipher key.

The AES encryption scheme is given below:

```
AddRoundKey

for round = 1 to Nr
    SubBytes
    ShiftRows
    MixColumns
    AddRoundKey
end

SubBytes
ShiftRows
AddRoundKey
```

The Key Expansion is typically performed interleaved with the rounds in software. The number of rounds Nr depends on the key size. If the key size is 128, 192 or 256 bits 10, 12 or 14 rounds are used, respectively. All AES transformations but SubBytes are linear. Hence, only SubBytes requires special attention with regard to masking. This articles intensely focuses on a secure yet efficient software implementation of SubBytes.

3   Related Work

In a typical software implementation, the SubBytes operation is implemented as a table look-up. Hence, for an input value in of a SubBytes operation, the output is derived as $out = S(in)$. As there are 16 8-bit chunks in the AES state, 16 table look-up operations have to be performed in one encryption round (not taking the key schedule into account).

When we mask the SubBytes operation with a value m (the mask), $i.e.$, when we add a random value m' (the mask) to its input, we have to re-compute the table S such that $out = S(in) + m$, where in is masked, $i.e.$, $in = x + m'$. Hence, we need a table $MSubBytes()$ such that

$$\mathbf{MSubBytes(x + m') = SubBytes(x) + m.}$$

The **MSubBytes()** table for the masks m and m' (for simplicity, m is often chosen to be equal to m') is calculated according to Algorithm 1. The exclusive-or (short: XOR) operation is denoted by $+$ in this article.

When more than one mask m is to be used, more $MSubBytes()$ tables need to be computed. For example, when using 16 masks m, 16 tables are needed.

Algorithm 1. Computation of Masked **SubBytes**

Require: m, m'
Ensure: MaskedSubBytes(x + m') = SubBytes(x) + m,
1: **for** $i = 0$ to 255 **do**
2:    $MaskedSubBytes(i + m') = $ **Subbytes(i)** $+ m$
3: **end for**
4: Return($MaskedSubBytes$)

As stated in [GT03], the usage of the same mask for all 16 s-boxes represents a serious threat, because intermediate variables (e.g. the s-box outputs) are masked with the same mask and their mutual correlation can be used to apply second order DPA attacks.

For this article, we consider the scenario where AES is implemented on an 8-bit smart card. We assume that AES is not used for bulk encryption. Instead, AES is used for example in a challenge-response protocol, where only one instance of the algorithm is typically computed at a time.

For every mask m, a masked table needs to be computed. There are several strategies an implementor can follow. Either all 256 masked tables are pre-computed and stored in a memory, or, only t tables for the t 8-bit masks are pre-computed at the beginning of the AES algorithm and stored in memory. Another option is to compute the masked table on the fly whenever it is needed during the encryption algorithm.

We argue that in practice the second method is the most attractive one, because it gives the best tradeoff between the amount of memory and the number of operations. Remember that the size of one table is 256 bytes. Counting the number of operations for this algorithm for t masks shows that in total an amount of $2 \times t \times 256$ table look-ups read/write operations and $2 \times t \times 256$ XOR operations are needed. In total, $(t + 1) \times 256$ bytes of memory are used. In typical AES implementations, a separate mask for each 8-bit chunk would be used. That amounts then to 8192 table look-ups, 4352 bytes of memory and 8192 XOR operations.

Many algorithmic countermeasures have been proposed for the AES algorithm, see [AG01], [GT03], [TSG03], [TK04], [BGK05] and [OMPR05]. They are all based on masking the intermediate value, *i.e.*, adding a random number (the mask) to the intermediate AES values. However two of them, [AG01] and [TSG03], are both susceptible to a certain type of (first-order) differential side-channel attack, the zero-value attack. The latter one has turned out to be vulnerable even to standard differential side-channel attacks [ABG04].

The countermeasure presented in [GT03] leads to very costly implementations. This is due to the fact that in order to circumvent the zero-value problem, the authors propose to embed the inversion operation (which is part of SubBytes) into a larger algebraic structure such that the zero-value is mapped to different non-zero values. Although this construction is mathematically elegant, implementations thereof, especially on 8-bit platforms, are not.

The countermeasure presented in [TK04] uses pre-computed discrete logarithm and exponentiation tables to realize the SubBytes operation (*i.e.*, the inversion operation that is part of the mathematical description of SubBytes). This approach is based on the fact that a non-zero element in a finite field can be inverted by computing the logarithm of the element to a particular base[1] and exponentiating the base again with the negated logarithm. The inversion of the zero element has to be carefully taken into account by using a conditional check, e.g. the authors suggest to manipulate the discrete logarithm and exponentiation tables in such a way that the zero element is inverted correctly to itself. Unfortunately, we believe that this approach has a flaw which is linked to the inversion of the zero element. In their work, the authors state that conditional branching for the zero element can be avoided by changing two table elements: $log[0] = 2^n - 1$ and $alog[2^n - 1] = 0$. However, because an inversion is defined as

$$\alpha^{-1} = alog[(2^n - 1) - log[\alpha]]$$

the inversion of zero will result in $0^{-1} = alog[0] = 1 \neq 0$ and, moreover, the inversion of 1 will result in $1^{-1} = alog[(2^n - 1) - log[1]] = alog[2^n - 1] = 0 \neq 1$. As a matter of fact, by setting $log[0] = 0$, $log[1] = 2^n - 1$ and $alog[2^n - 1] = 0$, we found a possibility to correct the log and $alog$ tables in such a way that both inversions will work properly, again. In their paper, a multiplication of two elements is defined as

$$\alpha \cdot \beta = alog[log[\alpha] + log[\beta] \bmod 2^n - 1]$$

However, when using this method a multiplication with zero will only always result in zero, if conditional branching is used. Based on the inversion and multiplication with the log and $alog$ tables the authors propose two different masking schemes which are supposed to provide a secure inversion. We have carefully implemented and tested both schemes. We observed that in both schemes there occur special cases when the s-box input, the mask or masked, intermediate variables are equal to zero and which will result in a faulty behavior of the proposed masking schemes. We believe that a correction of their approach is only possible with the use of conditional branches, which makes it susceptible to power-analysis attacks.

The countermeasures presented in [BGK05] and [OMPR05] are based on a similar idea. In both papers, the authors assume that the inversion operation is computed step-by-step, either as exponentiation or with composite field arithmetic. The exponentiation method is advertised for software implementations and described in [BGK05]. The composite-field method is advertised for hardware implementations and is described in detail in [OMPR05]. Both methods do not seem to be particularly suited for 8-bit software implementations. However, as we will show in this article, especially the composite-field method can be adapted in such a way that it is suitable for 8-bit platforms.

4 A New Scheme for Efficiently Masking AES in Software

The only difficult part in masking AES is to mask the SubBytes operation. The SubBytes operation is composed of two parts: an inversion in $GF(2^8)$ and an

---

[1] i.e. for a chosen generator.

affine mapping. Again, masking the affine part is easy, so we focus on the non-linear inversion operation only. Our goal is that all input and output values in the computation of the inverse are masked. According to [OMPR05], a masked input can be transformed to the composite field $GF(2^4) \times GF(2^4)$ with an isomorphic mapping, where it can be securely and efficiently inverted, and finally transformed back to the $GF(2^8)$. The inversion operation in the composite field can be computed as follows:

$$((a_h + m_h)x + (a_l + m_l))^{-1} = (a'_h + m'_h)x + (a'_l + m'_l) \tag{1}$$

$$\begin{aligned} a'_h + m'_h &= f_{a_h}((a_h + m_h), (d' + m'_d), m_h, m'_h, m'_d) \\ &= a_h \times d' + m'_h \end{aligned} \tag{2}$$

$$\begin{aligned} a'_l + m'_l &= f_{a_l}((a'_h + m'_h), (a_l + m_l), (d' + m'_d), m_l, m'_h, m'_l, m'_d) \\ &= (a_h + a_l) \times d' + m'_l \end{aligned} \tag{3}$$

$$\begin{aligned} d + m_d &= f_d((a_h + m_h), (a_l + m_l), p_0, m_h, m_l, m_d) \\ &= a_h^2 \times p_0 + a_h \times a_l + a_l^2 + m_d \end{aligned} \tag{4}$$

$$\begin{aligned} d' + m'_d &= f_{d'}(d + m_d, m_d, m'_d) \\ &= d^{-1} + m'_d \end{aligned} \tag{5}$$

The functions f_{a_h}, f_{a_l}, f_d and $f_{d'}$ are functions on $GF(2^4)$.

This calculation of a masked inversion operation is based on the composite field approach that is described in detail in [WOL02].

Whereas in [OMPR05] this approach is applied to hardware implementations and has been extended to work in so-called tower fields, we pursue a different approach. We show that these formulae can be mapped to a sequence of table look-ups and XOR operations. We show how to define tables which only require little space in memory. Furthermore, we show that only a small number of table look-ups are required to calculate the formulae.

4.1   Pre-computed Tables

We compute a number of tables that do the operations in $GF(2^4)$ and store them in memory:

$$T_{d_1} : ((x + m), m) \mapsto x^2 \times p_0 + m$$
$$T_{d_2} : ((x + m), (y + m')) \mapsto ((x + m) + (y + m')) \times (y + m')$$
$$T_m : ((x + m), (y + m')) \mapsto (x + m) \times (y + m')$$
$$T_{inv} : ((x + m), m) \mapsto x^{-1} + m.$$

All tables (or functions) take two elements of $GF(2^4)$ as inputs and give an element of $GF(2^4)$ as output.

With those 4 Tables, we can compute formulas (2)-(5). In order to map $GF(2^8)$ elements to $GF(2^4) \times GF(2^4)$ elements and vice versa, we need two more tables $Map : x \mapsto z$ and $Map^{-1} : z \mapsto x$. Map takes an element x of $GF(2^8)$ as input and gives an element z of $GF(2^4) \times GF(2^4)$ as output. Map^{-1} works vice versa. We assume that for all tables the input masks and the output masks are identical. Hence, the size of one table is at most 256 bytes and so we can pre-compute all tables and store them in read-only memory (ROM), since there is no need to compute them during run-time. This is a significant advantage over the use of $MSubBytes()$ tables. They have to be computed for every new mask m during run-time or at least at the invocation of a new AES encryption run.

4.2   Masked Inversion

First, we have to compute the masked value of d, i.e., $d+m_d = d+m_h$ according to (4):

$$
\begin{aligned}
f_d(a_h + m_h, a_l + m_l, m_h, m_l, m_h) = {} & T_{d_1}(a_h + m_h, m_h) \\
& + T_{d_2}((a_h + m_h), (a_l + m_l)) \\
& + T_m((a_h + m_h), m_l) \\
& + T_m((a_l + m_l), m_h) + T_m((m_h + m_l), m_l).
\end{aligned}
\tag{6}
$$

It is easy to check that the result will be indeed $a_h^2 \times p_0 + a_h \times a_l + a_l^2 + m_h$. For this computation we need five table look-up operations (TLs), four XOR operations and an additional XOR operation to compute $(m_h + m_l)$ which is used as input in $T_m((m_h + m_l), m_l)$. Note that the results of $T_m((a_h + m_h), m_l)$ and $T_m((a_l + m_l), m_h)$ are used again in (8) and (9), respectively, therefore it is a good idea to store these results and reuse them later on in order to save these two look-up operations.

In the next step we compute the inverse of the masked d with one more table look-up operation:

$$
f_{d'}(d + m_h, m_h, m_h) = T_{inv}(d + m_h, m_h).
\tag{7}
$$

In order to derive $f_{a_h}()$, we first compute $d^{-1} + m_l$ by one XOR addition with the term $(m_h + m_l)$. Then $f_{a_h}(a_h + m_h, d^{-1} + m_l, m_h, m_h, m_l)$ can be computed as follows:

$$
\begin{aligned}
f_{a_h}(a_h + m_h, d^{-1} + m_l, m_h, m_h, m_l) = {} & T_m(a_h + m_h, d^{-1} + m_l) \\
& + m_h + T_m(d^{-1} + m_l, m_h) \\
& + T_m(a_h + m_h, m_l) + T_m(m_h, m_l).
\end{aligned}
\tag{8}
$$

This computation gives as output $a_h \times d^{-1} + m_h$. For this computation, we need three new table look-up operations and four XOR operations in total.

In the last step we derive $f_{a_l}(a_h \times d^{-1} + m_h, a_l + m_l, d^{-1} + m_l, m_l, m_h, m_l, m_l)$. Hence, we calculate:

$$f_{a_l}(a_h \times d^{-1} + m_h, a_l + m_l, d^{-1} + m_l, m_l, m_h, m_l, m_l)$$
$$= T_m((a_l + m_l), (d^{-1} + m_h)) + m_l + T_m(d^{-1} + m_h, m_l)$$
$$+T_m(a_l + m_l, m_h) + f_{a_h} + m_h + T_m(m_h, m_l). \tag{9}$$

This gives $a_l \times d^{-1} + a_h \times d^{-1} + m_l$ as a result. Note that the term $T_m(m_h, m_l)$ occurs in the computation of f_{a_h} and f_{a_l}.

Hence, by also storing $f_{a_h} + T_m(m_h, m_l)$ during the computation of f_{a_h} and using this term during the computation of f_{a_l}, one additional table look-up and one XOR can be saved. Therefore, for this computation we only need two additional table look-ups and five XOR operations.

Prior to the inversion in $GF(2^4) \times GF(2^4)$ we need to map the 8-bit values (elements in $GF(2^8)$) to 2×4-bit values (elements in $GF(2^4) \times GF(2^4)$). This is done by a table look-up as well. Mapping back from $GF(2^4) \times GF(2^4)$ to $GF(2^8)$ can be achieved with an additional look-up table. Moreover, it makes sense to combine the isomorphic mapping from $GF(2^4) \times GF(2^4)$ to $GF(2^8)$ with the affine transformation that is part of SubBytes and use only one table for both.

Total Costs of a Masked Inversion. If we review the number of table look-ups (TLs) and XOR additions required for an entire masked AES SubBytes operation, we need five TL operations and four XOR additions in (6), one TL operation in (7), three TL operations and four XOR additions in (8), two TL operations and five XOR additions in (9). Furthermore, we need three TL operations for the isomorphic transformations: two TL operations to map the masked inversion input and the mask to $GF(2^4) \times GF(2^4)$ and one TL operation to map the masked result of the inversion back to $GF(2^8)$ and perform the affine transform.

This sums up to a total of 14 table look-up operations and 15 XOR operations.

4.3 Theoretical Security Analysis

In this section we show that all data-dependent intermediate masked values that are computed during the masked inversion operation are statistically independent from the unmasked values.

Hence, we follow the definition of security that was introduced in [CJRR99] and strengthened in [BGK05].

The values that we have to investigate are the outputs of the functions (tables) T_{d_i}, T_m, T_{inv}, Map, Map^{-1} and all intermediate values that occur after an XOR operation. In [OMPR05] it has been shown in Lemma 5 that a sum of independent masked values will again be independent from the unmasked values as long as an independent mask is used during the summation. Furthermore, in Lemmas 1–4 it has been shown that the XOR operation, as well as the masked multiplication and the masked squaring are secure in the sense that their output is statistically independent from the plaintext input.

Lemma 1. *Let $x \in GF(2^n)$ be arbitrary and let $p_0 \in GF(2^n)$ be an arbitrary but fixed value. Let $m \in GF(2^n)$ be independently and uniformly distributed in $GF(2^n)$. Then $T_{d_1}(x + m, m) = x^2 \times p_0 + m$ is uniformly distributed regardless of x. Therefore, the distribution of $x^2 \times p_0 + m$ is independent of x.*

Proof. As x is an element of the binary extension field, the element $x^2 = (\sum_i a_i \alpha^i)^2 = \sum_i a_i \alpha^{2i}$ with $a_i \in \{0,1\}$ is in $GF(2^n)$ as well. Hence, all elements of $GF(2^n)$ are quadratic residues and thus x^2 is uniformly distributed on $GF(2^n)$. Consequently, also $x^2 \times p_0$ and $x^2 \times p_0 + m$ are uniformly distributed.

For the independency of the output of T_{d_2} we reuse Lemma 2 of [BGK05].

Lemma 2. *Let $x, y \in GF(2^n)$ be arbitrary. Let $m, m' \in GF(2^n)$ be independently and uniformly distributed in $GF(2^n)$. Then the probability distribution of $T_m(x + m, y + m') = (x + m) \times (y + m')$ is*

$$\Pr((x + m) \times (y + m') = i) = \begin{cases} \frac{2^{n+1}-1}{2^{2n}} , if \, i = 0, \, i.e., \, if \, m = x \, or \, m' = y \\ \frac{2^n - 1}{2^{2n}} , if \, i \neq 0. \end{cases}$$

Therefore, the distribution of $(x + m) \times (y + m')$ is independent of x and y.

Lemma 3 follows directly from Lemma 2 and the observation that all elements of $GF(2^n)$ are quadratic residues.

Lemma 3. *Let $x, y \in GF(2^n)$ be arbitrary. Let $m, m' \in GF(2^n)$ be independently and uniformly distributed in $GF(2^n)$. Then the probability distribution of $T_{d_2}(x + m, y + m') = (x + m) \times (y + m') + (y + m')^2$ is*

$$\Pr((x+m) \times (y+m') + (y+m')^2 = i) = \begin{cases} \frac{2^{n+1}-1}{2^{2n}}, if \, i = 0, \, i.e., \, if \, m = x \, or \, m' = y \\ \frac{2^n - 1}{2^{2n}}, if \, i \neq 0. \end{cases}$$

Therefore, the distribution of $(x + m) \times (y + m')$ is independent of x and y.

The independence of $T_{inv}(x + m, m) = x^{-1} + m$ is clear as the inversion operation is bijective (note that the zero element is mapped to the zero element) and the XOR of any $a + m$ is independent from a. The mappings between $GF(2^8)$ and $GF(2^4) \times GF(2^4)$ are bijections and therefore their masked output is independent from the unmasked input in a statistical sense.

Based on these results we may conclude that the algorithm for computing masked inversion complies to the definition of security used in [BGK05].

Recently it was discovered, see [MPG05] and [SSI04], that glitches in CMOS circuits make masked implementations vulnerable to standard DPA attacks. Our masking scheme is also secure when glitches occur in a circuit as we only use table look-ups and XOR operations. For both operations it has been shown that glitches do not have an effect on their security, see [MPG05].

5   Implementation of the New Scheme

In our following analysis we regard the implementation of the SubBytes transformation in assembly on a smart card based on the 8-bit RISC architecture. In total, we require six pre-computed tables which can be stored in read-only memory (ROM). Table T_{d_1} takes two $GF(16)$ elements as input and gives one

$GF(16)$ element as output. The same holds for T_{d_2}, T_m and T_{inv}, as well. Hence, these four tables map an 8-bit input to a 4-bit output value.

In a practical software implementation there are two possibilities how the tables T_{d_1}, T_{d_2}, T_m and T_{inv} can be stored in memory on an 8-bit architecture. In a compact representation, each byte of these four tables stores two 4-bit output values, hence, each table requires 128 bytes in ROM and the four tables altogether require $4 \times 128 = 512$ bytes in ROM. The disadvantage of this compact representation is based on the fact that a few instructions are required after each table look-up to either erase the unwanted upper 4-bit half or to shift the upper 4-bit half by four bits to the right in order to erase the unwanted lower 4-bit half. These instructions are not required, if each byte of the tables T_{d_1}, T_{d_2}, T_m and T_{inv} only stores a single 4-bit result and the upper 4-bit half is always set to zero. This representation is more efficient in terms of clock cycles, but requires $4 \times 256 = 1024$ bytes in ROM. In the following we will only regard the efficient representation. The two isomorphic mappings from $GF(2^8)$ to $GF(2^4) \times GF(2^4)$ and back from $GF(2^4) \times GF(2^4)$ to $GF(2^8)$ deliver a $GF(2^4) \times GF(2^4)$ and a $GF(2^8)$ element as output, i.e. these two tables map an 8-bit input to an 8-bit output. Hence, in total we need $4 \times 256 + 2 \times 256 = 1536$ bytes to store all six tables in ROM.

The smart card architecture is a RISC design and provides 32 internal registers. A TL operation which reads an 8-bit value from a table stored in ROM to an internal register takes five clock cycles. A TL operation which reads an 8-bit value from a table stored in RAM to an internal register or writes an 8-bit value to a table stored in RAM takes four clock cycles. The XOR addition of two internal registers requires only a single clock cycle.

In an unmasked AES software implementation every SubBytes step would only require a single TL operation. If a standard masked table look-up, such as described in Sect. 3 is used, the SubBytes table would be stored in ROM and the masked tables would be derived from it prior to an AES encryption/decryption and then stored in RAM. If only one encryption is performed, this pre-computation would very likely be done for the 16 masks, only, and thus require $16 \times 256 = 4096$ bytes in RAM. During the encryption/decryption of AES only a single TL operation would be required for each SubBytes step. However, the pre-computation of the each masked table in RAM would require 256 XOR additions to mask the table index, 256 TL operations to read the unmasked table entries from ROM, 256 XOR additions to mask the table entries and finally 256 TL operations to store the masked table in RAM. If tables are generated in such a way for 16 different masks, this will result in pre-computational costs of $16 \times (256 + 256 \times 5 + 256 + 256 \times 4) = 45056$ clock cycles. If several encryption operations would be performed after each other and the same set of masks is used over and over again, the pre-computational costs occur only once. However, from a security point of view it is advisable to update the masks as often as possible. Another possibility is to store all masked tables in ROM. However, this would require $256 \times 256 = 64$ KB in ROM which might exceed the limitations in constrained environments such as smart cards.

Table 1. Comparison of various AES software implementations with regard to code size and speed for a single encryption

	ROM	RAM	PRE-TL	PRE-XOR	TL	XOR	cycles
unmasked	256	0	0	0	160	0	800
256 fixed masks	64 KB	0	0	0	160	0	800
single mask	256	256	512	512	160	0	3456
16 masks	256	4096	8192	8192	160	0	45696
MOS-box	1536	0	0	0	2240	2400	13600

As stated in Sect. 4, when using our proposal an entire SubBytes step for an arbitrary mask requires 14 TL operations and 15 XOR additions which results in $14 \times 5 + 15 = 85$ clock cycles. For an entire AES encryption this results in $10 \times 16 \times 85 = 13600$ clock cycles. Our method requires 1536 bytes in ROM and no RAM, moreover, no pre-computation needs to be performed. In Tab. 1 the costs of various masked and unmasked AES implementations are compared. Our proposal is referred to as "'New"' in Tab. 1.

Hence, the complexity of our proposal is lower in terms of memory and operations for a single encryption. If only a single mask is used, our proposal is about four times slower for a single encryption, however, our approach does not require any RAM. Furthermore, it has been pointed out in [GT03] that the usage of a single mask in AES may allow simple second-order DPA attacks, which can be avoided by the usage of 16 different masks in each round. If encryptions are repeated several times with the same set of 16 masks, our proposal will be slower after four encryptions, but will always require less memory.

6   Power Analysis of the New Scheme

In order to confirm the security claims that we made in Sect. 4 and to assess the practical security of our implementation, we performed DPA attacks on an AES

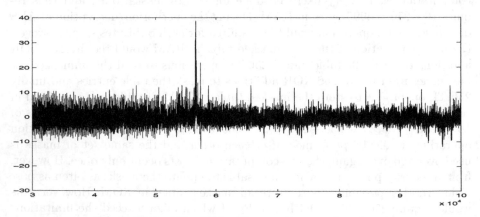

Fig. 1. DPA of the AES with no active countermeasure

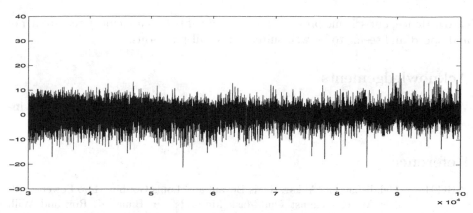

Fig. 2. DPA of the AES with our new masked s-box scheme

implementation based on our new inversion scheme. The target hardware was an 8-bit smart card. DPA attacks were performed in two independent experiments. The first time we performed DPA attacks on the implementation with the masking countermeasure switched off, i.e. all mask were fixed to zero. The second time we performed DPA attacks on the implementation with the masking countermeasure being active, i.e. all masks were randomly generated. In both experiments 1000 random plaintexts were encrypted and the corresponding power traces were measured using a digital oscilloscope with a sampling rate of 100 MSa/s and a current probe. The resulting differential traces are shown in Fig. 1 and Fig. 2.

It is obvious that the DPA of the unprotected AES implementation is successful, since a distinct correlation peak is contained in Fig. 1 for the correct key hypothesis. However, as shown in Fig. 2 the DPA of our new protected AES scheme was not successful.

7   Conclusion

In this article we have presented a new masking scheme for software implementations of AES on 8-bit platforms. Our scheme is based on computing the inverse operation, which is part of SubBytes, with composite-field arithmetic. All steps that are needed throughout the computation are done via table look-ups and XOR operations. We have proven that all intermediate masked values that occur during the computation are independent from unmasked intermediate values. We have confirmed our theoretical proof with actually performed DPA attacks. Our scheme is even secure when glitches in the underlying CMOS circuit occur because it only uses table look-ups and XOR operations. The strong point of our scheme is based on the fact that it is possible to use different masks for all 16 SubBytes operations with no RAM requirements. We believe that this is important, since RAM is generally very sparse on embedded devices such as smart cards. Hence, our scheme provides a nice tradeoff between memory requirements and speed and seems to be well suited for small platforms.

Acknowledgements

We would like to thank Andreas Krügersen for implementing the new AES inversion scheme in assembly on the smart card.

References

[ABG04]   Mehdi-Laurent Akkar, Régis Bevan, and Louis Goubin. Two Power Analysis Attacks against One-Mask Methods. In Bimal K. Roy and Willi Meier, editors, *Fast Software Encryption, 11th International Workshop, FSE 2004, Delhi, India, February 5-7, 2004, Revised Papers*, volume 3017 of *Lecture Notes in Computer Science*, pages 332–347. Springer, 2004.

[AG01]   Mehdi-Laurent Akkar and Christophe Giraud. An Implementation of DES and AES, Secure against Some Attacks. In Çetin Kaya Koç, David Naccache, and Christof Paar, editors, *Cryptographic Hardware and Embedded Systems – CHES 2001, Third International Workshop, Paris, France, May 14-16, 2001, Proceedings*, volume 2162 of *Lecture Notes in Computer Science*, pages 309–318. Springer, 2001.

[BGK05]   Johannes Blömer, Jorge Guajardo, and Volker Krummel. Provably Secure Masking of AES. In Helena Handschuh and M. Anwar Hasan, editors, *Selected Areas in Cryptography, 11th International Workshop, SAC 2004, Waterloo, Canada, August 9-10, 2004, Revised Selected Papers*, volume 3357 of *Lecture Notes in Computer Science*, pages 69–83. Springer, 2005.

[CJRR99] Suresh Chari, Charanjit S. Jutla, Josyula R. Rao, and Pankaj Rohatgi. Towards Sound Approaches to Counteract Power-Analysis Attacks. In Michael J. Wiener, editor, *Advances in Cryptology - CRYPTO '99, 19th Annual International Cryptology Conference, Santa Barbara, California, USA, August 15-19, 1999, Proceedings*, volume 1666 of *Lecture Notes in Computer Science*, pages 398–412. Springer, 1999.

[GT03]   Jovan D. Golić and Christophe Tymen. Multiplicative Masking and Power Analysis of AES. In Burton S. Kaliski Jr., Çetin Kaya Koç, and Christof Paar, editors, *Cryptographic Hardware and Embedded Systems – CHES 2002, 4th International Workshop, Redwood Shores, CA, USA, August 13-15, 2002, Revised Papers*, volume 2535 of *Lecture Notes in Computer Science*, pages 198–212. Springer, 2003.

[KJJ99]   Paul C. Kocher, Joshua Jaffe, and Benjamin Jun. Differential Power Analysis. In Michael Wiener, editor, *Advances in Cryptology - CRYPTO '99, 19th Annual International Cryptology Conference, Santa Barbara, California, USA, August 15-19, 1999, Proceedings*, volume 1666 of *Lecture Notes in Computer Science*, pages 388–397. Springer, 1999.

[MPG05]   Stefan Mangard, Thomas Popp, and Berndt M. Gammel. Side-Channel Leakage of Masked CMOS Gates. In Alfred Menezes, editor, *Topics in Cryptology - CT-RSA 2005, The Cryptographers' Track at the RSA Conference 2005, San Francisco, CA, USA, February 14-18, 2005, Proceedings*, volume 3376 of *Lecture Notes in Computer Science*, pages 351–365. Springer, 2005.

[Nat99]   National Institute of Standards and Technology (NIST).   FIPS-46-
             3: Data Encryption Standard, October 1999.   Available online at
             http://www.itl.nist.gov/fipspubs/.
[Nat01]   National Institute of Standards and Technology (NIST).   FIPS-197:
             Advanced Encryption Standard, November 2001.   Available online at
             http://www.itl.nist.gov/fipspubs/.
[OMPR05]   Elisabeth Oswald, Stefan Mangard, Norbert Pramstaller, and Vincent Rij-
             men. A Side-Channel Analysis Resistant Description of the AES S-box. In
             Helena Handschuh and Henri Gilbert, editors, *Fast Software Encryption,
             12th International Workshop, FSE 2005, Paris, France, February 21-23,
             2005, Proceedings*, volume 3557 of *Lecture Notes in Computer Science*,
             pages 425–435. Springer, 2005. to appear.
[SSI04]   Daisuke Suzuki, Minoru Saeki, and Tetsuya Ichikawa. Random Switch-
             ing Logic: A Countermeasure against DPA based on Transition Proba-
             bility. Cryptology ePrint Archive (http://eprint.iacr.org/), Report
             2004/346, 2004.
[TK04]   Elena Trichina and Lesya Korkishko. Secure and efficient aes software
             implementation for smart cards. In Chae Hoon Lim and Moti Yung,
             editors, *Information Security Applications, 5th International Workshop,
             WISA 2004, Jeju Island, Korea, August 23-25, 2004, Revised Selected Pa-
             pers*, volume 3325 of *Lecture Notes in Computer Science*, pages 425–439.
             Springer, 2004.
[TSG03]   Elena Trichina, Domenico De Seta, and Lucia Germani. Simplified Adap-
             tive Multiplicative Masking for AES. In Burton S. Kaliski Jr., Çetin
             Kaya Koç, and Christof Paar, editors, *Cryptographic Hardware and Em-
             bedded Systems – CHES 2002, 4th International Workshop, Redwood
             Shores, CA, USA, August 13-15, 2002, Revised Papers*, volume 2535 of
             Lecture Notes in Computer Science, pages 187–197. Springer, 2003.
[WOL02]   Johannes Wolkerstorfer, Elisabeth Oswald, and Mario Lamberger. An
             ASIC implementation of the AES SBoxes. In Bart Preneel, editor, *Topics
             in Cryptology - CT-RSA 2002, The Cryptographer's Track at the RSA
             Conference 2002, San Jose, CA, USA, February 18-22, 2002*, volume 2271
             of *Lecture Notes in Computer Science*, pages 67–78. Springer, 2002.

Secure Multi-attribute Procurement Auction

Koutarou Suzuki[1] and Makoto Yokoo[2]

[1] NTT Information Sharing Platform Laboratories, NTT Corporation,
1-1 Hikari-no-oka, Yokosuka, Kanagawa 239-0847, Japan
suzuki.koutarou@lab.ntt.co.jp
[2] Faculty of Information Science and Electrical Engineering, Kyushu University,
6-10-1 Hakozaki, Higashi-ku, Fukuoka 812-8581, Japan
lang.is.kyushu-u.ac.jp/~yokoo/
yokoo@is.kyushu-u.ac.jp

Abstract. In this paper, we develop a secure multi-attribute procurement auction, in which a sales item is defined by several attributes called quality, the buyer is the auctioneer (e.g., a government), and the sellers are the bidders. Our goal is to develop a protocol in which acting honestly is a dominant strategy for sellers and that does not leak the true cost of the sellers, which is highly classified information that the sellers want to keep private. We first present a Vickrey-type protocol that can be used for multi-attribute procurement auctions. Next, we show how this protocol can be executed securely.

Keywords: Procurement auction, Vickrey auction, security, privacy.

1 Introduction

Internet auctions have become an integral part of Electronic Commerce and a promising field for the application of game-theory and information security technologies. Also, electronic bidding via networks has become popular for procurement auctions. Since these auction procedures can be efficiently carried out, they have been introduced very rapidly and will be used more widely in the future.

However, the widespread research on auctions has focused mostly on models in which price is the unique strategic dimension. However, in many situations, it is necessary to conduct negotiations on multiple attributes of a deal. For example, in the case of allocating a task, the attributes of the deal may include starting time, ending deadline, accuracy level, etc. A service can be characterized by its quality, supply time, and risk involved, in case the service is not supplied on time. Also, a product can be characterized by several attributes, such as size, weight, supply date, etc.

In this paper, we investigate a model of multi-attribute procurement auctions that can handle such situations. In this model, a sales item is defined by several attributes called quality, the buyer is the auctioneer (e.g., a government), and the sellers are the bidders.

J. Song, T. Kwon, and M. Yung (Eds.): WISA 2005, LNCS 3786, pp. 306–317, 2006.
© Springer-Verlag Berlin Heidelberg 2006

We assume that the preference/type of the buyer is known and set our goal to develop a protocol in which acting honestly is a dominant strategy for sellers. This assumption is natural for the case of procurement by a government. Except for this assumption, our model is quite general. For example, the quality of a task can have arbitrary dimensions. Also, there is no restriction on the cost function of the seller.

We first present a Vickrey-type protocol that can be used for multi-attribute procurement auctions. In this protocol, acting honestly is a dominant strategy for sellers and the resulting allocation is Pareto efficient. Since truth-telling is a dominant strategy in our procurement auction, bids contain highly sensitive information, such as the true cost of sellers, which they want to keep private as much as possible. Thus, secrecy of the bids is required. We then show how this protocol can be executed securely, i.e., the secure protocol does not leak the true cost of the winner. The proposed protocol is the first procurement auction protocol that achieves the security of bids.

The rest of this paper is organized as follows. We show related works in section 2. We describe our auction model in section 3. We apply a Vickrey-type protocol to the problem in section 4. We show how to execute this protocol securely in section 5. We present our conclusions in section 6.

2   Related Works

So far, very little theoretical work has been conducted on multi-attribute auctions. One notable exception is the work of Che [7], where bidders bid on both price and quality, and bids are evaluated by a scoring rule designed by the buyer. In addition, first score and second score sealed bid auctions have been proposed. However, the quality was assumed to be one-dimensional.

Protocols and strategies of a multi-attribute English auction were proposed in [9], and strategies with a deadline were studied in [10]. In these studies, the value of the quality is extended to two dimensions.

In these works, the quality is assumed to have one or two dimensions, and the possible types of cost functions of bidders are limited. On the other hand, these works consider the incentive issues of the buyer, while we assume that the type of the buyer is public. Also, these works propose non-direct revelation mechanisms, which require less exposure of private information than direct revelation protocols. In this paper, we use a direct revelation protocol but the proposed protocol can keep the private information of the bidders hidden by utilizing information security techniques.

Suyama and Yokoo [19] have developed combinatorial multi-attribute procurement auctions, in which multiple correlated tasks are assigned. However, privacy/security issues were not considered. In this paper, we concentrate on a special case in which only a single task is assigned.

Bichler [3] carried out an experimental analysis of multi-attribute auctions. He showed that the utility scores achieved in multi-attribute auctions were higher than those of single-attribute auctions by the experiment.

To keep the bidding prices secret, many works have been carried out for secure sealed-bid auctions[1, 2, 4, 5, 11, 13, 14, 15, 16, 17, 18, 20, 21, 23]. However, as far as the authors are aware, there is no work on secure multi-attribute procurement auctions. Our proposed protocols are basically based on the M+1-st price auction in [1] but it is modified to handle multi-attribute procurement auctions.

3   Model

In this section, we describe the model of a multi-attribute procurement auction. This model is a special case of [19], in which multiple tasks are assigned.

- There exists a single buyer (auctioneer) 0, a set of sellers (bidders) $N = \{1, 2, \ldots, n\}$, and a task to be assigned to a seller. (For instance, in procurement by a government, a single buyer is the government, sellers are suppliers, and a task is public construction, supply of convenience goods, etc.)
- For the task, quality $q \in Q$ is defined. We assume there is a special quality $q_0 \in Q$, which represents the fact that the task is not performed at all. (For instance, q is a vector $\{q^1, q^2, \ldots\}$. Each element represents the ending deadline, accuracy level, etc.)
- Each seller i privately observes his type θ_i, which is drawn from set Θ. The cost of seller i for performing the task when the achieved quality is q is represented as $c(\theta_i, q)$. We assume c is normalized by $c(\theta_i, q_0) = 0$. (The private cost function $c(\theta_i, q)$ represents the real cost of seller i for performing the task with quality q. This is a highly sensitive information for the seller.)
- The gross utility of buyer 0 when the obtained quality is q is represented as $V(q)$. We assume V is normalized by $V(q_0) = 0$. Also, we assume V is public. (The gross utility $V(q)$ represents the utility of the buyer without considering the payment. In a procurement auction by a government, it is natural to assume the gross utility is public.)
- The payment from the buyer to the winning seller i is represented as p_i. We assume each participant's utility is quasi-linear, i.e., for winning seller i, his utility is represented as $p_i - c(\theta_i, q)$. Also, for the buyer, her utility is $V(q) - p_i$. (Such a utility is called quasi-linear since it can be decomposed into a linear part (money) and a non-linear part.)

Please note that although only one parameter q is used to represent the quality of the task, it does not mean our model handles only one-dimensional quality. We don't assume q is one-dimensional. For example, q can be a vector of multiple attributes.

An auction protocol is *individually rational* if no seller suffers any loss in a dominant-strategy equilibrium, i.e., the cost never exceeds the payment. In a private value auction, where each seller knows the exact cost of performing a task with a certain quality, individual rationality is indispensable; no seller wants to participate in an auction where he might be paid less than he would spend in performing the task. Therefore, in this paper, we restrict our attention to individually rational protocols.

We say an auction protocol is *Pareto efficient* when the sum of all participants' utilities (including that of the buyer), i.e., the social surplus, is maximized in a dominant-strategy equilibrium. In our model, the obtained social surplus is represented as $V(q) - c(\theta_i, q)$.

We assume that there is no collusion/bid-rigging. This is a standard assumption in most of the auction research.

4   Vickrey-Type Protocol

In this section, we develop a protocol that is based on the well-known Vickrey auction protocol [22]. We can consider this protocol to be a special case of the Vickrey-Clarke-Groves-based protocol presented in [19]. However, in the protocol described in [19], a seller needs to fully expose his private information θ_i. Our protocol, on the other hand, avoids the full exposure of types. By this modification, the protocol becomes easier to implement securely.

4.1   Basic Ideas

For a Vickrey auction in a standard auction setting, where multiple buyers and a single seller exist, we assume that seller i has a type θ_i, which determines the valuation $v(\theta_i)$ of the auctioned good. Each seller declares v_i, which can be different from his true valuation $v(\theta_i)$. The seller i^* with the highest valuation v_{1st} wins the good, and pays the amount that is equal to the second-highest valuation v_{2nd}.

The intuition behind the Vickrey auction is that, the winner needs to compensate the decrease of the social surplus caused by his participation, i.e., if the winner i^* did not participate the auction, the seller with the second-highest valuation v_{2nd} would have won. In this case, the social surplus except for i^* is equal to v_{2nd}. If the winner does participate, he takes the good and the social surplus except for i^* is 0. Therefore, the winner i^* is required to pay $v_{2nd} - 0 = v_{2nd}$.

In our model, since the bidders are sellers, a seller can increase the social surplus except for the seller, by performing the task at lower cost. In our newly developed protocol, the allocation of the task and its quality is determined so that the obtained social surplus is maximized. Accordingly, the winner is awarded with the amount that is equal to the increase of the social surplus, except for the winner, caused by the participation of the winner.

4.2   Details of the Protocol

The proposed Vickrey-type protocol is described as follows.

- Each seller i submits a pair (q_i, b_i), which means that if he performs the specified task with quality q_i, the resulting social surplus is b_i. If the seller acts honestly, he should choose $q_i = \arg\max_q V(q) - c(\theta_i, q)$ and $b_i = V(q_i) - c(\theta_i, q_i)$.

- Buyer 0 chooses i^* so that b_i is maximized, i.e., $i^* = \arg\max_i b_i$. Buyer 0 allocates the task to seller i^* with quality q_{i^*}.
- The payment p_{i^*} to seller i^* is defined as: $p_{i^*} = V(q_{i^*}) - b_{2nd}$, where $b_{2nd} = \max_{j \neq i^*} b_j$.

Please note that if all sellers act honestly, payment p_{i^*} is equal to $V(q^*) - [V(q^*_{\sim i}) - c(\theta_{j^*}, q^*_{\sim i})]$, where $(q^*_{\sim i}, j^*) = \arg\max_{j \neq i^*, q} V(q) - c(\theta'_j, q)$, i.e., $(q^*_{\sim i}, j^*)$ is the second-best choice when the task is not allocated to seller i^*. We can assume that the payment to seller i^* is equal to the increase of the social surplus, except for i^*, caused by the participation of i^*.

Example 1. Let us assume q is one-dimensional. Assume $V(q) = \sqrt{q}$. There are two sellers 1 and 2. The cost of seller 1, i.e., $c(\theta_1, q)$ is given by $q/4$, and the cost of seller 2, i.e., $c(\theta_2, q)$ is given by $q/2$.

Clearly, seller 1 is more efficient than seller 2. The buyer allocates the task to seller 1 with quality 4. Then, the resulting social surplus is 1. The second-best choice (excluding seller 1) is to allocate the task to seller 2 with quality 1. Therefore, the payment is given by $2 - (1 - 1/2) = 3/2$. The utility of seller 1 is $3/2 - 1 = 1/2$. The utility of the buyer is $2 - 3/2 = 1/2$.

4.3   Characteristics of the Protocol

The following theorem holds.

Theorem 1. *In the multi-attribute procurement auction protocol, for each seller i, acting honestly, i.e., reporting $q_i = \arg\max_q V(q) - c(\theta_i, q)$ and $b_i = V(q_i) - c(\theta_i, q_i)$, is a dominant strategy.*

Proof: We first show that for winner i^*, his utility is maximized when he acts honestly. i.e., declaring $q_i = \arg\max_q V(q) - c(\theta_i, q)$ and $b_i = V(q_i) - c(\theta_i, q_i)$.

From the assumption that a seller's utility is quasi-linear, the utility of seller i^* is represented as follows:

$$p_{i^*} - c(\theta_{i^*}, q_{i^*}) = V(q_{i^*}) - b_{2nd} - c(\theta_{i^*}, q_{i^*})$$
$$= [V(q_{i^*}) - c(\theta_{i^*}, q_{i^*})] - b_{2nd}$$

The second term is determined independently of i^*'s declaration. Therefore, seller i^* can maximize his utility by maximizing the first term. Clearly, the first term, $V(q_{i^*}) - c(\theta_{i^*}, q_{i^*})$ is maximized by choosing q_{i^*} as $\max_q V(q) - c(\theta_i, q)$, i.e., acting honestly. The declaration of b_{i^*} does not affect the utility of i^* as long as the seller wins. Therefore, seller i^* has no incentive to lie about b_{i^*}. Therefore, for i^*, acting honestly, i.e., declaring $q_i = \arg\max_q V(q) - c(\theta_i, q)$ and $b_i = V(q_i) - c(\theta_i, q_i)$, is the best strategy.

Next, we show that if $j \neq i^*$ cannot win when j acts honestly, i.e., by declaring $q_i = \arg\max_q V(q) - c(\theta_i, q)$ and $b_i = V(q_i) - c(\theta_i, q_i)$, then he cannot obtain a positive utility anyway. Let us assume that j declares (b'_j, q'_j) to be a winner. Then, the second best bid becomes b_{i^*}, where $b_j \leq b_{i^*} \leq b'_j$.

The utility of j is:

$$p_j - c(\theta_j, q_j') = V(q_j') - b_{i*} - c(\theta_j, q_j')$$
$$= [V(q_j') - c(\theta_j, q_j')] - b_{i*}$$

Since $b_j = \max_q V(q) - c(\theta_i, q)$, the first term is smaller than (or equal to) b_j. Also, since we assume $b_j = < b_{i*}$, the utility of seller j cannot be positive. Therefore, seller j has no incentive to lie. The above argument shows that in this protocol, acting honestly is a dominant strategy.   □

Furthermore, the following theorem holds.

Theorem 2. *The multi-attribute procurement auction protocol is individually rational for both the sellers and the buyer.*

Proof: If a seller cannot win, his utility is 0. For winner i^*, his utility is given as:

$$[V(q_{i*}) - c(\theta_{i*}, q_{i*})] - b_{2nd} = b_{i*} - b_{2nd}$$

Clearly, the first term is larger than the second term, so the utility of i^* is non-negative.

Furthermore, the utility of the buyer is given as:

$$V(q_{i*}) - p_{i*} = V(q_{i*}) - [V(q_{i_*}) - b_{2nd}]$$
$$= b_{2nd}$$

Each seller j can choose to perform a task with quality q_0, i.e., not performing the task. In this case, $V(q_0) - c(\theta_j, q_0) = 0 \le b_{2nd}$. Therefore, b_{2nd} is non-negative. Therefore, the utility of the buyer is non-negative.   □

Furthermore, the following theorem holds.

Theorem 3. *The multi-attribute procurement auction protocol is Pareto efficient in the dominant strategy equilibrium where each agent acts honestly.*

Proof: From Theorem 1, each seller acts honestly in a dominant strategy equilibrium. This protocol chooses the allocation and the quality so that the social surplus is maximized according to the declared (q_i, b_i), i.e., b_{i*} is chosen as $\arg\max_i \max_q V(q) - c(\theta_i, q)$. Therefore, if each seller acts honestly, the result of this protocol is Pareto efficient.   □

5   Secure Protocol

In this section, we provide a cryptographic protocol based on [1] to realize our procurement auction. We provide security requirement of auction protocol. We summarize cryptographic tools used in our protocol. We then propose our secure procurement auction protocol, discuss security and efficiency of our protocol.

5.1   Security Requirement of Auction

To achieve a fair auction, secure procurement auction must satisfy requirements: secrecy of bids, and public verifiability.

Since truth telling is a dominant strategy in our procurement auction, bids contain an information that the sellers want to keep private, e.g., the true cost of the sellers. Thus, secrecy of bids are required.

Secrecy of Bids: All bid information except auction result, i.e., winning seller and his payment, must be kept secret, even from the buyer.

Due to the secrecy requirement, only the result of the auction can be known. Accordingly, it is necessary to convince all sellers that anyone can verify the correctness of the result of the auction.

Public Verifiability: Anyone must be able to verify the correctness of the result of the auction.

5.2   Cryptographic Tools

We summarize the cryptographic tools used in our protocol. We denote a ciphertext of ElGamal encryption with public key $g, y = g^x$ by $E(m) = (G = g^r, M = my^r)$, and decryption function by D. We use the proof of equality of logarithms [6] and these proof of OR of statements [8]. By using the proofs, we have the following verifiable encryption, decryption, powering, mix [1], and mix and match [12] processes.

Proof of Encryption: We can prove that ciphertext $E(m) = (G = g^r, M \doteq my^r)$ is an encryption of m without revealing the secret random r by proving $\log_g G = \log_y M/m$.

Proof of Decryption: We can prove that plaintext $m = M/G^x$ is the decryption of $E(m) = (G, M)$ without revealing the secret key x by proving $\log_G M/m = \log_g y$.

Proof of Powering: We can prove that ciphertext $E'(m^r) = (G' = G^r, M' = M^r)$ is a power of $E(m) = (G, M)$ without revealing the secret random r by proving $\log_G G' = \log_M M'$.

Verifiable Mix [1]: The publicly verifiable mix randomizes and permutes its input ciphertexts without revealing the randomization and the permutation to hide the correspondence between inputs and outputs; a proof of the correctness of the mixing can be given.

First, we construct a publicly verifiable 2-input mix that randomizes and permutes two inputs in a publicly verifiable manner. We can prove that ciphertext $E'(m) = (G' = Gg^r, M' = My^r)$ is a randomization of $E(m) = (G, M)$ without revealing the secret random r by proving $\log_g G'/G = \log_y M'/M$. By combining this with the OR proof, we can prove that the 2-input mix randomizes and swaps OR randomizes and does not swap two inputs. We then can construct a publicly verifiable n-input mix by combining $n \log_2 n - n + 1$ 2-input mixes based on Waksman's permutation network.

Mix and Match [12]: By using mix and match, one can examine whether the decryption $D(c)$ of ciphertext c belongs to a specific set $S = \{p_1, p_2, \ldots, p_n\}$ of plaintexts.

First, we construct n ciphertexts $c_i = c/E(p_i)$ $(0 \le i \le n)$. We then take the power $c_i^{r_i}$ of them using a secret random factor r_i, mix them, and decrypt the mixed n ciphertexts in a publicly verifiable manner. If there exists one plaintext 1, we are convinced that $D(c) \in S$. If there exists no plaintext 1, we are convinced that $D(c) \notin S$.

5.3   Proposed Secure Procurement Auction

We securely realize our procurement auction based on the M+1-st price auction in [1].

There are n sellers $1, \cdots, n$, a single buyer 0, and trusted authority T. Buyer 0 plays the role of a bulletin board. Trusted authority T generates a secret key and a public key in the preparation phase. In the opening phase, it receives ciphertexts from buyer 0, performs mix and match, and decrypts them.

Notice that trusted authority T can be built in a distributed way, to make it trustful in a threshold sense. Plural servers generate secret and public key in threshold manner in the preparation phase, and decrypt a ciphertext in threshold manner in the opening phase. This threshold implementation prevents authority T from illegal decryption.

For simplicity, we assume there are no ties. If there exists a tie, then one seller is randomly chosen as the winner, but he needs to perform the task without making any profit.

Preparation: Trusted authority T generates a secret key and a public key for ElGamal encryption E, and publishes the public key. He also publishes a generator z of the cyclic group used for encryption.

Buyer 0 publishes a price list $P = \{1, 2, \cdots, p\}$, a quality list $Q = \{1, 2, \cdots, q\}$ (hereafter, we assume Q is finite), for the auctioned task, and her gross utility function $V(\cdot)$.

Each seller i obtains his private cost function $c(\theta_i, \cdot)$, and keeps it private.

Bidding: Each seller i decides his quality $q_i = \arg\max_q V(q) - c(\theta_i, q) \in Q$ and $b_i = V(q_i) - c(\theta_i, q_i) \in P$.

He computes encrypted vector $(c'_{1,i}, ..., c'_{p,i})$ of b_i where

$$c'_{j,i} = \begin{cases} E(z) & \text{if } j = b_i \\ E(1) & \text{if } j \ne b_i \end{cases}.$$

He then creates proof of correctness of the encrypted vector, i.e., "$D(c'_{1,i} \cdots c'_{p,i})$ $= z$ AND $(D(c'_{1,i}) = z$ OR $D(c'_{1,i}) = 1)$ AND...AND $(D(c'_{p,i}) = z$ OR $D(c'_{p,i}) = 1)$" using the homomorphic property of E, the proof of equality of logarithms [6], and the proof of OR of statements [8]. (This can be done with cost $O(p)$. $D(c'_{1,i} \cdots c'_{p,i}) = z$ implies product of all plaintexts is equal to z because of homomorphic property of E. $D(c'_{j,i}) = z$ OR $D(c'_{j,i}) = 1$ implies plaintext of $c'_{j,i}$

is equal to z or 1. So, we are convinced that exact one plaintext is equal to z and all other plaintexts are equal to 1.) He then publishes the encrypted vector and the proof.

He computes the encryption $e_i = E(q_i)$ of his quality q_i. He then creates proof of correctness "$D(e_i) \in Q$" of the encryption, i.e., "$D(e_i) = 1$ OR...OR $D(e_i) = q$", using the proof of equality of logarithms [6], and the proof of OR of statements [8]. (This can be done with cost $O(q)$.) He then publishes the encryption and the proof.

Opening: Buyer 0 publicly computes $c_{n,i} := c'_{n,i}$ and $c_{j,i} := c_{j+1,i} \cdot c'_{j,i}$ for $j = n - 1, n - 2, ..., 1$. Notice that by the homomorphic property now we have

$$c_{j,i} = \begin{cases} E(z) & \text{if } j \leq b_i \\ E(1) & \text{if } b_i < j \end{cases}.$$

He publicly computes products $c_j = c_{j,1} \cdots c_{j,n}$ $(1 \leq j \leq p)$. From the homomorphic property, we have the encrypted vector $(c_1, ..., c_p)$ where

$$c_j = E(z^{n(j)}), \quad n(j) = \#\{i \mid j \leq b_i\}.$$

By applying the mix and match technique [12] to c_j, we can examine whether $n(j) \leq 2$ or not, i.e., we can examine whether $D(c_j) \in \{1, z, z^2\}$ or not. To determine the 2-nd maximal $b_{2nd} = \max_{j \neq i^*} b_j$, i.e., b_{2nd} s.t. $n(b_{2nd}) \geq 2$ and $n(b_{2nd} + 1) \leq 1$, we perform a binary search using the examination by mix and match; buyer 0 sends c_j to trusted authority T for $\lceil \log p \rceil$ rounds, and trusted authority T performs mix and match.

To determine winning seller i^*, we decrypt $c_{b_{2nd}+1,i}$ $(1 \leq i \leq n)$ and find winning seller i^* with $D(c_{b_{2nd}+1,i^*}) = z$; buyer 0 sends $c_{b_{2nd}+1,i}$ $(1 \leq i \leq n)$ to trusted authority T, and trusted authority T decrypts them.

To determine q_{i^*} of the winning seller i^*, we decrypt $E(q_{i^*})$; buyer 0 sends $E(q_{i^*})$ to trusted authority T, and trusted authority T decrypts it.

Finally, buyer 0 publishes the payment $p_{i^*} = V(q_{i^*}) - b_{2nd}$ where V is the public utility of buyer 0, and the winning seller i^*.

5.4 Security

We discuss security of the proposed protocol.

Secrecy of Bids: The protocol leaks no information except $\max_{j \neq i^*} b_j, i^*, q_{i^*}$. In bidding phase, bidding price is encoded into the encrypted vector that leaks no information, since the underlying encryption scheme is indistinguishable. In opening phase, mix and match process leaks whether $D(c_j) \in \{1, z, z^2\}$ or not, however, this provides no more information than $\max_{j \neq i^*} b_j$. Illegal decryption by authority T is prevented by distributed decryption.

The protocol leaks information $\max_{j \neq i^*} b_j$ and q_{i^*} besides auction result $i^*, V(q_{i^*}) - \max_{j \neq i^*} b_j$. However, this is not serious, since the true costs of 1-st and 2-nd highest seller, these are what they want to conceal, cannot be found from the leaked information. Actually, to compute cost $c(\theta_i, q_i)$ of the highest seller i, we need b_i, and to compute cost $c(\theta_j, q_j)$ of the 2-nd highest seller j, we need q_j.

Public Verifiability: The protocol is publicly verifiable, since all steps, i.e., encryption, mix and match, and decryption, are publicly verifiable.

Moreover, the protocol is robust, since invalid bid can be detected because of public verifiability, and even if some sellers do not send their bids, buyer can compute the auction result correctly.

In the bidding step, the malicious seller can bid at any price relative to the bidding price of other seller. He can construct a encrypted vector of any price by shifting and randomizing another seller's encrypted vector. To avoid this, each seller commits the whole encrypted vector and its poof, and opens it after all sellers commit.

5.5   Efficiency

We discuss efficiency of the proposed protocol.

Communication and Computational Complexity: The communication and computational complexity of buyer 0 is $O(n(p+q))$, because of n sellers, the encrypted vector and its proof of length p, and proof of correctness of encrypted quality of length q. The communication and computational complexity of authority T is $O(n + \log p)$. The communication and computational complexity of seller i is $O(p + q)$.

It follows that the protocol is efficient for large n, but it is costly for large $\log p$ or large $\log q$.

Round Complexity: The round complexity of buyer 0 is $O(n + \log p)$, since there are n sellers and buyer 0 and authority T must interact for $\lceil \log p \rceil$ rounds. The round complexity of authority T is $O(\log p)$. The round complexity of seller i is 1, this means that the proposed protocol achieves "bid and go" concept.

It follows that the protocol is efficient for large n, large $\log p$, and large $\log q$ from the viewpoint of round complexity.

6   Conclusions

In this paper, we investigated a secure multi-attribute procurement auction in which each sales item is defined by several attributes, called quality, the buyer is the auctioneer (e.g., a government), and the sellers are the bidders.

We first developed a Vickrey-typo protocol in which acting honestly is a dominant strategy for sellers based on [19]. However, in the protocol described in [19], a seller needs to fully expose his private information θ_i. Our protocol, on the other hand, avoids the full exposure of types. By this modification, the protocol becomes easier to implement securely.

We then constructed secure protocol of the multi-attribute procurement auction that does not leak the true cost of the winner, which is highly classified information that the winner wants to keep private. We provide cryptographic protocol based on [1] to realize our procurement auction.

Acknowledgments

The authors would like to thank the anonymous referees for valuable comments.

References

1. Masayuki Abe and Koutarou Suzuki. M+1-st price auction using homomorphic encryption. In *Proceedings of Public Key Cryptography 2002*, pages 115–124, 2002.
2. Olivier Baudron and Jacques Stern. Non-interactive private auctions. In *Proceedings of Fifth International Financial Cryptography Conference (FC-01)*, pages 364–378, 2001.
3. Martin Bichler. An experimental analysis of multi-attribute auction. *Decision Support Systems*, 29(3):249–268, 2000.
4. Felix Brandt. Fully private auctions in a constant number of rounds. In *Proceedings of Seventh International Financial Cryptography Conference (FC-2003)*, pages 223–238, 2003.
5. Christian Cachin. Efficient private bidding and auctions with an oblivious third party. In *Proceedings of 6th ACM Conference on Computer and Communications Security*, pages 120–127, 1999.
6. David Chaum and Torben P. Pedersen. Wallet databases with observers. In *Proceedings of CRYPTO 1992*, pages 89–105, 1992.
7. Yeon-Koo Che. Design cometition through multidimensional auctions. *RAND Journal of Economics*, 24(4):668–680, 1993.
8. Ronald Cramer, Ivan Damgård, and Berry Schoenmakers. Proofs of partial knowledge and simplified design of witness hiding protocols. In *Proceedings of CRYPTO 1994*, pages 174–187, 1994.
9. Esther David, Rina Azoulay-Schwartz, and Sarit Kraus. Protocols and Strategies for Automated Multi-Attribute Auctions. In *International Joint Conference on Autonomous Agents and Multiagent systems*, pages 77–85, 2002.
10. Esther David, Rina Azoulay-Schwartz, and Sarit Kraus. Bidders' Strategy for Multi-Attribute Sequential English Auction with a Deadline. In *The Second International Joint Conference on Autonomous Agents and Multiagent systems*, pages 457–464, 2003.
11. Michael Harkavy, J. D. Tygar, and Hiroaki Kikuchi. Electronic auctions with private bids. In *Proceedings of Third USENIX Workshop on Electronic Commerce*, pages 61–74, 1998.
12. Markus Jakobsson and Ari Juels. Mix and match: Secure function evaluation via ciphertexts. In *Proceedings of ASIACRYPT 2000*, pages 162–177, 2000.
13. Ari Juels and Michael Szydlo. A two-server, sealed-bid auction protocol. In *Proceedings of Sixth International Financial Cryptography Conference (FC-02)*, pages 72–86, 2002.
14. Hiroaki Kikuchi, Michael Harkavy, and J. D. Tygar. Multi-round anonymous auction protocols. In *Proceedings of first IEEE Workshop on Dependable and Real-Time E-Commerce Systems*, pages 62–69, 1998.

15. Helger Lipmaa, N. Asokan, and Valtteri Niemi. Secure Vickrey auctions without threshold trust. In *Proceedings of Sixth International Financial Cryptography Conference (FC-02)*, pages 87–101, 2002.
16. Moni Naor, Benny Pinkas, and Reuben Sumner. Privacy preserving auctions and mechanism design. In *Proceedings of the First ACM Conference on Electronic Commerce (EC-99)*, pages 129–139, 1999.
17. Kazue Sako. Universally verifiable auction protocol which hides losing bids. In *Proceedings of Public Key Cryptography 2000*, pages 35–39, 2000.
18. Stuart G. Stubblebine and Paul F. Syverson. Fair on-line auctions without special trusted parties. In *Proceedings of Third International Financial Cryptography Conference (FC-99)*, pages 230–240, 1999.
19. Takayuki Suyama and Makoto Yokoo. Strategy/false-name proof protocols for combinatorial multi-attribute procurement auction. In *Proceedings of the Third International joint Conference on Autonomous Agents and Multiagent Systems (AAMAS-2004)*, 2004.
20. Koutarou Suzuki and Makoto Yokoo. Secure combinatorial auctions by dynamic programming with polynomial secret sharing. In *Proceedings of Sixth International Financial Cryptography Conference (FC-02)*, pages 44–56, 2002.
21. Koutarou Suzuki and Makoto Yokoo. Secure Generalized Vickrey Auction using homomorphic encryption. In *Proceedings of Seventh International Financial Cryptography Conference (FC-03)*, pages 239–249, 2003.
22. William Vickrey. Counter speculation, auctions, and competitive sealed tenders. *Journal of Finance*, 16:8–37, 1961.
23. Makoto Yokoo and Koutarou Suzuki. Secure multi-agent dynamic programming based on homomorphic encryption and its application to combinatorial auctions. In *Proceedings of the First International Conference on Autonomous Agents and Multiagent Systems (AAMAS-2002)*, pages 112–119, 2002.

Oblivious Conjunctive Keyword Search*

Hyun Sook Rhee, Jin Wook Byun, Dong Hoon Lee, and Jongin Lim

Center for Information Security Technologies (CIST),
Korea University, Anam Dong, Sungbuk Gu, Seoul, Korea
{math33, byunstar, donghlee, jilim}@korea.ac.kr

Abstract. We study the problem of keyword search in which a server
contains various multimedia contents and a user of server wishes to retrieve some multimedia item containing specific keywords without revealing to the server which item it is. Recently, Ogata and Kurosawa
introduced an interesting keyword search scheme called oblivious keyword search by using the notion of oblivious transfer. However, only one
keyword can be searched in each query, hence the scheme cannot provide a conjunctive keyword search which finds items containing each of
several keywords. In this paper, we firstly design a conjunctive keyword
search by using the oblivious transfer, and present *oblivious conjunctive keyword search* (for short, OCKS). We prove that OCKS protocol
is secure under the intractability of RSA known target inversion problem.

Keywords: Conjunctive Keyword Search, Storage system, Oblivious
Transfer, Anonymity, Privacy.

1 Introduction

As the amount of information to be stored and managed on the Internet rapidly
increases, the importance of storage system such as a database is increasingly
growing. As a result, ensuring privacy for the stored data on the storage system
is becoming one of the most urgent challenges in database research and industry.

Today, there are two important privacy issues in database research. The first
important issue is that a user needs to be assured that his data stored on the
database is protected against data thefts from outsiders. To simply resolve this
problem, we may implement a cryptographic encryption module in the database
management system (DBMS), and the module in the DBMS performs encryptions and decryptions for the stored data. Actually, the most real database systems such as `Oracle` 8i and `MS Access` provide themselves a cryptographic module in their DBMS, hence the first issue can be resolved without any additional
implementation costs such as private key management module certainly.

The second issue is that the data need to be protected even from an insider
system manager such as a system administrator of database if the database system cannot be trusted. When the storage system is not trustworthy, users may

* This research was supported by the MIC(Ministry of Information and Communication), Korea, under the ITRC(Information Technology Research Center) support
program supervised by the IITA(Institute of Information Technology Assessment).

J. Song, T. Kwon, and M. Yung (Eds.): WISA 2005, LNCS 3786, pp. 318–327, 2006.
© Springer-Verlag Berlin Heidelberg 2006

ensure the privacy of their data by storing it encrypted. The users of system should securely manage its encryption keys without revealing to the insider system manager. Originally, storing data in an encrypted form was proposed in Blaze's Cryptographic File System (CFS) [2], and expanded on later systems [2, 8, 23, 13]. If data are stored in an encrypted form, it can be protected from leaking by the server because it does not know the decryption key. In addition, there is no need to encrypt data again for confidentiality when it is sent on the public network. However, secure encryption makes documents look random, and unreadable to anyone other than the users holding the decryption keys, hence the server is unable to determine which encrypted documents contain specific keywords. To resolve this problem, many efficient search protocols over encrypted data have been suggested in various scenarios [4, 7, 10, 12, 17, 18, 21, 22].

In this paper, we study the problem of keyword search in a setting where a database supplier uploads data onto its database. Hence a system manager is also a database supplier and has no motivation to be an inside attacker. For example, consider a setting of keyword search where a server itself contains various multimedia contents and a user of server wishes to retrieve some multimedia item containing specific keywords without revealing to the server which item it is. Recently, in this setting, Ogata and Kurosawa first introduced an interesting keyword search scheme called oblivious keyword search (for short, OKS) by using the notion of oblivious transfer (for short, OT) [17]. Originally, the notion of OT was introduced by Rabin [20], and have been subsequently defined in different forms [9].[1] The OT protocol is a two party protocol between a sender S and a receiver R. S has two bits, and R wishes to get one of them satisfying the followings properties: (1) S does not know which bit R obtained and (2) R does not know any information about the bit that he did not obtain. The OKS protocol is also a two party protocol between a database supplier T and a user U based on the above properties. By the property of (1), the user U is able to search and retrieve the data containing keyword w chosen by user U without revealing the keyword w to T. On the other hand, the user U learns only the data containing keyword by the property (2).

1.1   Our Contributions

As mentioned by Ogata and Kurosawa themselves, the number of keywords for searching in their OKS protocol is restricted by only one. Hence a user cannot use boolean combinations of keywords, which should be an available functionality. One may think that a conjunctive keyword search can be derived from the multiple executions of only single keyword search scheme. In this case, however, the server should find all documents containing each individual keyword by using the single keyword search, check the intersection set of all documents, then return the results to the user. This approach requires the server high computational cost and redundancy due to duplicated comparisons and search, hence the design of conjunctive keyword search ensuring efficiency and security is never an easy task.

---

[1] All these OT variants were shown to be equivalent to one another [9, 5].

In this paper, we propose an oblivious conjunctive keyword search protocol(OCKS) by using the notion of OT. First, we present a new security model for OCKS, and define its security for OCKS. We then prove that our suggested OCKS protocol is secure if the RSA known target inversion problem [6] is hard.

1.2   Organization

This paper is organized as follows. In Section 2, we overview an OKS protocol presented by Ogata and Kurosawa. In Section 3, we describe our security model, security definition and computational assumption for constructing OCKS protocol. In Section 4, we present an OCKS protocol and show that the OCKS protocol is secure based on the hardness of RSA known target inversion problem. We conclude in Section 5.

2   OKS Protocol

Now we review the OKS protocol proposed by Ogata and Kurosawa [17], which is a building block of the proposed scheme.

2.1   Description of k-out-of-n OKS

The OKS protocol is based on the k-out-of-n OT protocol (OKS_k^n) suggested in [17]. The OKS_k^n protocol consists of database supplier $\mathcal{T}$ and a user $\mathcal{U}$. Let W be the set of keywords and l be a security parameter. The OKS_k^n protocol consists of a commit phase and a transfer phase.

In the commit phase, $\mathcal{T}$ commits n data $B_1, ..., B_n$ such that

$$B_i = (w_i, c_i)$$

where $w_i \in W$ and c_i is an encrypted data. We define the search result for a keyword w by

$$\mathrm{Search}(w) = \{c_i \, | w_i = w \ \text{for some} \ i \, \}$$

The transfer phase consists of k subphases. At each subphase j $(1 \leq j \leq k)$, $\mathcal{U}$ can choose a keyword $w_j^* \in W$ adaptively and learn $Search(w_j^*)$. However, $\mathcal{T}$ should gain no information on w_1^*, w_2^*, ..., w_k^* and $\mathcal{U}$ should not learn anything except the result of $Search(w_j^*)$. Let G be a pseudo-random generator and H be a cryptographic secure hash function. The OKS_k^n protocol works as follows.

- **[Commitment Phase]**. $\mathcal{T}$ generates a public key (N, e) and a secret key d of RSA. $\mathcal{T}$ publishes (N, e). Next, $\mathcal{T}$ computes $\mathcal{C}_i = \{K_i, E_i\}$ for $1 \leq i \leq n$, as follows.
$$\mathcal{C}_i = \begin{cases} K_i = (H(w_i))^d \ mod \ N \\ E_i = (G(w_i \| K_i \| i)) \oplus (0^l \| c_i) \end{cases}$$

  where $\|$ denotes concatenation and 0^l is a l-bit string with 0's. $\mathcal{T}$ sends $E_1, ..., E_n$ to $\mathcal{U}$.

- [**Transfer Subphase**]. At each transfer subphase j $(1 \leq j \leq k)$, $\mathcal{U}$ performs the followings.
  (1) $\mathcal{U}$ chooses a keyword w_j^*.
  (2) $\mathcal{U}$ chooses a random element r and computes Y where,

$$Y = r^e H(w_j^*) \bmod N.$$

$\mathcal{U}$ sends Y to $\mathcal{T}$.
  (3) $\mathcal{T}$ computes $K' = Y^d \bmod N$ and sends it to $\mathcal{U}$.
  (4) $\mathcal{U}$ computes K as follows.

$$K = K'/r = H(w_j^*)^d \bmod N.$$

For $i = 1, ..., n$, $\mathcal{U}$ computes $G(w_j^* \| K \| i)$, and gets the following.

$$(a_i \| b_i) = E_i \oplus G(w_j^* \| K \| i)$$

If $a_i = 0^l$ $(1 \leq i \leq n)$ then $\mathcal{U}$ succeeds and gets $c_i = b_i$. Otherwise, $\mathcal{U}$ outputs a failure message.

3   Security Definitions

In this section, we describe the security definitions for OCKS protocol. We slightly extend the security model of [17] to be suitable for conjunctive keyword search. In order to treat several keywords, we assume an untrusted storage system has an actual database which has several records, each of which contains keyword fields. We assume that there are m keyword fields for each encrypted documents.

3.1   Security Definition of OCKS

We define two security goals based on the definition of [17]. One is a user security. It guarantees that an untrusted database supplier $\mathcal{T}$ should not learn any information about keywords from the user's requesting query in the i-th subphase $(1 \leq i \leq k)$. The other is a database security. It guarantees that a malicious user $\mathcal{U}$ should get nothing except any search results. We formally define as follows.

Definition 3.1.1 [User Security in OCKS protocol]. Suppose that $\boldsymbol{w_i} = w_{ij_1}, w_{ij_2}, ..., w_{ij_{d_i}}$ and $\boldsymbol{w_i^*} = w_{ij_1}^*, w_{ij_2}^*, ..., w_{ij_{d_i}}^*$ are arbitrary keyword strings in the i-th subphase and $(\boldsymbol{w_1}, \boldsymbol{w_2}, ..., \boldsymbol{w_k}) \neq (\boldsymbol{w_1^*}, \boldsymbol{w_2^*}, ..., \boldsymbol{w_k^*})$. The OCKS protocol is secure for the user if for any malicious database supplier $\mathcal{T}$, the view of $\mathcal{T}$ for any keyword strings $\boldsymbol{w_1}, \boldsymbol{w_2}, ..., \boldsymbol{w_k}$ and the view of $\mathcal{T}$ for any keyword strings $\boldsymbol{w_1^*}, \boldsymbol{w_2^*}, ..., \boldsymbol{w_k^*}$ are computationally indistinguishable.

Definition 3.1.2 [Database Security in OCKS protocol]. Consider the following *ideal world*. A trusted third party (TTP) first receives $(B_1, B_2, ..., B_n)$ from $\mathcal{T}$. TTP next tells the user $\mathcal{U}$ the search result $\bigcap_{t=1}^{d_j} Search(w_{j_t}^*)$ on the request $\boldsymbol{w_j^*} = w_{j_1}^*, w_{j_2}^*, ..., w_{j_{d_j}}^*$ for any $(1 \leq j \leq k)$. We say that a protocol is secure for the database if the following condition is satisfied:

- **[Indistinguishability]**. For any malicious user $\tilde{\mathcal{U}}$, there exists a simulator $\triangle_S$ that plays the role of a user in the ideal world such that for any polynomial time distinguisher $\mathcal{D}$,

$$|Pr(\mathcal{D}(\text{the output of } \tilde{\mathcal{U}}) = 1) - Pr(\mathcal{D}(\text{the output of } \triangle_S) = 1)| < \epsilon(l).$$

where $\epsilon(l)$ is a negligible function and l is a security parameter.

Definition 3.1.3 [OCKS Security]. We say that a protocol is a secure OCKS protocol if it satisfies both user and database security in OCKS protocol.

Ogata and Kurosawa use the RSA blind signature scheme to hide keywords in the transfer phase. Thus, the user's requesting keywords are blinded from the malicious database supplier $\mathcal{T}$. We also use the RSA blind signature scheme in each transfer subphase.

3.2 Security of RSA Blind Signature and Its Related Problem

In [6], Bellare et al. proved that the RSA-blind signature scheme is secure as long as the RSA known-target inversion problem is hard [6, 19]. The following is a definition about the security of RSA-blind signature scheme. The function H is an one-way hash function, where $H : \{0,1\}^* \longrightarrow Z_N^*$. We let KeyGen be the RSA key generation algorithm which takes k as input and returns the values N, e and d, where N is a k-bit RSA modulus.

Definition 3.2.1 [Blind Signature Security]. Let $k \in \mathsf{N}$ be the security parameter, and let $m, h : \mathsf{N} \to \mathsf{N}$ be functions of k. Let $\mathcal{F}$ be a *forger* who has access to RSA-inversion oracle and a hash oracle, denoted $(\cdot)^d \bmod N$ and $H(\cdot)$, respectively. Consider the following experiment.

Experiment. $\mathsf{EXP}_{\mathcal{F},h,m}^{rsa\text{-}omf}(k)$.

$(N, e, d) \xleftarrow{R} \mathsf{KeyGen}(k)$

$((M_1, x_1), ..., (M_{m(k)+1}, x_{m(k)+1})) \longleftarrow \mathcal{F}^{(\cdot)^d mod N, H(\cdot)}(N, e, k)$

If the following are all true, return 1 else return 0:

- $\forall i \in \{1, ...t, m(k) + 1\}$: $H(M_i) = x_i^e \bmod N$
- Message strings $M_1, M_2, ..., M_{m(k)+1}$ are all distinct.
- $\mathcal{F}$ makes at most $m(k)$ quries of message to its RSA-inversion oracles.
- The number of hash-oracle queries made in this experiment is at most $h(k)$

We define the advantage of the forger $\mathcal{F}$ via

$$\mathbf{Adv}_{\mathcal{F},h,m}^{rsa\text{-}omf}(k) = \Pr[\mathsf{EXP}_{\mathcal{F},h,m}^{rsa\text{-}omf}(k) = 1].$$

The RSA blind signature scheme is *polynomial-secure against one-more forgery* if the function $\mathbf{Adv}_{\mathcal{F},h,m}^{rsa\text{-}omf}(\cdot)$ is negligible for any forger $\mathcal{F}$ whose time-complexity is polynomial in the security parameter k.

In RSA known target inversion (for short, **RSA-KTI**) problem, the number of oracle calls allowed to the adversary is just one fewer than the number of target points, so that to win it must compute the RSA-inverse of all target points. The following is a notion of **RSA-KTI** problem in [6]. We denote by $(\cdot)^d$ mod N the oracle that takes input $y \in Z_N^*$ and returns its RSA-inverse y^d. An adversary solving the known-target inversion problem is given oracle access to $(\cdot)^d$ mod N and is given $m(k) + 1$ targets where $m : N \longrightarrow N$. Its task is to compute the RSA-inverses of all the targets while submitting at most $m(k)$ queries to the oracle.

Definition 3.2.2 [Hardness of RSA-KTI problem]. Let $k \in N$ be the security parameter, and let $m, h : N \to N$ be functions of k. Let $\mathcal{A}$ be an adversary who has access to an $(\cdot)^d$ mod N. Consider the following experiment:

Experiment. $\mathsf{EXP}_{\mathcal{A},m}^{rsa\text{-}kti}(k)$.

$(N, e, d) \xleftarrow{R} \mathsf{KeyGen}(k)$
For $i = 1$ to $m(k) + 1$ do $y_i \xleftarrow{R} Z_N^*(N, e, k, y_1, ..., y_{m(k)+1})$
If the following are both true then return 1 else teturn 0

- $\forall i \in \{1, ..., m(k) + 1\}$: $y_i = x_i^e$ mod N
- $\mathcal{A}$ makes at most $m(k)$ oracle queries.

We define the advantage of $\mathcal{A}$ via

$$\mathbf{Adv}_{\mathcal{A},m}^{rsa\text{-}kti}(k) = \Pr[\mathsf{EXP}_{\mathcal{A},m}^{rsa\text{-}kti}(k) = 1]$$

The **RSA-KTI** problem is said to be hard if the function $\mathbf{Adv}_{\mathcal{A},m}^{rsa\text{-}kti}(k)$ is negligible for any adversary $\mathcal{A}$ whose time-complexity is polynomial in the security parameter k.

Proposition 3.2.3 [6]. If **RSA-KTI** is hard, then **RSA** blind signature scheme is polynomially-secure against one-more *forgery*. $\square$

4   OCKS Protocol

In this section, we construct an OCKS protocol. We show that OCKS protocol is secure if the one-more RSA-inversion problem is hard. The OCKS protocol is illustrated in Fig.1, and works as follows.

- [Commitment Phase]. $\mathcal{T}$ generates a public key (N, e) and a secret key d of RSA. We assume that the value k_i is a decryption key of encrypted data $c_i = E_{k_i}(D_i)$, where $D_i = \{w_{i1}, ..., w_{im}\}$. Let $keygen_i(x) = (x - r_{i1}) \times \cdots \times (x - r_{im}) + k_i$ be a key generation function which provides a decryption key k_i corresponding to data c_i, where m is the number of keyword fields. Let $leng : Z_N \longrightarrow Z_q$ is an ideal hash function and $f_k : Z_N \longrightarrow Z_N$ is a

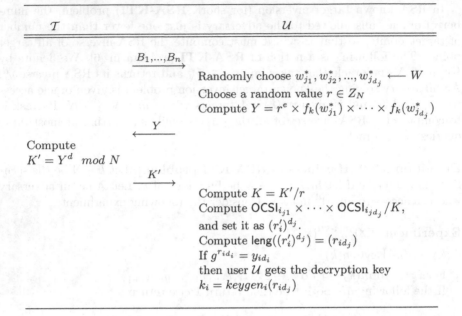

Fig. 1. OCKS Protocol

pseudo random function. For every $i = 1, ..., n$ and $j = 1, ..., m$, $\mathcal{T}$ computes the followings.

(**Step 1**) $\mathcal{T}$ randomly chooses $r_i' \in Z_N$.

(**Step 2**) $\mathcal{T}$ makes $\mathsf{OCSI}_{ij} = f_k(w_{i,j})^d r_i' \mod N$, where OCSI_{ij} is the oblivious conjunctive keyword searchable information for w_{ij}.

(**Step 3**) $\mathcal{T}$ computes $\mathsf{leng}(r_i'^j) = r_{ij}$ and sets $y_{ij} = g^{r_{ij}}$.

(**Step 4**) $\mathcal{T}$ constructs $B_i = c_i \parallel y_{i1}, y_{i2}, ..., y_{im} \parallel keygen_i(x) \parallel \mathsf{OCSI}_{i1}, ..., \mathsf{OCSI}_{im}$. $\mathcal{T}$ commits $B_1, B_2, \cdots, B_n$.

- [**Transfer Phase**]. The transfer phase consists of k subphases. $\mathcal{U}$ learns a conjunctive keyword search result $\bigcap_{t=1}^{d_j} search(w_{j_t}^*)$ as follows.

(**Step 1**) $\mathcal{U}$ choose d_j keywords $\boldsymbol{w}^* = w_{j_1}^*, w_{j_2}^*, ..., w_{j_{d_j}}^*$ on W adaptively

(**Step 2**) $\mathcal{U}$ chooses a random element $r \in Z_N$ and computes Y as follows. $\mathcal{U}$ sends Y to $\mathcal{T}$.

$$Y = r^e \times f_k(w_{j_1}^*) \times \cdots \times f_k(w_{j_{d_j}}^*).$$

(**Step 3**) $\mathcal{T}$ computes $K' = Y^d \mod N$ and sends it to $\mathcal{U}$.

(**Step 4**) $\mathcal{U}$ computes $K = K'/r$.

(**Step 5**) For every i from 1 to n, $\mathcal{U}$ computes r_{id_j} as follows.

$$\begin{cases} \mathsf{OCSI}_{ij_1} \times \cdots \times \mathsf{OCSI}_{ij_{d_i}} / K \Longrightarrow (r_i')^{d_j}. \\ \mathsf{leng}((r_i')^{d_j}) \Longrightarrow r_{id_j}. \end{cases}$$

If the following equation (1) is satisfied, then we determine that the data D_i contains the keywords $w_{j1}^*, w_{j2}^*, ..., w_{jd_j}^*$.

$$g^{r_{id_j}} = y_{id_j}. \tag{1}$$

And $\mathcal{U}$ can get a decryption key k_i for c_i by the equation (2).

$$k_i = keygen_i(r_{id_j}). \tag{2}$$

User $\mathcal{U}$ can get data D_i as decrypting the data c_i with k_i.

4.1   Security of OCKS Protocol

Theorem 1. The above OCKS protocol satisfies *user security* if the security of RSA blind signature scheme.

Proof. For every subphase i ($i = 1, 2, ..., k$), $\mathcal{T}$ has no information on $\boldsymbol{w_1^*}, \boldsymbol{w_2^*}, \cdots, \boldsymbol{w_k^*}$, where $\boldsymbol{w_i^*} = w_{ij_1}, w_{ij_2}, ..., w_{ij_{d_i}}$ since they are blinded by the RSA blind signature scheme. Therefore, user security is satisfies under an intractability of RSA known target inversion problem.   □

Theorem 2. The above OCKS protocol satisfies *database security* if the **RSA-KTI** is hard.

Proof. We next prove the database security by assuming that **RSA-KTI** is hard. We show that there exists a simulator $\triangle_S$ that plays the role of a user in ideal world as follows.

[Commitment Phase]. $\triangle_S$ generates (N, e, d) and sends (N, e) to $\tilde{u}$. $\triangle_S$ also chooses $B_1, ..., B_n$ and sends them to $\tilde{u}$.

- For every $i = 1, ..., n$, $\triangle_S$ randomly chooses c_i and $\mathsf{OCSI}_{i1}, ..., \mathsf{OCSI}_{im}$.
- For every i, j ($1 \leq i \leq n$, $1 \leq j \leq m$), $\triangle_S$ randomly chooses r_{ij} and decryption key k_i, and computes $y_{ij} = g^{r_{ij}}$ and sets $keygen_i(x) = (x - r_{i1}) \times \cdots \times (x - r_{im}) + k_i$.
- $\triangle_S$ commits $B_i = c_i \parallel y_{i1}, y_{i2}, ..., y_{im} \parallel keygen_i(x) \parallel \mathsf{OCSI}_{i1}, ..., \mathsf{OCSI}_{im}$.

[Transfer Phase]. $\triangle_S$ can perfectly simulate $\mathcal{T}$ because $\triangle_S$ knows (N, e, d).

$\triangle_S$ simulates f_k as follows. If $\tilde{u}$ queries $w_{ij_1}^*, w_{ij_2}^*, ..., w_{ij_{d_i}}^*$ to f_k for the first time, then $\triangle_S$ chooses a random value over Z_N, return it as the value of $f_k(w_{ij_1}^*) *$ $f_k(w_{ij_2}^*) * \cdots * f_k(w_{ij_{d_i}}^*)$, where the vector of keywords $\boldsymbol{w_i} = w_{ij_1}^*, w_{ij_2}^*, ..., w_{ij_{d_i}}^*$ In i-th subphase.

We assume that $\boldsymbol{QA\text{-}list}$ contains the pair of query and the set of result $(\boldsymbol{w_i}, \bigcap_{t=1}^{d_i} Search(w_{ij_t}^*))$ ($1 \leq i \leq k$). To simulate an ideal hash function leng, we need a $\boldsymbol{QA\text{-}list}$. $\triangle_S$ simulates an ideal hash function leng as follows.

- Let $cnt = 0$.
- If $cnt = 0$ then **QA-list** is empty.
- WLOG, before $\tilde{u}$ queries Y to $\mathcal{T}$, $\tilde{u}$ queries $w^*_{ij_t}$ to f_k, for every $t = 1, ..., d_i$.
  - (a) If $(\boldsymbol{w_i}, \bigcap_{t=1}^{d_i} Search(w^*_{ij_t})) \in$ **QA-list**, then go to step (c).
    else $cnt = cnt + 1$
  - (b) If $cnt > cnt + 1$, then a simulator $\triangle_S$ sets $\bigcap_{j=1}^{d_i} Search(w^*_{ij})$ at random.
    Otherwise, $\triangle_S$ queries $\boldsymbol{w_i}$ to the *TTP* and receives $\bigcap_{j=1}^{d_i} Search(w^*_{ij})$.
    $\triangle_S$ adds $(\boldsymbol{w_i}, \bigcap_{j=1}^{d_i} Search(w^*_{ij}))$ to **QA-list**.
  - (c) For i $(1 \leq i \leq n)$, if c_i is included in $\bigcap_{j=1}^{d_i} Search(w^*_{ij})$, then sets the values of *leng* as follows.
    - $\triangle_S$ computes $(r'_i)^t = \mathsf{OCSI}_{ij_1} \times \mathsf{OCSI}_{ij_2} \times \cdots \times \mathsf{OCSI}_{ij_{d_i}} / (f_k(w_{ij_1}))^d \times (f_k(w_{ij_2}))^d \times \cdots (f_k(w_{ij_{d_i}}))^d$ and then $\triangle_S$ sets $\mathsf{leng}((r'_i)^{j_t}) = r_{ij_t}$.
    - For all $t = d_{i+1}, ..., m$, $\triangle_S$ sets $\mathsf{leng}((r'_i)^j t)$ at random.
    Otherwise, $\triangle_S$ sets the value leng at random.

Let **BAD** be the event that $cnt > cnt + 1$. If **BAD** dose not occur, then $\triangle_S$ simulates hash function leng perfectly. Note that $\Pr(\textbf{BAD})$ means the probability that $\tilde{\mathcal{U}}$ succeeds in the one-more forgery attack on the **RSA** blind signature scheme. From Proposition 3.2.3, it is negligible if the **RSA-KTI** is hard. Consequently, the output of $\triangle_S$ and $\tilde{u}$ are indistinguishable if the **RSA-KTI** is hard. □

5   Concluding Remarks

In this paper, we first gave an oblivious conjunctive keyword search to the scheme of [17] in the random oracle model. We prove its security under the RSA known target inversion problem. It would be a good future work to design a secure OCKS protocol without random oracle assumption.

Acknowledgement

We deeply thank Hyun-A Park for helpful discussions of an earlier version of this paper. We also very thank anonymous referees of WISA05' for valuable comments.

References

1. R. Agrawal and R. Srikant,"Privacy-Preserving Data Mining", *In Proceedings of the 2000 ACM SIGMOD International Conference on Management of Data*, pp. 439-450, 2000.
2. M. Balze, "A Cryptographic file system for UNIX.", *Processings of 1st ACM Conference om Communications and Computing Security*, 1993.
3. S. Bellovin , W. Cheswick, "Privacy-enhanced searches using encrypted bloom filters", *Cryptology ePrint Archive*, Report 2004/022, Feb 2004.

4. D. Boneh, G. D. Crescenzo, R. Ostrovsky, and G. Persiano, "Public key Encryption with Keyword Search", *EUROCRYPT'04*, 2004.
5. D. Brassard, C. Crepeau, and J. M. Robert, "All-or-Nithing Disclosure of Secrets", *Crypto'86*, Springer-Verlag, 1987, pp. 234-238.
6. M. Bellare, C. Namprempre, and D. Pioncheval, "The Power of RSA Onversion Oracles and the Security of Chaum's RSA-Based Blind Signature Scheme", *Proc. of Finandcial Cryptography 2001*, LNCS vol. 2339, pp. 319-338.
7. Y. C. Chang, M. Mitzenmacher, "privacy preserving keyword searches on remote encrypted data", *ePrint*, October 7th 2003.
8. G. Cattaneo, G. Persiano, A. Del Sorbo, A. Cozzolino, E. Mauriello, and R. Pisapia, "Design and implementation of a transparent cryptographic file system for UNIX", *Techincal Report, University of Salerno*, 1997.
9. S. Even, O. Goldreich, and A. Lempel, "A Randomized Protocol for Signing Contracts", *comm. of ACM*, 28:637-647, 1985.
10. E. J. Goh, "secure index", *ePrint*, October 7th 2003.
11. P. Golle, M. Jakobsson, A. Juels, and Paul Syverson, "Universal Re-encryption for Mixnets", *In proceedings of CT-RSA 2004*, 2004.
12. P. Golle, J. Staddon and B. Waters, "Secure Conjunctive Keyword Search Over Encrypted Data", *Proccedings of the Second International Conference on ACNS:Applied Cryptography and Network Security*, 2004.
13. J. Hughes and D. Corcoran, "A nuiversal access, smart-card-based, secure fiel system.", *Atlanta Linux Showcase* , October 1999.
14. A. John , R. Peter, "Electric Communication Development", *Communications of the ACM* ,40,May 1997, pp. 71-79. 48-63, 2002.
15. K. Kurosawa, "Multi-recipient Public-Key Encryption with Shortened Ciphertext", *In proceedings of PKC 2002*, LNCS 2274, pp. 48-63, 2002.
16. M. Noar and B. Pinkas, "Efficient Oblivious trnasfer protocols", *12th Annual Symposium on Discrete Algorithms(SODA)*, pp 448-457(2001).
17. W. Ogata and K. Kurosawa, "Oblivious Keyword Search", *Journal of complexity'04*, Vol 20. April/Jun 2004.
18. D. Park, K. Kim, and P. Lee, "Public key Encryption with Conjunctive Field Keyword Search", *WISA'04*, LNCS 3325, pp73-86, 2004.
19. D. Pointcheval and J. P. Stern, "Provably secure blind signature schemes", *Proc. of Asiacrypt'96*, LNCS Vol. 1163, pp 252-265, 1996.
20. M. Rabin, "How to exchange secrets by oblivious transfer", *Technical Report TR 81*, Aiken computation Lab, Harvard University.
21. D. Song, D. Wagner, and A. Perrige, "Practical Techniques for searches on Encrypted Data", *In Proc. of the 2000 IEEE Security and Privacy Symposium*, May 2000.
22. B. R. Waters, D. Balfanz, G. Durfee, and D. K. Smetters, "Building an Encrypted and Searchable Audit Log", *11th Annual Network and Distributed Security Symposium (NDSS '04)*; 2004.
23. E. Zadok, I. Badulescu, and A. Shender, "Cryptfo : A stackable vnode level encryption fiel system.", *Technical Report CUCS-021-98*: 1998.

Efficient, Non-optimistic Secure Circuit Evaluation Based on the ElGamal Encryption

Go Yamamoto, Koji Chida, Anderson C.A. Nascimento,
Koutarou Suzuki, and Shigenori Uchiyama

NTT Information Sharing Platform Laboratories,
NTT Corporation 1-1, Hikarinooka, Yokosuka,
Kanagawa, Japan

Abstract. We propose a protocol for implementing secure function evaluation based on the homomorphic threshold ElGamal encryption scheme. To the best of our knowledge, our solution is more efficient in terms of computational complexity than previous solutions existent in the literature.

1 Introduction

1.1 Background

Two-party secure function evaluation consists of a protocol which allows n players, to compute a function $f(\cdot)$, which depends on inputs from the players, such that at the end of the protocol: the parties are sure that the result of the computation is correct; no party has learned more about each other's input than what can be computed from the output itself; dishonest players did not obtain significant knowledge about the output of the protocol while preventing the honest parties from receiving the result of the computation.

Secure function evaluation (SFE) is a central problem in the theory of cryptography and has received considerable attention since its introduction in [19]. Several different solutions, based on a wide range of models and assumptions, were proposed, e.g. [2, 11, 19].

However, it is still a big challenge to design protocols which are *secure* and *efficient*. Most of the proposed works till now aimed at proving the impossibility/possibility of SFE in principle, rather than in practice.

With the advent of ubiquitous computing and the bigger role played by low-computational powered devices in security protocols, the search for efficient protocols, in terms of computational complexity, for implementing SFE becomes a crucially important topic.

In this contribution, we give an efficient protocol for implementing secure function evaluation based on the DDH assumption which, to the best of our knowledge, possesses better computational and communication complexities than previous solutions in the literature attaining a similar level of security.

J. Song, T. Kwon, and M. Yung (Eds.): WISA 2005, LNCS 3786, pp. 328–342, 2006.

1.2 Previous Work

Many function evaluation protocols were presented in the literature in several different forms and flavors. The problem was first considered by Yao in [19], who proved that given the existence of one-way functions, any distributed computation can be securely implemented.

Subsequently, several researchers tried to obtain more efficient protocols by using different computational assumptions.

In [5], Cramer et al. proposed a generic and very efficient protocol, in terms of communication complexity, implementing secure distributed computation based on homomorphic encryption. They also proved that their protocol is secure when implemented with the Paillier encryption scheme.

It would be desirable to replace the Paillier encryption used in [5] by the elliptic ElGamal encryption since the latter can be implemented with much less computational effort and its key generation process is much simpler and efficient. This goal was achieved in [17], where a SFE protocol was proposed which has its security based on the homomorphic ElGamal encryption. The proposed scheme is secure against active adversaries, and the computational and communication complexities of the protocol are linear in the number of players. However, two prices were paid to obtain this improvement: (*i*) the round complexity of the protocol depends on the number of players (what is not a big problem if the number of players is not large) and (*ii*) the scheme of [17] is optimistic, that is, its performance degrades if the parties engaged in the protocol misbehave.

1.3 Our Contribution

This paper proposes a protocol for secure function evaluation which is as secure as the protocol proposed in [17], but achieves an improved communication and computational complexities while being *non-optimistic*.

We achieve this improvement by modifying the original protocol for computing conditional gates proposed in [17] so as to remove cheating parties from the computation without any need to re-start it and by using slightly modified versions of known zero-knowledge proofs ([6], [3], and [16]).

1.4 Road Map

Our paper is organized as follows. In Section 2 we present our security model, definitions and assumptions. In Section 3 we present our protocol, its security and performance analysis. Conclusions and open problems are given in Section 4. Some proofs of knowledge used in the main protocol are stated in an Appendix.

2 Security Model

Our model is very similar to the ones presented in [5] and [17].

We assume that there are n players connected by authenticated channels and a broadcast channel. We assume synchronous communications among the players. No more than $t < n$ players are corrupted by a static malicious adversary (thus, the adversary has to choose which parties are to be corrupted before the beginning of the protocol and does not corrupt any more players once the protocol starts). All the parties, including the adversary, are polynomial time Turing machines.

The goal of the protocol is to evaluate a certain function F represented as a binary circuit composed of addition and multiplication gates.

To define security, we introduce a trusted third party, which is connected by private and synchronous channels to all other players. A protocol secure in the *ideal* world is one where all the players give their respective inputs to the trusted party which them computes the outputs of all the players and distribute them to the respective parties.

A protocol secure in the *real* world is one which efficiently emulates the ideal protocol previously described. That is, any adversary attacking the real protocol can be simulated in polynomial time, given only the view of an adversary attacking the ideal protocol. For further details we refer to [5].

We assume the hardness of the decisional Diffie-Helmann problem (DDH problem) and the existence of random oracles, as in [17].

We note here that, in the case a majority of the players is dishonest, there are certain attacks which are unavoidable. For instance, if $t > n/2$ players are dishonest, always a subset $n-t$ of players will be able to abort the protocol. Thus, in the case of dishonest majority we always consider a non-aborting adversary. Moreover, if $t > n/2$ nothing prevents cheating parties from leaving the protocol after they have obtained their desired output, even if the honest parties have not yet received theirs. Thus, *strong* fairness is never achieved in this scenario. Therefore, in our work, in case of dishonest majority, we aim at a weaker form of fairness, where cheating parties can leave the protocol with some, but not significant, advantage over honest parties.

3   Proposed Protocols

3.1   Preliminary

In our protocol we use the threshold ElGamal encryption scheme. For the sake of simplicity, we first introduce its non-threshold version.

Consider a cyclic group $\mathcal{G}$ of order q generated by G where the DDH problem is hard. Consider the ElGamal public key $(G, H = uG)$ and its secret key u.

An encryption of $a \in \{0, 1\}$ is defined as:

$$E(a, r) \overset{\text{def}}{=} (rG, (a + r)H), \tag{1}$$

where $r \in_R \mathbb{Z}/q\mathbb{Z}$.

a can be obtained from $E(a, r)$ by dividing $(a + r)H$ by urG and then computing the discrete logarithm of the result. This is infeasible in general. However, in our case, because a is always taken from a small (binary) domain, this task can be performed efficiently.

Note that this encryption scheme is homomorphic, that is, $E(a,r) \times E(\tilde{a}, \tilde{r})^\lambda = E(a + \lambda\tilde{a}, r')$, for a publicly known value λ. Thus, linear operations are easily implementable on ciphertexts. Also, it is easy to see that, given $E(a,r)$, $E(\tilde{a}, \tilde{r})$ and λ, a party A can prove in zero-knowledge to a verifier B that $E(a + \lambda\tilde{a}, \tilde{r})$ is indeed a valid encryption of $a + \lambda\tilde{a}$. For further details, please see Appendix 1.

In the multi-party setting in this paper, players keep shares of the secret key u in advance. We can use key generation schemes as the ones proposed in [14] and k-out-of-n verifiable secret sharing schemes as [8] to securely distribute shares of an unknown and randomly chosen secret key u.

Our goal in the subsequent sections is to securely implement an operation $\oplus$ on $a \in \{0,1\}$ and $b \in \mathbb{Z}/q\mathbb{Z}$ taken not necessarily from a binary domain, such that:

$$a \oplus b \stackrel{\text{def}}{=} \begin{cases} b & (a = 0) \\ 1 - b & (a = 1) \end{cases}$$

It is obvious that $\oplus$ stands for the ordinary XOR if $a, b \in \{0,1\}$, which together with addition gates, can be used to obtain any secure function evaluation. A gate implementing $a \oplus b$ was called a conditional gate in [17]. In the next section we give a new, more efficient protocol for obtaining conditional gates.

3.2   Proposed Protocol for Implementing Conditional Gates

Here we give a new, more efficient protocol for implementing conditional gates. Compared to the protocol proposed in [17] our solution is non-optimistic while presenting a slightly better computational performance.

Hereafter, $E(\cdot)$ stands for the threshold homomorphic ElGamal encryption with its secret key shared among n players. We start with input bits $a, b \in \{0,1\} \subset \mathbb{Z}/q\mathbb{Z}$ (not necessarily known to any of the players) and random numbers $r, s \in_R \mathbb{Z}/q\mathbb{Z}$. The proposed protocol uses $E(a,r)$ and $E(b,s)$ as input, and computes $E(a \oplus b, t)$ for some $t \in_R \mathbb{Z}/q\mathbb{Z}$ while keeping a and b secret through its entire execution. Denote the n players participating in the protocol by $P_1, P_2, \cdots, P_n$.

The basic idea of the protocol is close to that of [17], but the scheme is different. The proposed protocol requires no translation from $\{0,1\}$ to $\{-1,1\}$ for input/output bits, and no Pedersen commitments in the process, what overall results in a more efficient protocol. We assume that at a setup phase, the players generated a public key π and secret shares of a private key σ of an ElGamal encryption scheme, for instance, by using the protocols proposed in [14].

The Protocol Z in Figure 1 illustrates our protocol. The Protocol B is described in Figure 2, that illustrates an honest verifier zero-knowledge proof of knowledge for a witness on the membership of ANDORDL, where

---

Parties: players $\{P_i\}_{i=1,2,\cdots,n}$.
Common input: ciphertexts $E(a,r)$, $E(b,s)$, where $a \in \{0,1\}$, $b \in \mathbb{Z}/q\mathbb{Z}$
Output: ciphertext $E(a \oplus b, r'')$ for some random r''.

1. Let $E(a_0, r_0) \overset{\text{def}}{=} E(a,r)$, $E(b_0, s_0) \overset{\text{def}}{=} E(b,s)$.
2. Repeat the following steps for $i = 1, 2, ..., n$.
   (a) P_i generates a random bit e_i and a random number $t_i, u_i \in_R$ $\{0, 1, 2, \cdots, p-1\}$.
   (b) P_i takes $E(a_{i-1}, r_{i-1})$, $E(b_{i-1}, s_{i-1})$ as input, computes $E(a_i, r_i) = (A', B')$, $E(b_i, s_i) = (X', Y')$ according to the equations below. If $i \neq n$ then P_i sends this result to P_{i+1}, otherwise move to Step 3. Denote $(A, B) = E(a_{i-1}, r_{i-1})$, $(X, Y) = E(b_{i-1}, s_{i-1})$.

$$(A', B') = \begin{cases} (A, B) + (t_i G, t_i H) & (e_i = 0) \\ (-A, -B) + (t_i G, (t_i + 1)H) & (e_i = 1) \end{cases} \tag{2}$$

$$(X', Y') = \begin{cases} (X + Y) + (u_i G, u_i H) & (e_i = 0) \\ (-X, -Y) + (u_i G, (u_i + 1)H) & (e_i = 1) \end{cases} \tag{3}$$

   (c) P_i proves in zero knowledge (by using protocol B described in Figure 2) that he has acted honestly in the previous step. Set

$$((G, H), (G_0, H_0), (G_1, H_1),$$

$$(G'_0, H'_0), (G'_1, H'_1), (b, s, t)) \leftarrow$$

$$((G, H), (A' - A, B' - B), (A + A', B + B' - H),$$

$$(X' - X, Y' - Y), (X + X', Y + Y' - H), (e_i, t_i, u_i)).$$

   (d) In case P_i fails to prove he acted honestly in the previous step set his output to $E(a_{i-1}, r_{i-1})$, $E(b_{i-1}, s_{i-1})$ and exclude him from the remaining of the protocol.
3. The players decrypt $E(a_n, r_n)$ using verifiable ElGamal distributed decryption, and open a_n publicly.
4. Define $(X, Y) = E(b_n, s_n)$. (C, D), the output of the protocol, is:

$$(C, D) = \begin{cases} (X, Y) & (a_n = 0) \\ (-X, -Y - H) & (a_n = 1) \end{cases} \tag{4}$$

Fig. 1. Protocol Z (Conditional Gate)

$$\text{ANDORDL} = \{(G, H, G_0, H_0, G_1, H_1, G'_0, H'_0, G'_1, H'_1) \in \mathcal{G}^{10} \mid$$
$$(\log_G G_0 = \log_H H_0 \wedge \log_G G'_0 = \log_H H'_0) \vee$$
$$(\log_G G_1 = \log_H H_1 \wedge \log_G G'_1 = \log_H H'_1)\}.$$

The proofs for Protocol B are described in Appendix.

It is easy to verify the correctness of Protocol Z. First check that

$$e_1 \oplus (e_2 \oplus b) = (e_1 \oplus e_2) \oplus b,$$

where $e_1, e_2 \in \{0, 1\}$, $b \in \mathbb{Z}/q\mathbb{Z}$, and $\oplus$ stands for

$$a \oplus b = \begin{cases} b & (a = 0) \\ 1 - b & (a = 1). \end{cases}$$

The output of Protocol Z is $E(a_n \oplus b_n, r'')$ for some r''. Since $a_n = e_1 \oplus e_2 \oplus \cdots \oplus e_n \oplus a$ and $b_n = e_1 \oplus e_2 \oplus \cdots \oplus e_n \oplus b$, thus

$$
\begin{aligned}
a_n \oplus b_n &= (e_1 \oplus e_2 \oplus \cdots \oplus e_n \oplus a) \oplus (e_1 \oplus e_2 \oplus \cdots \oplus e_n \oplus b) \\
&= (e_1 \oplus e_2 \oplus \cdots \oplus e_n \oplus a \oplus e_1 \oplus e_2 \oplus \cdots \oplus e_n) \oplus b \\
&= a \oplus b,
\end{aligned}
$$

hence $E(a_n \oplus b_n, r'') = E(a \oplus b, r'')$.

Protocol B:

Common input: $(G, H, G_0, H_0, G_1, H_1, G'_0, H'_0, G'_1, H'_1) \in \mathcal{G}^{10}$.
Private input to P: $b \in \{0, 1\}$, $s, t \in \mathbb{Z}/q\mathbb{Z}$ s.t. $G_b = sG$, $H_b = sH$, $G'_b = tG$, and $H'_b = tH$.
Statement to prove: $(G, H, G_0, H_0, G_1, H_1, G'_0, H'_0, G'_1, H'_1) \in$ ANDORDL.

1. P chooses $r, v, c_{1-b} \in_R \mathbb{Z}/q\mathbb{Z}$ and computes $R^b_G = rG$, $R^b_H = rH$, $R^{1-b}_G = vG + c_{1-b}(eG_{1-b} + G'_{1-b})$, $R^{1-b}_H = vH + c_{1-b}(eH_{1-b} + H'_{1-b})$, $c_b = \mathcal{H}_1(R^0_G \| R^0_H \| R^1_G \| R^1_H) - c_{1-b}$, $z_b = r - c_b(se + t)$, and $z_{1-b} = v$, where $e = \mathcal{H}_0(G \| H \| G_0 \| H_0 \| G_1 \| H_1 \| G'_0 \| H'_0 \| G'_1 \| H'_1)$ and $\mathcal{H}_0$ and $\mathcal{H}_1$ are hash functions that map $\{0, 1\}^* \to \mathbb{Z}/q\mathbb{Z}$. It then sends (z_0, z_1, c_0, c_1) to V.
2. V verifies
$c_0 + c_1 = \mathcal{H}_1(z_0 G + c_0(eG_0 + G'_0) \| z_0 H + c_0(eH_0 + H'_0) \| z_1 G + c_1(eG_1 + G'_1) \| z_1 H + c_1(eH_1 + H'_1))$ and returns **accept** or **reject**.

Fig. 2. A protocol for honest verifier zero-knowledge proof of knowledge for a witness on the membership of ANDORDL

3.3 Security Analysis

Theorem 1. *In protocol Z, when less than $t < n$ players are corrupted, the adversary does not learn any non-negligible information about a, b under the DDH assumption and the random oracle model.*

Proof. (Sketch) Since we assume that, in the case $t > n/2$ corrupted adversaries do not abort the protocol, and the threshold of the ElGamal encryption is always set to be larger than t, we know that protocol Z does not abort and that unauthorized ciphertexts are never decrypted.

The proof will follow from two facts: the security of the proofs of knowledge presented in the appendix and the fact that during the entire protocol, only data indistinguishable from random is presented to the adversary. In detail, the input for Protocol B is computationally indistinguishable from a random input from the point of view of the adversary because $((G_0, H_0), (G_1, H_1), (G_0', H_0'), (G_1', H_1')) = ((A' - A, B' - B), (A + A', B + B' - H), (X' - X, Y' - Y), (X + X', Y + Y' - H))$, while A, A', X, X' are randomly chosen and we have that DDH assumption holds. So according to Proposition 4, if the active adversary corrupts a player, and the corrupted player generates input/output with no knowledge of e_i, t_i, u_i, Protocol B will reject this player. Since the rejected player is immediately excluded from protocol, the only action that the active adversary can take is to control the choices of (e_i, t_i, u_i). It is obvious that Protocol Z outputs $E(a \oplus b, r'')$ even when some of the players are corrupted.

Without loss of generality we assume that a single player j is uncorrupted.

To see that Protocol Z leaks no information on a, b, we configure a simulator for the protocol that has no decryption oracle but takes $E(a, r)$, $E(b, s)$, $E(a \oplus b, r'')$ as input. Without loss of generality we may assume all players are corrupted except for a player j.

For the simulation of corrupted players, the simulator execute the protocol as described in Protocol Z, while setting e_i, t_i, u_i as the adversary chooses.

For the simulation of player j, the only uncorrupted player, the simulator choose $e_j \in_R \{0, 1\}$ and outputs $E(e_j, t_j)$, $E(e_j \oplus a \oplus b, s_j)$ in place of $E(a_j, r_j)$, $E(b_j, u_j)$ respectively, where $E(e_j \oplus a \oplus b, s_j)$ is obtained by

$$
E(e_j \oplus a \oplus b, s_j) = \begin{cases} E(a \oplus b, r'') + (u_j G, u_j H) & (a = 0) \\ -E(a \oplus b, r'') + (u_j G, (u_j + 1)H) & (a = 1). \end{cases}
$$

To authenticate its input/output by Protocol B, the simulator execute the simulation of Protocol B as in Proposition 1.

For simulating the decryption stage, the simulator outputs $\tilde{a}_n = \bigoplus_{i=j}^n e_i$, and generates the proof by executing the simulation for the verifiable decryption protocol.

Since the output of the simulated player k is $E(\bigoplus_{i=j}^n e_i, r_n)$ and $E(a \oplus b \oplus \bigoplus_{i=j}^n e_i, s_n)$, one obtains $E(a_n \oplus b_n, r'') = E(a \oplus b, r'')$ as the output of the simulation, successfully simulating Protocol Z.

To see the simulated view of the adversary is indistinguishable from that of the real protocol it suffices to see

$$
\text{view}_R = (\{(E(a_i, r_i), E(b_i, s_i), \Pi_i\}, \Pi', a_n),
$$

and

$$
\text{view}_S = (\{(\tilde{E}(a_i, r_i), \tilde{E}(b_i, s_i), \tilde{\Pi}_i\}, \tilde{\Pi}', \tilde{a}_n),
$$

are indistinguishable. Here Π_i is the proof of protocol Z in Step 2, and Π' is the proof in Step 3, $\tilde{E}(a_i, r_i), \tilde{E}(b_i, s_i)$ are the outputs of simulated players, $\tilde{\Pi}, \tilde{\Pi}'$ are simulated proofs for Step 2 and Step 3 respectively.

It is obvious that $E(a_i, r_i)$ and $\tilde{E}(a_i, r_i)$ are computationally indistinguishable because of the DDH assumption and so for $E(b_i, s_i)$ and $\tilde{E}(b_i, s_i)$. Π_i and $\tilde{\Pi}_i$ for each i, Π' and $\tilde{\Pi}'$ are zero-knowledge proofs, thus they cannot help distinguish view_R and view_S. a_n is a random bit since at least one of the players in the real protocol is not corrupted. $\tilde{a}_n = \bigoplus_{i=j}^{n} e_i$ is also a random bit because player j is not corrupted in the simulation. Hence view_R and view_S are computationally indistinguishable under the DDH assumption. $\blacksquare$

3.4   Secure Function Evaluation

First note that in the case we restrict our inputs a and b to be binary in protocol Z, it is easy to show that conditional gates can be used to securely evaluate any logic gate, while keeping the the logic gate itself hidden.

Consider a "quadratic form"

$$f_{x,y,z,w}(a, b) = (a \oplus x) + (b \oplus y) + (a \oplus b) \oplus z + w, \tag{5}$$

where $x, y, z, w \in \mathbb{Z}/q\mathbb{Z}$.

It is easy to see that $f_{x,y,z,w}$ can be configured to be any logic gate if one choose $x, y, z, w \in \mathbb{Z}/q\mathbb{Z}$ appropriately.

By having encrypted values $E(x, r_x)$, $E(y, r_y)$, $E(z, r_z)$, and $E(w, r_w)$ the inputs $E(a, r)$, $E(b, s)$, $E(x, r_x)$, $E(y, r_y)$, $E(z, r_z)$, and $E(w, r_w)$, one can securely evaluate f_{xyzw}. Additions are performed by exploiting the homomorphism of the underlying encryption scheme, whereas XOR operations can be performed by using our protocol Z. Thus one can apply any logic gate to encrypted plaintexts while hiding the gate itself.

Informally speaking, a computation is said to be secure if it is private, correct and fair [12], informally these properties are:

Private: No party learns anything more than what can be computed from the output.

Correct: The output received by each party is guaranteed to be the output of the specified function.

Fair: Corrupted parties should receive an output iff honest parties do.

The fairness requirement is usually relaxed in the faulty majority scenario. We assume that the additional unfair information a corrupted party has about the computation's output can be made arbitrarily small in a security parameter k.

A secure computation usually has three stages:

Input Stage: Here the parties enrolled in the protocol commit to their inputs.

Computation Stage: In the computational stage, the parties evaluate the circuit which describes the function to be evaluated gate by gate. We consider only AND and negation gates, since they are universal.

Output Stage: In this stage, the parties receive their correspondent outputs.

In our protocol we assume an extra stage which happens before the input stage, it is called Setup phase.

Setup Phase: During the setting phase, the players generate the public/private keys for the threshold ElGamal encryption scheme used subsequently in the computation stage.

A Protocol Implementing Secure Multi-Party Computation: Our protocol is similar to the one presented in [5] and the security analysis there presented can be straightforwardly modified to show the security and correctness of our protocol.

1. **Setup Phase:** In this stage, all the players generate the private/public keys of the threshold encryption schemes used in the subsequent stages.
2. **Input Stage:** Each player encrypts his own input by using the ElGamal threshold encryption scheme agreed on during the Setup phase. The players prove in zero-knowledge that they have behaved correctly.
3. **Computation Stage:** During the computation stage, the players evaluate the circuit being computed gate by gate. AND gates can be evaluated by using protocol Z. Negation gates can be easily implemented by exploiting the linearity of our encryption scheme (the players should prove in zero knowledge that they behave correctly).
4. **Opening Stage:** Here, all the players reconstruct the result of the computation. If the number of corrupted players is larger or equal to a half of the players, then fairness becomes an important issue. However, we note that a solution proposed in [17] equally applies to our setting and can be straightforwardly used here to achieve weak fairness.

3.5   Performance Analysis

In this section, we study the performance of the proposed protocol in terms of computational and communication complexities.

We compare our protocol with the other protocols possessing linear communication and computational complexities in the literature that are secure against active adversaries, namely [5] and [17]. We compare the costs of implementing a conditional gate with our protocol and the protocol proposed in [17] to the cost of implementing a multiplication with the protocol proposed in [5].

Table 1 shows a comparison of the required computational effort, and Table 2 shows a comparison of the communications complexities for each XOR gate (multiplication gate in the case of [5]). Here n is the number of participants in the protocol, MLT is the amount of computational effort required for computing XOR (multiplication gates) with honest-but-curious adversaries (without any kind of verification), PRF is the computational cost of the proofs for making the XOR (multiplication) secure against active adversaries and VRF is the cost of verifying those proofs. $M_{\mathbf{Pai}}$, $M_{\mathbf{EIG}}$ are the times required for computing the modular exponentiation operation in the Paillier encryption and the elliptic multiplication by scalars in the elliptic ElGamal encryption, respectively. We take the protocol proposed in [10] as the distributed decryption scheme in [5].

Table 1. Computation time for XOR gate(worst case)

	MLT	PRF	VRF
[5]	$4nM_{\mathbf{Pai}}$	$15nM_{\mathbf{Pai}}$	$13nM_{\mathbf{Pai}}$
[17]	$6nM_{\mathbf{EIG}}$	$18nM_{\mathbf{EIG}}$	$27nM_{\mathbf{EIG}}$
ours	$5nM_{\mathbf{EIG}}$	$10nM_{\mathbf{EIG}}$	$16nM_{\mathbf{EIG}}$

Table 2. Communications traffic for XOR gate(outbound, worst case)

	MLT	PRF
[5]	$3n|N^2|$	$4n|N^2|$
[17]	$6n(|p^k|+1)$	$11n|q|$
ours	$5n(|p^k|+1)$	$6n|q|$

The modular exponentiation in Paillier encryption is executed on $\mathbb{Z}/N^2\mathbb{Z}$, the bit length of N is 1024. The elliptic ElGamal encryption is executed on an elliptic curve over $\mathbb{F}_{p^k}$. q is the order of the base point. We consider that the resulting primitives have about the same level of security. Regarding elliptic exponentiation on OEF(Optimal Extension Fields), 174 bit elliptic multiplication by scalars is computed in 0.254 ms on a 500 MHz Alpha 21264 processor if we optimize it according to [1] etc. Regarding modular exponentiation, the library evaluation by [18] indicates that 1.6 GHz AMD Opteron processor took 28.41 ms to compute 2048 bits RSA decryption. If we take this value as a rough approximation, we may consider $M_{\mathbf{Pai}} \sim 200M_{\mathbf{EIG}}$. Hence the proposed protocol seems to be the most efficient homomorphic encryption based scheme in terms of computational communication complexities (but it should be remarked that [5] has a better round complexity).

4   Conclusions and Future Works

In this paper, we proposed a protocol to perform secure distributed computations based on the DDH assumption. The performance of our protocol was superior when compared to a previous construction [17] while, at the same time, being *non-optimistic*. Our solution seems applicable when the number of players engaged in the computational is no so large, e.g. secure two-party computations.

The biggest open problem left by this work is to improve the round complexity of the protocol, while preserving its computational efficiency.

References

1. K. Aoki, F. Hoshino, and T. Kobayashi, "A Cyclic Window Algorithm for ECC Defined over Extension Fields," S. Qing, T.Okamoto, and J. Zhou (Eds.), Proceedings of International Conference on Information and Communication Security (ICICS 2001), LNCS 2229, pp. 62–73, Springer-Verlag, 2001.

2. D. Chaum, C. Crépeau, and I. Damgård, "Multiparty unconditionally secure protocols," STOC '88.
3. D.L. Chaum and T.P. Pedersen, "Wallet databases with observers," Advances in Cryptology - CRYPTO '92, LNCS 740, pp. 80–105, Springer-Verlag, 1993.
4. H. Cohen, A. Miyaji, and T. Ono, "Efficient elliptic curve exponentiation using mixed coordinates," K. Ohta and D. Pei (Eds.), Advances in Cryptology - ASIACRYPT '98, LNCS 1514, pp. 51–65, Springer-Verlag, 1998.
5. R. Cramer, I. Damgård and J.B. Nielsen, "Multiparty computation from threshold homomorphic encryption," Basic Research in Computer Science (BRICS) RS-00-14, Jun. 2000.
6. R. Cramer, I. Damgård and B. Schoenmakers, "Proofs of partial knowledge," Advances in Cryptology - CRYPTO '94, LNCS 839, pp. 174–187, Springer-Verlag, 1994.
7. Y. Desmedt and Y. Frankel, "Threshold cryptosystems," G. Brassard (Ed.), Advances in Cryptology - CRYPTO '89, LNCS 435, pp. 307–315, Springer-Verlag, 1990.
8. P. Feldman, "A practical scheme for non-interactive verifiable secret sharing," In Proc. of the 28th IEEE Symposium on the Foundations of Computer Science (FOCS), pp. 427–437, IEEE Press, Oct. 1987.
9. A. Fiat and A. Shamir, "How to Prove Yourself: practical solutions of identification and signature problems," A. M. Odlyzko (Eds.), Advances in Cryptology - CRYPT '86, LNCS 263, pp. 186–194, Springer-Verlag, 1987.
10. P.-A. Fouque, G. Poupard, and J. Stern, "Sharing decryption in the context of voting or lotteries," Financial Cryptography '00, LNCS 1962, pp. 90–104, Springer-Verlag, 2000.
11. O. Goldreich, S. Micali, and A. Widgerson, "How to play any mental game," STOC '87, pp. 218–229, 1987.
12. O. Goldreich, "Secure Multi-Party Computation," Working Draft, Version 1.1, 1998. Available at
    http://www.wisdom.weizmann.ac.il/~oded/pp.html.
13. D. Grigoriev and I. Ponomarenko, "Homomorphic public-key cryptosystems over groups and rings," arXiv:cs.CR/0309010 v1, 8 Sep. 2003.
14. T. P. Pedersen, "A threshold cryptosystem without a trusted party," Advances in Cryptology - EUROCRYPT '91, LNCS 547, pp. 522–526, Springer-Verlag, 1991.
15. T. P. Pedersen, "Non-interactive and information-theoretic secure verifiable secret sharing," J. Feigenbaum (Ed.), Advances in Cryptology - CRYPTO '91, LNCS 576, pp. 129–140, Springer-Verlag, 1991.
16. D. Pointcheval and J. Stern, "Security Proofs for Signature Schemes," U. Maurer (Ed.), Advances in Cryptology - EUROCRYPTO '96, LNCS 1070, pp. 387–398, Springer-Verlag, 1996.
17. B. Schoenmakers and P. Tuyls, "Practical Two-Party Computation Based on the Conditional Gate," P.J.Lee (Ed.), ASIACRYPT 2004, LNCS 3329, pp. 119–204, Springer-Verlag, 2004.
18. W. Dai, http://www.eskimo.com/~weidai/benchmarks.html, 2004.
19. A.C. Yao, "How to generate and exchange secrets," In Proc. of the 27th IEEE Symp. on Foundations of Computer Science (FOCS '86), IEEE Press, pp. 162–167, 1986.

Appendix

In this appendix our goal is to present Protocol B, which is essential to prove the security of Protocol Z. Roughly speaking, through Protocol B the players engaged in Z can prove in zero-knowledge that they acted correctly. Our protocol is a modification of earlier results in the literature (mostly [6], [3], and [16]).

We first describe Protocol A (OR-Proof) which is an important module of protocol B.

Underlying OR-Proof. Let G^{DL} be a probabilistic polynomial-time algorithm that outputs an instance of a discrete logarithm problem $(\mathcal{G}_q, G, H)$ by taking security parameter κ, where $\mathcal{G}_q$ is a cyclic group of order q, G is a generator of $\mathcal{G}_q$, and H is an element of $\mathcal{G}_q$. We assume the bit-length of q is κ.

Let $R \subset \{0,1\}^* \times \{0,1\}^*$ be a binary relation where there exists a polynomial-time machine that decides whether given (x,w) is in R or not with non-negligible probability in the length of x. Let $L_R \overset{\text{def}}{=} \{x \mid \exists w \text{ s.t. } (x,w) \in R\}$ be a language. Note that when $(x,w) \in R$, w is called a witness of x.

Now consider the language defined by

$$\mathsf{ORDL} \overset{\text{def}}{=} \{(G,H,G_0,H_0,G_1,H_1) \in \mathcal{G}_q^6 \mid \log_G G_0 = \log_H H_0 \lor \log_G G_1 = \log_H H_1\}.$$

This is the language that the discrete logarithm of G_b to the base G is equal to the discrete logarithm of H_b to the base H for $b \in \{0,1\}$.

Below Protocol A illustrates an honest verifier zero-knowledge proof of knowledge for a witness on the membership of ORDL.

Protocol A:

Common input: $(G,H,G_0,H_0,G_1,H_1) \in \mathcal{G}_q^6$, where $(\mathcal{G}_q, G, H) \leftarrow \mathsf{G}^{\mathsf{DL}}(1^\kappa)$.
Private input to P: $b \in \{0,1\}$, $s \in \mathbb{Z}/q\mathbb{Z}$ s.t. $G_b = sG$ and $H_b = sH$.
Statement to prove: $(G,H,G_0,H_0,G_1,H_1) \in \mathsf{ORDL}$.

1. P chooses $r, v, c_{1-b} \in_R \mathbb{Z}/q\mathbb{Z}$ and computes $R_G^b = rG$, $R_H^b = rH$, $R_G^{1-b} = vG + c_{1-b}G_{1-b}$, $R_H^{1-b} = vH + c_{1-b}H_{1-b}$, $c_b = \mathcal{H}(R_G^0\|R_H^0\|R_G^1\|R_H^1) - c_{1-b}$, $z_b = r - c_b s$, and $z_{1-b} = v$, where $\mathcal{H}$ is a hash function that maps $\{0,1\}^* \rightarrow \mathbb{Z}/q\mathbb{Z}$. It then sends (z_0, z_1, c_0, c_1) to V.
2. V verifies $c_0 + c_1 = \mathcal{H}(z_0G + c_0G_0\|z_0H + c_0H_0\|z_1G + c_1G_1\|z_1H + c_1H_1)$ and returns accept or reject.

Fig. 3. A protocol for honest verifier zero-knowledge proof of knowledge for a witness on the membership of ORDL

The following lemma can be obtained regarding ORDL.

Lemma 1 (Indistinguishability). The hardness of deciding whether $ins \overset{\text{def}}{=} (G,H,G_0,H_0,G_1,H_1) \in \mathsf{ORDL}$ or not is equivalent to the DDH problem over $\mathcal{G}_q$, where $G_0, H_0, G_1, H_1 \in_R \mathcal{G}_q$ if $ins \notin \mathsf{ORDL}$.

Furthermore, by combining the OR-proof [6] and the proof of equality of discrete logarithms [3], we obtain a Σ-protocol. To make it non-interactive, one can follow [16], as it is proven in the following lemmas.

Lemma 2 (Simulatability). Define $\text{view}_R = (z_0, z_1, c_0, c_1)$. There exists a simulator that, on input $(G, H, G_0, H_0, G_1, H_1) \in \text{ORDL}$, outputs view_S which is perfectly indistinguishable from view_R in expected polynomial time in κ under the random oracle model.

Lemma 3 (Soundness). If P is successful in producing (z_0, z_1, c_0, c_1) accepted by V, P has witnesses $b \in \{0, 1\}$ and $s \in \mathbb{Z}/q\mathbb{Z}$ s.t. $G_b = sG$ and $H_b = sH$ under the random oracle model.

AND-OR Proof Consider the language defined by

$$\text{ANDORDL} \overset{\text{def}}{=} \{(G, H, G_0, H_0, G_1, H_1, G_0', H_0', G_1', H_1') \in \mathcal{G}_q^{10} \mid$$

$$(\log_G G_0 = \log_H H_0 \wedge \log_G G_0' = \log_H H_0') \vee$$

$$(\log_G G_1 = \log_H H_1 \wedge \log_G G_1' = \log_H H_1')\}.$$

This is the language that the discrete logarithms of G_b and G_b' to the base G are respectively equal to the discrete logarithms of H_b and H_b' to the base H for $b \in \{0, 1\}$.

The Protocol B illustrates an honest verifier zero-knowledge proof of knowledge for a witness on the membership of ANDORDL. For the convenience of the readers here we describe Protocol B again, where $(\mathcal{G}, G, H)$ is generated by G^{DL}.

Protocol B:

Common input: $(G, H, G_0, H_0, G_1, H_1, G_0', H_0', G_1', H_1') \in \mathcal{G}_q^{10}$, where $(\mathcal{G}_q, G, H) \leftarrow \mathsf{G}^{\mathsf{DL}}(1^\kappa)$.
Private input to P: $b \in \{0, 1\}$, $s, t \in \mathbb{Z}/q\mathbb{Z}$ s.t. $G_b = sG$, $H_b = sH$, $G_b' = tG$, and $H_b' = tH$.
Statement to prove: $(G, H, G_0, H_0, G_1, H_1, G_0', H_0', G_1', H_1') \in \text{ANDORDL}$.

1. P chooses $r, v, c_{1-b} \in_R \mathbb{Z}/q\mathbb{Z}$ and computes $R_G^b = rG$, $R_H^b = rH$, $R_G^{1-b} = vG + c_{1-b}(eG_{1-b} + G_{1-b}')$, $R_H^{1-b} = vH + c_{1-b}(eH_{1-b} + H_{1-b}')$, $c_b = \mathcal{H}_1(R_G^0 \| R_H^0 \| R_G^1 \| R_H^1) - c_{1-b}$, $z_b = r - c_b(se + t)$, and $z_{1-b} = v$, where $e = \mathcal{H}_0(G\|H\|G_0\|H_0\|G_1\|H_1\|G_0'\|H_0'\|G_1'\|H_1')$ and $\mathcal{H}_0$ and $\mathcal{H}_1$ are hash functions that map $\{0, 1\}^* \to \mathbb{Z}/q\mathbb{Z}$. It then sends (z_0, z_1, c_0, c_1) to V.
2. V verifies
$c_0 + c_1 = \mathcal{H}_1(z_0 G + c_0(eG_0 + G_0')\|z_0 H + c_0(eH_0 + H_0')\|z_1 G + c_1(eG_1 + G_1')\|z_1 H + c_1(eH_1 + H_1'))$ and returns accept or reject.

Fig. 4. A protocol for honest verifier zero-knowledge proof of knowledge for a witness on the membership of ANDORDL

Proposition 1 (Simulatability). Define $\mathrm{view}_R = (z_0, z_1, c_0, c_1)$. There exists a simulator that, on input $(G, H, G_0, H_0, G_1, H_1, G'_0, H'_0, G'_1, H'_1) \in$ ANDORDL, outputs view_S which is perfectly indistinguishable from view_R in expected polynomial time in κ under the random oracle model.

Proof. A simulator performs the following procedure for input $(G, H, G_0, H_0, G_1, H_1, G'_0, H'_0, G'_1, H'_1) \in$ ANDORDL.

1. Choose $\tilde{r}, \tilde{v}, \tilde{c}_0, \tilde{c}_1 \in_R \mathbb{Z}/q\mathbb{Z}$.
2. Generate $e = \mathcal{H}_0(G\|H\|G_0\|H_0\|G_1\|H_1\|G'_0\|H'_0\|G'_1\|H'_1)$.
3. Compute $\tilde{R}^0_G = \tilde{r}G + \tilde{c}_0(eG_0 + G'_0)$, $\tilde{R}^0_H = \tilde{r}H + \tilde{c}_0(eH_0 + H'_0)$, $\tilde{R}^1_G = \tilde{v}G + \tilde{c}_1(eG_1 + G'_1)$, $\tilde{R}^1_H = \tilde{v}H + \tilde{c}_1(eH_1 + H'_1)$, $\tilde{z}_0 = \tilde{r}$, $\tilde{z}_1 = \tilde{v}$.
4. Output $\mathrm{view}_S \overset{\text{def}}{=} (\tilde{z}_0, \tilde{z}_1, \tilde{c}_0, \tilde{c}_1)$.

Here we assume $\mathcal{H}_0$ is an ideal random function that maps $\{0,1\}^*$ to $\mathbb{Z}/q\mathbb{Z}$. We also assume $\mathcal{H}_1$ is a random function that maps $\{0,1\}^*$ to $\mathbb{Z}/q\mathbb{Z}$, however, it returns $\tilde{c}_0 + \tilde{c}_1$ when the string $\tilde{R}^0_G\|\tilde{R}^0_H\|\tilde{R}^1_G\|\tilde{R}^1_H$ is input. Then it is clear view_S is accepted by V and view_R and view_S are perfectly indistinguishable. ∎

Proposition 2 (Soundness). If P is successful in producing (z_0, z_1, c_0, c_1) accepted by V, P has witnesses $b \in \{0,1\}$ and $s, t \in \mathbb{Z}/q\mathbb{Z}$ s.t. $G_b = sG$, $H_b = sH$, $G'_b = tG$, and $H'_b = tH$ with overwhelming probability assuming the hardness of discrete logarithm problem under the random oracle model.

Proof. Set $\alpha_i = \log_G G_i$, $\beta_i = \log_H H_i$, $\alpha'_i = \log_G G'_i$, and $\beta'_i = \log_H H'_i$ for $i = 0, 1$. Then, it is considered the following three cases;

Case 1: $\alpha_b = \beta_b(= s) \wedge \alpha'_b = \beta'_b(= t)$ for $b \in \{0,1\}$, that is, P is honest.
Case 2: $(\alpha_0 \neq \beta_0 \wedge \alpha_1 \neq \beta_1) \vee (\alpha'_0 \neq \beta'_0 \wedge \alpha'_1 \neq \beta'_1)$, but $\alpha_b e + \alpha'_b = \beta_b e + \beta'_b$ for $b \in \{0,1\}$.
Case 3: $(\alpha_0 \neq \beta_0 \wedge \alpha_1 \neq \beta_1) \vee (\alpha'_0 \neq \beta'_0 \wedge \alpha'_1 \neq \beta'_1)$ and $\alpha_0 e + \alpha'_0 \neq \beta_0 e + \beta'_0 \wedge \alpha_0 e + \alpha'_0 \neq \beta_0 e + \beta'_0$.

In Case 3, it is obvious from Lemma 4 that V rejects the proof generated by P. In Case 1, if the proof generated by P is accepted, b and $se + t$ can be extracted by the knowledge extractor in Lemma 3. Thus we separate the analysis of Case 1 in two subcases. The first is the case where P has all of witnesses b, s, and t. The other is when P does not have s and t though it has $se + t$. We show that a probabilistic polynomial-time adversary $\mathcal{A}$ breaks the discrete logarithm problem using $\tilde{P}$ who outputs the correct proof for ANDORDL assuming the latter case.

Let $(\mathcal{G}_q, G, \tilde{G}) \leftarrow \mathsf{G}^{\mathsf{DL}}(1^\kappa)$ be an instance of the discrete logarithm problem. Denote $\log_G \tilde{G}$ by x. Let $\mathcal{H}_0$ be an ideal random function that maps $\{0,1\}^*$ to $\mathbb{Z}/q\mathbb{Z}$. $\mathcal{A}$ and $\tilde{P}$ are allowed to access to $\mathcal{H}_0$. Without loss of generality, we can see that $\tilde{P}$ is an oracle that inputs

$$(G, H, G_0, H_0, G_1, H_1, G'_0, H'_0, G'_1, H'_1) \in \text{ANDORDL}, \tag{6}$$

which is the input of Protocol B, and $e \in \mathbb{Z}/q\mathbb{Z}$ and outputs $w = se + t$ with non-negligible probability in κ, where $s = \log_G G_b = \log_H H_b$, $t = \log_G G'_b = \log_H H'_b$, and $b \in \{0,1\}$. $\mathcal{A}$ performs the following procedure.

1. Inputs $(\mathcal{G}_q, G, \tilde{G})$.
2. Chooses $\tilde{b} \in_R \{0, 1\}$ and $\tilde{z}, \tilde{z}', \tilde{s}, \tilde{t} \in_R \mathbb{Z}/q\mathbb{Z}$.
3. Computes $\tilde{H} = \tilde{z}G$, $\tilde{G}_{\tilde{b}} = \tilde{s}G$, $\tilde{H}_{\tilde{b}} = \tilde{z}\tilde{G}_{\tilde{b}}$, $\tilde{G}'_{\tilde{b}} = \tilde{t}G$, and $\tilde{H}'_{\tilde{b}} = \tilde{z}\tilde{G}'_{\tilde{b}}$.
4. Chooses $\tilde{G}_{1-\tilde{b}}, \tilde{H}_{1-\tilde{b}}, \tilde{G}'_{1-\tilde{b}}, \tilde{H}'_{1-\tilde{b}} \in_R \mathcal{G}_q$.
5. Sends $ins_{\mathcal{A}} \stackrel{\text{def}}{=} (G, \tilde{H}, \tilde{G}_0, \tilde{H}_0, \tilde{G}_1, \tilde{H}_1, \tilde{G}'_0, \tilde{H}'_0, \tilde{G}'_1, \tilde{H}'_1)$ to $\mathcal{H}_0$ and obtains $\tilde{e} \in \mathbb{Z}/q\mathbb{Z}$ from it.
6. Sends $ins_{\mathcal{A}}$ and $\tilde{e}$ to $\tilde{P}$ and obtain $\tilde{w} \in \mathbb{Z}/q\mathbb{Z}$ from it.

Then, since $\tilde{w}$ is equal to $(\tilde{s}x)\tilde{e} + \tilde{t}x$ with non-negligible probability, $\mathcal{A}$ can obtain x with high probability. $\tilde{P}$ always works because $ins_{\mathcal{A}} \in$ ANDORDL and e and $\tilde{e}$ are perfectly indistinguishable.

Finally, we show the success probability of probabilistic polynomial-time adversary $\mathcal{A}'$ that aims at generating Case 2 is negligible. Let $\mathcal{O}_B$ be an oracle that executes Protocol B. We denote by q_H the maximum number of access that $\mathcal{A}'$ has to $\mathcal{O}_B$. Note that, q_H is polynomially bounded in κ. Since challenge e is randomly chosen by $\mathcal{H}_0$ after $\alpha_b, \beta_b, \alpha'_b$, and β'_b are publicly committed, the success probability of an adversary $\mathcal{A}'$ that is allowed to access $\mathcal{O}_B$ only once is exactly $1/q$. Namely, the success probability, $\text{Win}_{\mathcal{A}'}$, of $\mathcal{A}'$ that access to $\mathcal{O}_B$ q_H-times is at most $1 - (1 - \frac{1}{q})^{q_H}$. Thus, it is obtained

$$
\begin{aligned}
\text{Win}_{\mathcal{A}'} = \quad & 1 - (1 - \tfrac{1}{q})^{q_H} \\
= \; & 1 - (1 - \tfrac{q_H}{q} + \tfrac{q_H(q_H-1)}{2q^2} - \cdots) \\
< \; & \tfrac{q_H}{q},
\end{aligned}
$$

and this is negligible.   ∎

New Concept of Authority Range for Flexible Management of Role Hierarchy

Sejong Oh

Dept. of Computer Science, Dankook University, San 29 Anseo-dong,
Cheonan, 330-714, Korea
sejongoh@dankook.ac.kr
http://home.dankook.ac.kr/sejong

Abstract. Most of DBMS adopt Role-Based Access Control (RBAC) model. Administrative Role-Based Access Control (ARBAC) model intends to decentralize authority management with plural security administrators. They have their work range on the role hierarchy. One problem with this is that legal modification of a role hierarchy may induce unexpected side effects. The Role-Role Assignment 97 (RRA97) model introduced some geometry-based integrity principles to prevent unexpected side effects. They are complex and ambiguous. We analyze the reasons of shortcoming of RRA97 model, and introduce a new concept of authority range for flexible management of role hierarchy.

1 Introduction

The Role-based access control (RBAC) model [1-4] is well known for large-scale organizations and information systems. The central idea of RBAC is to prevent users from accessing company information at their own discretion. Instead, access rights are associated with roles, and users are assigned to appropriate roles. The notion of role is an enterprise or organizational concept. Therefore, RBAC allows security to be modeled from an enterprise perspective. Since the security modeling can be aligned to the roles and responsibilities within the organization, this greatly simplifies the management of access rights. In the real world, a role can be defined as a job position within an organization that describes the authority and responsibility conferred on a user assigned to that role. Role hierarchies are natural means for structuring roles to reflect an organization's lines of authority and responsibility, and are defined as a partial-order relationship of related roles. As role hierarchies are similar to authorization systems, they are suitable for modeling of enterprise organization structures.

In large-scale organizations or information systems, there are numerous roles and users and managing these can be a formidable problem. One solution is to decentralize role management. The administrative RBAC (ARBAC) model [5, 6] adds decentralized RBAC administration to the RBAC model. In the ARBAC model, there are two role hierarchies, a (general) role hierarchy and an administrative role hierarchy. Fig.1 shows two role hierarchies examples. A security administrator is assigned to proper administrative role, and each administrative role has its own administration

J. Song, T. Kwon, and M. Yung (Eds.): WISA 2005, LNCS 3786, pp. 343–353, 2006.

range. In the ARBAC model, the *can-modify* relation describes the administration range of each administrative role. Table 1 shows an example of the *can-modify*. (*Note*. In a role hierarchy, if role X is parent of role Y, X inherits all access rights of Y. As a result the set of access rights for Y is a subset of access rights for X).

Under the *can-modify* relation, user-role assignment and permission-role assignment work well, but role-role assignment is not straightforward. Role-role assignment changes the structure of the role hierarchy, and may create unexpected side effects. For example, if administration role PSO1 deletes role 'E1' in the role hierarchy, administration range (E1, PL1) becomes unavailable. Another example is shown

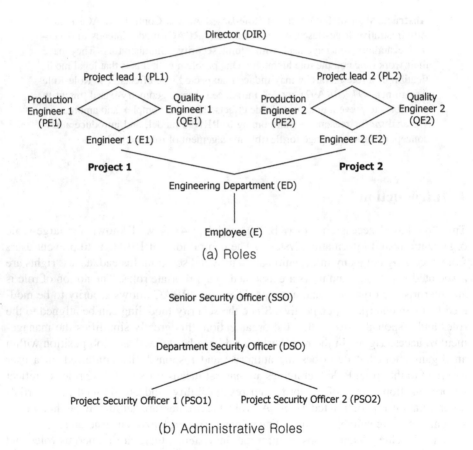

(a) Roles

(b) Administrative Roles

Fig. 1. An example Role and Administrative Role Hierarchy

Table 1. An example of *can-modify*

Administrative Role	Admin. Range
DSO	(ED, DIR)
PSO1	(E1, PL1)
PSO2	(E2, PL2)

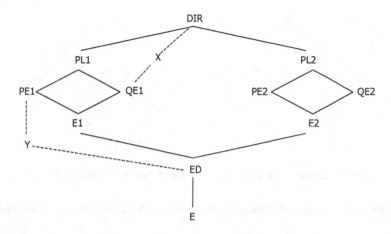

Fig. 2. An example Out of Range Impact

in Fig.2. Suppose administration role DSO adds two roles 'X' and 'Y' as shown. If administration role PSO1 adds an edge between PE1 and QE1, then the access rights of 'Y' are inherited to 'X'. Although 'X' and 'Y' do not belong to the administration range of PSO1, PSO1 can change the access rights of 'X'. To overcome these problems, the ARBAC model introduces some restrictions, called integrity principles. We will discuss these in section 2.

ARBAC use a geometric approach, together with several other concepts for describing integrity principles. While we understand each principle, it is not possible to deduce the reason for each of them. In this paper, we analyze the origin of ambiguity and shortcoming included in RRA97 model. The origin is definition of authority range in *can-modify* relation. We also show the way of flexible management of role hierarchy by redefinition of authority range. This paper is organized as follows. Section 2 reviews integrity principles for the role hierarchy management of ARBAC. This is well described in the RRA97 model. Section 3 introduces the origin of shortcoming of RRA97, and propose new authority range concept, and the paper is then conclusion in Section 4.

2 Integrity Principles of the ARBAC Model

ARBAC97 model consists of URA97, PRA97, and RRA97 model. The RRA97 model [7] describes integrity principles for role hierarchy management. Role hierarchy management has four types of operation – add a role, delete a role, add an edge between roles, and delete an edge between roles. We begin by reviewing some definitions and integrity principles grouped by these four operations.

Definition 1. A **range** of roles is defined by giving the lower bound x and upper bound y, where y > x. Formally $(x, y) = \{z \in role \mid x < z < y\}$. We say x and y are the endpoints of the range. (A range as defined here does not include the endpoints).

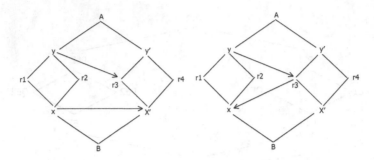

Fig. 3. Encapsulated Range(x,y)   **Fig. 4.** Non-Encapsulated Range (x,y)

Definition 2. Any range referenced in the *can-modify* relation is called an **authority range**.

Definition 3. A range (x, y) is said to be **encapsulated** if $\forall r1 \in (x, y) \land \forall r2 \notin (x, y)$ we have $r2 > r1 \Leftrightarrow r2 > y$ and $r2 < r1 \Leftrightarrow r2 < x$.

Definition 4. A range (x', y') is said to be **junior** to range (x, y) if (x', y') is a subset of (x, y).

Definition 5. The **immediate authority range** of a role r written $AR_{immediate}(r)$ is the authority range (x, y) such that $r \in (x, y)$ and for all authority ranges (x', y') junior to (x, y) we have $r \notin (x', y')$.

Definition 6. The range (x, y) is a **create range** if $AR_{immediate}(x) = AR_{immediate}(y)$ or x is an endpoint of $AR_{immediate}(y)$ or y is an endpoint of $AR_{immediate}(x)$.

IP1. All authority ranges must be encapsulated.

IP2. (Integrity Principle for Role Creation). The immediate parent and child of a new role must be a create range in the hierarchy before a new role can be created.

IP3. (Integrity Principle for Role Deletion). Roles referred in *can-assign*, *can-revoke*, and *can-modify* relationships cannot be deleted. This is a more restrictive constraint, but is required to maintain the referential integrity of ranges.

IP4. (Integrity Principle for Edge Insertion). A new edge A-B can be inserted between incomparable roles A and B if

- $AR_{immediate}(A) = AR_{immediate}(B)$, or
- (x, y) is an authority range such that $(A = y \land B > x) \lor (B = x \land A < y)$, then insertion of AB must then preserve encapsulation of (x, y).

IP5. (Integrity Principle for Edge Deletion). i) if edge A-B is not in the transitive reduction then it cannot be deleted. ii) if the edge being deleted is between the end points of an authority range, this operation is disallowed.

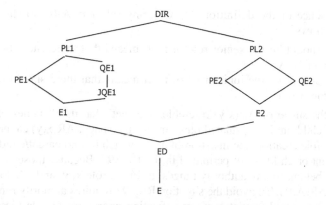

Fig. 5. Modified role hierarchy of Fig. 1

Though above integrity principles are clear and useful, there are insufficiencies as follows:

- **IP1** restricts the topology of authority range. Section 3.1 describes it in detail.
- **IP2** is to prevent potential risks such as those shown in Fig.2. However, the case shown in Fig.2 is allowable. Only the operation of adding an edge from PE1 to QE1 should be restricted. **IP2** is therefore overly restrictive.
- The principles above are based on several concepts; incomparable range, encapsulated range, immediate authority range, and crate range. From a practical point of view, this leads to a difficult implementation.
- Each principle has a vague rationale, and appears to be part of an ad-hoc approach. If we can find a new case that current principles cannot cover, we must create a new principle.
- Role insertion (deletion) leads to edge insertion (deletion) or vice versa. Therefore, we must consider integrating principles **IP2 – IP5**.
- We should treat role creation, role deletion, edge insertion, and edge deletion with different way. It makes complex work of managing role hierarchy.

Crampton [8] points out shortcomings of ARBAC97 such like lack of applicability, flexibility, coherence, and robustness. To overcome the shortcomings he proposed the concept of 'administrative scope'. In spite of its advantages there exists complexity of integrity rules. Section 3 presents our new approach to relieve shortcomings of RRA97 and complexity of Crampton's approach.

3   New Concept of Authority Range

3.1   The Origin of Shortcomings of RRA97

RRA97 model includes an important shortcoming. Large part of integrity principles of RRA97 is caused by the shortcoming; it is the authority range in *can-modify* relation. RRA97 defines an authority range AR(a,b) as follows:

$$AR(x,y) = \{ r \in R | x < r < y \} \text{ (by Definition 1).}$$

As a consequence of the definition AR(x,y), any role r ∈ AR(x,y) should keep the features as follows:

i) role y should be the senior role of r . It means that there should exist an edge line from r to y

ii) role x should be the junior role of r . It means that there should exist an edge line from x to r.

As a result, the shape of AR(x,y) resembles the 'net' that its all nodes have edges to parent and to children. Encapsulated range means the shape. AR(x,y) cannot be a 'tree'. In the case of role creation, the insertion of a role which has no parent/child or has more than one parent or child is not permitted in the RRA97. Because those cases make the role does not belong to any authority ranges. In Fig.6, role x, y, and z belong to neither AR(a,b) nor AR(A,B). To avoid the situation RRA97 requires authority ranges maintain encapsulated range and restrict some modification operations of role hierarchy. It is a too strong restriction for composition and modification of a role hierarchy.

3.2 New Definition of Authority Range

If we can find reasonable method making that role x, y, and z in Fig.6 belong to some authority range, we can modify RRA97 to more flexible model. To achieve the purpose we redefine authority range named NAR(x,y).

Definition 7. New authority range written NAR(x, y) is defined by the notion below

$$NAR(x,y) = S \cup T \cup U$$

where

- $S = \{r \in R \mid x < r < y \}$
- $T = \{r \in R \mid x < r < B\} - \{r \in R \mid A < r \leq y \}$
- $U = \{r \in R \mid A < r < y\} - \{r \in R \mid x \leq r < B \}$
- (A,B) is an immediate senior range of (x,y).

If x is the minimum role and y is the maximum role of the role hierarchy,

$NAR(x,y) = \{ r \in R \mid r > x \} \cup \{ r \in R \mid r < y \}$.

Note. There are the other definitions of new authority range

$$NAR[x,y) = \{r \in R \mid x \leq r < y \} \cup T \cup U$$
$$NAR(x,y] = \{r \in R \mid x < r \leq y \} \cup T \cup U$$
$$NAR[x,y] = \{r \in R \mid x \leq r \leq y \} \cup T \cup U$$

Definition 8. The new **immediate authority range** of a role r written $NAR_{immediate}(r)$ is the new authority range (x, y) such that $r \in NAR(x, y)$ and for all new authority ranges (x', y') junior to (x, y) we have $r \notin NAR(x', y')$.

The idea of NAR(x,y) is that we let every roles belong to 'nearest' authority range. As a result, role x, y, and z belong to NAR[x,y] in Fig.7. It contrasts with that AR(x,y) cannot contain x,y, and z in Fig.6. Now we prove NAR(x,y) has soundness and clearness through Property 1.

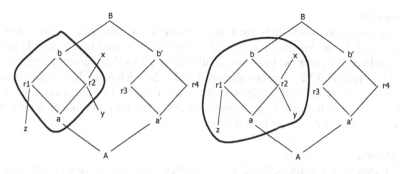

Fig. 6. AR[a,b]   **Fig. 7.** NAR [a,b]

Property 1. For any role r on a role hierarchy, there exists one only one $NAR_{immediate}(r)$.

Proof. First we prove there exists at least one $NAR_{immediate}(r)$.

Let minR is the minimum role and maxR is the maximum role on a role hierarchy. Then (minR,maxR) is the largest role range of the role hierarchy. If role r is on the role hierarchy, r has parent or child role. If r has parent role, r < maxR and has child role(s), r < minR. By definition 7, r belongs to NAR(minR,maxR). If there is no other NAR(x,y) that r ∈ NAR(x,y), NAR(minR,maxR) is the $NAR_{immediate}(r)$. Thus there exist at least one $NAR_{immediate}(r)$.

Now we prove there exists only one $NAR_{immediate}(r)$.

Suppose there exists r ∈ NAR(a,b) and r ∈ NAR(c,d). By the basic requirement of authority range, NAR(a,b) and NAR(c,d) can not be partially disjointed. If NAR(a,b) ⊂ NAR(c,d), then NAR(a,b) is a candidate of $NAR_{immediate}(r)$ else NAR(c,d) is a candidate of $NAR_{immediate}(r)$. Suppose NAR(c,d) is chosen as a candidate of $NAR_{immediate}(r)$. If there is no NAR(e,f) that NAR(e,f) ⊂ NAR(c,d) and r ∈ NAR(e,f), NAR(c,d) is the $NAR_{immediate}(r)$ else NAR(e,f) can be chosen as a new candidate of $NAR_{immediate}(r)$. If we continue this process until we cannot find new candidate, the last candidate is the $NAR_{immediate}(r)$.

3.3 The Effects of New Authority Range

Property 1 shows that new authority concept NAR(x,y) is clear and has no ambiguity. If we replace AR(x,y) in *can-modify* relation with NAR(x,y), we can relieve some restrictions of RRA97. (For convenience we call RRA97 model using our new authority range by the name of 'RRA-NAR').

Encapsulated Range
In the RRA97 model, encapsulated range is a base concept for integrity principles. **IP1** requires all authority ranges should be encapsulated, or some roles may exist out of authority range. But RRA-NAR has no need of encapsulated range concept because every role on a role hierarchy belongs to one NAR(x,y). Thus we can ignore **IP1**.

Role Creation

RRA97 requires two conditions for role creation. First, new role should have both parent and child role. Second, the immediate parent and child of a new role must be an encapsulated range or be in an encapsulated range in the hierarchy before a new role can be created. **IP2** describes the conditions. But RRA-NAR requires new role should have parent or child role and the parent or child role should be in the NAR(x,y) (which belongs to an administration role executing the role creation). RRA-NAR is more relievable model than RRA97.

Role Deletion

RRA97 requires that roles referred in *can-assign*, *can-revoke*, and *can-modify* relationships cannot be deleted through **IP3**. If they are deleted, we cannot control authority of administration roles. RRA-NAR maintains **IP3**.

Edge Insertion

RRA97 has two rules for edge insertion. The roles, between which the edge is inserted, must have same immediate authority range; or if the new edge connects a role in one authority range to a role outside the range, encapsulation of the authority range should not be violated. RRA-NAR requires the roles, between which the edge is inserted, should have same immediate NAR(x,y). RRA-NAR does not require second rule of RRA97 because RRA-NAR does not have encapsulated concept.

Edge Deletion

RRA97 requires a compensatory operation before edge deletion. For example, if we want to delete an edge QE1-JQE1 in Fig.5, we need to insert two edges E1-QE1 and JQE1-PL1. And RRA97 disallows an edge deletion if the edge being deleted is between the end points of an authority range. RRA-NAR allows that we delete an edge A-B without compensatory operation if role A has no child or role B has no parent. For example, edge z-r1, y-r2, and r2-x in Fig. 6 can be deleted without any compensatory operation.

As we can see RRA-NAR model is more flexible than RRA97. **IP1** and **IP2** are ignored; **IP4** and **IP5** are relieved in the RRA-NAR model. Further, RRA-NAR supports various topologies of authority range that RRA97 cannot do. Fig.8 shows the fact. Finally, authority range of RRA-NAR can be dynamically changed by senior administration role's activity. For example, NAR(a,b) is changed after two edge insertions in Fig.9. It shows strong flexibility of RRA-NAR.

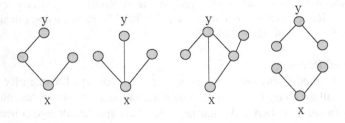

Fig. 8. Possible topologies of NAR(X,Y)

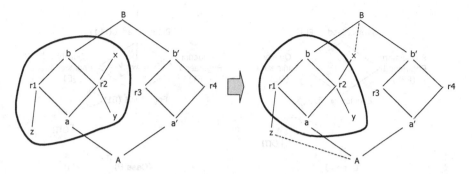

Fig. 9. Adjustment of NAR(a,b) after two edge insertions

4 Application Examples of New Authority Range

Our new authority range concept is useful for real world applications. In this chapter we show real application examples of new authority range.

Separation of Duty (SOD)
SOD is a security principle used in formulating multi-person control policies, requiring that two or more different people be responsible for the completion of a task or set of related tasks. The purpose of SOD is to discourage fraud by separating the responsibility and authority for an action, or task, over many people. One of difficulty of ARBAC model is that SOD cannot be implemented on the role hierarchy. Let's suppose Sales_clerk and Salesman have a SOD relationship (Case A of Fig.10). Both Sales_clerk and Salesman should have parent role, such like Sales_manager, by the role hierarchy principle of ARBAC model. As a result Sales_manager inherits authority of both Sales_clerk and Salesman, and can violate SOD principle. ARBAC model cannot solve the problem. If we adopt our new authority concept, we can make role hierarchy as shown in Case B of Fig.10, and Sales_manager cannot inherit authority of Sales_clerk and Salesman. Our new authority range brings ability of implementing SOD to ARBAC model.

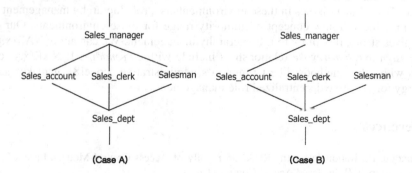

Fig. 10. SOD and role hierarchy

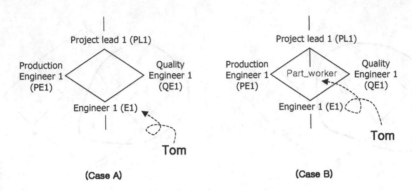

Fig. 11. Temporal role insertion

Temporal Role Creation

Suppose that a project team wants to employ Tom as a part time worker for two months. Security manager John for the project team wants to give minimum authority of the project team. He wants to give partial authority of role E1 to Tom, and tries to make junior role of E1 for assigning partial authority of E1. But it is impossible job because it is out of authority range of John. The best choice is that John assigns Tom to E1 role (Case A of Fig.11). As a result, Tom owns extra authority, and it is undesirable situation. If we bring our new authority range to ARBAC model, John can make junior role 'Part_worker' under PL1, and assign Tom to 'Part_worker'. John can give partial authority of E1 to 'Part_worker'. As a result Tom owns partial authority of E1 (Case B of Fig.11).

This situation may apply to delegation. Most of delegation model on ARBAC model, delegator makes sub role and assigns delegatee to the sub role. The sub role is regarded as special role because role hierarchy cannot contains the sub role on ARBAC model. If we adopt our new authority range, we can regard the sub role as general role.

5   Conclusion

In large organizations or information systems, decentralized role management is required. One of main issues in these environments is a role hierarchy management. We have introduced a new concept of authority range for those environments. Our concept gives strong flexibility to role hierarchy management. We can apply NAR(x,y) to *can-assign* and *can-revoke* relationships include with *can-modify*. If NAR(x,y) combines with other methods, like Crampton's administrative scope[8], it makes strong synergy for effective decentralized role management.

References

1. Sandhu, R.: Rationale for the RBAC96 Family of Access Control Models. Proc. of ACM Workshop on Role-Based Access Control (1995)
2. Ferraio, D., CuginiJ., Kuhn, R.: Role-based Access Control (RBAC): Features and motivations. Proc. of 11th Annual Computer Security Application Conference (1995)

3. Sandhu, R., Coyne, E., Feinstein, H., Youman,C.: Role-Based Access Control Models. IEEE Computer, Vol.29, No.2 (1996)
4. Gavrila, S.I., Barkley, J.F.: Formal Specification for Role Based Access Control User/Role and Role/Role Relationship Management. Proc. of the 3rd ACM workshop on Role-Based Access Control (1998)
5. Sandhu, R., Bhamidipati, Munawer, Q.: The ARBAC97 Model for Role-Based Administration of Roles. ACM Trans. on Information and Systems Security (TISSEC), Vol.2 (1999)
6. Sandhu, R. Munawer, Q.: The ARBAC99 Model for Administration of Roles. Proc. of Annual Computer Security Applications Conference (1999)
7. Sandhu, R., Munawer, Q.: The RRA97 Model for Role-Based Administration of Role Hierarchies. Proc. of Annual Computer Security Applications Conference (1998)
8. Crampton, J., Loizou, G.: Administrative scope: A foundation for role-based administrative models. ACM Transactions on Information and System Security (TISSEC), Vol.6 , Issue 2 (2003)

Role-Based Access Control Model for Ubiquitous Computing Environment

Song-hwa Chae[1], Wonil Kim[2,*], and Dong-kyoo Kim[3]

[1] Graduate School of Information and Communication,
Ajou University, Suwon, Korea
portula@ajou.ac.kr
[2] College of Electronics and Information Engineering,
Sejong University, Seoul, Korea
wikim@sejong.ac.kr
[3] College of Information and Computer Engineering,
Ajou University, Suwon, Korea
dkkim@ajou.ac.kr

Abstract. Ubiquitous computing is characterized by freedom of movement in both time and location, which means users expect to receive services anytime and anywhere. Therefore, the security service should consider the factor of *location* and *time*. As a basic authorization service mechanism, RBAC has been used in the security community for access control model. In order to apply RBAC to ubiquitous computing environment, it is necessary to add both location and time dimension. In this paper, we propose new access control model supporting time and location dimensions. The proposed access control model can effectively support various ubiquitous computing environments.

1 Introduction

As wireless networking has become more common, ubiquitous computing begins to receive increasing attention as new paradigm after Internet [1]. Invisible and ubiquitous computing aims at defining environments where human beings can interact in an intuitive way with surrounding objects [2]. In order to accommodate user's frequent movement and accessing resources anytime and anywhere, the complexity of security is increased and the security service should consider the factors of *location* and *time*. As with security services in wired network, it is essential for service providers to know user's information such as *who connect* and *what is user's rights*. It can be supported by proper authentication and authorization methods [11]. Role-Based Access Control (RBAC) is one of famous access control model [3][4]. RBAC has shown to be policy neutral [5] and supports security policy objectives as the least privilege and static and dynamic separation of duty constraints [6]. In order to protect abusing rights, the user must have the least privilege. For that reason, several models with constraints - time and location are suggested for the least privilege service such as

---

* Author for correspondence +82-2-3408-3795.

J. Song, T. Kwon, and M. Yung (Eds.): WISA 2005, LNCS 3786, pp. 354–363, 2006.

TRBAC (Temporal RBAC) [5] and SRBAC (Spatial RBAC) [8]. However, these models consider just one dimension, either temporal or spatial. For the ubiquitous computing environment, both dimensions should be supported for RBAC model. These constraints are provided as a peculiar feature of environment. In this paper, we propose an access control model for ubiquitous computing environment that supports temporal and spatial dimensions. We call these factors *situation information*. We suggest new expression of RBAC with *situation information*. This paper is organized as follows. Chapter 2 surveys related works. Chapter 3 formally presents the access control model for ubiquitous computing environment. Chapter 4 discusses example scenarios and we compare the proposed model with other models in Chapter 5. Chapter 6 concludes with future works.

2 Related Works

2.1 Role-Based Access Control (RBAC)

RBAC uses the concept of *role*. It does not allow users to be directly associated with permissions, instead each user can have several roles and each role can have multiple permissions. There are three components of RBAC: users, roles, and permissions. Each group can be represented as a set of user *Users*, a set of role *Roles*, and a set of permission *Permissions*. Two different types of associations must be managed by the system; one is the association between user and role, the other is the association between role and permission. It is characterized as user-role (UA) and role-permission (PA) relationships.

Definition 1 (RBAC Model). *The RBAC model consists of the following components [6]:*

- *Users, Roles, Permissions, Sessions*
- *User_assignment : $UA \subseteq Users \times Roles$*
- *Permission_assignment : $PA \subseteq Permissions \times Roles$*
- *Session_Users(s : Sessions) $\rightarrow$ Users*
- *Session_Roles(s : Sessions) $\rightarrow 2^{Roles}$*
- *Role_hierarchy : $RH \subseteq Roles \times Roles$*

2.2 Temporal RBAC (TRBAC)

There are many situations that roles may be available to users at certain time periods, and unavailable at others. TRBAC is an extension of RBAC that has time constraint. It supports periodic role enabling and disabling [5]. It provides temporal dependencies among the enabling and disabling of different roles, expressed by means of role triggers. Role trigger actions may be either immediately executed, or deferred by an explicitly specified amount of time. For example, $\{(PE).([1/1/2000, \infty], night\text{-}time, VH:enable\ doctor\text{-}on\text{-}night\text{-}duty)\}$ presents that *doctor-on-night-duty* role must be enabled during the night. $\{(RT).enable\ doctor\text{-}on\text{-}night\text{-}duty\ H:enable\ nurse\text{-}on\text{-}night\text{-}duty\}$ means that the role *nurse-on-night-duty* must be enabled whenever the role *doctor-on-night-duty* is.

2.3 Generalized Temporal RBAC (GTRBAC)

GTRBAC is an extension of the TRBAC [9]. TRBAC provides constraints only on role enabling and triggers, considerably limiting its use in many diverse real world application requirements. The GTRBAC model incorporates a set of language constructs for the specification of various temporal constraints on roles, including constraints on their activations as well as on their enabling times, user-role and role-permission assignment. It introduces the separate notions of the enabled and activated states of role, and provides constraints and event expressions associated with both these states. An enabled role indicates that a user can activate it, whereas an activated role indicates that at least one subject has activated a role in a session. For example, *((10am,3pm),assignu Carol to DayDoctor)* indicates that Carol can assume the *DayDoctor* role everyday between 10am and 3pm. *c1 =(6 hours, 2 hours, enable NurseInTraining)* specifies a duration constraint of 2 hours on the enabling time of the *NurseInTraining* role, but this constraint is valid for only 6 hours after the constraint *c1* is enabled. *enable DayNurse enable c1)* presents that constraint *c1* is enabled once the *DayNurse* is enabled, which means now the *NurseInTraining* role can be enabled within the next 6 hours [10]. Although this model is well defined by mathematical expression, it does not consider location constraint.

2.4 Spatial RBAC (SRBAC)

The mobile computing devices and wireless networks are dramatically utilized by many organizations. The users frequently access to networked computer resources anywhere and anytime, through their mobile terminals. For that reason, the system should be able to base its access decisions depending on the spatial dimension in which the user in situated. SRBAC [8] is an extension of the RBAC model. It is able to specify spatial constraints on enabling and disabling of roles. It defines the concept of *Zone* for location. *Zone* is a similar concept to the cell of cellular network and logical location domain. Permissions are assigned to *Zone* in a role by a Location Permission Assignment List (LPAL) that is presented by matrix. As this model supports spatial dimension, it has some problems. It represents assignment among role, location and permissions by matrix. In real environment, there are a lot of locations so that this model should have matrix. It is also difficult to divide an area into *Zones*. The proposed access control model solves these shortcomings by employing hierarchy structure for expressing location information.

2.5 Other Researches

There are some other researches to extend RBAC model for various environments. H. F. Wedde et al.[14] suggests extended RBAC model for distributed authorization and authenication. Although this model consider location structures, it focuses on modeling the authorization process with in highly distrubuted yet predefined organizational relationships. S. Fu et al.[15] researches Shared

Resource Access Language(SRAL) for the specification of access patterns by a mobile device. They only focues on user mobility problem that is shared resource when mobile client relates their networks.

3 Role-Based Access Control Model for Ubiquitous Computing Environment

3.1 The Proposed Access Control Model

In order to incorporate RBAC model in a mobile environment such as ubiquitous computing environment, the role for each location in an organizational domain has to be defined [8]. In many organizations, functions may have limited or periodic temporal duration [5]. SRBAC, which is an extension of RBAC, incorporates location information associated with roles in order to permit location-based definition of security policy. TRBAC, which is another extension of RBAC, considers time dimension. In spite of many researches on TRBAC and GTRBAC (Generalized TRBAC) [7], they still have some problems such as inappropriate in representing situation information. On the other hand, certain domains have to consider both temproal and spatial dimensions at the same time. We propose new access control model that support the ubiquitous computing environment. It can support not only temporal and spatial dimension alone but also two dimensions together.

3.2 Location Hierarchy

Most of location information is consists of leveled information. For example, a room in a university is a part of a building and the building is a part of the university. As shown in Figure 1, room 202 is a room in the second floor, which is one of floor in the Engineering-building, one of building of university A. If a user A has access permission in all rooms of Engineering-building, the expression should include all names of each room. In set expression that is normally used in ubiquitous computing model, the expression is {*Auditorium, #201, #202,*

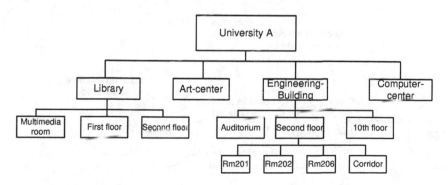

Fig. 1. An example of location hierarchy

#206, Corridor,, 10th floor}. The elements of location set increases in geometric progression when the number of permitted location is increased. However, the hierarchical expression is able to represent this by a simple way. In the proposed model, A's location information is *{Engineering-Building}*. It reduces the number of expression and operation. The proposed model also supports an expression for a few excluding locations in big permitted area. For example, a user B is able to access student data in all of university area except Multimedia room in Library. Common set expression should represent all location names without Multimedia room. However, the proposed model has easy expression method such as *{ UniversityA\-\ UniversityA@Library\MultimediaRm}*. The expression '\ − \' means exception. The detail of expression is discussed in 3.5. In addition, common set expression needs unique name for all location in global area but the proposed model needs it just in small local area.

3.3   Role States

The proposed access control model supports *situation information* that consists of time and location constraints for ubiquitous computing environment. The *situation information* consists of three role states. We defined three role states such as *Assign, Disable* and *Enable*. The user's role state is changeable during a session. When a user logs into system, the system assigns roles to user. At this point in time, the role state is *Assign*. The system checks time and location constraints, and then the role state is changed to *Disable* or *Enable*. Figure 2 shows role states of the proposed access control model.

- *Assign* : A role is assigned to a user.
- *Disable*: The role is deactivated when constraints are unsatisfied and the resources are not accessible at this state. The state transits to *Enable* when both location and time are satisfied.
- *Enable*: The role is activated when constraints are satisfied. By this activation, the user is able to access resources at this state. The state transits to *Disable* when location or time constraints are unsatisfied.

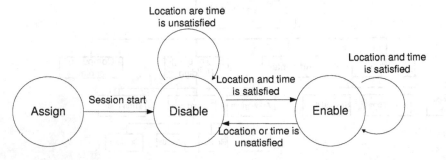

Fig. 2. The role states of the proposed model

3.4 Components

We define *Locations, Times, Constraints* and *EnableRoles* that represents the set of locations, times, constraints and enabled roles. The proposed model consists of the following components.

- *Users, Roles, Permissions, Sessions, Locations, Times, Constraints, EnableRole*
- *User_assignment* : $UA \subseteq Users \times Roles$
- *Permission_assignment* : $PA \subseteq Permissions \times Roles$
- *Session_Users*(s : *Sessions*) $\rightarrow Users$
- *Session_Roles*(s : *Sessions*) $\rightarrow 2^{Roles}$
- *Role_hierarchy* : $RH \subseteq Roles \times Roles$
- *Location_hierarchy* : $LH \subseteq Locations \times Locations$
- *Constraints_UA*(c : *Constraint*) $\rightarrow UA$
- *Constraints* = *Locations|Times|Locations* $\times$ *Times*
- *Assigned_users*(r : *Roles*) $\rightarrow 2^{Users}$
- *Assigned_permissions*(r : *Roles*) $\rightarrow 2^{Permissions}$

3.5 Syntax and Semantics

In this section, we present the proposed model by introducing its syntax and semantics.

Definition 2 (Discrete Location Expression). *Given locations* $l_1, l_2, l_3, ...,$ l_j *where j is integer, a location expression L is defined as* $L = \{l_1, l_2, l_3, ..., l_j\}$, *e.g. L={ResearchCenterBuilding A, Student Building} represents the set of locations which is research center building A and student building.*

Definition 3 (Adjacent Location Expression). *Given locations* $l_i, l_{i+1}, l_{i+2},$ *..., l_k where i and k are integer, a location expression L is defined as* $L = \{l_i : l_k\}$, *e.g. $L = \{ResearchCenterBuilding\ A : StudentBuilding\}$ represents the set of all locations which is from research center building A to student building.*

Definition 4 (Location Hierachy Expression). *Location information l is defined as* $l = l_1@l_2\backslash l_3\backslash l_4$ *where l_1 is the highest level in location structure and* $l_2 \leqq l_3 \leqq ... \leqq l_k$. *e.g. $l = UnivA@Engineering - building\backslash SecondFL\backslash Rm202$ represents room 202 in Engineering-building of University A.*

Definition 5 (Exception Location Expression). *Given location l excepting in location l_1, a location expression L is defined as* $L = \{l\backslash - \backslash l_1\}$. $\backslash - \backslash$ *means location exception. e.g. $L = \{UnivA@reserchbuilding\backslash - \backslash SecondFL\}$ represents the set of locations which is research center building without second floor in university A.*

Definition 6 (Discrete Time Expression). *Given times* $t_1, t_2, t_3, ..., t_j$ *where j is integer, a time expression T is defined as* $T = \{t_1, t_2, t_3, ..., t_j\}$, *e.g. $T = \{Monday, Friday\}$ represents the set of times as Monday and Friday.*

Definition 7 (Continuous Time Expression). *Given times $t_i, t_{i+1}, t_{i+2}, ...,$ t_k where i and k are integer, a location expression T is defined as $T = \{t_i : t_k\}$, e.g. $T = \{Monday : Friday\}$ represents the set of all times from Monday to Friday. Therefore, $T = \{Monday : Friday\} = \{Monday, Tuesday, Wednesday, Thursday, Friday\}$*

Definition 8 (Location Constraint Expression). *Given location values, a location constraint expression L_C is defined as $L_C = \{l_1, l_2, l_3, ..., l_j | l_i : l_k\}$ where i, j and k are integer.*

Definition 9 (Time Constraint Expression). *Given time values, a time constraint expression T_C is defined as $T_C = \{t_1, t_2, t_3, ..., t_j | t_i : t_k\}$ where i, j and k are integer*

Definition 10 (Constraint Expression). *Given a role, a constraint expression C is defined as $C = L_C | T_C | L_C \times T_C$*

Definition 11 (Role Status Expression). *Given a role R, we represent three kinds of role status S such as assign, enable and disable. Role status expression S is defined as $S = \{Assign, Enable, Disable\}$. The role's status is defined as $R_S = \{assignR, enableR, disableR\}$*

Definition 12 (User/Role/Constraint Expression). *Given a user u, roles r and constraints c, the proposed RBAC assignment expression is defined as $u : \{c, R\}$ where u Users, c Constraints, e.g. $A : \{UnivA@studentbuilding, 11 : 00 : 13 : 00, GradStudentUser\}$ represents that user A has gradate student role in Student building when it is from 11:00 to 13:00.*

4   Scenarios

The proposed access control model can be applied to the following three cases of environment such as with only time constraint, only location constraint, and both constraints. In this section we will discuss the three scenarios in detail.

The first scenario is where the time constraint alone is required. For instance, the role of part-time staff in a hospital is to be authorized to work only on certain days or times. The time constraint can enable or disable roles at certain time periods. In this model, constraint expression is $C = T_C$ and $T_C = \{t_1, t_2, t_3, ..., t_j | t_i : t_k\}$ where i, j and k are integer. Alice is a part-time nurse of the hospital and works from 1 p.m. to 6 p.m. on workday. Bob is also a part-time nurse of the same hospital and works from 6 p.m. to 10 p.m. on workday. Alice's role, *part-timeNurse* is *Disable* state at first time, and then it is changed to *Enable* state from 1 p.m. to 6 p.m. The Alice's role state moves to *Disable* except this time. In this case, the expression is as follows.

- Alice: { *13:00 : 18:00, enable part-timeNurse* }
- Bob : { *18:00 : 22:00, enable part-timeNurse* }

The second scenario is where the location constraint alone is required in organizations. It normally happens in the following cases in ubiquitous computing environment. For example, the case of a doctor that has permission to access a patient record that is only accessed in designated area. The location constraint can enable or disable roles at assigned locations. The constraint expression is $C = L_C$ and $L_C = \{l_1, l_2, l_3, ..., l_j | l_i : l_k\}$ where i, j and k are integer. Alice is a physician who can access patient records in her office. Bob is a surgeon who can access patient records in his office and operating rooms. The expression for this case is as follows.

– Alice : { Room301, enable accessPatientRecords }
– Bob : { Room302, OperatingRooms, enable accessPatientRecords }

The last scenario is where the time and location constraints are required. In reality, most ubiquitous computing environment should consider both time and location factors. For instance, the case of part-time nurse who works in the operation room is authorized only on working days or times. It is necessary to apply both time and location constraints. Time and location constraints can restrict in his/her permissions. The constraint expression is $C = L_C \times T_C$. Alice is a part-time nurse during nighttime in the operation room. The expression of the proposed access control model is the following:

– Alice:{ OperationRoom, 20:00 : 4:00 , part-timeNurse}

5 Comparison

We compare the proposed model with GTRBAC and SRBAC in the following business scenarios. Alice works with Bob from company's partner. When Bob needs to access some resource such as printer in meeting room at restricted time periods from 10 a.m. to 3 p.m. In this case, Bob's role has to restrict time and

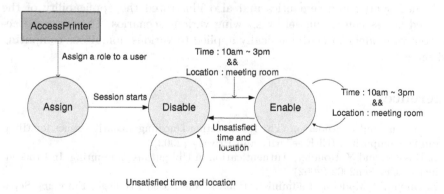

Fig. 3. The role states of accessPrinter

Table 1. The proposed model, GTRBAC and SRABC

Support	GTRBAC	SRBAC	The proposed model
Temporal dimension	Yes	No	Yes
Spatial dimension	No	Yes	Yes
Location hierarchy	No	No	Yes

location dimensions. In GTRBAC, it is represented as the following expression. *([10am, 3pm], assignU Bob to accessPrinter)*. There is no way to represent location restriction together. In SRBAC, they use location permission assignment list that contains role name, locations and permission. Therefore, it also does not have time expression. On the other hand, the proposed model is able to represent location and time constraints together as following. *Bob:{MeetingRoom, 10:00:15:00, Enable accessPrinter}*.

Figure 3 shows states diagram of the above example.

In the table 1, the proposed model is compared with GTRBAC and SRBAC about supporting factors such as temporal and spatial dimensions and location hierarchy.

6   Conclusion and Future Works

Nowadays, as wireless networking became more common, ubiquitous computing is receiving increasing attention. In this environment, the system should be able to accommodate the user's temporal movement. Consequently, adapting security service is more difficult than common network, since it has to consider user's situation. RBAC is widely used access control method for authorization. In order to adapt to these changing environment, it is necessary to adjust time and location dimensions for more efficient and secure RBAC model. We propose new access control model that supports *situation information* for ubiquitous computing environment. It is provided as a peculiar feature of environment. In this paper, we defined syntax and semantics and also illustrated the applicability of the proposed access control model by showing various scenarios. The proposed access control model can be dynamically applied to various ubiquitous computing environments.

References

1. F. Stajano and R. Anderson, The Resurrecting Duckling: Security Issues for Ubiquitous Computing, IEEE security and Privacy (2002)
2. L. Bussard and Y. Roudier, Authentication in Ubiquitous Computing, In Proceedings of UbiCom2002 (2002)
3. E. Choun, A Model and administration of Role Based Privileges Enforcing Separation of Duty. Ph.D. Dissertation, Ajou University (1998)
4. G. Ahn and R. Sandhu, Role-Based Authorization Constraints Specification, ACM Transactions on Information and System Security, Vol3, No4 (2000) 207-226

5. E. Bertino, P. A. Bonatti and E. Ferrari, TRBAC: A Temporal Role-Based Access Control Model. ACM Transactions on Information and System Security, Vol4, No3 (2001) 191-223
6. D.F.Ferraiolo, R.Sandhu, E.Gavrila, D.R.Kuhn and R.Chandramouli, Proposed NIST Standard for Role-Based Access Control, ACM Transactions on Information and System Security, Vol4, No3 (2001) 224-274
7. J.B.D. Joshi, E. Bertino, U. Latif and A. Ghafoor, A Generalized Temporal Role Based Access Control Model, IEEE Transactions on Konwledge and Data Engineering, Vol17, No1 (2005) 4-23
8. F. Hansen and V. Oleshchuk, SRBAC: A Spatial Role-based Access Control Model for Mobile Systems, In Proceedings of Nordec 2003, Gjovik, Norway (2003)
9. J.B.D. Joshi, E. Bertino, and A. Ghafoor, Hybrid Role Hierarchy for Generalized Temporal Role Based Access Control Model, In Proceedings of the 26th Annual International Computer Software and Application Conference (2002)
10. J.B.D. Joshi, E. Bertino, and A. Ghafoor, Temporal Hierarchy and Inheritance Semantics for GTRBAC, In proceedings of 7th ACM Symposium on Access Control Models and Technologies, Monterey, CA (2002)
11. S. Chae, W. Kim and D. Kim, Efficient Role Based Access Control Method in Wireless Environment, Lecture Notes in Computer Science 3260 (2004) 431-439
12. S. Chae, W. Kim, and D. Kim, A Novel Approach to Role-Based Access Control, Lecture Notes in Computer Science 2660 (2003) 1060-1068
13. S. Chae, W. Kim, and D. Kim, Role-based Access Control using Neural Network, In Proceedings of SCI2003 Vol2 (2003) 36-40
14. H.F. Wedde and M. Lischka, Role-based Access Control in Ambient and Remote Space, In Proceedings of the 9th ACM symposium on Access control models and technologies (2004)
15. S. Fu and C. Xu, A Coordinated Spatio-Temporal Access Control Model for Mobile Computing in Coalition Environments, In Proceedings of 19th IEEE International Parallel and Distributed Processing Symposium (2005)

Designing Security Auditing Protocol
with Web Browsers

Ho Jung Lee and Jung Hwan Song

Department of Mathematics, Hanyang University,
17 Haengdang-dong, Seongdong-gu, Seoul 133-794, Korea
camplab@ihanyang.ac.kr, camp123@hanyang.ac.kr
http://math.hanyang.ac.kr/camp

Abstract. The most of users of personal computer use web browsers such as MS(Microsoft) Internet Explorer, Mozilla Firefox, and so on for accessing to internet. Especially MS Internet Explorer which is used for internet access is a module to execute local files and to install softwares that are activated by install shield. Also Explorer is the same as Shell. Analyzing "index.dat" log which is the history of executing files and accessing web sites makes security audit effective. In this paper, by analyzing Windows "index.dat" and Mozilla Firefox cache files with time analysis, we suggest a method to perform auditing of cyber crimes such as information leakage and hard disk vulnerability.

1 Introduction

Since highly efficient computers and high speed networks have been popularized, lots of information are easily shared through internet. Also most of hard copied documents are converted into electronic documents, and it is easy for someone to transfer electronic documents from his computer to the others by e-mail, P2P, ftp, and so forth. Particularly public agencies and companies lead this work, but there are risks such as information leakage and data hijackings against it's convenience. "Information Leakage" is defined as "The accidental or intentional release of information to someone before it is made available to the general public." [1], and if someone who illegally flow out some information is in conflict with the laws or regulations as the follows[2].

- Disclosure of secret
- Interference of duty
- Interference of execute of public duty
- Larceny
- Breech of duty

By the statistical data, the rate of intentional information leakage is 80% by inside and 20% by trespassers[3]. It is important not only preventing information leakages, but also gathering evidences after crimes so that we take appropriate action against the crimes. So the recognition of information leakage is an important category of security auditing. Mostly security auditing on personal computer seems to depend on auditor's abilities, which make indefinite amount of time and human resources. Thus it is easy

J. Song, T. Kwon, and M. Yung (Eds.): WISA 2005, LNCS 3786, pp. 364–376, 2006.

for expert user to avoid auditing by perfect deleting log files and killing links of file on disk for a short time. In this paper, we suggest a security auditing protocol, against intentional information leakage through internet with analyzing web browser's log files. And, we deal with analyzing MS Explorer log files that are History "index.dat", Temporary "index.dat" and Cookie "index.dat" using Computer Forensics[4][5][6] and MAC times. In addition, the security auditing protocol contains the case of using other web browser Mozilla Firefox.

2   Logs of Web Browser in Windows

The log is defined as a record that describes events that occur during an operation, and log file means a file in which system record special events[7]. In this section, we analyze "index.dat" log for MS Internet Explorer and cache files for Mozilla Firefox.

2.1   "Index.dat" Log

The "index.dat" is a binary format log containing information about internet sites accessed by MS internet explorer and Windows. So this "index.dat" must be paid attention at security auditing. The "index.dat" is recorded history information of MS Internet Explorer, internet cache, cookies, user data and special events on Explorer. Note that the size of space for private information of user is 128 Kbytes per record, there are sensitive information besides cookies, such as use, modify, copy, distribute, transfer, publicly display, publicly perform, reproduce, publish, sublicense, create derivative works and so on.

It is impossible to delete "index.dat" in Explorer or Command windows, and trying to delete "index.dat" brings down "Access violation error" in Windows. It means that "index.dat" is used in operating system. By the above reason, we know that "index.dat" always exists in Windows. As the above, our security auditing protocol with using "index.dat" is able to be applied in the most of Windows system.

2.1.1   Specification of "Index.dat"
There are three different types "index.dat" with the same filename and extension in several folders. They have different roles in each others as the follows.

1) *Temporary "index.dat"* : The most of information about address of accessed sites and image files in web pages are recorded in this "index.dat". The information in "index.dat" can not be deleted even if user executes "Delete temporary internet files" Explorer command and only temporary internet files are deleted.
2) *Cookies "index.dat"* : The contents in this type of "Index.dat" are information in the cookie list which contains cookies of accessed sites by MS internet explorer.
3) *History "index.dat"* : Every information about URL which is accessed by MS Explorer is recorded in this type of "index.dat". URL contains following two parts. The one indicates what kind of resource it is addressing, such as http, ftp, file, and so on. The other contains the address of the computer where it is located as well as the path to the file. History "index.dat" is created in every week and is backed up every two month.

2.1.2 Structure of "Index.dat"

The header of "index.dat" contains data which verify "index.dat" has been made up by specified information of version such as "Client UrlCache MMF Ver 5.2", and the fixed length of data with 0x0 (zero) after information of version. Thus we cannot open "index.dat" with usual application such as Notepad and Wordpad, because they regard zero sequence as the end of file.

Thus the usual applications such as Notepad and Wordpad can open only header because they regard zero sequence as the end of file. The body of "index.dat" is connected after end of zero sequence. It is hard to recognize the start and the end of data by the structure.

Temporary, Cookie and History "index.dat" contain the following data as in the Table 1. The column "offset bytes" in the Table 1 indicates size of bytes from starting tag of URL information.

Table 1. Public specification in "index.dat"

Offset bytes	Description
0x00	Starting tag of URL
0x04	Length in stored block
0x08	Last modified time
0x10	Last accessed time
0x38	Cache directory index
0x3c	Offset to file name
0x44	Offset to URL header
0x64	"OBADFOOD" sign
0x68	URL

History, Temporary and Cookies "index.dat" have different data in each other, but they have same following 5 data areas.

1) *URL* : In this data area, URL of sites and URL of files that explorer has accessed are recorded.
2) *REDR*(Redirect) : This data area is a kind of secondary storage which contains the information about accessed sites that has not been stored in folder of temporary internet files. It is also called dynamic file and contains sensitive information such as ID, password, and so on. Also, there are information about redirected pages form URL.
3) *LEAK* : Same as REDR.
4) *HASH* : Hash values are used for fast indexing.
5) *BADFOOD* : The "BADFOOD" marks that are stored in the last records of the information, are called "OBADFOOD" because they have the hexadecimal values as the form "0D F0 AD 0B". This is managed only by some memory management process but does not permit any other applications to refer it. It cannot be referred from security auditing.

The History "index.dat" contains 3 additional data with the data as described above in the Table 1 and starting addresses of each data are not fixed. The additional data are follows.

1) *File name* : The accessed file names in URL
2) *URL header* : URLs and URLs type which consist of HTTP, FTP, TELNET, MAILTO, MSINST, FILE
3) *Padding* : Padding bytes which consist of the form"0D F0 AD 0B"

Temporary "index.dat" contains different information from History "index.dat". The header of Temporary "index.dat" contains addresses of hidden cache folders which have html of sites, images, and web loading files accessed by Explorer. For example, it looks as in the Fig. 1, and names of hidden cache folders can be extracted to the Table 2 by the Fig. 1. All information of Temporary "index.dat" are equal to History "index.dat" except information of hidden cache folder. The name of hidden cache folder is made by random.

The URLs information of Cookies "index.dat" is similar to the URLs information of History "index.dat", and the URLs area which is located at a distance of 68 bytes is changed to "cookie" in the Table 1. Cookies "index.dat" contains following three more information except information of these and the starting addresses of each data are not fixed.

Address	Hexadecimal value																Statement
000000	43	6C	69	65	6E	74	20	55	72	6C	43	61	63	68	65	20	Client UrlCache
000010	4D	4D	46	20	56	65	72	20	35	2E	32	00	00	00	72	00	MMF Ver 5.2...r.
000020	00	50	00	00	80	E3	00	00	BF	2B	00	00	00	00	00	00	.P.......+......
000030	00	60	11	27	00	00	00	00	00	A0	3D	07	00	00	00	00	.`.'......=.....
000040	00	00	00	00	00	00	00	00	14	00	00	00	A1	00	00	00	....
000050	39	44	4D	33	47	31	4D	5A	A1	00	00	00	53	48	36	37	9DM3G1MZ....SH67
000060	38	31	41	37	A0	00	00	00	4B	56	30	4C	59	52	34	48	81A7....KV0LYR4H
000070	A0	00	00	00	57	4C	38	37	43	46	4F	44	A0	00	00	00	....WL87CF0D....
000080	48	38	30	56	54	54	53	44	A0	00	00	00	41	58	39	41	H80VTTSD....AX9A
000090	5A	32	4C	53	A0	00	00	00	58	46	56	5A	35	39	53	45	Z2LS....XFVZ59SE
0000a0	9F	00	00	00	53	42	35	4A	41	51	33	58	A0	00	00	00	....SB5JAQ3X....
0000b0	50	57	47	5A	44	50	57	44	A0	00	00	00	45	4C	31	49	PWGZDPWD....EL1I
0000c0	4A	51	48	4B	A0	00	00	00	4A	56	58	46	42	54	34	57	JQHK....JVXFBT4W
0000d0	A0	00	00	00	30	56	50	46	51	49	4E	50	A0	00	00	00	....0VPFQINP....
0000e0	31	4F	4F	4E	35	4C	53	48	A1	00	00	00	59	44	4C	51	100N5LSH....YDLQ
0000f0	52	32	39	34	A0	00	00	00	46	46	48	5A	52	44	57	57	R294....FFHZRDWW
000100	A0	00	00	00	4B	46	46	56	59	47	48	31	A0	00	00	00	....KFFVYGH1....
000110	4D	33	49	5A	59	31	59	37	A0	00	00	00	4B	48	34	54	M3IZY1Y7....KH4T
000120	45	56	30	50	A1	00	00	00	45	50	53	52	32	44	41	35	EV0P....EPSR2DA5
000130	A0	00	00	00	57	44	36	37	4B	54	36	4A	00	00	00	00	....WD67KT6J....
000140	00	00	00	00	00	00	00	00	00	00	00	00	00	00	00	00	....

Fig. 1. Example of header of Temporary "index.dat"

Table 2. Information of cache folder in Temporary "index.dat"

Hidden cache folder
9DN3G1HZ , SH6781A7 , KV0LYR4H , WL87CF0D, H80VTTSD
AX9AZ2LS , XFVZ59SE , SB5JAQ3X, PWGZDPWD , EL1IJQHK
JVXFBT4W , 0VPFQINP, 100N5LSH , YDLQR294 , FFHZRDWW
KFFVYGH1, M3IZY1Y7 , KH4TEV0P , EPSR2DA5 , WD67KT6J

1) *URL header* : The URLs of sites which distribute the cookies
2) *File name* : Cookie file name
3) *Padding* : Padding bytes which consist of the form "0D F0 AD 0B"

The MAC times("last modified time", "last accessed time" and so on) in History, Temporary and Cookie "index.dat" are recorded by the forms in hexadecimal, and these are specified with a special type of "NT timestamp". The type has been used after Windows NT first issued, and the hexadecimal values are encoded with a method which has not been publicized. For decoding this hexadecimal values to GMT times, we use the "w32tm.exe" program supported by Windows. For example, if the hexadecimal value of the form "F0 DE 36 5A 14 3E C4 01" is decoded by "w32tm.exe" in the DOS mode command window, "147332 02:44:20.7030000 - 2004-05-20 AM 11:44:20 (local time)" is returned. The first 6 digits of return value is not important information because it is just a hashed value. We know that the time is expressed in minimum unit of which CPU can indicate. When we construct tools for security auditing, we use "COleDateTime" class(supported by Windows SDK), "FILETIME" structure and "SYSTEMTIME" structure[8][9] instead of using "w32tm.exe", because "w32tm.exe" uses much resources compared to the others.

2.1.3 Locations of "Index.dat"

The "index.dat" is stored in different folders by each version of Windows. The locations of "index.dat" are shown in the Table 3 and 4 by the version of Windows. However "index.dat" of MS internet explorer 4 or older version is included in explorer and there are some files of similar function called "mm256.dat" or "mm2048.dat". In this paper, we consider MS internet explorer 5.x or more. The location of "index.dat" depends on not only version of Windows but also whether or not user profiles act. Windows make it difficult to find "index.dat". Every folder contains "index.dat" also contains "desktop.ini" which has some information about the location of "index.dat" but Windows hide "index.dat" by force so explorer can never find "index.dat".

In the Table 3 and 4, underbar ("__") indicates dates, so we know Windows have been backed up periodically. And the folder typed "<USER>" indicates the name of Windows user account.

Table 3. Locations in Windows 95+, NT+, Me

```
C:\Windows\Cookies\
C:\Windows\History\
C:\Windows\History\MSHist_____\    ( __ is some variable)
C:\Windows\History\History.IE5\
C:\Windows\History\History.IE5\MSHist_____\
C:\Windows\Temporary Internet Files\      (Explorer 4.x)
C:\Windows\Temporary Internet Files\Content.IE5\
C:\Windows\UserData\
C:\Windows\Profiles\<USER>\Cookies\
C:\Windows\Profiles\< USER>\History\
C:\Windows\Profiles\< USER>\History\MSHist_____\
C:\Windows\Profiles\< USER>\History\History.IE5\
C:\Windows\Profiles\< USER>\History\History.IE5\MSHist_____\
C:\Windows\Profiles\< USER>\Temporary Internet Files\    (Explorer 4.x)
C:\Windows\Profiles\< USER>\Temporary Internet Files\Content.IE5\
C:\Windows\Profiles\< USER>\UserData\
```

Table 4. Locations in Windows 2000+, XP

C:\Documents and Settings\<USER>\Cookies\
C:\Documents and Settings\< USER >\Local Settings\History\History.IE5\
C:\Documents and Settings\< USER >\Local Settings\History \History.IE5\MSHist_____\
C:\Documents and Settings\< USER >\Local Settings\Temporary Internet Files\Content.IE5\
C:\Documents and Settings\< USER >\UserData\

Table 5. URL information of "Index.dat"

Header	Information
HTTP	Visited Web site
FTP	Accessed ftp folder
FILE	Used file
TELNET	Accessed Telnet
MAIL TO	Sent e-mail by outlook
MS INST	Installed program by MS install shield

Table 6. Location of Firefox cache files

C:\Documents and Settings\<USER>\Application Data\Mozilla\Firefox\Profiles_____\Cache (___ is some variable)

2.1.4 Comprehensive Information of "Index.dat"

We know that "index.dat" include URLs of accessed data, MAC(Modified, Accessed, Created) times, and locations of URLs caches. The information about URL can be represented as Table 5, and we proceed to audit with these information.

2.2 Log Files of Firefox

Now, we deal with log files of Mozilla Firefox that is other popular internet web browser besides MS Internet Explorer. The Firefox stores cache folder with log files by the forms of cache file. Now we call this log files cache files.

The Firefox cache files on our system are located on the following path as described in the Table 6.

In the cache folders of Firefox, there are three types of caches files as Cache Map file, Cache Block files, and Cache Data files.

First, the Cache Map file is named "_CACHE_MAP" and is the main file used to reconstruct Firefox's cached internet accessed data. The Cache Map file has the 8,192 records mapping information to the cached data and contains hashed number, data locations, metadata locations fields.

Firefox either saves the information inside a Block file or creates a Data files. The hashed number is used to name the separate file if that is how a specific cache instance was saved. The other two fields used to reconstruct the cache data are the are the data locations and metadata locations. Each instance of cache data has metadata information and cache contents. But, Cache Map file don't have any information of accessed sites. Thus, we don't care about this file for security auditing.

Second, the Cache Block files named "CACHE_00X_", where 'X' is a number from 1 to 3. Cache block files contain cache content and metadata information for each instance of cache activity. It can be identified using the method presented as follows.

1) *Start block* : "bitwise AND" the metadata location/data location with 0x00FFFFFF.
2) *Number of data block* : "bitwise AND" the metadata location/data location with 0x03000000 and right shifting the result 24 bits. (the data blocks mean contiguous blocks comprising the cache metadata/data.)
3) *Size of data block* : Left shifting the number 256 by the following number of bits(Subtract one from the cache block file number and then multiply the result by two. Therefore, X=1 → 256 bytes, X=2 → 512 bytes, X=3 → 1,024 bytes).

Finally, if the cache content of metadata is too large to be embedded in the Cache Block files, then the information is saved into a Cache Data files. The file names are identified by the following format.

<Hashed Number> <Type> <Generation number>

The hashed number is available from the Cache Map file. The "Type" is either 'd', for cache content, or 'm', for cache metadata. The "Generation number" is an integer that identified by "bitwise AND" the metadata location and data location with 0x000000FF.

Both of Cache Block file and Cache Data file have cached data files which are hyper text, picture, script, and so on.

3   Security Auditing with "Index.dat"

In this section, we assume that there is only one user account in windows and the user uses MS Internet Explorer to access internet. In the case of using Mozilla Firefox, we suggest an optional protocol in section 6. The security auditing of personal computer is represented by the following process, and it records necessary information in "Parameters" in each step.

3.1   Simple Flowchart of Security Auditing

We suggest a security auditing protocol as described in the flowchart in Fig. 2. The security auditors can gain result of auditing, which is described in the below through the protocol.

1) Document files.
2) Destination of document files to be transferred.
3) Time of document files to be transferred.
4) Way of document files to be transferred.

3.2   Detailed Protocol of Security Auditing

First of all, we must fully compose domain database of websites which support webmail. We select addresses obtained by connecting the webmail accounts for domain database which has the following URLs.

- www.hotmail.com (www.hotmail.com)
- mail.naver.com (naver.com)
- kr.f901.mail.yahoo.com (www.yahoo.co.kr) and so forth

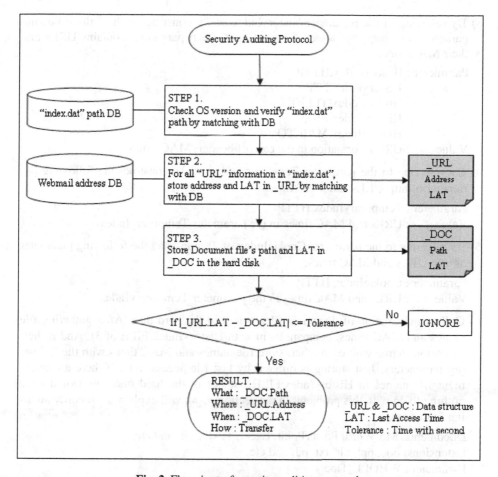

Fig. 2. Flowchart of security auditing protocol

In the following stages from 1) to 10), "Parameter" is representing a storage for data, and "Value" is representing data in "Parameter". Above information of webmail address is represented parameter as MAIL_Domain.

1) Store parameter VER with the current operating Windows version.

    Parameter : VER
    Value   : Windows 95+
                  Windows 2000+
                  Windows XP

2) Find all "index.dat" in a case of parameter VER of 1) within "index.dat" courses of Table 3 or 4, and store in following parameters with all contents of "index.dat".

    Parameter : HistoryIndex, TemporaryIndex, CookieIndex
    Value   : Store each parameters with contents of "index.dat"

3) By referring to the parameter HistoryIndex of 2), construct each of the following parameters of http, ftp, telnet, file, and mail. Each parameter contains URLs and their MAC times.

Parameter : HistoryIndex.HTTP
     HistoryIndex.FTP
     HistoryIndex.TELNET
     HistoryIndex.FILE
     HistoryIndex.MAILTO
Value : URL information in the case of header, MAC times

4) By referring to the parameter TemporaryIndex of 2), construct the following parameter of http URLs and MAC times.

Parameter : TemporaryIndex.HTTP
Value : URLs and MAC times in the parameter TemporaryIndex

5) By referring to the parameter CookieIndex of 2), construct the following parameter of http URLs and MAC times.

Parameter : CookieIndex.HTTP
Value : URLs and MAC times in the parameter TemporaryIndex

6) Collect information of document files stored in the hard disk. After gathering file names and MAC times, compare them with HistoryIndex.FILE of 3). And if their extensions agree with each other, store file names and MAC times with the following parameters. Just storing is ordered by last file access time. If there are document file names in HistoryIndex.FILE but not in the hard disk, we would have nothing to do with this problem. In the section 5, we will explain the security auditing in this case.

Documents: MS Word, PowerPoint, Excel, Text, PDF and etc.
Extensions: doc, ppt, xls, txt, pdf and etc.
Parameter : WHOLE_Doc
Value : file names, last file access times

7) Compare HistoryIndex.HTTP of 3), TemporaryIndex.HTTP of 4) and CookieIndex.HTTP of 5) with the above MAIL_Domain. And if their URLs agree with each other, store URLs and MAC times with the following parameter.

Parameter : MAIL_Access
Value : URLs and MAC times

After all, additionally updates the parameter MAIL_Access with collecting "send mail information" by MS outlook in the HistoryIndex.MAILTO.

8) Construct following parameter WHOLE_Access with HistoryIndex.FTP, HistoryIndex.TELNET of 3) and MAIL_Access by referring and concatenating. After all, there are all URLs information and MAC times supposed to transfer files in target computer of being audited. Just storing is ordered by URL access time.

Parameter : WHOLE_Access
Value : URLs and MAC times for each parameters

9) In the following procedure a) through c), make out final report by comparing parameter WHOLE_Access of 8) with WHOLE_Doc of 6). Store the following parameter REPORT with final report.

Parameter : REPORT

    a) Verify one URL information in the WHOLE_Access.

    b) Compare access time of URL in a) with last access time of WHOLE_Doc, and select file name in the case of "within access time ± 120 seconds". After this, store file name of WHOLE_Doc for URL in WHOLE_Access and ordered by access time.

    c) Perform a) and b) for all URLs in WHOLE_Access.

Additionally, above "120 seconds" is predicted by the elapsed time from accessed webmail account to browse files, and by the average elapsed time to send file with FTP, TELNET. It is calculated by measuring the average time from saving document to sending it by e-mail.

10) There are URLs information of being suspected to transfer some document files and file information of being suspected to be transferred to URLs in the parameter REPORT. And it is ordered by access time. Thus we proceed to audit for illegal outflow of important document.

The above protocol efficient by using specified file name in 6). For example, if security auditing is proceeded with specified word "a plan of operations", "confidence", or "Secret".

4 Extensions of Security Audit

More information are required for gaining high accuracy through the security auditing in the section 5. Consider the following four cases for more accurate security auditing.

- In the case of backed up "Index.dat"
- In the case of undeleted "Index.dat"
- In the case of recovered "Index.dat" in the case of being undeleted imperfect
- In the case of using Mozilla Firefox web browser

4.1 Use of Backed Up "Index.dat"

As we described "Location of "Index.dat"" in the section 2.1.3, "index.dat" is periodically backed up in "MSHist<backup date>" folder. In addition to currently used "index.dat", we proceed to audit for past period with using backed up "Index.dat". It means that the backed up "index.dat" can be replaced by section 3 "Security Auditing with "Index.dat""

4.2 Use of Deleted "Index.dat"

Notice that, it is difficult to undelete the removed "index.dat", because it looks like a folder with being deleted after backup period. After undeleting "index.dat", we proceed to audit in section 3.

4.3 Use of Damaged "Index.dat"

In the case that "index.dat" is partly damaged through undeleting, we recover "in-dex.dat" with Windows inline completion ability in the Windows registry. Windows supports automatic correction ability by used URLs when user types wrong URLs. The URLs of inline completion ability recorded in following Windows registry ordered by accessed time.

HKEY_CURRENT_USER\Software\Microsoft\InternetExplorer\TypedURLs

First, we store the following parameter with URLs in the above registry to recover damaged "index.dat".

Parameter : REGISTRY_URL
Value   : URLs information(except first and last stage domain)

And we compare "Value" of REGISTRY_URL with damaged "index.dat" by the following steps from 1) to 2).

1) We create "Templates" for one URL in the parameter REGISTRY_URL. In this way, "Templates" means much similar information are generated through one URL information. For Example,
   URL   : hotmail
   Templates : hotmai_, hotma_l, ~ , __tmail, h__mail and so forth.

   If the sequence of "Templates" has blanks("_") too much, the performance would be remarkably fallen down.
2) In the case that the one of created "Templates" in 1) is equal to URLs information of damaged "index.dat", the corresponded imperfect URL can be recovered to selected URL in 1) which selected for creating "Templates".
3) For all about URLs in parameter REGISTRY_URL, we proceed steps 1) and 2).
4) At the end of 3), the security audit protocol in section 3 is proceeded.

4.4 Use of Deleted Document Files

In the case that document files exist in the parameter HistoryIndex.FILE but not in the hard disk, we proceed to audit with undeleting these files. Undeletable document files are used in the protocol 6) in the section 3.2 with being undeleted.

In general, the deleted files on Windows are not perfectly removed but lost their links from file header. Thus, it can be undeleted by recovering of damaged link. Methods of recovering of deleted files will be omitted in this paper, because there are already many methods and tools for recovering of deleted files[10]. The possibilities of recovering of deleted files by using MS-DOS "undelete.exe" are described in the following Table 7, by our experiments.

The MS-DOS "undelete.exe" supports almost the minimum recovery ability of known undelete techniques. There are lots of undelete methods besides it. Thus even if any kinds of undelete methods are used in the Section 3, it will offer better results than MS-DOS "undelete.exe".

Table 7. Possibility of recovery for deleted files by using MS-DOS "undelete.exe"

Deleted before	Probable possibility of recovery
1 day	99 %
5 days	95 %
7 days	90 %
10 days	80 %
30 days	40 %
60 days	Under 10 %

4.5 Use of Firefox Cache Files

As the analysis of Firefox cache files in the section 2.2, abilities of Firefox cache file are almost same to "index.dat" logs. Because Cache Map file contains only mapping to the other cache files, just we consider information of Cache Block files and Cache Data files. The cache files can be categorized by the domain names from which they were retrieved by the method of section 2.2. After categorizing the cache files, we define the parameter Firefox.HTTP and store it with URLs and MAC times. And then, we apply additionally the parameter Firefox.HTTP to stage 7) of security auditing protocol in the section 3.2.

4.6 Forgery and Alteration of "Index.dat"

Recently, there are no ways to indicate alteration and forgery of "index.dat". Thus it is hard to use the result of our protocol as legal fact, because our protocol does not guarantee the integrity and indication of alteration and forgery of "index.dat". But it is fitted to use the result of our protocol as adminicle and reference to examination of a suspected person.

5 Conclusions

In this paper, we analyze the MS Explorer log "index.dat" and Mozilla Firefox cache files. The "index.dat" gives us the information about most of URLs accessed by explorer of Windows on personal computer and suggests a security auditing protocol with using "index.dat". And, the most popular web browser except MS Explorer, Firefox has cache files like "index.dat". The principal purpose of security auditing protocol we have suggested, gathers access information about URLs and document file information from "index.dat". Since auditor does not directly access document files, and proceed to security audit with high performance. Moreover, with the protocol 5) and 9) in section 3.2, we can find the suspected document to be flow out. As a result of analysis of "index.dat", we find out that there are use, modify, copy, distribute, transfer, publicly display, sublicense, so it is important to protect log "index.dat" from cracking or hacking. If the logs are deleted from personal computer, auditor can proceed to audit with the method in the section 4.3, "Use of Damaged 'Index.dat'". In this case, some errors can be occurred in recovering and the confidence level

Table 8. Confidence of security auditing

Illegal outflow	The rate of confidence
1 day ago	90 %
5 days ago	85 %
7 days ago	81 %
10 days ago	72 %
30 days ago	36 %
60 days ago	Under 5 %

becomes lower, so perfect recovering method for "index.dat" is needed to reduce errors and increases in confidence of security audit.

The future works are improvement of section 4.3, "Use of Damaged "index.dat"" and section 4.5 "Use of Firefox Cache Files", and development of software on our protocol.

Finally, we calculate the rate of confidence of security auditing for MS Explorer logs. This for Firefox is not tested, and it remains to be future work. Not all URLs are recorded in "index.dat" and the confidence after recovering damaged "index.dat" is not guaranteed. The "index.dat" has 90% of all URLs information and be backed up every week for 8 weeks. Also The probability of recovering the deleted "index.dat" within 4 weeks after being deleted is under 50%. The rate of confidence of security audit for illegal outflow occurred in about 2 months is shown in Table 8, and the probability can be calculated with the probabilities of recovering in the section 3 and above. Since errors can be occurred in comparing with access time to webmail and FTP accounts and access time to document files, accidental errors of the protocol 9) in section 3.2 is not considered.

References

[1] http://www.investorwords.com/2747/leakage.html
[2] http://www.moleg.go.kr/. Korea Ministry of Government Legislation.
[3] FBI/CSI 2004 Computer Crime and Security Survey, FBI/CSI, http://www.gocsi.com (2004)
[4] Warren G. Kruse II, Jay G. Heiser : Computer Forensics incident Response Essentials. Addison Wiley(2001)
[5] Eoghan Casey : Handbook of Computer Crime Investigation. Academic Press(2001)
[6] Shon Harris : CISSP Certification. McGraw-Hill (2001)
[7] Solomon, David A. Russinovich, Mark : Inside Microsoft Windows 2000. Microsoft Press(2000)
[8] Microsoft : http://msdn.microsoft.com. Microsoft Development Network

Author Index

Lecture Notes in Computer Science

For information about Vols. 1–3773

please contact your bookseller or Springer

Vol. 3819: P. Van Hentenryck (Ed.), Practical Aspects of Declarative Languages. X, 231 pages. 2005.

Vol. 3818: S. Grumbach, L. Sui, V. Vianu (Eds.), Advances in Computer Science – ASIAN 2005. XIII, 294 pages. 2005.

Vol. 3817: M. Faundez-Zanuy, L. Janer, A. Esposito, A. Satue-Villar, J. Roure, V. Espinosa-Duro (Eds.), Nonlinear Analyses and Algorithms for Speech Processing. XII, 380 pages. 2006. (Sublibrary LNAI).

Vol. 3816: G. Chakraborty (Ed.), Distributed Computing and Internet Technology. XXI, 606 pages. 2005.

Vol. 3815: E.A. Fox, E.J. Neuhold, P. Premsmit, V. Wuwongse (Eds.), Digital Libraries: Implementing Strategies and Sharing Experiences. XVII, 529 pages. 2005.

Vol. 3814: M. Maybury, O. Stock, W. Wahlster (Eds.), Intelligent Technologies for Interactive Entertainment. XV, 342 pages. 2005. (Sublibrary LNAI).

Vol. 3813: R. Molva, G. Tsudik, D. Westhoff (Eds.), Security and Privacy in Ad-hoc and Sensor Networks. VIII, 219 pages. 2005.

Vol. 3811: C. Bussler, M.-C. Shan (Eds.), Technologies for E-Services. VIII, 127 pages. 2006.

Vol. 3810: Y.G. Desmedt, H. Wang, Y. Mu, Y. Li (Eds.), Cryptology and Network Security. XI, 349 pages. 2005.

Vol. 3809: S. Zhang, R. Jarvis (Eds.), AI 2005: Advances in Artificial Intelligence. XXVII, 1344 pages. 2005. (Sublibrary LNAI).

Vol. 3808: C. Bento, A. Cardoso, G. Dias (Eds.), Progress in Artificial Intelligence. XVIII, 704 pages. 2005. (Sublibrary LNAI).

Vol. 3807: M. Dean, Y. Guo, W. Jun, R. Kaschek, S. Krishnaswamy, Z. Pan, Q.Z. Sheng (Eds.), Web Information Systems Engineering – WISE 2005 Workshops. XV, 275 pages. 2005.

Vol. 3806: A.H. H. Ngu, M. Kitsuregawa, E.J. Neuhold, J.-Y. Chung, Q.Z. Sheng (Eds.), Web Information Systems Engineering – WISE 2005. XXI, 771 pages. 2005.

Vol. 3805: G. Subsol (Ed.), Virtual Storytelling. XII, 289 pages. 2005.

Vol. 3804: G. Bebis, R. Boyle, D. Koracin, B. Parvin (Eds.), Advances in Visual Computing. XX, 755 pages. 2005.

Vol. 3803: S. Jajodia, C. Mazumdar (Eds.), Information Systems Security. XI, 342 pages. 2005.

Vol. 3802: Y. Hao, J. Liu, Y.-P. Wang, Y.-m. Cheung, H. Yin, L. Jiao, J. Ma, Y.-C. Jiao (Eds.), Computational Intelligence and Security, Part II. XLII, 1166 pages. 2005. (Sublibrary LNAI).

Vol. 3801: Y. Hao, J. Liu, Y.-P. Wang, Y.-m. Cheung, H. Yin, L. Jiao, J. Ma, Y.-C. Jiao (Eds.), Computational Intelligence and Security, Part I. XLI, 1122 pages. 2005. (Sublibrary LNAI).

Vol. 3799: M. A. Rodríguez, I.F. Cruz, S. Levashkin, M.J. Egenhofer (Eds.), GeoSpatial Semantics. X, 259 pages. 2005.

Vol. 3798: A. Dearle, S. Eisenbach (Eds.), Component Deployment. X, 197 pages. 2005.

Vol. 3797: S. Maitra, C. E. V. Madhavan, R. Venkatesan (Eds.), Progress in Cryptology - INDOCRYPT 2005. XIV, 417 pages. 2005.

Vol. 3796: N.P. Smart (Ed.), Cryptography and Coding. XI, 461 pages. 2005.

Vol. 3795: H. Zhuge, G.C. Fox (Eds.), Grid and Cooperative Computing - GCC 2005. XXI, 1203 pages. 2005.

Vol. 3794: X. Jia, J. Wu, Y. He (Eds.), Mobile Ad-hoc and Sensor Networks. XX, 1136 pages. 2005.

Vol. 3793: T. Conte, N. Navarro, W.-m.W. Hwu, M. Valero, T. Ungerer (Eds.), High Performance Embedded Architectures and Compilers. XIII, 317 pages. 2005.

Vol. 3792: I. Richardson, P. Abrahamsson, R. Messnarz (Eds.), Software Process Improvement. VIII, 215 pages. 2005.

Vol. 3791: A. Adi, S. Stoutenburg, S. Tabet (Eds.), Rules and Rule Markup Languages for the Semantic Web. X, 225 pages. 2005.

Vol. 3790: G. Alonso (Ed.), Middleware 2005. XIII, 443 pages. 2005.

Vol. 3789: A. Gelbukh, Á. de Albornoz, H. Terashima-Marín (Eds.), MICAI 2005: Advances in Artificial Intelligence. XXVI, 1198 pages. 2005. (Sublibrary LNAI).

Vol. 3788: B. Roy (Ed.), Advances in Cryptology - ASIACRYPT 2005. XIV, 703 pages. 2005.

Vol. 3787: D. Kratsch (Ed.), Graph-Theoretic Concepts in Computer Science. XIV, 470 pages. 2005.

Vol. 3786: J. Song, T. Kwon, M. Yung (Eds.), Information Security Applications. XI, 378 pages. 2006.

Vol. 3785: K.-K. Lau, R. Banach (Eds.), Formal Methods and Software Engineering. XIV, 496 pages. 2005.

Vol. 3784: J. Tao, T. Tan, R.W. Picard (Eds.), Affective Computing and Intelligent Interaction. XIX, 1008 pages. 2005.

Vol. 3783: S. Qing, W. Mao, J. Lopez, G. Wang (Eds.), Information and Communications Security. XIV, 492 pages. 2005.

Vol. 3782: K.-D. Althoff, A. Dengel, R. Bergmann, M. Nick, T.R. Roth-Berghofer (Eds.), Professional Knowledge Management. XXIII, 739 pages. 2005. (Sublibrary LNAI).

Vol. 3781: S.Z. Li, Z. Sun, T. Tan, S. Pankanti, G. Chollet, D. Zhang (Eds.), Advances in Biometric Person Authentication. XI, 250 pages. 2005.

Vol. 3780: K. Yi (Ed.), Programming Languages and Systems. XI, 435 pages. 2005.

Vol. 3779: H. Jin, D. Reed, W. Jiang (Eds.), Network and Parallel Computing. XV, 513 pages. 2005.

Vol. 3778: C. Atkinson, C. Bunse, H.-G. Gross, C. Peper (Eds.), Component-Based Software Development for Embedded Systems. VIII, 345 pages. 2005.

Vol. 3777: O.B. Lupanov, O.M. Kasim-Zade, A.V. Chaskin, K. Steinhöfel (Eds.), Stochastic Algorithms: Foundations and Applications. VIII, 239 pages. 2005.

Vol. 3776: S.K. Pal, S. Bandyopadhyay, S. Biswas (Eds.), Pattern Recognition and Machine Intelligence. XXIV, 808 pages. 2005.

Vol. 3775: J. Schönwälder, J. Serrat (Eds.), Ambient Networks. XIII, 281 pages. 2005.

Vol. 3774: G. Bierman, C. Koch (Eds.), Database Programming Languages. X, 295 pages. 2005.